Continued on back

THE ASSESSMENT
OF PSYCHOTHERAPY
OUTCOME

THE ASSESSMENT OF PSYCHOTHERAPY OUTCOME

Edited by

MICHAEL J. LAMBERT
EDWIN R. CHRISTENSEN
STEVEN S. DeJULIO

A WILEY-INTERSCIENCE PUBLICATION
JOHN WILEY & SONS
New York • Chichester • Brisbane • Toronto • Singapore

Library of Congress Cataloging in Publication Data:
Main entry under title:

The Assessment of psychotherapy outcome.

    (Wiley series on personality processes, ISSN
0195-4008)
    Includes indexes.
    1. Psychotherapy—Evaluation. I. Lambert, Michael J.
II. Christensen, Edwin R. III. DeJulio, Steven S.
IV. Series. [DNLM: 1. Outcome and process assessment
(Health care) 2. Psychotherapy. WM 420 A8463]
RC480.5.A88   1983   616.09′14′0287   82-21831
ISBN 0-471-08383-6

Printed in the United States of America

10 9 8 7 6 5 4 3 2 1

For Dick and Mary,
Linda, Rick, Kent, and Chris

Contributors

D. A. ANDREWS, PH.D.
Associate Professor
Department of Psychology
Carleton University
Ottawa, Ontario, Canada

JONATHON ARONOFF, M.A.
Clinical Research Assistant
Department of Psychology
Brigham Young University
Provo, Utah

ARTHUR AUERBACH, M.D.
Professor of Psychiatry
Hospital of University of
   Pennsylvania
Philadelphia, Pennsylvania

MICHAEL BERGER, PH.D.
Research Psychologist
Davis County Mental Health Center
Ogden, Utah

LARRY BEUTLER, PH.D.
Professor of Psychology and
   Psychiatry
Department of Psychiatry
University of Arizona
   School of Medicine
Tucson, Arizona

EDWIN R. CHRISTENSEN, PH.D.
Staff Psychologist
Salt Lake City Mental Health
   Center
Salt Lake City, Utah

MARJORIE CRAGO, PH.D.
Research Assistant
Department of Psychiatry
University of Arizona
   School of Medicine
Tucson, Arizona

CHRISTINE V. DAVIDSON, PH.D.
Director, Section of
Psychiatric Consultation
Liaison to Inpatient Pediatrics,
Department of Psychiatry,
Cook County Hospital,
Chicago, Illinois

RONALD H. DAVIDSON, PH.D.
Chief, Adolescent Inpatient Unit
Illinois State Psychiatric Institute,
Chicago, Illinois

STEVEN S. DeJULIO, PH.D.
Psychologist
Westworld Community Health
   Care, Inc.,
Lake Forest, California

MICHAEL G. EPPINGER, PH.D.
Staff Psychologist
U.S.A.F.
Reese Air Force Base
Lubbock, Texas

BEVERLY HAAS, B.A.
Staff Research Associate
Rehabilitation Medicine Service
Brentwood Veterans
    Administration Medical Center
Los Angeles, California

JAY JENSEN, B.S.
Clinical Research Assistant
Department of Psychology
Brigham Young University
Provo, Utah

MARILYN JOHNSON, PH.D.
Assistant Professor
Department of Psychology and
    Social Science
Rush–Presbyterian–St. Luke's
    Medical Center
Chicago, Illinois

RONETTE L. KOLOTKIN, PH.D.
Associate Professor
Department of Psychology and
    Social Science
Rush-Presbyterian–St. Luke's
    Medical Center
Chicago, Illinois

MICHAEL J. LAMBERT, PH.D.
Professor
Department of Psychology
Brigham Young University
Provo, Utah

CHRISTINE A. MAISTO, M.S.
Graduate Student
Peabody College
John F. Kennedy Center for
    Research on Education and
    Human Development
Nashville, Tennessee

STEPHEN A. MAISTO, PH.D.
Assistant Professor and Director of
    Graduate Studies on Alcohol
    Dependence
Department of Psychology
Vanderbilt University
Nashville, Tennessee

PETER W. MORAN, PH.D.
Staff Psychologist
Moriarty Clinic
Shrewsbury, Massachusetts

FREDERICK L. NEWMAN, PH.D.
Associate Professor of Community
    and Preventive Medicine
Medical College of Pennsylvania
Philadelphia, Pennsylvania

DONALD T. REICK, B.S.
Management Information Specialist
Salt Lake County, Division of
    Health
Salt Lake City, Utah

SUE ROBERTS, M.S.
Clinical Research Assistant
Department of Psychology
Brigham Young University
Provo, Utah

ROBERT F. SABALIS, PH.D.
Associate Professor
Department of Neuropsychology
  and Behavioral Sciences
University of South Carolina School
  of Medicine
Columbia, South Carolina

STEVEN D. SHERRETS, PH.D.
Director Day Hospital Program
Bradley Hospital
Assistant Professor
Section of Psychiatry and Behavior
Brown University
East Providence, Rhode Island

GEORGE STRICKER, PH.D.
Professor and Assistant Dean
Institute for Advanced
  Psychological Studies
Adelphi University
Garden City, New York

MICHAEL G. TRAMONTANA, PH.D.
Director of Psychology, Bradley
  Hospital
Assistant Professor
Section of Psychiatry and Human
  Behavior
Brown University
East Providence, Rhode Island

CHARLES J. WALLACE, PH.D.
Director of Program for Social
  Independent Living Skills
Brentwood Veterans
  Administration Medical Center
Associate Clinical Professor
Neuropsychiatric Institute
University of California at
  Los Angeles

Series Preface

This series of books is addressed to behavioral scientists interested in the nature of human personality. Its scope should prove pertinent to personality theorists and researchers as well as to clinicians concerned with applying an understanding of personality processes to the amelioration of emotional difficulties in living. To this end, the series provides a scholarly integration of theoretical formulations, empirical data, and practical recommendations.

Six major aspects of studying and learning about human personality can be designated: personality theory, personality structure and dynamics, personality development, personality assessment, personality change, and personality adjustment. In exploring these aspects of personality, the books in the series discuss a number of distinct but related subject areas: their nature and implications of various theories of personality; personality characteristics that account for consistencies and variations in human behavior; the emergence of personality processes in children and adolescents; the use of interviewing and testing procedures to evaluate individual differences in personality; efforts to modify personality styles through psychotherapy, counseling, behavior therapy, and other methods of influence; and patterns of abnormal personality functioning that impair individual competence.

IRVING B. WEINER

University of Denver
Denver, Colorado

Preface

The idea for a book on measuring psychotherapy outcome came about as a result of our study of research into the effects of psychotherapy and behavior change techniques. As students of the literature on psychological treatments, we became aware of the many problems associated with measuring changes in patients following treatment interventions. Clearly, measurement problems added considerable ambiguity and uncertainty to the already nearly insurmountable methodological problems inherent in the study of psychotherapy. The obvious lack of agreement over those instruments that were selected as dependent variables was confusing and even disheartening. Could we facilitate the discovery of causal treatment variables by focusing on the problems and techniques of assessment?

We felt certain that the time was right for a volume dealing with the problems, methods, and instruments used in outcome studies. It seemed ideal to make this volume atheoretical, as its appeal was to be broad and unconstrained by theoretical conceptions. Furthermore, it seemed important to invite contributions that would not necessarily have allegiance to certain scales. Thus, the contributors list does not include authors who played a central role in the development of the measures they recommend. We felt that this would leave authors more free to offer critical suggestions and independent recommendations.

It seemed desirable to approach the organization of this book with due attention to the necessity of making assessments disorder specific. This approach would result in many diverse symptom-specific assessments rather than a general battery appropriate for all patients. It recognized the need for both greater variety in assessment batteries and less divergence in devices that are applied to patients with a relatively homogeneous set of problems. The ideal result of these scholarly efforts would be the identification of a large number of assessment batteries appropriate for unique patient populations. Although it is not practical to cover every conceivable patient population, many of the most common and relevant disorders were included. Notable exceptions include inpatient schizophrenics and alcoholics.

We also recognized the value-laden aspects of psychotherapy outcome measurement and the tendency for disagreements between data sources. The book contains, therefore, recommendations for instruments and procedures to be used when assessing outcome from the perspective of several typical data sources. These recommendations and procedures, along with the theories and issues in assessment, discussed in the introduction chapter, were thought to provide a relatively balanced and comprehensive coverage of current trends for assessing changes in patients undergoing psychotherapy.

It is our hope that the material in the text will be appropriate for researchers and clinicians. We attempted to encourage authors to attend to both theoretical and pragmatic issues. To a great extent this goal was achieved. Our belief was that, at the very least, this volume would provide a stimulus to future research and development. It will be some time before our success at reaching this particular goal can be assessed.

We were aided by many helpful people in our effort. We would like to acknowledge those whose contribution has been immediate and remote. Some of these people were helpful by being fine teachers and stimulating thinkers: Ted Packard; Addie Fuhriman; Bob Finley; Ernst Beier; and Allen Bergin. Others contributed more directly to the text: Logan Zemp; Jeff Clark; Audry Goddard; Robert Hill; Ted Asay; Brenda Merrill; Reed Olsen; Valerie Bentley; and Rebecca Jewell, by their careful reading of manuscripts and related scholarly and technical assistance. We should also like to thank Mary Eppinger, Laurie Leishman, Melissa Peterson, and Sherie Lewis for their assistance in the preparation of manuscripts.

MICHAEL J. LAMBERT
EDWIN R. CHRISTENSEN
STEVEN S. DEJULIO

Provo, Utah
Salt Lake City, Utah
March 1983

Contents

Introduction to Issues in Assessing Psychotherapy Outcome and Program Evaluation

CHAPTER 1

Introduction to Assessment of Psychotherapy Outcome: Historical Perspective and Current Issues

MICHAEL J. LAMBERT

In a recent review of psychotherapy outcome studies, Bergin and Lambert (1978) concluded that psychotherapy in general has been demonstrated to have a modestly positive effect on patients. This conclusion, based on a thorough reading of an extensive literature dating back to the 1930s, is generally accepted today. Although our past sophistication in measuring changes following psychotherapy has been adequate to allow this general conclusion in response to questions as to whether psychotherapy is effective, more contemporary questions remain beyond our reach. These questions deal with the comparative effectiveness of different treatment methods; the effective matching of patient, technique, and therapist; and perhaps most important, the identification of specific effective causal agents that are operative during psychotherapy. To explore such specific questions, it is necessary to measure psychotherapy outcome with greater accuracy than in the past. Unless more accurate measurement of psychotherapy outcome is obtained, it is unlikely that we will make much progress in unraveling the complex causal relationships that exist between treatments and outcomes.

In addition to accuracy and precision in measurement, advances in understanding the effects of treatment will be fostered by greater convergence in the kinds of device and method of assessment used in outcome studies. The accumulation of knowledge in the area of treatment effects is bound to proceed very slowly. This is a result of the highly complex nature of treatment effects and the impossibility of designing and carrying out critical and complete experiments in this field. Reasonable progress in understanding causal relationships in this area will depend on the ability to integrate the results of a variety of experiments carried out in numerous locations by diverse researchers. Greater uniformity in the selection and use of dependent measures would go a long way toward making the results of these diverse studies comparable, thereby facilitating the comparison and integration of results.

The problems created by the current lack of uniformity or agreement as to what constitutes adequate outcome measurements are apparent when scholars attempt to reconcile conclusions drawn from psychotherapy research literature based on different or ambiguous criteria of success [see Bergin (1971), in which Eysenck was shown to have drawn quite misleading conclusions about the comparative effects of psychoanalysis]. This lack of agreement in the selection of outcome measures is both historical and contemporary, as the example in the following paragraph illustrates. It is widely believed that the success rates (following therapy) for patients with a circumscribed sexual dysfunction such as premature ejaculation range somewhere between 75 and 90%. Yet one can find substantial differences between individual studies and their reported "success rates." This is especially interesting given the relatively uniform treatment techniques that have been employed. On careful examination of these studies, it would appear that the differences between rates of successful outcome are possibly not so much a function of using different treatments as they are the result of applying differential definitions of success.

This conclusion was dramatized in a recent report by Levine and Argle (1978), who studied the treatment outcome of 16 male patients who were diagnosed "chronic secondary psychological impotence." The authors noted that this dysfunction could be viewed as a performance problem only, but that it was more realistic to consider the sexual life of patients more broadly. As a result, they not only collected outcome on changes in performance, but also on sexual desire and emotional satisfaction with sexual relations. Functioning in these three broad areas was evaluated prior to therapy, at termination, and at 3, 6, 9, and 12 months following treatment. These later data added a fourth dimension to those already discussed: How stable were the observed changes?

The authors noted that the outcome data collected could be summarized to show conservative and liberal views of improvement. Thus if one were to consider the criterion of success to be "better erectile functioning at one-year follow-up than at initial evaluation—regardless of any interim relapses," then 68.8% of the men could be considered improved. Although this figure is nearly identical to that reported by Masters and Johnson's reversal rate of 69%, therefore suggesting a replicable finding, this figure is misleading in the sense that a substantial portion of these patients continued to have "profound" disturbances in their sexual lives.

If a more conservative estimate of improvement, "Improvement in sexual functioning and satisfaction plus stability over time," is used, only one couple, 6.3% of the cases, was improved. This couple achieved the characteristics of good sexual functioning and was able to maintain this comprehensive and substantial improvement. Since the criterion of improvement used by Masters and Johnson (1970) was highly ambiguous, it is impossible to replicate their findings. The 69% improvement rate found by Levine and Argle (1978) is no more a confirmation of the Masters and Johnson figure than is the 6% improvement figure a refutation of it. Clearly, the careful (but fallible) work of Levine and Argle demonstrates the importance of specifying improvement rates (something Masters and Johnson failed to do), if not the value of developing uniform criteria for success to allow one to compare alternative treatments. Within a single study, a variety of success rates can be offered and defended. This emphasizes the (1) need to provide operational definitions of success, (2) the varied definitions that are possible, (3) the possibility of drawing misleading conclusions by using only simple indices of change, and (4) the value of standardizing definitions across studies so that comparisons between these studies can be made. This uniformity in outcome measurement, coupled with comparable measurement techniques, research design, and sample population, will result in more rapid advances in our knowledge about effective treatments.

A BRIEF HISTORICAL OVERVIEW

In this chapter an attempt is made to discuss important issues in assessing the impact of treatment on patients. First, the enterprise of outcome assessment is placed in a historical context. This will be followed by a review of assessment practices as reflected in published research over the past few years. The reader will become familiar with typical devices and patterns of assessing psychotherapy outcome. Following the review of past and present assessment procedures, a discussion of ways of conceptualizing the task of evaluating psychotherapy outcome is presented. The purpose of such a presentation is to help researchers and examiners of research gain a broad perspective on their work. Finally, this chapter elaborates on current issues in assessing the effects of psychotherapy.

Although measurement and qualification are central properties of empirical science, the earliest attempts at quantifying treatment gains lacked scientific rigor. Early attempts at evaluating therapeutic outcome were based solely on therapist ratings. Frequently these ratings were not based on a published rating scale with operationally defined anchor points, but rather on impressionistic conclusions. Seldom were the same definitions applied from one study to the next, nor were any steps taken to ensure the reliability of ratings. A next step in early assessments resulted in some standard rating scales of general improvement. Typical of these, and a method that came to enjoy widespread use, were Knight's criteria (Knight, 1941). Therapists rated patients at the termination of treatment on a five-point scale (cured, improved, etc.), in which each scale point had a general definition. Researchers studying a variety of patient populations were able to apply Knight's rating scale and bring some consistency into outcome ratings. Data based on this or similar rating scales became controversial because of the scale's ambiguous nature, its difficult replicability, and its gross or general nature. The ratings derived from these scales were useful in calculating the percentage of cases who were improved but failed to specify the nature of improvements. They also seemed to reflect final status rather than improvement per se.

The aforementioned scales were then replaced or supplanted by patient self-reports. Early on, these self reports took the form of satisfaction ratings and global judgments of the value of therapy. Usually they were improvement ratings or general evaluations of therapy rather than ratings gathered before and after treatment. Later they included a host of structured personality tests, symptom rating scales, and the like, typically collected on a pretest, posttest basis. Many problems were apparent with these patient evaluation scales, as well as self-report personality tests for evaluating outcome. These problems included the intentional distortion of data for personal and sociopolitical reasons, as well as less consciously intended distortions, such as the desire to reward the therapist. As a means of overcoming these problems and as a result of theoretical and professional development, the use of persons not involved in the therapy encounter was attempted. Experts blind to treatment status thus employed "objective" ratings of both a specific and global nature. In addition, numerous attempts were made to rate changes in actual behavior. These latter procedures were especially important in behavioral therapies.

The search for adequate outcome or change measures also led researchers to evaluate the usefulness of physiological indices of improvement—from measures of anxiety such as galvanic skin response to the chemical content of urine or blood. In addition, data generated in the environment such as college grades, employment records, hospital readmissions, and income were also considered appropriate as indicators of effective treatment and were frequently included among outcome data. In every case the clear fallibility of each of these specific or more "objective" approaches became apparent. Researchers learned that some patients improved subjectively but remained unchanged on "objective" physiological measures. Release and readmission to hospitals, rather than being objective and unbiased, were often found to be more a function of policy decisions than of patient status. These and a host of similar concerns left researchers with a more conservative and tentative stance toward these dependent variables.

Attempts at evaluating psychotherapy have usually reflected current, in-vogue theoretical positions. Thus early studies of psychotherapy applied devices that developed from Freudian dynamic psychology. Not at all uncommon was the use of projective methodologies, including the Rorschach Inkblot Test, the Thematic Apperception Test (TAT), Draw-A-Person, and sentence-completion methods. Problems with the psychometric qualities of these tests, their reliance on inference, and derivation from a theoretical position based on the unconscious all resulted in the waning use of these tests as indices of outcome. Rarely today does one hear the virtues of such tests for outcome measurement. Changes in the quality of fantasy material as produced on the TAT simply do not convince most researchers that significant improvement has occurred in the actual lives of patients. Projective methodology gave way to assessment devices derived from other theories. Client-centered psychology, for example, concentrated on measures of perceived-self–ideal-self discrepancies based on the Q-sort technique. These and related measures of self-concept proved only slightly better than projective techniques. The disappearance of such devices in outcome research thus must be viewed as a sign of progress and an acceptance of the idea that the effects of psychotherapy should extend into the daily functioning of patients. These theoretically derived devices have been replaced by atheoretical measures of such factors as measures of adequate role performance, symptom and behavioral checklists, and the direct observation of target behaviors. Perhaps it is only a contemporary perspective that leads us to conclude that current methods of assessment are improvements over the past methods. Yet contemporary assessment methods seem to focus more on the assessment of actual symptoms and behaviors. Although there are many problems with current measurement methods, there is an excitement about the continued refinement and development of assessment devices. Despite the current optimistic attitude toward outcome assessment, there is a long way to go before consensus will be reached on the type of yardstick to apply in measuring the results of psychotherapy and behavior-change techniques.

To give the reader an informed perspective on outcome assessment, we now provide an overview of recent outcome studies and the nature of devices used to measure improvement. Following this, ways of organizing outcome assessment procedures and some of the issues facing those who design and conduct outcome studies are discussed.

COMMONLY USED PSYCHOTHERAPY OUTCOME MEASURES

Hall (1979) reviewed every article published in the *British Journal of Psychiatry* between 1945 and 1975 to determine the methods that had been used to assess outcome in studies of "long-stay patients." Of the 129 relevant studies, the most frequently used assessment device was the ad hoc psychiatric rating scale. Of all studies, 42% used an unstandardized procedure consisting of either clinical notes or an ad hoc assessment method based on an unpublished scale. Unfortunately, this type of device has no published reliability or validity data to support it. As was already noted, reliance on this type of scale makes replication of a study very difficult, if not impossible. It is disappointing to find that, at least with this population, this type of evaluation not only persists but is prevalent. It is clear that journals should adopt more rigorous editorial policies with regard to the nature of dependent measures used in this type of outcome study.

Hall's review can be compared with an earlier report in which Meltzoff and Kornreich (1970) reviewed devices used in controlled outcome research published prior to 1970. The patients included both inpatients and outpatients treated with a wide variety of group and individual psychotherapies. These authors reported that 39% of the studies used "observed behavior," 27%

personality inventories, 27% "rated behavior," 19% projective techniques, and 10% the Q-sort technique, whereas 9% used "objective performance tools" and 8% studied physical signs. Notable was the low frequency of global ratings made by the patient (6%) and the therapist (7%). Important also was the finding that about 50% of the studies examined used more than one of the above types of criterion.

To examine more recent trends in outcome measurement, we undertook a study of commonly used devices. Our survey was limited to all issues of the *Journal of Consulting and Clinical Psychology*, published during 1976 through 1980. In all, we identified 216 outcome studies published during this five-year period. Next, we classified specific outcome measures into five source categories: *self-report, trained observer, significant other, therapist,* and *instrumental*. We then computed frequency data on the usage of specific instruments and on the usage of instrument sources across studies. Table 1.1 presents data on the frequency with which research studies have employed outcome measures from different sources. It is also a tabulation of the number of studies using one or more sources for assessing outcome. To properly interpret this table, the reader should keep in mind that cell entries refer to the number of studies rather than the number of outcome measures.

In order of preference, researchers are employing devices from the five source categories listed in the previous paragraph. Clearly, therapist ratings and reports from "significant others" were not considered primary sources of data in outcome studies, as they were employed in only 3% of the studies as a single data source. In contrast, self-report methods employed as a single source were used in more than three times as many studies (34%) as its closest competitor, the trained observer. Appropriately, the patient was the primary source of data in outcome studies.

Table 1.1 also illustrates how rarely researchers combined dependent measures from certain sources. Not a single study, for example, combined assessments from more than three sources. Studies employing significant-other ratings alone or in combination with all other sources were relatively infrequent, occurring in about 10% of the studies. This same trend held true for therapist ratings, which alone and in combination were employed in approximately 9% of the studies examined. On the other hand, the most popular combination of assessment sources combined self-reports and ratings by trained observers. This combination was present in 19% of the studies reviewed.

As can be seen in Table 1.1, nearly 75% of the studies reviewed used from two to six outcome measures. This finding indicates that, to a great extent, researchers are indeed using multiple outcome indices in their research. Still, the data would indicate that between 20 and 25% of the studies published during the time period considered used only a single dependent measure. This latter finding is even more sobering when column totals are considered. One-third of the studies reviewed limited their assessment procedures to self-report devices only. Fifty-one (24%) of the 216 studies examined used two or more

TABLE 1.1. Frequency of Outcome Studies Using Different Types of Assessment "Sources" and Differing Numbers of These "Sources"

Sources of Outcome Data

Number of Sources per Study	Self[a]	Trained Observer[b]	Significant Other[c]	Therapist[d]	Instrumental[e]	Self and Trained Observer	Self and Significant Other	Self and Therapist	Self and Instrumental
1	22	15	1	4	6	22	6	7	14
2–3	26	7	1	1	3	13	5	2	7
4–6	24				1	7			
>6	1								
Total	73	22	2	5	10	42	11	9	21
Percentage of grand total (%)	33.8	10.2	0.9	2.3	4.6	19.4	5.1	4.2	9.7

Number of Sources per study	Trained Observer and Significant Other	Trained Observer and Therapist	Trained Observer and Instrumental	Self and Trained Observer and Significant Other	Self and Trained Observer and Therapist	Self and Trained Observer and Instrumental	Self and Significant Other and Therapist	Self and Significant Other and Instrumental	Trained Observer and Significant Other and Instrumental	Grand Total
1										48 (22.2%)
2–3	1	1	1	1	2	1		2	1	94 (43.5%)
4–6	1			3		5	3			61 (28.2%)
>6		1	1			2	1		1	13 (6.7%)
Total	2	2	1	4	2	8	4	2	2	216
Percentage of grand total (%)	0.9	0.9	0.5	1.9	0.9	3.7	1.9	0.9	0.5	100

[a]Self-reports are instruments such as the Minnesota Multiphasic Personality Inventory (MMPI), where patients evaluate and rate their own symptoms.
[b]Trained observers are ratings based on standardized scales (e.g., Psychiatric Status Schedule), where symptoms or behaviors are rated by trained judges.
[c]Significant-other ratings are made by fellow patients, relatives, or friends of the patient.
[d]Therapist ratings are usually based on therapist ratings of symptoms or improvements on Lickert-type scales.
[e]Instrumental devices include those where such factors as physiological monitoring devices are used to assess changes in status.

self-report measures in their assessment. And in all, 52% of the studies relied on assessment devices from single *sources* of outcome (e.g., self-report, trained observer). We can conclude from these data that multiple criteria are being used but researchers have not sufficiently represented the full range of data sources available. The extent to which this tendency generalizes to other journals and to psychotherapy outcome research in general is unknown. These figures, however, may represent a conservative estimate of current practice since the acceptance standards of the *Journal of Consulting and Clinical Psychology* (JCCP) are relatively high.

To give the reader a more concrete view of the variety of outcome measures currently employed in research, a listing of specific approaches and devices seemed in order. Table 1.2 is a listing of instruments in current use as derived from our review. It should be noted that the review procedures probably do not accurately reflect current program evaluation procedures routinely used in mental health agencies. Table 1.2 does give the reader an idea of the most popular outcome measures employed in research by "source" of data. The most frequently used of these measures are listed along with the relative frequency that they appeared in the studies examined.

In the 216 studies examined, 254 different self-report measures were used. This listing of the most commonly used self-report procedures shows that researchers have a continuing interest in the MMPI and related paper–pencil tests. These instruments, by and large, focus on feeling states (and symptoms), mostly anxiety and depression. In the domain of self-report, the 13 most frequently used inventories accounted for 41% of the total self-report scales. This suggests that there are a few popular instruments that are being employed with high frequency. The value of these popular instruments for outcome assessment is a debatable issue to be dealt with in more detail in later chapters. However, one can't help but wonder about the possibility and value of reducing the number of acceptable dependent measures even further. Although diversity across problem (patients) categories is to be expected and the use of diverse self-report measures is thus desirable, some reduction in the number of similar instruments may be feasible. If we can reduce the number of high-frequency scales, it would seem even more desirable to reduce the number of rarely used, "homemade" scales that are often employed in outcome studies.

From Table 1.2 it is apparent that there were relatively few physiological indicators being employed in the outcome studies reviewed. The use of physiological indices as outcome measures appears rather straightforward (although attempts to use devices from different companies quickly convinces researchers that much of this data are not totally objective), given the relative ease and reliability of such measures, their use could be expected to increase. The limited variety of separate measures within this source of assessment results in data that can be easily compared across treatment settings and research reports. In contrast, the lack of specific commonly used scales is apparent when measuring outcome from the view of the therapist or significant others. Not only are assessments by these sources relatively rare, but apparently no stan-

TABLE 1.2. Commonly Used Inventories and Methods of Assessment[a]

Self-Report (N = 254)	Number of Times Used	Percent of Total (%)	Instrumental (N = 67)	Number	Percent (%)	Significant Others (N = 25)	Number	Percent (%)
State-Trait Anxiety Inventory	22	8.7	Heart rate	17	25.4	Informant on specific behavior	8	32
Minnesota Multiphasic Personality Inventory	13	5.1	Skin conductance	15	22.4	Problem checklist—informant	2	8
Rotter's Internal–External Locus of Control Scale	10	3.9	Electromyogram	10	14.9	Single use of measures of family functioning, e.g., Family Life Questionnaire, Family Environment Scale, Family Adjustment	5	20
S–R Inventory of Anxiousness	7	2.8	Respiration	8	11.9			
Achievement Anxiety Test	7	2.8	Pulse rate	5	7.5			
Marital Adjustment Scale	7	2.8						
Rathus Assertiveness Schedule	6	2.4						
Social Avoidance and Distress Scale	6	2.4						
Fear of Negative Evaluation Scale	6	2.4						
Beck Depression Inventory	5	2.0						
Pleasant Events Schedule	5	2.0						
Multiple Affect Adjective Checklist	5	2.0						
Fear Thermometer	5	2.0						

Therapist (N = 22)	Number	Percent (%)	Trained Observer (N = 106)	Number	Percent (%)
Interview—global or level of functioning ratings	19	86.4	Frequency of specific behavior	27	25.5
			Behavioral Role-Playing Test	13	12.3
			Weight Loss	10	9.4
			Behavioral Avoidance Test	7	6.6
			Timed Behavioral Checklist	5	4.7
			Marital Interaction Coding System	3	2.8

[a]Based on 216 outcome studies published in the *Journal of Consulting and Clinical Psychology* between 1976 and 1981.

11

dardized devices have gained widespread acceptance. This finding suggests that measurement in this area is in an even more primitive state than in other areas of assessment. Finally, Table 1.2 indicates the preference researchers have shown for rating specific behaviors. Trained observers have been used in recent studies, by and large, to assess frequencies of specific behaviors rather than to make diagnostic judgments. Our review of current outcome measurement practices suggests the tendency for researchers to employ an unnecessarily large number of dependent measures.

Clearly, a review of past and current practices for assessing psychotherapy outcome indicates that the field is maturing. Assessment procedures are becoming more complex and are also relying more heavily on standardized instruments that deal with specific kinds of change. One has the impression that very little systematic work has been done in making comprehensive assessments of change. Researchers are not prone to clarify the limits of their assessment practices. They do not discuss the general philosophy underlying choice of instruments or the implications of such choices. In the following section an attempt is made to discuss some of the important unspoken conceptual issues that have guided and should guide the selection of instruments for assessing the effects of psychotherapy.

CURRENT ATTEMPTS TO CONCEPTUALIZE OUTCOME ASSESSMENT: THE NEED FOR A PARADIGM

The simplest way to organize outcome assessment is to place it in one of a number of dichotomies. The most typical conceptualization of this sort divides outcome into changes in either internal states or behavior.

In our view, outcome studies would ideally assess both changes in behavior and changes in internal states of experience. This issue emerges directly from the theoretical and technical controversies surrounding the confrontation between behavioral and more traditional therapies (Lambert & Bergin, 1973; Wachtel, 1977). Changes in overt behavior when targeted as criteria are currently very popular and, because they are more directly observed and thereby more easily assessed, tend to be more impressive than phenomenological changes, although not necessarily more important. The problem of measuring experiential phenomena with adequacy and precision remains a crucial task for future research in criterion development. There is also a growing awareness of the inadequacies of behavioral assessment and the need for more systematic and thorough analysis of assessment procedures in this area (Ciminero et al., 1977). Truax and Carkhuff (1967), for example, reviewed a number of studies of patient characteristics and patient change and found that certain apparent contradictions in outcome could be resolved by distinguishing between internal and behavioral criteria. They point out, for example, that initial level of inner disturbance is positively correlated with outcome whereas initial level of behavioral disturbance is negatively related to outcome.

Malan (1976) and his associates have taken this concept one step further and devised what they call an assessment of internal or dynamic change as opposed to symptomatic or behavioral change. The distinction between dynamic and symptomatic criteria has proved valuable in the interpretation of change data. In their analysis, an assessment is made at treatment termination and follow-up to determine how the patient has handled situations that were initially predicted to be the cause of regression and symptom formation. That is, to be dynamically improved, the patient must increase the capacity to cope with specific stress-precipitating events. In their study the spontaneous remission rate for untreated subjects was between 33 and 50% on dynamic criteria as opposed to 60 to 70% on symptomatic criteria.

From a somewhat different perspective, Cattell (1966) argues in favor of two major sets of factors: source traits and surface traits. Source traits refer to the underlying source of behavior or symptoms and are rated by his 16-Personality-Factor Questionnaire. Surface traits refer to constellations of syndromes or symptoms like those that are measured by the MMPI. Factor-analytical studies also reflect this dichotomy when they derive factors representing self-evaluation or TAT factors and behavioral and other concrete factors based on posttherapy achievement or life functioning (Cartwright et al., 1963).

Since "internal" and "external" criteria measure different human characteristics that are significant since changes frequently occur in both domains during therapy and since important decisions regarding the value of different techniques continue to be based on the extent of change induced by them, it is recommended that future studies include representative measures derived from this dichotomy. It is further suggested that therapy process measures be correlated with each of these kinds of criteria to determine more precisely how differing types of change are effected and whether single techniques have multiple effects. Energy might also be more vigorously devoted to specifying which type of client change is more crucial in a given case, thus laying the groundwork for eventually providing the kind of therapy that is most appropriate for the change desired. To merely dichotomize outcome measures into one of two categories and leave it at that is to oversimplify the issues involved in assessing change. Such dichotomies as internal–external, experiential–behavioral, dynamic–symptomatic, and surface–source are important and have clear theoretical implications. Nevertheless, there are other useful ways of conceptualizing outcome measures and their characteristics.

Meltzoff and Kornreich (1970) organized methods of measuring changes in patients into four categories based on the process that created the data: judgmental data, descriptive data, performance data, and status data. They suggest that before picking specific measures one must evaluate the kind of data desired from one or more of the available processes. *Judgmental data* are based on direct appraisals of the results of psychotherapy. These include patient, therapist, and outside evaluation of treatment. Data of this type are difficult if not impossible to cross-validate because they are by definition highly subjective and are a more or less gross evaluation of improvement. *Descriptive data*, on the other hand, may be collected from these same informants, but they are transformed into evaluative data by someone not involved in the therapy process. Descriptive data are "factual," for example, "How many drinks did you have today?" Factual information once obtained can be cross-validated and then placed on a rating scale. *Performance data* are observed rather than self-reported as in observations of therapy behavior or in situational tests. This would include behavior ratings by judges and the like. Finally, *status data* refer to physiological data and other data obtained from appropriate status examinations such as body weight. As Meltzoff and Kornreich point out, each of these sources of data involve problems with bias and require appropriate procedures to control for these extraneous biasing influences. Furthermore, it is likely, that some outcome measures call for a mixture of processes in creating data and thus make this conceptualization for categorizing outcome measures less clear-cut than it appears.

Unfortunately, the logic of Meltzoff and Kornreich's particular method of categorizing outcome data and its actual relevance to research results is not clear from their discussion, nor is a full elaboration of devices that fall in one or another category provided. However, one bit of logic that supports such a conceptualization is that measures so classified vary on the dimension of reactivity to experimental demand characteristics. Judgmental data to a great degree, and descriptive data as well as performance data to lesser degrees, can be exaggerated by the patient to reward and please therapists and researchers. This is less true of status data, such as physiological measurements that cannot be very well feigned by patients. This means that data generated through different processes vary in credibility and that judgmental data are the least convincing evidence of improvement.

Various other methods of conceptualizing outcome measures have been provided in several books published on the topic. Cone and Hawkins (1977) edited *Behavioral Assessment: New Directions in Clinical Psychology*. This volume reviewed a variety of topics and methods in behavioral assessment. Included are self-report and other "indirect" assessment methods, behavioral checklists, behavioral monitoring, physiological assessment, behavioral interviews, and computer-assisted behavioral assessment. Cone and Hawkins (1977) attempted to expand on methodological difficulties of behavioral assessment, elaborate on the advantages and disadvantages of various techniques, and identify new developments and future trends in assessment. The book is relevant to the widest variety of patient populations, educational settings, and age ranges. It should be of greatest interest to behavior therapists and researchers but also provides a valuable reference device for a wider variety of persons planning research into the effects of interventions on diverse patient populations.

Psychological Measurements in Psychopharmacology, edited by Pichot and Olivier-Martin (1974), describes and evaluates some of the more popular outcome measures used in psychopharmacology research. The volume was intended to review popular instruments and raise some problems with their use. Contributions including presentations of reliability and validity data were from the authors or creators of the instruments studied. This edited volume reviews instruments used for rating observable behaviors, mostly of psychotic inpatients (e.g., Nurse Observation Scale, Inpatient Multi-dimensional Psychiatric Scale, Brief Psychiatric Rating Scale); self-report symptom checklists, dealing mostly with neurotic patients (e.g., Hopkins Symptom Checklist, Middlesex Hospital Questionnaire), and ratings of moods and anxiety (e.g., Clyde Mood Scale, Beck Depression Inventory, Self-Rating Depression Scale).

The interested reader will find this a worthwhile although somewhat out of date volume that fails to include criticism from persons other than those who created the instruments considered. Even so, it remains a valuable source of reference materials on the evaluation of treatment methods.

Behavioral Assessment: A Practical Handbook, edited by Hersen and Bellack (1976), provides the reader with a comprehensive guide to instruments used in the evaluation of behavioral therapies. The book attempted to summarize methods of diagnosis and outcome assessment unique to behavioral interventions. The authors emphasized the need to assess motoric, physiological, and cognitive systems as well as to identify useful strategies for consulting room practice, outcome research, and single-case experimental research.

Although written by behavior therapists for behavior therapy, this book has clear application for the assessment of psychotherapy applied from a broad range of theoretical positions. Included in this volume are chapters on the assessment of anxiety and fear, depression, psychosis, addiction, retardation, marital and sexual dysfunction, and a variety of childhood disorders. The authors deal extensively with populations and problems where behavior therapy has been most frequently applied. Unfortunately, it emphasized behavioral problems (e.g., the development of social skills) to the exclusion of a more comprehensive view of patients and their symptoms. Nevertheless, it is an excellent reference text and should supply the researcher or practitioner with valuable suggestions and guidelines for assessing the effects of (especially behavioral) treatments.

The Handbook of Behavioral Assessment, edited by Ciminero et al. (1977), is another important text that attempts to summarize, organize, and evaluate devices used to assess treatment outcomes. The organization of this text allows the editors to emphasize (1) general issues in behavioral assessment, (2) general approaches to assessment (interviews, self-report schedules, self-monitoring, direct observation, and psychophysiological instrumentation), and (3) the measurement of outcomes with specific problem behaviors such as anxiety, sexual and marital conflict, addictive behaviors, and social skills.

As did Hersen and Bellack (1976), these authors chose to limit their focus to behavior therapy rather than a broader focus on less homogenous problems and treatments. Among the more unique and interesting chapters is one dealing with the use of analogue measures for outcome assessment. The focus is on identifying methods of data collection in the "laboratory" that approximate the type of data that it generalizes to in the natural environment (Nay, 1977). The methods employed represent creative attempts to solve the difficult measurement problems currently abounding in the field. These include paper–pencil measures, role playing, videotape presentations, and the use of confederates. For example, in an interesting test of the effects of assertiveness training, a person describing himself as a classmate of the treated client phoned the client at home some time after treatment termination and made increasingly inappropriate requests for help with a homework assignment. The level of inappropriateness at which the client refused to help the confederate was used as a dependent variable.

Behavioral Assessment of Adult Disorders, edited by Barlow (1981), considers behavioral assessment in neuropsychological disorders, schizophrenia, affective disorders, phobia, obsessive–compulsive disorders, psychophysiological disorders, alcohol abuse, sexual behaviors, eating disorders, social inadequacy, and marital dysfunction. Each chapter deals with DSM-III classification, tries to develop a model for assessment that emphasizes what should be assessed, and presents specific procedures for assessment. The greatest strength of this book seems to be its emphasis on diagnosis and conceptualization of problem areas. The reader desiring recommendations for specific devices will be left wanting. The fact that it emphasizes only behavioral assessment procedures also limits its suitability for directing researchers to a comprehensive and perhaps most viable assessment approach.

In all, this book is an important contribution to the field of outcome measurement, even though it is limited to behavior therapies and related perspectives. The interested researcher from any orientation can find much of value in this text.

Another text that has focused on behavioral assessment was also published in the 1970s, a "bumper" decade in behavioral assessment. *Behavior Therapy Assessment*, edited by Marsh and Terdal (1976), took an approach somewhat different from that in the aforementioned texts. It was organized around four general topics, going into great detail about a few specific devices. The chapters deal with (1) self-report measures such as the College Self-Expression Scale (a measure of assertiveness) and measures of fear and anxiety (2) the assessment of potential reinforcers such as the Reinforcement Survey Schedule and the Positive Reinforcement Observation Schedule, (3) observational assessment including the Classroom Observation Code and the Response–Class Matrix (a procedure for recording parent-child interactions), and (4) methods of behavioral interviewing such as the Drinking Profile.

Several of the contributions to this book were not original but consisted of "classic papers," albeit a bit out of date by present standards. The focus of this book was also very broad in that it included a greater emphasis on behavior modification with children in the classroom. In addition, its emphasis on diagnosis and measurement planning rather than specific assessment procedures makes it the least valuable of the behavioral assessment collection for guiding outcome research. Even so, it does bring together technical data on several popular measurement devices and methods and thus continues to be of some value.

Waskow and Parloff (1975) attempted to tap the resources of expert consultants in a National Institute of Mental Health (NIMH)-sponsored project aimed at unifying psychotherapy research by recommending a core battery for outcome assessment. Their conceptualization of outcome measurement divided measures on the basis of source of ratings: patient measures, therapist measures, relevant other measures, and independent clinical evaluations. Within each of these broad headings, such devices as paper–pencil test batteries, behavioral ratings, and psychophysiological data were considered. This project, which is discussed later in this chapter, provided a variety of opinions on ideal assessment procedures.

It is clear from the preceding review that a variety of methods have been employed to categorize outcome measures. Interestingly, most of the books on outcome assessment published in recent years have dealt with behavioral therapies and "behavioral" strategies. Most categorizations of outcome measures have been based on practical grounds emphasizing the source providing the data or have been derived directly from existing psychotherapy interventions. Researchers have had difficulty in finding a unified frame of reference from which to view outcome measures. Shall we consider outcome from the point of view of source of data, type of rating scale, aim of assessment, type of patient problem, process producing the data, or some other point of view?

A central issue in choosing a way of conceptualizing outcome measures is whether the guiding organizational principle should be based on a theory of mental health and adaptive functioning (i.e., tackle the problem of values) or on a pragmatic view of how devices are indeed related to one another. As the preceding discussion implies, it seems that little agreement will be reached on what constitutes an adequate assessment of psychotherapy outcome from the point of view of values. Certainly we are not now, nor may we ever arrive, at a point where we can reach widespread agreement on a definition of ideal mental health. Until such a point arrives, we will probably function with a pragmatic view of comprehensive outcome assessment. Such a conception places due emphasis on the fact that different *sources* of ratings correlate only at modest levels but seem to provide separate information that is important to consider. It also recognizes that the data can be collected by various *methods*. It can take the form of behavioral observations, psychophysiological monitoring, judgments, descriptions, and the like. Each of these methods of data collection presents a different view of the change process, and perhaps each should be represented in outcome assessment. For the sake of convergent validity, at least two different methods ought to be employed.

Finally, in addition to source and method, one must consider range of *content*. The focus of evaluation could be on such varied content areas as mood, symptoms (psychopathology), self-concept, role performance, self-regulation or self-control, and physical performance. The content is to be determined by the presenting problem or diagnosis and by therapist conceptions of mental health. Proper outcome assessment must cover a reasonable range of relevant content. Yet a single outcome study, using a wide variety of assessment sources and multiple "methods" of assessment, can hardly hope to adequately assess improvement in all relevant content areas. The result of this dilemma is that progress will be slow, and without systematic efforts at understanding the interrelationship of sources, methods, and content areas, progress will most likely be even slower.

Two implications of this situation are (1) research needs to be directed toward a more comprehensive understanding of outcome assessment devices and their interrelationships, (2) researchers, laypersons, and those formulating public policy need to exercise more caution in interpreting the findings of psychotherapy outcome studies. Surely the lack of comprehensive outcome assessment will lead to faulty overgeneralized conclusions. Future research into the interrelationships of outcome measures will go a long way toward clarifying the meaning of results from studies that of necessity must limit the number and type of outcome measures.

Progress toward adequate outcome assessment depends to a degree on our ability to conceptualize outcome measurement. To facilitate this process, we propose the following scheme as a method of ordering the selection of future outcome measures. Outcome measures vary on three dimensions that must be considered when choosing or evaluating the appropriate measures (Table 1.3).

TABLE 1.3. Three Critical Dimensions of Therapy Outcome Measures

Content[a]	Process	Source
Affective	Evaluational	Self-Report
Cognitive	Descriptive	Therapist Rating
Conative	Observational	Relevant Other
	Status	Trained Observer
		Instrumental

[a]For a more extensive justification and the philosophical roots of such a conceptualization, see Chapter 11 in this volume.

The content of measurement can be reduced to three functions of the individual—feelings, thoughts, and behavior. Since in reality individuals function as a "whole" rather than in mechanistic and compartmentalized ways, this conceptualization may cause some distortion of reality as information about the patient is collected. For example, when we collect data on grade point average, we are largely evaluating behavior, but these data also reflect feelings and thinking. Of considerable importance in planning and evaluating outcome research is a careful examination of the degree to which measures represent all three areas of content, rather than emphasizing a single domain.

In addition to variations in content, outcome measures vary in the "process" or the *manner* in which data come into existence. Thus data at the most subjective level are the result of judgments by one or more participants in the treatment. At a less subjective level they represent descriptions of past behavior or observations of ongoing behavior. The process through which data come into being has a serious impact on their credibility and meaningfulness.

Finally, researchers will want to attend to the perspective or source from which data are collected. The need to consider this factor is elaborated on elsewhere. At the root of this need, however, seems also to be the trustworthiness, meaning, and credibility of the data produced.

Despite the rather comprehensive nature of the three factors mentioned, there are other dimensions of obvious importance and interest in outcome assessment. A partial list of these and an excellent discussion was published by Gelso (1979). The conscientious researcher would not want to ignore the statistical properties of outcome measures, their degree of finality (extent to which they measure immediate versus ultimate consequences), the degree to which they are theory bound, their inclusiveness (versus global nature), or the extent to which they are meaningful to the particular patients who are being treated and studied.

ISSUES IN OUTCOME ASSESSMENT

Despite advances in methodology and the technical quality of assessment measures, scientifically sound conclusions are still severely hampered by a lack of sophistication in the application and interpretation of outcome measures. Nevertheless, some general principles for assessing change have been formulated and may be used to guide future research.

Change is Multidimensional

Clearly, one of the more important conclusions to be drawn from past psychotherapy outcome research is that the results of studies can be easily misunderstood and even misrepresented through failure to appreciate the multidimensionality of the change process. It has proved far too simplistic to expect clients to show consistent and integrated improvement as a result of therapy. The now necessary and common practice of applying multiple criterion measures in research studies has made it obvious that multiple measures of even simple fears do not yield unitary results. For example, we find in studies using multiple criterion measures (Mylar & Clement, 1972; Ross & Proctor, 1973; Wilson & Thomas, 1973) that a specific treatment used to reduce seemingly simple fears may result in a decrease in behavioral avoidance of the feared object while not affecting the self-reported level of discomfort associated with the feared object. Likewise, a physiological indicator of fear may show no change in response to a feared object as a result of treatment whereas improvement in subjective self-report will be marked. This means that divergent processes are occurring in therapeutic change, that people themselves embody divergent dimensions or phenomena, and that divergent methods of criterion measurement must be used to match the divergency in human beings and in the change processes that occur within them. This conclusion is further supported by factor analytic studies that have combined a variety of outcome measures.

The main factors derived from factor analytic data tend to be closely associated with the measurement method or the source of observation used in collecting data rather than being identified by some theoretical or conceptual variable that would be expected to cut across techniques of measurement. Among the most typical factors are (1) client self-evaluation, (2) therapist evaluation, (3) independent clinical judgment, (4) TAT or other fantasy evaluation, (5) indices of concrete overt behaviors, and (6) a miscellany of factors associated with specific instruments such as interest inventories, sentence completions, personality inventories (e.g., subsets of MMPI and CPI scales), and the like (Cartwright et al., 1963; Forsyth & Fairweather, 1961; Gibson et al., 1955; Nichols & Beck, 1960; Shore et al., 1965).

Numerous other studies report intercorrelations among two or more outcome measures; and, although the results sometimes appear to confirm the factor-analytic findings, they are highly variable and difficult to interpret cogently (Dietze, 1966, 1967; Ends & Page, 1957; Knapp, 1965; Parloff, et al., 1954, Paul, 1966; Shore et al., 1965; Shostrom & Knapp, 1966). A puzzling aspect of these studies is that significant correlations between different criteria occur consistently across studies in contradiction to the factor evidence, but they do not occur consistently within studies. It has not been determined whether this is because of chance fluctuations in the diverse data or is the result of some more substantial factors.

A recent study by Berzins et al. (1975) was addressed directly to the issue of consensus among criterion measures. The authors studied the relationship among outcome measures in 79 client-therapist dyads, using the MMPI, the Psychiatric Status Schedule, and the Current Adjustment Rating Scale. Sources of outcome measurement involved the client, therapist, and trained outside observers. Data from all three sources and a variety of outcome measures showed generally positive outcomes for the treated group as a whole at termination. There was the usual lack of consensus between criterion measures.

Their primary thesis, however, was that problems of intersource consensus can be resolved through the application of alternatives to conventional methods of analysis. The principal components analysis showed four components: (1) changes in patients' experienced distress as reported by clients on a variety of measures; (2) changes in observable maladjustment as noted by psychometrist, client, and therapist (an instance of intersource agreement); (3) changes in impulse expression (an instance of intersource disagreement between psychometrist and therapist); and (4) changes in self-acceptance (another type of client-perceived change). The practical implication of these findings is that a single criterion might suffice for measuring changes in observable maladjustment, whereas this practice would be misleading if "impulse control" were the outcome criterion. When outcome measures were partitioned into patient sources and other sources and analyzed with canonical analysis, further specification of areas of agreement between sources of outcome were identified. For example, considerable agreement between patient and psychometrist regarding changes in psychoticism were found.

Analysis of homogeneous subgroups allowed for yet another examination of the data by focusing on patients who showed similar patterns of change according to all three sources of data. About half the sample of clients were clustered in this way in four homogeneous but distinct classes. The largest group of clients (19) showed improvement agreed on by all sources, with increased self-acceptance probably the most characteristic change. Eleven clients formed the second cluster with the opposite pattern—namely, consensual deterioration. The last two cluster types were composed of six and five patients, and within each cluster a different pattern of criterion disagreement emerged.

The lack of consensus across sources of outcome evaluation, especially when each source is presumably assessing the same phenomena, has been viewed as a threat to the veracity of data. Indeed, it appears that outcome data do provide evidence about changes made by the individual as well as information about the differing value orientations and unconscious motivations of the individuals providing outcome data. This issue has been dealt with in several ways ranging from discussions of "biasing motivations" and ways to minimize bias to discussions of the value orientation of those involved.

The multiple assessment of outcome was also discussed in an article by Green et al. (1975). These authors compared final status scores, pretreatment to posttreatment difference scores, and direct ratings of global improvement in 50 patients seen in brief crisis-oriented psychotherapy. The Hopkins Symptom Checklist was filled out by the patient while a research psychiatrist rated the patient on the Psychiatric Evaluation Form and the Hamilton Depression Rating Scale. Ratings of global improvement were made by the patient and the therapist.

Green and colleagues concluded that the type of rating scale used has a great deal to do with the percentage of patients considered improved; more so, in fact, than improvement per se! They also suggested that outcome scores have more to do with the "finesse" of rating scales than whether ratings are "objective." Global improvement ratings by therapists and patients showed very high rates of improvement with no patients claiming to do worse. However, when patients had to rate their symptoms more specifically, as with the Hopkins Symptom Checklist, they were likely to indicate actual intensification of some symptoms and to provide more conservative data than estimates of change.

Additionally, patient and therapist global ratings correlated with final status but not initial status. This reinforces the claim that global improvement ratings primarily reflect final status rather than actual change in status. Even so, the results suggest that regardless of source, clients, therapists, and research psychiatrist were all focusing on similar variables, that is, a decrease in symptomatology and improvement in daily functioning.

The least efficient use of information seemed to result from difference scores. These scores were less reliable than status scores. The authors suggest that when a battery of scores is used to evaluate outcome, comparisons among groups or individuals should be made for sets of scores that have been corrected by multiple regression for initial values rather than correcting each scale by its own initial value.

This chapter underscores the importance of paying careful attention to the outcome measure used in a particular set of measures. Similar implications are apparent in several other recent studies. Willer and Miller (1978), for example, correlated three measures of client satisfaction with client demographic variables and outcome measures, such as client-rated goal attainment and length of stay in the hospital. The Client Satisfaction Scale, but not the other measures of satisfaction, correlated with client outcome. The authors suggest that more attention be paid to developing adequate satisfaction indices.

Green et al. (1979) studied the relationship between three measures of assertiveness: self-report; role playing, *in vivo*; and a standardized personality inventory. While there was a relationship between the two measures of self-reported assertiveness, these did not correlate highly with *in vivo* ratings of assertiveness. Thus outcomes assessed by means of these different methods and sources of outcome data did not produce the same picture of the individual.

Ellsworth et al. (1979) reported data from a Veterans Administration Cooperative study that sought to identify the ward milieu characteristics of effective psychiatric programs. This large-scale study examined 79 programs on 191 characteristics. Rather than treatment qualities that could be manipulated, the study dealt with so-called setting variables. The major finding was that patients on wards with a mixture of acute and chronic cases had better outcomes. Of interest here is the discovery that the data that were collected from patients, staff, and significant others showed little agreement in judging ward adjustment or the effectiveness of treatment. In addition, they report that ward return rates did not correlate with measures of community adjustment obtained from veterans or others.

In yet another study showing poor agreement between outcome variables, Boroto et al. (1978) examined the differences between judges and "clients" ratings of counselor effectiveness in an analogue study. They reported a high degree of reliability within rating systems but discrepancies between ratings when "clients" provided ratings. They question the advisability of throwing out clients as a rating source.

Major research effort should continue to be expended to more carefully delineate the divergent processes of change that take place as a result of the various therapies. This may best be done by studying more extensively the relationships among client characteristics, change techniques, and the specific kinds of change that occur (Fiske, 1971; Garfield et al. 1971a, b; Luborsky, 1971). Researchers and therapists must study specific kinds of change instead of general multiform change. A correlated activity would be a more rigorous and extensive development of measures for tapping different kinds of change. Measures based directly on factor analytic work would involve more rigorous specification of the variables underlying clients', therapists', and others' ratings of outcome to determine whether differences are due to different dimensions of the change process or are the result of differing values (Mintz et al., 1973).

Outcome Reflects Value Orientation

Several recent articles that have relevance to these issues have considered an underlying dilemma in assessing outcome: the question of values.

Strupp and Hadley (1977) have emphasized the importance of values in the assessment of therapeutic outcomes. Yet they also noted the lack of consensus on what constitutes mental health and how changes that occur in psychotherapy are to be evaluated. They emphasized the need to consider multiple perspectives in order to derive a comprehensive evaluation of psychotherapy outcome. To foster greater understanding of the effects of psychotherapy, these authors suggested taking into account three major points of view. As they note, these points of view concern value orientations that may at times be in conflict, although it is also possible for a consensus to be reached on what is valued.

The three perspectives from which they suggest we view change include society, the individual patient, and the mental health professional. With regard to society, these authors argue that one must take into account the need for society and its agents to view change in relation to the degree to which treatments effect the maintenance of social relations, institutions and prevailing standards. Thus the researcher would be concerned with such activities as criminal behavior, occupational stability, and related social role behavior. Outcome from the point of view of the individual often involves distinctly different criteria. Of more concern to the patient are subjective feelings of well-being, contentment, satisfaction, and even fulfillment. These feelings can exist in individuals who lack adequate role performance by societal values or can even be absent in individuals who are by most standards functioning well in society. Finally, Strupp and Hadley noted that mental health professionals impose their own conception of adequate and ideal functioning. Thus psychotherapy may be viewed as more or less successful at moving a person toward goals of ideal adjustment. Examples might include the client-centered conceptions of the fully functioning person or psychoanalytic models of integration.

Conclusions that follow such a conception of outcome include the idea that individuals may be viewed as improved and deteriorated when judged by several points of view. Judgments made from a single perspective are quite possibly only reflecting one of the three possible value orientations. This may result in a less than accurate picture of the entire result of treatment and, therefore, lead to faulty conclusions and decisions. The authors go on to suggest the development of standardized and generally accepted criteria of "good functioning" in the areas of behavior (society), feelings (individuals), and psychological structure (mental health practitioners).

The value of this discussion of outcome measurement seems to be its emphasis on the inclusion of different perspectives for evaluation of therapy. However, although there is an agreement between patients on subjective reactions after therapy, little agreement can be reached between those providing societal and professional perspectives. For example, rather than a distinct unitary point of view, professionals have much to disagree about when it comes to statements of ideal mental health and ideal outcomes. These discrepancies were highlighted by a recent series of articles discussing the place of values in psychotherapy.

Bergin (1980) argues that religion and value systems should in essence be the central focus of psychology. He states that psychotherapy presupposes implicit moral doctrines and that therapists thus are somewhat akin to "secular moralists." In lieu of their position as "secular moralists," he contends that therapists often promote change based on their own values and not those that are valued by the client or the community. He then pinpoints differences between theistic and clinical–humanistic values characteristic of therapist and societal value systems, which would implicitly belie different therapeutic objectives and evaluations. Some examples of these differences would be as follows (the former examples of each set represent the theistic view and the latter, the clinical–humanistic view as proposed by Bergin): (1) God is supreme versus the human is supreme; (2) one's relationship with God defines self-worth versus one's relationship with humans defines self-worth; (3) strict morality versus flexible morality; (4) marital commitment versus an open or no marriage at all; and (5) personal responsibility for ones own actions versus others being responsible for ones own actions.

Bergin contends that since value systems are implicit even within non-directive psychotherapeutic techniques, personal value systems must be faced openly by the psychotherapist and likewise be made known to the community. Bergin also contends that the personal belief factors of the client are possibly central to the process of therapeutic change and that it is thus important that psychotherapists respect the value systems of both the client and the community.

Bergin suggests that the value systems intuitively and experientially espoused by himself and his contemporaries be openly tested and evaluated as a means of justifying that particular system's cliental as well as communal value. For example, he proposes as a testable hypothesis for future consideration that religious communities providing the combination of a viable belief structure and a network of loving, emotional support, would manifest lower rates of emotional and social pathology and physical disease.

In summation, Bergin states that inasmuch as psychotherapy is directed toward goals that are selected in value terms, values and religion should become the rightful "cynosure" and not the so-called derelict of psychology.

Ellis (1980), in response to Bergin's article, "Psychotherapy and Religious Values," contends that dogmatic religion or orthodox values are significantly correlated with human pathology. He argues that human disturbance is often the result of absolutistic thinking, or what Eric Hoffer refers to as "true believerism." Ellis contends that personality types with inclinations toward absolutism or extreme devoutism best minimize these tendencies by discarding orthodox philosophies. He argues that those people suffering from pathologies related to "extreme religiosity" might best benefit from consultation with a therapist who adheres to less orthodox values than they themselves do and, most important for our discussion, has goals more closely associated with humanism than theism.

Rather than defining self-worth as either one's relationship with God (as defined in Bergin's paradigm as the theistic view) or as one's relationship with people (as defined in Bergin's paradigm as the clinical–humanistic view), Ellis (in conjunction with his definition of the clinical–humanistic–atheistic view) defines self-worth as something that can be had for the asking, independent of either God or humans. Another example of the clinical–humanistic–atheistic view would be the acceptability of choosing either a conventional marriage, an open marriage, or no marriage, as opposed to the presumed preference for a conventional marriage arrangement espoused by Bergin and typical of traditional societal values. Clearly, mental health professionals show great divergence in their value orientations.

Returning to the Strupp and Hadley (1977) position, we cannot assume that patients' judgments of outcome represent distinct judgments of only subjective discomfort. Although they may represent primarily this factor, they may well represent some notions of theoretically idealized mental health. They may also incorporate to some degree social values about cooperation and conformity. Finally, criteria that represent societal interests may also reflect ideal notions of mental health. For example, both Freudians and "society" may consider divorce as a poor outcome, although for different reasons. From one perspective it is seen as a failure to maintain a satisfying, intimate relationship with a person of the opposite sex (resolving the oedipal complex), whereas from the other it may be seen as a poor outcome because it leads to numerous expensive failures in functioning for the individual and other family members. Strupp and Hadley's conceptualization of outcome assumes far too much uniformity in the values it associates with "society," "mental health practitioners," and "patients." Although the Strupp and Hadley (1977) position is helpful in showing the subjectivity and value-laden issues inherent in change assessment, it is not a perspective that leads to the selection of a battery of outcome measures. Also, it is not an organization that does much to conceptualize the variety of outcome measures that can be applied (e.g., it completely ignores physiologically based change measures). It does not provide a satisfactory base for guiding instrument choice in outcome measurement.

Can Individualized Outcome Criteria Be Effectively Used?

In assessing changes in groups of patients, it is common for researchers to apply a single criterion such as the MMPI to all the patients in treatment regardless of their diagnosis. By giving all clients the same scales while considering movement in opposite directions for different clients' improvement, or by using diverse standardized measures tailored to the individual client, more precision can be brought into outcome studies. The possibility of tailoring change criteria to each individual in therapy is being mentioned with increasing frequency, and the idea offers intriguing alternatives for resolving several recalcitrant dilemmas in measuring change.

This notion strongly supports the development of a general trend toward specific rather than global improvement indices. Thus, if a person seeks help for severe depression and shows little evidence of pathological anxiety, we would emphasize changes in depression rather than changes in anxiety level or global psychological status. Taken together, the trends to specify and individually tailor criteria offer a strong antidote to the sometimes vague and unimpressive conclusions so often reported in the outcome literature.

An example of this trend that is receiving widespread attention and increased use is Goal Attainment Scaling (GAS) (Kiresuk and Sherman, 1968). Goal Attainment Scaling requires that a number of mental health goals be set up prior to treatment. These goals are formulated by an individual or a combination of clinicians, client, and/or a committee assigned to the task. For each goal specified, a scale with a graded series of likely outcomes, ranging from least to most favorable, is devised. These goals are formulated and specified with sufficient precision that an unfamiliar observer can determine the point at which the patient is functioning at a given time. The procedure also allows for transformation of the overall attainment into a standard score.

In using this method for the treatment of obesity, for example, one goal could be the specification and measurement of weight loss. A second goal could be a reduction of depressive symptoms as measured by a scale from a standardized test such as the MMPI. The particular scale examined could be varied from patient to patient, and, of course, other specific types of diverse measures from additional points of view could also be added. The value of such a procedure becomes even more obvious when one reads examples of traditional research procedures that assume unidirectional changes to be valuable for all. Vosbeck, for example [reported by Volsky et al. (1965)] found that in using "grade-getting" and "degree-getting" behaviors as criteria for effectiveness of college counseling, counselors were often working "against" themselves by encouraging some individuals to seek alternatives to a college degree. In the same way, an increase in anxiety instead of a decrease could be the most beneficial goal of some therapy.

Woodward et al. (1978) examined the role of GAS in studying family therapy outcome. The authors used content analysis to analyze the nature of the goals that were set and the types of goal set by therapists of different types. In their study, which focused on termination and six-month follow-up goals, 270 families were considered. This resulted in an analysis of 1005 goals. The authors, who seem to be advocates of GAS, reported that the ratings were reliable and reflected diverse changes in the families studied. They also noted that GAS correlated with other measures of outcome and thus seemed to be valid. This interesting although somewhat uncritical report is a good demonstration of the flexibility and wealth of information resulting from the use of these procedures.

Recently, Calsyn and Davidson (1978) reviewed and assessed GAS as an evaluative procedure. These authors suggest that GAS has poor reliability in that there is insufficient agreement between raters on the applicability of predefined content categories to particular patients. In addition, the interrater agreement for goal attainment ranged from $r = .51$ to .85, indicating variability between those making ratings (e.g., therapist, client, expert judge). No studies were found dealing with the temporal stability of GAS, whereas at least one study suggested that ratings obtained through telephone interviews had some similarity ($r = .66$) to those obtained in person. Simons et al. (1978) examined the relationship between GAS scores based on patient records and independent phone interviews, client global improvement, and satisfaction ratings. The authors found a significant relationship between phone ratings and case record ratings and concluded that this relatively simple method of data collection may be quite useful. The method used did not require therapist time and provided an independent assessment of outcome. Surprisingly, global satisfaction with treatment reported by the client did not correlate with any GAS scores or with therapist global ratings of improvement.

In general, studies that have correlated GAS improvement ratings with other ratings of improvement such as MMPI scores, client satisfaction, and therapist improvement have failed to show substantial agreement and are quite disappointing. (Frequently, coefficients have been below .30.) As Calsyn and Davidson (1978) point out, the use of GAS also frequently eliminates the use of statistical procedures, such as covariance, that could otherwise be used to correct for sampling errors. The authors feel that because of this problem, as well as the unknown effects of poor reliability, it is inappropriate to use GAS as the sole outcome measure. They suggest that GAS be used in conjunction with standard scales applied to all patients.

Given the above problems, the likelihood that units of change derived from individually tailored goals are unequal and therefore hardly comparable, the likelihood that different goals are differentially susceptible to psychotherapy influence, the fact that some therapies have a unitary goal or set of goals, and the improbability of treating samples with a homogeneous problem, the status of individually tailored goals is tenuous. The findings thus far reported are not highly supportive of GAS methodology. Effective individualization of goals remains an ideal rather than a reality.

Status of Traditional Personality Assessment

Currently, there is considerable skepticism about the value of personality assessment devices as applied in outcome studies. This skepticism comes from various quarters, including (1) the popularity of behavioral approaches and corresponding lack of interest in standard assessment methods that lead to assigning people to diagnostic categories, identifying static traits, or elaborating on internal dynamics, (2) the humanistically derived belief that the traditional testing and diagnostic enterprise is itself an unhelpful way of relating to persons seeking help, and (3) the belief that personality tests don't work very well and have unimpressive validity coefficients because they largely measure personality traits to the exclusion of situational variables (Mischel, 1972, 1977) and the environment in general.

Although traditional psychological tests should not be considered as abandoned, the practice of assessing situation-specific behaviors rather than global qualities that are viewed as signs or indirect manifestations of important general tendencies (e.g., that human movement in Rorschach responding indicates creativity or impulse control) should be emphasized. Assessments that attempt to measure situation-specific behavior, such as social anxiety related to skill deficiency in heterosexual relationships rather than traditional personality tests (especially projective tests), should be used in outcome research.

Standard Assessment Procedures Do Seem Desirable Although Not Yet Feasible

Waskow and Parloff (1975) published a report of their NIMH-sponsored attempt to recommend a battery of assessment devices that could form the core of assessment in psychotherapy outcome studies. A routinely given set of measures could go a long way toward coordinating and accelerating the advancement of knowledge about change endeavors. They were able to draw on the expertise of several well-known psychotherapy researchers and thereby develop a standard test battery. This battery includes the Hopkins Symptom Checklist (Derogatis et al., 1973, 1974); Target Complaints (Battle et al., 1966); the Psychiatric Status Schedule (Spitzer et al., 1967, 1970), the MMPI (Dahlstrom et al., 1972), and either the Katz Adjustment Scales (Katz & Lyerly, 1963) or the Personal Adjustment and Role Skills Scales (Ellsworth, 1975).

Of course, much controversy is bound to develop over the appropriate devices to be included in such a battery, and at present it is not possible to reach agreement. Our impression of the recommendations of the Waskow–Parloff consultants is that they seem to recommend good measures that have wide, but not universal appeal, especially among behavioral researchers. The value of the battery as a whole has not been demonstrated. Now that these recommendations have been in existence for a reasonably long period of time, we can conclude that they have not had the desired impact on the field. Diverse treatment samples, differences concerning valued directions of change, and theoretical and conceptual preferences, all make the possibility of an effectively applied, single-core battery doubtful.

The approach of this book, in contrast to the core battery approach, is to develop several alternative batteries centered around diagnostic criteria and varied sources of data. Although it still appears that agreement may not be reached, perhaps the alternatives for effective assessment in outcome evaluation will be reduced. In addition, problems related to evaluating outcome will be clarified and recommended solutions proposed. At any rate, the possibility of unifying assessment efforts and thus accelerating the acquisition of knowledge about treatment effects is exciting.

REFERENCES

Barlow, D. H. *Behavioral assessment of adult disorders*. New York: Guilford Press, 1981.

Battle, C. C., Imber, S. D., Hoehn-Saric, R., Stone, A. R., Nash, C., & Frank, J. D. Target complaints as criteria of improvement. *American Journal of Psychotherapy*, 1966, **20**, 184–192.

Bergin, A. E. The evaluation of therapeutic outcomes. In A. E. Bergin & S. L. Garfield (Eds.), *Handbook of psychotherapy and behavior changes*. New York: Wiley, 1971.

Bergin, A. E. Negative effects revisited: A reply. *Professional Psychology*, 1980, **11**, 93–100.

Bergin, A. E., & Lambert, M. J. The evaluation of therapeutic outcomes. In S. L. Garfield, & A. E. Bergin (Eds.), *Handbook of psychotherapy and behavior change: An empirical evaluation* (2nd ed.). New York: Wiley, 1978.

Berzins, J. I., Bednar, R. L., & Severy, L. J. The problem of intersource consensus in measuring therapeutic outcomes: New data and multivariate perspectives. *Journal of Abnormal Psychology*, 1975, **84**, 10–19.

Boroto, D. R., Kalafat, J. D., & Cohen, L. H. Client vs. rater judgments of counselor effectiveness. *Journal of Clinical Psychology*, 1978, **34**, 188–193.

Calsyn, R. J., & Davidson, W. S. Do we really want a program evaluation strategy based solely on individualized goals? A critique of goal attainment scaling. *Evaluation of Study Revised Annual*, 1978, 700–713.

Cartwright, D. S., Kirtner, W. L., & Fiske, D. W. Method factors in changes associated with psychotherapy. *Journal of Abnormal and Social Psychology*, 1963, **66**, 164–175.

Cattell, R. B. Evaluating therapy as total personality change: Theory and available instruments. *American Journal of Psychotherapy*, 1966, **20**, 69–88.

Ciminero, A. R., Calhoun, K. S., & Adams, H.E. (Eds.). *Handbook of behavioral assessment*. New York: Wiley, 1977.

Cone, J. D., & Hawkins, R. P. (Eds.). *Behavioral assessment: New directions in clinical psychology*. New York: Brunner/Mazel, 1977.

Dahlstrom, W. G., Welsh, G. A., & Dahlstrom, L. E. *An MMPI handbook: Volume I. Clinical applications*. (Rev. ed.). Minneapolis: University of Minnesota Press, 1972.

Derogatis, L. R., Lipman, R. S., & Covi, L. SCL-90: An outpatient psychiatric rating scale (preliminary report). *Psychopharmacology Bulletin*, 1973, **9**, 13–27.

Derogatis L. R., Lipman, R. S., Rickels, K., Uhlenhuth, E. H., & Covi, L. The Hopkins Symptom Checklist (HSCL): A measure of primary symptom dimensions. In P. Pichot & R. Olivier-Martin (Eds.), *Psychological measurements in psychopharmacology*. Basel, Switzerland: Karger, 1974.

Dietze, D. Staff and patient criteria for judgments of improvement in mental health. *Psychological Reports*, 1966, **19**, 379–387.

Dietze, D. Consistency and change in judgment of criteria for mental health improvement. *Journal of Clinical Psychology*, 1967, **23**, 307–310.

Ellis, A. Psychotherapy and atheistic values: A response to A.E. Bergin's "Psychotherapy and Religious Values." *Journal of Consulting and Clinical Psychology*, 1980, **48**, 635–639.

Ellsworth, R. B. Consumer feedback in measuring the effectiveness of mental health programs. In E. L. Struening & M. Guttentag (Eds.), *Handbook of evaluation research*. Beverly Hills, Calif.: Sage Publications, 1975.

Ellsworth, R. B., Casey, N. A., Hickey, R. H., Twenlar, S. W., Collins, J. F., Schoolover, R. A., Hylar, L., & Hesselroade, J. R. Some characteristics of effective psychiatric treatment programs. *Journal of Consulting and Clinical Psychology*, 1979, **47**, 799–817.

Ends, E. J., & Page, C. W. Functional relationships among measures of anxiety, ego strength, and adjustment. *Journal of Clinical Psychology*, 1957, **13**, 148–150.

Fiske, D. W. The shaky evidence is slowly put together. *Journal of Consulting and Clinical Psychology*, 1971, **37**, 314–315.

Forsyth, R., & Fairweather, G. W. Psychotherapeutic and other hospital treatment criteria. *Journal of Abnormal and Social Psychology*, 1961, **62**, 598–605.

Garfield, S. L., Prager, R. A., & Bergin, A. E. Evaluation of outcome in psychotherapy. *Journal of Consulting and Clinical Psychology*, 1971, **37**, 307–313. (a)

Garfield, S. L., Prager, R. A., & Bergin, A. E. Evaluating outcome in psychotherapy: A hardy perennial. *Journal of Consulting and Clinical Psychology*, 1971, **37**, 320–322. (b)

Gelso, C. J. Research in counseling: Methodological and professional issues. *Counseling Psychologist*, 1979, **8**, 7–35.

Gibson, R. L., Snyder, W. U., & Ray, W. S. A factor analysis of measures of change following client-centered psychotherapy. *Journal of Counseling Psychology*, 1955, **2**, 83–90.

Green, B. L., Burkhart, B. R., & Harrison, W. H. Personality correlates of self-report, role-playing and in vivo measures of assertiveness. *Journal of Consulting and Clinical Psychology*, 1979, **47**, 16–24.

Green, B. L., Gleser, G. C., Stone, W. N., & Siefert, R. F. Relationships among diverse measures of psychotherapy outcome. *Journal of Consulting and Clinical Psychology*, 1975, **43**, 689–699.

Hall, J. N. Assessment procedures used in studies on long-stay patients: A survey of papers published in the British Journal of Psychiatry. *British Journal of Psychiatry*, 1979, **135**, 330–335.

Hersen, M., & Bellack, A. *Behavioral assessment: A practical handbook*. New York: Pergamon, 1976.

Katz, M. M., & Lyerly, S. B. Methods for measuring adjustment and social behavior in the community: 1. Rationale, description, discriminative validity and scale development. *Psychological Reports*, 1963, **13**(4), 1503–1555.

Kiresuk, T. J., & Sherman, R. E. Goal attainment scaling: A general method for evaluating comprehensive community mental health programs. *Community Mental Health Journal*, 1968, **4**, 443–53.

Knapp, R. R. Relationship of a measure of self-actualization to neuroticism and extroversion. *Journal of Consulting Psychology*, 1965, **29**, 168, 172.

Knight, R. P. Evaluation of the results of psychoanalytic therapy. *American Journal of Psychiatry*, 1941, **98**, 434–446.

Lambert, M. J., & Bergin, A. E. Psychotherapeutic outcomes and issues related to behavioral and humanistic approaches. *Cornell Journal of Social Relations*, 1973, **8**, 47–61.

Levine, S. B., & Argle, D. The effectiveness of sex therapy for chronic secondary psychological impotence. *Journal of Sex and Marital Therapy*, 1978, **4**, 235–258.

Luborsky, L. Perennial mystery of poor agreement among criteria for psychotherapy outcome. *Journal of Consulting and Clinical Psychology*, 1971, **37**, 316–319.

Malan, D. H. *Toward the validation of dynamic psychotherapy: A replication*. New York: Plenum Press, 1976. (b)

Marsh, E. J., & Terdal, L. G. (Eds.). *Behavior therapy assessment*. New York: Springer Publishing Company, 1976.

Masters, W. H. & Johnson, V. E. *Human sexual inadequacy*. Boston: Little, Brown, 1970.

Meltzoff, J., & Kornreich, M. *Research in psychotherapy*. New York: Atherton Press, 1970.

Mintz, J., Auerbach, A. H., Luborsky, L., & Johnson, M. Patient's therapist's, and observers' views of psychotherapy: A "Rashomon" experience or a reasonable consensus. *British Journal of Psychology*, 1973, **46**, 83–89.

Mischel, W. Direct versus indirect personality assessment: Evidence and implications. *Journal of Consulting and Clinical Psychology*, 1972, **38**, 319–324.

Mischel, W. On the future of personality research. *American Psychologist*, 1977, **32**, 246–254.

Mylar, J. L., & Clement, P. W. Prediction and comparison of outcome in systematic desensitization and implosion. *Behavior Research and Therapy*, 1972, **10**, 235–246.

Nay, W. R. Analogue measures. *Handbook of behavioral assessment*. New York: Wiley, 1977.

Nichols, R. C., & Beck, K. W. Factors in psychotherapy change. *Journal of Consulting Psychology*, 1960, **24**, 388 399.

Parloff, M. B., Kelman, H. C., & Frank, J. D. Comfort, effectiveness and self-awareness as criteria of improvement in psychotherapy. *American Journal of Psychiatry*, 1954, 3, 343–351.

Paul, G. L. *Effects of insight, desensitization, and attention placebo treatment of anxiety*. Palo Alto, California: Stanford University Press, 1966.

Pichot, P., & Olivier-Martin, R. (Eds.). *Psychological measurement in psychopharmacology*. Basel, Switzerland: Karger, 1974.

Ross, S. M. & Proctor, S. Frequency and duration of hierarchy item exposure in a systematic desensitization analogue. *Behavior Research and Therapy*, 1973, **11**, 303–312.

Shore, M. F., Massimo, J. L., & Ricks, D.F. A factor analytic study of psychotherapeutic change in delinquent boys. *Journal of Clinical Psychology*, 1965, **21**, 208–212.

Shostrom, E. L., & Knapp, R. R. The relationship of a measure of self-actualization (POI) to a measure of pathology (MMPI) and to therapeutic growth. *American Journal of Psychotherapy*, 1966, **20**, 193–202.

Simons, L. S., Morton, T.L., Wade, T. C., & McSharry, D. M. Treatment outcome and follow-up evaluation based on client case records in a mental health center. *Journal of Consulting and Clinical Psychology*, 1978, **46**, 246–261.

Spitzer, R. L., Endicott, J., & Cohen, G. *The Psychiatric Status Schedule: Technique for evaluating social and role functioning and mental status*. Biometrics Research, New York State Psychiatric Institute, 1967.

Spitzer, R. L., Endicott, J., Fleiss, J. L., & Cohen, J. The psychiatric status schedule: A technique for evaluating psychopathology and impairment in role functioning. *Archives of General Psychiatry*, 1970, **23**, 41–55.

Strupp, H. H., & Hadley, S. W. A tripartite model of mental health and therapeutic outcomes: With special reference to negative effects in psychotherapy. *American Psychologist*, 1977, **32**, 187–196.

Truax, C. B., & Carkhuff, R. R. *Toward effective counseling and psychotherapy*. Chicago: Aldine, 1967.

Volsky, T., Jr., Magoon, T. J., Norman, W. T., & Hoyt, D. P. *The outcomes of counseling and psychotherapy*. Minneapolis: University of Minnesota Press, 1965.

Wachtel, P. L. *Psychoanalysis and behavior therapy: Toward integration*. New York: Basic Books, 1977.

Waskow, I. E., & Parloff, M. B. *Psychotherapy change measures*. Washington, D.C.: DHEW, No. 74–120, 1975.

Willer, B., & Miller, G. H. On the relationship of client satisfaction to client characteristics and outcome of treatment. *Journal of Clinical Psychology*, 1978, **34**, 157–160.

Wilson, G. T., & Thomas, M. G. W. Self versus drug-produced relaxation and the effects of instructional set in standardized systematic desensitization. *Behavior Research and Therapy*, 1973, **11**, 279–288.

Woodward, C. A., Santa-Barbara, J., Levin, S., & Epstein, N. B. The role of goal attainment scaling in evaluating family therapy outcome. *American Journal of Orthopsychiatry*, 1978, **48**, 464–475.

CHAPTER 2

Meta Analysis in Mental Health Treatment Outcome Evaluation

EDWIN R. CHRISTENSEN AND DONALD T. REICK

Meta analysis, or "the analysis of analyses" (Glass, 1976), may be defined as the use of data analytic procedures, practices, or techniques where multiple studies or sets of data are used. Research methods utilizing these techniques have been found in the fields of educational research, social psychology research, psychotherapy outcome research, program evaluation research, and mental health outcome research. Until recently, absolute frequencies or other gross numerical indicators have been used for literature reviews in behavioral and social sciences. This type of review remains a valuable tool in the array of discovery methods. However, because of the large volume of studies and data accruing in various fields of the social and behavioral sciences, the potential for statistical analyses of multiple data sets, per se, cannot be ignored. Most recently, investigators from different fields (Glass, 1976; Kulik et al., 1979; Rosenthal, 1978; Smith & Glass, 1977) have espoused the aggregation of the large amounts of data from past evaluations or research studies with different dependent measures as sources of discovery.

While admitting the potential for broad application, the discussion here is necessarily limited to (1) a brief illustrative review of meta analysis in educational research, social psychology research, program evaluation research, and psychotherapy outcome research, (2) a review of efforts utilizing techniques previously tried in mental health outcome research, and (3) for the investigator concerned with the practical logistics of obtaining various levels of data, indications of what level of data is needed with the various techniques. This review of techniques and indications of data required assumes that meta analysis is a group of methods for aggregating data from different sets of data with different dependent measures. This view of meta analysis is consistent with the recent meta analyses in psychotherapy outcome literature (Shapiro & Shapiro, 1981; Smith & Glass, 1977, 1980).

META ANALYSES IN BEHAVIORAL SCIENCE RESEARCH

Under the leadership of Gene V. Glass and Mary Lee Smith, some educational research has been conducted using meta analysis techniques. For example, Glass (1976) illustrated the use of meta analysis in educational research by referring to a doctoral thesis by White (1976) on the relationship between socioeconomic status and achievement. Areas where there is abundant research such as class size related to achievement, reading research, programmed instruction, and instructional television were also suggested by Dr. Glass as fields that could profitably use a meta analysis approach. As examples of work in these areas, Glass and Smith (1978) cited two unpublished doctoral dissertations in educational research entitled "The Effects of Individually Paced Instruction in Mathematics" (Hartley, 1977) and "The Effects of Television on Social Behavior" (Hearold, 1978). A further example of this type of analysis is the work of Kulik et al. (1979), who published a study in which they evaluated the research on Keller's personalized instruction system. They analyzed 75 comparative studies of this instruction approach with the use of meta analysis techniques. Light (1979) has also written on methods and procedures to use under given situations such as "conflicting research findings" in education. The potential for using meta analysis in educational research is great, particularly where threats of making uninformed legislative decisions are present. For example, the governor of Minnesota recently used Glass and Smith's (1979) meta analysis on "the relationship of class size and achievement" to influence funding decisions. Meta analysis in educational research has only recently been attempted, and hence is currently underutilized.

Some investigators have capitalized on the volumes of previous research in social psychology by applying meta analysis techniques. Rosenthal (1976) accomplished a meta analysis of findings in over 300 studies on interpersonal expectations His results showed that expectations have clear effects on the outcome of experimental studies. An associate of Rosenthal's (Hall, 1978) studied the effects of gender on the decoding of nonverbal cues by use of a meta analysis approach. Her results showed that females in the typical study are moderately superior at judging nonverbal cues. Strube (1980) suggested the use of meta analysis techniques in cross-cultural social psychology along with limitations and cautions. Several issues for consideration in combining statistical probabilities and in the use of "effect sizes" were elucidated for this type of research. Strube and Garcia (1980) also conducted a meta analysis of Fiedler's Contingency Model of Leadership Effectiveness, showing that the model is able to predict group performance with a high degree of success.

A fair amount of work has been done in the field of program evaluation research with meta-analytic-type techniques. Empirical "meta evaluations" were reviewed by Cook and Gruder (1978), who identified seven different models of "meta evaluation." They were categorized into two broad classes, with the first class comprising those studies that use data subsequent to the primary evaluation and the second class comprising those studies that use data simultaneously with the primary evaluation. Their work provided hints to the program evaluator for where and how the different models might apply.

Other fields where meta analyses have been used are the related fields of psychotherapy outcome research and mental health outcome evaluation. These are reviewed in the next section.

PSYCHOTHERAPY OUTCOME RESEARCH AND MENTAL HEALTH OUTCOME EVALUATION

Since Eysenck's negative assertions concerning the efficacy of psychotherapy (Eysenck, 1952, 1966), there have been a number of other works written using studies with different methodologies and different outcome measures to draw conclusions in addition to and at variance with Eysenck. Meltzoff and Kornreich (1970) made comparisons from studies with different methodologies and different measures on variables such as therapist–client match versus therapist–client nonmatch and the efficacy of different types of therapy. Bergin (1971), Lambert (1976), and Bergin and Lambert (1978) drew conclusions regarding the general efficacy of psychotherapy, the relative difference in schools of psychotherapy, and other variables from studies with different outcome measures and different methodologies. Luborsky et al. (1975) studied different variables relating to psychotherapy and arrived at both specific and general conclusions from studies with different methodologies and different outcome measures. All these reviews used methods where frequency of studies with given results indicated the preponderance of one conclusion over another. Only elementary analyses were used, such as calculations of percentages and medians. For example, Eysenck (1952) reviewed several studies and reported median and mean estimates of spontaneous remission. Lambert (1976), in response to this, reviewed the same studies plus additional ones and arrived at conclusions markedly different from those of Eysenck. Both investigators, however, used essentially the same procedures, that is, calculations of percentages and medians.

Glass (1976) suggested the use of more sophisticated data analytic methods in the analyses of educational research. Glass illustrated the kind of techniques to be used by displaying analyses of psychotherapy outcome studies conducted by himself and Dr. Mary Lee Smith. Smith and Glass (1977) used techniques suggested in the earlier paper (Glass, 1976) to further explain their analysis of psychotherapy outcome. They calculated the statistic "effect size" (ES) based on posttest experimental group mean minus posttest control group mean divided by the standard deviation of the control group or $ES = (M_e - M_c)/SD_c$. Smith and Glass (1977) drew conclusions about the validity of psychotherapy, differences between schools of psychotherapy, and other variables thought to affect psychotherapy outcome. They also used a more sophisticated data analytic technique where regression analysis provided some statistical control of variables influencing effect sizes.

These findings triggered anew the storm of controversy over Eysenck's earlier assertions regarding psychotherapy (Eysenck, 1978; Gallo, 1978; Glass & Smith, 1978; Lambert, 1979). Shapiro and Shapiro (1981) showed results from a meta analysis that agreed with the general conclusion on psychotherapy efficacy in Smith and Glass (1977). Their meta analysis of 143 outcome studies was designed to account for previous criticism (Rachman & Wilson, 1980) of the Smith and Glass (1977, 1980) work. The results showed an average "effect size" similar to that obtained by Smith and Glass and indications of technique accounting for only 10% of total variance.

There have been at least two previously published efforts to compare data sets from outcome measures with different scale definitions and different scale metrics in mental health outcome research and evaluation. Newman and Carter (1975) used therapist ratings of patient "level of functioning" with different scale definitions and different metrics to conduct a comparative analysis of some community mental health facilities. A special method for developing statistical control was used in the analysis of the data.

In the State of Utah the community mental health centers and the State Hospital have used a meta analysis approach when analyzing sets of data with different outcome measures from the different mental health facilities. The results of the meta analyses of program outcome measures in Utah are included in evaluation reports by Geertsen (1979, 1980). Some of the analysis methods, illustrated in the next section, yielded results included in these reports. Evaluation and research on outcomes of mental health intervention is a domain where a meta analysis approach could often be useful.

TECHNIQUES AND PROCEDURES FOR MENTAL HEALTH OUTCOME EVALUATION AND RESEARCH

The balance of this chapter is devoted to a discussion and elaboration of some data aggregation methods or techniques that may be useful in various evaluation situations. In the investigation of many research "questions," the cost-effective use of data becomes paramount. For instance, when planning a meta analysis, what data will be required for the techniques chosen should be reviewed because the practicalities and costs of data retrieval influence methodology decisions. The availability of raw data versus the availability of descriptive statistics, to the investigator, will affect which data aggregations can be computed. Since this issue influences which techniques will be used, the methods illustrated in this chapter are categorized by what level of data is required. Some situations, with different levels of data required, may be conceptualized as follows: (1) literature review of studies where written conclusions or basic numerical indicators are used to indicate the relative stability or instability of findings across studies; (2) situations where previously calculated descriptive statistics of studies or of data sets are used as the metrics of analysis; and (3) circumstances in which original raw data are transformed or manipulated to expose or elaborate across data set or across-study findings. These situations are respectively illustrative of three levels of data required in various data aggregations or types of meta analysis. Combinations of these situations are often found in different meta analysis investigations.

The first group of procedures to be reviewed, is that group used in situations where traditional hypothesis tests exist and lend themselves to aggregation.

COMBINATION OF STATISTICAL PROBABILITIES

In research and elementary statistics literature, testing for differences between two groups with *t* tests has long been recognized as a method for estimation of the probability of the result being a chance finding. Where study or evaluation results based on two group comparisons exist for two or more samples with differing dependent measures, the actual probability levels may be combined across dependent measures to examine the generalizability or stability of findings on given hypotheses. To illustrate, the case may be used where posttreatment experimental group scores are compared to posttreatment control group scores and probabilities of the results being chance are generated. The resulting *p* levels could then be combined with *p* levels of other studies testing the same hypothesis, but using different measures. The final result would be a combined *p* level for studies or data sets *x* through *y*. These studies might be using the same treatment, while not using the same measures, subject pools, or treatment staff. The combination of *p* levels in this manner is an aggregation method espoused by Rosenthal (1978) and others (Strube, 1980; Strube & Garcia, 1980).

Following the work of Smith and Glass (1977), Rosenthal (1978, 1979) published techniques to be used when combining the probabilities of independent studies where two groups are compared at a time. Rosenthal's (1978) paper elucidated nine techniques for combining statistical probabilities indicating advantages, limitations, and applicability of techniques. A serious bias or threat to this procedure (and all meta analysis) was the possibility that studies that verify the null hypothesis may not be published at an equally high rate as studies not verifying the null hypothesis. Also, trends in what is popular may influence what is published, thereby creating uncontrolled bias in what studies or data sets are available for use in meta analysis. Methods for estimating the probability of this kind of bias were discussed by Rosenthal (1978, 1979).

After reviewing previous efforts to determine the validity of Fiedler's leadership effectiveness model, Strube and Garcia (1980) used a meta analysis approach that combined probabilities of significance tests. They used one of the methods discussed by Rosenthal (1978) and presented in Mosteller and Bush (1954). The method was to translate actual one-tailed probabilities into Z scores. These Z values were then combined using Stouffer's (Mosteller & Bush, 1954) formula.

In another paper Strube (1980) discusses the use of combined probabilities, gives an illustrative formula, and also discusses a technique for estimating the probability of bias. The number of additional hypothesis tests necessary to change the combined P level in a given analysis to a desired level was the method used. An advantage of this determination was that it provided a way to estimating the validity of the combined findings in "relation to the felt completeness of the literature review."

These techniques would be useful where there is more than one hypothesis test. For example, they could be used in mental health outcome research where the evaluator is faced with data from different outcome measures and/or different programs. If the question to be answered dealt with overall or aggregative results, these techniques would be especially useful. In addition, an advantage of these techniques from a cost and logistics point of view is that only group descriptive statistics are required in most instances. Thus the expense and time involved in gaining access to raw data and in storing raw data is rarely required if the hypothesis tests have already been calculated when the evaluator receives the data.

CONVERSIONS TO STANDARD METRICS

There are several circumstances where the conversion of raw data into standard metrics would be advantageous. For example, in the Kulik et al. article (1979), the authors indicated that one of the issues faced when conducting a meta analysis is the need to convert data into a common metric. These authors used five-point rating scales for conversion of ratings into common metrics. They also used percentage correct as a common metric for final examination scores.

The following example of standard score conversions in our current research illustrates the value of these procedures. The Utah Mental Health Program Evaluation Committee has conducted statewide meta analyses of mental health outcomes for two years, using sets of data from different programs with different pre- and posttreatment measurement systems. Some of these analyses are found in Geertsen (1979, 1980). Additional results are published here for the first time. Since several of the mental health facilities in Utah use different outcome measures, and because there is very little agreement as to what the best criterion is for measuring treatment outcome, a meta analysis approach was used. In both the 1979 and 1980 evaluations, standard score conversions were experimentally used. In 1979, seven mental health facilities submitted pre- and posttreatment data. The n sizes and outcome measures used varied among facilities with each facility employing a single outcome measure. Four different staff rating scales were used: the Global Assessment Scale; a Level of Functioning Scale; a Problem Severity Scale; and a Behavior Rating Scale. One client self-report scale (Symptom Checklist 90-R) was used. The Global Assessment Scale was used by four facilities, and the other scales were each used by one facility. Client populations for the studies were restricted to individuals 18 years of age or older who were seeking treatment for mental health or related problems. Pre- and postratings were included in the studies if the client ended treatment during the given fiscal year period.

In the 1979 study a standard score conversion of each mental health center's raw data was experimentally employed to test the significance of differences between mental health facilities (or mental health centers). To convert raw scores to the same metric for all mental health centers, each raw posttreatment observation score was converted into a T score based on each center's pretreatment, standard deviation, and mean. The formula for converting post-observations into T scores was $T = 50 + 10(X_{post} - M_{pre})/SD_{pre}$, where X_{post} = a posttreatment observation score, M_{pre} = the mean of the pretreatment observation scores, and SD_{pre} = standard deviation of the pretreatment observation scores.

If the different centers' raw posttreatment means and standard deviations had been used to calculate scores, the means and standard deviations for the data sets would all have been respectively 50 and 10. However, with the use of pretreatment means and standard deviations in the calculation of the converted posttreatment scores, the changes in the observation after treatment were reflected in the derived distributions of scores. The results of these conversions were that the postobservation T score means and standard deviations for each data set represented the change from a statistically common base for all the sets of data.

Before scores could be converted, two centers' raw postobservation scores had to be reversed in terms of the direction of their deviation from their pretreatment observation score. This was done to make the direction of positive or negative change consistent with the other center's sets of data. After direction of change was made consistent across centers, each postobservation was converted into the pretest distribution derived T scores (see formula above). Means and standard deviations of each center's postobservation T scores were calculated. This enabled statistical tests of differences between the various centers converted postobservations to be conducted. The Utah group tested all possible differences between independent means. Other typical inferential statistics tests could have been used (e.g., analysis of covariance), provided the underlying assumptions were met.

This method of preparing and testing data indicated statistically significant differences between one center's data set and all other centers' data sets. Three centers' data sets were not significantly different from each other but were significantly different from three other centers' data sets. This technique thus allowed for comparisons of patient outcome despite the use of divergent outcome measures. There are some dangers inherent in this approach. Under certain conditions the assumption that the pretest standard deviations for the different data sets are equal may not hold. The problem here is that it may be difficult to test this assumption because the different distributions are in different metrics. This leaves the researcher assuming homogeneity where visual inspection of the distribution or other subjective methods are the only checks. There are also many research design issues (too extensive for discussion here) that could influence bias in this type of statistical comparison. Some accounting or control for the sources of error would have to be introduced; ideally, experimental designs with randomization and other features would be used. However, the mental health evaluator is more often than not faced with situations where such controls are not feasible or cost-effective.

In 1980, the Utah group did attempt some statistical control of this type of data, with mixed results (Geertsen, 1980). A similar posttreatment score conversion procedure to that given above was used; Z scores were derived in place of T scores. The derived posttest scores, called "adjusted" posttest scores, were used in some interesting attempts to control for measurement error between the different mental health centers' data sets. "Adjusted" posttest scores were used as the criteria against which the pretest scores and other variables thought to effect "reactivity" (Smith & Glass, 1977) were regressed in an attempt to "wash out" some of the sources of error. Each mental health center's data set was given a score on a rationally developed group of "reactivity" criteria hypothesized to account for measurement error. The criteria selected were degree of specificity of the measure, whether the measure was staff ratings or client ratings, whether the ratings were performed only at admission and termination or at each session, and whether the same person did the rating at admission and at termination. Approximately 13% of the variance was accounted for by scores on these criteria, in addition to about 20% of the variance being accounted for by the pretreatment observation scores. Attempts at graphically displaying derived changes in the "adjusted" posttest means, caused by introducing these controls, were unsuccessful because variances around the means were not homogeneous. Another problem was that the correlation of ordinal data (reactivity rankings) with interval data (adjusted posttest score) created a situation where some changes in means due to the introduction of controls exceeded the grand mean in the opposite direction. However, this methodology experiment serves as an illustration of potential uses for this type of score conversion.

Of the two standard score systems used, the authors prefer T scores because Z score conversions can sometimes equal zero. A score conversion to distribution based scores where there are no zeros is advantageous since some computer programs treat zeros as though they are missing data. Data processing headaches can be saved by using conversions that do not have zeros as actual scores. There are some computer programs where the investigator can derive their own standard score system. When taking advantage of such an option, it may be best to avoid score systems with zeros and use one of the more frequently encountered score systems such as T scores for the sake of ease in interpretation.

When conversions of raw data are required, another possibility is the use of percentile scores. Conversion of scores to percentile ranks could be an appropriate technique under certain conditions. Percentile conversions would be particularly advantageous in situations where rank data are all that is needed and the distance in the distribution of one score from another is not important. It is sometimes advantageous to use percentile ranks where distributions of scores are not normal. However, there are some situations where this score conversion would not be appropriate; for example, if the Utah group had converted their posttest scores in the illustration above into percentiles of the pretest scores, there would have been some posttest score percentiles above 100.

The examples and illustrations given here were concerned with a special case where "adjusted" posttest scores were derived. It would more often be the case that standard score or percentile conversions would be based on their own means and standard deviations instead of means and standard deviations of other related distributions. An obvious limitation in the use of standard score conversions is that direct access of raw data is required as in the third level of meta analysis given in the previous sections of this chapter. In situations where access can be found only in some data sets and not others, one has to assume or examine evidence for the assumption that there is no selection bias operating in data sets where raw data are available as opposed to not available. Sometimes the logistics of obtaining raw data can be difficult, especially where studies are old or computer equipment is not readily available.

In some evaluation situations there are circumstances where data with different independent measures can best be compared or aggregated by categorizing cases into predefined groups, as described in the next section.

STATISTICALLY DERIVED GROUPS

It is sometimes convenient to put data into categories or groupings either for descriptive purposes or for further analysis. For example, to express their pre- and posttreatment data in terms of percentage of cases having positive change versus maintenance versus deterioration, the Utah group (Geertsen, 1980) reviewed a formula to help in determining the percentage of clients having shown reliable change during treatment [adapted from Anastasi (1966)]. The formula gives the standard error of a difference between test or behavioral observation scores:

$$SE_{\text{diff}} = \sqrt{\left(SD \sqrt{1 - r_{xx_{\text{pre}}}}\right)^2 + \left(SD \sqrt{1 - r_{xx_{\text{post}}}}\right)^2}$$

This formula gives the standard error of a difference between pre- and postobservation scores. Results from this formula would provide a cutoff above or below which each mental health center's outcome data could be tallied. The improvement group would be the percent of the n of a given mental health center that have postobservation scores one or more standard errors of a difference in the positive direction from the preobservation score. The maintenance group would be the percentage of the n that has postobservation scores within plus or minus one standard error of the difference from the preobservation score. The deterioration group would be the percentage of the n value that has postobservation scores at least one standard error of the difference in the negative direction from the preobservation score. By calculating the standard error of the difference for each center's data set and tallying each center's data into the three groups, an aggregation for all centers could be computed.

If more rigorous definitions of positive change and negative change were desired, the standard error of the difference would be multiplied by 1.28 or

1.96, which would give respective probabilities of .9 and .95 that scores beyond these cutoffs would evidence genuine change. For most analyses, the use of either the raw standard error of the difference or multiplication of the standard error of the difference by 1.28 would be preferable in order to avoid excessive categorization errors in the negative direction.

An advantage of such categorization is that the data could be presented in an intuitively interpretable fashion for individuals relatively naive in statistics. Another advantage is that this procedure appears to control for the problem of low reliability of raw difference scores. Disadvantages of these procedures are that (1) for devices with multiple items, internal consistency reliability r values for both pre- and posttests must be obtained, (2) for rating devices, interrater reliability r values must be obtained, and (3) the magnitude or amount of client change is not given. An illustration of this method is presented in Figure 2.1 for hypothetical Symptom Checklist 90-R data at admission and after termination.

$$SE_{diff} = \sqrt{(SD \sqrt{1 - r_{xx_{pre}}})^2 + (SD \sqrt{1 - r_{xx_{post}}})^2}$$

$$SE_{diff(.05)} = 1.96(SE_{diff})$$

Pretest			Posttest		
r_{xx}	=	.95	r_{xx}	=	.96
SD	=	.73	SD	=	.69
$1 - .95$	=	.05	$1 - .96$	=	.04
$\sqrt{.05}$	=	.223	$\sqrt{.04}$	=	.2
$.223 \times .73$	=	$.162 = s_{meas_{pre}}$	$.2 \times .69$	=	$.138 = s_{meas_{post}}$

$$s^2 = .026 \qquad\qquad s^2 = .019$$

$$\sqrt{.026 + .019} = \sqrt{.045} = .212 = SE_{diff}$$
$$.212 \times 1.96 \text{ for } .05 \text{ level} =$$
$$.415 = SE_{diff} \text{ at } .05$$

Number .415 or more above pretest score
$$71 = 39\% \text{ improved}$$
Number within + or −.415 from pretest score
$$99 = 54\% \text{ maintained}$$
Number .415 or more below pretest score
$$14 = 7.6\% \text{ deteriorated}$$

Figure 2.1.   Illustration of pre- and posttreatment data categorization technique.

In actual use of a method similar to this, the Utah group (Geertsen, 1980) aggregated 2405 mental health cases from nine different mental health facilities pre- and posttreatment observations into three groups. Results showed that

67% had "improved level of functioning," 23% had "stabilized/maintained level of functioning," and 10% had "declined level of functioning." These groups were derived by using the method described above, except that the standard error of posttreatment minus pretreatment difference scores was used instead of the standard error of difference between test scores. The formula used was $SD_{diff}/\sqrt{N-1}$, where SD_{diff} = standard deviation of the posttreatment minus pretreatment difference scores and N = the number of difference scores. Results for each mental health center were multiplied by 1.28 so that the .10 level of confidence was used, and data for each center were tallied (by computer) into the three groups derived from their data set. Percentages of mental health clients in the groups where then ready for display to individuals not sophisticated in statistics. One apparent advantage of this method over the former proposed method was that reliability data were not required.

This kind of statistically derived group membership lends itself to further analysis of the characteristics of the population of the derived groups. The three groups defined above were analyzed for which client characteristics were found in greater or lesser proportion among the members of the groups. Chi square values were calculated on several variables, and some significant χ^2s were found (Geertsen, 1980), yielding indicators of client characteristics that could be associated with the different groups. In reviewing these data, there were at least two possibilities for serious questions about the interpretation of the findings. The first question concerned the situation where a small number of data sets with grossly different n values contribute to a total N value. The question was, "How much of a given proportion in the total sample is due to one data set with special proclivities or due to more than one data set with similar proclivities?" Similarly, it might be asked whether this finding is due to one large data set representing some special characteristic or to more than one data set representing similar special characteristics.

Another potential concern with this type of analysis was that the method of determining group membership was based on pre- and posttreatment change scores. Although the use of such change scores was defensible for indicating the gross percentage of clients actually changing, it was not defensible for analyzing what is characteristic of the individuals in the groups. For example, on some measurement scales the lower the functioning of a client at admission, the larger the change score might be, because the lower ratings are further away from the scale ceiling. As an example, the profoundly disturbed psychotic may show a much larger change score because their pretreatment score does not reach the scale ceiling. A mildly disturbed situational-reaction patient may have a pretreatment score closer to the scale ceiling, thereby restricting the size change score to one smaller than that of the disturbed psychotic. However, if a theoretical scale without a ceiling were used, the mildly disturbed patient might show a change score larger than that of the psychotic.

Methods for controlling this latter problem by calculating various "residual" scores were discussed by Cronbach and Furby (1970). They indicate that none of these methods are satisfactory and that research designs not requiring these methods be used. However, under certain conditions some research questions lend themselves to the use of implied pre- and postresidual scores in a regression analysis approach. Hummel-Rossi and Weinberg (1975) indicate that the use of multiple regression techniques where the posttest score is the criterion (with the pretest score inserted in the regression equation in front of other client or measurement variables) is an acceptable technique for some applied research situations. This approach could be used to control the problem of restrictive scale ceilings discussed above.

Sources of bias or other possible distortions such as those just discussed are of paramount concern in most meta analyses. Therefore, attempts to account for these distortions are necessary if data are to be understood correctly. As an illustration, one of the authors, under the guidance of the Utah Mental Health Program Evaluation Committee, attempted to account for the two problems mentioned in the preceding discussion. Pre- and posttreatment scores for each set of data from the different mental health facilities were transformed into "residual scores," which were derived by first determining the predicted posttreatment score. The predicted score was based on linear regression of the pretreatment scores against the posttreatment scores. Next, the difference between each predicted posttreatment score and each actual posttreatment score was obtained, giving residual scores. Thus the residual scores represented the deviation of the actual score from what would statistically be predicted for the given pretreatment score. Because certain distortions can become problematic when using residual scores (Cronbach & Furby, 1970), the Utah data residual scores were grouped without using absolute values (only group membership was used in the analysis). As a result, some potential distortions were minimized.

In the Utah investigation, three groups were formed for each data set. One group labeled "high changers" was defined as individuals with residual scores one standard deviation or more above the mean of residual scores for the given data set. Another group called "average changers" was defined as individuals with residual score within + 1 or – 1 standard deviation of the mean of residual scores for the given set of data. The final group was defined as individuals with residual scores – 1 standard deviation or more below the mean of residual scores in the data set. These residual score groupings introduced some statistical control to the problem of differentially disturbed patients who had unequal potential change scores. After group membership was determined for each case in relation to their respective data set, a discriminant function analysis designed to maximally discriminate between groups (Klecka, 1975) was conducted on the given set. There were two groups of analyses, respectively, using characteristics of the group members and amount by type of service as the variables of discrimination. Variables that proved to be useful in discriminating between the three groups were then examined in terms of whether they consistently discriminated across data sets. This was done by accomplishing discriminant function analysis on the three groups aggregated across data sets from mental health centers with different pre- and posttreatment measures. The total number of cases on seven mental health centers, for the analysis of service delivery variables, was 2306 (see Table 2.1). The total number of cases for the patient characteristics analysis was 2375 for eight data sets. In all these analyses, individual cases were placed in one of the three groups according to their residual score in the set of data from which the score was derived.

An idea of the different data sets relative contribution to the overall findings can be ascertained by using the tables (see Tables 2.1 & 2.2). These tables were constructed to investigate and account for what proportions of the aggregate findings were influenced by proclivities of one special data set as opposed to findings from more than one data set. This gives a starting point for determining the generalizability of the aggregate results. It is interesting to note that the findings may have genuine interest to the investigator concerned with what variables tend to predict the effectiveness of mental health interventions.

The results indicate that the service delivery variables, client admission mode, number of inpatient days, number of other residential treatment days, number of partial-care days, and number of outpatient contacts significantly discriminate between the three "change groups." However, number of outpatient contacts and the client admission mode were most highly related to group membership. The findings regarding number of outpatient contacts are illustrative of the problem of differing data sets relative contributions in overall findings. It will be noticed in Table 2.1 that the findings for one mental health center's data were opposite in direction from the others. This is confusing until one reviews the means of the data sets on this variable. All centers where the variable discriminated like the aggregate showed the highest mean number of contacts in the high change group. The means for these centers were tightly grouped around 13 contacts. However, for the one center that showed differing results, the highest mean number of 30 contacts was in the low-change (i.e., low degree of change) group. This disparity of highest mean number of contacts adds an interpretive dimension to why one center's data are opposite.

Results of the client variables surprisingly indicate that diagnostic variables are more related to membership in the three groups than are demographic variables. However, variability among different data sets relative contribution is noticeable. There remains a question as to what accounts for this variability. Would measurement error, differences in diagnostic practices, or other variables account for it?

One problem with this type of analysis is that cause–effect relationships can only be surmised. One way to examine cause and effect would be to determine group membership where residual scores, with measurement and diagnostic variables controlled, are used in a path analysis of client and service delivery variables. This would make possible an examination of the effect client and service delivery variables have on outcome when controlled for differing outcome measures and differing diagnostic practices.

TABLE 2.1. Individual Data Set Results Compared to Aggregate Discriminant Function Results on Service Delivery Variables

	Number of Data Sets Where Variable Discriminated Like Aggregate	Number of Data sets with $\bar{n} \leq 5$ on the Variable	Number of Data Sets Variable Not a Discriminator of Group Membership	Number of Data Sets Where Variable Discriminated Different from Aggregate	Aggregate Discriminant Function Results on Service Delivery Variables
Admission mode	4	2	1	0	More clients enter mental health system through crises and intensive services in low-change group, next most in high-change group[a]*
Inpatient days	3	2	3	0	Clients have more inpatient days in low-change group[b]*
Residential days	1	6	1	0	Clients have more residence days in high-change group and least in average-change group[c]*
Partial-care days	3	3	2	0	Clients have more partial-care days in low-change group, next most in high-change group, least in average-change group[c]*
Outpatient contacts	5	0	1	1	Clients have more outpatient contacts in high-change group[a]*

[a]Largest standardized canonical discriminant function coefficient.
[b]Next largest standardized canonical discriminant function coefficient.
[c]Smallest standardized canonical discriminant function coefficient.
* F is significant at .05 or beyond for one-way analysis of variance (ANOVA) of the three groups on the given variable.

As with standard score conversions, these methods have at least one significant limitation; raw data must be readily accessible. These procedures are also representative of level three meta analysis where raw data are manipulated.

EFFECT SIZE

Since the introduction of effect size statistics in psychotherapy outcome research, there have been several explanations and amplifications of these techniques; therefore, it is not necessary to thoroughly examine this issue here. There has been very little or nothing written on the use of effect size statistics in mental health outcome evaluation. Yet mental health outcome evaluation represents one area where the use of such statistics could be beneficial. In typical outcome evaluation efforts, a control group is not practical or feasible, and under some conditions it is not legal. Often, outcome data are presented as some form of behavioral observation or test at one time and are compared to subsequent observations at a later time. An evaluator is sometimes presented with outcome data where different measures were used. Effect size statistics may have potential benefit to the evaluator in these situations.

An example illustrating the use of effect size statistics in outcome evaluation efforts is presented for situations where these conditions were present. In this example seven mental health centers with different outcome measures used effect size formulas to experiment with possible comparison methodologies (Geertsen, 1979). A formula in which the mean of the pretest was subtracted from the mean of the posttest and the result was divided by the standard deviation of the pretest, or $ES = (M_{post} - M_{pre})/SD_{pre}$, was used. This formula was selected according to the assumption that pretreatment data would be analogous to the control group data in the denominator of the Smith and Glass (1977) formula. The practicality and ethics of no-treatment control groups for the mental health facilities were viewed as prohibitive.

In the initial analysis it became apparent that four of the posttest standard deviations were significantly larger than the pretest standard deviations. Because the unequal standard deviations did not meet the assumption of common variance for the two distributions, another formula for calculating effect size was used to minimize distortions:

$$ES = \frac{M_{post} - M_{pre}}{\sqrt{(SD_{post}^2 + SD_{pre}^2)/2}}$$

This formula was obtained from Jacob Cohen's work (Cohen, 1977) in which he developed several derivatives of a statistic labeled d, which is an index of effect size. Cohen recommended this formula as being applicable when standard deviations of two groups are not equal. Figure 2.2 compares the results of the two different effect size formulas using the data in the Utah report. The difference between the two formulas was not very great, except in center 7,

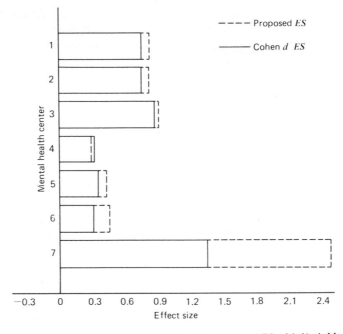

Figure 1.2   A comparison of the proposed ES and the Cohen d ES with Utah Mental Health Center data.

which had the largest effect size and the largest difference between pre- and posttreatment standard deviations.

If effect size were to be used as displayed here, there would be some serious problems with these comparisons. Factors influencing effect sizes other than treatment effects would have to be controlled or "washed out." Methods of controlling effect size by using regression analyses and Baysian statistics have been proposed, experimented with, and implemented. A brief review of these methods is appropriate here.

Smith and Glass's (1977) use of effect size in their work on psychotherapy outcome has been labeled "brilliant" (Rosenthal, 1979). Their basic formula, $ES = (\overline{M}_e - \overline{M}_c)/SD_c$, makes appropriate use of studies where control groups are available. Statistical control of variables influencing effect size was possible because there was a sufficient number of effect sizes to permit the use of regression analysis. In Smith and Glass's (1977, 1980) work, regression analysis was used to control for some of the measurement variance called "reactivity." Additionally, Strube (1980) summarized another method for controlling variables influencing effect size presented in Schmidt and Hunter (1977). According to Strube (1980), the approach is to use Baysian statistics in accounting for the sources of variance in succeeding steps. The final result, if all variance is not accounted for, is to develop confidence intervals around average effect size. In Strube's commentary on this approach, he states that it may be impractical in situations where data on control variables are not available. Also, the procedures for another method were presented earlier in this chapter in the section on conversions to standard metrics. An illustration was given that showed a regression analysis in which attempts were made to account for measurement variance. Because the total number of effect sizes was only seven, the approach used employed raw data of individual subject scores instead of effect sizes as criterion variables. The results showed that more work and experimentation is needed before comparisons of the type attempted in this last approach can be relied on in decision making.

Effect size measures have some advantages over alternatives for comparison or aggregation of data from different mental health programs using different measures. Some of these advantages are: (1) effect size statistics are generally easy to calculate, and hence there is less work, time, and expense involved; (2) where pre- and posttreatment effect sizes are used, there is intrinsic control for the problem of poor reliability of individual raw gain scores (Cronbach & Furby, 1970) because all change scores are pooled to yield one metric; (3) there is general familiarity with and more advanced development of the concept of effect size as in Cohen's (1977) contributions; and (4) effect size statistics are unique in that they reflect both the number of individuals having changed and the average magnitude of change in these individuals.

Effect size averaging or comparison is usually associated with our second level of meta analysis where previously calculated descriptive statistics are used as the metrics of analysis. This means that the time and expense of obtaining raw data can be avoided where standard deviations and means have already been given.

SUMMARY AND CONCLUSIONS

Meta analysis has been used in educational research, social psychology research, and psychotherapy outcome research with some degree of success. It is reasonable to assume that these techniques would also have applicability in an area so clearly related to psychotherapy outcome research as mental health program evaluation. Mental health outcome evaluation could benefit from the techniques of meta analysis since the evaluator is usually confronted with data from different programs, using different treatment philosophies, with different objectives and utilizing different measures. Although some of the illustrations imply experimental attempts at comparison, present levels of sophistication in these techniques do not lend themselves to comparison. The aggregation of data from different sources to form general conclusions about variables related to outcome or effectiveness appears to have merit at this time. If the evaluator is compulsive and creative, the possibility of valid comparison methodologies does exist in the near future. Caution and peer review in the area of pioneering endeavors such as these are important.

Traditional statistical techniques can be brought to bear in situations where data aggregation from different sources is being attempted. Regression analysis and discriminant function analysis are used in illustrations in this chapter.

TABLE 2.2. Results on Individual Data Sets Compared to Aggregate Discriminant Function Results on Client Variables

	Number of Data Sets Where Variables Discriminated Like Aggregate	Number of Data sets with $\bar{n} \leq 5$ on the Variables	Number of Data Sets Not Variables Not Discriminator of Group Membership	Number of Data Sets Where Variables Discriminated Different from Aggregate	Aggregate Discriminant Functional Results on Client Delivery Variables
Gender	3		5		More clients in the low-change group were males[b]*
Age	3		4	1	Clients had lowest mean age average-change group and highest mean age in low-change group[c]*
Education	4		4		Clients had lowest mean years of education in low-change group, next lowest mean in average-change group, and highest mean in high-change group[c]*
Prior mental health	6		2		Move clients with a prior mental health treatment in low-change group[b]*
Court referred		1	5	2	Did not discriminate
White	2	1	5		Fewest white clients in low-change group[c]*
Black	3	5			More black clients in high-change group[c]*
Spanish	2	2	4		More Hispanic clients in low-change group[c]*
Other minority		5	4		Did not discriminate

Variable				Group differences
Single—never married	1	5	2	Did not discriminate
Married	1	7		Fewest married clients in low-change group, more married clients in average-change group[c*]
Widowed	2	4	2	Did not discriminate
Divorced or separated	1	7		Did not discriminate
OBS	2	1	5	Did not discriminate
Substance abuse	3	4	1	Did not discriminate
Schizophrenic	4	1	3	Many more schizophrenic clients in low-change group[a*]
Depressive	3	5		More in high-change group, fewest in low-change group[a*]
Other psychotic		1	7	Did not discriminate
Anxiety neurosis		7	2	Did not discriminate
Personality disorder	4	4		Fewest in high-change group[c*]
Situation reaction adjustment	5	3		Fewest in low-change group, more in high-change group[a*]

[a] Largest standardized canonical discriminant function coefficient.
[b] Next largest standardized canonical discriminant function coefficient.
[c] Smallest standardized canonical discriminant function coefficient.
[*] F is significant at .05 or beyond for one way ANOVA of the three groups on the given variable.

TABLE 2.3. Summary Matrix of Meta Analysis Types with Levels of Data Required

Type of data \ Type of analysis	Combination of Statistical Probabilities	Effect Size Averaging and Comparisons	Conversions of Individual Scores to Standardized Metrics	Statistically Derived Groupings	Traditional Literature Reviews
Narrative conclusions and basic numerical presentations are used in analysis					X
Previously calculated descriptive statistics of whole studies or data sets are used as metrics of analyses	X	X_r^a			
Raw data are directly transformed or manipulated for further analysis			X_r	X_r	

[a]Subscript r = regression analysis, analysis of variance, or other traditional statistical techniques can be used.

Analysis of variance is also used in other meta analysis literature (Kulik et al., 1979), and its use in mental health outcome evaluation has also been suggested (Bartko, 1980). It is important to note that as time passes and more data accumulate, the use of these data for validation, alteration, and understanding of mental health intervention is essential. However, the often used maxim of "poor data" being better than "no data" is not true when the techniques of aggregation are flawed or misleading. Therefore, it is vital that (in new developments where data usage is the "guinea pig") a great deal of energy and thought be put into the method. The use of established techniques as part of a new set of evaluation tools is seen as a very appropriate direction in meta analysis.

We have attempted to review and illustrate five types of meta analysis or data aggregation techniques. These are summarized in Table 2.3.

The combining of statistical probabilities is a technique that so far has been used mostly in social psychology research, although its potential usefulness in outcome evaluation is obvious, especially when aggregate findings are to be used. These techniques should be explored and utilized when possible because of their relative simplicity. Effect size averaging and the resulting comparisons are an area with a high degree of potential for use. Extreme caution is advised where effect sizes are used for comparison and where control groups do not exist. Raw data conversions have existed for a long time. Extensive use is made of various standard score conversions in psychological testing literature and elsewhere. The T scores with a mean of 50 and a standard deviation of 10 have been used often as they avoid zeros, which would create problems from a data processing point of view. Statistically derived groups such as "high-," "low-," and "average-change" groups are an area not yet exploited, with apparent potential if one can accept arbitrary cutoffs for group membership.

Meta analysis is an evolving group of methodologies. As with any evolving methodology, there comes a point in its evolution when the original designs become outmoded. Simple ABA designs utilized in within-subject design research are often not viewed as adequate in and of themselves. In group data statistical designs, T tests are often viewed as inadequate in and of themselves. As meta analysis or other data aggregation techniques evolve, we must look beyond the pioneering methods and design other techniques. Their development will follow as the need for such technology becomes more clear.

REFERENCES

Anastasi, A. *Psychological testing*. London: Macmillan, 1966.

Bartko, J. Untitled paper presented at the National Conference on Mental Health Statistics, Williamsburg, 1980.

Bergin, A. E. The evaluation of therapeutic outcomes. In A. E. Bergin & S. L. Garfield (Eds.), *Handbook of psychotherapy and behavior change*. New York: Wiley, 1971.

Bergin, A. E., & Lambert, M. J. The evaluation of therapeutic outcomes. In A. E. Bergin & S. L. Garfield (Eds.), *Handbook of psychotherapy and behavior change: An empirical evaluation* (2nd ed.). New York: Wiley, 1978.

Cohen, J. *Statistical power analysis for the behavioral sciences.* New York: Academic Press, 1977.

Cook, T. D., & Gruder, C. L. Meta evaluation research. *Evaluation Quarterly*, 1978, **2**, 5–51.

Cronbach, L. J., & Furby, L. How we should measure "change"—Or should we. *Psychological Bulletin*, 1970, **74**, 68–70.

Eysenck, H. J. The effects of psychotherapy: An evaluation. *Journal of Consulting Psychology*, 1952, **16**, 319–324.

Eysenck, H. J. *The effects of psychotherapy.* New York: International Science Press, 1966.

Eysenck, H. J. An exercise in mega-silliness. *American Psychologist*, 1978, **5**, 517.

Gallo, P. S. Meta-analysis—A mixed meta-phor? *American Psychologist*, **5**, 1979, 515–517.

Geertsen, D. G. *State Mental Health Program Evaluation in Utah* (Executive Summary). 1979.

Geertsen, D. G. *State Mental Health Program Evaluation in Utah* (Executive Summary). 1980.

Glass, G. V. Primary, secondary, and meta-analysis of research. *The Educational Researcher*, 1976, **5**(10), 3–8.

Glass, G. V., & Smith, M. L. Reply to Eysenck. *American Psychologist* 1978, **5**, 517–519.

Glass, G. V., & Smith, M. L. Meta-analysis of research on the relationship of class-size and achievement. *Evaluation and Policy Analysis*, 1979, **1**, 2–15.

Hall, J. A. Gender effects in decoding nonverbal cues. *Psychological Bulletin*, 1978, **85**, 845–857.

Hartley, S. S. *Meta-analysis of the effects of individually paced instruction in mathematics.* Unpublished doctoral dissertation, University of Colorado, 1977.

Hearold, S. L. *Meta-analysis of the effects of television on social behavior.* Unpublished doctoral dissertation, University of Colorado, 1978.

Hummel-Rossi, B., & Weinberg, S. L. Practical guidelines in applying current theories to the measurement of change. *Journal Supplement Abstract Service-Catalog of Selected Documents in Psychology*, 1975, **5**, 226. (MS. No. 916)

Klecka, W. Discriminant analysis. In N. H. Nie et al., *Statistical package for the social sciences* (2nd ed.). New York: McGraw-Hill, 1975.

Kulik, J. A., Kulik, C. C., & Cohen, P. A. A meta-analysis of outcome studies of Keller's personalized system of instruction. *American Psychologist*, 1979, **34**, 304–318.

Lambert, M. J. Spontaneous remission in adult neurotic disorders: A summary and revision. *Psychological Bulletin*, 1976, **83**, 107–119.

Lambert, M. J. Psychotherapy outcome research. *American Psychologist* 1979, **1**, 91.

Light, R. J. Capitalizing on variation: How conflicting research findings can be helpful for policy. *Educational Researcher*, 1979, **8**, 8–11.

Luborsky, L., Singer, B., & Luborsky, L. Comparative studies of psychotherapies. *Archives of General Psychiatry*, 1975, **32**, 995–1008.

Meltzoff, J., & Kornreich, M. *Research in psychotherapy*. New York: Atherton Press, 1970.

Mosteller, F. M., & Bush, R. R. Selected quantitative techniques. In G. Lindsey (Ed.), *Handbook of social psychology:* Volume I. *Theory and method*. Cambridge, Mass.: Addison-Wesley, 1954.

Newman, L. F., & Carter, D. *A strategy for studying clinical judgement and therapeutic outcome in community mental health settings*. Paper presented at the meeting of the Society for Psychotherapy Research, Boston, June, 1975.

Rachman, S. J., & Wilson, G. T. *The effects of psychological therapy* (2nd enlarged ed.). New York: Pergamon, 1980.

Rosenthal, R. *Experimenter effects in behavioral research* (Enlarged ed.). New York: Irvington, 1976.

Rosenthal, R. Combining results of independent studies. *Psychological Bulletin*, 1978, **85**, 185–193.

Rosenthal, R. The "file-drawer problem" and tolerance for null results. *Psychological Bulletin*, 1979, **86**, 638–641.

Schmidt, F. L., & Hunter, J. E. Development of a general solution to the problem of validity generalization. *Journal of Applied Psychology*, 1977, **62**, 529–540.

Shapiro, D. A., & Shapiro, M. P. *Meta-analysis of comparative therapy outcome studies: A replication and refinement*. Paper presented at the Annual Meeting of the Society for Psychotherapy Research, Aspen, Colorado, June, 1981.

Smith, M. L., & Glass, G. V. Meta-analysis of psychotherapy outcome studies. *American Psychologist*, 1977, **32**, 752–760.

Smith, M. L., & Glass, G. V. *The benefits of psychotherapy*. Baltimore: Johns Hopkins University Press, 1980.

Strube, M. J. *Meta-analysis as an approach to cross-cultural comparison: Advantages and limitations*. Paper presented at Fifth International Association for Cross-Cultural Psychology Congress, Bhubaneswar, India, December 1980.

Strube, M. J., & Garcia, J. E. *A meta-analytic investigation of Fiedler's contingency model of leadership effectiveness*. Paper presented at the Annual Meeting of the American Psychological Association, Montreal, August, 1980.

White, K. R. *The relationship between socioeconomic status and academic achievement*. Unpublished doctoral dissertation, University of Colorado, 1976.

CHAPTER 3

Toward Maximizing the Utility of Consumer Satisfaction as an Outcome

MICHAEL BERGER

Consumer satisfaction has gained in usage and sophistication over the last five years. In writing an overview of client satisfaction techniques five years ago, Sorenson et al. (1976) included client satisfaction as one of the four As: acceptability, availability, accessibility, and awareness measures. He listed client satisfaction techniques for assessing the first of the four As—acceptability. One year later, Hagedson et al. (1976, p. 230) wrote: "When client satisfaction is known, it tells the evaluator something about the acceptability of services being evaluated; but the specifics of client satisfaction also offer a useful measure of treatment outcome, which is why the subject is included in this chapter." Writing in 1981, Schulberg notes the complete evolution: "The prevailing framework presently guiding client outcome is to obtain change measures of the client's (1) psychiatric status of distress level; (2) social functioning; and (3) satisfaction with treatment" (Schulberg, 1981, p. 132).

Despite the advancements in measurement technology and the improvements in instruments, consumer satisfaction has not achieved the status of other outcome measures. Sorenson et al. (1979) conducted an extensive survey of the extent, nature, and utility of client satisfaction in federally funded mental health centers. In the 366 mental health center surveys they found that 50% of the mental health centers used a form of consumer satisfaction. Their conclusion from the review was that until evaluators developed clear, standardized methods, client satisfaction would continue to be of limited utility.

A number of researchers and evaluators argue for client satisfaction as an outcome instrument. Larsen et al. (1980) list a number of references and arguments for using client satisfaction. Their most potent argument suggests that when client satisfaction is not included, findings tend to become biased toward the provider of services in a perspective already dominated by the provider's point of view. Their point is that consumer satisfaction provides a check against internal rating systems of client outcome and valuable feedback from a source different from that of the therapist and the providing agency. Waskow and Parloff (1975) suggested an increasingly popular view of client satisfaction: consumer satisfaction measures another dimension of treatment outcome. This dimension has demonstrated consistent low to moderate correlations with other measures of outcome (Berger & Callister, 1981).

Historically, the focus of research on psychotherapy has been dominated by the view of therapy as the 50-minute hour. In many community mental health centers, therapy is far different from this traditional perspective. Consider the client's gestalt. Treatment in a mental health center may include a separate intake, an orientation session, several 50-minute hours, a weekly therapy group, attending client socials, being driven to the local college to register for a class, or being introduced to the interviewer at the local job service office. This gestalt also includes bills for services, long waits in waiting rooms, missed appointments, paperwork, and red tape. Somehow a *T* score on the depression scale of the MMPI or a GAS score fail to represent the many diverse aspects of this approach to therapy. Clearly, therapy is multidimensional. Traditionally, research on psychotherapy has focused on the therapist–client interaction dimension of therapy. Client satisfaction is a research tool designed to measure other dimensions in therapy.

When the focus of outcome is broadened, client satisfaction assumes increasing importance. For example, a mental health center administrator might be concerned about the quality of treatment or with methods of service delivery, treatment modality, or therapist burnout. With any of these concerns, client satisfaction would provide valuable information and in some cases would be the instrument of choice.

Most researchers would agree that evaluation is not the same esoteric sciencing that takes place in university laboratories. The goal of evaluative efforts is to provide information for understanding and improving services. Client satisfaction provides data about the outcome of therapy untapped by other outcome measures.

ISSUES RELATED TO CONSUMER SATISFACTION

To begin to maximize the utility of client satisfaction, the evaluator must first understand the limitations associated with the methods. Besides instrument and psychometric considerations, logistics, cost, and application of feedback are problematic to client satisfaction. When the researcher has a clear understanding of these limitations, methods can be developed to overcome the problems and to produce usable, high-quality data.

The problems underlying client satisfaction may be grouped into three categories: theoretical philosophical issues, measurement issues, and practical issues. Each is discussed in turn.

Theoretical Issues

The techniques of client satisfaction rest on four basic assumptions: (1) individuals are capable of evaluating their own feelings and making judgments about those feelings; (2) individuals can and are willing to accurately express their judgment about experiences; (3) a given stimulus situation will elicit identical or at least similar responses across individuals (e.g., similar therapy given by the same therapist in the same therapeutic situation will elicit similar responses across several clients); and (4) judgments about subjective experience have some correspondence with a system used to quantify these judgments.

From a practical viewpoint, these assumptions may seem self-evident. Deeper inspection, however, makes it clear that these assumptions are of practical as well as philosophical importance. Nunnally and Wilson (1975) examined assumption 2. They listed social pressures, liking and respect for the therapist, low- or no-fee services, and cognitive dissonance as factors that induce subjects to provide *nonvalid* information about themselves. Locke (1976) suggests that the mechanism of defensiveness plays a role in this assumption. Locke points out that clients who receive services may pass the responsibility for failure of the services to factors external to themselves. He further suggests that for many, the easiest way to preserve personal integrity is to evaluate therapy in the best possible light. Additional problems relating to high-positive responding are listed by Levois et al. (in press). If the problems cannot be assuaged, the second assumption that people *can* and *will* report judgments about their impressions and feelings is not justified and the measurement of consumer satisfaction becomes an exercise in futility. Similar arguments can be made for the other three assumptions.

With improvements in client satisfaction methods, data can be brought to bear on each criticism. It is well to remember that client satisfaction is a form of self-report and as such suffers from its own version of Heisenberg's uncertainty principle; specifically, bringing empirical data to bear on any one of these assumptions requires making one or more of the other assumptions. Thus one can never escape the problem of empirically verifying all the assumptions simultaneously. It is the analogue of trying to solve for four unknowns with three simultaneous equations.

Measurement Issues

There are many significant measurement issues with client satisfaction. Several major articles have dealt with these issues at length (Lebow, 1981; Ware, 1978). Perhaps the most crucial of the measurement issues relates to assumption 4 in the previous section; that is, some scaling method can be devised that will correspond in some way to the subjective self-report of the client. Scaling issues are paramount in the measurement of client satisfaction. Most researchers would agree that the data produced by most client satisfaction ratings are ordinal. In the past this would mean that the variety of parametric statistical procedures and arithmetic computations applied to this level of data are not justified. Several scales that have been developed have attempted to overcome scaling problems by using the Lickert scales, Thurstone's method of equal-appearing intervals, and factor analytic scales (Ware, 1978). Still, most scales have made little attempt beyond a Lickert format to develop rigorous scaling.

With the coming of age of the computer and the ability to inspect data, many evaluators consider the old argument about levels of measurement to be passé. The current thinking is that the procedures are "robust" and have been shown empirically to produce meaningful findings at both the interval and ordinal levels.

Unfortunately, the word "robust" creates two problems as it (1) provides a false sense of security about data and (2) suggests that further refinements beyond a Lickert scale are unnecessary. These are the least preferable meanings that the term "robust" should imply. The fact that Lickert scales exist does not relieve the researcher or clinician of the responsibility of examining distribution data and analyzing residuals. An excellent overview of residual analysis is given by SPSS (1981). Data, to be valuable, must be of high quality. Quality of data is based on the appropriate scaling of items and on the degree to which the assumptions underlying sampling and statistical procedures are met. Robust is not a substitute for perspiration.

It may be helpful to follow this rule of thumb: When the findings are descriptive only, robust may be used. When you are hypothesis testing and making inferences, further analysis of assumptions is required.

A second measurement issue with client satisfaction is the operation of various biases in the data. Typically, two types of bias have been reported; (Justice & McBee, 1980; Larsen et al., 1980). The types of bias documented by these studies are high rate of positive responding (positive-response bias) and sample bias.

The general level of reported satisfaction is between 80 and 95% (Balch et al., 1977; Geertsen, 1979; Hartman, 1977; McFee et al., 1975; Noel & Block, 1979). These studies report the range of satisfaction clustering around 85%, suggesting a very strong positive response bias operating. There are several explanations other than positive response bias for the consistency of this 85% level. The first alternative suggests that poor scaling procedures produced this level as an artifact, and the second hypothesis is that 85% is a general baseline level of satisfaction.

The most crucial of the biases reported in the literature is that of sample bias. Response rates to mailed questionnaires, including a second mailed reminder, range from 30 to 50%. It is not uncommon to report client satisfaction response rates as low as 15 to 20% (Christensen, 1980, Reference Note 1 at end of chapter). The rates of responding are higher for both telephone and face-to-face survey methods. It is not uncommon to have response rates near 80% with telephone or face-to-face interviews (Berger, 1980).

Sample bias has two potent effects on research. First, it raises the noise level in the data; specifically, the researcher can no longer rely on randomization to cancel error terms. The means of the error components can no longer be assumed to be zero, and the nature of the statistical procedures changes when the condition of randomization is not met.

The second effect is more of a practical one than theoretical. Suspected sample bias reduces the level of trust in the data. For a review of sample bias, see Larsen et al. (1980) and Owen and Goza (Reference Note 2). Traditionally, low return rates have eroded the quality of the data, and many writers have supposed that a majority of nonresponders are highly dissatisfied with services. This group may not be as forboding as envisioned. In fact, some of the data highlighted in the next section suggest quite the opposite.

Practical Issues

Practical issues in client satisfaction are many and varied. They range from cost-effectiveness to logistics to the use of data. Three broad issues are discussed here: (1) mistrust and resistance to client satisfaction measurement; (2) who, what, where, when, and why considerations and their implication for logistics; and (3) political realities and the use and abuse of data.

Mistrust and Resistance

The data generated by client satisfaction seem to be stable across time. Unless programs undergo severe change, the levels of reported satisfaction tend to remain constant from month to month. Data reported by Kelner illustrate this point (Reference Note 3). These data demonstrate that even under the severe changes of a major reorganization, with numerous mental health staff reassigned or terminated, consumer satisfaction remains relatively constant. This stability might suggest measures that are too gross to be sensitive to even major changes in organizational variables. On the other hand, it may point out a fact critical to research in general: procedural changes in research may be as important, if not more so, than changes in independent variables.

There has proved to be some resistance by therapists to the collection of client satisfaction data. Their resistance is not without merit. The typical argument claims that therapy and client satisfaction are incompatible; specifically, to produce changes in the client, the therapist must use confrontive or even aversive procedures. This will produce good therapy but poor client satisfaction. Resistance is discussed further in the section on recommendations.

There is often mistrust of client satisfaction data among those receiving reports of findings. This mistrust is rarely based on a thorough understanding of the techniques and procedures. This is due to the consistently high levels of reported satisfaction. Like the old saying, medicine must taste bad to be good for you; so must research be critical and stress negative feedback to gain attention and acceptance. The section on recommendations offers several suggestions to overcome this problem.

Who, What, Where, When, and Why Considerations

These problems are of practical importance. The who and what questions are partially answered in the next two sections, and the others are addressed in the section on recommendations. For those who may be beginning to use client satisfaction or are considering revisions, Pandiani and Kessler (1981) offer a practical guide to help the evaluator think through most of the basic questions.

Political Issues

Practical issues of great importance are political considerations. Evaluations, including client satisfaction, do not take place in a vacuum. If item analysis and improvements in scaling yield a better instrument but also reduce the apparent level of satisfaction, how can or should such efforts be justified to an administrator who is fighting the dollar crunch? This is the type of refinement that an administrator doesn't need when talking with a legislator about mental health appropriations.

Perhaps the most crucial of all practical issues is the use of client satisfaction data as an index in individual performance appraisal. Most evaluators would agree that client satisfaction presents little problem when used for planning service delivery, assessing training needs, or suggesting improvements in intake, orientation, and so on. Major problems come when client satisfaction is used to evaluate the individual therapist. Much of a client's satisfaction level is outside the direct control of the therapist and as such is a poor performance appraisal tool. A therapist in a candid remark summed up the problem, "If you equate pay raises and promotions to client satisfaction, in three months you will have all your therapists providing satisfaction instead of therapy." It should be emphasized that client satisfaction is a poor index of individual performance when cross-therapist comparisons are made. A compromise that seems workable for the administrator who insists on using these data involves three steps: (1) giving adequate warning that client satisfaction is multidimensional and the therapist may have direct control of one-third (estimated from variance accounted for from the literature) of a total client satisfaction rating; (2) providing time samples on a single therapist (e.g., last year's mean ratings as a baseline, compared to last month's ratings); and (3) providing raw data without client or therapist. These steps will usually satisfy the supervisor or administrator who is seeking information on which to base personnel decisions.

Salient Findings

The literature on client satisfaction is now sufficiently extensive to provide conclusions from the data that are consistently reported. Several excellent reviews of the literature exist, so a very general review is presented here. In the general medical area the reviews by Ware (1978) and Lebow (1982) are both comprehensive and well organized. In the area of job satisfaction from industrial psychology, the review by Locke (1976) is excellent.

The following section frequently cites the work of Attkisson and his colleagues and their attempts to standardize a single instrument across settings and their attempts to control the error component in their instruments. The section also cites the work of the Utah Mental Health Program Evaluation Committee. The reference to the Utah data is twofold: (1) as an illustration that individual centers, private clinics, and so on can conduct viable research in addition to service delivery; and (2) the data are on a clinical population, and the number of cases available for analysis (nearly 4000) is extremely large.

Client Satisfaction is Multidimensional

It is clear that client satisfaction is multidimensional. Ware and Snyder (1975) found 20 dimensions (factors) using factor analysis of an extensive client satisfaction survey. The Utah data yield two sets of factors: (1) those intrinsic to therapy (e.g., therapist interest, therapist communication, improvement, and ability to cope with future problems) and (2) those extrinsic to therapy (e.g., fees, orientation, and friendliness of nontherapy staff). Richer factor structures were generated in the Utah analysis when centers were considered individually. Global satisfaction scales have utility; however, they must be used only when their underlying dimensions are known.

Level of Satisfaction

As mentioned previously, the levels of reported satisfaction range between 80 and 95%. High levels of satisfaction have typically been treated as a fault in the psychometric properties of the satisfaction instruments. The consistency of the findings suggests an alternative hypothesis: 85% satisfaction may be a baseline of satisfied clients in mental health treatment. Ware (1981) has suggested that the distribution of satisfaction may be normalized by item analysis. Ware's research, however, was conducted on a general population. His work needs to be extended to a clinical population.

Dwarshuis and Kolton (1976) suggest that clients are much more optimistic in their ratings than are staff members. In their studies, clients rated staff and staff rated clients. There was considerable discrepancy between these two sets of ratings. Leicht and Levy (1979) also report differences between client and staff ratings. This suggests that clients may hold a generalized positive set about the helping professions that may contribute to the high levels of reported satisfaction. On the other end of the scale, LeVois et al. (in press) found moderate correlations, .45, $p < .01$, between a life satisfaction instrument and a service delivery satisfaction instrument. Similarly, the present author (Berger, 1980) found that there is a generalized set for satisfaction among certain clients. The sample included 100 subjects selected from active clients of the mental health center. These clients were asked to rate their feelings about four areas of American life: (1) the quality of workmanship in American automobiles; (2) the quality of food in restaurants; (3) medical care; and (4) their present jobs. The correlation between these items scored on a Lickert-type scale and an eleven-question client satisfaction instrument (see Appendix A p. 633) was .41, $p < .01$.

Dissatisfied Clients

Dissatisfaction has been reported in the 10 to 25% range, with 15% as a general average across the studies that were reviewed. This level of dissatisfaction is consistent with the findings in job satisfaction (Gilmer, 1971). Gilmer states, "The average figure of job dissatisfaction found in varying industries is around 13 percent" (Gilmer, 1971, p. 347). A variety of variables correlate with dissatisfaction. In the study cited by the author above, some clients tend to have a generalized dissatisfaction about life that transfers to client satisfaction. Analysis of the scatterplot suggested that much of the moderate correlation (.41) was due to those subjects who were highly dissatisfied with the four life items and also reported a low degree of client satisfaction. Sorenson et al. (1976) point out the dissatisfied clients return fewer mailed surveys than do satisfied clients. These findings are also consistent across several studies (Balch, 1977; Berger & Callister, 1981).

Vroom (1964), in his extensive work on job satisfaction, reports that male workers at lower levels in the organization who are between the ages of 25 and 30 and who are nonwhite show strong tendencies toward dissatisfaction with their jobs.

Client Characteristics

Larsen et al. (1980) present a finding that nonwhite males and those who drop out of therapy after a few sessions report lower levels of satisfaction. This is consistent with the findings of Kline et al. (1974); Read (1980), and Berger & Callister (1981).

Ware (1978) lists the following from the literature:

1. *Age.*   Older persons tend to be more satisfied. This is confirmed in clinical populations by three years of analysis of nearly 5000 cases by UMHPEC (1979, 1980, 1981).
2. *Education.*   Less educated persons tend to be less satisfied. This was also confirmed by the UMHPEC studies.
3. *Family size.*   Persons in large families tend to be less satisfied.
4. *Income.*   Lower-income persons tend to be less satisfied. This was confirmed by the UMHPEC data.
5. *Marital status.*   Ware reports no clear trend. However, UMHPEC found clear trends in marital status. Married persons tend to return more questionnaires and to report higher levels of satisfaction.
6. *Occupational levels.*   Individuals in higher levels of occupation tend to report greater satisfaction. No UMHPEC data are available on this point. This is consistent with a majority of the literature in job satisfaction.
7. *Race.*   Ware reports no clear trend. The UMHPEC data show a clear pattern of whites reporting higher levels of satisfaction.

8. *Sex.*   All sources agree that females tend to be more satisfied.

9. *Social class.*   No clear trend is evident.

Therapist Interest

In research on dissatisfaction, Kline et al. (1974) report therapist interest as a potent variable in dissatisfaction in clients. Salvman (1967) found that negative interest or angry feelings were associated with early dropout and reduced satisfaction levels. Hill (1974) reports that satisfaction levels tend to increase when the therapist sets specific goals with the client. Even when the therapist's goals were different from those of the client, the resultant satisfaction was more positive than for clients who did not receive goal setting. In an excellent study by Brown (1979), therapist-related variables accounted for 50% of the common variance that was being studied in consumer satisfaction. The importance of the therapist as a satisfier and dissatisfier seems to be well grounded in the literature.

Data Collection

Numerous studies have compared the various methods of collecting data. The most recent are consistent with earlier studies in the area. Warner (1981) presents an extensive study contrasting three survey procedures. These procedures involve mailed questionnaires, face-to-face interviews, and telephone interviews. Warner lists advantages for each method but concludes that for the return on the investment of time, effort, and expense, mailed questionnaires were by far the most efficient technique for assessing client satisfaction.

Concerning data collection, it seems clear that the normal response rate for mailed questionnaires seems to be in the range of 40% (UMHPEC, 1979, 1980). This number is slightly higher when the unknown deliverable instruments are eliminated from the calculations. It is not uncommon in face-to-face interviews for the response rate to jump to the 60 to 70% level (Berger, 1980). Several practical suggestions are given in the section on recommendations to help improve the general level of responding.

It is generally found that both telephone and face-to-face interviews produce slightly more positive responses than do mailed questionnaires. The general reported figure seems to be in the range of 5 to 10% higher for both procedures. The data reported by UMHPEC indicate that surveys mailed after a two-month period from termination clearly show a decrease in the level of satisfaction reported.

Client Expectation

Client expectation is also a powerful variable. Studies by Greenberg (1970) demonstrate that clients can be strongly influenced by initial orientation sessions. Clients who are told that their therapists are warm and experienced evaluated therapy more favorably than did control groups. Christensen (Reference Note 4) varied the type of information about therapy given to incoming clients. The control group was given a general lecture on mental health services

and organization structure. The experimental group received specific information about the average length of stay and what to expect in therapy. The
experimental group remained in services significantly longer than the control
group and reported greater satisfaction. Leishman (1980) found in a case study
approach to 12 troubled families that the majority of the conflicts between
social workers and families resulted from misunderstanding that took place in
the initial meeting.

Number of Visits

Satisfaction tends to increase with the number of visits (Berger & Callister,
1981). Figure 3.1 gives the relationship for the UMHPEC data. These findings
are consistent with those of both Ware (1978) and Lebow (1982). This is not
surprising since the number of visits is itself a criterion of satisfaction.

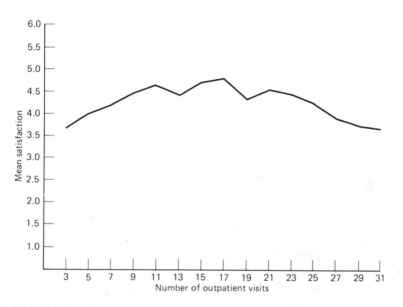

Figure 3.1.   Relationship between number of visits and level of satisfaction.

Initial Diagnosis

LeVois et. al. (in press) report moderate correlations between certain diagnostic categories and client satisfaction. They report that total symptom score
accounts for 16% of the variance with the use of the SCL-90 and the Client
Satisfaction Questionnaire (CSQ). A major development in this area has been
by Nguyen and Attkisson (1981). They have attempted to standardize their
instrument, the Service Evaluation Questionnaire (SEQ), across a variety of
clinical settings (see Appendix B p. 634 for a copy of the SEQ).

   In the UMHPEC data diagnosis was an important independent variable.
Initial cononical analysis suggests a simple dichotomy of psychotic versus non-

psychotic as the best combination of DSM codes. This variable accounted for 7% of the variance. It entered third in the stepwise regression analysis behind postscore on a measure of client outcome and behind the therapist variable, warm and empathetic.

Other Therapist Variables

Findings from numerous studies agree on the potency of therapist variable in predicting client satisfaction (Cornely & Bigman, 1963; Doyle & Ware, 1977; Fisher, 1971). Ware and Snyder (1975) found that therapist variables accounted for more variance than did any other set of variables. His factor analytic study did not distinguish between therapist competence and warmth. Ware reports a zero-order correlation of .644 and an r^2 of .414 for the therapist factor.

With the UMHPEC data a variety of therapist variables were tried in a multiple regression equation with total score clients satisfaction dependent. Therapist warmth and empathy entered second in the stepwise analysis with a simple R of .36, accounting for 13% of the variance. Other therapist variables were disappointing. The combination of therapist age, sex, race, years of education, years of experience, and number of clients in the therapist's case load accounted for another 5% of the total variance.

Organizational Variables

Considerable emphasis has been placed on organizational variables in the past. The 18-item CSQ provides an example. Seven of the 18 items refer to organizational factors. These include procedures, location, nontherapy staff, fees, confidentiality, intake, and help offered by secretarial staff. The assumption has been that organizational variables tend to act as satisfiers or dissatisfiers. In a study reported by Greenly and Schoenherr [(1981), the organization variable], the authors examined the role of the organization's autonomy, communications with other agencies, staff role discretion, delay or rejection of services, and unhelpful services. In their regression model, client characteristics accounted for 34% of the variance, whereas the organizational variables accounted for an additional 20% of the variance.

This study was listed because it attempts to probe beyond the typical reports of frequency counts of percentages with organizational factors.

The Utah data are sketchy at this point, but there is some evidence to suggest that organizational variables tend to act as dissatisfiers more frequently than as satisfiers. The process is, however, not that simple in that the role of such factors as fees, collections, orientation methods, and location of clinic are strongly interactive with both client characteristics and situational stress variables operating in clients' lives.

Situational Stress Variables

A review of the literature fails to list any studies where this variable is reported with client satisfaction as the criterion variable. In the Utah study, when life stress factors such as separation, divorce, and loss of employment are added to the regression equation, they entered in fifth position, accounting for 6% of the variance. The scale used consisted of 15 negative life stress questions suggested by Holmes and Rahe (1967).

Community Impact

The work of Ellsworth must certainly occupy a place in a review of client satisfaction. Although Ellsworth (1975) cites much research to demonstrate the low level of correlation between self-report and external criterion, his work serves both as a caution and as a starting point for the long overdue process of testing client satisfaction data against measures of social and community adjustment. For those practicing community psychology, his point is terse: "It matters little if the client learns to adjust well to the hospital setting or in relating to his clinic therapist if the behavior at work or his relationship to family members is not satisfactory" (Ellsworth, 1975, p. 239).

Ellsworth points out a crucial hidden assumption in much clinical work. This assumption states that people behave consistently in different settings. This assumption is contrary to the 20 years of work in the area of behavioral settings by Barker (1968) and the current emphasis of social ecology (Moos, 1976).

Ellsworth's work is cited because it extends the view of therapy outcome beyond the point of symptom reduction. If client satisfaction is to assume increased stature as an outcome measure, it must ask community impact questions and verify the results.

Findings From Other Domains

An extensive analysis of marketing or industrial-oriented satisfaction is beyond the scope of this chapter. The reader is directed to the review by Locke et. al. (1976) and to the *Journal of Marketing Psychology.*

The current literature in marketing psychology is dominated by the constructs of consonance and dissonance. Satisfaction with a product is the congruence of product characteristics with consumer expectations. An interesting concept suggested by Kashwath argues that a warranty on an appliance will not influence anyone to choose that product. The absence of a warranty, however, discourages many consumers from considering a particular product. Whether a product is eliminated from consideration depends on the importance of the warranty to the consumer. The warranty acts as a go/no-go decision point for some, whereas to others, lack of a warranty is a minor irritant that has little effect on the final choice of products. An analogy is apparent with the client who is told to pay a fee. To some in financial difficulty, this would terminate therapy. To a wealthy client, it would be a minor irritant.

The history of job satisfaction is dominated by the work of Herzberg et al. (1957). Herzberg proposed the famous "two-factor theory." Herzberg and associates analyzed data generated by 200 scientists and engineers. They asked the subjects to report what events and conditions produced satisfaction and dissatisfaction. Herzberg found that two factors emerged from the data. The work itself, which included accomplishment, recognition for accomplishment, and so on, produced satisfaction, whereas their famous hygiene factor (e.g., company policy, working conditions, pay) tended to produce dissatisfaction.

Whereas Herzberg's work is largely discredited, many studies still report two factors emerging from job satisfaction data. The problem with the two-factor theory is that no simple relationship between these factors and satisfaction exists, as Herzberg suggests.

The many parallels between job satisfaction literature and client satisfaction literature are fascinating (viz., accomplishment and therapy, supervisor and therapist, client characteristics and worker characteristics, organization climate and clinic atmosphere). The parallels need more exploration.

Toward a Global Definition of Client Satisfaction

Client satisfaction can be defined as a set of positive and/or negative feelings resulting from receiving mental health services. Although most researchers would agree on this definition, it lacks the precision needed for a measurement system. This definition does not define client or satisfaction. Much of the reported research does an inadequate job of stating an operational definition of either what is a client or what is satisfaction.

Definition of what constitutes a client is not as trivial as it seems. Most studies exclude large numbers of clients from their data. Groups often excluded are brief visits (one or two visits), children, chronically ill or disabled clients who cannot respond, clients in inpatient units, court-ordered clients who report low levels of satisfaction, those in alcohol treatment programs, and quasi-clients who receive direct service, but through an affiliation agreement with other agencies or adjunct groups. Client satisfaction seems to be an excellent instrument for adult outpatients. If this is the population being studied, an explicit statement to that effect is necessary.

One of the major problems with the measurement of client satisfaction in the past has been a lack of an operational definition of satisfaction. There seems to be as many operational definitions of satisfaction as there are instruments that have been developed to measure it. The Utah studies presented earlier use either a total score or the added score of questions 7 and 8 to operationally define client satisfaction. The questions were:

1. Would you return for services?
2. Would you refer others?

The Services Evaluational Questionnaire (SEQ) contains eight items. These items are currently undergoing standardization across the country and represent an attempt to standardize client satisfaction. The authors have provided three items in a short form to measure satisfaction:

1. To what extent has our program met your needs?

2. In an overall general sense, how satisfied are you with the services you received?

3. If you were to seek help again, would you come back to our program?

These questions are the operational definition of the SEQ (Larsen et al., 1980). The research by Larsen and colleagues indicates that there is only one underlying factor in the larger 31-item scale and that the SEQ also contains only one unidimensional factor. The logical conclusion would be that each of the three short-form questions measure a slightly different version of the basic dimension. Their definition is that satisfaction is a unidimensional outcome that can be represented by the three questions above. Ware (1981) points out that a major problem attendant to measuring satisfaction with a global scale is the inability of instruments to make fine gradations of levels of satisfaction. This factor alone may be the cause of high-positive responding among respondents. The global consumer satisfaction instrument may elicit responses from the client that require no discrimination; For example, they force no judgments on the respondent's part. Perhaps if more rigorous questions and techniques were available, the cases would distribute in a normal distribution. Ware (1981) has suggested that the distribution of satisfaction is linear; there is no point inflection in the line indicating a natural break between those who are satisfied and dissatisfied. Ware has used factor analysis as a means of selecting questions and item analysis to improve the questions' psychometric properties. Another scaling suggestion is offered by Bechtel (1980), who suggests improvements through the use of successive interval scaling theory.

Satisfaction is an affective reaction. Scaling might also be improved and anchors established by using *The Taxonomy of Educational Objectives: The Affective Domain* (Bloom et al., 1964) to define the range of the satisfaction variable. By use of the levels suggested by Bloom in his affective taxonomy, the highly positive consumer satisfaction could be distributed and a minimal threshold established. Presently, UMHPEC members are evaluating a consumer satisfaction questionnaire that attempts to make this type of minimal level of satisfaction and spread the responses over a wider range. Their (yes/no) questions include the following: (1) I would like the name of someone to tell about my complaints; (2) I desire no further contact with the mental health center; (3) if the mental health center published a monthly bulletin, I would like to receive it; (4) if I needed help in the future, I would return for services; (5) I would be willing to help out occasionally with mental health activities if I were called; (6) I would be willing to sign a petition that would raise taxes to support mental health activities; and (7) I would donate money to help support mental health activities.

This item pool was drawn from a sample of 40 items that were tested in a telephone survey conducted by the Weber Mental Health Center. Fifty-five clients of the center were contacted and asked to respond to the entire item pool and the Utah client satisfaction instrument. The above items were selected on the basis of intercorrelations of the items with total score on the Utah instrument (See Appendix C p. 635).

A principal problem with the satisfaction definition proposed by the Bloom hierarchy is that consumer satisfaction is multidimensional. The value of this single index would be its reduction of data and its reliance on items that can be empirically verified.

Questions such as "Would you refer a friend for services?" have no way of being verified in reality. Respondents may be adamant about their answers, but may never have friends with problems that would require referral. On the other hand, "Would you sign a petition to raise taxes for support of mental health activities?" can be verified directly.

Toward a Conceptual Model of Client Satisfaction

Several approaches to developing a conceptual model of client satisfaction hold promise. Larsen et. al. (1980) have tacitly implied an expectancy model. Building a model of this type could borrow from the rich literature in consumer satisfaction in marketing. The author does not lean in this direction for two reasons: (1) much of the data in this area are self-reports, which only compound the present problems of client satisfaction; (2) most econometric models are decision oriented. They assume that the individuals act in their own interest to maximize the utility of their decisions. The work of Webster and Sobiestrek (1974) on significant others makes it clear that the econometric assumption is not justified with self-report data.

A second approach that holds great appeal is the work of the environmental psychologists. An excellent overview of this approach is found in the Psychological Bulletin article. Pervin (1968, p. 57) wrote: "A 'match' or 'best fit' of an individual to the environment is viewed as expressing itself in high performance, satisfaction and little stress in the system."

The author has not felt that this was the best model for purely philosophical reasons. This approach has much of its philosophical roots in phenomenological psychology, which the author considers antithetical to an empirical approach:

> Within the framework of this paper, it is assumed that individuals vary in their sensitivity to different stimuli and in the nature of their responses to these stimuli. Behavior is represented as a function of the interaction or transaction between the individual and his environment. (Pervin, 1968, p. 57)

The author, in turn, suggests the model diagrammed in figure 3.2.

This causal path analysis should provide a functional model that can be tested and refined. The technique represents a method of decomposing linear relationships. In the model, X_1 represents client characteristics, such as sex, age, income, education, race, and marital status. This also includes the more stable characteristics such as previous mental health services. The X_2 factor represents pretreatment, psychosocial stressors acting on the individual at the time of intake. Stress instruments such as the one proposed by Holmes and Rahe (1967) might prove useful.

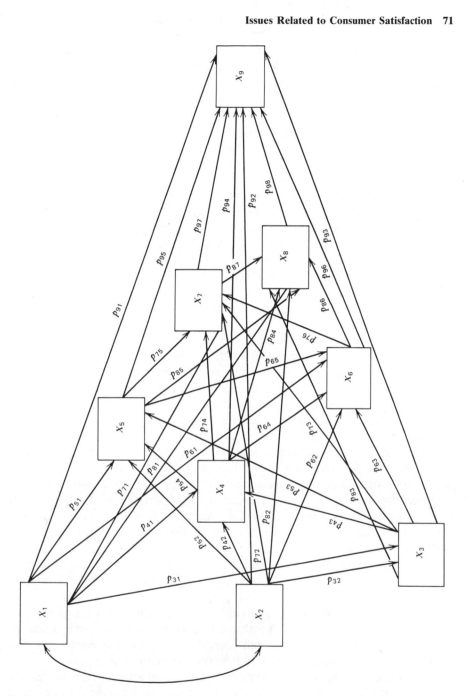

Figure 3.2. Hypothetical Path analysis.

The X_3 measure represents a diagnostic factor. It might include categories of disability as well as severity. Simple dichotomies such as psychotic versus nonpsychotic are possibilities for inclusion. Other systems using the DSM III could be valuable predictors, including items such as depressed versus non-depressed, acute or inpatient admissions versus standard outpatient admission, and so on. Severity would be measured by some pretreatment instrument such as the global assessment scale or the SCL-90. The author has tried a series of multiplicative scales combining dichotomous categories with measures of severity. The results have been disappointing. The combined scales have typically accounted for less variance than those in which a single variable was used. The X_3 factor represents direct diagnosis.

The hygiene factor, X_4, would include in the regression equation such variables as orientation, friendliness of center staff, location of center, distance of travel to obtain therapy, fees, billing timeliness, and accuracy.

The X_5 factor would include as much information about therapists as possible, including standard demographic data such as age and race. In addition, self-report or rating data by others might include philosophical orientation, use of relationship as opposed to structure (Mejia, 1981, Reference Note 5). Additional data such as years of experience, attitude toward the change process (optimistic or pessimistic) and burnout might add to the explained variance in this factor.

The X_6 factor would include the number of visits from admission to termination or until the date of response for active clients. It would be important to separate visits by service modality (e.g., namely outpatient, inpatient, partial care, emergency services, and residential). Another useful variable for regression is the construct of treatment density, which is the total number of visits divided by the length (in days) of service; length is usually defined as the time from admission to the last treatment contact.

The X_7 measure could be a repetition of the X_2 measure made at or near termination. In the case of active clients at the point of observation, the author would hope that much of the elimination of stress might be found in path p_{82} and that the second psychosocial stressors might be examined in the light of community impact. It is recognized that community impact has been traditionally viewed as an outcome rather than a mediating variable. One could argue, however, that adjustment to family, friends, work, and so on may be viewed as part of the process of therapy as well as an outcome. This argument acquires a certain cogence when the view of therapy is expanded beyond the 50-minute hour.

The X_8 measure could be a postscore on a standard instrument or a community adjustment score. An alternative would again be a multiplicative variable, multiplying a symptom scale score by a community adjustment score.

The topic of the X_9 measure was discussed in the previous section.

Some question may be raised as to the relative positioning in the model; the position of the hygiene factor is an example. It was placed in the framework at this point to account for the economic notion of "importance" and to explain premature terminations and their effect on the level of satisfaction. It is hypothesized that paths $p_{42} + p_{94}$, $p_{42} + p_{64} + p_{96}$, and $p_{42} + p_{64} + p_{86} + p_{98}$ will account for a high percentage of dissatisfied clients reporting satisfaction. The hygiene factor, aggravated by the stress factor, will raise the level of importance of the hygiene variables. As importance rises, these variables will have an all-or-none influence on client satisfaction.

Cronkite and Moos (1981) reported a path analysis indicating a total explained variance of 19.0 to 46.3%, depending on the criteria used in their study to define alcohol abuse improvement. This is not significantly different from the 37.2% variance explained in the Utah studies for client satisfaction; however, Cronkite and Moos also reported an increase of 21% explained variance by adding an additional factor in their path analysis. The decomposition of the path analysis should answer various questions about the model and the placement of the factors. The author's analysis is in process at this writing.

Recommendations

Client satisfaction stands at a point where it must move on from its adolescence into a more mature posture. Rather than reporting the standard findings of 85% satisfaction with the program, evaluators must now address certain basic issues with client satisfaction. These involve developing a better understanding of what is being measured, reducing the error or unknown component in the measurement of satisfaction, and relating measurements to external criteria. The following recommendations are offered to move the measurement of satisfaction in that direction.

Recommendation 1

The construct of client satisfaction has not been fully defined or conceptualized. There is evidence to suggest that client satisfaction is a continuous linear function. Evidence suggests that client satisfaction includes two separate phenomena, satisfaction and dissatisfaction. The author's recommendation is to accept the measurement as a single continuous variable. This recommendation is based on three separate arguments: (1) the idea that satisfaction is a single, continuous, linear variable is appealing from the measurement standpoint; (2) the author has great respect for the effort involved in the approach of Ware and his attempts to normalize the distribution—no such attempt was made with the Utah data, and thus the distribution of Ware's data should perhaps be more viable from this perspective; and (3) Ware's findings are based on a generalized population of which a clinical population would be a subset. It would seem logical to accept the more generalized approach that should lead to broader applications of research.

Work should begin immediately to apply the techniques developed by Ware in normalizing his distribution to normalizing the distribution in the mental health setting. A sharing of item pools and analysis would save reinventing the satisfaction wheel.

Recommendation 2

A model of the nature suggested by the author should be adopted to gain a clearer understanding of the influences on satisfaction of the known factors that influence client satisfaction. Although this model does not represent a comprehensive model, it does help to conceptualize client satisfaction in terms of an empirical relationship rather than a more speculative and less empirical notion.

Recommendation 3

Findings are functions of questions asked. The range of questions in client satisfaction instruments need to be broadened to include items dealing with validity issues—namely, community impact, reduction of criminal or aberrant behavior, improved role functioning, and improved self-concept.

Recommendation 4

Clinicians and researchers need to adopt a more rigorous operational definition of client satisfaction. It would be well advised for anyone who is constructing such a research instrument to capitalize on the work previously done, including data base generated by Larsen et al. (1980). To this end, any research questionnaire might include the three short scale items suggested by ·these authors as reference points in the research scale.

Recommendation 5

One difficulty that the author has experienced and suspects that other researchers have encountered and not fully taken into consideration is the problem of between-site variance. When data are aggregate, there seems to be an interactive effect between the data and the sites. The process of aggregation tends to increase the intercorrelations between data items. It is strongly recommended that multiple-site data be transformed to data with common means and variance. This reduces between-group variance, which tends to confound certain data analysis techniques.

Recommendation 6

It is strongly recommended that both terminated and active clients be included in the sample procedure for client satisfaction. The following methodology has worked well across several centers in Utah and provides an added dimension. Client satisfaction instruments should be mailed to all terminated cases as they terminate and all who have four months of service. Excluded from this group would be those who have had only one visit. If a person has not terminated in the first four months, they would automatically receive a client satisfaction questionnaire as an active client of the mental health center on the anniversary of their fourth month in service. This particular methodology has several advantages: (1) it increases the response or return rate of questionnaires; (2) it includes data on both active and terminated clients that can be compared; and (3) it maximizes the feedback function of the data. You are collecting recent data as opposed to ancient history.

Recommendation 7

The time interval between when the client leaves service and is surveyed for client satisfaction should be held to a minimum. It has been found by the Utah centers that where the time interval is less than two weeks from the time of termination, the response rate has an attendant increase of 5 to 7%. It is also recommended that a follow-up letter be sent before two weeks after the original mailing. This should be a routine part of the sampling procedure. The Utah data demonstrate that a timely follow-up letter will increase the percentages of responses by 25 to 35%.

Recommendation 8

It is recommended that certain routine statistics be kept on client satisfaction. Unless the number of terminated clients exceeds 500, a continuous sampling of all cases is recommended for research purposes. If extensive multivariate analysis is to be used, 100% sampling is also indicated to keep cell sizes viable. When the total number exceeds 500, a sampling procedure is recommended (Pandiani & Kessler, 1981). Routine statistics should include the rate of return, means and standard deviations of the individual questions, a Pearson correlation between client satisfaction, and other outcome measures that have been found to be of use to evaluate the outcome of psychotherapy.

Recommendation 9

It is recommended that a separate survey be used for brief contacts, inpatients, and agency consultations. Brief contact data (one visit only) provide a rich source of data about the operation of dissatisfiers. The standard instruments are not oriented toward these brief visits. The author has included a brief contact instrument in Appendix D p. 636.

Recommendation 10

The researcher who intends to do detailed analysis is not the only one who should develop an extensive satisfaction data base. The data base should include facility for the selection of subgroups for which client satisfaction can be analyzed separately. It is valuable to have data that can be isolated, such as ethnic groups or groups that have been in service for over one year, subgroups within certain diagnostic categories, or subgroups or different divisions or satellite facilities. Construction of the analysis procedures with the use of a standard statistical package such as the SPSS is not difficult provided the information is available in the data base.

Recommendation 11

Clinician resistance to client satisfaction can usually be overcome by three basic steps: (1) including clinicians in the planning of client satisfaction measurement; (2) giving clinicians the assurance that client satisfaction data will not be used as a means of individual evaluation; and (3) providing immediate feedback from client satisfaction instruments. This feedback should be nonpunitive whenever negative comments are received. It is recommended that the evaluator follow a rule of thumb: for each level that the findings rise in an organization, the data should undergo a corresponding level of aggregation. At the clinician level, raw (unaggregated) data can be given to the worker directly.

Data that go to a first-level supervisor should undergo one level of aggregation so that the supervisor does not receive any information on the individual worker personally nor any individual client. Data going to higher levels are reaggregated to simplify the data for management use and to de-identify the individual client and the clinician.

Recommendation 12

It is important that the comment section of the evaluation forms not be overlooked. The comments provide a separate dimension unmeasured by most client satisfaction questions. If the distinction between quantitative and qualitative research in client satisfaction is valid, comments become the qualitative side of the research paradigm. In dealing with top-level administrators as well as people outside the agency, it has been found that a well-rounded package of comments is often worth a year's accumulation of data. Comments provide a richness that the numbers cannot. The inclusion of a liberal sample of comments, including negatives along with empirical data, raises the trust level and reduces resistance to reports.

Recommendation 13

It has been suggested that satisfaction measures are also worth measuring because they are predictive of behavior; that is, they may be viewed as an independent variable. Is the behavior of more satisfied clients different from that of dissatisfied clients? If so, are the differences in behavior important? Does satisfaction relate to recidivism, better community adjustment, and so on? These questions need to be placed in the high-priority category for research in this area.

Recommendation 14

The model suggested by the author in the preceding section (on a conceptual model of client satisfaction) provides some insight into the methods of increasing patient satisfaction. One is to concentrate on the crucial areas of pretherapy orientation. The author feels that better therapy and improved satisfaction will result from the improvement of orientation procedures. Better role induction, more specific information about what to expect from therapy, and the development of positive expectations of therapy are all methods of enhancing therapeutic outcome and satisfaction.

Recommendation 15

More research must be done to eliminate the error component inherent in all client satisfaction instruments. Of immediate need is a study of nonresponders to mailed surveys to determine the degree to which sample bias is operating. Those who are attempting to reduce error in their measurement of satisfaction may well look at item analysis and develop better item pools and better techniques of behaviorally anchoring scales and individual items to examine the possibility of general response sets as artifacts in the data.

Much work needs to be done in further defining and refining client satisfaction as a therapeutic outcome. Those who are just beginning to use client satisfaction as an outcome measure need not wonder about its advisability on the basis of state-of-the art questions. Client satisfaction has evolved into a viable outcome measure. Researchers, center evaluators, and administrators realize that satisfaction data present a dimension of the outcome of therapy as viable as symptom reduction.

REFERENCE NOTES

1. Christensen, E., Salt Lake County Mental Health, Salt Lake City, Utah. Data reported in an oral presentation to the Utah Program Evaluation Meeting, Spring, 1980.
2. Owen, W., Davis Mental Health Center, Farmington, Utah, and Goza, B., Granite Mental Health Center, Salt Lake City, Utah. The data report findings of two centers that isolate significant factors between responders and nonresponders.
3. Kelner, G., Salt Lake County Mental Health, Salt Lake City, Utah. An oral report of data following a major revision and consolidation of services at three mental health centers.
4. Christensen, E., and Shepard, J. S., Salt Lake County Mental Health, Salt Lake City, Utah. A report of unpublished findings reported by Christensen by telephone conversation.
5. Mejia, J., Utah Division of Mental Health. Unpublished Doctoral Dissertation: "The Role of Structure vs. Relationship in Marital Counseling."

REFERENCES

Balch, P., Ireland, J. F., McWilliams, S., & Lewis, B. Client evaluations of community mental health services. *American Journal of Community Psychology*, **5**, 1977, 243–247.

Barker, R. *Ecological Psychology*. Los Angeles: Stanford University Press, 1968.

Bechtel, G.G. A scaling model for survey monitoring. *Evaluation Review*, 1980, **4**, 5–41.

Berger, M. A study of failures of follow through for mental health services. *Rural Connections*, Spring 1980.

Berger, M., & Callister, S. *A review of comments from consumer satisfaction instruments*. Ogden, Utah: Weber Mental Health Center, 1981.

Bloom, B. S., & Krathwohl, M. D. *A Taxonomy of educational objectives*: Handbook II. *The affective domain*. New York: David McKay, 1964.

Brown, E. D. The role of expectancy in ratings of consumer satisfaction with mental health services. Doctoral Dissertation, Florida State University, 1979.

Cornely, P., & Bingham, S. Some consideration in changing health attitudes. *Children*, 1963, **10**, 23–28.

Cronkite, R. C., & Moss, R. H. Determinants of the posttreatment functioning of alcoholic patients: A conceptual framework. *Journal of Consulting and Clinical Psychology*, 1981, **48**, 305–316.

Dwarshuis, L., & Kolton, M. S. Evaluating staff and client perceptions. *Evaluations in Practice*. Rockville, Md.: NIMH publication, 1976.

Doyle, B. J., & Ware, J. E. Physician conduct and other factors that affect consumer satisfaction with medical care. *Journal of Medication Education*, 1977, **52**, 793.

Ellsworth, R. B. Consumer feedback in measuring the effectiveness of mental health programs. *Handbook of program evaluation publications*. Beverly Hills, Calif.: Sage Publications, 1975, 239–274.

Fisher, A. N. Patient evaluation of outpatient medication care. *Journal of Medical Education*, 1971, **46**, 238.

Geertsen, D. C. Client awareness and accessibility. *Evaluations in Practice*. Rockville, Md.: NIMH publication, 1979.

Gilmer, B. *Industrial and organizational psychology*. New York: McGraw-Hill, 1971.

Greenberg, R. P. The influence of referral information upon patient perception in psychotherapy analogue. *Journal of Nervous and Mental Disorders*, 1970, **150**, 31–36.

Greenly, J. F., & Schoenherr, R. A. Organizational effects on client satisfaction with humaneness of services. *Journal of Health & Social Behavior*, 1981, **22**, 2–18.

Hagedson, H. J., Beck, K. J., Newbert, S. F., & Werlin, S. H. Editorials, *A working manual of simple program evaluation techniques for community mental health centers*. Rockville, Md.: NIMH publication, 1976.

Hartmen, P. F. Survey finds need for improved consumer satisfaction measures. *Evaluation*, 1977, **4**, 59–60.

Herzberg, F., Mausner, B., Peterson, R. O., & Campbell, D. F. *Job attitudes*. Pittsburgh: Psychological Services of Pittsburgh, 1957.

Hill, J. A. Therapist goals, patient aims and patient satisfaction in psychotherapy. *Journal of Clinical Psychology*, 1974, **25**, 455–459.

Holmes, T. H., & Rahe, R. H. The social readjustment rating scale. *Journal of Psychometric Research*, 1967, **11**, 213–218.

Justice, B., & McBee, G. A client survey as one element of evaluation. *Community Mental Health Journal*, 1980, **14**, 248–252.

Kline, F., Adrian, A., & Spevak, M. Patients evaluate therapists. *Archives of General Psychology*, 1974, **31**, 113–116.

Larsen, D. L., Attkisson, O., Hargreaves, W. A., & Nguyen, T. D. Assessment of client/patient satisfaction: Development of a general scale. *Evaluation Program Planning*, 1980, **2**, 197–207.

Lebow, J. L. Consumer satisfaction with mental health treatment. *Psychological Bulletin*, 1982, **91**, 244–259.

Leicht, P. O., & Levy, S. J. Client and staff perception of a day treatment program. *Evaluation in Practice*. Rockville, Md.: NIMH publication, 1979.

Leishman, J. A clash in perspectives. *British Journal of Social Work*, 1980, **10**, 251–257.

Levois, M., Nguyen, T., & Attkisson, C. Artifact in client satisfaction assessment: Experience in community mental health settings. *Program Planning and Evaluation*, in press.

Locke, E. A. The nature and causes of job satisfaction. *The Handbook of Industrial and Organization Psychology*. New York: Rand McNally College Publications, 1976, 1297–1350.

McFee, C. B., Suesman, J., & Joss, R. H. Measurement of patient satisfaction: A survey of practices in community mental health centers. *Comprehensive Psychiatry*, 1975, **16**, 399–404.

Moos, R. Sources of variance in response to questionnaires in behavior. *Journal of Abnormal Psychology*, 1976, **74**, 405–412.

Nguyen, T. D., & Attkisson, C. C. *Assessment of client/patient satisfaction: Development and standardization of a service evaluation questionnaire*. A paper presented at the American Psychological Association Convention, Los Angeles, August 1981.

Noel, G., & Block, B. Client evaluations of outpatient mental health services: Three telephone surveys. *Evaluation in Practice*. Rockville, Md.: NIMH publication, 1979.

Nunnally, J. C., & Wilson, W. H. Method and theory for developing measures in evaluation research. *Handbook of program evaluation*. Beverly Hills, Calif.: Sage Publications, 1975.

Pandiani, J. A., & Kessler, R. *Monitoring client satisfaction, political, practical and empirical issues*. A paper presented to the National Council of Community Mental Health Centers, Dallas, April 1981.

Pervin, L. A. Performance and satisfaction as a function of individual–environment fit. *Psychological Bulletin*, 1968, **69**, 56–68.

Read, P. *Consumer perspectives of social services: A study in the measurement of consumer satisfaction*. Unpublished doctoral dissertation, Ohio State University, 1980.

Salvman, K. Interviewer anger and patient dropout in walk-in clinics. *Comprehensive Psychiatry*, 1967, **2**, 267–273.

Schulberg, H. C. Outcome evaluations in mental health field. *Community Mental Health Journal*, 1981, **17**, 132–142.

Sorensen, J. L., Hammer, R., & Windle, C. The four A's: Acceptability, availability, accessibility, awareness. *Evaluation in Practice*. Rockville, Md.: NIMH publication, 1976.

Sorensen, J. L., Cantor, L., Margolis, R. A., & Galano, J. The extent, nature and utility of evaluating consumer satisfaction in community mental health centers. *American Journal of Community Psychology*, 1979, **3**, 329–337.

SPSS. Analyzing residuals. *Keywords for Users of SPSS #25*, Chicago, Il.: SPSS Inc., 1981.

UMHPEC. *The executive summary of mental health programs in Utah*, 1979, 1980 and 1981, Utah State Division of Mental Health.

Vroom, V. H. *Work and motivation*. New York: Wiley, 1964.

Ware, J. E. Effects of acquiescent response set on patient satisfaction ratings. *Medical Care*, 1978, **16**, 327–336.

Ware, J. E. *The behavior of dissatisfied patients*. A paper presented to the annual meeting of the American Psychological Association, Los Angeles, August 1981.

Ware, J. E., & Snyder, M. K. Dimensions of patient attitudes toward doctors and medical care services. *Medical Care*, 1975, **13**, 669–682.

Warner, J. L. Alternative methods for collecting data on mental health treatment outcome. Reported in the Organization for Program Evaluation in Colorado, *Program Evaluation Bulletin*, Spring 1981.

Waskow, I. E., & Parloff, M. B. (Eds.). *Psychotherapy change measures*. Washington, D.C.: DHEW, No. 74–120, 1975.

Webster, M., & Sobiestrek, B. *Sources of self-evaluation*. New York: Wiley, 1974.

PART TWO

Assessing Outcome in Select Mental Health Settings

CHAPTER 4

Outcome Assessment in a Private Practice Setting

GEORGE STRICKER

Before the problems and promise of research in a private practice setting can be considered, it is necessary to define what is meant by the term "private practice." The private sector is often contrasted with the public sector, with the distinction between the two based on the source of funds contributing to the support of treatment. This is a murky distinction since many agencies charge patients on a sliding scale and are also subsidized by public funds, so that they do not fit neatly into either category. Furthermore, many patients who enter into private arrangements with therapists meet their bills through third-party payments, so that the source of funds is neither public nor from personal resources. Finally, although many fee-for-service agencies rely entirely on private or third-party funds, they are not generally considered to be part of the private practice community. The more appropriate contrast, then, is not private versus public but, rather, private practice versus institutional practice. Regardless of source of funds, a therapist functioning under the aegis of a responsible organization, whether it be a hospital, a university, an agency, or a community mental health center, would be considered to be in institutional practice. On the other hand, a therapist assuming sole responsibility for the patient, whether paid by the patient, an insurance company, or public funds, is considered to be in private practice. Blau (1981, Reference Note 1 at end of chapter) prefers the term "independent practice" to "private practice" because "private" connotes some restriction of clientele. Additionally, the term "independent" also underlines the lack of shared responsibility for the patient. The term "private practice" is used in this chapter because of common parlance; however, "independent practice" does come closer to capturing the meaning of the topic under consideration. Because the focus of this chapter is on outcome, the concentration is on the patient and little attention is given to the rich lode of data derived from private therapists concerning their attitudes and practices.

UNIQUE PROBLEMS AND POTENTIAL

No outcome measures are unique to a private practice setting. The appropriate gauge of change in a patient does not vary as a function of the setting but, rather, as a function of the characteristics of the patient. The uniqueness in a private practice setting rests with some of the methodological issues raised, and it is these that lend the distinctive quality to the research done in this arena. As a backdrop to this discussion of methodology, it should be noted that the responsibility for the research in a private practice setting falls squarely on the therapist, as do all other responsibilities, and cannot be shunted to an institution. Thus every decision and consequence, from research design to consent procedures to reactive effects, rests with the therapist, and it may be the weight of this burden that explains, in part, the paucity of research in private practice. In this section many of the unique features of research in private practice are considered, along with a number of features that also apply to research in other settings but that may have particular meanings in private practice.

The first issue to be considered is whether therapists in private practice would agree to be involved in data collection for a research project. This removes the burden of research design from the practitioner and asks only whether the therapist would cooperate with an established research protocol. An attempt to answer a related question was made by the American Psychological Association–Civilian Health and Medical Program for Uniformed Services (APA–CHAMPUS) project, pursuant to a different concern (Shueman, 1981, Reference Note 2). A brief questionnaire was sent to 100 randomly selected providers listed in the National Register. It asked if they would be willing to participate in a study of the validity of peer review that might involve such methods as completion of treatment reports describing care of the patient, interviewing and other surveying of the patient, and taping of psychotherapy sessions. A fairly high return rate of 51% was obtained, although seven subjects were eliminated because they were not in private practice. The majority of the respondents had more than 10 years of postdoctoral experience, worked in an urban setting, and described themselves as eclectic in orientation. Of the 44 respondents in private practice, 13 indicated that they would probably participate in the project and an additional 22 were willing to consider participation. Of this group, half felt that they would not have any trouble convincing some of their patients to participate.

The major portion of the questionnaire listed a variety of data collection procedures and asked whether they would be acceptable. By far the highest rate of endorsement (over 80%) was given to the preparation of written treatment reports by the provider and written survey responses by the patient. A majority also agreed to the audiotaping of selected sessions (65%) and interviewing of the patient by another clinical psychologist (55%). Methods that were found unacceptable by a majority of the respondents included telephone interviews with the patient by the research staff (63%), videotaping of selected sessions (60%), and face-to-face interviews with the patient by the research staff (53%). An additional method that did not appear acceptable, although there was no clear majority, was a survey of the patient's significant others. It is of some interest that the reported study found no differences in acceptable methods of intervention that were related to the orientation of the provider. In a similar vein, even though Kazdin and Wilson (1978) indicate that one of the two basic defining characteristics of all behavior therapies "is a commitment to scientific method, measurement, and evaluation" (Kazdin & Wilson, 1978, p. 7), behavior therapists have not been particularly responsive to participation in research projects (Gold, 1980; Norcross & Wogan, Reference Note 3).

The project summarized above falls in the general category of cooperative research, an approach in which a single project is conducted with central coordination, but with data collected in a variety of settings. This has a marked advantage in terms of generalizability since therapists can be widely dispersed geographically and chosen because of specified features of their orientation or their patient's characteristics. It also relieves the provider of responsibility for the research design and, therefore, is likely to be the modal approach to research in this setting. It does seem clear that a psychologist wishing to coordinate a study utilizing private practitioners, depending on the inherent interest and soundness of the project, could expect cooperation from a substantial minority of providers. The advantages regarding generalizability that would accrue from the distribution of therapists would be partially counterbalanced by the selectivity of the volunteer process. Clearly, the broader the participation, the more valuable the study would be, and the less intrusive methods are more likely to encourage cooperation. The method of data collection employed, then, would be a determining factor in the breadth of therapists' cooperation that, in turn, would be integrally related to the generalizability and external validity of the project. Methods involving therapist or patient reports would be more acceptable, whereas methods involving direct contact with the patient or significant others would be less acceptable.

This leads to a consideration based on prior therapy research (Bergin & Lambert, 1978) that has indicated the lack of correspondence among data sources. Outcome measures can be gathered directly from the patient, in the form of self-reports, projective tests, or behavioral observations, or they can be in the form of reports about the patient from the therapist, an independent clinician, or significant others. Process measures can be obtained from patient or therapist reports or derived from a variety of instruments ranging from audiotapes to physiological recording devices. Because these various measures seldom correlate highly, the findings of a study will be a function of the dependent variables chosen. This does not cast doubt on the value of an individual study as much as it reflects the multifaceted nature of therapeutic change. In any case, since private practice research is only likely to employ a selected subgroup of the available dependent measures, findings will reflect only a restricted band of the many facets of psychotherapy. Since this same problem obtains with most studies, regardless of site, it serves to emphasize the need to seek multiple measurements and converging operations in order to provide a full description of the nature of psychotherapy.

There is increasing recognition that there is no universally appropriate dependent variable. Rather, just as each patient presents different problems and thus requires treatment directed toward different goals, each therapy study would do well to capture this aspect of treatment by individualizing the dependent measure. Of course, this leads to psychometric complications, and it is far easier, even if less veridical, to seek a unitary measurement. A single measure can be utilized if it is of an abstract and overarching dimension, like health–sickness, but this choice lacks specificity and loses information. It is also possible to retain a single measure and gain greater specificity by restricting the range of patients, so that exercising selection in defining the patient population can make it more appropriate to use a single, highly focused measure. This choice, of course, restricts the generalizability of the findings.

Fortunately, developments in fields as distant as behavior modification, psychoanalysis, and program evaluation all point to the possibility of retaining specificity without restricting range by individualizing the treatment measure. Workers in behavior modification have a long history of evaluating treatment with an $N = 1$ model (Hersen and Barlow, 1976) in which target behaviors are selected for modification and carefully monitored, either by the therapist, the patient, or a significant other. A replicated $N = 1$ design could deal with some of the problems raised by limited statistical power and restricted generalizability. It is possible to vary target behaviors and combine data, assessing whether established criteria have been met. This is the general approach taken within the psychodynamic model in the work of Malan (1976), who establishes individual therapy goals for each patient after a lengthy initial evaluation. The success of the treatment is then judged according to whether these initial goals were met, so that the overall efficacy of Malan's short-term treatment approach can be evaluated even though each patient may present a different set of problems and require a different set of changes. Finally, the most fully articulated method of individualizing the dependent variable has been developed for program evaluation by Kiresuk (Kiresuk and Sherman, 1968). In his Goal Attainment Scaling approach, each patient and therapist jointly construct a series of dimensions on which change is desired, along with a definition of the various steps of change. This method allows not only each patient to select the relevant dimensions but also for the quantification of degree of change by defining specific points on the continuum. These three methods differ in that the behavioral approach and Goal Attainment Scaling are keyed to specific behavioral change, whereas the psychodynamic approach allows for the consideration of more unconscious motivational factors, but they share a recognition of patient differences that will contribute to the veridicality of therapy research.

The approaches described to this point, whether general or specific, can be utilized in therapy research regardless of the setting where it is performed, and are all superimposed on the treatment process. There is also a valuable data source that is an inherent part of therapy and can be utilized in evaluating either the process or outcome of treatment. In institutional settings elaborate records are often kept, many of which conform to standard guidelines as a result of the requirements of either governmental authorities such as state health departments or quasi-governmental structures such as the Joint Commission for the Accreditation of Hospitals. The requirements in private practice are not as rigidly specified, and record-keeping habits are often a matter of individual comfort and conscience. Both professional standards and many state codes of professional conduct require the maintenance of adequate records, but the definition of adequacy is vague and the monitoring is nonexistent. Nevertheless, to the extent that such records are both maintained and accessible, they constitute a rich source of information about the process of psychotherapy, and a content analysis could provide a unique view of the progress of a therapeutic encounter. As a sole source it would present many methodological problems, but as a converging source, it would add a dimension, the therapist's immediate and unstructured associations, which is rarely tapped.

In psychotherapy research, regardless of venue, it is necessary to obtain the cooperation of the patient if any of the measures are going to be derived from that patient. In institutional settings, such cooperation even if given grudgingly, can be built into the established procedures of the facility. Some settings are even described as research centers, and treatment is offered at a low cost in return for cooperation during research activities. Patients who seek a private practitioner, regardless of the fee that they pay, do not feel any compulsion to participate in any activity that does not contribute immediately to their welfare. In many cases they choose to pay a premium to consult a private practitioner in order to receive the increased attention and freedom from bureaucratic requirements that they feel, rightly or wrongly, are integral to private practice. This does not mean that patients in private practice will not cooperate with a request that they participate in a research project, but it does point out that they feel a greater freedom to decline such participation.

Any therapy research, regardless of the site or dependent measure employed, should obtain the informed consent of the patient. The initial therapeutic contract calls for complete confidentiality and privacy. Any deviation from this contract, whether for clinical or research purposes, must be explicitly stated so that the patient has the opportunity to withdraw consent, or even to withdraw from the relationship. Even patients not being asked to participate directly in any information gathering process should realize that they are objects of study and should give permission for the use of data resulting from such studies. There is much ambiguity in determining what constitutes sufficient information for the consent to be considered informed. It is clearly more than a mere statement that research is being conducted, and usually less than a copy of the research proposal and outline. A handy rule of thumb is that the patient should be given as much information as a reasonable person would require in order to make an informed decision. This is hardly operational and does not reduce the ambiguity, but it can serve as a guideline that can be used in consulting with colleagues to make a determination. In institutional settings, an institutional research board will exercise some judgment in order to protect the patient. In private practice the therapist has the sole responsibility, short of a court of law, for deciding how much information is sufficient and, therefore, would be well advised to confer with peers to ascertain that a fair decision has been reached.

It seems reasonable that, other things being equal, patients will be more willing to give permission for research that requires less effort on their part. It also seems reasonable that patients will be less likely to give permission for research that will lead to the disclosure of sensitive personal data. We have already seen that therapists anticipate this and protect their patients by resisting intrusive studies, and we can guess that they will also be reluctant to participate in studies that require a great deal of their effort. Extrapolation from the Civilian Health and Medical Program For the Uniformed Services (CHAMPUS) survey, crude as it was, revealed that only about one-third of the therapists initially contacted indicated any wish to cooperate and, of these, about half felt that they would have difficulty in convincing patients to cooperate. The exact figures are of little consequence at this point, but the clear principle is that very selective sampling will be an integral problem in private practice research. The problem will be more pronounced for some studies than for others, but no study will achieve exhaustive sampling. The sampling problems will always have to be considered in the interpretation of the research findings and may be sufficiently great as to discourage the performance of some particularly interesting studies. On the other hand, the value of access to this population is such that it may counterbalance the unique problems, and many studies can be performed with little sampling restriction beyond that ordinarily encountered in the institutional setting.

Much of the research that has been described is concerned with the outcome of psychotherapy. It is also of value to consider the potential of process research. Some process recording devices are highly intrusive, such as physiological measurement, and they may be uncomfortable for either the therapist or the patient. Other methods, such as patient or therapist post-session rating forms, require additional work and may be resisted for that reason. There are, however, some data sources relevant to process that may be an integral part of routine clinical procedure. Some therapists maintain detailed process notes, whereas others routinely audio tape sessions. Both of these can be productive sources of information about treatment, if used with the patient's permission.

There is also an enormous value to follow-up research, which is rarely conducted over any meaningful span of time. Follow-up research is patient centered since it involves contacting the patient after treatment has terminated, either with a request to fill out a questionnaire or, more rarely, to return for an evaluation. For research to be meaningful, it is necessary to receive the cooperation of a significant proportion of the patients. Private practice may provide a particularly good opportunity for this. Most patients seen in private practice enjoy some economic advantages and, as a result, often are more geographically stable. This will reduce the loss of patients due to failure to be able to locate them. Once having found the patient, it is possible that a higher return rate would be achieved on the basis of a relationship developed with a single provider, rather than the more diffuse relationship characteristic of many institutional settings. In any case, it is highly probable that the response rate would be increased if the patient had been properly prepared during the termination session to anticipate follow-up contact.

Perhaps the most important issue, and one that applies to the matters already discussed, is the potential reactive effects of the measurement process. One critical form this may take is the effect of the measurement on the patient's behavior. It is well known that the very process of monitoring one's own behavior will often serve to increase the frequency of desirable responses while decreasing the frequency of undesirable responses (Kazdin, 1974). It is also possible that the use of questionnaires will direct the patient's attention to some critical areas and, by so doing, modify the likelihood of change in those areas. Additionally, there is a possibility that the therapist's behavior will be affected by the knowledge that the treatment is under external scrutiny. In many cases these effects are of more profound research than clinical consequence. If a patient is more likely to reduce undesirable behaviors when self-monitoring is initiated, the use of such a dependent variable confounds our understanding of the nature of the change and requires appropriately chosen control procedures to disentangle effects. Clinically, however, the acceleration of change is to the advantage of the patient, regardless of the source, so that a research procedure may eventually be incorporated as part of a clinical method.

All reactive effects, however, are not necessarily salutary. Although the effect on the patient's behavior may often be constructive, there are also effects on the therapeutic relationship, and these may not be as desirable. There are orientations to treatment which proscribe any therapeutic behavior that may ask the patient to do something for the therapist (Langs, 1976). This can include matters as seemingly innocuous as changing an appointment time for the therapist's convenience and as potentially powerful as asking for a personal favor. Whereas some therapists view such requests as contributing toward mutuality, others view them as exploitative. In any case, it is clear that the therapeutic relationship will be affected, and if that relationship is seen as an integral part of the treatment process, the therapist is likely to resist any unnecessary sources of influence.

Although a request to participate in a research project will affect the patient–therapist relationship to varying degrees, depending on the nature of the project, this does not mean that the request should not be made. All therapists but the most orthodox of psychoanalysts will occasionally change an appointment time for reasons of personal convenience, and most therapists find that the pristine nature of the patient–therapist relationship is often sullied by reality factors. Even with a psychodynamic orientation, which would be most concerned with relationship factors, the impact of a request to participate in research can be considered grist for the mill. Thus, although the therapeutic meaning of such a request cannot be ignored, it is also not sufficient grounds to avoid making the request.

The therapist must balance the potential value of the research against the possible reactive effect on the relationship and reach a decision as to which side carries the greater weight. In private practice, this decision will be reached by each therapist, individually, with no institutional pressure to participate, and so the burden will be on the investigator to convince the therapist of the inherent value of the project. There is an additional complication if the investigator and the therapist are one and the same person. In this case the potential for exploitation increases since the patient does not have any ally other than the therapist's conscience. In cooperative research, it appears as though the private practice patient has more protection than does the institutional one since the therapist will resist undue influence and represent the best interests of the patient in reaching a decision about participation. On the other hand, in independent research the private practice patient may have less protection since there are no institutional safeguards to serve as a buffer between the patient and the therapist, and in such a case the therapist would be well advised to seek collegial review to ensure that an exploitative process has been avoided.

SELECTED EXAMPLES OF PRIVATE PRACTICE RESEARCH

A comprehensive review of studies employing private practice patients would pose a difficult problem as far as a literature search was concerned, since the source of patients is not always identified clearly, but it probably would not consume a great deal of space. An informal review of journals in both psychology and psychiatry for the past five years did not reveal as many as a dozen empirical studies that clearly identify their subjects as private practice patients. This presents some real difficulty for the field of psychotherapy research, which is discussed in a later section. In this section, however, a single exemplar is chosen for a number of different approaches to therapy research. This will serve to show the promise, rather than the sum and substance, of work with private practice patients.

Before reviewing any individual study, attention should be called to a summary review of dependent measures prepared by Nelson (1981). Although her paper is not restricted to the private practice arena, it has already been noted that measures are not unique to sites, and the principles that apply in one setting are likely to pertain in others as well. Several of the points made earlier in this chapter were among the guidelines suggested by Nelson. These include the use of specific rather than general measures, the individualization of dependent measures, and the use of multiple measures. A large number of specific approaches to measurement are viewed, and it would be instructive for the prospective researcher to refer to this summary.

Stiles (1980) has demonstrated the value of outcome research with a concentration on the single session rather than the entire course of treatment. Of the

16 therapists sampled in the study, 12 studied patients from their private practice. A Session Evaluation Questionnaire (SEQ) was developed, consisting of 22 bipolar adjective scales, and was filled out by therapist and patient following a series of consecutive sessions. The SEQ was mailed anonymously by the patient directly to the researcher, who was available to respond to any questions about the study. Although factor analyses were performed, they did not form the basis of the scales that were developed. For patient and therapist, ratings were tabulated on the depth and value of the session, the smoothness and ease of the session, and positive feelings following the session. The two session rating scales did not correlate with each other, and both correlated with overall positive feelings. The most interesting finding resulted from the intercorrelation of patient and therapist ratings. Positive feelings correlated moderately, so there was only a limited extent to which patient and therapist felt satisfied after the same session. Perhaps this was because therapist positive feelings correlated with patient and therapist ratings of session depth and value, whereas patient positive feelings were correlated with patient and therapist ratings of smoothness and ease. This may suggest that patients feel satisfied after comfortable sessions, whereas therapists feel satisfied after productive sessions. Although the relationship between SEQ and overall outcome was not assessed, the next logical research step is to do so and to determine the cumulative nature of sessions in a successful therapeutic experience.

Koss (1979) did focus on a specific treatment outcome variable. She studied the length of psychotherapy for all 100 patients seen by seven psychotherapists in a single private psychology clinic. Although the study explicity refers to the subjects as "clients seen in private practice," it is unclear as to whether the clinic meets our definition of private practice or is more nearly an institutional setting. The purpose was to determine whether a private practice setting would produce a greater preponderance of long-term patients than has been noted in the literature. For example, Garfield (1978), after reviewing the literature, has reported a median treatment length of six sessions, a number out of keeping with the basic assumptions of most psychodynamic theorists. Koss found the median length of treatment to be eight sessions, with only 20% of the patients remaining in therapy for longer than 25 sessions and only 7% remaining in therapy for over 60 sessions. These data are quite consistent with those obtained in studies based on public agencies. In a similar vein, Langsley (1978) also found great similarity in session length for private and clinic psychiatrists, but that study was biased methodologically toward short-term patients. Data of this type, collected in a more geographically diverse manner, would be crucial for mental health planning. The implications of data of this sort for insurance reimbursement are profound and would be most meaningful if collected in the private practice settings that are most likely to rely on third-party payments.

One of the primary potential advantages of research in private practice is the increased opportunity for follow-up studies. Gold (1980) studied the experience of patients seen by behavior therapists, a study modeled after earlier work in a psychodynamic setting by Strupp et al. (1964, 1969). A group of 20 behavior therapists contacted 211 former patients, 80 of whom returned the study materials. It is not clear how many of the patients were seen privately, but it is reasonable to assume that most of them had been. The 37.9% return rate is roughly comparable to that in the two earlier studies by Strupp and his colleagues and demonstrates that even relatively involved patients are not available in great numbers for long-term follow-up. Interpretation of the results must be tempered by knowledge of the selective nature of the returns. In any case, Gold found that the great majority of patients rated their treatment as successful and satisfying, and both therapists and patients linked success with positive perceptions of the therapeutic relationship. Changes in intrapsychic or interpersonal functioning were indicated as key therapeutic gains more often than symptom relief. The results had a number of parallels with Strupp's work with psychodynamic patients, which also emphasized relationship factors over technique, and pointed to the potential value of an integrative model of psychotherapy (Wachtel, 1977).

Finally, Mintz, et al. (1971) attended to a variety of process variables. In an attempt to determine the major dimensions of an observer's perspective of psychotherapy, they had three raters listen to tape recordings of entire sessions. Fifteen psychotherapists tape-recorded sessions with two of their patients, and of the 30 patients, 17 were being seen privately. Ratings were made initially on 110 patient and therapist variables, and these were reduced to 27 by cluster analytic techniques. Factor analysis then revealed four major dimensions, three of which related to therapist's behavior. The therapist's dimensions were named optimal empathic relationship, directive mode, and interpretive mode, whereas the patient's dimension related to health versus distress. These results were related to two outcome variables with little success, a finding that may have been due to the small number of subjects and the difficulty of predicting long-term outcome from a single early session.

It is particularly interesting to note that none of the four exemplar studies was exclusively performed in a private practice setting. Stiles (1980), Gold (1980), and Mintz et al. (1971) all used both private and clinic patients, and Koss (1979) used a private clinic. Although the results of the individual studies are of some interest, they also serve to underline the paucity of studies based on private practice patients.

ACCOUNTABILITY, PEER REVIEW, AND RESEARCH

Nelson (1981) lists three reasons why a practicing clinician might collect dependent measures on patients regularly, one of which was the demand for accountability that might originate within a service delivery setting or from a governmental agency or third-party payer. Clinicians in private practice are not responsible to any institution but may wish to gauge progress for their own information and certainly will be called on with increasing frequency to supply data to third-party payers to justify continued financial support. The American

Psychological Association (APA) has engaged in a major endeavor with third-party payers, and that effort is described in this section [for further information, see Stricker (1980)]. After the program is outlined, the research potential of the data is also discussed.

In 1977, in response to questions raised in Congress about the continued funding of mental heath services, CHAMPUS signed contracts with the American Psychological Association and the American Psychiatric Association to establish criteria for the review of outpatient mental health services. The Civilian Health and Medical Program for the Uniformed Services is the largest health plan in the world. It has over 7 million beneficiaries and covers retired military personnel, dependents of active duty military personnel, and, in some instances, active-duty servicemen.

The contracts ask each professional association, independently, to establish standards to guide review decisions so that a determination as to the appropriateness of professional services could be made on a professional basis. The CHAMPUS regulations established a number of constraints that influenced the plans devised by the National Advisory Panels appointed to discharge the contract. This chapter describes the efforts of psychology's panel because the author has served as the chair of that panel since its inception, but there are many areas in which the products of psychology and psychiatry were in substantial agreement. In any case, CHAMPUS regulations required that a review system be retrospective and direct its attention to services that have already been offered. Theoretically, the panel felt that prospective review, which would authorize services in advance on the basis of a treatment plan, would be more advisable. Similarly, CHAMPUS regulations mandate that review must occur at the eighth, twenty-fourth, fortieth, and sixtieth sessions, with peer review required at 60 sessions and whenever a patient is seen more than twice a week. The panel has felt that later, and perhaps less frequent, review would be equally efficacious, but had to follow the requirements of CHAMPUS regulations.

Because of the enormous flow of cases within the CHAMPUS system, the panel opted for an exceptions review program rather than reviewing each case, except where mandated by CHAMPUS regulations. This system asked for treatment plans to be filed at each of the mandated review points, examined by reviewers within the office of the fiscal intermediary, and then sent to professional peer reviewers only if they fell outside explicit criteria (Stricker, 1979) that were developed by the panel.

The criteria constructed by the panel were solely for the purpose of guiding reviewers within the office of the fiscal intermediary. All decisions reached by the peer reviewers were made on the basis of individual professional judgment. The criteria served to isolate those cases that appeared to fall in an area that suggested the need for professional review but allowed for the possibility that reviewers would recognize the rationale of the provider's approach and would approve payment.

The treatment report requires that the provider submit a description of the progress since the last review point, the current problem, the goals of treatment, and the interventions planned to reach those goals. There are no requirements for extensive historical material or psychodynamic formulations, but there is a need for sufficient explicit information to allow a reviewer to arrive at a decision about the need for service and the appropriateness of service delivery.

Although the program was initially funded by CHAMPUS, the first implementation of a review program was with a private insurance company, Aetna. In 1979 Aetna signed a contract with APA that provided for the review of cases by psychologists' peer reviewers on the basis of criteria established by the insurance company. In 1980 the full review program utilizing the criteria for reviewers established by the panel was implemented by CHAMPUS. Since that date, other carriers have adopted portions of the program, often on a pilot basis. Although it is not at all clear what direction this general program will take, it does seem apparent that there will be increased demands on psychologists for accountability.

Payment for psychotherapy in over half the cases currently being seen in the United States is made by a party other than the patient or the patient's immediate family (Dörken and Webb, 1978, Reference Note 4). Although mental health professionals have welcomed the advent of third-party payment because it allows services to become available to a broader segment of the population, there also has been some reluctance to share information about the services for fear that the confidentiality of the relationship would be disrupted. It is becoming increasingly clear that no source of payment, whether private or governmental, will continue to pay large sums of money without some indication of the basis for such payment. If decisions about the payment of claims are not made by professionals on a professional basis, they will be made by third-party payers, probably on the basis of actuarial criteria.

The systems that have been implemented to date differ as to the basis for peer review. They are similar, however, in their demands for the submission of information on a regular basis in a systematic fashion. The recognition that information will need to be submitted places demands on the provider to maintain orderly records so as to be prepared to comply with such requests. These records, once compiled, can form the basis of very important and significant research undertakings.

If every practitioner begins to collect a uniform data set that indicates the nature of the problems, goals, and progress within treatment, the opportunity for systematic research would be unparalleled. The possibility of determining which types of treatment produce what types of effects with which patients would become realistic. Cooperative research would have to be undertaken, so that a central research team could collect this information, properly doctored so that confidentiality would be protected. This being done, however, the statistical compiling of the information would not be very difficult.

In the absence of such a central research unit, the insurance companies are in a position to request systematic information on a regular basis. These files, also handled properly so as to protect confidentiality, can be made the basis of research exploration with very little additional work called for on the part of the individual provider. To date such research has not yet been undertaken, largely because the technical implementation of the system has been the major focus of effort, but we can look forward to the time when a gold mine of data will become available for research inquiry.

The suggestion that clinicians' records, and particularly their insurance claims, be used as data leads to one striking potential problem. The various motivations that underlie the selection of information for retention in a patient's file for submission to an insurance company and for scientific data collection are not always consistent, and truth may find itself at cross-purposes with economics. Distortions in claims material will reduce the scientific value of the information and will jeopardize the validity of the review procedure. The more specific the requirement for information is, the more sound the data are likely to be, except in the case of fraud, whereas more open-ended requirements for information invite more highly selected and creative submissions.

There is a staggering implication of an approach in which data collected for the purpose of accountability will allow us to determine which treatments are most efficacious in which circumstances. We would then be in a position to make recommendations to providers about preferred approaches on the basis of information rather than theoretical predilection. A feedback loop could be established in which practice would provide information for research analysis, and the research could, in turn, inform practice. This is an ideal situation that is embodied in a scientist professional model, but very rarely in the specifics of either the science or the profession of psychology.

CONCLUSIONS

Meehl (1954) stated that the use of statistics by clinicians was unavoidable. He was referring to the need to determine which inferences and approaches were more likely than chance to be correct and helpful and to the use of statistics to make this determination. The implication was that no responsible clinician would function with the use of techniques without some certainty as to their efficacy and that statistics were the only method to provide that certainty. Leaving aside some possible methodological and philosophical questions, clinicians have indeed demonstrated that it is quite possible for them to avoid statistics and yet to retain their conviction about their procedures.

One possible explanation lies in a sense that many clinicians claim that research is irrelevant to clinical practice. For example, Barlow (1981) introduced a very important series of papers on research and practice with the statement "at present clinical research has little or no influence on clinical practice" (Barlow, 1981, p. 147). One possible reason for this may lie in the separation between research and practice. Research requires too much skill and knowledge to be conducted as a hobby by a busy clinician; thus, with a few exceptions, researchers do not practice and practitioners do not do research. As a result, the research that is done is often seen as irrelevant to the issues of practice, whereas the relevant papers by practitioners are justly criticized for their methodological inadequacies. The theoretical loop between research and practice is rarely found, and proponents of each find it easier to mock the other than to seek rapprochement.

A second possible reason for the gap is one that is not frequently considered but is a natural consequence of the circumstances that separate research and practice. The theory underlying clinical practice, for the most part, is developed by clinicians who work in a private practice setting seeing private patients. Research testing this theory is often conducted in an institutional setting, using patients who may differ in systematic ways from those seen privately. Neither the essentially healthy students seeking counseling in a college psychological services center or the markedly impaired psychotic residents of state hospitals are at all comparable to the patients seen in private practice, yet they are frequent subjects in psychotherapy research. When the research is inconsistent with theory, the clinician is given the choice of rejecting the theory, which has an intuitive and heuristic appeal, or rejecting the research. The choice that is made is reflected by Barlow's comment, but another choice is possible. It is possible to do research that is more in keeping with clinical reality, so that the findings will be of more value to the practitioner.

In our description of the problems and potential of psychotherapy research, one factor that was mentioned repeatedly was generalizability. The key to the value of any therapy research is in its generalizability. This relates to the issue of internal and external validity (Campbell and Stanley, 1966). Research that is not methodologically sound is lacking in internal validity and will not be generalizable because there are no sound findings to generalize. Research which has internal validity, however, may or may not have external validity as well. When research is considered irrelevant, frequently that refers to a study whose findings cannot be generalized to a common clinical situation. To promote generalizability, we need to employ representative design (Hammond, 1964) in which we sample therapists, patients, and settings rather than work within a specific setting and, by so doing, restrict the therapists and patients that can be sampled. To make matters worse, the choice of setting usually leads to the selection of therapists who are relative novices and patients who are atypical. The inclusion of the private practice setting in the research domain will allow for a wider variety of therapists and patients to be sampled and will be a big step toward the ultimate generalizability of the body of findings.

Once a decision has been made to do research in private practice settings as well as in other settings, generalizability relies on the sampling in that setting. This is a consideration for research in an institutional setting as well, but the greater freedom of the private patient and the private practitioner to refuse to participate will multiply the sampling problem in the private setting. If only the rare private practitioner agrees to participate, and if only the rare patient in that practitioner's case load agrees as well, we will have done little to make research more generalizable and relevant. For this reason, there is some value in designing research that will encourage participation, and this implies the use of minimally intrusive methods and measures. Capitalizing on existing data, such as case records, is a particularly good way of finding information without inconveniencing subjects, as long as these records are relatively uniform as to the information they contain. The use of rating scales by both therapist and patient seems to be the least intrusive and, therefore, most acceptable form of data collection other than that that is inherent in ordinary clinical practice and record keeping.

It should be clear that private practice is not a panacea, and even a maximum expansion in this direction will not solve all of the problems of psychotherapy research. For one thing, just as results from institutional settings do not generalize to private practice, we can assume that research in private practice may not generalize to institutional settings. Furthermore, the limitations in methodology and data sources in private practice suggest the incremental value of studying more accessible patients and therapists. As the mass of psychotherapy research expands, some findings will be identified as unique to particular combinations of therapist, patient, and setting, whereas other findings will converge and form the core of our understanding of the general process of treatment. In this way our research will be more relevant to our practice and our understanding of the phenomenon of psychotherapy enhanced.

REFERENCE NOTES

1. Blau, T. H. Personal communication, January 2, 1981.
2. Shueman, S. A. Personal communication, March 4, 1981.
3. Norcross, J. C. and Wogan, M. *Characteristics and activities of psychotherapists.* Paper presented at the meeting of the Eastern Psychological Association, Hartford, April 1981.
4. Dörken, H., and Webb, J. P. *Health service practice of licensed/certified psychologists: Training, mobility, clientele, fee-for-service practice and hospital practice.* Paper presented at the meeting of the Southeastern Psychological Association, Atlanta, April 1978.

REFERENCES

Barlow, D. M. On the relation of clinical research to clinical practice: Current issues, new directions. *Journal of Consulting and Clinical Psychology*, 1981, **49**, 147–155.

Bergin, A. E., & Lambert, M. J. The evaluation of therapeutic outcomes. In S.L. Garfield & A. E. Bergin (Eds.), *Handbook of psychotherapy and behavior change: An empirical analysis* (2nd ed.). New York: Wiley, 1978.

Campbell, D. T., & Stanley, J. C. *Experimental and quasiexperimental designs for research*. Chicago: Rand McNally, 1966.

Garfield, S. L. Research on client variables in psychotherapy. In S. L. Garfield & A. E. Bergin (Eds.), *Handbook of psychotherapy and behavior change: An empirical analysis* (2nd ed.). New York: Wiley, 1978.

Gold, J. *A retrospective study of the behavior therapy experience*. Unpublished doctoral dissertation, Adelphi University, 1980.

Hammond, K. R. Representative and systematic design in clinical psychology. *Psychological Bulletin*, 1964, **51**, 150–159.

Hersen, M., & Barlow, D. H. *Single-case experimental designs: Strategies for studying behavior change*. New York: Pergamon Press, 1976.

Kazdin, A. E. Reactive self-monitoring: The effects of response desirability, goal setting, and feedback. *Journal of Consulting and Clinical Psychology*, 1974, **42**, 704–716.

Kazdin, A. E., & Wilson, G. T. *Evaluation of behavior therapy: Issues, evidence, and research strategies*. Cambridge, Mass.: Ballinger, 1978.

Kiresuk, T. J., & Sherman, R. E. Goal attainment scaling: A general method for evaluating comprehensive community mental health programs. *Community Mental Health Journal*, 1968, **4**, 443–453.

Koss, M. P. Length of psychotherapy for clients seen in private practice. *Journal of Consulting and Clinical Psychology*, 1979, **47**, 210–212.

Langs, R. *The bipersonal field*. New York: Jason Aronson, 1976.

Langsley, D. G. Comparing clinic and private practice of psychiatry. *American Journal of Psychiatry*, 1978, **135**, 702–706.

Malan, D. H. *The frontier of brief psychotherapy*. New York: Plenum Press, 1976.

Meehl, P. E. *Clinical vs. statistical prediction*. Minneapolis: University of Minnesota Press, 1954.

Mintz, J., Luborsky, L., & Auerbach, A. H. Dimensions of psychotherapy: A factor-analytic study of ratings of psychotherapy sessions. *Journal of Consulting and Clinical Psychology*, 1971, **36**, 106–120.

Nelson, R. O. Realistic dependent measures for clinical use. *Journal of Consulting and Clinical Psychology*, 1981, **49**, 168–182.

Stiles, W. B. Measurement of the impact of psychotherapy sessions. *Journal of Consulting and Clinical Psychology*, 1980, **48**, 176–183.

Stricker, G. Criteria for insurance review of psychological services. *Professional Psychology*, 1979, **10**, 118–122.

Stricker, G. Peer review of outpatient psychological services. In A. G. Awad, H. B. Durost, & W. O. McCormick (Eds.), *Evaluation of quality of care in psychiatry*. Toronto: Pergamon Press, 1980.

Strupp, H. H., Fox, R. E., & Lessler, K. *Patients view their psychotherapy*. Baltimore: Johns Hopkins Press, 1969.

Strupp, H. H., Wallach, M. S., & Wogan, M. Psychotherapy experience in retrospect: Questionnaire survey for former patients and their therapists. *Psychological Monographs*, 1964, **78** (11, Whole No. 588).

Wachtel, P. L. *Psychoanalysis and behavior therapy*. New York: Basic Books, 1977.

CHAPTER 5

Assessing Outcome in Chronic Populations Treated in Day-Treatment Programs

CHARLES J. WALLACE AND BEVERLY J. HAAS

The purpose of this chapter is to review the instruments suitable for measuring the functioning of the more chronically ill patients in day-treatment–day-hospital programs. The instruments are summarized in detail, including evaluative statements about the advantages and disadvantages of each. Additionally, several promising but less well developed instruments are mentioned. Before proceeding to the review, however, it seems appropriate to examine the several studies that have evaluated the effectiveness of day-treatment–day-hospital programs. In particular, a look at the outcome measures used in these studies should reflect the range of functioning that is affected by these programs and that should be addressed by the instruments to be reviewed.

STUDIES OF DAY-TREATMENT–DAY-HOSPITAL PROGRAMS

In spite of the many enthusiastic testimonials about the beneficial effects of day-hospital–day-treatment programs, there are relatively few studies that have systematically compared these programs with alternative services. Twelve of the more recent studies involving seven such comparisons are summarized in Table 5.1. Focusing on the techniques used to measure outcome, we discuss the studies as follows.

Hogarty et al. (1968) compared the characteristics of patients referred to the Baltimore Psychiatric Day Center with the characteristics of patients referred to either inpatient or outpatient facilities. Using measures of psychopathology (Mental Status Schedule, Brief Psychiatric Rating Scale, Springfield Symptom Index, Hopkins Distress Index, and the Katz Adjustment Scale Forms R1 and S1) and community functioning (Katz Adjustment Scale Forms R2 to R5), the authors found that schizophrenic patients referred to the day center were

TABLE 5.1. Seven Day-Treatment Studies

Author(s)	Study	Number of Subjects	Diagnosis	Outcome Measures
Herz et al., 1971	Inpatient care vs. day treatment	45 inpatients, 45 day treatment	Inpatients Organic brain syndrome 2% Schizophrenic 57% Involutional psychoses 9% Neuroses 9% Personality disorders 5% Other 18% Day treatment Organic brain syndrome 2% Schizophrenic 40% Involutional psychoses 7% Neuroses 22% Personality disorders 11% Other 17%	Psychiatric Status Schedule, Psychiatric Evaluation Form, Time-to-discharge rates, Readmission rates
Guy et al., 1969; Hogarty et al., 1968, 1969	Outpatient care (medication only) vs. day treatment	25 outpatients, 31 day treatment	Schizophrenic 39.5%, depression 32.5%, neurosis and other 27.8%	Mental Status Schedule, Brief Psychiatric Rating Scale, Springfield Symptom Index, Hopkins Distress Index, Katz Adjustment Scale (Forms R1 and S1, R2–R5) Hospitalization rates
Linn et al., 1979	Outpatient care (medication only) vs. day treatment	152 (both groups, V. A. multicenter study)	Schizophrenic	Brief Psychiatric Rating Sale, Personal Adjustment and Role Skills Scale III, Community tenure, Cost of treatment, Attitudes toward work, self, family, hospital, and people-in general
Michaux et al., 1972, 1973	Inpatient care vs. day treatment	56 inpatients 50 day treatment	Inpatients Schizophrenic 54%	Discharge Readiness Inventory, Inpatient Multidimensional

Study	Comparison	Sample	Diagnoses	Measures
			Major affective disorder 9% Neurosis 15% Other nonpsychotic disorders 11% Day treatment Schizophrenic 44% Major affective disorder 20% Neurosis 20% Other nonpsychotic disorders 15%	Psychiatric Rating Scale, Minnesota Multiphastic Personality Inventory, Global ratings of overall severity of illness, adaptability, and discomfort, Michaux Stress Index, Katz Adjustment Scale, Rehospitalization rates, Employment
Penk et al., 1978	Inpatient care vs. day treatment	24 inpatients 24 day treatment	Schizophrenic 48%	Personal Adjustment and Role Skills Scale III
Washburn et al., 1976	Inpatient care vs. day treatment	30 inpatients 29 day treatment	Schizophrenic 50%, affective psychosis 12%, personality disorders 20% borderline personality 18%	Psychiatric Status Schedule (informant & subject versions), Psychiatric Evaluation Form, Community Adjustment Questionnaire, Family Adjustment Questionnaire, Burden Evaluation Line, Number of attempted roles,
Weldon et al., 1979	Outpatient care vs. day treatment	15 outpatients 15 day treatment	Schizophrenic	Profile of Mood States, Symptom Checklist 90, Community Adaptation Schedule, Rehospitalization rates, Employment

moderately to severely disordered with less perceptual–conceptual distur-bance and more social competence than their inpatient counterparts. No such differences were noted for patients with affective disorders.

The majority of these patients were then randomly assigned to receive either medication only dispensed at the Springfield Outpatient Clinic or medication plus milieu therapy conducted at the Baltimore Psychiatric Day Center. Post-treatment ratings on the measures of psychopathology indicated that schizo-phrenic patients benefitted significantly more from treatment at the day center. Nonschizophrenic patients improved equally well under either regimen (Guy et al., 1969). There were no differences in hospitalization rates, although the day center patients required significantly shorter hospitalizations. Follow-up measurements taken at 2 and 12 months after treatment indicated that schizo-phrenic patients maintained their gains only if they were involved in aftercare activities with the day center staff. Without aftercare, schizophrenic patients' functioning deteriorated over time. For nonschizophrenic patients, improve-ment continued over time regardless of the treatment (Hogarty et al., 1969).

Linn et al. (1979) evaluated the effects of day treatment for patients referred after an initial period of hospitalization. The study was conducted under the auspices of the Veterans Administration and included 10 hospitals and 10 day-treatment centers. Patients, all of whom were schizophrenic, were ran-domly assigned after discharge from the inpatient phase to receive either medication only or medication plus day treatment. The effects of treatment were evaluated with measures of community tenure, psychopathology (Brief Psychiatric Rating Scale), community functioning (Personal Adjustment and Role Skills Scale III), cost of treatment, and attitudes toward work, self, family, hospital, and people in general. All measures were administered at the point of entry into the study and at 6, 12, 18, and 24 months thereafter. Results indicated that social functioning improved for all patients in all centers, whereas some centers (those characterized by more occupational therapy and a nonthreatening environment) were effective in forestalling relapse, changing attitudes, and reducing symptoms.

Weldon et al. (1979) also evaluated the effects of day treatment for schizo-phrenic patients referred after an initial period of hospitalization. Thirty pa-tients, randomly assigned to either day or outpatient treatment, were adminis-tered measures of psychopathology (Profile of Mood States and Symptom Checklist 90) and community functioning (Community Adaptation Schedule). Also monitored were rates of rehospitalization and employment. Results indicated no significant differences for any measure except employment, which favored the day-treatment group.

In a series of studies, Michaux and her colleagues (Michaux et al., 1969, 1972, 1973; Sappington & Michaux, 1975) compared the effects of day treat-ment with those of hospitalization. A total of 106 patients were nonrandomly assigned to either day treatment (50 patients) or hospital care (56 patients). The effects were evaluated in terms of psychopathology (Discharge Readiness

Inventory, Katz Adjustment Scale Forms R1 and S1, Inpatient Multidimensional Psychiatric Rating Scale, Minnesota Multiphasic Personality Inventory, and global ratings of overall severity of illness, adaptability, and discomfort), community functioning (Katz Adjustment Scale, Discharge Readiness Inventory, and Michaux Stress Index), and rates of rehospitalization and employment. Result indicated that symptom reduction was significantly greater for schizophrenic patients receiving hospital treatment, although the differences virtually disappeared at 2 and 12 months after treatment. There were no differences between the two treatments in the amount of symptom reduction for nonschizophrenic patients. However, nonschizophrenic patients receiving day treatment were significantly better in rate of employment and community functioning 2 and 12 months after treatment. No such differences were noted for schizophrenic patients.

Herz et al. (1971) randomly assigned 90 patients to receive either day or hospital care. The effects of the two treatments were evaluated with the Psychiatric Status Schedule and the Psychiatric Evaluation Form, both measures of psychopathology and community functioning. Time-to-discharge and readmission rates were also calculated. Interestingly, both treatments were administered in the hospital by the same staff; the only difference was that the day-care patients returned to their homes in the evening. Results indicated that not only did day-care patients return to the community at a significantly more rapid rate than hospital patients, but a significantly smaller proportion relapsed. Both groups experienced significant reductions in psychopathology, with the few differences between treatments favoring the day-care group. The contrast between these results and those of Michaux and her colleagues is likely due to the different selection procedures of the two studies that excluded many schizophrenics from the Herz et al. (1971) study.

Washburn et al. (1976) randomly assigned 59 patients to either day or hospital care after an initial one- to six-week period of inpatient evaluation. Patients were periodically administered measures of psychopathology (Psychiatric Status Schedule S, Psychiatric Evaluation Form, Community Adjustment Questionnaire, and Family Adjustment Questionnaire). Patients' significant others were also administered measures of patients' psychopathology (Psychiatric Status Schedule I) and community adjustment (Psychiatric Status Schedule I, Family Adjustment Questionnaire, Burden Evaluation Line, and number of attempted roles). Results indicated that day-treatment patients experienced significantly more reduction in psychopathology and improvement in community functioning, although these differences virtually disappeared by 18 to 24 months after treatment.

Penk et al. (1978) compared the effects of day treatment with 24 patients who were matched on a post hoc basis with 24 patients receiving hospital care. The effects of the treatments were evaluated with the Personal Adjustment and Role Skills Scale III, a measure of both psychopathology and community functioning administered to patients' significant others. Results indicated that both groups experienced significant reductions in psychopathology, with greater improvement noted for day treatment clients in depression, social activities, and employment.

It is apparent in reviewing these studies that although there are differences in the "place" of day-treatment–day-hospital programs in the delivery of clinical services, there is a unanimity of opinion that these programs should be evaluated in terms of rates of rehospitalization, degree of psychopathology, and level of community functioning. Perhaps this is an indication that these programs function:

> (1) as an alternative to inpatient treatment, (2) as a transitional facility for patients who have been hospitalized, (3) as a locus for intermediate term rehabilitation of persons who have social and vocational deficits resulting from or related to mental illness, and (4) as a service for patients, so seriously impaired that but for the support and maintenance of the day program, long-term hospitalization would be required. (Glasscote et al., 1969, p. 5)

Thus measures of the outcomes of day-treatment–day-hospital programs must address all these functions. Furthermore, careful attention should be paid to diagnosis since the impact of treatment varies with different diagnostic groups.

REVIEW OF INSTRUMENTS

Summarized below are 12 instruments that have been frequently used to measure the functioning of chronically ill patients. Several have already been noted as measures of the effects of day-treatment–day-hospital programs; the others have proven to be useful in studies of the treatment of chronically ill patients. Excluded are instruments with primarily "historical" value such as the Social Adjustment Inventory Method (Berger et al., 1964), the Normative Social Adjustment Scale (Barrabee et al., 1955), and the Social Ineffectiveness Scale (Parloff et al., 1954). Also excluded are instruments designed either for use only in a particular study [e.g., the follow-up interview schedule by Freeman and Simmons (1963)] or for use with a wide variety of patient populations (e.g., the Minnesota Multiphasic Personality Inventory, the Symptom Checklist 90, and the California Psychological Inventory). Descriptions of the latter are widely available.

The 12 instruments are divided into two groups. For the first nine, information is obtained from the patients to determine their level of functioning; for the remaining three, information is obtained from the patients' significant others. As noted in the summaries and in Table 5.2, several of the instruments have forms for both patients and significant others, although only one of these forms is likely to have been widely used. Capsule summaries of many of these instruments have appeared in Weissman (1975), Weissman et al. (1981a), Hogarty (1975), and Fiske (1975).

Patients as Informants

For eight of the nine instruments for which patients are the primary source of information, the information is obtained by means of structured or semistructured interview. Information for the ninth is obtained by means of a questionnaire.

Social Dysfunction Rating Scale (SDRS)

The SDRS (Linn, et al., 1969) consists of 21 items designed to measure patient functioning in three areas: feelings about self, relationships with significant others, and performance in community-related activities. Each item is phrased as a global characteristic (e.g., lack of goal, overdependence) that is rated on a six-point scale of severity. Information to rate the items is obtained during a semistructured interview with the patient. Considering that the items are globally defined and that the interview is only partially structured, the instrument would be best used by relatively experienced interviewers.

Scores for each of the 21 questions can be treated as separate variables or can be summed to obtain an overall measure of functioning. Alternately, scores from the items can be summed to reflect totals on five factors obtained from a factor analysis of the responses of 80 psychiatric and nonpsychiatric patients. These five factors are apathetic–detachment, dissatisfaction, hostility, health–finance concern, and manipulative–dependence.

Psychometrically, the agreement between two raters about the adjustment of 40 schizophrenics was found to be acceptable for all but two of the items (intraclass correlation coefficients of .54 to .86). Similarly, the agreement among 7 raters about the overall adjustment of 10 schizophrenics was acceptable (Kendall's w of .91). All but three of the items significantly differentiated between normals and schizophrenics, and the total score was significantly correlated ($r = .89$) with social workers' global ratings of adjustment (Goodman et al., 1969).

The advantages of the SDRS are its relative brevity and simplicity of scoring. The disadvantages are the high cost of obtaining information by means of an interview (particularly conducted by an experienced interviewer), the lack of precise definitions of each of the 21 items that may limit generalizability across studies, the lack of separate coverage of certain roles such as spouse and parent, and the rather limited interrater reliability data (only nine raters).

Social Adjustment Scale (SAS, SAS-SR, SAS-II)

The SAS (Weissman et al., 1971), a modification of the Structured and Scaled Interview to Assess Maladjustment (Gurland et al., 1972), consists of 42 items that measure patients' general performance, interpersonal performance, and satisfactions during the past two months in six broad social roles: work, social and leisure activities, extended family, relationships with spouse, parental relationships, and general family unit. All items are rated on a five-point scale of severity; information to rate each is obtained during a 45- to 90-minute struc-

TABLE 5.2. Twelve Instruments Used for Measuring Psychopathology and Community Functioning with Chronically Ill or Disabled Populations

Instrument and Reference(s)	Coverage	Assessment Period	Number of Items	Factors or Summary Scales	Type of data Collection	Information Source–Participant	Completion Time
Community Adaptation Schedule (CAS); Roen et al. (1966)	Community functioning (in "six communities")	Present	212 items	none	Questionnaire	Patient	30–50 minutes
Current and Past Psychopathology Scales (CAPPS); Endicott and Spitzer (1972b)	CAPPS and community functioning (5 instrumental roles)	Past month and age 12 to the last month	171 items	Current section, 8 factors; past section, 18 factors	Optional interview	All available sources (patient, significant other, case notes, nursing observations)	With interview, 1–2 hours; without interview; 15–20 minutes
Denver Community Mental Health Questionnaire (DCMHQ); Ciarlo et al. (1977)	Community functioning	Past 24 hours to the past month	51 items	12 summary scales	Semistructured interview	Patient	30–50 minutes
Katz Adjustment Scales (KAS); Katz (1963)	Psychopathology and community functioning	Past 3 weeks	338 items	Form 1 of the KAS-R: 13 first-order factors and 3 second-order factors	Questionnaire	Patient version (KAS-S), significant-other version (KAS-R)	25–45 minutes
Personal and Role Adjustment Scale (PARS); Ellsworth (1968)	Community Functioning	Past month	PARS-V: 39 items (male form), 37 items (female form)	7 factors	Questionnaire	Significant other	10–20 minutes

Instrument	Focus	Time frame	Items	Factors/Scales	Method	Sources	Administration time
Psychiatric Evaluation Form (PEF); Endicott and Spitzer (1972a)	Psychopathology and community functioning (5 instrumental roles)	Past week and month	25 items	5 factors, 1 summary role performance scale	Optional interview	All available sources (patient, significant other, case notes, nursing observations)	With interview; 20–40 minutes; without interview; 2–4 minutes
Psychiatric Status Schedule (PSS); Spitzer et al. (1970)	Psychopathology and community functioning (five instrumental roles)	Past week and month	321 items	15 first-order factors, 4 second-order factors	Structured interview	Patient version, significant other version (PSS-1)	30–50 minutes
Schedule for Affective Disorder and Schizophrenia (SADS); Spitzer and Endicott (1968)	Current and past psychopathology	Past week and past psychiatric history	436 items	Current section, 8 summary scales	Structured interview	Patient plus all available sources	1½–2 hours
Social Adjustment Scale (SAS II); Schooler, et al. (1969)	Community functioning	Past 2 months (SAS, SAS-II), past 2 weeks (SAS–SR)	SAS 11, 52 items; SAS and SAS-SR, 42 items	SAS, 6 factors	SAS and SAS-11, structured interview; SAS-SR, Questionnaire	Patient	SAS and SAS-II, 45–90 minutes; SAS-SR, 15–20 minutes

(continued)

TABLE 5.2. *(continued)*

Instrument and Reference(s)	Coverage	Assessment Period	Number of Items	Factors or Summary Scales	Type of data Collection	Information Source– Participant	Completion Time
Social Behavior Assessment Schedule (SBAS); Platt et al. (1980)	Psychopathology and community functioning	Past month	329 items	6 summary scales	Structured interview	Significant other	60–90 minutes
Social Dysfunction Rating Scale (SDRS); Linn et al. (1969)	Community functioning	Present or past week	21 items	5 factors	Semistructured interview	Patient	30–45 minutes
Social Stress and Functioning Inventory for Psychotic Disorders (SSFIPD); Serban (1978)	Community functioning and subjectively experienced stress	Not indicated	304 items	None	Structured interview	Patient version, significant-other version	45–90 minutes

tured interview with the patient. Five additional items measure global adjustment in all of the six roles except general family unit. One final item measures global adjustment across all six roles. The scores on the 42 items can be combined to yield an average per role by omitting items that do not apply to a particular patient. However, the more commonly used scoring system involves summing 33 items to obtain scores of each of six factors: work performance, interpersonal friction, inhibited communications, submissive dependency, family attachment, and anxious rumination (Paykel et al., 1971).

Psychometrically, Weissman et al. (1971) and Paykel et al. (1971) reported that the scale had adequate interrater reliability (average r of .80 across 31 interviews with 86% of the items differing by no more than one scale point) but, according to their criteria, an insufficient degree of internal consistency reliability. The latter finding prompted their factor analysis of the SAS, which resulted in the more frequently used scoring procedures. The SAS was designed primarily to measure the adjustment of depressed women; as such, almost all the questions have been found to significantly discriminate between carefully matched samples of depressed and normal women (Weissman et al., 1971). The scale has proved to be sensitive to the impact of psychotherapy and/or medication with acutely depressed women (Weissman et al., 1974; 1981b). Interestingly, the SAS did not prove to be predictive of relapse, although work performance and anxious rumination were significantly worse during relapse. Although SAS scores were not significantly correlated with the severity of symptoms during depression (Paykel et al., 1978), the correlations were significant eight months after treatment (Weissman et al., 1974).

A self-report version has been developed [SAS-SR (Weissman and Bothwell, 1976)] that is identical to the SAS, except for the rating period which includes the past two weeks rather than the past two months. The form requires only 15 to 20 minutes to complete and correlates from .40 to .76 with scores derived from the interview-based scales. Internal consistency reliabilities (coefficient α) of the SR scales average .737, with test-retest reliabilities ranging from .716 to .820 (Edwards et al., 1978). Like the SAS, the SR form has been found to be sensitive to the impact of drugs and/or psychotherapy with acutely depressed women (Prusoff et al., 1980) and has been administered to a variety of individuals including undergraduates, women attending consciousness raising groups, patients receiving day-treatment–day-hospital services, and patients recovering from cardiac surgery (Weissman et al., 1978).

Weissman et al. (1978) have noted a problem in using either the SAS or SAS-SR with marginally adjusted individuals. These individuals have not participated in several of the roles assessed by the SAS (e.g., spouse, parent), and yet the instructions specify that scores be based on the average of the applicable items, thus yielding an overestimate of these individuals' adjustment. To correct this discrepancy, Schooler et al. (1979) developed the 52-item, interview-based SAS-II. The SAS-II provides coverage of instrumental and interpersonal performance in five areas of functioning: wage earner, homemaker, or student roles; relationships with household members; relationships with relatives not in the immediate household; performance of social and leisure activities; and personal well-being. Glazer et al. (1980) reported significant correlations between patients' and significant others' reports of adjustment with a range of .27 to .81.

An advantage of both the SAS and the SAS-SR is that they have proved their ability to discriminate among contrasted groups and to be sensitive to the impact of various interventions. Thus either would be a good choice for use with somewhat higher-functioning patients. The SAS-SR has the further advantage that it is less costly to administer than the SAS. Unfortunately, neither is entirely appropriate for use with more chronically ill, marginally adjusted patients. The SAS-II is appropriate for such patients, although it has the disadvantage of the high cost associated with collecting information by means of an interview. Furthermore, far less information has been reported about its psychometric characteristics.

Psychiatric Status Schedule (PSS, Subject and Informant Versions)

The PSS [second edition; Spitzer et al., (1970)] consists of 321 items designed to measure both patients' community functioning and the kind and degree of their psychopathology. Information to rate the items is obtained during a 30- to 50-minute structured interview with the patient that focuses on behavior and events during the interview and during the past week (except for items concerned with community functioning, which focus on the past month). Each of the 321 questions is scored as either true or false; each is worded with such specificity that only a modicum of interviewer judgment is required to score each.

The items that measure psychopathology are variations of those on the Mental Status Examination (Spitzer et al., 1964) and yield scores on 15 first-order and four second-order factors. The first-order factors are depression–anxiety, social isolation, suicide–self-mutilation, somatic concern, speech disorientation, inappropriate affect–appearance–behavior, agitation–excitement, interview belligerence–negativism, disorientation–memory impairment, retardation–lack of emotion, antisocial impulses or acts, reported overt anger, grandiosity, suspicion–persecution–hallucinations, and denial of illness. Three more "factors" can be scored, although they do not have statistical confirmation; daily routine–leisure time impairment, alcohol abuse, and drug abuse. The four second-order factors are subjective distress, behavioral disturbance, impulse-control disturbance, and reality-testing disturbance. Nineteen supplementary scales can be scored and are used to obtain DSM-II diagnoses.

The questions about community functioning yield information, as applicable, about the adequacy of patients' performance in five roles: wage earner; housekeeper; student or trainee; mate; and parent. Scores on all five can be combined into a summary role scale score.

An interesting feature of the PSS is that computer programs, written in FORTRAN, are available to assist in scoring and analyzing both group and individual data (Fleiss & Spitzer, 1967; Spitzer & Endicott, 1968). The programs convert raw scores to standard scale scores and provide not only a DSM-II diagnosis, but also a graph of the results and, if appropriate, a graph of group differences.

Psychometrically, the reliability and validity of the PSS have been thoroughly investigated. For example, Spitzer et al. (1970) reported that the internal consistency reliabilities (coefficient α) of the four second-order symptom factors range from .80 to .89, of the 18 first-order factors from .34 to .93, and of the role scales from .65 to .80. Interrater reliabilities (intraclass correlation coefficients) of the four second-order symptom factors range from .90 to .98, of the 18 first-order symptom factors from .57 to .99, and of the six role scales from .66 to .98. Test-retest reliabilities determined with a rather stringent methodology (different raters for the two testings, one week test-retest interval occurring just after hospital admission) were lower than the other reliability coefficients, although still acceptable.

First- and second-order factor scores have discriminated not only between inpatients, outpatients, and nonpatients, but also between different psychiatric groups. Factor scores have been shown to be sensitive to symptom changes expected after four weeks of hospitalization and have correlated significantly with other measures of psychopathology such as the MMPI, the Inpatient Multidimensional Rating Scale, the Brief Psychiatric Rating Scale, the Zung Self-Rating Depression Scale, the Hamilton Depression Rating Scale, the Beck Depression Inventory, and the Cornell Medical Index (Spitzer et al., 1967a). The correlations of the role scales with other instruments are somewhat less clear-cut suggesting, as Spitzer et al. (1970, p. 54) note that these scales "are of limited value for assessing role impairment in highly disorganized patients."

One of the major advantages of the PSS is its comprehensiveness. Not only does it yield detailed descriptions of psychopathology, but it covers both the affective and instrumental aspects of patients' performances of five major roles. The interview is sufficiently structured and specific to even include four items to measure patients' grooming, five items to measure orientation, and 37 items to measure the quality and quantity of speech and spontaneous physical movement during the interview. A version is available for use with significant others (PSS-I), but little has been reported about its psychometric characteristics. The data clearly reflect the psychometric adequacy of the patient version of the PSS; importantly, the data are based on large samples gathered in different locales by different investigators. Perhaps the major disadvantage of the PSS is the cost associated with gathering data by means of an interview, although it is not necessary that the interviewer be an experienced professional.

The Psychiatric Evaluation Form (PEF)

The PEF (Endicott & Spitzer, 1972a) consists of 25 items designed to measure both patients' community functioning and the kind and degree of their psychopathology. Each item is rated on a six-point scale of severity; information to rate each is obtained from all available sources including the patient, significant others, and case notes (a guide for interviewing patients is available, although it is assumed that the interview will be conducted by an experienced professional). Nineteen of the items measure psychopathology evidenced in the past week and are quite similar in meaning to the first-order factors of the PSS. The 19 are narcotic–drug abuse, agitation–excitement, suicide–self-mutilation, grandiosity, somatic concerns, antisocial attitudes–acts, speech disorganization, hallucinations, social isolation, belligerence–negativism, disorientation–memory impairment, alcohol abuse, anxiety, inappropriate behavior, suspiciousness–persecution, impairment of daily routine and leisure time, denial of illness, depression, and retardation–lack of emotion. One item measures the overall severity of illness. The remaining five items measure impairment in the roles of housekeeper, employed wage earner, student–trainee, mate, and parent. Three additional items, used only with new admissions, ask for ratings of the degree of precipitating stress, the reason for admission in terms of the 19 psychopathology and the five role-impairment items, and the duration of the present episode. Scores on the 19 pathology items can be combined into six factor analytically derived summary scales: disorganization, subjective distress, antisocial behavior, withdrawal, alcohol abuse, and grandiosity–externalization. A primary role performance score can also be calculated by summing scores on the applicable roles.

Psychometrically, the interrater reliability of the PEF has been investigated with three types of raters differing in their level of experience with psychiatric patients. The intraclass correlation coefficients were almost all acceptable, particularly those for the summary scales. As would be expected, better agreement was achieved among the more experienced raters (psychiatrists). The PEF discriminated among outpatients, inpatients, and nonpatients, particularly the summary role and the overall severity scores. Different diagnostic groups (e.g., depressive, paranoid schizophrenics, alcoholics) were also differentiated on the appropriate items, and changes were shown in the symptomatology of both manic-depressives and schizophrenics as the result of either hospital or day-care treatment. Correlations with the similar PSS scales have been generally positive, although not always so (e.g., r of .05 between retardation–lack of emotion on the PEF and the identical scale on the PSS). Endicott and Spitzer (1972a) note that the PSS and the PEF differ in the source of the rating information, and the PSS may be somewhat less accurate since it is based only on the interview behavior and responses.

A major advantage of the PEF is its relative brevity and simplicity, although this is achieved at the expense of the specificity and detailed comprehensiveness of the PSS. The PEF is clearly designed to be administered by an experienced interviewer, a costly method of collecting data. The coverage of the items that measure role impairment is rather limited, and several important aspects of psychopathology are not included (e.g., phobia, conversion reaction, thought disorder). Like the PSS, the psychometric adequacy of the PEF has been well documented with large samples gathered in different locales by different investigators.

Current and Past Psychopathology Scales (CAPPS)

The CAPPS (Endicott & Spitzer, 1972b) consists of 171 items designed to measure not only psychopathology and impaired role functioning in the past month (current section, 41 items), but also personality characteristics, social adjustment, and psychopathology from age 12 years to the last month (past section, 130 items). Information to rate the items is obtained from all available sources such as patients (a guide for interviewing patients is available, although it is assumed that the interview will be conducted by an experienced professional), significant others, case notes, and nursing observations. The current section of the CAPPS is the complete PEF (including the five role impairment items) plus 13 items that measure additional areas of psychopathology not separately covered in the PEF (e.g., guilt, elated mood, phobia, conversion reaction, disassociation). The 41 items are combined into eight factor-analytically derived summary scales: reality testing–social disturbance, depression–anxiety, impulse control, somatic concern, disorganization, obsessive–guilt–phobic, elation–grandiosity, and summary role performance.

The past section of the CAPPS is the complete Psychiatric History Schedule (Spitzer et al., 1967a). The 130 items are combined into 18 factor analytically derived summary scales: depression–anxiety, impulse control, social–sexual relations, reality testing, dependence, somatic concern, obsessive–compulsive, anger–excitability, manic, sexual disturbance, memory–orientation, disorganized, organicity, neurotic childhood, phobia, retardation–stubborn, hysterical symptoms, and intellectual performance. As with the PSS, a computer program is available to determine the appropriate DSM-II diagnosis.

Psychometrically, interrater reliabilities (intraclass correlation coefficients) have been determined only with experienced raters and have been found to range from .68 to 1.0 for individual items and from .74 to 1.0 for the summary scales. Almost all of the eight current and 18 past summary scales significantly differentiated inpatients from outpatients; all but eight of the scales differentiated nonpatients from either patient group. Different diagnostic groups were also differentiated on the appropriate scales, and correlations between the MMPI scales and the 26 summary scales were generally as expected.

Compared to the PEF and the PSS, a major advantage of the CAPPS is its detailed coverage of past psychopathology. Like the PEF, the CAPPS is relatively brief, although this is achieved at the expense of the specificity and detailed comprehensiveness of the PSS. The coverage of impairment in role functioning is rather limited, and the cost of obtaining information by means of an interview conducted by an experienced interviewer is high. Like the PSS and the PEF, the psychometric adequacy of the CAPPS has been thoroughly documented.

The Schedule for Affective Disorder and Schizophrenia (SADS)

The SADS (Endicott & Spitzer, 1978) consists of 436 items designed to measure patients' current and past psychopathology. The schedule is divided into two parts: Part 1 measures the severity of psychopathology both at the worst point of the current episode and during the past week, and Part 2 measures the type and severity of psychopathology prior to the current episode. The Global Assessment Scale is also included as an overall measure of the severity of the current episode at its worst, for the week prior to the hospital admission, and for the past week. Information to rate the items is obtained from all available sources, although it is expected that a 1½- to 2-hour interview will be conducted by an individual with considerable experience "in making judgments about manifest psychopathology" (Endicott & Spitzer, 1978, p. 838). The items are structured so that the answers result in assignment of a diagnosis according to Research Diagnostic Criteria [RDC; Spitzer et al., (1978)]. Unlike the PSS and CAPPS, the diagnosis is assigned without the necessity of a computer program. Information from Part 1 can also be combined into eight content-based summary scales: depressive mood and ideation; endogenous depression features; features associated with depression, suicidal ideation, and behavior; anxiety; manic syndrome; delusions–hallucinations; and formal thought disorder. In addition, two variations of the SADS are available; the SADS-Lifetime (SADS-L) and the SADS-Change (SADS-C). The SADS-L is much the same as Part 2 of the SADS, except for the time frame which is changed to include the present as well as past episodes. The SADS C is the subset of items from Part 1 of the SADS that are rated both for severity at the worst point of the current episode and during the past week. Monitoring of these items throughout the course of the current episode yields a measure of improvement.

Psychometrically, the interrater and internal consistency reliabilities of the eight summary scales of Part 1 are acceptable (intraclass correlation coefficients of .82 to .97; α coefficients of .75 to .97). The test–retest reliabilities of the scales (same patient interviewed at different times by different interviewers) are also acceptable with a range of .49 to .93. The scales correlate as expected with Form 1 of the KAS-R, Forms 2 and 3 of the KAS-S, and with scores on the summary factors of the Symptom Checklist 90. These correlations are, however, sufficiently low to suggest that somewhat different constructs are being measured by each of the tests.

A major advantage of the SADS is its comprehensive and systematic coverage of severe psychopathology using items whose results allow assignment of an RDC diagnosis (RDC diagnoses are quite similar to those of DSM-III). An unusual feature, necessary for correct diagnosis, is the measurement of psychopathology both during the week before the interview and at the worst point during the current episode. This also provides a choice of baseline measurements from which to estimate improvement during treatment. Like the other instruments produced by Spitzer, Endicott, and their colleagues (PSS, PEF, CAPPS, Global Assessment Scale), the psychometric adequacy of the SADS has been thoroughly documented. The disadvantages of the SADS are its almost exclusive focus on psychopathology and the high cost of obtaining data by means of such a lengthy interview conducted by an experienced professional. However, the SADS could be useful for standardizing diagnostic procedures in any treatment facility, greatly assisting in comparing results across different facilities and treatment modalities.

The Social Stress and Functioning Inventory for Psychotic Disorders (SSFIPD; Patient and Informant Versions)

The SSFIPD (Serban, 1978) consists of 304 items designed to measure patients' level of functioning (174 items) and subjectively experienced stress (130 items) in each of 21 areas of adjustment. The 21 include six areas of instrumental performance (education, work, housekeeping, dependence on welfare, management of finances, general living circumstances); four areas of family interaction (parents, relatives, marriage, children); seven areas of social interaction (dating, sex, friends, neighbors, others, leisure activities, religion), and four areas of social maladjustment (drinking, addictive drugs, psychedelic drugs, antisocial acts). The 174 functioning items measure five variables: actual level of functioning, comparison of the level of functioning with that of significant others, attempts at self-improvement, impairment due to uncontrolled events, and personal appraisal of one's own behavior. The 130 stress items measure the degree to which patients are distressed by their own level of functioning and by the problems they face in each of the 21 areas of adjustment. Separate summary scores of functioning and stress are calculated for each area by averaging the ratings for all applicable items. Almost all of the 304 items are rated on three-point scales of severity or improvement; information to rate them is obtained during a 45- to 90-minute structured interview with patients. A version is available for which information is obtained from significant others.

Psychometrically, the interrater reliability determined with 25 cases ranged from 85 to 91% agreement. Unfortunately, no mention is made of the "units of analysis"; that is, the unit could be functioning and/or stress scores per item, per area, or across all areas. Test–retest reliabilities (six-month interval with different interviewers at each testing) range for seven areas from .43 to .77, with four less than .60. Correlations between informants' and patients' ratings of functioning were significant for 18 areas for chronic patients and 13 areas for acute patients. Correlations for ratings of stress were significant for only six areas for both chronic and acute patients (Serban, 1980). Comparisons of the functioning of normals, acute, and chronic patients indicated that normals functioned significantly better than chronic patients on 13 areas and had significantly less stress than acute patients on six areas (Serban, 1975). Poor functioning in certain areas was associated with subsequent rehospitalization for both chronic and acute patients (for chronics, antisocial behavior and poor interpersonal relationships with neighbors and the opposite sex; for acutes, poor interpersonal relationships with parents and friends). High levels of stress did not seem to be associated with rehospitalization.

The advantages of the SSFIPD are its comprehensive coverage of the 21 areas of social adjustment and its thorough definition of functioning in terms of the five variables indicated previously. The scoring system tends to "mask," however, these five variables by averaging them to obtain a summary score of functioning per area. The major disadvantages of the SSFIPD are that the psychometric adequacy of the instrument is not thoroughly documented and the usefulness of the stress section has yet to be demonstrated.

Denver Community Mental Health Questionnaire (DCMHQ)

The DCMHQ (Ciarlo & Reihman, 1977) consists of 61 items designed to measure the quality of patients' functioning in 12 broad, primarily community-based scales: psychological distress; interpersonal isolation–family; interpersonal isolation–friends; productivity; public system dependence; alcohol abuse; drug use; client satisfaction; interpersonal aggression with friends; and legal difficulties. All items are rated on a four-point scale with different anchor points for each item. Information to rate the items is obtained during a 30- to 60-minute semistructured interview with the patient that covers the past 24 hours to the past month, depending on the item.

Psychometrically, the 12 scales, based on a cluster analysis of an original pool of 79 items, have been shown to have adequate internal consistency reliability (coefficient α of .52 to .96). Interrater reliability based on ratings of 18 patients ranged from .85 to 1.0 for 10 of the 12 scales (2 were not measured). Ratings made by significant others correlated from .59 to .87 with scores based on patients' responses for 9 of the 12 scales (3 were not measured), whereas similar ratings made by clinicians correlated from –.03 to .63 with patients' responses for 11 of the scales. The latter are lower primarily because the clinicians making the ratings were intake workers with only limited contact with the patients. Norms have been calculated on the basis of the response of a carefully selected sample of 212 community residents in the Denver area; all scales but interpersonal aggression with friends significantly discriminated between residents and patients. (The client satisfaction, hard-drug use, and soft-drug use scales were not administered.) The scales have reflected the improvement expected from treatment.

One advantage of the DCMHQ is its simplicity in both scoring and administration. It "was designed to be a tool for assessing any and all mental health center clients capable of communication." Thus it quite comprehensively covers certain areas such as drug and alcohol abuse (22 items), legal difficulties, and dependence on public agencies. It is unique in including a scale for assessing client satisfaction with services; this clearly reflects its primary development and use in a community mental health center. It does not, however, afford comprehensive coverage of performance in instrumental roles such as parent, spouse, student, and homemaker. It is expensive to administer, as are all measures that gather information by means of an interview. Indeed, Ciarlo and Reihman (1977) estimate the cost of each interview at $30.00 (1977 U.S. dollars), which includes the time necessary to locate patients after discharge and persuade them to participate in the interview. Interestingly, an initial cost of $45.00 resulted in a successful interview rate of 70%; $30.00 resulted in a rate of only 50%.

Community Adaptation Schedule (CAS)

The CAS [revised edition; Burnes and Roen (1967)] consists of 212 items designed to measure patients' "relationships with six communities": work community; family community; social community; larger community; commercial community; and professional community. The six "communities" are divided into 34 "subsections" such as employment, work potential, spouse, neighbors, recreation, and transportation. Three types of item are included in the 212. One type measures behavior (e.g., "How many different organizations and clubs do you belong to?"), another measures affect (e.g., "How do you feel about participating in groups?"), and the third measures perception or belief (e.g., "Would you join more organizations or clubs if you were invited to?"). The items are presented in questionnaire format; patients respond using a six-point scale with each point defined differently from item to item. The responses are summed to obtain a total per subsection, per community, and across all communities. Total scores are also obtained for the behavior, affect, and belief questions.

Psychometrically, the scale has been found to have acceptable one-week and one-month test–retest reliability for both normals [average r per subsection of .75 (Burnes & Roen, 1967; Cook & Josephs, 1970)] and psychiatric inpatients [average r per subsection of .73 (Burnes & Roen, 1967)]. Normal subjects were significantly better adapted than posthospital psychiatric patients on the majority of the original CAS communities and subsections (Roen et al., 1966) and on the total for the behavior questions. Similarly, there were significant differences among the scores of 79 inpatients, 58 outpatients, and 54 mental health professionals on all six communities, 18 subsections, and all three types of question of the revised CAS (Burnes and Roen, 1967). In contrast, there were essentially no significant differences in adjustment between 23 inpatients and 23 outpatients matched for sex, age, race, and marital status (Cook et al., 1973). Correlations between the California Psychological Inventory for 57 undergraduates generally indicated that higher adaptation was associated with higher personal adjustment (Cook & Josephs, 1970). Similar results were reported for correlations between the Adjective Checklist and the CAS for 46 inpatients and outpatients (Cook et al., 1973). However, the CAS was not generally correlated with scores on the Personal Orientation Inventory administered to 40 volunteers for a mental health paraprofessional training program (Harris & Brown, 1974). Importantly, the CAS scores were significantly correlated with scores on the Marlowe–Crowne Social Desirability Scale (Harris & Brown, 1974) and with the Good Impression Scale of the California Psychological Inventory (Cook & Josephs, 1970).

The major advantages of the CAS are its comprehensive coverage of community roles and its ease of administration. An unusual feature is its tripartite division of items into measures of affect, behavior, and perception. Unfortunately, the value of this division has yet to be conclusively shown. The psychometric adequacy of the CAS is not as well documented as that of the

PSS, for example, and the scale could undoubtedly be shortened as the result of a more intensive study of its internal consistency reliability (Harris & Brown, 1974). Interestingly, this was done with the original CAS (Roen et al., 1966). The correlations of the CAS with the Marlowe–Crowne Social Desirability Scale and with the Good Impression Scale of the California Psychological Inventory suggest that the scale may be seriously affected by a respondent's set to answer in a socially desirable manner, at least for nonpsychiatric respondents.

Significant Others as Informants

As Hogarty (1975) and Ellsworth et al. (1968) note, ratings made by significant others have often been considered suspect because of a presumed bias related to the emotional closeness between the patient and the significant other. However, significant others' ratings have been found to be as reliable as those of clinicians and patients (Ellsworth et al., 1968; Katz & Lyerly, 1963), and correlations among the ratings of significant others, patients, and clinicians have generally been significant (Ciarlo & Reihman, 1977; Ellsworth et al., 1968; Vestre & Zimmerman, 1969). Agreement between the ratings made by different significant others with equally extensive information about patients' behavior have been found to be substantial, particularly for more behaviorally based items (Berger et al., 1964; Ciarlo & Reihman, 1977; Crook et al., 1980).

Katz Adjustment Scales (KAS)

The KAS (Katz & Lyerly, 1963) consists of 338 items designed to measure both patients' community functioning and the kind and degree of their psychopathology. There are two versions of the KAS: the KAS-R (205 items) is administered to significant others, and the KAS-S (133 items) is administered to patients. The items of each version are grouped into five forms. For the first form of the KAS-S (55 items), which is a modified version of the Johns Hopkins Symptom Distress Checklist, patients are asked to indicate the degree of discomfort they experience as a result of their symptoms. For the first form of the KAS-R (127 items), significant others are asked to indicate the frequency with which various psychopathological and interpersonal behaviors (e.g., talks to self, is dependable) have occurred during the "past few weeks." Scores on the items can be combined to obtain measures of the severity of minor psychiatric symptoms, major psychiatric symptoms, and interpersonal disturbance. Alternately, and far more typically, scores on 86 of the items can be combined to obtain measures of the severity of 13 clusters of symptoms and disturbed interpersonal behaviors (Hogarty & Katz, 1971; Katz & Lyerly, 1963): belligerence, verbal expansiveness, negativism, helplessness, suspiciousness, anxiety, withdrawal–retardation, general psychopathology, nervousness, confusion, bizarreness, hyperactivity, and stability (additional items can also be combined to yield a score on a content-based scale of depression). Cluster scores can then be combined to yield scores on three second-order factors: social obstreperousness, acute psychoticism, and withdrawal depression. Cluster scores can also be used to assign patients to one of six patterns of symptomatology (Katz, 1966): agitated–belligerent–suspicious; withdrawn–periodically agitated; acute panic state; withdrawn–helpless–suspicious; agitated–helpless; and agitated–expansive–bizarre–suspicious.

For Form 2 of the KAS-R (16 items), a modification of a scale used by Freeman and Simmons (1958), relatives are asked to indicate the frequency with which patients perform each of 16 "socially expected" activities such as working, going to church, visiting friends, and getting along with family members. The items are summed to obtain a total score. For Form 2 of the KAS-S, patients are asked to provide the same information about themselves.

For Form 3 of the KAS-R (16 items), the Form 2 items are used and relatives are asked to indicate their expectations about the frequency with which patients should be performing these socially expected activities. The items are summed to obtain a total score; this can be subtracted from the score obtained on Form 2 to yield a measure of the relatives' dissatisfaction with patients' performance of the activities. For Form 3 of the KAS-S, patients are asked to provide the same information about themselves.

For Form 4 of the KAS-R (23 items), a modification of a scale used by Cavan et al. (1949), relatives are asked to indicate the frequency with which patients perform each of 23 leisure-time and self-improvement activities such as going to the library, shopping, and working in and around the house. The items are summed to obtain a total score. For Form 4 of the KAS-S, patients are asked to provide the same information about themselves.

For Form 5 of the KAS-R (23 items), the Form 4 items are used and relatives are asked to indicate their satisfaction with the patients' frequency of performance of the activities. The items are summed to obtain a total score. For Form 5 of the KAS-S, patients are asked to provide the same information about themselves.

Psychometrically, the reliability and validity of the KAS, particularly Form 1 of the KAS-R, have been thoroughly investigated. [Indeed, the KAS is the most frequently used scale of social adjustment, and Katz (personal communication, October 1981) is currently preparing an updated bibliography that will list more than 200 references]. Katz and Lyerly (1963) reported that the reliability (coefficient α) of 12 of the 13 clusters (the stability cluster was a later addition) ranged from .41 to .81 and that all scores derived from both the KAS-R and KAS-S (except form 5 of the KAS-S) significantly discriminated between small samples of patients judged by experienced clinicians to be well and poorly adjusted. Katz (1968) and Katz et al. (1966) found that the six patterns of symptomatology described by relatives were not only corroborated by data gathered by experienced clinicans (although only a maximum of 63% of the patients could be classified into one of the six types), but also reflected the differential effectiveness of antipsychotic medication. Vestre and Zimmerman (1969) found that the KAS-R correlated significantly, although weakly, with ratings of patient behavior made by inpatient nurses. Crook et al. (1980) reported substantial agreement between mothers and fathers of recently hospitalized schizophrenic sons for the more behaviorally based clusters (e.g., r of .84 for belligerence), with less agreement on the more inferential clusters (e.g., r of .33 of nervousness).

Hogarty and Katz (1971) normed the KAS with 450 nonpsychiatric community residents and found that all scores significantly differentiated between residents and patients. The KAS-R has been used cross-culturally (Katz et al., 1969) and with nonpsychotic psychiatric patients (Shaffer et al., 1972). The KAS has been found to reflect the changes to be expected as the result of either outpatient or day-hospital treatment with or without medication (Goldberg et al., 1977; Hogarty et al., 1969; Michaux et al., 1969b).

Major advantages of the KAS-R and KAS-S include its ease of administration and extensive coverage of symptomatic behaviors. Certain role areas are only partially surveyed (e.g., spouse), and the scales would seem most appropriate for the more chronically ill patients. The measurement of dissatisfaction with the performance of socially expected and leisure-time activities is useful and unique to the KAS, although it is approximated by the stress questions of the SSFIPD. The psychometric adequacy of primarily the KAS-R, Form 1 has been quite well documented, and the scales have proved to be useful in numerous studies involving a variety of treatment techniques and patient populations.

Personal and Role Adjustment Scale (PARS)

Five versions of the PARS have been published since the initial version was described by Ellsworth et al. (1968). Each has been designed as a questionnaire to be completed by a significant other about patients' community adjustment within the previous month. The PARS-I (originally named the Community Adjustment Scale) consisted of 39 items rated on a four-point scale of occurrence and designed to measure the treatment outcome of male veterans with a diagnosis of schizophrenia. Items were summed to obtain scores on the factor analytically derived dimensions of dependent–confusion, agitation–depression, unacceptable behavior, friendship skills, participation in organizations, and employment.

To widen the scale's applicability to all psychiatrically disabled male veterans, 50 items were added to the PARS-I to make the PARS-II. Of the total of 89 items, 79 proved to be stable and to discriminate between pre- and posttreatment adjustment. A factor analysis indicated that the 79 items measured interpersonal involvement, confusion, anxious–depression, agitation, alcohol abuse, outside social involvement, and employment.

To even further widen the applicability of the PARS to male and female veteran or nonveteran patients treated in either hospital or clinics, the PARS-III was developed. The response scale was expanded to five points and separate forms of 115 items for males and 120 items for females were developed. Analyses of the reliability and the discriminative validity of the items (differences between pre- and posttreatment) resulted in final versions of a 57-item form for males and a different 57-item form for females. Factor analyses of the male form yielded results quite similar to that of the PARS-II. Factor analyses of the female form indicated that the items measured interpersonal involvement, confusion, agitation, alcohol and drug abuse, household management, outside social activities, and employment (if applicable). For both males and females, parenthood skills (if applicable) could be scored as a separate dimension, although the results of the factor analysis indicated that these items were actually included in the interpersonal involvement factor.

A PARS-IV was then developed for a large-scale investigation of the program characteristics associated with successful treatment outcomes for psychiatrically disabled male veterans. Twenty-five items of the PARS-III were selected for the PARS-IV, four items were added to reflect male performance of household chores, and the response scale was contracted to its original four points.

Finally the current PARS-V was developed for both male and female veterans or nonveteran patients treated in either community clinics or hospitals. The male form consists of 39 items selected from the PARS-III on the basis of their factor loadings, reliabilities (stability and internal consistency), and discriminative validity (significant differences between pre- and postratings and between clinic, hospital, and nondisabled populations). The female form consists of 37 similarly selected items. The same factors are apparent on the PARS-V as on the PARS-III. A useful feature of the PARS-V is the provision of norms for prepost change as well as norms for the total scores on each factor.

Psychometrically, the reliability and validity of the five versions have been thoroughly investigated. The internal consistency of the PARS-V factors (coefficient α) ranges from .77 to .94 for females and .60 to .94 for males. Test–retest reliabilities (interval not stated) range from .72 to .97 for females and .80 to .92 for males. Residual change scores on the more symptom based factors of the PARS-III were significantly correlated with patients' judgments of their own improvement made one month and six months after hospital treatment. Fontana and Dowds (1975) found significant agreement between relatives' and patients' ratings of PARS-II adjustment, particularly on the employment and alcohol–drug abuse factors. Agreement on the degree of pretreatment symptomatology was low; however, the agreement on posttreatment symptomatology was high. The same results were reported for the PARS-III (Ellsworth, 1975). As has been found with other scales, there was little relationship between one-month PARS-III posthospital adjustment and rehospitalization within six months. Nor did the PARS I factors discriminate between patients who were rehospitalized and a set of carefully matched patients who did not relapse (Arthur et al., 1968).

Extensive research has been conducted by Ellsworth and his colleagues using the versions of the PARS as measures of treatment effectiveness. For example, Ellsworth (1970, 1973) found that feedback to hospital units about the relationships between posttreatment adjustment of their patients and several program characteristics such as time spent with patients could lead to program changes and increased treatment effectiveness. Ellsworth (1978) reported that PARS-V adjustment indicated no differences in posttreatment effectiveness for patients treated in the hospital compared to those treated in community clinics in spite of the fact that hospitalized patients were significantly more maladjusted at pretreatment. Indeed, hospital treatment resulted in significantly greater improvement for females even when initial differences were covaried. Results on the PARS-IV have indicated that certain "setting" variables discriminate between effective and ineffective hospital units (Ellsworth et al., 1979).

Among the major advantages of the various versions of the PARS (particularly the PARS-III and PARS-V) are their ease of administration and relatively extensive coverage of symptomatic behavior and community functioning. Of course, given their brevity, the coverage is not in depth and certain instrumental roles such as spouse are not at all covered. Thus they seem most appropriate for measuring the functioning of the more chronically ill patients. Their psychometric adequacy has been well documented; in particular, they have been shown to be sensitive to the impact of both hospital and clinic treatment.

Social Behavior Assessment Schedule (SBAS)

The SBAS [revised edition (Platt et al., 1980)] consists of 329 items designed to measure patients' community functioning and the kind and degree of their psychopathology. Information to rate the items is obtained during a 60- to 90-minute structured interview with a significant other that surveys the patient's behavior in the month prior to administration of the schedule. The items are divided into six sections. For the first section (22 items), the significant other is asked for demographic information about the patient. The second section (66 items) measures 22 symptoms such as misery, irritability, and self-neglect in terms of their severity, onset, and degree of distress to the significant other. The third section (48 items) measures 12 socially expected activities such as child care, interpersonal relationship with the significant other, and work–study behaviors in terms of the quality of performance, changes in performance, onset of changes, and distress to the informant. The fourth section (104 items) measures 25 activities and "states" of household members such as the emotional health of the significant other in terms of the quality of the activities or states, the onset of poor performances or states, the degree to which the poor performances or states were related to the patient's symptoms, and the degree of distress to the significant other. The fifth section (66 items) measures 11 life events such as death, unemployment, and legal problems in terms of to whom they occurred (patient, significant other, relatives, or close friends), their onset, and the degree to which they were related to the patient's symptoms. The sixth section (23 items) measures the degree of relief experienced by the significant other as the result of assistance received from relatives, friends, neighbors, and social services. The sixth section also asks for information about the informant's housing situation such as type of dwelling and number of different types of room. Scores on the sections are combined to yield measures of disturbed behavior, social performance, objective burden, distress caused by the disturbed behavior, distress caused by the social performance, and distress caused by the objective burden.

Psychometrically, Hirsch et al. (1979) found that the first edition of the SBAS reflected significant changes in patients' behaviors, particularly symptomatology, as the result of either brief or extended hospital treatment. Similar changes were found on the Present State Examination and were maintained at a three-month follow-up. Interestingly, there were no differences in improvement between the extended (median = 22 days) and brief stay (median = 9 days) patients. Interrater reliability of the first edition of the SBAS determined with four raters listening to interviews of nine significant others (four conducted by one of the raters and five by another) ranged from .92 to .99 for the six summary scales (intraclass correlation coefficient). Analysis of the interrater reliabilities of each item indicated that the weighted kappa value of 83% of the items exceeded .70 averaged across all possible pairings of raters. However, only 53% of the items measuring distress caused by disturbed behavior and 66% of the items measuring distress caused by social performance exceeded averaged weighted kappa values of .70. Platt et al. (1980) indicate that the revised edition has been constructed to remove the sources of the unreliability of these items.

The major advantage of the SBAS is its extremely comprehensive coverage of psychopathology, instrumental role performance, life events, and distress experienced by the informant. Although its psychometric adequacy remains to be sufficiently demonstrated, the initial results are promising. Additionally, a version is being prepared in which information will be obtained from the patients themselves (Platt et al., 1980). The major disadvantage is the high cost of collecting data by means of an interview.

Other Instruments

There are several other instruments that may be useful, although they are not currently as well developed or as widely applicable or as readily available as the previous 12. For example, Clare and Cairns (1978) designed the 48-item Social Maladjustment Scale to measure three aspects of patients' community functioning (material conditions, instrumental performance, satisfaction) in each of six major areas (housing, occupation and social role, economic situation, leisure and social activities, family and domestic relationships, marital relationships). Information to measure functioning is obtained from either patients or significant others during a 45-minute semistructured interview. In studies with patients of general practitioners, neurotic patients, and gynecologic patients with premenstrual tension, interrater reliability has been found to be satisfactory, and scores on the scale have significantly discriminated between individuals judged psychiatrically disturbed and those judged psychiatrically healthy. A unique feature of the schedule is that the rating of material conditions is made in terms of objective standards of housing, income, and so on.

The Strauss–Carpenter Outcome Scale (Strauss & Carpenter, 1972) consists of four items that measure functioning in four areas: work performance; social relationships; symptoms; and duration of hospitalization. The scale was designed for use in the International Pilot Study on Schizophrenia. Information to measure functioning is obtained during a semistructured interview with the patient. Each item is rated on a five-point scale, with each point specifically anchored in terms of the variable being measured (e.g., percentage of time employed, number of social contacts per week). Interrater reliability has been found to be acceptable, and the results of a two-year follow-up of patients in the International Pilot Study indicated that the four areas are relatively independent of one another. However, the results of a five-year follow-up of the same patients indicated that the area of social relationships was significantly related to all other areas (Strauss & Carpenter, 1977). Although lacking detailed information, the scale would seem to be useful as a brief, low-cost measure of outcome.

Willer and Biggen (1976) designed the 55-item Self-Assessment Guide not only to measure patients' community functioning in seven areas (physical health, general affect, interpersonal skills, personal relations, use of leisure time, control of aggression, employment), but also to assist in developing individualized treatment plans. The 55 items are administered to patients pre- and posttreatment. The results are entered into a computer-assisted, Goal-Oriented Record (Willer, 1977; Willer & Howard, 1974) whose format is based on the Problem-Oriented Medical Record. The guide has been found to significantly discriminate between patients who were rehospitalized within six months after treatment and those who were not, and the use of individualized treatment plans resulted in significantly better functioning in five of the seven areas compared to traditional treatment. Unfortunately, no data about the reliability of the guide have been reported in the published literature.

Similar to the Self-Assessment Guide, the 98-item Community Adjustment Profile System (Evanson et al., 1974) was designed to fit with computer-assisted documentation of ongoing clinical services. The 98 items are administered as a questionnaire to patients' significant others. The items are scored to provide information about patients' hostility, alcohol abuse, depression, work problems, assault, peculiarity, previous treatment contact, drug use, suicidal behavior, police contact, early deprivation, early maladjustment, and family pathology. Norms have been developed on the basis of data from 748 patients. Internal consistency reliabilities have been found to range from .70 to .92, and the system has been used primarily to evaluate inpatient services in the State of Missouri.

Perhaps even more directly tied to the documentation of clinical services is Goal Attainment Scaling (Kiresuk & Sherman, 1968). This is a method of evaluating the effectiveness of treatment in terms of the attainment of a set of measurable goals that have been specified by therapists and/or patients. The method is relatively content free; that is, specification of the goals and the means by which they are to be measured is left to the discretion of the individuals involved in planning the delivery of services. This flexibility is a major advantage of Goal Attainment Scaling since the heterogeneity of patients' needs and therapeutic techniques can easily be accommodated. However, this flexibility introduces serious complications in the comparison of outcomes across different types of patients, treatments, and facilities [although it can be done (Austin et al., 1976)]. Wilson (1977) has described a method for standardizing some aspects of Goal Attainment Scaling, including specification of 700 goal statements grouped into five basic categories: symptoms; self-concept; patient-initiated interaction; other-initiated interaction; and disposition. Patients, therapists, and significant others can select goals and record them on special forms that result in computer-produced graphs that present the level of attainment achieved by comparable patients. The data have been used to provide evaluative feedback to clinicians and to calculate cost-benefit ratios for various types of patients and treatments (Halpern, 1977).

Recommendations

The recommendation of one instrument over another is rather difficult since the required information and the resources available to obtain it vary from situation to situation. Nevertheless, certain guidelines can be suggested. Collection of data by means of an interview, although costly, potentially yields the most accurate and comprehensive information. The only interview-based instrument designed for use with significant others is the SBAS. It is an excellent instrument that provides detailed and comprehensive information about patients' psychopathology, social functioning, and burden to the family. Its psychometric characteristics are good, and it has proved to be sensitive to changes in patients' symptoms. However, the interviewers must be thoroughly trained to make the fine discriminations required by the items, and they must be continually monitored to ensure that their competencies do not wane.

Of the interview-based instruments designed for use with patients, the PSS would make an excellent choice. Not only does it provide detailed and comprehensive information about patients' psychopathology and community functioning, but the items are well specified and do not require the interviewing skills needed for the SBAS, PEF, and CAPPS. Its psychometric characteristics are quite good, and its value has been proved in numerous studies. If more experienced interviewers are available, the CAPPS may be a good choice. It is less detailed than the PSS, but the inclusion of a social and psychiatric history schedule may be useful in standardizing clinical record keeping procedures.

Collecting information by means of a questionnaire, although potentially yielding information that is less accurate and/or comprehensive than that obtained from interviews, is convenient and low in cost. Of the questionnaires designed for use with significant others, either the KAS or the PARS-III and PARS-V would make excellent choices. Both scales have good psychometric characteristics and have proved their usefulness in numerous studies. A choice between them should be made on the basis of the information required and on the differences in time required to complete each.

Of the questionnaires designed for use with patients, none is entirely satisfactory. The CAS is the best, but its psychometric characteristics and usefulness have not been thoroughly documented.

It should be noted that all instruments should be considered in making the choice to use one of them. A particular instrument may fit the limitations of resources and the requirements for information in a particular situation. Perhaps the most important step in selecting an instrument is to thoroughly specify the needed information, its use, and the cost of obtaining it. These specifications should guide the user in selecting the appropriate instrument.

REFERENCES

Arthur, G., Ellsworth, R. B., & Kroeker, D. Readmission of released mental patients: A research study. *Social Work*, 1968, **13**, 78–84.

Austin, N. K., Liberman, R. P., King, L. W., & DeRisi, W. J. A comparative evaluation of two day hospitals: Goal attainment scaling of behavior therapy vs. milieu therapy. *Journal of Nervous and Mental Disease*, 1976, **163**, 253–262.

Barrabee, P., Barrabee, E. L., & Finesigner, J. E. A normative social adjustment scale. *American Journal of Psychiatry*, 1955, **112**, 252–259.

Berger, D. G., Rice, C. E., Sewall, L. G., & Lemkau, P. V. The posthospital evaluation of psychiatric patients: The social adjustment inventory method. *Psychiatric Studies and Projects*, 1964, **3**, 1–30.

Burnes, A. J., Roen, S. R. Social roles and adaptation to the community. *Community Mental Health Journal*, 1967, **3**, 153–158.

Cavan, R. S., Burgess, E. W., Havighurst, R. J., & Goldhammer, H. *Personal adjustment in old age*. Chicago: Science Research Association, 1949.

Ciarlo, J., & Reihman, J. The Denver Community Mental Health Questionnaire: Development of a multidimensional program evaluation. In R. D. Coursey, G. A. Specter, S. A. Murrell, & B. Hunt (Eds.), *Program evaluation for mental health: Methods, strategies, and participants*. New York: Grune and Stratton, 1977.

Clare, A. W., & Cairns, V. E. Design, development and use of a standardized interview to assess social maladjustment and dysfunction in community studies. *Psychological Medicine*, 1978, **8**, 589–604.

Cook, P. E., & Josephs, P. O. The Community Adaptation Schedule and the California Psychological Inventory: A validational study with college students. *Community Mental Health Journal*, 1970, **6**, 366–373.

Cook, P. E., Looney, M. A., & Pine, L. The Community Adaptation Schedule and the Adjective Check List: A validational study with psychiatric inpatients and outpatients. *Community Mental Health Journal*, 1973, **9**, 11–17.

Crook, T., Hogarty, G. E., & Ulrich, R. F. Inter-rater reliability of informants' ratings: Katz Adjustment Scales R Form. *Psychological Reports*, 1980, **47**, 427–432.

Edwards, D. W., Yarvis, R. M., Mueller, O. P., Zingale, H. C., & Wagman, W. J., Test-taking and the stability of adjustment scales: Can we assess patient deterioration? *Evaluation Quarterly*, 1978, **2**, 275–291.

Ellsworth, R. B. Evaluating and applying information about treatment outcome. *Hospital and Community Psychiatry*, 1970, **21**, 115–117.

Ellsworth, R. B. Feedback: Asset or liability in improving treatment effectiveness? *Journal of Consulting and Clinical Psychology*, 1973, **40**, 383–393.

Ellsworth, R. B. Consumer feedback in measuring the effectiveness of mental health programs. In M. Guttentag & E. L. Struening (Eds.), *Handbook of Evaluation Research* (Vol. 1). Beverly Hills, Calif.: Sage Publications, 1975.

Ellsworth, R. B. The comparative effectiveness of community clinic and psychiatric hospital treatment. *Journal of Community Psychology*, 1978, **6**, 103–111.

Ellsworth, R. B., Collins, J. F., Casey, N. A., Schoonover, R. A., Hickey, R. H., Hyer, L., Twemlow, S. W., & Nesselroade, J. R. Some characteristics of effective psychiatric treatment programs. *Journal of Consulting and Clinical Psychology*, 1979, **47**, 799–817.

Ellsworth, R. B., Foster, L., Childers, B., Arthur, G., & Kroeker, D. Hospital and community adjustment as perceived by psychiatric patients, their families, and staff. *Journal of Consulting and Clinical Psychology*, 1968, **32**, 1–41.

Endicott, J., & Spitzer, R. L. A diagnostic interview: Schedule for Affective Disorders and Schizophrenia. *Archives of General Psychiatry*, 1978, **35**, 837–844.

Endicott, J., & Spitzer, R. L. What! Another rating scale? The Psychiatric Evaluation Form. *Journal of Nervous and Mental Disease*, 1972, **154**, 88–104. (a)

Endicott, J., & Spitzer, R. L. Current and Past Psychopathology Scales (CAPPS): Rationale, reliability, and validity. *Archives of General Psychiatry*, 1972, **27**, 678–687. (b)

Evanson, R. C., Sletten, I. W., Hedlund, J. L., & Faintich, D. M. CAPS: An automated evaluation system. *American Journal of Psychiatry*, 1974, **131**, 531–534.

Fiske, D. W. The use of significant others in assessing the outcome of psychotherapy. In I. E. Waskow, & M. B. Parloff (Eds.), *Psychotherapy change measures: Report of clinical research branch, N.I.M.H. Outcome Measures Project*. Washington, D.C.: U. S. Government Printing Office, 1975.

Fleiss, J. L., & Spitzer, R. L. A FORTRAN IV program for the analysis of demographic, item and scale data. *Educational and Psychological Measurement*, 1967, **27**, 187–194.

Fontana, A. F., & Dowds, B. N. Assessing treatment outcome: I. Adjustment in the community. *The Journal of Nervous and Mental Disease*, 1975, **161**, 221–230.

Freeman, H. E., & Simmons, O. G. Mental patients in the community: family settings and performance levels. *American Sociologcal Review*, 1958, **23**, 147–154.

Freeman, H. E., & Simmons, O. G. *The mental patient comes home.* New York: Wiley, 1963.

Glasscote, R. M., Kraft, A. M., Glassman, S. M., & Jepson, W. W. *Partial hospitalization for the mentally ill: A study of programs and problems.* Washington, D.C.: Joint Information Service of the American Psychiatric Association and the National Association for Mental Health, 1969.

Glazer, W. M., Aaronson, H. S., Prusoff, B. A., & Williams, D. H. Assessment of social adjustment in chronic ambulatory schizophrenics. *Journal of Nervous and Mental Disease*, 1980, **168**, 493–497.

Goldberg, S. C., Schooler, N. R., Hogarty, G. E., & Roper M. Prediction of relapse in schizophrenic outpatients treated by drug and sociotherapy. *Archives of General Psychiatry*, 1977, **34**, 171–184.

Goodman, S. P., Schulthorpe, W. B., Euve, M., Slater, P., & Linn, M. W., Social dysfunction among psychiatric and non-psychiatric outpatients. *Journal of the American Geriatrics Society*, 1969, **17**, 694–700.

Gurland, B. J., Yorkston, N. J., Stone, A. R., Frank, J. D., & Fleiss, J. L. The Structured and Scaled Interview to Assess Maladjustment (SSIAM): I. Description, rationale, and development. *Archives of General Psychiatry*, 1972, **27**, 259–264.

Guy, W., Gross, M., Hogarty, G. E., & Dennis, H. A controlled evaluation of day hospital effectiveness. *Archives of General Psychiatry*, 1969, **20**, 329–338.

Halpern, J. Program evaluation, systems theory, and output value analysis: A benefit/cost model. In R. D. Coursey, G. A. Specter, S. A. Murrell, & B. Hunt (Eds.), *Program evaluation for mental health: Methods, strategies, and participants*. New York: Grune and Stratton, 1977.

Harris, D. E., & Brown, T. R. Relationship of the Community Adaptation Schedule and the Personal Orientation Inventory: Two measures of positive mental health. *Community Mental Health Journal*, 1974, **10**, 111–118.

Herz, M. I., Endicott, J., Spitzer, R. L., & Mesnikoff, A. Day versus inpatient hospitalization: A controlled study. *American Journal of Psychiatry*, 1971, **127**, 1371–1382.

Hirsch, S. R., Platt, S., Knights, A., & Weyman, A. Shortening hospital stay for psychiatric care: Effect on patients and their families. *British Medical Journal*, 1979, **1**, 442–446.

Hogarty, G. E. Informant ratings of community adjustment. In I. E. Waskow & M. B. Parloff (Eds.), *Psychotherapy change measures: Report of N.I.M.H. Outcome Measures Project*. Washington, D.C.: U.S. Government Printing Office, 1975.

Hogarty, G. E., & Katz, M. M. Norms of adjustment and social behavior. *Archives of General Psychiatry*, 1971, **25**, 470–480.

Hogarty, G. E., Dennis, H., Guy, W., & Gross, G. G. "Who goes there?"–A critical evaluation of admissions to a psychiatric day hospital. *American Journal of Psychiatry*, 1968, **124**, 934–944.

Hogarty, G. E., Guy, W., Gross, M., & Gross G. G. An evaluation of community-based mental health programs: Long-range effects. *Medical Care*, 1969, **7**, 271–280.

Katz, M. M. A typological approach to the problem of predicting response to treatment. In J. R. Wittenborn & P. R. A. May (Eds.), *Prediction of response to pharmacotherapy*. Springfield, Ill.: Thomas, 1966.

Katz, M. M. A phenomenological typology of schizophrenia. In M. M. Katz, J. O. Cole, & W. E. Barton (Eds.), *The role and methodology of classification in psychiatry and psychopathology*. Washington, D.C.: U.S. Government Printing Office, 1968.

Katz, M. M., Gudeman, H., & Sanborn, K. Characterizing differences in Psychopathology among ethnic groups: A preliminary report on Hawaii-Japanese and Mainland-American schizophrenics. In W. Caudill & T. Lin (Eds.), *Mental health research in Asia and the Pacific*.

Katz, M. M., Lowery, H. A., & Cole, J. O. Behavior patterns of schizophrenics in the community. In M. Lorr (Ed.), *Explorations in typing psychotics*. New York: Pergamon Press, 1966.

Katz, M. M., & Lyerly, S. B. Methods for measuring adjustment and social behavior in the community: I. Rationale, description, discriminative validity and scale development. *Psychological Reports*, 1963, **13**, 502–535.

Kiresuk, T. J., & Sherman, R. E. Goal attainment scaling: A general method for evaluating comprehensive community mental health programs. *Community Mental Health Journal*, 1968, **4**, 443–453.

Linn, M. W., Caffey, E. M., Klett, C. J., Hogarty, G. E., & Lamb, H. R. Day treatment and psychotropic drugs in the aftercare of schizophrenic patients. *Archives of General Psychiatry*, 1979, **36**, 1055–1066.

Linn, M. W., Schulthorpe, W. B., Evje, M., Slater, P. H., & Goodman, S. P. A social dysfunction rating scale. *Journal of Psychiatric Research*, 1969, **6**, 299–306.

Michaux, M. H., Chelst, M. R., Foster, S. A., & Prium, R. J. Day and full-time psychiatric treatment: A controlled comparison. *Current Therapeutic Research*, 1972, **14**, 279–292.

Michaux, M. H., Chelst, M. R., Foster, S. A., Prium, R. J., & Dasinger, E. M. Post-release adjustment of day and full time psychiatric patients. *Archives of General Psychiatry*, 1973, **29**, 647–651.

Michaux, M. H., Garmize, K., Rossi, J. A., Schoolman, L. R., & Gross, G. M. A controlled comparison of psychiatric day center treatment with full time hospitalization. *Current Therapeutic Research*, 1969, **11**, 190–204.

Michaux, W. W., Katz, M. M., Kurland, A. A., & Gansereit, K. H. *The first year out: Mental patients after hospitalization*. Baltimore: John Hopkins Press, 1969.

Parloff, M. B., Kelman, H. C., & Frank, J. D. Comfort, effectiveness, and self-awareness as criteria of improvement in psychotherapy. *American Journal of Psychiatry*, 1958, **111**, 343–351.

Paykel, E. S., Weissman, M. M., & Prusoff, B. A. Social maladjustment and severity of depression. *Comprehensive Psychiatry*, 1978, **19**, 121–128.

Paykel, E. S., Weissman, M., Prusoff, B. A., & Tonks, C. M. Dimensions of social adjustment in depressed women. *Journal of Nervous and Mental Disease*, 1971, **152**, 158–172.

Penk, W. E., Charles, H. L., & Van Hoose, T. A., Comparative effectiveness of day hospital and inpatient psychiatric treatment. *Journal of Consulting and Clinical Psychology*, 1978, **46**, 94–101.

Platt, S., Weyman, A., Hirsch, S., & Hewett, S. The Social Behavior Assessment Schedule (SBAS): Rationale, contents, scoring, and reliability of a new interview schedule. *Social Psychiatry*, 1980, **15**, 43–55.

Prusoff, B. A., Weissman, M. M., Klerman, G. L., Rounsaville, B. J. Research diagnostic criteria subtypes of depression as predictors of differential response to psychotherapy and drug treatment. *Archives of General Psychiatry*, 1980, **37**, 796–801.

Roen, S. R., Ottenstein, D., Cooper, S., & Burnes, A. Community adaptation as an evaluative concept in community mental health. *Archives of General Psychiatry*, 1966, **15**, 36–44.

Sappington, A. A., & Michaux, M. H. Prognostic patterns in self-report, relative report, and professional evaluation measures for hospitalized and day-care patients. *Journal of Consulting and Clinical Psychology*, 1975, **43**, 904–910.

Schooler, N., Hogarty, G., & Weissman, M. M. Social Adjustment Scale II. (SAS II) In W. A. Hargreaves, C. C. Attkisson, & J. E. Sorenson (Eds.), *Resource materials for community mental health program evaluators*. Washington, D.C.: DHEW, No. 79–328, 1979.

Serban, G. Relationship of mental status, functioning and stress to readmission of schizophrenics. *British Journal of Social and Clinical Psychology*, 1975, **14**, 291–301.

Serban, G. Social Stress and Functioning Inventory for Psychotic Disorders (SSFIPD): Measurement and prediction of schizophrenics' community adjustment. *Comprehensive Psychiatry*, 1978, **19**, 337–347.

Serban, G. *Adjustment of schizophrenics in the community*. New York: SP Medical and Scientific Books, 1980.

Shaffer, J. W., Perlin, S., Schmidt, C. W., & Himelfarb, M. Assessment in absentia: New directions in the psychological autopsy. *Johns Hopkins Medical Journal*, 1972, **130**, 308–316.

Spitzer, R. L., & Endicott, J. DIAGNO: A computer program for psychiatric diagnosis utilizing the differential diagnostic procedure. *Archives of General Psychiatry*, 1968, **18**, 746–756.

Spitzer, R. L., Endicott, J., & Fleiss, J. L. Instruments and recording forms for evaluating psychiatric status and history. Rationale, method of development and description. *Comprehensive Psychiatry*, 1967, **8**, 321–343.

Spitzer, R. L., Endicott, J., Fleiss, J. L., & Cohen, J. The Psychiatric Status Schedule: A technique for evaluating psychopathology and impairment in role functioning. *Archives of General Psychiatry*, 1970, **23**, 41–55.

Spitzer, R. L., Endicott, J., & Robins, E. *Research Diagnostic Criteria (RDC) for a selected group of functional disorders* (3rd ed.). New York: New State Psychiatric Institute, 1978.

Spitzer, R. L., Fleiss, J. L., Burdock, E. I., Hardesty, A. A. (1964). The Mental Status Schedule: Rationale, reliability and validity. *Comprehensive Psychiatry*, 1964, **5**, 384–395.

Spitzer, R. L., Fleiss, J. L., Endicott, J., & Cohen, J. Mental Status Schedule: Properties of factor-analytically derived scales. *Archives of General Psychiatry*, 1967, **16**, 479–493.

Strauss, J. S., & Carpenter, W. T., Jr. The prediction of outcome in schizophrenia: I. Characteristics of outcome. *Archives of General Psychiatry*, 1972, **27**, 739–746.

Strauss, J. S., & Carpenter, W. T., Jr. Prediction of outcome in schizophrenia: III. Five-year outcome and its predictors. *Archives of General Psychiatry*, 1977, **34**, 159–163.

Vestre, N. D., & Zimmerman, R. Validity of informants' ratings of the behavior and symptoms of psychiatric patients. *Journal of Consulting and Clinical Psychology*, 1969, **33**, 175–179.

Washburn, S., Vannicelli, M., Longabaugh, R., & Scheff, B. A controlled comparison of psychiatric day treatment and inpatient hospitalization. *Journal of Consulting and Clinical Psychology*, 1976, **44**, 655–675.

Weissman, M. M. The assessment of social adjustment: A review of techniques. *Archives of General psychiatry*, 1975, **32**, 357–365.

Weissman, M. M., & Bothwell, S. The assessment of social adjustment by patient self-report. *Archives of General Psychiatry*, 1976, **33**, 1111–1115.

Weissman, M. M., Klerman, G. L., Paykel, E. S., Prusoff, B., & Hanson, B. Treatment effects on the social adjustment of depressed patients. *Archives of General Psychiatry*, 1974, **30**, 771–778.

Weissman, M. M., Klerman, G. L., Prusoff, B. A., Sholomskas, D., & Padian, N. Depressed outpatients: Results one year after treatment with drugs and/or interpersonal psychotherapy. *Archives of General Psychiatry*, 1981, **38**, 51–55.(b)

Weissman, M. M., Paykel, E. S., Siegel, R., & Klerman, G. L. The social role performance of depressed women: Comparisons with a normal group. *American Journal of Orthopsychiatry*, 1971, **41**, 390–405.

Weissman, M. M., Prusoff, B. A., Thompson, W. D., Harding, P. S., & Myers, J. K. Social adjustment by self-report in a community sample and in psychiatric outpatients. *Journal of Nervous and Mental Disease*, 1978, **166**, 317–326.

Weissman, M. M., Sholomskas, D., & John, K. The assessment of social adjustment. *Archives of General Psychiatry*, 1981, **38**, 1250–1258.(a)

Weldon, E., Clarkin, J. E., Hennessy, J. J., & Frances, A. Day hospital versus outpatient treatment: A controlled study. *Psychiatric Quarterly*, 1979, **51**, 144–150.

Willer, B. S. Individualized patient programming: An experiment in the use of evaluation and feedback for hospital psychiatry. *Evaluation Quarterly*, 1977, **1**, 587–608.

Willer, B., & Biggen, P. Comparison of rehospitalized and nonrehospitalized psychiatric patients on community adjustment: Self-Assessment Guide. Psychiatry, 1976, **39**, 239–244.

Willer, B., & Howard, P. Development of a computer assessted progress record for psychiatry. In G. Garwick (Ed.), *Goal Attainment Review*, **1**, Minneapolis: Program Evaluation, Resource Center, 1974.

Wilson, N. C. The automated tri-informant goal-oriented note: One approach to program evaluation. In R. D. Coursey, G. A. Specter, S. A. Murrell, & B. Hunt (Eds.), *Program evaluation for mental health: Methods, strategies, participants*. New York: Grune and Stratton, 1977.

CHAPTER 6

Crisis Intervention and Measurement of Treatment Outcome

RONETTE L. KOLOTKIN AND MARILYN JOHNSON

Betty's husband has abandoned her and their three young children.

Jack, a 52-year-old steel worker, has been laid off.

Ed lost his home and all of his material possessions in the Mt. Saint Helen eruption.

Nancy, a seventh grader, has just found out she's pregnant.

Agnes has recognized that, 5 months after being discharged from the state hospital, she can't cope outside on her own.

Barney's children have announced that they can no longer care for him at home and have made arrangements to place him in a local nursing home.

What do these diverse situations have in common? They all represent what most experts define as crises in the lives of individuals. Other questions can be raised about these situations: Is each of them appropriate for crisis intervention? What are the goals of such interventions? If crisis intervention is undertaken with each of these individuals, can the outcomes of these treatments be compared? How should these comparisons be made?

This set of questions guides the direction of this chapter. We begin with a discussion of the sociopsychological context (to determine why crisis intervention has developed) and an examination of the definition problem (to define what crisis intervention is). Next, we offer an analysis of measurement problems occurring in crisis intervention research. After reviewing current literature and discussing some issues arising from that literature, we conclude with a number of recommendations for outcome evaluation of crisis intervention.

GROWTH AND DEVELOPMENT OF CRISIS INTERVENTION

Crisis intervention services have expanded rapidly in recent years. Although crisis intervention may have begun as a brief treatment for survivors of physical disasters (Lindemann, 1944) and is still widely used for dealing with victims of disaster (Blaufarb & Levine, 1972; Sank, 1979; Zarle et al., 1974), currently any of the following services might describe themselves as offering crisis intervention treatment: short-term psychotherapy clinics, walk-in counseling agencies, youth emergency services, rape counseling centers, child abuse hotlines, programs for battered women and incest victims, psychiatric inpatient wards with short lengths of stay, various types of information–referral agency, emergency social services, crisis-oriented alcoholism–chemical dependence treatment programs, emergency homemakers, and 24-hour suicide hotline centers. In addition, crisis intervention services are now offered in a variety of settings (e.g., hospitals, community mental health agencies, "storefront" clinics), with widely varying client populations and staff (Stelmachers, 1978, Reference Note 2 at end of chapter).

A number of factors contribute to the rapid growth and expansion of crisis intervention services. The first involves changes in the nature of consumers and healers. The social forces of the past 20 years have sensitized professionals to the needs of special groups of consumers. In addition, the civil rights movement, the war on poverty, the women's movement, and other social action forces have led many individuals to organize themselves in groups to seek psychological assistance. Abused women and children, children of divorce, victims of sudden catastrophic illness, alienated war veterans, and former mental hospital patients—these groups have always existed, but only recently have they become the focus of attention by the mental health community. Their problems are construed as justifiable reasons for psychological intervention.

The effects of change can also be seen in the nature of the healers sought by those in crisis. The mental health professional has, in many ways, replaced not only the family doctor, but also the family member or friend formerly contacted by individuals in crisis. There is a tendency to seek professional advice for problems that formerly were viewed as pains to be endured with the help of loved ones. A parallel trend is the emphasis on peer assistance arising out of the self-help movement (Alcoholics Anonymous, Parents Anonymous, cancer patient groups, etc.). Both the professional and the peer are felt to possess an expertise that intimate others do not have (or at least cannot muster in a crisis).

Changes in mental health policy and treatment have also influenced the growth and development of crisis intervention services. The growth of the community mental health center movement has contributed to a change of focus in much of the psychotherapy practiced today. Most community mental health center clients seek crisis intervention rather than self-actualization, and in fact their crises often *require* rapid intervention (Garfield, 1978). Also, wider acceptability of psychotherapy by the entire population has resulted in increased stress on existing resources, making it impractical to provide extensive long-term psychological treatment to all who seek it. Another treatment change has been the growth of the number of treatment modalities that can be implemented in brief psychotherapeutic interventions. Variants of behavioral and cognitive therapies can be used to help patients restore a sense of mastery within a relatively brief period of time.

There is a final factor in mental health policy change that relates to the future of crisis intervention. The imminence of national health insurance makes it indisputable that critical attention will be given to discovering those methods of brief therapeutic intervention that are most effective for specific presenting problems. There is already a good deal of attention given to this topic, and emphasis on the cost efficiency of therapeutic services is here to stay. It seems safe to predict that crisis intervention will receive careful scrutiny as a cost-beneficial solution to a number of social and emotional problems. As a result, the role of outcome evaluation will be of extreme importance.

THE PROBLEM OF DEFINITION

An unfortunate side effect of the rapid expansion of crisis intervention services has been the creation of confusion about the meaning of the term "crisis intervention." This confusion has prompted the author of a recent textbook on crisis intervention to conclude that "the concept itself is in a state of 'crisis' . . . . Even among professionals approaching crisis intervention with similar goal or intentions, there remains much confusion and controversy over what the concept means" (Ewing, 1978, p. 3). Unfortunately, this confusion may have serious implications for crisis intervention researchers. It is difficult to evaluate crisis intervention research if studies differ from each other with respect to how the terms "crisis" and "crisis intervention" and their treatment goals are conceptualized.

Adding to the confusion surrounding the term "crisis intervention" is the lack of a generally accepted classification system of crises. Baldwin (1978) has argued for a classification of crises that examines anticipated life transitions, traumatic situations, maturational and developmental factors, psychopathology, and other emergencies as sources of stress that are not mutually exclusive. Similarly, Golan (1978) suggests different crisis intervention strategies depending on whether the crisis is a developmental–maturational crisis, a natural–artificially produced disaster, or an acute, situational crisis. Crises have been further classified in a number of ways, such as the exhaustion crisis versus the shock crisis (Korner, 1973), the generic versus the individual crisis (Jacobson et al., 1968), and internal versus external crisis (Butcher & Herzog, 1982).

It is clear that the many different ways of viewing crisis and crisis intervention further confuse the picture. Although most crisis intervention clinicians and researchers agree that crisis intervention treatment goals should be limited, the exact nature of these goals tends to vary somewhat. Most crisis intervention clinicians and researchers would agree that the two primary goals of crisis intervention are symptom relief and a return to the precrisis state of functioning. However, other stated treatment objectives of crisis intervention have included understanding the precipitating circumstances, connecting current stresses to past experience and conflicts, teaching more adaptive coping responses, and innoculating the client against future similar problems (Butcher & Koss, 1978; Golan, 1978). Rapoport (1970) believes that treatment goals should vary (depending on the favorableness of the personality and social situation) from return to precrisis functioning and basic symptom relief to creation of new modes of perceiving and feeling. Others (Kiresuk & Sherman, 1968) believe that crisis intervention treatment goals are so variable from person to person that they should be separately identified and specified for each individual. In any case, it is clear that one's belief about the goals of crisis intervention can clearly affect treatment outcome and should be taken into account when different crisis intervention outcome studies are compared.

The discussion in this chapter is focused on crisis intervention rather than brief therapy; however, we realize that one person's brief therapy may be another's crisis intervention. It is not uncommon to combine crisis intervention and brief therapy because of their similarities (Butcher & Kolotkin, 1979; Butcher & Koss, 1978). Both crisis intervention and brief therapy are similar in terms of their limited goals, present-day focus, therapist directiveness, rapid early assessment, and prompt intervention. There is general agreement that "brief therapy" is the broader term, encompassing crisis intervention and other interventions of a time-limited nature (Butcher and Koss, 1978). We use the term "crisis intervention" to represent brief, problem-focused treatment of individuals who are experiencing a high level of emotional distress. It is this intense distress and its self-limiting nature that define the situation as a crisis, and the distress is often, but not always, the result of a specific event or situation. We make no attempt to differentiate between crisis intervention, crisis intervention therapy, and crisis therapy since others have tended to use these terms interchangeably and no doubt will continue to do so.

UNIQUE PROBLEMS IN CRISIS INTERVENTION RESEARCH

The difficulties inherent in the measurement of treatment outcome in any psychotherapeutic endeavor are great and are discussed at length elsewhere in the psychotherapy outcome literature (Bergin & Lambert, 1978; Lambert, 1979). However, there are certain methodological problems unique to crisis intervention outcome research. We first address these issues and then examine other measurement issues that are shared by both crisis intervention and other forms of therapy. The unique issues fall into two categories: (1) the nature of the crisis intervention client population and (2) the nature of crisis intervention itself.

Nature of the Client Population

Unlike other psychotherapy services, many crisis intervention centers permit and even encourage client anonymity. Of course, it is impossible to collect follow-up data and to conduct outcome studies on crisis clients if the clients are unidentifiable. Furthermore, crisis counselors are seldom attuned to the importance of research and may fear that the data collection process will impinge on treatment or will invade the client's privacy. Several investigators, however, report that none of these adverse effects occur (Murphy et al., 1969; Slaikeu et al., 1975).

Another serious methodological problem in outcome studies of crisis intervention is the mobility of the population. Many users of crisis services are transients or otherwise rather mobile individuals with unstable life patterns. Consequently, it is often difficult to locate crisis clients for follow-up information, resulting in a larger sample loss than is typically found in traditional mental health settings (Stelmachers, 1978, Reference Note 2). For example, Lowy et al. (1971) reported that nearly half of their follow-up sample was unavailable because the subjects had died, moved, or given false names. Furthermore, it was believed that this unreachable group contained more physically ill people, more alcoholics, and more people in trouble with the police than the successfully contacted portion of the sample. Similarly, Williams et al. (1972) lost 25% of their initial treatment sample due to client dropout and refusal; Williams and Polak (1979) lost 49% of their treatment sample as a result of client refusal alone.

Another characteristic of crisis intervention clients that creates difficulties in collecting treatment outcome data is that users of crisis intervention services are often too disturbed, psychotic, uncooperative, or confused to cooperate with the necessary procedures (Stelmachers, 1978, Reference Note 2). A substantial number of clients are unable to remember the contact and thus cannot provide any feedback regarding the intervention. Stelmachers et al. (1977, Reference Note 3) report that at one point 65% of their crisis intervention center's client population had to be excluded from the follow-up evaluation for these reasons.

A further methodological problem in crisis intervention research is the extreme heterogeneity of the population. Target symptoms vary so greatly from client to client that often the only commonality among clients is that they have contacted a crisis intervention agency (Auerbach and Kilmann, 1977). In a description of their crisis intervention service, Stelmachers et al. (1977, Reference Note 3) noted that the most frequent presenting complaints (i.e., reported by at least 20% of the clients) covered a wide variety of problems. The nine most frequently reported problems included anxiety, physical complaints, depression, interpersonal relationships, psychopathological symptoms, family and marital difficulties, suicide, alcohol use, and aggression. The diagnostic breakdown in their population (using DSM-II) also demonstrated heterogeneity: 29% had personality disorders, 25% were psychotic, 18% had transient situational disturbances, and 17% were chemically dependent. Although target complaints may vary considerably from client to client within a particular agency, they may also differ a great deal from setting to setting. Given the variety of crisis intervention agencies and settings, it is not unusual to find a great deal of heterogeneity among crisis intervention clients.

As more crisis intervention agencies specialize in particular crisis populations—for example, rape, battery, sexual abuse, abortion, marital transition, widowhood, occupational upheaval, death of a child, aging, terminal illness, and childbirth (Zukerman, 1979)—some of the problems of client heterogeneity may be resolved. That is, the general crisis client population will be categorized into more homogeneous subgroups and then can be studied as such. Stelmachers et al. (1977, Reference Note 3) have already begun to divide their diverse population into relatively homogeneous subgroups and to use different evaluation methods for each subgroup. Agencies that specialize in a particular type of crisis (e.g., a rape counseling center) are fortunate in that they begin with an already relatively homogeneous population (i.e., all rape victims). Some of the more recent, better designed outcome studies on crisis intervention evaluate crisis clients who have all experienced the same type of crisis [e.g., see Bordow and Porritt (1979) on victims of road trauma].

By studying the typical effects that similar crises tend to produce in most individuals experiencing these crises, it will be possible to produce a data base of normative reactions to particular crises. In this way, client responses to crisis intervention can be compared to victims of similar crises who have not received crisis intervention services. Unfortunately, there is currently a lack of normative data on most crises against which to evaluate treatment gains in crisis intervention (Auerbach & Kilmann, 1977). Normative data are difficult to obtain because individuals in crisis who are not seeking treatment tend to refuse to be evaluated for research purposes. For example, 43% of Williams and Polak's (1979) untreated bereavement sample refused to return research questionnaires. Similarly, 30% of persons contacted following a death of a family member refused to be evaluated for research purposes (Williams et al., 1972).

Thus the frequent use of client anonymity in crisis intervention, as well as the mobility, high level of disturbance, and heterogeneous nature of crisis clients, lead to difficulties that must be addressed by crisis intervention researchers.

Nature of Crisis Intervention

Another problem with evaluating treatment outcome in crisis intervention is that crises are generally considered to be self-limiting in nature. Most individuals suffering from life crises recover spontaneously within six weeks regardless of the kind of care that they receive (Caplan, 1964). If crises tend to be self-limiting, it is difficult to demonstrate that crisis intervention techniques actually produce greater recovery from crises.

In addition, outcomes in crisis intervention are difficult to evaluate because of the relationship that exists between the transitional pathology of the crisis state and psychopathology in general. It is assumed that individuals who contact a crisis intervention agency are in crisis, acutely distressed, and experiencing transitory psychopathology, and that in time they will return to a precrisis level of functioning. Although this may indicate a return to adequate functioning for most crisis intervention clients, what about clients whose precrisis level of functioning was already disordered and psychopathological? Is a return to their precrisis level desirable or to be considered a treatment success?

Butcher and Herzog (1982) caution that crisis intervention treatment strategies work best with individuals who are experiencing transitory pathology and that these strategies are generally less effective with individuals who have chronic personality problems or neuroses that result in repetitive crises. These authors argue for the the importance of accurate initial assessment of clients so that one can determine whether the client's symptomatology is a function of the immediate stressful situation or whether the client's problems actually result from chronically poor life adjustment. Others (Conroe et al., 1978; McKenna et al., 1975; Stelmachers et al., 1977, Reference Note 3) suggest that crisis intervention may be used with chronically disturbed individuals, but that the expected goals of treatment will vary according to the precrisis level of functioning of the client. In the McKenna et al. study, for example, differences were found between "acutely suicidal" and "chronically suicidal" individuals in response to crisis intervention treatment. This study suggests the possibility of different treatment goals for different client subpopulations.

These factors—the self-limiting nature of crises and the sometimes unclear boundary between an individual's psychological response to stress and typical behavior—must be considered by the crisis intervention researcher.

PROBLEMS IN CRISIS INTERVENTION AND THERAPY OUTCOME RESEARCH

In addition to having its own unique measurement difficulties, research on crisis intervention is also subject to some of the same measurement problems found in psychotherapy outcome research in general. Three such methodological issues that are accentuated in the crisis intervention setting are discussed: collateral interventions, deterioration effects, and subsequent therapy.

Collateral Interventions

The question arises as to whether there is greater likelihood that crisis clients, more than other therapy clients, will seek collateral interventions. To our knowledge, this specific question has not been investigated. However, it would seem that the nature of crisis intervention as well as particular characteristics of individuals in crisis would promote a greater possibility of collateral interventions. Crisis intervention is conducted with individuals who are experiencing intense emotional feelings; the time limitation and the directive and confrontative nature of treatment tend to enhance the emotional arousal. This heightened arousal is likely to be accompanied by increased motivation to resolve the crisis and to return to the precrisis state. As a result, the crisis client may be so eager to resolve the crisis as to intentionally or unintentionally seek out other help givers in the environment, in addition to the crisis therapist. Even if there is no difference between crisis clients and other therapy clients in terms of the *frequency* with which they seek collateral interventions, the *effects* of collateral intervention may be greater in crisis clients than in other therapy clients. The crisis client's sense of urgency may well render that client especially susceptible to a number of extraneous factors, including collateral interventions.

The crisis therapist may also, in both direct and indirect ways, encourage collateral interventions since, in crisis intervention, the therapist encourages the clients to keep a sense of urgency during the treatment (Butcher & Kolotkin, 1979). This sense of urgency is demonstrated by the therapist through the brevity of the treatment, the limitations of the goals, and the promptness and rapidity of the assessment and intervention process. In encouraging a prompt return to emotional equilibrium, the crisis therapist may be indirectly encouraging crisis clients to seek help simultaneously from outside sources. At other times, the crisis therapist will directly encourage involvement of other individuals and agencies in the environment. Butcher and Herzog (1982) suggest that crisis intervention is best conducted in the context of the individual's life situation and that it may be necessary to enlist the aid of family or community resources to help the individual deal with existing problems. Although the involvement of outside individuals and agencies may serve to promote more rapid resolution of crises, this may tend to cloud the picture in terms of which aspect of crisis intervention was most related to treatment outcome.

It is important for researchers to address the issue of collateral interventions and their influence on treatment outcome. One study on treatment outcome in crisis intervention (Gottschalk et al., 1973) provides some support for the easy availability and profound effects of collateral interventions. In this study 78 clients who came voluntarily to a crisis intervention clinic were randomly assigned to either an immediate treatment condition or a six-week waiting-list condition. By the end of six weeks, both groups had improved considerably and there was no significant difference between the groups on the Psychiatric Morbidity Scale. In attempting to account for these results, the authors suggested that collateral intervention from friends and relatives may have accounted for the considerable improvement in the wait-list group. They also proposed other possible explanations for their results.

Deterioration Effects

A great deal of attention has been directed to the possible negative effects of psychotherapy (Hadley & Strupp, 1976; Lambert et al., 1977). If deterioration is a possible outcome of psychotherapy, it is certainly also a possible outcome of crisis intervention. In fact, it has been suggested that brief treatment methods such as crisis intervention might be particularly susceptible to negative effects (Butcher & Kolotkin, 1979; Butcher & Koss, 1978). The relatively fast pace and the need for prompt therapeutic intervention may result in premature or inadequate initial assessments, as well as incorrect efforts at therapeutic intervention.

Furthermore, the intensity of crisis intervention treatment and the directive, somewhat authoritarian style of many crisis therapists may lead to negative reactions in clients. Negative effects may be even more likely if the therapist both confronts and directs the client to engage in activities for which the client may not be prepared. Although advice giving is an acceptable practice in crisis intervention therapy, advice that is either prematurely given or unsound can result in undesirable consequences. Finally, the brief and intense nature of the interaction in crisis intervention may render this form of therapy more susceptible to the effects of the therapist's experience level. Since crisis therapists are often paraprofessionals or trained lay persons, therapist training or inexperience may be even more an issue in crisis intervention than in other methods of therapy.

It is clear that the evaluation of therapeutic outcome in crisis intervention practice and research requires that possible negative effects be given consideration. At least two studies of crisis intervention services have indicated deterioration following crisis intervention treatment (Gottschalk et al., 1967; Green et al., 1975). The question of whether crisis intervention lends itself to more deterioration effects than other methods of therapy may also be a valuable issue for researchers to consider.

Subsequent Therapy

Another issue of concern in psychotherapy outcome research that may also be a concern in crisis intervention outcome research is the issue of subsequent therapy (i.e., additional therapy following the completion of a course of crisis intervention therapy). The question arises as to whether crisis clients seek subsequent therapy more often than do clients receiving other types of psychotherapy. If users of crisis intervention services do receive more subsequent therapy than other clients, this may have important implications for follow-up assessment in outcome research.

Given the brevity of crisis intervention treatments and their limited focus, it is likely that not all of a client's problems are resolved by the end of treatment. Butcher and Herzog (1982) indicate that crisis intervention may leave some work unfinished, so that the individual must deal with residual problems at a later date when the crisis has abated. It is possible that the client who is ready to deal with those deferred problems will desire outside assistance in the form of additional psychotherapy.

A recent study suggests that crisis clients frequently seek subsequent therapy following termination of crisis treatment. Maris and Connor (1973) evaluated the effects of crisis therapy on 200 psychiatric emergency room outpatients. Follow-up measures were administered 8 to 12 months posttreatment. In the interim between intake and follow-up, 78% of the clients had received some form of subsequent therapy. In a study conducted by Patterson et al. (1977), 60% of clients received additional therapy following termination of a brief (one- to eight-session) therapy intervention (not specifically crisis intervention). It was difficult to predict which clients tended to seek subsequent therapy. There were no differences between those clients who did and those who did not seek subsequent therapy on outcome measures taken at the termination of brief therapy. It is obvious that if a substantial number of crisis clients receive additional therapy at some point following termination of crisis intervention, it will be difficult to interpret the results of a follow-up assessment. The improvement may be attributed either to the crisis intervention, or the subsequent therapy, or the combination of both.

It is also difficult to judge whether the act of seeking additional treatment is to be perceived as a crisis intervention success or a crisis intervention failure. It could be that the individual has made considerable progress and is, after a time, ready to make further progress in additional therapy. On the other hand, the individual may not have improved as a result of crisis intervention (or may have deteriorated) and is thus seeking subsequent therapy. A study by McKenna et al. (1975) addressed this issue. In this study 18 persons identified as either chronically suicidal or acutely suicidal were evaluated one month after a telephone contact with a crisis intervention agency. Whereas the majority of the chronically suicidal individuals continued to feel suicidal at the time of the follow-up, the majority of the acutely suicidal individuals no longer did. Despite the difference between these two groups in terms of treatment outcome, they did not differ with respect to receptiveness to subsequent long-term therapy. Therefore, the presence of further therapy in the McKenna et al. study did not seem to be indicative of progress made in brief crisis intervention treatment. A substantial number of crisis clients seem to receive additional therapy some time after the completion of the crisis intervention treatment. This is an issue that crisis intervention researchers would be well advised to consider when evaluating treatment outcome.

In summary, crisis intervention outcome evaluation can be compromised by potent collateral interventions and by further experience in psychotherapy. It may also be more susceptible to deterioration effects than are other therapies. We view these factors as challenges faced by all psychotherapy researchers.

REVIEW OF OUTCOME RESEARCH ON CRISIS INTERVENTION

In spite of the popularity and widespread availability of crisis intervention treatment approaches, the number of studies on treatment outcome in crisis intervention is actually quite small. Few new outcome studies have appeared since Auerbach and Kilmann's (1977) review of community-oriented suicide prevention programs, crisis intervention programs in psychiatric settings, and studies with surgical patients. Many of the existing studies deal more with brief therapy than with crisis intervention per se. Furthermore, many studies suffer from methodological weaknesses such as failure to employ adequate control groups, failure to clearly specify the treatment procedures, failure to clearly define the client population, and failure to clearly define meaningful outcome criteria. We discuss some of the research on crisis intervention treatment outcome below, attempting to focus on the most methodologically sound studies.

In general, evidence thus far suggests that crisis-oriented therapies produce positive results (Auerbach & Kilmann, 1977). In their survey on research in brief and crisis-oriented therapies, Butcher and Koss (1978) found that 70 to 80% of the treated cases showed measured improvement. They noted slightly lower rates of improvement (60 to 70%) when considering only the best designed studies.

In a comparative treatment study, Greer and Bagley (1971) conducted a long-term ($\bar{x}$ = 18 months) follow-up of 204 clients who had previously attempted suicide. Forty-seven untreated individuals were compared with 76 persons who received one to two sessions of crisis intervention, as well as 88 persons who received long-term therapy. The investigators found that subsequent suicide attempts occurred significantly more often among untreated than among treated patients and that prolonged treatment was associated with the best prognosis. The results of this study, however, are to be regarded with caution. Since subjects were not randomly assigned to treatment but were self-selected or referred by a psychiatrist depending on unspecified criteria, the treatment groups were not equivalent initially. As a result, posttreatment changes may have been more a function of subject selection than of type of treatment.

Decker and Stubblebine (1972) conducted another outcome study, comparing 225 clients who received crisis intervention prior to a psychiatric hospitalization with 315 clients who received only a traditional psychiatric hospitalization. Follow-up evaluation was conducted 2½ years posttreatment, using length of hospital stay and number of readmissions as outcome criteria. Those individuals who received crisis intervention therapy spent less time in the hospital during their initial and subsequent hospitalizations and were readmitted less often than were the other patients who had not received crisis intervention.

Gottschalk and his colleagues conducted two crisis intervention outcome studies. In the first study (Gottschalk et al., 1967), acutely disturbed psychiatric clients who had been treated with emergency psychotherapy (up to a maximum of six sessions) were compared with clients who had discontinued this treatment. The outcome criterion utilized in this study was a rating of psychiatric morbidity made by a separate evaluation team. In general, treated clients showed more improvement than treatment dropouts, both at posttreatment and at follow-up (three to seven months later). Another finding of this study was that some clients experienced negative effects of therapy.

In a later study (Gottschalk et al., 1973), 61 individuals who came voluntarily to a crisis intervention clinic were randomly assigned to either an immediate intervention condition or a wait list-group. Persons in the wait-list condition underwent a diagnostic evaluation but were placed on a waiting list for six weeks prior to receiving treatment. Persons in the crisis-treatment group received an average of 2.7 treatment sessions. The primary outcome measure in this study was the same psychiatric morbidity rating scale employed in the previous study. An evaluation that took place six weeks after therapy revealed no differences between the groups. These results suggested that individuals in crisis may respond as well to a brief diagnostic contact as they do to formal crisis intervention. The authors offered a variety of alternative explanations for the results they obtained, including spontaneous remission and collateral interventions.

Maris and Connor (1973) evaluated the effects of crisis intervention on 200 psychiatric emergency room outpatients. Clients were evaluated at 8 to 12 months posttreatment on several outcome measures (self-reports of self-satisfaction, depression, and chief complaints). In the interim between intake and follow-up, 78% of the clients received some form of subsequent psychotherapy. Approximately 60% of the clients showed improvement in the measures of self-satisfaction and depression. The nature of the clients' complaints changed over time as well; whereas originally complaints tended to be related to depression and a general low level of satisfaction, later complaints were focused on specific complaints such as financial and work problems.

Another study on the effects of crisis intervention was conducted by Green et al. (1975). Following six weeks of brief crisis-oriented treatment, evaluations were made by the clients ($N = 50$), the therapists, and a research team on a variety of measures (viz., the Hamilton Depression Rating Scale, The Psychiatric Evaluation Form, global ratings of improvement, and a self-rating symptom checklist). In general, ratings made by both the client and the research team indicated improvement for most patients. Final status measures tended to correlate highly with each other. Whereas global ratings of improvement made by the therapist indicated that 95% of the clients had improved, similar ratings made by the clients themselves indicated that only 74% of the clients had experienced improvement. The findings also revealed that some of the treated clients experienced deterioration by the time of follow-up testing.

Calsyn et al. (1977) also examined the efficacy of crisis intervention. The participants in this study were 305 clients who had been seen for one to six sessions of crisis intervention. Records of subsequent hospitalization and subsequent outpatient treatment were employed as outcome criteria; unfortunately, any hospitalization or outpatient treatment taking place at either a private or out of state facility went undetected. Calsyn et al. found that approximately 30% of the clients had received subsequent treatment within three years after they were in the crisis intervention program. One-half of these clients received only outpatient treatment, one-third received only inpatient treatment, and one-sixth of these clients received both inpatient and outpatient treatment. Current precipitating events as well as prior hospitalization and suicidal behavior were predictive of subsequent treatment, whereas demographic variables and therapist characteristics were not predictive of subsequent treatment. Although we cannot assume that the remaining 70% of the clients improved, the results of this study support the efficacy of crisis intervention.

In the previously reported studies, clients were quite heterogeneous with respect to the type of crisis precipitant. The following studies investigated crisis intervention with homogeneous populations. Bordow and Porritt (1979) assessed 70 male victims of road trauma who had been hospitalized for at least one week following their accidents. Individuals in this study were randomly assigned to one of three treatment conditions. In the "delayed contact" condiction, clients received no intervention but were contacted for follow-up and outcome assessment three months after their accidents. In the "immediate review" group, clients were given a one session structured intake interview (which provided minimal emotional support and instead reviewed the traumatic events and clients' reactions to them) and were followed up three months later. Individuals in the "full intervention" group received the same initial structured interview as well as 2 to 10 hours of crisis intervention (defined as emotional, practical, and social support) by an experienced social worker specifically trained in techniques of crisis intervention. At follow-up, all subjects completed a battery of health and adjustment measures. The findings indicated that individuals in the delayed contact condition remained generally distressed, that some persons in the immediate review condition were able to benefit from the one session structured interview, and that the most favorable outcomes occured in the full intervention treatment condition.

Three related studies on response to bereavement reported negative results (Polak et al., 1975; Williams & Polak, 1979; Williams et al., 1972). Crisis intervention services were offered to families immediately after death of a loved one. These families were compared on a number of measures with two control groups: one group of families experiencing sudden death and receiving no crisis intervention and another group of families with no recent death and receiving no crisis intervention. The three groups were compared at 6 and 18 months following the initial contacts.

In no case did the crisis intervention show evidence of aiding the families with respect to physical or mental health factors. The bereaved families, treated and untreated, usually indicated more psychological distress at followup than did the nonbereaved group. These studies have certain methodological limitations (e.g., nonrandom assignment to treatment groups in the 1975 study and rather high rates of subject refusal) that compromise the findings. Perhaps the most critical flaw in these studies is the fact that the families did not actively seek therapeutic intervention, so the results cannot be generalized to a helpseeking bereaved population.

To summarize the outcome studies reviewed here, the efficacy rate is about 50%. The results of Greer and Bagley (1971), Decker and Stubblebine (1972), Gottschalk et al., (1967), Maris and Connor (1973), Bordow and Porritt (1979), and Calsyn et al. (1977) suggest that crisis intervention can be useful in a variety of settings. Mixed results are reported by Gottschalk et al. (1973) and Green et al. (1975). The bereavement studies by Williams and Polak and their colleagues (1972, 1979) indicated no effect from crisis intervention.

These studies on the efficacy of crisis intervention suggest that, in general, brief crisis-oriented therapy can facilitate client improvement and return to precrisis functioning. Although these studies tend to be among the best available, some methodological weaknesses are nonetheless apparent. Perhaps the most obvious weakness is the total lack of consistency across studies. A great deal of variability was present in the length of treatment, timing of follow-up evaluations, type of crisis intervention setting, treatment outcome measures, and nature of crisis populations. It is fortunate that some of the later studies attempted to control some of the variability by carefully specifying and limiting the ranges of variables within the study (e.g., the study by Bordow and Porritt evaluated the first 70 male victims of road trauma who had been hospitalized for at least one week following their accidents).

Another conclusion to be drawn from this review is that further studies of special crisis populations (i.e., persons confronted by a common stressor or aversive event) are needed, rather than additional studies of populations of mixed stress reactions. A number of special crisis populations have been identified and the stress reactions associated with these crises examined; these include response to surgical interventions (Auerbach & Kilmann, 1977); death of a spouse (Baler & Golde, 1964); response of mothers to the birth of premature children (Caplan et al., 1965); rape (Burgess & Holmstrom, 1979; Freiberg & Bridwell, 1976); battery (Martin, 1976); breast cancer (Schain, 1976); problem pregnancy (Baldwin, 1973); abortion (Bracken et al., 1973); widowhood (Hiltz, 1975); and geriatric crises (Grauer & Frank, 1978). Unfortunately, most of these authors emphasize subjective case histories, program description, and anecdotal reports, rather than experimental research on crisis intervention with these populations.

Furthermore, there tends to be an emphasis on understanding the nature of *responses to crises* rather than *responses to interventions*. Burgess and Holmstrom (1979) have made an in-depth study of the variables that affect a person's response to rape. Similar studies are under way into personality and situational characteristics of battered women and their assailants. Walker (1980) has formulated a theory that delineates a number of stages undergone by victims and batterers. Golan (1978) outlined stages that occur in a number of different kinds of crisis. Horowitz and his colleagues have developed the most carefully detailed theory of the trauma response syndrome (Horowitz, 1976). If these stages in fact do occur as described, clinicians may derive benefit from this work. It should be possible to plan specific interventions to aid victims in the various stages. In any case, the state of the art may be such that we have to formulate theories first before learning the best ways to help individuals in crisis.

ASSESSMENT OF OUTCOME IN CRISIS INTERVENTION

In this section we discuss three aspects of outcome assessment: criteria; timing; and instruments.

Criteria

It is generally agreed that psychotherapeutic outcomes are complex and multi-faceted, requiring multidimensional evaluation of both positive and negative outcomes on the basis of information obtained from the client, the therapist, and other members of society (Bergin & Lambert, 1978; Butcher & Kolotkin, 1979; Lambert, 1979; Strupp & Hadley, 1977; Waskow & Parloff, 1975). As a result, analyses of treatment outcome generally are based on a wide range of outcome criteria that are measured by a variety of test instruments and indices. That this situation also exists in research on crisis intervention is evident from the previous review of outcome studies. A great deal of variability exists across studies of crisis intervention with respect to the manner in which treatment outcome is evaluated. This variability makes comparisons across studies difficult. Butcher and Herzog (in press), for example, listed 19 different assessment instruments that have been employed in crisis intervention and brief therapy.

Crisis intervention research employs traditional means of outcome assessment (i.e., self-report measures of symptom relief, personality test scores, therapist's ratings, independent rater's judgments, observations by family members, and external indices of behavior) and also other methods (e.g., measurements of referral success, subsequent therapy, hospitalization rate, suicide rate, and client satisfaction). Some of these latter methods of measurement fall within the realm of "remote criteria" or "pseudocriteria" discussed by Butcher and Kolotkin (1979) and consequently are not particularly useful as outcome criteria. These criteria tend also to be based on the erroneous assumption that positive outcomes are unidirectional. These and other problems associated with the use of these indices of change are discussed next.

Several studies have utilized referral success as an indication of treatment outcome (Paul & Turner, 1976; Slaikeu et al., 1973, 1975; Tapp et al., 1974). In these studies a positive treatment outcome is assumed to have occurred if a client returns to the crisis center for an in-person appointment following a referral made during a telephone crisis call, or if a client keeps outpatient therapy appointments that have been recommended by the crisis therapist. However, research by Slaikeu and colleagues indicates that a large number of clients who are noncompliant with referrals either take some specific action to solve their problems or find help at another agency and thus can be considered treatment successes rather than treatment failures (Slaikeu et al., 1973, 1975).

Because it is difficult to evaluate reasons for noncompliance with a referral, perhaps this measure is not a useful outcome criterion in crisis intervention.

The use of either hospital admission rates or subsequent outpatient therapy as indicators of the failure of crisis intervention is also questionable. These indices were employed in a study by Calsyn et al. (1977). Whereas the reduction of hospital admission rates may be an appropriate goal for some clients, for other clients the intended goal of crisis intervention may be the rapid hospitalization of a client. Similarly, the reasons for seeking treatment subsequent to termination may represent a positive outcome for some, whereas for others it may indicate a poor response to crisis intervention. With regard to hospital admission rates as an outcome measure, Stelmachers (1977, Reference Note 2) suggests that the more appropriate criterion of successful crisis intervention might be the early and accurate *discrimination* of clients needing hospitalization from those who require other methods of treatment.

It is apparent that the above three indices of change (referral success, subsequent therapy, and subsequent hospitalization) are based on the erroneous assumption that positive treatment outcomes are unidirectional and consistent across persons. Researchers must be careful to avoid use of outcome criteria that are erroneously assumed to indicate improvement whereas in fact they may indicate treatment success for one person and treatment failure for another.

Although many crisis intervention studies utilize suicide rate as an outcome measure (Bagley, 1968; Greer & Bagley, 1971; Lester, 1974), the utility of this measure has been criticized (Auerbach & Kilmann, 1977). These authors suggest that suicide is an impractical measure since it deals only with the relatively atypical event of suicide, rather than with the typical problems found in crisis intervention settings. Furthermore, suicide rate varies considerably depending on the length of follow-up interval employed and the criteria utilized by coroners.

Another often used outcome measure in crisis intervention studies (Stelmachers, 1977, Reference Note 2) is the client satisfaction measure. Unfortunately, this is an unstandardized measure that may be artificially inflated as a result of the client's desire to please the therapist. Client satisfaction measures are also not useful measures to employ with involuntary clients who are resistant or uncooperative.

Timing

Another related methodological issue concerns the point of final measurement. Since most crisis intervention is brief, highly focused, and not directed to *all* the client's problems, the client may have more residual anxiety and uncertainty during the termination phase than other clients. Furthermore, the crisis client is not expected to be completely changed immediately following this minimal treatment interaction. Research by Frank (1974) suggests that, after termination, clients consolidate the gains resulting from brief treatment, continuing to improve, and eventually approaching life problems more effectively. Patterson et al. (1977) found that clients demonstrated considerable differences in amount of improvement following brief treatment depending on whether they were assessed at the end of the eight-session contact, three months later, or one year later (with later assessments indicating greater improvement).

An important issue is the point at which clients receiving crisis intervention should be evaluated. The length of the follow-up period becomes a critical variable in crisis intervention research. Whereas shorter follow-up periods may more accurately reflect the types of change that have actually taken place during the period of contact with the crisis clinic and may tend to minimize the effects of extraneous factors, longer follow-up periods may more accurately reflect the types of long-term change made possible by the earlier gains that took place during the crisis intervention therapy. Unfortunately, follow-up periods tend to vary a great deal from study to study: six weeks (Gottschalk et al., 1973); 12 months (Lowy et al., 1971); and up to 34 months (Decker & Stubblebine, 1972). Follow-up periods also vary within studies: 0 to 28 days and 67 to 290 days (Gottschalk et al., 1967) and 8 to 12 months (Maris & Connor, 1973). Stelmachers et al. (1977, Reference Note 3) deliberately vary the follow-up period in their routine evaluations of crisis clients. They select a follow-up period of from 14 to 30 days based on differences observed among various subgroups of their clinic population.

Instead of a simple pretest–posttreatment model, Butcher and Kolotkin (1979) recommend a repeated measures design that allows for ongoing assessment during and after therapy. This type of ongoing assessment enables the therapist to be aware of any relatively rapid symptom changes associated with the crisis state, as well as to examine whether clients are able to consolidate gains over a period of time.

Instruments

Among the plethora of standardized instruments to measure treatment outcome, there are only two instruments specifically designed for use in crisis intervention settings: the Halpern Crisis Scale (Halpern, 1973) and the Impact of Events Scale (Horowitz et al., 1979, 1980).

The Halpern Crisis Scale was devised to validate a cognitive model of crisis state behavior based on the theories of Caplan and Lazarus. The scale examines ten dimensions of crisis behavior: tiredness, helplessness, inadequacy, confusion, physical symptoms, anxiety, disruption of social activities, and disorganization in work, family, and social relationships. This 60-item scale was validated on four different crisis groups: individuals getting divorced, students experiencing identity crises, newly admitted psychiatric patients entering a hospital, and persons experiencing bereavement. Unfortunately, the Halpern Crisis Scale has not been widely used, and little information is available on its psychometric properties.

The Impact of Event Scale (Horowitz et al., 1979) is a 15-item self-report scale that measures current subjective distress subsequent to a particular traumatic life event. Items cluster into two subscales, intrusion and avoidance. Intrusion items tend to deal with unbidden thoughts and images, strong waves of feeling, and repetitive behavior; avoidance items relate to ideational constriction, behavioral inhibition, blunted sensation, and denial of the meanings and consequences of the event. The Impact of Event Scale has been demonstrated to have high test–retest reliability (.87) as well as high internal-consistency reliability (.78 for intrusion and .82 for avoidance). This scale has been used with individuals experiencing bereavement, as well as with persons experiencing injuries resulting from accidents, violence, illness, and surgery.

All other instruments to assess outcome in crisis intervention have been "borrowed" from psychotherapy evaluation research, rather than being specifically designed for use with crisis intervention. This raises the issue of whether it is appropriate to transpose measures from one setting to another. Given the unique characteristics of crisis intervention, it may be inappropriate to utilize measures traditionally employed in psychotherapy outcome research. On the other hand, crisis intervention is not so dissimilar from other interventions. What instruments should we use to evaluate outcome in crisis intervention? In answering this question, a number of issues must first be explored as they relate to crisis intervention: subjective and objective personality assessment, state versus trait measurement, symptom reduction versus pattern change, and idiographic versus nomothetic measurement.

OBJECTIVE AND SUBJECTIVE PERSONALITY ASSESSMENT

For a variety of reasons, many crisis intervention researchers and clinicians object to the use of personality tests to evaluate treatment outcome. Most personality tests, particularly projective tests like the Rorschach, take a good deal of time to administer and interpret. In a crisis intervention setting where time pressures are great, it may not always be feasible or desirable to conduct extensive, formal personality testing. Furthermore, much of the information derived from personality testing (i.e., measures of personality traits or intrapsychic events) may be irrelevant with respect to the focus of crisis intervention (i.e., attainment of specific goals) or may be greatly exaggerated due to the nature of crises. In addition, many crisis intervention therapists may not be trained to administer or interpret psychological instruments (e.g., paraprofessionals, social workers, and physicians).

In spite of the above objections, Butcher and Herzog (1982) argue that, if time and interpretive skill allow, information derived from objective personality assessment may provide valuable information about the chronicity and severity of the client's problems, as well as about the effectiveness of the intervention techniques. They strongly support the use of the MMPI in brief and crisis therapies and report MMPI changes occurring after only five treatment sessions. Certain MMPI scales (e.g., D, Pt, and Sc) that have been useful as change indices in other psychotherapy research (Garfield et al., 1971) may be sensitive enough to measure short-term changes resulting from crisis intervention. The sum of clinical scales as well as the number of critical items endorsed may also be useful indices of change in crisis intervention, as both of these reflect overall distress to a greater degree than specific personality dimensions. If the time and staff criteria cannot be met, we would suggest using one of the shorter versions of the MMPI (Kincannon, 1968), keeping in mind that these short forms have not yet been specifically validated on a crisis population (Stevens & Reilley, 1980). Furthermore, the use of short forms in individual prediction is somewhat controversial (Hoffman & Butcher, 1975). The development of a valid short form of the MMPI for use in crisis intervention settings is certainly an important area for further research.

STATE VERSUS TRAIT MEASUREMENT

Since crises are considered to be time-limited states of transitory pathology, it may be more appropriate in crisis intervention research to utilize measures that reflect changes in the "state" of the client rather than changes in that client's "traits." Three instruments designed to assess specific client states (i.e., anxiety, depression, and suicidal ideation) are discussed, and their utility in crisis intervention research is examined.

The State–Trait Anxiety Inventory (Spielberger et al., 1970) is a self-report inventory that distinguishes between current feelings of anxiety (i.e., state anxiety) and general characteristics associated with anxiety-prone individuals (i.e., trait anxiety). Because the State Anxiety Inventory instructs individuals to rate the level of anxiety experienced over the previous week, the state portion of the inventory may be administered repetitively following brief intervals and, as a result, may be a useful indicator of change over the course of crisis intervention treatment. The State–Trait Anxiety Inventory is easy to administer, and the score is psychometrically sound and has wide applicability across all crisis clients.

The Beck Depression Inventory (Beck et al., 1961) is another device designed to assess the state of a client's functioning. It is a very short inventory (21 items) that assesses an individual's current level of depression (i.e., the level of depression experienced during the previous week). Like the State Anxiety Scale, the Beck Depression Inventory may be administered repetitively at brief intervals and is capable of measuring rapidly occurring changes. For this reason, it is particularly useful in crisis intervention research. Furthermore, the Beck Depression Inventory is very easy to administer and score, it has wide applicability across all crisis clients, and its psychometric properties have been investigated in well over 150 published studies (Butcher and Herzog, 1982).

The Scale for Suicidal Ideation (Beck et al., 1979) is a 19-item inventory that measures current, conscious suicidal thoughts of clients. The scale is completed by a clinician, based on the client's responses to a semistructured interview. Unlike the previous two measures (i.e., the State–Trait Anxiety Inventory and the Beck Depression Inventory), the Scale for Suicidal Ideation is not generally applicable for all crisis clients (since all crisis clients do not necessarily experience suicidal ideation). The relatively low correlation (.51) between pre- and posttreatment scores for 90 self-destructive patients suggests that this scale may be sensitive to changes over time resulting from treatment. Butcher and Herzog (1982) point out that the Scale for Suicidal Ideation has yet to be studied in a crisis center population and that its predictive validity is not yet established.

Symptom Reduction Versus Type of Change

A reduction in symptomatology is usually expected to occur following crisis intervention. Unfortunately, since crises tend to resolve themselves within six weeks with or without treatment, a similar reduction in symptomatology may be found in individuals not receiving crisis intervention. How are we to know, then, whether crisis intervention is effective? Instead of measuring the amount of posttreatment symptomatology, perhaps researchers should measure the *duration* of the distress period or the reported ease of recovery from the crisis. In this way, if crisis intervention is effective, the effectiveness may be observed as a decreased recovery time (compared to recovery time without treatment).

Perhaps researchers should examine the *type* of symptomatology, as opposed to intensity and frequency of symptoms. It may be that successful outcome is associated more with some reported symptoms than with others. Future research needs to direct attention to the issue of whether some symptoms are prognostically "better than" other symptoms. Another way of viewing symptom change is to look at *patterns* of change, as opposed to change in specific symptoms. Kaltreider and colleagues (Kaltreider et al., 1981a) have studied such patterns of change in a bereaved population and have developed the Patterns of Individual Change Scale Battery for use with this population. Similar patterns of change inventories could be developed for use with other populations.

Idiographic Versus Nomothetic Measurement

The conflict between idiographic and nomothetic approaches to the measurement of behavior is an old one, dating back at least as far as 1937, when Allport was arguing for an individualized approach to the study of personality (Allport, 1937). An idiographic approach to measurement assumes that individuals are too unique to be studied nomothetically with standardized instruments. Generalized instruments are felt to obscure individual differences; instead, in an idiographic approach individualized measures that allow for the observation of individual differences are emphasized.

Most of the current research on outcomes in psychotherapy is based on nomothetic measurement. Similarly, most outcome research on crisis intervention utilizes nomothetic measuring devices (e.g., all the above reported research). Several investigators have recognized the value of tailoring outcome criteria to individuals, and at least two idiographic instruments to assess treatment outcome have been developed: Goal Attainment Scaling and Target Complaints. [See Kaltreider et al. (1981b) for an excellent discussion of individualized approaches to outcome assessment.]

Goal Attainment Scaling (Kiresuk & Lund, 1978; Kiresuk & Sherman, 1968) assesses client change on several unique scales specifically designed for each individual by mutual agreement between client and therapist. For each treatment goal, a scale with a graded series of likely outcomes, ranging from least to most favorable, is devised. The number of scales utilized varies from client to client. Each scale is behaviorally anchored at a minimum of three points, so that an unfamiliar observer would be able to rate client functioning on these goals at any given point in time. Scores may be derived from individual scales, and/or a total summary score may be computed. Comparison across persons is possible with Goal Attainment Scaling by counting the number of people who reach their expected goals. Goal Attainment Scaling also permits rapid assessment of a client's progress, including the assessment of deterioration effects.

Although Goal Attainment Scaling is generally considered to be a valuable measuring device, it is not without its disadvantages. Because this method is completely individualized, starting points and units of change are different for each individual, making interindividual comparisons difficult. In addition, the development of individualized scales may also be more time consuming than utilizing generalized scales. Kaltreider and colleagues (1981a) found that using generalized scales rather than unique scales cut judging time in half for independent raters of treatment outcome. Lambert (1979) criticizes Goal Attainment Scaling because the goals are based on subjective decisions, are often difficult to state, and are written at various levels of abstraction.

Another idiographic approach to the measurement of change involves the instrument Target Complaints (Battle et al., 1966). This measure asks the clients to identify one, two, or three principal complaints and to indicate the severity of each on a 13-point scale. At posttreatment assessment, the client again notes the severity of each complaint. In addition, each complaint can be rated on a five-point scale indicating the amount of change. The same pre- and posttreatment ratings can be made by the therapist. Target Complaints have been found to be sensitive to change in a number of studies (Waskow & Parloff, 1975). The Behavioral Target Complaints form (Nichols, 1974) is a refinement of Target Complaints, in which goals are operationally defined in terms of concrete behavioral subgoals as a means of increasing interrater reliability.

Most measures are clearly based on either nomothetic or idiographic principles. Yet Kaltreider and colleagues (1981a) have developed a set of scales [Patterns of Individual Change Scales (PICS)] that seem to be simultaneously individualized, standardized, and objective. Unlike Goal Attainment Scaling, which is tailored to the given *individual* being assessed, the PICS is tailored to the particular *population* being assessed. At the present time the PICS is based on dimensions common to individuals undergoing bereavement. The PICS still allows for individualized assessment by enabling the rater to (1) select only those scales that are appropriate for a given person or (2) develop special unique scales for dimensions not otherwise assessed. Because the PICS battery is not totally individualized, cross-study comparisons are easily made. Initial analyses of PICS interrater reliability indicate moderate reliability (at least .60) on 8 of 14 scales. There are also some preliminary data to support the validity of the PICS.

One of the values of this type of combined individualized–generalized approach to measurement is that it may be easily applied to other populations. Another crisis group (e.g., rape victims) may be studied, and through a similar process, homogeneous scales tailored to the assessment of rape victims can be developed.

A CORE BATTERY

Several years ago, a group of experienced psychotherapy researchers met to evaluate existing outcome measures and to recommend a core battery of the best instruments for use in measuring psychotherapy outcome (Waskow & Parloff, 1975). The battery contained measures to be completed by the client, the therapist, an independent evaluator, and the client's significant others. The relevance of the core battery for use in crisis intervention outcome measurement is discussed below.

Client Measures

The recommended measures were the Hopkins Symptom Checklist (Derogatis et al., 1973), the Target Complaints (Battle et al., 1966), and the MMPI (Dahlstrom et al. 1972). The use of the MMPI and Target Complaints in crisis intervention research has already been discussed. It is likely that the somatization and anxiety scales of the Hopkins Symptom Checklist would be important for describing individuals in crisis. The advantage of the Hopkins Symptom Checklist and Targets Complaints is the brevity of time required to complete each of them. In the case of client measures, then, we would recommend all of the three named in the core battery (if time permits).

Therapist Measures

The experts could recommend only one therapist measure: Target Complaints. We agree that is is useful to have target complaints defined by both the client and the therapist and thus would want to use this measure in evaluating crisis intervention outcome. The same dearth of therapist measures pointed to by Waskow and Parloff persists today.

In addition, we think it is critical to assess the therapist's interventions. What therapeutic techniques are being applied to help the client? We know those nonspecific factors that create a therapeutic milieu for most individuals, but we do not know the impact of specific interventions on clients in crisis. For example, if the crisis team offers cognitive–behavioral treatment, it is important to be able to assess which cognitive behavioral interventions are applied and with what effect. This seems a more promising avenue for further research than does additional work on therapist characteristics.

Independent Evaluator Measures

Recommended in the core battery was the Psychiatric Status Schedule (PSS) (Spitzer et al., 1970), both its symptom scales and the role scales. Although we appreciate the value of an independent clinical assessment, the nature of crisis intervention often makes such an assessment a luxury. It is highly unlikely that a crisis intervention service can provide time and/or staff to undertake the lengthy interview required to complete the PSS. Even if an independent evaluation were undertaken, it is doubtful whether the PSS would be the optimal instrument as it inquires into a number of areas reflective of severe psychopathology. Given the brief tenure of most crisis intervention, we would not recommend an emphasis on independent evaluation measures.

Significant-Other Measures

Two instruments were recommended in the core battery: The Katz Adjustment Scales (Katz & Lyerly, 1963) and the Personal Adjustment and Role Skills Scales (Ellsworth,1975). Like the PSS, both of these measures were developed from research on individuals with severe psychopathology. This suggests that their application in a crisis intervention setting may be inappropriate. The brevity of crisis intervention makes it unlikely that the client's family would be included in the measurement process, but the acute nature of the crisis may involve the family to a greater degree than does traditional psychotherapy. We believe that efforts should be made to obtain significant other's evaluations (using either the Katz or the PARS) because of their usefulness, especially at follow-up; however, we recognize that the data loss may be so severe as to make the effort worthless. We believe that the client and therapist should be the recipients of our strongest efforts at evaluation as they are most involved and most accessible. The economic feasibility of procuring independent evaluators and staff to obtain data from relevant others is uncertain at best.

We find many of Waskow and Parloff's (1975) recommendations for a core battery relevant for crisis intervention research. Initially, we considered proposing a core battery for use in crisis intervention research, but we could not devise an ideal battery for use in all crisis situations. We agree with Lambert's (1979) proposal that researchers not rely on a single battery, but rather develop several core batteries to meet the demands of various treatment situations. Such batteries might be organized around symptom type, level of psychological mindedness, chronicity or acuteness of problem, and other variables. Length of proposed treatment might also be an organizing principle. For crisis centers providing only one or two sessions, a limited battery of Target Complaints (client and therapist forms) and Symptom Checklist 90R administered pre- and posttreatment would seem adequate. For centers offering more extended treatment, other measures could be added to these, and ongoing assessment could be conducted.

Our final recommendations would be that crisis intervention researchers follow the lead of those psychotherapy researchers who are studying the effects of specific interventions on specific populations (NIMH Psychotherapy of Depression Collaborative Research Program, Reference Note 1; Strupp & Hadley, 1979) and that more emphasis be given to the development of instruments that combine the best qualities of the nomothetic and idiographic approaches. As we noted earlier, crisis intervention is growing in importance as the most efficient treatment mode in many areas; we believe that the assessment of its efficacy is just as important.

REFERENCE NOTES

1. NIMH Psychotherapy of Depression Collaborative Research Program (Pilot Phase), 1980.
2. Stelmachers, Z. T. *Crisis intervention: Quo vadis?* Unpublished manuscript, 1978.
3. Stelmachers, Z. T., Ellenson, G. M., & Baxter, J. *Quality control system of a crisis center: Method and outcome results.* Unpublished manuscript, 1977.

REFERENCES

Allport, G. W. *Personality: A psychological interpretation.* New York: Holt, Rinehart and Winston, 1937.

Auerbach, S. M., & Kilmann, P. R. Crisis intervention: A review of outcome research. *Psychological Bulletin,* 1977, **84,** 1189–1217.

Bagley, C. The evaluation of a suicide prevention schema by an ecological method. *Social Science and Medicine,* 1968, **2,** 1–14.

Baldwin, B. Problem pregnancy counseling: General principles. In R. R. Wilson (Ed.), *Problem pregnancy and abortion counseling.* Saluda, N. C. Family Life Publications, 1973.

Baldwin, B. A paradigm for the classification of emotional crisis: Implications for crisis intervention. *American Journal of Orthopsychiatry,* 1978, **43,** 538–551.

Baler, L. A., & Golde, P. J. Conjugal bereavement. *Working Papers in Community Mental Health*, 1964, **2**, 1–18.

Battle, C. C., Imber, S. D., Hoehn-Saric, R., Stone, A. R., Nash, E. R., & Frank, J. D. Target complaints as criteria of improvement. *American Journal of Psychotherapy*, 1966, **20**, 184–192.

Beck, A. T., Kovacs, M., & Weissman, A. Assessment of suicidal intention: The scale for suicide ideation. *Journal of Consulting and Clinical Psychology* 1979, **47**, 343–352.

Beck, A. T., Ward, C. H., Mendelson, M., Mock, J. E., & Erbaugh, J. K. An inventory for measuring depression. *Archives of General Psychiatry*, 1961, **4**, 561–571.

Bergin, A. E., & Lambert, M. J. The evaluation of therapeutic outcomes. In S. L. Garfield & A. E. Bergin (Eds.), *Handbook of psychotherapy and behavior change: An empirical analysis*. New York: Wiley, 1978.

Blaufarb, H., & Levine, J. Crisis intervention in an earthquake. *Social Work*, 1972, **17**, 16–19.

Bordow, S., & Porritt, D. An experimental evaluation of crisis intervention. *Social Science and Medicine*,1979, **13A**, 251–256.

Bracken, M. B., Grossman, G., Hackamovikin, M., Sussman, D., & Schrieir, D. Abortion counseling: An experimental study of three techniques. *American Journal of Obstetrics and Gynecology*, 1973, **117**, 10–20.

Burgess, A. W., & Holmstrom, L. L. *Rape: Crisis and recovery*. Bowie, Md.: Robert J. Brady Co., 1979.

Butcher, J. N., & Herzog, J. G. Individual assessment in crisis intervention: Observation, life history, and personality approaches. In C. D. Spielberger & J. N. Butcher (Eds.), *Advances in personality assessment* (Vol. 1). New York: Lawrence Erlbaum Associates, 1982.

Butcher, J. N., & Kolotkin, R. L. Evaluation of outcome in brief psychotherapy. *Psychiatric Clinics of North America*, 1979, **2**, 157–169.

Butcher, J. N., & Koss, M. P. Research in brief and crisis-oriented therapy. In S. Garfield & A. Bergin (Eds.), *Handbook of psychotherapy and behavior change: An empirical analysis*. New York: Wiley,1978.

Calsyn, R. J., Pribyl, J. F., & Sunukjian, H. Correlates of successful outcome in crisis intervention therapy. *American Journal of Community Psychology*, 1977, **5**, 111–119.

Caplan, G. *Principles of preventive psychiatry*. New York: Basic Books, 1964.

Caplan, G., Mason, E. A., & Kaplan, D. M. Four studies of crises in parents of prematures. *Community Mental Health Journal*, 1965, **2**, 149–161.

Conroe, R. M., Cassata, D. M., & Racer, H. J. A systematic approach to brief psychological intervention in the primary care setting. *The Journal of Family Practice*,1978, **7**, 1137–1142.

Dahlstrom, W. G., Welsh, G. S., & Dahlstrom, L. E. *An MMPI handbook*. Minneapolis: University of Minnesota Press, 1972.

Decker, J. B., & Stubblebine J. M. Crisis intervention and prevention of psychiatric disability: A follow-up study. *American Journal of Psychiatry*, 1972, **129**, 725–729.

Derogatis, L. R., Lipman, R. S., & Covi, L. SCL-90: An outpatient psychiatric rating scale (preliminary report). *Psychopharmocology Bulletin*, 1973, **9**, 13–27.

Ellsworth, R. B. Consumer feedback in measuring the effectiveness of mental health programs. In E. L. Struening & M. Guttentag (Eds.), *Handbook of evaluation research*. Beverly Hills, Calif.: Sage Publications, 1975.

Ewing, C. P. *Crisis intervention as psychotherapy*. New York: Oxford University Press, 1978.

Frank, J. D. Therapeutic components of psychotherapy: A 25-year progress report of research. *Journal of Nervous and Mental Disease*, 1974, **159**, 325–342.

Freiberg, P., & Bridwell, M. W. An intervention model for rape and unwanted pregnancy. *The Counseling Psychologist*,1976, **6**, 50–53.

Garfield, S. Research on client variables in psychotherapy. In S. Garfield & A. Bergin (Eds.), *Handbook of psychotherapy and behavior change: An empirical analysis*. New York: Wiley. 1978.

Garfield,S. L., Prager, R. A., & Bergin, A. E. Evaluation of outcome in psychotherapy. *Journal of Consulting and Clinical Psychology*,1971, **37**, 307–313.

Golan, N. *Treatment in crisis situations*. New York: The Free Press, 1978.

Gottschalk, L. A., Mayerson, P., & Gottlieb, A. A. Prediction and evaluation of outcome in an emergency brief psychotherapy clinic. *Journal of Nervous and Mental Disease*, 1967, **144**, 77–96.

Gottschalk, L. A., Fox, R. A., & Bates, D. E. A study of prediction and outcome in a mental health crisis clinic. *American Journal of Psychiatry*, 1973, **130**, 1107–1111.

Grauer, H., & Frank, D. Psychiatric aspects of geriatric crisis intervention. *Canadian Psychiatric Association Journal*, 1978, **23**, 201–207.

Green, B. L., Gleser, G. C., Stone, W. N., & Seifert, R. F. Relationships among diverse measures of psychotherapy outcome. *Journal of Consulting and Clinical Psychology*, 1975, **43**, 689–699.

Greer, S., & Bagley, C. Effect of psychiatric intervention in attempted suicide: A controlled study. *British Medical Journal*, 1971, **1**, 310–312.

Hadley, S. W., & Strupp, H. H. Contemporary views of negative effects in psychotherapy: An integrated account. *Archives of General Psychiatry*, 1976, **33**, 1291–1302.

Halpern, H. A. Crisis theory: A definitional study. *Community Mental Health Journal*, 1973, **9**, 342–349.

Hiltz, S. R. Helping widows: Group discussions as a therapeutic technique. *The Family Coordinator*, 1975, **24**, 331–335.

Hoffman, N. G., & Butcher, J. N. Clinical limitations of three MMPI short forms. *Journal of Consulting and Clinical Psychology*, 1975, **43**, 32–39.

Horowitz, M. J. *Stress response syndromes*. New York: Jason Aronson, 1976.

Horowitz, M., Wilner, N. & Alvarez, W. Impact of event scale: A measure of subjective stress. *Psychosomatic Medicine*, 1979, **41**, 209–218.

Horowitz, M. J., Wilner, N., Kaltreider, N., & Alvarez, W. Signs and symptoms of posttraumatic stress disorder. *Archives of General Psychiatry*, 1980, **37**, 85–92.

Jacobson, G. F., Strickler, M., & Morley, W. E. Generic and individual approaches to crisis intervention. *American Journal of Public Health*,1968, **58**, 338–343.

Kaltreider, N., DeWitt, K., Lieberman, R., & Horowitz, M. Individualized approaches to outcome assessment: A strategy for psychotherapy research. *Journal of Psychiatric Treatment and Evaluation*, 1981, **3**, 105–111.(b)

Kaltreider, N., DeWitt, K., Weiss, D., & Horowitz, M., Patterns of individual change scales. *Archives of General Psychiatry*, 1981, **38**, 1263–1269.(a)

Katz, M. M., & Lyerly, S. B. Methods for measuring adjustment and social behavior in the community: I. Rationale, description, discriminative validity and scale development. *Psychological Reports*, 1963, **13**, 1503–1535.

Kincannon, J. C. Prediction of the standard MMPI scale scores from 71 items: The mini-mult. *Journal of Consulting and Clinical Psychology*, 1968, **32**, 319–325.

Kiresuk, T. J., & Lund, S. H. Goal attainment scaling. In C. C. Attkisson, W. A. Hargreaves, M.J. Horowitz, & J. Sorenson (Eds.), *Evaluation of human service programs*. New York: Academic Press, 1978.

Kiresuk, T. J., & Sherman, R. E. Goal attainment scaling: A method for evaluating comprehensive community mental health programs. *Community Mental Health Journal*, 1968, **4**, 443–453.

Korner, I. N. Crisis and the psychological consultant. In G. A. Specter & W. A. Claiborn (Eds.), *Crisis intervention*. New York: Behavioral Publications, 1973.

Lambert, M. J. *The effects of psychotherapy* (Vol. 1). Montreal: Eden Press, 1979.

Lambert, M. J., Bergin, A. E., & Collins, J. L., Therapist-induced deterioration in psychotherapy. In A. S. Gurman & A. M. Razin (Eds.), *Effective psychotherapy: A handbook of research*. New York: Pergamon Press, 1977.

Lester, D. Effect of suicide prevention centers on suicide rates in the United States. *Public Health Reports*, 1974, **89**, 37–39.

Lindemann, E. Symptomatology and management of acute grief. *American Journal of Psychiatry*, 1944, **101**, 141–148.

Lowy, F. H., Wintrob, R. M., Borwick, B., Garmaise, G., & King, H. O. A follow-up of emergency psychiatric patients and their families. *Comprehensive Psychiatry*, 1971, **12**, 36–47.

Maris, R., & Connor, H. E. Do crisis services work? A follow-up of a psychiatric outpatient sample. *Journal of Health and Social Behavior*, 1973, **14**, 311–322.

Martin, D. *Battered wives*. San Francisco: Glide Publications, 1976.

McKenna, J., Nelson, G., Chatterson, J., Koperno, M., & Brown, J. H. Chronically and acutely suicidal persons one month after contact with a crisis intervention centre. *Canadian Psychiatric Association Journal*, 1975, **20**, 451–454.

Murphy, G. E., Wetzel, R. D., Swallow, C. S., & McClure, J. N. Who calls the suicide prevention center: A study of 55 persons calling on their own behalf. *American Journal of Psychiatry*, 1969, **126**, 314–324.

Nichols, M. P. Outcome of brief cathartic psychotherapy. *Journal of Consulting and Clinical Psychology*, 1974, **42**, 403–410.

Patterson, V., Levene, H., & Breger, L. A one-year follow-up of two forms of brief psychotherapy. *American Journal of Psychotherapy*, 1977, **31**, 76–82.

Paul, T. W., & Turner, A. J. Evaluating the crisis service of a community mental health center. *American Journal of Community Psychology*, 1976, **4**, 3.

Polak, P. R., Egan, D., Vandenbergh, R., & Williams, W. V. Prevention in mental health: A controlled study. *American Journal of Psychiatry*, 1975, **132**, 146–148.

Rapoport, L. Crisis intervention as a mode of brief treatment. In R. W. Roberts & R. H. Nee (Eds.), *Theories of social casework*. Chicago: University of Chicago Press, 1970.

Sank, L. I. Community disasters: Primary prevention and treatment in a health maintenance organization. *American Psychologist*, 1979, **34**, 334–338.

Schain, W. S. Psychosocial issues in counseling mastectomy patients. *The Counseling Psychologist*, 1976, **6**, 45–49.

Slaikeu, K., Lester, D., & Tulkin, S. R. Show versus no show: A comparison of referral calls to a suicide prevention and crisis service. *Journal of Consulting and Clinical Psychology*, 1973, **40**, 481–486.

Slaikeu, K., Tulkin, S. R., & Speer, D. C. Process and outcome in the evaluation of telephone counseling referrals. *Journal of Consulting and Clinical Psychology*, 1975, **43**, 700–707.

Spielberger, C. D., Gorsuch, R. L., & Lushene, R. *STAI Manual*. Palo Alto, Calif.: Consulting Psychologists, 1970.

Spitzer, R. L., Endicott, J., Fleiss, J. L., & Cohen, J. The psychiatric status schedule: A technique for evaluating psychopathology and impairment in role functioning. *Archives of General Psychiatry*, 1970, **23**, 41–55.

Stevens, M. R., & Reilley, R. R. MMPI short forms: A literature review. *Journal of Personality Assessment*, 1980, **44**, 368–376.

Strupp, H. H., & Hadley, S. A tripartite model of mental health and therapeutic outcome. *American Psychologist*, 1977, **32**, 187–196.

Strupp, H., & Hadley, S. Specific vs. nonspecific factors in psychotherapy: A controlled study of outcome. *Archives of General Psychiatry*, 1979, **36**, 1125–1136.

Tapp, J. T., Slaikeu, K. A., & Tulkin, S. R. Toward an evaluation of telephone counseling: Process and technical variables influencing "shows" and "no-shows" vs. a clinical referral. *American Journal of Community Psychology*, 1974, **2**, 357–364.

Walker, L. Battered women. In A. Brodsky & R. Hare-Mustin (Eds.), *Women and psychotherapy*. New York: Guilford Press, 1980.

Waskow, I. E., & Parloff, M. B. *Psychotherapy change measures*. Washington, D.C.: DHEW, No. 74-120, 1975.

Williams, M. V., and Polak, P. R. Follow-up research in primary prevention: A model of adjustment in acute grief. *Journal of Clinical Psychology*, 1979, **35**, 35–45.

Williams, W. V., Polak, P., & Vollman, R. R. Crisis intervention in acute grief. *Omega*, 1972, **3**, 67–70.

Zarle, T., Hartsough, D., & Ottinger, D. Tornado recovery: The development of a professional–paraprofessional response to a disaster. *Journal of Community Psychology*, 1974, **4**, 311–321.

Zukerman, E. *Changing directions in the treatment of women: A mental health bibliography*. Rockville, Md.: National Institute of Mental Health, 1979.

CHAPTER 7

Assessment of Outcome in Correctional Samples

D. A. ANDREWS

The preparation of this chapter was facilitated by grants No. 410-80-0729 and No. 410-78-0027 from the Social Sciences and Humanities Research Council of Canada and by the support of the Community and the Research Divisions of the Ontario Ministry of Correctional Services (the Assessment and Evaluation Project). The opinions expressed are those of the author. Thanks are extended to Susan Mickus and Wendy Watkins for their great assistance in the preparation of the manuscript.

Most agencies in the human and social services share a number of objectives: humane and ethical practice; fairness; cost-efficiency and cost-effectiveness; the promotion of human welfare; social development; social protection; the satisfaction of clients and significant others, workers, and managers and representatives of other agencies; and the satisfaction of accountants, lawyers, politicians, and the public at large. Providing a classic illustration of "agency centrism," criminologists have recently proclaimed these nonspecific concerns "criminal justice objectives." A concern unique to corrections is the management of criminal penalties imposed on individual offenders by the courts (Haley & Lerette, 1981). An objective associated with that concern is specific deterrence or the control of recidivism: reduction of the probability of future law violations on the part of those whose sentences are managed. The assessment of that objective is the primary focus of this chapter, with special reference to those variations in outcome that may be attributed to psychosocial interventions. Variations in the level and type of psychosocial services offered those imprisoned or on probation and parole represent variations in the management of the sentence (Andrews, 1981, Reference Note 1 at end of the chapter). A related problem is the assessment of changes in those attributes of offenders and their situations that are thought to mediate subsequent variations in criminal activity. There are practical, methodological, and theoretical reasons for consumers of evaluation studies to insist that researchers monitor not only effects on criminal behavior but also document the extent to which interventions succeed in influencing intermediate targets (Andrews, 1981, Reference Note 1; Andrews & Kiessling, 1980).

A first step, perhaps best employing the small-scale designs typical of the psychotherapy literature, is to document that effects on intermediate targets can be achieved (Andrews, 1980). A focus on the objective of specific deterrence requires a few preliminary comments. To focus on crime control is not to imply that the concerns of fairness, cost-efficiency, and consumer satisfaction are unimportant. Interventions and assessments of outcomes are value-laden efforts in any context, and where possible, evaluations will monitor indices relevant to those values. In fact, inequalities in the distribution of power within correctional agencies require that special attention be paid to the ethical issues of intervention and assessment.

Second, it is likely that psychosocial professionals in corrections spend most of their time not on the crime-control objective, but on attempts to reduce the human misery and administrative entanglements that a penalty such as incarceration carries. In brief, efforts to assist at the level of offender (and staff) "adjustment" to the prison environment, including the redesign of that environment and the development of alternate environments, are worthy objectives that need not be linked to crime control for their justification. Finally, it is necessary that evaluators and consumers of evaluations not confuse recidivism rates with crime rates; the former refer to the criminal activity of individuals, whereas the latter are measures of the extend of criminal activity within a geographically or socially defined unit. As is noted later, a major policy issue is whether the pursuit of the correctional objective of controlling recidivism rates is a cost-effective means of controlling community-wide crime rates. Rhetoric to the contrary (Martinson, 1976), the relationship between recidivism and crime rates, has simply not been the object of systematic empirical exploration. It remains to be seen whether prevention programs (broadly defined), correctional programs, or some combination of both may influence crime rates in socially significant ways.

RECIDIVISM

Recidivism: an offense or some offenses committed during a specified follow-up period by a person who has previously been convicted for an offense or, by a person whose future offensive conduct has been judged of interest in preventive or descriptive studies.

The definition is a modification of one preferred by Waldo and Griswold (1979, p. 229). Four aspects of the definition are noteworthy because they avoid some problems associated with alternate definitions.

1. The definition specifies that a longitudinal design is necessary for the assessment of recidivism. This is obvious, perhaps, but some of the

more widely accepted and grossly inflated estimates of recidivism rates were derived from cross-sectional surveys of the criminal records of current prisoners (Glaser, 1964, Chapter 2).

2. The definition avoids terms such as "habitual," "tending toward repetition," and "proneness to continue to crime" (Waldo & Griswold, 1979). Such phrases may describe "risk assessments," but assessments of risk, like assessments of offense history, are nominally and analytically distinct from assessments of recidivism.

3. The definition is not tied to any particular conception of the essence of crime. Whether crime is viewed as a "disease" or "an assertion of human dignity within a corrupt state," the definition applies equally well.

4. The definition may be applied in descriptive studies as well as evaluations of both correctional and prevention programs. When intake samples include both offenders and nonoffenders, what must be avoided are the sorts of definitional games documented by Hawkins et al. (1977) in the following example.

Where a program serves some persons without an offense history, there is a tremendous opportunity to confuse and mislead consumers of outcome research through the selective inclusion or exclusion of "offense history" in the computation of "recidivism" rates. For illustrative purposes, Hawkins et al. (1977) seized the opportunity and showed how "recidivism" rates could be manipulated in their sample of 510 juveniles, only 142 of whom had been "arrested" prior to program contact. If recidivism referred only to the postintake arrests of those with an arrest history, the overall recidivism rate was 3.3% (17 of 510). If recidivism referred to postintake arrests regardless of arrest history, the rate was 5.5% (28 of 510). Neither estimate is particularly useful because it hides the important differences in rates that exist as a function of arrest history. Those with an arrest history were recidivating at rates (12%; 17 of 142) higher than those without an arrest history (3.0%; 11 of 368). The important point is that offense history, like type of intervention, is a potential source of variance in recidivism, and not an appropriate element of the operational definition of recidivism. Moreover, the inclusion of offense history as a factor in an evaluation will allow any offense history-by-treatment interactions to emerge as illustrated by O'Donnell et al., (1979) in the following example.

O'Donnell et al. (1979) reported that their "buddy system" program was associated with reduced recidivism among those with an offense history (56% "buddy system" vs. 78% controls), but with increased recidivism among those without an offense history (22% vs. 16%). Had O'Donnell and colleagues chosen to define recidivism as the proportion of those with both an offense history and a rearrest, they would have concluded that the recidivism rates for the experimentals and controls were identical at 8% each. Had they ignored offense history completely, they would have concluded that the buddy system was tending to be associated with increased (27% vs. 23%) recidivism. When the analytic distinction between offense history and recidivism is lost, so is the opportunity to explore an important source of variability in recidivism.

The two fundamental operational problems are the specification of the follow-up period and the definition of "offenses." The operational choices may be guided by the specific goals of any correctional effort, by political or theoretical preferences, and by the application of psychometric criteria such as the implications of our choices for reliability, validity, utility, and sensitivity to intervention efforts. The intercorrelations among operational definitions and the possibility of differential validities become intriguing questions for empirical exploration.

Operational Specifications of the Follow-up Period

Commencement of Follow-Up

Operational choices regarding the follow-up period are two: when it begins and when it ends. For reasons to be developed, it is strongly recommended that the beginning of the follow-up period coincide with the implementation of intervention decisions. The implications for randomized group designs are obvious. For purposes of pseudoexperimental evaluations, the recommendation suggests that it is inappropriate to sample from lists of "graduates" of the programs to be compared; rather, sampling *must* be done from lists of those who enter the programs, from lists compiled before "dropouts," and in-program "failures" are deleted. The only exceptions to this guideline occur when the investigator can document that "dropouts" were distributed proportionally across programs; that the dropout phenomenon was unrelated to any prescores that are predictive of recidivism, or that may interact with the program factor on recidivism; and that the recidivism rates of dropouts were equivalent across programs. The latter, of course, requires that the investigator monitor the recidivism of dropouts, including both in-program and postprogram recidivism. Thus there are, in effect, no conditions under which the choice of an alternate starting point can yield accurate estimates of the effects of intervention decisions on recidivism.

Rationales for ignoring in-program recidivism—for beginning follow-up at the termination of treatment rather than at the initiation of treatment—include the argument that it is unreasonable to monitor recidivism before treatment has had an opportunity to impact. Thus it was, for example, that Quay and Love (1977) chose to ignore the in-program recidivism of participants in a diversion program. An outstanding feature of the Quay and Love report is that they provide sufficient information to allow an inspection of the implication of their choice relative to the decision to include in-program recidivism. With in-program recidivism ignored, they report an impressive and statistically significant difference of 13% in the recidivism rates of participants and control subjects. However, when the in-program recidivism of the participants is included, the effect drops to an unimpressive and statistically untested difference of 5%. The latter difference best reflects the effects of implementing the program.

The serious problem with the Quay and Love rationale for ignoring in-program recidivism is that investigators do not have advance knowledge of when or even if interventions will begin to impact. A strategy more justifiable than the ignoring of in-program data involves the appropriate employment of control groups (preferably random). Repeated measures over successive follow-up periods will allow group-by-periods interactions to emerge if, in fact, they do exist. That strategy is a standard and universally acceptable means of discounting the effects of any predispositional or nontreatment factors on outcome—a means that does not require assumptions about when treatment efforts will emerge and hence a manipulation of the start of follow-up.

Another rationale for playing with the beginning of follow-up is to suggest that there are "obvious" differences in the extent to which participants of different programs are "incapacitated" or "at risk." For example, it is judged only "fair" that institution- and community-based programs be compared when participants are equally at risk: thus the follow-up period for participants in the community-based program begins with the initiation of that program, whereas the follow-up period for the more incapacitated sample begins post-program. Such a practice ensures that any incapacitation effects associated with the institutional program are ignored. The point is not that "obvious" incapacitation effects are always present; in fact, there are indications in the juvenile literature that incarceration does not suppress recidivism even in-program (Empey & Erickson, 1972; Fixsen et al., 1976). The point is that the incapacitation elements of a program are highly relevant treatment dimensions when the objective is specific deterrence. Incapacitation effects can be detected only by monitoring recidivism during the in-program phase. Any negative effects of incapacitation on cost and social validity criteria may be detected by monitoring indices of cost and social validity, but such effects should not be confused with effects on recidivism.

A particularly problematic rationale for manipulating the beginning of follow-up is based on the suggestion that the effects of treatment received are more interesting than the effects of treatment planned. Thus follow-up begins with the successful completion of treatment, and the recidivism of those who fail to "graduate" or to "successfully complete treatment" are either ignored or analyzed separately from the data of the successes. (The problems are compounded when, as is very often the case, the criteria for "failure" includes evidence of inprogram recidivism.) Table 7.1 presents some hypothetical outcome data, data deliberately constructed to illustrate some logical extremes when in-program data are ignored and when "successes" and "failures" are analyzed separately, with or without inprogram data included in the estimates of effects on recidivism. During the in-program phase, assignment to Program A was associated with higher levels of recidivism overall than was assignment to Program B. This overall effect was evident even though the "successes" of A

TABLE 7.1. Intervention Effects as a Function of Follow-Up: In-Program, Postprogram, and Total Follow-Up Period

	In-Program	Postprogram	In and Postprogram	Comments
Percentage arrested (Quay and Love, 1977)				
Participants (n = 436)	16%	32%	40%	On average, participants followed for 89 days (in-program) and 311 days (postprogram); controls followed for 450 days
Controls (n = 132)	(45%)	(45%)	45%	
Percentage reconvicted (hypothetical)				
Program A				
Successes (n = 30)	0%	50%	50%	A data set constructed to illustrate some logical extremes
Failures (n = 70)	40%	60%	90%	
Overall (n = 100)	28%	57%	78%	
Program B				
Successes (n = 70)	0%	60%	60%	
Failures (n = 30)	60%	70%	70%	
Overall (n = 100)	18%	63%	63%	
Pearson r (n = 44) (Andrews et al., 1981, Reference Note 2)				
Authority	-.38	-.12 (NS)	-.24	Objective measures of supervision practices in relation to recidivism (0–1)
Modeling	-.42	-.34	-.36	
Problem solving	-.29	-.05 (NS)	-.15 (NS)	
Advocate–broker	.13 (NS)[a]	-.23 (NS)	-.26	
Percentage reconvicted (Stephenson & Scarpitti, 1974)				
Prison	0% (n = 100)	53% (n = 100)	53% (n = 100)	Postprogram includes only "in-program successes"
Group centers	27% (n = 67)	41% (n = 49)	57% (n = 67)	
Essex fields	23% (n = 100)	48% (n = 77)	60% (n = 100)	
Probation	28% (n = 926)	15% (n = 671)	38% (n = 926)	

[a]NS = not significant

and B did not differ in recidivism rates and the recidivism rate of A "failures" was actually lower than that of the B "failures." During the postprogram phase, the overall rates favored program A, as did the rates for both the in-program successes and the in-program failures. However, often there is little reason to believe that the postprogram effects are a better estimate of ability of programs to influence recidivism than are in-program effects. The crucial question relates to the relative position of groups at the end of the *total* follow-up period, with the in-program and postprogram data sets combined. The tabulated values for the end of the total follow-up period, overall and for the failures, favor Program B. However, if policymakers only had access to a follow-up of program successes, they would conclude that Program A was the program to be promoted. If successfully promoted, Program A would result in an overall increase in recidivism. Initiating follow-up at the time that treatment is successfully completed is an operationalization of recidivism to be avoided.

While the data of Andrews et al. 1981, (Reference Note 2) are less extreme than the hypothetical data set, they represent another example of the preceding conclusion. Reinspection of Table 7.1 reveals that the additional data set reinforces the conclusions regarding the critical importance of considering in-program recidivism when making conclusions regarding the ultimate impact of interventions. The tabulated values from Andrews and colleagues are point biserial correlations between objective measures of the supervision practices of probation officers and the recidivism (0 to 1) of their probationers. Neither the in-program nor postprogram correlations need yield conclusions similar to those derived from correlations involving the combined in-program and post-program data: one measure, anticriminal modeling, demonstrated predictive validity across the board; the predictive validity of another measure, advocate-broker activity, emerged only by the end of the total follow-up period; the early evidence of the predictive validity of problem-solving had faded by the end of follow-up; the early predictive validity of authority was not evident at post-program but was evident over the total follow-up period.

Finally, Table 7.1 presents the recidivism rates from Stephenson and Scarpitti (1974), recomputed for illustrative purposes with all inprogram failures included as recidivists at the end of the total follow-up period. (Stephenson and Scarpitti reported in-program and postprogram results separately; whereas all inprogram failures had committed a new offense, it is not clear whether these new offenses would meet the definition of recidivism employed at postprogram. Thus we ask the reader to note that the recomputation is for illustrative purposes only.) Inclusion of the inprogram data resulted in a reordering of the groups from that found postprogram: the two group homes, rather than appearing more effective than prison, now appear less effective in controlling crime.

Termination of Follow-Up

Choices regarding the beginning of follow-up are more fundamental than choices regarding when follow-up ends. The latter limits the ability to generalize over time; the former, as just reviewed, limits the ability to produce accurate estimates of the effects of intervention decisions, regardless of the duration of follow-up. Paradoxically, the duration issue has attracted the most attention in the evaluation literature. Reviewers of the intervention literature generally agree on the following: *most evaluations have involved follow-up periods judged too brief; they recommended a duration of at least two or three postprogram years.* The limiting conditions of this recommendation remains to be established (Waldo and Griswold, 1979), but, on average, the majority of those who will recidivate appear to do so within two or three postprogram years. Across a variety of correctional samples and across a variety of specific measures of recidivism, 80 to nearly 100% of those who recidivate within three or four postprogram years have been identified by the end of the second year (Andrews et al., Reference Note 2; Empey & Erickson, 1972; Gendreau & Leipciger, 1978; Stephenson & Scarpitti, 1974; Waldo & Chiricos, 1977).

The three-year recommendation is only a rule of thumb, albeit a rule with some support in the literature. There is no substitute for the investigator knowing the sample, knowing the data, and making decisions appropriate to that knowledge. A few general guidelines are possible regarding when it is sensible to suspend follow-up without loss of information. One guideline is fairly straightforward: If cumulative measures of recidivism have reached their upper limit or reached levels where changes in relative outcome would be impossible to detect statistically, follow-ups may be suspended with no loss of information. For example, if 100% of the 15 members of group A have been registered as recidivists and if only three of the 15 members of group B are still at risk, follow-ups may be suspended; with the Fisher exact test, the p is already greater than .05 and could not possibly take a lower value in the future. Considerations of sample size, the magnitude of error terms, the logically possible changes in recidivism measures, and the power of available statistical tests may well yield the reasonable conclusion that no further changes could be detected statistically.

Additional follow-up is unlikely to yield new information once the cumulative differences among programs remains *stable* over three successive postprogram periods of at least six months each. In other words, when the relative outcomes stabilize, we likely have solid estimates of the ultimate relative outcomes. Glaser (1964) has suggested a guideline that is useful when one is satisfied to conclude that there was an effect as opposed to estimating the absolute magnitude of the ultimate effect: progressive *increases* in the estimate of an effect over successive follow-up periods suggest that an effect will be maintained in the future (Waldo & Griswold, 1979).

Other rules of thumb and guidelines aside, "the longer the better." Delayed effects require time to emerge and any effect requires time to allow conclusions regarding maintenance and any ultimate strengthening or weakening. So few long-term follow-ups have been conducted within the context of program evaluation that some basic parameters of assessments of recidivism are essentially unknown. Any investigator who has the resources to conduct long-term follow-ups is in a position to contribute substantially to the assessment issues. For example, the present author knows of no study in which the reliability of recidivism assessments was directly examined as a function of duration of follow-up. Following Epstein (1979), one may expect that the stability of assessments (over scorers, observers, and items or offenses) approach an asymptote as assessments are sampled over an increasing number of occurrences. Exploration and documentation of this in the situation of corrections will speak directly to two of the most common complaints about any measure of recidivism: some offenses occur but are undetected, and some persons may be falsely accused.

Type of Predictor and Length of Follow-Up

Little is known about the differential validities of recidivism measures as a function of duration of follow-up. Our own work, within both descriptive and experimental frameworks, has led us to expect that the "validity" of recidivism as a *criterion* measure (or dependent variable) does vary in systematic ways with both the duration of follow-up and the type of predictor or independent variables employed. Consider the case of time-constant predictors such as fixed sociohistorical or trait measures and the traditional problem that they tend to overpredict recidivism. With increasing duration of follow-up, the number of "false positives" can only decrease; that is, some of those who were incorrectly identified initially as recidivists will later become recidivists. It may be in the nature of some types of predictors that they, relative to other predictors, cannot be found to account for a reduced proportion of the variance in recidivism as the duration of follow-up increases.

The situation is quite the contrary for time-varying predictors, for assessments of those dynamic or less stable attributes of offenders and their situations: real changes on dynamic factors may occur over time, sometimes deliberately induced through intervention, sometimes inadvertently produced, and sometimes as a function of nontreatment factors. If those changes are not included in the prediction formula, the predictive validity of those factors, as originally assessed, is bound to appear relatively poor. However, if the changes themselves are unstable, the predictive validity of the original (pretested) measures will ultimately increase with increases in the duration of follow-up.

Table 7.2 presents an illustration of the interactions suggested. The predictive validity of fixed biosocial factors was clearly increasing with duration of follow-up. The predictive validity of prescores on a targeted dynamic factor also increased, but most notable is the fact that posttreatment (or change) scores were more predictive than prescorers over the short term. By the end of follow-up, both pre- and postscores on the targeted variables were making independent contributions to the predictability of recidivism. In this particular data set, the effect of treatment remained stable.

An understanding of the differential validities of person-based assessments as a function of duration of follow-up should increase our ability to predict recidivism. However, more important than simple predictive efficiency are the

TABLE 7.2.   Prediction of Recidivism with Fixed, Dynamic, and Treatment Variables by Duration of Follow-Up

Predictors	In-Program	End of Follow-Up	
Fixed biosocial factors[a]	.27	.41	(Pearson r)
"Targeted" factors[b]			
Prescores	.04	.11	(Pearson r)
Postscores	.17	.23	(Partial r, controlling for prescores)
Treatment factor[c]	.15	.14	(Beta values)

Source: Andrews et al. (1981, Reference Note 2).
[a] A sociohistorical Level of Supervision Inventory (Andrews, 1981).
[b] Identification with criminal others.
[c] Assignment to high-empathy–high-socialization probation officers versus other officers.

functions of assessments of persons and their situations in the context of evaluation research and how those functions may be more or less well performed depending on the duration of follow-up. Assessments of predictive attributes that have not themselves been targeted within intervention programs may function as control variables, reducing the magnitude of the error term and hence increasing the sensitivity of the test of intervention effects. The above paragraphs suggest that the control function of time-constant predictors will increase in importance with increasing duration of follow-up. The effects of treatment may weaken over time, and thus, just when the need for a sensitive test is greatest, the amount of variance subtracted from the error term by the use of control variables increases. Note that it would be unreasonable to select measures of targeted attributes for the control function since the treatment plan involves changing prescores on targeted attributes.

Assessments of stable and dynamic attributes of persons and their situations (including targeted attributes) may function as moderator variables, allowing the emergence of client-by-treatment interactions. Where treatments require different lengths of time to become effective (e.g., advocate–broker or referral activity as opposed to immediate problem solving on the part of the counselor, evidence of treatment-by-follow-up period interactions will be found (see Table 7.1).

Repeated assessments of those client-based attributes that represent the intermediate targets of intervention are strongly indicated to determine, independent of recidivism, whether intervention had its intended impact. Repeated assessments of nontargeted dynamic attributes are also indicated—particularly during an extended follow-up. A classic problem in the evaluation literature is that a weakening of an intervention effect on recidivism over time may or may not indicate a weakening of the effects on the intermediate factors targeted by the intervention program. For example, a program that targeted attitudes may have successfully modified attitudes and subsequent effects on recidivism may have been evident; two years later, offenses may recur, not because attitudes have again suddenly become procriminal, but because of a financial crisis. Another very serious reason for monitoring nontargeted dynamic factors is that an intervention program may inadvertently increase or decrease risk on such factors. Evidence of this is presented in the section on intermediate targets in this chapter. A full understanding of the effects of intervention, the persistence of those effects, and the role of nontreatment factors requires that recidivism and time-varying covariates be monitored over an extended follow-up period.

The mathematics of behavioral change are increasing in sophistication (Maltz & McCleary, 1977; Schmidt and Witte, 1980; Stollmack & Harris, 1974) and the analysis of recidivism data is currently a testing ground for the new measures and models. Essentially, two parameters of recidivism are considered in the new models: the ultimate recidivism level (binary) and the timing of recidivism. An advantage of this failure-rate methodology is the use of those variations in the duration of follow-up that often arise because persons are entering and leaving programs at differing times. One need not exclude recidivism data, where available for over a two-year period, just because not all the subjects have been followed up for more than two years.

Barton and Turnbull (1979) have recently demonstrated how both time-varying and fixed covariates may be introduced into failure-rate regression models. It appears that available models for the analysis of recidivism data are beginning to match existing conceptual systems in their sophistication. What remains is to generate data banks that include assessments of the factors judged important by theory. A note of caution regarding the emerging mathematical models: generally accepted tests of statistical significance have yet to be developed (Lloyd & Joe,1979) and the basic assumptions are topics of continuing debate. The present author's recommendation is to follow *Evaluation Quarterly* and *Evaluation Review* but never let your statistical consultant be more than a phone call away.

Operationalization of "Offenses": Official Process Measures[*]

The three most common measures of recidivism are derived from records or reports of rearrest, reconviction, and/or reincarceration (or arrest, conviction,

---

[*]Reflecting the state of the literature and in the interest of brevity, we refer to arrests, convictions and incarceration. However, any researcher entering into the criminal justice field for the first time should be aware that there is an increasing variety of dispositions possible at the court level. Technically, for example, it is possible to be found guilty and yet not be convicted (an "absolute discharge"). Similarly, probation may be a disposition but technically not a sentence. In many jurisdictions the number of pretrial and intrial diversionary alternatives are increasing. A review of any introduction to the criminal (or juvenile) justice systems is strongly recommended (Griffiths et al., 1980). In addition, Glaser (1964) and Stephenson and Scarpitti (1974) are recommended, with the latter providing a practical review of the factors that must be considered in the operationalization of recidivism.

and incarceration for prevention samples). These measures are reflections of official processing, and the typical sources of information are either official records or self-reports. The official sources include police files; court files; correctional files; and any local, state–provincial, or federal agencies that collect and store reports from the police, courts, and correctional agencies. The use of federal files (RCMP or FBI) does not guarantee that all offenses are detected, but it does cast a wider net than do local agencies. A wider geographic net does not, however, ensure that *more* cases of official processing will be identified. Reports from local agencies must first make their way to the central agency and must further meet any special criteria the central agency sets (e.g., supporting fingerprint evidence). The files of central agencies represent a standard source for investigators working in different geographically defined areas. On this basis their use, along with local sources, is highly recommended (Waldo & Griswold, 1979). Self-reports of official processing are collected through interviews and/or questionnaires, the validity of which are discussed later in conjunction with self-reports of officially undetected criminal activity.

Rearrest, reconviction, and reincarceration data may be represented as binary or "extent" measures. The binary measures are in the following form: the number, proportion, or percentage rearrested–reconvicted–reincarcerated over a specified follow-up period. The standard extent measures are the number of arrests and the number of convictions recorded or registered over a specified follow-up period. Preferable to "number of incarcerations" is "total follow-up time incarcerated" (in weeks or months, "percentage of total follow-up time incarcerated," of "percentage of total follow-up time spent in the community (not incarcerated)." A measure of total incarceration time is very attractive because it reflects reconvictions and the severity of court dispositions. It also likely reflects costs in the sense that institution-based programs are more expensive in both human and economic terms than are community-based programs. (We see later that this measure also seems particularly sensitive to intervention effects.)

Sometimes investigators choose to ignore rearrests or reconvictions for certain types of offense that are judged trivial. For example, O'Donnell et al. (1979) ignored arrests for juvenile status offenses (runaway, curfew, etc.) as well as technical violations of the conditions of probation and minor vice offenses. Although this is sensible within a given community, one community's (or investigator's) judgment of "trivial" may not be another's. It would seem most appropriate, therefore, for investigators to report both the total data set and any slices of that set they consider meaningful or of special importance for their specific purposes. Some attempts to scale seriousness of offense and severity of disposition are reviewed later.

Other involvements with the criminal justice system that have been employed in recidivism studies either as binary or extent measures include police contacts (unspecified; complaint received; suspect), court contacts (unspecified; an appearance), and police and court contacts (both unspecified). Waldo and Griswold (1979) distinguished between arrests and charges. Time to first (re)arrest or (re)conviction have been employed; for example, the California Youth Authority uses "rates of arrest for each month on parole in the community," with and without offenses of minor severity included (Palmer, 1974).

Parole (or probation) violations are particularly problematic official measures. The problems arise because violations of the formal conditions of parole or probation do not necessarily involve the recurrence of illegal acts. Technical violations are those that would not be illegal if the person were not on probation or parole. The point has been repeatedly made that technical violations may also interact with intervention; for example, technical violations are susceptible to differential decision making as opposed to "real" behavioral effects (Banks & Rardin, 1978; Gottfredson, 1979; Lerman, 1975). Technical violations may be highly meaningful outcome measures for correctional agencies, but they should not be considered to be the same as recidivism measures.

A related concern is the use of official ratings of outcome as recorded by correctional agencies. Depending on the agency, a "favorable discharge" or "a success" may or may not indicate the absence of rearrests, reconvictions, or reincarcerations. Similarly, an "unfavorable discharge" or an officially recorded "failure" may or may not have involved criminal activity. Hudson (1977) recounts the classic tale of one agency with an official "success" rate of 76%. Twenty-five percent of these "successes" had been convicted of at least one felony, including murder, rape, and robbery. It appeared that a "success" was not necessarily an individual who had not committed an offense, but one who had not committed an offense within the jurisdiction of the agency. This author has had similar experiences in adult probation. If the investigator were to rely on "regular terminations" as they are officially recorded, it is probable that some cases who served a significant portion of their probation term in prison for a new offense would be recorded as having a regular termination because the probation sentence may have been allowed to run its course. It is equally probable that an unfavorable termination represented a failure to "seek and maintain" employment. The inclusion of such as an "offense" not only strains the definition of recidivism, but would be considered by many to be morally unjustifiable.

Note that these cautions regarding the use of "official" ratings of outcome do not apply to the reports of probation and parole officers regarding the rearrests or reconvictions of their clients. Platt et al. (1980) reported nearly 100% agreement between parole reports and police records of arrest. A later section of this chapter cites several examples of the impressive predictive validity of probation officers' ratings of other aspects of the offenders' situations.

Alternatives to Official Records

Questions regarding the reliability and validity of official processing measures are many and include a number of standard objections. Stressing the criterion problem is the number one "treatment-destruction technique" (Gottfredson, 1979, p. 41) employed by those hell-bent on destroying a science of individual differences within criminology: "not all those engaged in illegal conduct are caught (or better yet, discovered); not all those arrested are guilty; not all those arrested are convicted." Official processing is not a function of *offense* characteristics, but of *offender* characteristics! Indeed, are we not all offenders? If so, is it not the work of scoundrels to label some "offenders" and others "nonoffenders"? This author once participated in a professional seminar in which the evidence was leading to the conclusion that certain types of interventions have been associated consistently with reduced recidivism, regardless of the specific outcome measures employed. A visibly shaken colleague in the social sciences asked for the floor and proclaimed in emotional tones that crime was a social necessity, necessary in order to define the boundaries of acceptable human conduct. It begins to appear that if corrections were to manage to show some modest impact on recidivism it would be accused of threatening the boundaries of human civilization. There *are* serious problems within the criminal justice system. There *is* a need for a constant monitoring of that system for abusive or unfair practices. A political economy and a sociology of the law and criminal justice are important and valued areas of investigation. However, none of these concerns should be considered sufficient evidence to dismiss official process measures as measures of recidivism for purposes of evaluation studies.

Serious questioning of the reliability and validity of official records have led to exploration of the use of self and even peer and family reports on criminal activity. Although few investigations of the reliability and validity of self-reports have been conducted within the context of outcome-evaluation research, a small but relevant literature does exist within the context of descriptive research. Nettler (1978) has provided an outstanding review of that literature and, always true to his style, calls self-reports "confessions":

1. "Almost everyone, by his or her own admission, has broken some criminal law" (p. 98).

2. "The amount of 'hidden crime' is enormous" (p. 98).

3. "Persistent and grave violations of the law are the experience of a minority" (p. 98).

4. "There is a [positive] relationship in both [confessions and official statistics] between being *persistent* as an offender and being a *serious* offender" (p. 98).

5. Official delinquents report more offenses and more serious ones than do nondelinquents.

6. "The policing process operates like a coarse net that is more likely to catch the repetitive, serious offender than the now-and-then, minor offender" (p. 78).

7. "[The policing process] is also more likely to catch the impulsive and stupid thief than the more deliberate and intelligent one" (p. 78).

8. "Confessions of delinquency, surveys of victims, test situations, direct and indirect observations, and official records point to similar social sites in both developing countries and industrialized states as producing

more murderers, muggers, rapists, robbers, burglars, and heavy thieves than others" (p. 117).

9. "A comparison of a new measure of uncertain validity (self-reports) with an old measure of moderate validity (official records) tells us nothing about their relative accuracy *unless there is assurance that both instruments are designed to measure the same thing*" (p. 116).

There is as yet little reason to believe that self-reports will add anything of real value to the assessment of recidivism relative to the costs of follow-up interviews. Self-reports may identify more of those less persistent and less grave offenders who tend to be missed by official records, but as already suggested and to be discussed further, in many evaluations the decision is made to ignore trivial offenses even where official processing has occurred. If in practice nearly 100% are recidivists according to self-report, the investigator is forced to set new definitions. An example of this is the proportion with two or more self-reported offenses or the mean number of offenses. Constants are of little value as outcome measures. The suggestion that self- and official reports are differentially sensitive to the offenses of the more intelligent and less impulsive offender has important implications for the assessments of programs that may be increasing functional intelligence or self-control and indirectly increasing the ability to evade official processing. This is one of the limited conditions where self-reports may prove highly valuable.

It is important that estimates of reliability and validity of the traditional variety be derived within the context of the evaluation studies. The two essential issues are that subjects maintain their relative position in the absence of treatment effects and that the reliability of reports does not vary with treatment. Nettler noted that Hirschi found only modest interitem correlations and that Farrington found high rates of denial of earlier confessions in a two-year retest. Modest interitem correlations are the general rule (Epstein, 1979) for almost any assessment instrument. That is why multiple-item indices are standard recommendations in psychometrics. Reports of the proportion of subjects "changing their tune" with regard to an earlier confession are a particularly inappropriate method of reporting reliability since the relative position of respondents at Time 1 and Time 2 may be highly stable. In fact, the Nettler review includes several descriptive studies reporting very high test–retest reliabilities for self-reported criminality.

The importance of the specific items included in the self-report or peer or family report inventory will vary from study to study, sample to sample, and program to program. The Nye and Short (1957), Short (1957) and Hirschi (1969) scales are relatively well known, brief, and easily administered for the purpose of surveying young persons. They also sample a number of status or trivial offenses. Since relatively unexplored issues abound with regard to self-report, this author has opted for the Gold (Berger et al., 1975) approach, but with a comprehensive survey of illegal acts. We employ a structured interview with descriptions of each of 32 different offenses presented on one side of its own card and an offense identification number printed on the other side of the card. Respondents are asked to sort the cards into the most appropriate of five categories: never; at least once, but not in the last six months; once in the last six months; twice in the last six months; or three or more times in the last six months. Both respondents and interviewers appear to appreciate the fact that the respondent is not asked to confess directly to the interviewer. Rather, the respondent sorts the card and the interviewer simply records offense identification numbers. This protects the respondent from offering direct evidence of having committed an offense and the interviewer from being in a position of "aiding and abetting." (We are arguing appearances rather than real legal points here.)

Scaling Seriousness of Offense and Severity of Disposition

No matter the source—official records, self-report, or the reports of privileged observers such as family, peers, or correctional officers—numerous authors have suggested that outcome measures should reflect the seriousness of offenses and/or the severity of disposition (Gendreau & Leipciger, 1978; Glaser, 1964; Kellar & Carlson, 1977; Waldo and Griswold, 1979). The empirical evidence is remarkably clear and consistent on the following points [for a review, see Wellford (1975)]: the anthropological literature reveals high levels of cross-cultural agreement regarding the prohibition of murder, assault, and violations of private property rights; consensus is less for what may be called "status offenses"and "minor crimes"; when applied internationally and sub-nationally, citizen ratings of offense seriousness are highly correlated, and the seriousness judgments of citizens (students) and parole decision makers (professionals) are highly correlated (Carroll & Payne, 1977).

The Sellin and Wolfgang (1964) seriousness index is the most frequently cited measure in *discussions* of recidivism measures but much less evident in actual practice. The standard complaint is that the Sellin and Wolfgang measure requires more information on a given offense than is normally available to investigators [for an extended discussion, see Gendreau and Leipciger (1978)]. At this stage it appears crucial for practical purposes and general use that a seriousness scale be based on a simple description of offenses as opposed to detailed data on the circumstances of offense, amount of injury, and other factors. Such scales include Kellar and Carlson (1977) for adult samples and Hooke (1970) for juveniles. No matter the choice of extant seriousness scales, expect high levels of overall agreement on ratings but heated debates regarding some offenses.

Severity of disposition scales are an alternative or adjunct to seriousness of offense scales. Typically, they reflect level of penetration into the criminal justice system (Berger et al., 1975) with some additional attention to the amount of the fine or the length of probation or incarceration.The value or potential of "total time incarcerated" was noted earlier. The Moberg and Ericson (1972) outcome index does not have the ratio properties of "total time" measures, but it does provide an ordinal listing of various dispositions. Although this author has not yet seen the Moberg–Ericson scale employed in an American evaluation study, a Canadian version (Gendreau & Leipciger, 1978) has been employed (Andrews et al., 1981, Reference Note 2; Wormith, 1979). In *one* study the disposition index was more sensitive to both program and predictor variables than was a binary measure of recidivism, number of reconvictions, seriousness ratings, or total follow-up months in prison (Andrews et al., 1981, Reference Note 2).

A general problem with seriousness scales and severity scales is that the averages produced have little obvious meaning for policy makers. Both the senior author of the Canadian version of the Moberg–Ericson scale (Gendreau) and the agency that sponsored that revision (Ontario Ministry of Correctional Services) now appear to be using and advocating simple binary measures of reconviction and/or reincarceration. The development and use of seriousness scales is to be encouraged, but any developer or user will recognize that consumers will ultimately be more interested in binary or simple-extent measures. However, it is necessary to specify how choices were made to ignore certain offenses when computing the more policy relevant measures. The value of seriousness–severity scales will reside in their standard nature, and perhaps a committee of experts and consumers is required if there is to be any standardization (Waldo & Griswold, 1979). Investigators should be careful to outline the specifics by which they choose to ignore particular offenses or certain evidence of offenses.

Type of Offense

Conceptually and analytically distinct from seriousness ratings are considerations of type of offense. Where a program targets a specific type of offense, it is obvious that recidivism rates should be established for that specific type of offense, separate from equally valuable rates for nontargeted types of offense. It is appropriate that a program for chronic drunkenness offenders monitor alcohol and drug offenses and that a program with a focus on car thefts monitor car thefts. More generally, it has been suggested that recidivism be restricted to recurrences of offenses of the same type as the original offense.

The overall issue has not been of great significance in the evaluation literature to date. It will emerge as a serious issue if the effects of even general interventions prove to be specific to certain types of offense. The extant typologies distinguish among property offenses, person offenses with or without physical violence, victimless crimes, and so on. However, more sophisticated and perhaps more theoretically relevant classifications of offenses will emerge. For example, a program that targets alcohol and drug abuse would be well advised to make use of the advances in assessments in that area. Similarly, when "aggression" is targeted, evaluators should consider important distinctions such as "emotional" versus "instrumental" aggression (Berkowitz, 1962). Classifications that consider the role of the victim may be particularly relevant for the evaluation of psychosocial interventions. The potential of offense typologies is a wide-open question for empirical exploration in the context of evaluation research. The fact of "plea bargaining" appears to be a particularly relevant concern for those evaluators who are interested in specific types of offense.

Comparison of Measures of Recidivism

The number of recidivists identified will vary with sources of data, levels of involvement with the criminal justice system sampled, duration of follow-up, and the application of criteria such as seriousness of type of offense. Self-report sources will yield higher rates than will official sources (Nettler, 1978; Waldo & Griswold, 1979). More persons come in contact with the police than are arrested, charged, convicted, and then incarcerated. If this order is not found within a given data source, serious reliability problems are indicated. The cumulative proportion of recidivists and the absolute value of extent measures approach their asymptotes with increases in the duration of follow-up, but the number of new arrests and convictions decrease with successive follow-up periods. Finally, assessments of the occurrence and extent of recidivism may be manipulated by the application of minimal frequency and/or seriousness and/or typing criteria.

The fact that variations in the absolute levels of recidivism are a function of the selected operational definitions is well established. However, such variations are of little importance in outcome evaluation research except under certain conditions. The assessed levels of recidivism must not be so low (or so high) that intervention effects become impossible to detect statistically. The measures must be relevant to the specific concerns of the investigator or the concerns of the consumers of research (e.g., a program which aimed to reduce incarceration rates would monitor incarceration indices). The measure must not include any element of bias which might favor one treatment program over another. For example, prior dispositions tend to be predictive of future dispositions, and thus in any comparison of community- and prison-based programs it would be highly questionable to rely on a reincarceration measure of recidivism: participants in the prison program are, by virtue of their having been in prison, more likely to receive a new prison sentence for subsequent offenses than are community-based participants. Finally, the measures may be differentially sensitive to treatment effects.

The latter point is underinvestigated, but some tentative generalizations are possible from descriptive studies that have employed different measures of recidivism as criterion variables. This author has been impressed with the consistency of results when different measures of recidivism have been employed. The many recidivism studies of the research branch of the Ontario Ministry of Correctional Services have typically employed at least two measures of recidivism. In study after study, if measured attributes of offenders and/or situations predict reconviction, they will also predict reincarceration.

Gendreau et al. (1979) have reported very similar results across a variety of operational definitions of recidivism. In our own on-going work, the factors that correlate with or predict official processing tend to be the same factors that correlate with or predict self-reported criminal activity. It is certainly possible to dramatize differential validities of criterion measures (Hawkins et al., 1977), but agreement rates tend to be high. Although multivariate techniques that incorporate various operationalizations of recidivism have rarely been employed, they should help to pinpoint any systematic differences.

Differential validity estimates are most likely when the criterion measures vary in the source of data (official vs. self-report; local vs. central agency). This, however, may be more a question of reliability than validity, In other areas of research it is standard practice to combine observations (to average, or to use multivariate techniques) when different observers or sources are employed. Such a strategy seems equally appropriate in the analysis of recidivism when the reports of different agencies and even self- or peer-reports are available. Averaging over time as well as observers and items (offenses) should allow both reliability and validity estimates to approach their asymptotes.

In a direct attempt to examine differential sensitivity within the context of evaluation studies, Lipton et al. (1975) and the Ross and Gendreau (1980) collection were reviewed to obtain a set of studies all of which showed a statistically significant effect of intervention on recidivism. Thirty-four studies were found in which a comparison group was employed (Level 1 or 2 in the Lipton et al. methodology ranking) and in which there was a clearly evident statistically significant ($p < .05$) effect. The following is based on n values too small to yield estimates worthy of much confidence, but it is suggestive. It is not surprising that the binary measure of any arrests, convictions, or violations was the most frequently employed measure in the sample ($n = 20$), most often tested by χ^2. The hit rate for this simple and readily interpretable measure was an impressive 95%. The hit rate for the extent measures of number of arrests and convictions was also high (80%; $n = 10$). The hit rates for seriousness of offense ratings ($n = 6$), time to first arrest and conviction ($n = 5$), and proportion incarcerated ($n = 14$) were unimpressive at 67, 60, and 57% respectively. Indices of severity of disposition ($n = 8$) had a hit rate of 100%. Most notable, the p values associated with the analysis of disposition indices were, in every study but one, equal to or less than the p values reported for alternative measures of recidivism. Thus severity of disposition and/or "total follow-up time incarcerated" indices appear attractive, not only in their links with human and socioeconomic criteria, but also in terms of their sensitivity to treatment effects. One caution about the measure of "total time incarcerated": when employed with prison-based programs, it will also reflect the ability to achieve an early release or parole.

Another approach to comparison of recidivism measures is to explore the stability of the relative position of various estimates of recidivism in the absence of evidence of treatment effects. The Waldo and Chiricos (1977) study is of special value here. Their Table I (page 16) includes experimental-control comparisons on 15 different binary measures of recidivism. Depending on the specific measure employed, recidivism varied from a low of 19% to a high of 70%. However, the outstanding fact is that such variation was far from random: the correlation (Pearson r) was .95 (computed by this author). In other words, those measures that yield high rates for one randomly selected group were the measures that yielded high rates for the other randomly selected group. In the absence of treatment effects, the variation in rates associated with different measures are highly systematic. Waldo and Chiricos (1977, Table 2, page 95) also present comparisons with 15 different extent measures of recidivism: again, the correlation was .95.

Quite properly, investigators will choose the specific measure of recidivism most relevant to their particular situation, including considerations of subjects, the nature of specific targets of intervention, and the interests of the consumers of the evaluation study. However, if individual studies are to contribute to the general knowledge pool regarding the assessment of recidivism, the following recommendations appear appropriate:

1. The proportions reconvicted and the proportions reincarcerated should be routinely reported, with the proportions computed before and after the application of any seriousness or typology criteria.

2. The mean number of reconvictions and the mean "follow-up time incarcerated" should be reported routinely, including and excluding those with no reconvictions, and before and after the application of any seriousness criteria.

3. The intercorrelations among the measures of recidivism should be reported and, where possible, multivariate analyses conducted.

These recommendations are consistent with those of the National Advisory Commission on Criminal Justice Standards and Goals, 1973, a frequently cited body in the American literature (Banks & Rardin, 1978; Waldo & Griswold, 1979).

These recommendations obviously place a higher premium on reconviction data than on arrest data or police and court contact data. We reject outright the argument that arrest or police contact data are in some way more valid indicators of recidivism. The typical argument is that police data are closer to the original criminal act and that with higher levels of criminal justice processing, there is increasing distance from that act [see Waldo and Griswold (1979) for a review of this point]. Arrest data may provide a more accurate reflection of the total amount of crime in a community than do conviction data, but such is not the concern of evaluation studies in corrections. The arguments in favor of arrest data appear to be an inappropriate generalization of some classic arguments employed where the computation of crime rates was the major concern (Sellin, 1951). There are certain situations when arrest data, court contact data, police contact data, and self-report data are indicated. When the base rates of reconviction are very low, one must turn to alternate definitions of recidivism. Police data and/or self-report data are also indicated when there is solid reason to expect that intervention may be selectively influencing the likelihood of offenses being detected officially. Police and self-report data may also help to specify when an act occurred; this is sometimes a problem with reconviction data since there is often a great gap between the commission of an offense and date of conviction or sentence (Adams, 1975a).

Crime Rates

The objective of specific deterrence is conceptually distinct from the objective of reducing crime rates. However, where a program releases many graduates to a particular community, there is a logical and, it seems, reasonable possibility of documenting effects on crime rates. Both the self-report and official sources of data agree that a relatively small proportion of persons are responsible for a disproportional amount of criminal activity. A recent follow-up of adult probationers revealed that 24% of the probationers accounted for 85% of the total reconvictions recorded (Andrews et al., 1981, Reference Note 2). Within a juvenile diversion sample, 9% of the cases accounted for 52% of the rearrests (Quay & Love, 1977). Employing a different methodology, Erickson et al. (1977) report that a typical measure of community crime rates was largely a function of individual repeaters within the community. There is a dramatic suggestion that effective correctional interventions delivered to high-risk offenders have the potential of influencing crime rates in significant ways. Such remains to be documented. In the absence of any experimental evidence regarding the efficacy of community-wide structural or system change approaches to prevention (Mayer, 1972), it is an important issue for investigation.

An important consideration here is the employment of risk scales. Many offenders on probation and parole have very low probabilities of recidivism. It is, in a sense, a waste of resources to focus on such persons. The basic mathematics of behavior change actually work against a focus on very low risk cases; if there is any effect, there is only one way to move, and that is in the direction of an increased probability of recidivism. Rather, a focus on the moderate and higher-risk offenders is indicated. Those attributes of persons and situations that predict the fact of rearrest or reconviction are, for the most part, the same factors that predict multiple arrests and multiple reconvictions (Andrews et al., 1981, Reference Note 2; Quay & Love, 1977). If those skilled and knowledgeable in the area of psychosocial interventions do not pick up this challenge, there is the strong possibility that we will see considerations of "variations in the management of sentences" return to the level of variation in styles of leg irons, the width and strength of prison bars—two approaches that do not systematically open up noncriminal opportunity but remove the physical opportunity for any behavioral choice. The potential associated with the humane and ethical development and application of sociobehavioral knowledge is too great to allow corrections to maintain and/or revert to such practices unchallenged.

ASSESSMENT OF INTERMEDIATE CHANGE

That there are substantial individual differences in criminal behavior is the most firmly established empirical fact in criminology. Ideological and disciplinary interests have made that fact the focus of denial, dismissal, ridicule, and even charges of immorality (Schur, 1973). But the fact remains apparent in the original studies, if not always apparent from review articles and textbooks in criminology (Hirschi & Hindelang, 1977). Cross-sectional studies that employ a comprehensive psychosocial battery now readily yield multiple correlations with indices of problem behaviors in the 60s through 80s, and correct classification rates in the 80s and above are not unusual (Akers et al., 1979; Andrews et al., 1979; Donovan & Jessor, 1978; Jessor & Jessor, 1977; Renner, 1978; Wormith, 1977). Longitudinal studies cannot take advantage of reciprocal causation and avoid base–rate problems as in the case of cross-sectional studies. Still, multiple correlations in the 40s and even into the 60s are found and correct classification rates in the low to high 70s are reported (Andrews et al., 1981, Reference Note 2; Jessor & Jessor, 1977; Gendreau et al., 1979, 1980, Rogers, 1981; Wormith, 1978, 1979; Wormith et al., 1980). Evidence is slowly emerging that such levels of predictive efficiency are of practical significance even when the "false alarm" rate appears high (Andrews, 1981; Baird et al., 1979; Barton et al., 1973; Bonta, 1981; Jenkins & Sanford, 1972; Madden, 1978; Rogers, 1981).

The predictive estimates are especially impressive when the obvious limitations of the studies to date are noted: biophysical attributes have yet to be introduced within comprehensive psychosocial batteries; moderator variables are only rarely considered; relatively short term follow-up periods have been employed; perceived situational measures outnumber objective assessments of situations; clinical judgments and the ratings of privileged others have not been introduced into the prediction formulas to cover idiosyncratic factors; powerful statistical methods have not always been employed; and likely most important, time-varying attributes have rarely been monitored during the follow-up period.

The issues limiting predictive efficiency are trivial when compared with some of the other problems that exist in the literature regarding the attributes of persons and their situations that predict criminal activity. The network of intercorrelations among the correlates (or predictors) remains to be understood in relation to criminal behavior. The formal classification of predictors employed by Jessor and Jessor (1977) and path analytic work such as Johnson's (1979) represent important approaches to this issue. The construct validity of the majority of individual correlates remains to be explored, and such explorations will almost certainly result in modification of both the measures and the underlying construct. *Very* serious is that comprehensive and systematic evaluation of the measures of attributes have not been conducted on key methodological dimensions such as content (cognitive, physiological, motor), method (interviews, self-report, ratings by privileged others such as peers and/or independent observers of performance or situation), and reliability (scorer, internal consistency, temporal stability). Cone's (1978) grid system suggests the many questions to be explored. *Most* serious is that the derivation of concurrent and predictive validity estimates do not suggest functional significance. The factors associated with the acquisition of troubled or troublesome behavior may not be the most powerful factors, the most feasible factors, or even relevant factors when the issue is the modification of problem behavior.

An approach that suggests functional significance more directly than either concurrent or predictive validity is that of documenting that assessed *changes* in attributes are associated with *subsequent* variations in recidivism. Such documentation we now call *functional validity*, and evidence that the measures change along with theoretically relevant interventions we term *dependent validity* (Andrews, 1981, Reference Note 3). Naturally, the value of functional and dependent validity estimates vary with the methodological rigor of the longitudinal study (Howard, 1980). Confidence in the estimates will be greatest when the changes have occurred under controlled conditions and the effects of competing factors or changes can be discounted. For example, the predictive validity of prescores *must* be discounted in order to document the validity of post (or change) scores. Controlled program evaluations provide a unique meeting ground for theorists and practitioners since they share a basic interest in the identification of functional factors (Andrews, 1980). However, practitioners and evaluators must also consider the practical and ethical issues when choosing intermediate targets for intervention.

A major difficulty with the correctional outcome literature, and with predictive studies in general, is that so few studies have reported directly on the relationship between intermediate change and recidivism. Studies that document intermediate change tend to be the same studies that report effects on recidivism (Andrews, 1974). However, the aggregate fallacy limits the conclusions that can be drawn from interstudy comparisons: the establishment of individual differences requires the direct linking of measures, assessed at the individual level. Some studies have reported functional validity estimates, and they are noted shortly. An exhaustive survey of the outcome literature with reference to functional validity has yet to be conducted, and it appears that many promising functional variables have yet to be explored seriously. Thus this section of the chapter presents a classification of intermediate targets that, in theory and limited practice, appears reasonably comprehensive and promising.

The theoretical perspective is a broad social learning approach to deviant behavior that considers personal, interpersonal, and community antecedents and consequences for criminal and noncriminal behaviors (Andrews, forthcoming). Its roots reside in the work of Burgess and Akers (1966), Adams (1973), Glaser (1974), Bandura (1969), Hunt and Azrin (1973), Rotter (1966), Jessor and Jessor (1977), and Linden and Hackler (1973). In general terms, and certainly within the context of community standards and professional ethics, the task of intervention is to produce a shift in the density of rewards and the density of the costs for criminal and noncriminal behaviors such that the noncriminal are favored. One task of assessments is to monitor such shifts. The concept of density is important because it underscores the position that crime is multifunctional. That is, criminal acts (like noncriminal acts) may be under the control of many factors that vary in their importance both inter- and intra-individually. "Density" refers to the number, variety, magnitude, and quality of response consequences and to the immediacy, frequency, and regularity with which rewards or costs are delivered. Rewards and costs, and the antecedents that signal their delivery may be personally mediated (as suggested by the social learning and behavioral models of self-management), interpersonally mediated (requiring the immediate presence of others), socially contracted (as in the case of an employment situation), or the relatively automatic consequences of an act (in the sense that passing a check delivers money and ingestion of a drug relieves withdrawal distress for the physically dependent person). The rewards, costs, and antecedents that signal their delivery constitute either additions to or subtractions from the environment. Thus rewards and costs both may be of the additive ($+$) or subtractive($-$) variety. Assessments of persons and their situations provide indicators of these relatively immediate antecedents and consequences of action judged critical to understanding inter- and intraindividual variations in the probability of occurrence of a given class of behavior.

More specifically, the task of intervention is to effect one and preferably more of the following: (1) a reduction in the density of the rewards in effect or signaled for criminal behavior; (2) an increase in the density of the costs for criminal behavior; (3) an increase in the density of the rewards for noncriminal behavior; and (4) a decrease in the density of the costs for noncriminal behavior. Assessments of the following attributes of persons and their situations provide indicators of the reward–cost contingencies in effect or signaled for criminal behavior ("ties to crime"): (1) an early and extensive involvement in criminal activities; (2) possession of prerequisite skills for criminal activity; (3) personal endorsement of attitudes and beliefs supportive of deviance in general and specific illegal acts in particular; (4) value placed on outcomes more readily achieved by criminal than noncriminal behavior and devaluation of costs associated with crime; and (5) social support for criminal behavior, including resources, exposure to criminal models, and affective ties to offenders.

A complementary set of measures is required to tap "ties to convention" or the density of the rewards and costs in effect for noncriminal alternative behaviors. A comprehensive assessment of ties to convention samples the density of the rewards and satisfactions associated with a variety of noncriminal pursuits, especially those that occur in the company of anticriminal others and within anticriminal settings such as the home, school, work, recreation, neighborhood, and other social settings such as the church and unions. A middle-class bias need not limit the number or type of settings assessed. Ties to alternative life-style groups such as "hippies" and "surfers" (Marks & Glaser, 1980) may be found to function in an anticriminal direction.

Measures of ties to crime and ties to convention will share variance, both within and between the two sets of measures. However, the *fact* of intercorrelations does not indicate that the assessed factors will fail to make independent contributions to the predictability of criminal behavior. The theoretical perspective suggests that a *shift* in both attitude and patterns may have independent effects. If personal attitudes move in the anticriminal direction, the probability of self-reward or self-instructions supportive of criminal behavior decrease. Variations in association patterns suggest variations in the probability of interpersonal approval or disapproval of criminal activity. Moreover, interactions may be expected within the two sets of measures: under some conditions, strong social support for crime will increase the predictive and functional significance of criminal attitudes.

Interactions between the two sets of measures are likely to be of special significance. Ties to convention are suggested to be of particular importance in the analysis of criminal behavior under the following conditions: (1) the rewards delivered by noncriminal activities are the same as those delivered by crime (strong ties to convention reduce the motivational base for crime and increase the effectiveness of any extant costs for crime); (2) the rewards delivered by noncriminal activities are subject to withdrawal or interruption should criminal activity occur (the *subtractive* costs of crime increase); and (3) the noncriminal activities are, by virtue of their location or physical characteristics, simply incompatible with criminal activity (in the sense that time on the job is not time on the streets). In brief, the predictive and functional significance of ties to convention are greatest when the contingencies for crime and noncrime interlock. Moreover, increase in the density of the rewards for noncriminal alternatives may be the outstanding approach to influencing ties to crime.

Traditional personality factors are distributed across several categories of ties to crime and ties to convention. Intelligence, academic and vocational aptitude, interpersonal skills, social and life skills, and self-control are, in part, assessments of the prerequisite competencies and skills necessary for normative or rewarded performance in anticriminal and some criminal settings. The predictive and functional validity of many traditional personality measures is likely to be a function of the concomitant strength of ties to crime and convention. For example, the possession of behavioral self-management skills suggest that one is less likely to stumble into trouble at school, at work, or with the law. At the same time, variations in self-regulation skills suggest important variations in the ability to translate one's "good intentions" into performance. Those "good intentions" may be procriminal or anticriminal depending on the standards of conduct implied by one's personal sentiments or suggested by one's associates. Similarly, self-esteem may be a positive or negative correlate of criminal behavior depending on the standards of conduct. Preliminary runs with the data from an ongoing project along without overall social learning perspective are leading us to the position that one indeed does have to be "crazy" (or "unique" or "special") to commit crimes when ties to crime are weak and ties to convention are strong. In other words, the predictive and functional validity of traditional measures of personal distress and disturbance are greatest when the personal and social supports for crime are weak. The position does not suggest that all offenders are disturbed. *Variations on indices of disturbance are found regardless of ties to crime and ties to convention.* However, personality disturbance and skill deficits are more strongly related to criminality under some conditions than others.

The position suggests that some of the traditional psychological targets in correctional programming may have been very inappropriate when the ultimate goal was reduced recidivism. Consider the effects of increasing the feelings of self-worth and reducing the guilt of an offender personally and socially committed to crime. Consider the effect of increasing the functional intelligence and self-management skills of a "committed" offender. The suggestion is that not only may offenders consciously choose the deviant route (Taylor et al., 1973), but also that some of our interventions may succeed in smoothing the bumps along that route. Table 7.3 presents some concurrent validity estimates from the early returns of an ongoing study. Note the appar-

TABLE 7.3. Some Personality Correlates of Self-Reported Criminal Behavior by Criminal versus Conventional Orientation[a]: Pearson r Values

	Overall Orientation[b]	
	Conventional	Criminal
Personality factors[c]	($n = 41$)	($n = 52$)
Self-esteem (Bennett et al., 1971)	−.26[*]	.36[*]
Alienation (Dean, 1961)	.41[*]	.00
Neuroticism (Peterson et al., 1959)	.36[*]	−.14
Self-control	−.31[*]	.04
Socialization (Gough, 1969)	−.36[*]	−.03

[*]$p < .05$.
[a]From Addie (1980), based on the first 99 male probationers to be tested in the Andrews and Kiessling ongoing project.
[b]Median splits on a measure based on Harris (1975).
[c]The Andrews and Wormith (1981) versions of the indicated scales.

ent interaction of personality and ties to crime and convention. The point of all this has been to underscore several interrelated considerations that are more important in the assessment of correctional outcomes than present knowledge regarding the relative value of measure A over measure B.

1.   The intermediate targets of intervention *and* the methods of assessing those targets may be selected with explicit reference to the goal of reduced recidivism. This point has been made and remade by most every reviewer of the correctional-outcome literature (Adams, 1975a, 1975b; Andrews, 1974, 1979a, 1979b; Bailey, 1966; Cook & Scioli, 1975; Gendreau & Ross, 1979; Glaser, 1974; Kirby, 1954; Lipton et al.,

1975; Logan, 1972; Martinson, 1974; Palmer, 1975). However, there is little in the recent literature to suggest that programmers or evaluators are any more sensitive to the issue or any less sensitive to current fads in treatment approach and target.

2. The predictability of criminal behavior will increase with the reliable, valid, and *comprehensive* assessment of ties to crime, convention, personality and their potential interactions. Single-focus studies are doomed to failure, except for the most carefully selected samples. The careful selection of samples requires comprehensive assessment.

3. A construct–validation approach to assessments and program evaluation will facilitate the development of both the measures and the theoretical perspective in which the measures may be located.

4. For purposes of the assessment of intermediate targets, the currently favored methods of estimating reliability (temporal stability) and validity (concurrent and predictive validity) are less appropriate than internal consistency, temporal stability within treatment groups, and the derivation of estimates of dependent and functional validity.

5. Assessment of persons and their situations may also function as control and/or moderator variables in the context of evaluation research. Repeated measures of time-varying covariates, both targeted and nontargeted, will assist in gaining an understanding of the processes by which and conditions under which intervention effects on recidivism appear and fade or are maintained. Time-constant risk assessments will be particularly valuable as control and moderator variables.

6. The tapping of method and content variance in assessments—variance attributed to observers or to cognitive versus behavioral content—are crucial to comprehensive assessment. We may expect that self-reports will provide the most accurate indicators of the procriminal versus anticriminal direction of personally mediated antecedents and consequences. On the other hand, the reports of peers and/or independent observers may provide the most accurate indicators of the interpersonally mediated antecedents and consequences of action. Although cognitive controls are powerful (Bandura, 1977, 1981), there is no convincing evidence as yet that externally mediated consequences are incapable of having independent effects. Finally, content and method variance in assessments are likely to interact with the practice variance associated with intervention. Jesness (1975) provided rather clear evidence of treatment-by-assessment method interactions: a behavior-modification program tended to impact on behavioral measures of intermediate gain, whereas a program with a more cognitive orientation tended to impact on cognitive indices. Important to our more general point, both the behavioral and cognitive measures were related to recidivism.

The following review of specific scales is only a small sample of possible measures. Space limitations preclude a review of intermediate forecasters of outcome such as institutional adjustment [for a psychometric review of institutional indices, see Wormith (1977)].

Ties to Crime: Attitudes, Values, and Beliefs

Measures of attitudes, values, and beliefs supportive of crime are probably the single set of measures with the strongest theoretical and empirical support. The latter includes evidence of concurrent validity, predictive validity, dependent validity, and functional validity. The Andrews and Wormith (1981) self-report, paper-and-pencil measures are highly recommended given the amount and quality of psycho- and sociometric information available: both the potential of the scales and their limitation are fairly well known. Attitudes toward the law, courts and police, tolerance for law violations, and identification with criminal others are serious candidates for inclusion in the evaluation of any correctional program. The three scales also have a rich research history in their earlier Reckless version (Gendreau et al., 1979).

Additional evidence (although less direct and conceptually more cloudy) for the importance of criminal sentiments is suggested by selected scales of the CPI (Ferdinand, 1962), the MMPI (Persons, 1966), the Jesness Inventory and Checklist (Jesness, 1975), and the MCI (Truax et al., 1970). The pioneering work of Shelley and Johnson (1961) and Massimo and Shore (1963) with the TAT suggests that scoring for antisocial themes, including attitudes toward authority and aggression, are highly promising alternatives or adjuncts to the paper-and-pencil approaches. The predictive validity of the Buss and Durkee aggression scales (Gendreau et al., 1979) suggest the need for their exploration in the context of evaluation research. The procriminal expressions of offenders in the situation of counseling or interview sessions have been reliably assessed by independent observers (Andrews, 1980; Wormith, 1977). Some predictive validity is apparent, but functional validity is not as yet. Seidman et al., (1980) employed self-, peer-, and parent-evaluations of "deviant identification," but neither dependent nor functional validity were evident. By contrast, probation officer ratings of improvement versus deterioration on both "control of hostility" and "avoidance of new crime" show evidence of functional validity (Rogers, 1981).

Some specific value-level indices of ties to crime worthy of serious exploration include value excitement and thrills and sensation seeking (Platt et al., 1980; Zuckerman, 1978), value independence (Jessor & Jessor, 1977), and contempt for or rejection of the existing social order [or more mildly stated, social criticism (Jessor & Jessor, 1977)]. Assessments of the "expected value" of criminal activity appear particularly promising (Harris, 1975). In structured interview and/or paper-and-pencil formats, investigators may explore the value placed on the specific rewards and costs associated with crime. They may specify the rewards or allow the client to suggest rewards of individualized relevance. Additional ratings on the perceived chances that these rewards and costs would be delivered if one engages in criminal activity provide assessments relevant to personal efficacy. The measures distinguish between official offenders and nonoffenders and correlate with a self-reported criminal past within both official offender and nonoffender samples (preliminary findings from the author's ongoing studies).

Ties to Crime: Social Support

Indices of association with offenders are the only serious rivals to criminal sentiments in terms of the amount of empirical and theoretical attention received in the social sciences. In spite of this, this author is unaware of even one published and evaluated effort that explicitly targeted and monitored that objective of reduced association with offenders. Rather, there are many evaluated efforts that appear to have deliberately programmed an opening up of communication and interaction within offender groups, with the theoretically expected but unintended result of producing subsequent increases in criminal activity: Grant and Grant's (1959) low-maturity military offenders; Murphy's (1972) adult heroin addicts; Craft et al.'s (1964) young hospitalized psychopaths; Truax et al.'s (1970) incarcerated juveniles exposed to leaderless group sessions; Hackler and Hagan's (1975) work gangs with a nondirective leader; and Klein's (1971) street gangs. In this set of studies it was only Klein who linked an assessment of a group cohesiveness to the increased criminality. For a more complete review, see Andrews (1979a, 1979b, Chapter 3).

The two key dimensions for the assessment of interpersonal situations are the contingency (or normative dimensions) and the socioemotional (or relationship or control) dimension. The contingency dimension reflects the extent to which procriminal versus anticriminal expressions are modeled and reinforced or punished. The socioemotional or control dimension refers to the number, quality, and variety of rewards and costs available for delivery and the immediacy, frequency, and regularity with which they are delivered. In any interpersonal situation the quality of the interpersonal relationship, factors such as mutual liking and respect and/or openness and warmth are primary indicators of the effective rewards and costs available. Generally, the control dimension is related to the *strength* of effects and the contingency dimension, to the *direction* of effects [for experimental evidence, see Andrews (1980), and for an outstanding descriptive study, see Linden and Hackler (1973)].

Several examples of reasonably reliable and valid (concurrent and predictive) self-report measures of affective ties to offenders are available: Short (1957), Linden and Hackler (1973), Jessor and Jessor (1977), and Akers et al. (1979). Although association with peers or companions are the typical concern in the available literature, parents, siblings, relatives, and employers represent "others" who may express criminal sentiments and criminal behaviors. Our current assessment battery includes self-reports of access to criminal resources such as a "fence" and exposure to criminal models even in the absence of affective ties. We are also monitoring victimization as an index of exposure to crime. The relevance of these latter measures remains to be established.

Obvious alternatives and adjuncts to self-reports are peer, police, and other privileged observers' reports on the crime rate or the concentration of offenders in given neighborhoods or socially defined units. Roger's (1981) data suggest that the ratings of probation officers on improvement versus deterioration in terms of "peer relationships" and "suitability of accommodation" have functional validity.

Ties to Convention: General Attitudes, Values, and Beliefs

A traditional criminological concern is a person's sense of alienation and perceptions of the opportunity associated with conventional pursuits. Common measures of alienation in correctional situations are scales based on the work of Dean (1961), Struening and Richardson (1965), and Reckless (Andrews et al., 1979; Gendreau et al., 1979). Concurrent validity estimates tend to be impressive, and one measure, awareness of limited opportunity (based on Reckless) has been shown to distinguish between probationers with stable versus unstable employment records and to change with improvements in their vocational situation (Andrews et al., 1981). What we have yet to uncover in the literature is *any* evidence that reduced alienation is associated with subsequent reductions in recidivism. We expect that functional significance of alienation depends on extant levels of ties to convention and ties to crime. Variables that moderate the functional significance of alienation may well be found. At this stage, evaluation research like descriptive research (Johnson, 1979) suggest that the functional significance assigned alienation by anomie and strain theories has simply been overstated.

Our assessment battery incorporates the Harris (1975) expected value approach to the rewards and costs for noncriminal pursuits, including the rated chances that noncriminal pursuits would result in the delivery of those rewards and costs. Preliminary validity data with criminal indices as criteria suggest that the expected utility and disutility of conventional pursuits are not strongly related to criminal behavior. Even in relation to stability of employment history, the distinguishing factor between those with relatively stable and those with unstable records of employment was not the expected value of conventional activities, but the expected value of criminal activities. Those with an unstable record seem particularly attracted to the rewards unique to crime and to show a devaluation of the costs of crime. We further found that improvement in the employment situation of those with unstable records appeared to have the effect of opening their eyes to the relatively low rewards and the relatively high costs associated with the type of job they were able to find (Andrews et al., 1981).

Ties to Convention: Performance and Reward Levels at School and Work

Assessments of academic and vocational history are among the strongest predictors of criminal behavior. However, it is also clear that vocational history is only one of a highly intercorrelated set of predictors. Some of these predictors show functional validity, but at the present time, vocational functioning is not among these with the strongest evidence. Reports of successful intervention effects on "grade-point average," "school attendance," "dollars earned," and "days worked" are not infrequent in the evaluation literature. What we have not yet found is convincing evidence that such changes are linked to subsequent reductions in the probability of recidivism. Typically, controls for pretreatment or vocational history factors have not been introduced into the longitudinal studies, and the studies in the area almost invariably fail to assign offenders to treatment on a random basis.

Both the control and normative dimensions should be sampled in assessments of school and employment settings. Ratings of the level of rewards and satisfaction associated with school or employment (participation with performance, relationship with authority, and relationship with peers) are among the strongest correlates of a stable or unstable employment history (Andrews et al., 1981). Such ratings may prove more powerful than single-item indices such as grade-point average attendance, or simply obtaining a job. Friedlander and Greenberg (1971) have developed a scale that allows an independent assessment of the extent to which the employment situation is supportive of the individual. Such an assessment seems worthwhile if only to underscore the point that the objective situation of employment for offenders, as opposed to personal characteristics or reactions to employment, may be an important source of variance in outcome.

Ties to Convention: Family Functioning

With the limitations noted, the available literature supports the functional validity of indices of family functioning. Changes in self-reports of family conflict, a scale based on Peterson et al. (1959), have been shown to be associated with reduced recidivism in both probation (Andrews et al., 1981, Reference Note 2) and prison samples (Wormith, 1979). The Alexander and Parsons (1973) study provides an outstanding example of the assessment of family functioning by independent observers and documents a relationship with recidivism. The Patterson (1974) approach to contingency analysis also appears powerful, reinforced by evidence that impact on the families of delinquents had subsequent impact on nontargeted siblings. Among the many sobering reports on the assessment of outcome with families, the work of Bernal et al. (1980) especially warrants careful study.

Skills and Competencies

Although interpretations are controversial, it is widely accepted that offenders score more poorly on average than do nonoffenders on existing measures of intelligence and traditional indices of vocational–academic aptitude. However, even some of the better-known critics of correctional intervention programs (Lipton et al., 1975) agree that there is now little question that psychosocial interventions have succeeded in influencing skill levels. What continues to be unclear is that increased skill is associated with reduced recidivism. We expect that the link depends on the new skills having an opportunity to be demonstrated and rewarded in anticriminal employment situations. This requires getting a job and keeping it (Rogers, 1980).

Social and Interpersonal Skills

The positive results of early studies such as that of Sarason and Ganzer (1973) bode well for the success of programs that incorporate systematic social-skill training. Several studies have shown that ratings by correctional staff possess dependent validity (Daigle-Zinn & Andrews, 1980; Jesness, 1975; Wormith, 1977). Again, functional validity is less apparent. The careful background work in the development of assessments of skill deficits by Freedman et al. (1978) promises dynamic and functional validity under certain conditions.

   The assessment of interpersonal skills through self-report measures such as the Hogan (1969) Empathy Scale and the Berger (1952) Acceptance of Others Scale requires special comment. It is our experience that such measures readily distinguish between official offenders and nonoffenders. Their predictive validity is much less well established, except as moderator variables (Andrews et al., 1979, Reference Note 2). Most seriously, where there is any evidence of functional validity, the trend has been that reduced interpersonal sensitivity is associated with reduced recidivism. We expect that a moderator variable is functioning here, but at the present time, this author is unaware of any evidence that increased empathy is associated with reduced recidivism, where empathy has been assessed by self-report.

   One approach to the modification and measurement of empathy that demands replication is the fine study by Chandler (1973) using the Flavell egocentrism measure. A highly relevant program theoretically resulted in reduced egocentrism and reduced recidivism. Although changes on the egocentrism measure were not directly linked to recidivism, the effects were sufficiently large on both outcome measures that it is reasonable to expect that the link was there. The assessment of empathy as an intermediate change measure may prove to be as complex as the assessment of empathy as a counselor and practice factor (Lambert et al., 1978).

Self-Management and Self-Control

The available measures of self-control vary considerably at the levels of method and content. Not surprisingly, they share little common variance (Wormith & Hasenpusch, 1979). Such variations in content and method are probably very appropriate in terms of increasing predictive efficiency. As Wormith and Hasenpusch (1979) suggest, combined measures are strongly indicated. In terms of frequency of use and available validity data, the following deserve notation: the Mischel (1961) approach; the Porteus (1965) maze, the Gough (1969) self-control measure, and the many variations of the Rotter (1966) locus of control approach.

A major problem with the existing measures is that they reflect products of self-control deficits and/or cognitions supportive of self-control rather than the processes of self-control. In our own laboratory, the social-learning perspective on behavioral self-regulation is being employed as the base for the development of process-oriented assessment of self-management skills. One approach based on ratings of client statements during audiotaped counseling sessions has shown very impressive predictive validity (Andrews & Friesen, 1981, Reference Note 5; Friesen & Andrews, 1981, Reference Note 4). A feature of the self-management ratings strategy is that there was a clear distinction in the predictive validity of client expression of good intentions versus the application of those specific behavioral skills that help to align plans with performance.

Self-Esteem

This review of personality measures, potentially relevant as intermediate targets, closes with a classic variable in criminological theory and in counseling theory: attitudes toward self. Several self-report, paper-and-pencil measures have a rich tradition in corrections: the Rosenberg and Rosenberg (1978) scale, Bennett et al.'s (1971) self-esteem scale, and the Berger (1952) acceptance of self scale. Each of these measures has been shown to possess dependent validity, and each distinguishes between offenders and nonoffenders. Predictive validity and functional validity are another matter. Wormith (1979) has recently found that increases in self-esteem during periods of incarceration were associated with an increased probability of recidivism. He traced this effect to a concomitant increase in Identification with criminal others. This interaction, we think, is basic to the personal, interpersonal, and community-reinforcement perspective (Andrews, forthcoming). References to standards of conduct, whether based on personal sentiments or the external environment, are necessary to make any sense of the functional significance of self-esteem. This was evident in those early theories that emphasized self-esteem, but in practice and research, it seems to have been forgotten.

CONCLUSION

This chapter has focused on assessments of a unique and socially sanctioned objective of correctional agencies: achieving a reduction in the probability of recidivism on the part of those whose sentences are managed. Such an objective and its assessment are value laden, and it was stressed that both the pursuit of the goal and its assessment are conducted within a context with human, ethical, social, political, economic, and justice dimensions. It was noted that the delivery of psychosocial services may well serve functions that need not be linked to crime control for justification. It was also noted that there is a serious and underinvestigated question of how and whether the pursuit of the objective of specific deterrence is a relevant strategy when the broader goal of social protection is a reduction in community-wide crime rates.

Any reader familiar with correctional research will know that agencies have been, and some still are, very near the point of banning any research with adjudicated offenders. The situation is serious, for it appears that many are ready to freeze the knowledge-generating process just when the need for program decisions appears to be as great as it has ever been! Offenders and the community have a right to the "best possible validated" management of sentences. A responsible society can do no less than encourage the examination of the effectiveness of alternate programs (Davison & Stuart, 1975). To blindly maintain the *status quo* within a system under attack from many directions is ethically repugnant. Not to monitor the implications of naturally occurring variations in the management of sentences is wasteful. To prevent the application of the more powerful knowledge-generating methods, such as the experiment, is to suggest that human values should not be served by powerful methods.

Because of the inequalities in power that exist within correctional agencies, because what we influence or monitor may have implications for the future status of a client, it is crucial that assessments be conducted with both standard and special safeguards firmly in place. A review of the standard safeguards is impossible. But the issues of informed consent and the option of reversing a decision to participate are basic. With reference to informed consent, we now employ a two-tier system. Potential participants in an evaluated effort are at least twice exposed to an account of the objectives and methods to be employed. The first presentation occurs during the screening interview and an interview with a representative of the agency. The second review occurs at first meeting with the research staff. Also available are printed manuals describing the project and containing the same information. The distinction between what offenders are obliged to do in terms of their sentence and what they are being asked to do with respect to research is always drawn. Details are provided on how data are collected and stored and who has access to the data. Even with signed consent, we have a general rule that any participant who misses three assessment appointments is judged to have opted to reverse the original decision to participate. The disclosure sessions also include an appeal not to participate if they are uncertain of their desire to follow through. All of the above assumes a prescreening of evaluation plans with peers, formal committees at the university level and at the level of the funding agencies, and the host agency. We have worked with some correctional agencies that also have inmate committees established to review program plans. When a given agency does not have such a client committee, an evaluator may request that one be established for a review of plans. We have elsewhere discussed how relationships with host agencies may contribute to productive assessments (Gendreau & Andrews, 1979; Kiessling & Andrews, 1980; Russel et al., 1979). Overall, to reduce the number of victims of crime and to reduce the human and economic costs of managing sentences are worthy objectives, which cannot possibly be met without systematic research and evaluation.

REFERENCE NOTES

1. Andrews, D. A. *The supervision of offenders: Identifying and gaining control over the factors which make a difference.* Report submitted to the Ministry of the Solicitor General of Canada, June, 1981.
2. Andrews, D. A., Friesen, W., & Kiessling, J. J. *A three year postprogram follow-up of the CaVIC probationers: The effects of selection of officers, supervision by volunteers and supervision practices on recidivism.* Report submitted to the Ministry of the Solicitor General of Canada, 1981.
3. Andrews, D. A. *Functional validity: Increasing the theoretical and practical significance of descriptive research.* A paper in preparation for the Assessment and Evaluation Project, 1981.
4. Friesen, W., & Andrews, D. A. The behavioral assessment of self-management processes evident during counselling sessions. Unpublished manuscript. Psychology Department, Carleton University, Ottawa, Canada, 1981.
5. Andrews, D. A., & Friesen, W. The differential predictive validity of behavioral self-management assessment with low and high socialization probationers. Unpublished manuscript. Psychology Department, Carleton University, Ottawa, Canada, 1981.

REFERENCES

Adams, R. Differential association and learning principles revisited. *Social Problems*, 1973, **20**, 458–470.

Adams, S. *Evaluation research in corrections: A practical guide.* Washington, D.C.: U.S. Department of Justice, 1975 (a).

Adams, S. Evaluation: A way out of rhetoric. Paper presented at the Evaluation Research Conference, Seattle, Washington, 1975 (b).

Addie, D. *An exploration of the sex differences in the correlates of criminality.* Unpublished honors thesis, Carleton University, 1980.

Akers, R. L., Krohn, M.D., Lonza-Kaduce, L., & Radosevich, M. Social learning and deviant behavior: A specific test of a general theory. American Sociological Review, 1979, **44**, 635–655.

Alexander, J. F., & Parsons, B. V. Short-term behavioral intervention with delinquent families: Impact on family process and recidivism. *Journal of Abnormal Psychology*, 1973, **81**, 219–225.

Andrews, D. A. *Outcome evaluations of group counselling in corrections.* Paper presented at the Symposium on Corrections, Ontario Psychological Association Meeting, Ottawa, Feb., 1974.

Andrews, D. A. *The friendship model of voluntary action and controlled evaluations of correctional practices: Notes on relationships with behaviour theory and criminology.* Toronto: Ontario Ministry of Correctional Services, 1979 (a).

Andrews, D. A. *The dimensions of correctional counselling and of supervisory processes in probation and parole.* Toronto: Ontario Ministry of Correctional Services, 1979 (b).

Andrews, D. A. Some experimental investigations of the principles of differential association through deliberate manipulations of the structure of service systems. *American Sociological Review,* 1980, **45**, 448–462.

Andrews, D. A. *Report on the first year of the assessment and evaluation project.* Toronto: Ontario Ministry of Correctional Services, 1981.

Andrews, D. A. *A personal, interpersonal and community-reinforcement perspective (PIC-R) on deviant behaviour.* Toronto: Ontario Ministry of Correctional Services, forthcoming.

Andrews, D. A., & Kiessling, J. J. Program structure and effective correctional practices: A summary of the CaVIC research. In R. R. Ross & P. Gendreau (Eds.), *Effective correctional treatment.* Toronto: Butterworths, 1980.

Andrews, D. A., Kiessling, J. J., Russell, R. J., & Grant, B. A. *Volunteers and the one-to-one supervision of adult probationers: An experimental comparison with professionals and a field description of process and outcome.* Toronto: Ontario Ministry of Correctional Services, 1979.

Andrews, D. A., Pirs, S., & Hurge, A. *The Ottawa employment project.* Toronto: Ontario Ministry of Correctional Services, 1981.

Andrews, D. A., & Wormith, J. S. *Criminal sentiments and criminal behaviour: A construct validity approach.* Paper presented at the Canadian Congress for the Prevention of Crime, Winnipeg, Manitoba, June, 1981.

Bailey, W. Correctional outcome: An evaluation of 100 reports. *Journal of Criminal Law, Criminology and Police Science,* 1966, **57**, 153–160.

Baird, S. C., Heinz, R. C., & Bemus, B. J. *The Wisconsin case classification/staff development project: A two-year follow-up report.* Madison, Wis.: Division of Corrections, 1979.

Bandura, A. *Principles of behavior modification.* New York: Holt, Rinehart and Winston, 1969.

Bandura, A. *Social learning theory.* Englewood Cliffs, N.J.: Prentice-Hall, 1977.

Bandura, A. In search of pure unidirectional determinants. *Behavior therapy,* 1981, **12**, 13–40.

Banks, J., & Rardin, R. L. Measurement practice in intensive and special adult probation. *Evaluation Quarterly,* 1978, **2**, 127–140.

Barton, M., & Jenkins, W. O. *The Maladaptive Behavior Record (MBR): A scale for the analysis and prediction of community adjustment and recidivism of offenders.* Elmore, Ala.: National Technical Information Services,1973.

Barton, R. R., & Turnbull, B. W. Evaluation of recidivism data: Use of failure rate regression models. *Evaluation Quarterly,* 1979, **3**, 629–641.

Bennett, L. A., Sorensen, D. E., & Forshay, H. The application of self-esteem measures in a correctional setting: I. Reliability of the scale and relationships to other measures. *Journal of Research in Crime and Delinquency,* 1971, **8**, 1–9.

Berger, E. The relation between expressed acceptance of self and expressed acceptance of others. *Journal of Abnormal and Social Psychology*, 1952, **47**, 778–782.

Berger, R. J., Crowley, J. E., Gold, M., Gray, J., & Arnold, M. *Experiment in a juvenile court: A study of a program of volunteers working with juvenile probationers*. Ann Arbor, Mich.:Institute for Social Research, 1975.

Berkowitz, L. *Aggression: A social psychological analysis*. New York: McGraw-Hill, 1962.

Bernal, M. E., Kinnert, M. D., & Schultz, L. A. Outcome evaluation of behavioral parent training and client-center parent counseling for children with conduct problems. *Journal of Applied Behavioral Analysis*, 1980, **13**, 677–691.

Bonta, J. *Prediction of success in community resource centres*. Paper presented at the 34th Annual Convention of the Ontario Psychological Association, Toronto, 1981.

Burgess, R. L., & Akers, R. L. A differential association-reinforcement theory of criminal behavior. *Social Problems*, 1966, **14**, 128–147.

Carroll, J. S., & Payne, J. W. Crime seriousness, recidivism risk, and causal attributions in judgments of prison terms in students and experts. *Journal of Applied Psychology*, 1977, **62**, 595–602.

Chandler, M. J. Egocentrism and antisocial behavior: The assessment and training of social perspective-taking skills. *Developmental Psychology*, 1973, **9**, 326–332.

Cone, J. D. The Behavioral Assessment Grid (BAG): A conceptual framework and a taxonomy. *Behavior Therapy*. 1978, **9**, 882–888.

Cook, T. J., & Scioli, F. P. *The effectiveness of volunteer programs in courts and corrections: An evaluation of policy related research*. Washington, D.C.: National Science Foundation, 1975.

Craft, M., Stephenson, G., & Granger, C. A controlled trial of authoritarian and self-governing regimes with adolescent psychopaths. *American Journal of Orthopsychiatry*, 1964, **34**, 543–554.

Daigle-Zinn, W. J., & Andrews, D. A. Role playing versus didactic discussion in short-term interpersonal skill training with young incarcerated offenders. *Canadian Journal of Criminology*, 1980, **22**, 320–329.

Davison, G. C., & Stuart, R. B. Behavior therapy and civil liberties. *American Psychologist*, 1975, **30**, 755–763.

Dean, D. Alienation: Its meaning and measurement. *American Sociological Review*, 1961, **26**, 753–771.

Donovan, J. E., & Jessor, R. Adolescent problem drinking: Psychosocial correlates in a national sample study. *Journal of Studies on Alcohol*, 1978, **39**, 1506–1524.

Empey, L. T., & Erickson, M. L. *The Provo experiment: Evaluation community control of delinquency*. Lexington, Mass.: Lexington Books, 1972.

Epstein, S. The stability of behavior: On predicting most of the people much of the time. *Journal of Personality and Social Psychology*, 1979, **37**, 1097–1126.

Erickson, M. L., Gibbs, J. P., & Jensen, G. F. Conventional and special crime and delinquency rates. *The Journal of Criminal Law and Criminology*, 1977, **68**, 440–453.

Ferdinand, T. N. An evaluation of milieu therapy and vocational training as methods for the rehabilitation of youthful offenders. *Journal of Criminal Law, Criminology and Police Science*, 1962, **53**, 49–54.

Fixsen, D. L., Phillips, E. L., Phillips, E. A., & Wolf, M. M. The teaching-family model of group home treatment. In W. E. Craighead, A. E. Kazdin, & J. J. Mahoney (Eds.), *Behavior modifications: Principles, issues and applications*. Boston: Houghton Mifflin, 1976.

Freedman, B. J., Rosenthal, L., Donahoe, C. P., Schlundt, D. G., & McFall, R. M. A social-behavioral analysis of skill deficits in delinquent and nondelinquent adolescent boys. *Journal of Consulting and Clinical Psychology*, 1978, **46**, 1448–1462.

Friedlander, F., & Greenberg, S. Effect of job attitudes, training and organizational climate on the performance of the hard-core unemployed. *Journal of Applied Psychology*, 1971, **55**, 287–295.

Gendreau, P., & Andrews, D. A. Psychological consultation in correctional agencies: Case studies and general issues. In J. J. Platt & J. Wicks (Eds.), *The psychological consultant*. New York: Grune & Stratton, 1979.

Gendreau, P., Grant, B. A., Leipciger, M., & Collins, C. Norms and recidivism rates for the MMPI and selected experimental scales on a Canadian delinquent sample. *Canadian Journal of Behavioural Science*, 1979, **11**, 21–31.

Gendreau, P., & Leipciger, M. The development of a recidivism measure and its application in Ontario. *Canadian Journal of Criminology and Corrections*, 1978, **20**, 3–17.

Gendreau, P., Madden, P. G., & Leipciger, M. Predicting recidivism with social history information and a comparison of their predictive power with psychometric variables. *Canadian Journal of Criminology*, 1980, **22**, 328–336.

Gendreau, P., & Ross, R. R. Effective correctional treatment: Bibliotherapy for cynics. *Crime and Delinquency*, 1979, **25**(4), 463–489.

Glaser, D. *The effectiveness of a prison and parole system*. Indianapolis: Bobbs-Merrill, 1964.

Glaser, D. Remedies for the key deficiency in criminal justice evaluation research. *Journal of Research in Crime and Delinquency*, 1974, **10**, 144–154.

Gottfredson, M. R. Treatment destruction techniques. *Journal of Research in Crime and Delinquency*, 1979, **16**, 39–54.

Gough, H. *Manual for the California psychological inventory* (Rev. ed.). Palo Alto, Calif.: Consulting Psychologists, 1969.

Grant, J. D., & Grant, M. Q. A group dynamics approach to the treatment of non-conformists in the Navy. *Annals of the American Academy of Political and Social Science*, 1959, **322**, 126–135.

Griffiths, C. T., Klein, J. F., & Verdun-Jones, S. N. *Criminal justice in Canada: An introductory text*. Vancouver: Butterworth & Co., 1980.

Hackler, J. C., & Hagan, J. L. Work and teaching machines as delinquency prevention tools: A four-year follow-up. *Social Services Review*, 1975, **49**, 92–106.

Haley, H. J., & Lerette, P. *Correctional effectiveness project: Report #1—correctional objectives: A set of Canadian options*. A draft report prepared for the Ministry of the Solicitor General of Canada, July, 1981.

Harris, A. R. Imprisonment and the expected value of criminal choice: A specification and test of aspects of the labelling perspective. *American Sociological Review*, 1975, **40**, 71–87.

Hawkins, J. D., Cassidy, C. H., Light, N. B., & Miller, C. Interpreting official records as indicators of recidivism in evaluating delinquency prevention programs. *Criminology*, 1977, **3**, 397–423.

Hirschi, T. *Causes of delinquency*. Berkeley and Los Angeles: University of California Press, 1969.

Hirschi, T., & Hindelang, M. J. Intelligence and delinquency: A revisionist review. *American Sociological Review*, 1977, **42**, 571–587.

Hogan, R. Development of an empathy scale. *Journal of Consulting Psychology*, 1969, **33**, 307–316.

Hooke, J. E. Rating delinquent behavior. *Psychological Reports*, 1970, **27**, 155–158.

Howard, G. S. Response-shift bias: A problem in evaluating interventions with pre/post self-reports. *Evaluation Review*, 1980, **4**, 93–106.

Hudson, J. Problems of measurement in criminal justice. In L. Rutman (Ed.), *Evaluation research methods: A basic guide*. London: Sage Publications, 1977.

Hunt, G. M., & Azrin, N. H. A community-reinforcement approach to alcoholism. *Behavioral Research and Therapy*, 1973, **11**, 91–104.

Jenkins, W. O., & Sanford, W. L. *A manual for the use of the Environmental Deprivation Scale (EDS) in corrections: The prediction of criminal behavior*. Montgomery, Ala.: Rehabilitation Research Foundation, 1972.

Jesness, C. F. Comparative effectiveness of behavior modification and transactional analysis programs for delinquents. *Journal of Consulting and Clinical Psychology*, 1975, **43**, 758–779.

Jessor, R., & Jessor, S. L. *Problem behavior and psychosocial development: A longitudinal study of youth*. New York: Academic Press, 1977.

Johnson, R. E. *Juvenile delinquency and its origins*. Cambridge, England: Cambridge University Press, 1979.

Kellar, S. L., & Carlson, K. A. Development of an index to evaluate programs in a correctional setting. *Canadian Journal of Criminology and Corrections*, 1977, **19**, 273–277.

Kiessling, J. J., & Andrews, D. A. Behaviour analysis systems in corrections: A new approach to the synthesis of correctional theory, practice, management and research. *Canadian Journal of Criminology*, 1980, **22**, 412–427.

Kirby, B. C. Measuring effects of treatment of criminals and delinquents. *Sociology and Social Research*, 1954, **38**, 368–374.

Klein, M. W. *Street gangs and street workers*. Englewood Cliffs, N.J.: Prentice-Hall, 1971.

Lambert, M. J., DeJulio, S. S., & Stein, D. M. Therapist interpersonal skills: Process, outcome, methodological considerations and recommendations for future research. *Psychological Bulletin*, 1978, **85**, 467–489.

Lerman, P. *Community treatment and social control*. Chicago: University of Chicago Press, 1975.

Linden, E., & Hackler, J. Affective ties to delinquency. *Pacific Sociological Review*, 1973, **16**, 27–46.

Lipton, D. Martinson, R., & Wilks, J. *The effectiveness of correctional treatment: A survey of treatment evaluation studies*. New York: Praeger, 1975.

Lloyd, M. R., & Joe, G. W. Recidivism comparisons across groups: Methods of estimation and tests of significance for recidivism rates and asymptotes. *Evaluation Quarterly*, 1979, **3**, 105–117.

Logan, C. H. Evaluation research in crime and delinquency: A reappraisal. *Journal of Criminal Law, Criminology and Police Science*, 1972, **63**, 378–387.

Madden, P. G. *Factors related to level of supervision among probationers in Ontario.* Toronto: Ontario Ministry of Correctional Services, 1978.

Maltz, M. D., & McLeary, R. The mathematics of behavioral change: Recidivism and construct validity. *Evaluation Quarterly*, 1977, **1**, 421–438.

Marks, J. B., & Glaser, E. M. The antecedents of chosen joblessness. *American Journal of Community Psychology*, 1980, **8**, 173–201.

Martinson, R. California research at the crossroads. *Crime and Delinquency*, 1976, **22**, 178–191.

Martinson, R. What works?—Questions and answers about prison reform. *The Public Interest*, 1974, **35**, 22–54.

Massimo, J. L., & Shore, M. F. The effectiveness of a comprehensive vocationally-oriented psychotherapeutic program for adolescent delinquent boys. *American Journal of Orthopsychiatry*, 1963, **33**, 634–642.

Mayer, R. R. *Social planning and social change.* Englewood Cliffs, N. J.: Prentice-Hall, 1972.

Mischel, W. Preference for delayed reinforcement and social responsibility. *Journal of Abnormal and Social Psychology*, 1961, **62**, 1–7.

Moberg, D. D., & Ericson, R. L. A new recidivism outcome index. *Federal Probation*, 1972, **36**, 50–57.

Murphy, B. C. *A quantitative test of the effectiveness of an experimental treatment program for delinquent opiate addicts.* Ottawa: Information Canada, 1972.

Nettler, G. *Explaining crime* (2nd ed.). Toronto: McGraw-Hill, 1978.

Nye, F. I., & Short, J. F. Scaling delinquent behavior. *American Sociological Review*, 1957, **22**, 326–331.

O'Donnell, C. R., Lydgate, T., and Fo, W. S. O. The buddy system: Review and follow-up. *Child Behavior Therapy*, 1979, **1**, 161–169.

Palmer, T. The youth authorities community treatment project. *Federal Probation*, 1974, **38**, 3–13.

Palmer, T. Martinson revisited. *Journal of Crime and Delinquency*, 1975, **12**, 133–152.

Patterson, G. R. Interventions for boys with conduct problems: Multiple settings, treatments and criteria. *Journal of Consulting and Clinical Psychology*, 1974, **42**, 471–481.

Persons, R. W. Psychological and behavioral change in adolescents following psychotherapy. *Journal of Clinical Psychology*, 1966, **22**, 337–340.

Peterson, D. R., Quay, H. C., & Cameron, G. R. Personality and background factors on juvenile delinquency as inferred from questionnaire responses. *Journal of Consulting Psychology*, 1959, **23**, 395–399.

Platt, J. J., Perry, G. M., & Metzger, D. S. The evaluation of a heroin addiction program within a correctional environment. In R. R. Ross & P. Gendreau (Eds.), *Effective correctional treatment.* Toronto: Butterworths, 1980.

Porteus, S. D. *Porteus maze test: Fifty years application.* Palo Alto, Calif.: Pacific Books, 1965.

Quay, H. C., & Love, C. T. The effects of a juvenile diversion program on rearrest. *Criminal Justice and Behavior*, 1977, **4**, 377–396.

Renner, J. C. *The adult probationer in Ontario*. Toronto: Ontario Ministry of Correctional Services, 1978.

Rogers, S. *Factors related to recidivism among adult probationers in Ontario*. Toronto: Ontario Ministry of Correctional Services, 1981.

Rogers, S. *An examination of adult training centres in Ontario. 3. Community follow-up*. Toronto: Ontario Ministry of Correctional Services, 1980.

Rosenberg, F. R., & Rosenberg, M. Self-esteem and delinquency. *Journal of Youth and Adolescence*, 1978, **7**, 279–294.

Ross, R. R., & Gendreau, P. (Eds.). *Effective correctional treatment*. Toronto: Butterworths, 1980.

Rotter, J. B. Generalized expectancies for internal versus external control of reinforcement. *Psychological Monographs: General and Applied*, 1966, **80**, 1–28.

Russell, R. J., Andrews, D. A., & Kiessling, J. J. Some operational aspects of research in probation and parole. In D. A. Andrews, J. J. Kiessling, R. J. Russell, & B. A. Grant, *Volunteers and the one-to-one supervision of adult probationers: An experimental comparison with professionals and a field-description of process and outcome*. A CaVIC Module, Module II, Volume 2. Toronto: Ontario Ministry of Correctional Services, 1979.

Sarason, I. G., & Ganzer, V. J. Modeling and group discussions in the rehabilitation of juvenile delinquents. *Journal of Counseling Psychology*, 1973, **20**, 442–449.

Schmidt, P., & Witte, A. D. Evaluating correctional programs: Models of criminal recidivism and an illustration of their use. *Evaluation Review*, 1980, **4**, 585–600.

Schur, E. M. *Radical nonintervention: Rethinking the delinquency problem*. Englewood Cliffs, N.J.: Prentice-Hall, 1973.

Seidan, E., Rappaport, J., & Davidson, W. S. Adolescents in legal jeopardy: Initial success and replication of an alternative to the criminal justice system. In R. R. Ross & P. Gendreau (Eds.), *Effective correctional treatment*. Toronto: Butterworths, 1980.

Sellin, T. The significance of records of crime. *The Law Quarterly Review*, 1951, **67**, 489–504.

Sellin, T., & Wolfgang, M. E. *The measurement of delinquency*. New York: Wiley, 1964.

Shelley, E. L. V., & Johnson, W. F. Evaluating an organized counseling service for youthful offenders. *Journal of Counseling Psychology*, 1961, **8**, 351–354.

Short, J. F. Differential association and delinquency. *Social Problems*, 1957, **4**, 233–239.

Stephenson, R. M., & Scarpitti, F. R. *Group interaction as therapy: The use of small groups in corrections*. Westport, Conn.: Green Wood Press, 1974.

Stollmack, S., & Harris, C. M. Failure rate analysis applied to recidivism data. *Operations Research*, 1974, **22**, 1192–1205.

Struening, E. L., & Richardson, A. H. A factor analytic exploration of the alienation, anomia and authoritarianism domain. *American Sociological Review*, 1965, **30**, 768–776.

Taylor, I., Walton, P., and Young, J. *The new criminology: For a social theory of deviance*. London: Routledge, 1973.

Truax, C. B., Wargo, D. G., & Volksdorf, N. R. Antecedents to outcome in group counseling with institutionalized juvenile delinquents. *Journal of Abnormal Psychology*, 1970, **76**, 235–242.

Waldo, G. P., & Chiricos, T. G. Work release and recidivism: An empirical evaluation of a social policy. *Evaluation Quarterly*, 1977, **1**, 87–108.

Waldo, G. P., & Griswold, D. Issues in the measurement of recidivism. In L. Sechrest, S. White, & E. Brown (Eds.), *The rehabilitation of criminal offenders: Problems and prospects*. Washington, D.C.: The National Research Council, 1979, 225–248.

Wellford, C. Labelling theory and criminology: An assessment. *Social Problems*, 1975, **22**, 332–345.

Wormith, J. S. *Converting prosocial attitude change to behaviour change through self-management training*. Unpublished doctoral dissertation, University of Ottawa, 1977.

Wormith, J. S. *Parole decisions and recidivism scales: Cross-validation in the field*. Paper presented at the Correctional Services Conference (Prairie Region), Winnipeg, Manitoba, 1978.

Wormith, J. S. *Attitude and behaviour change of correctional clientele: A three year follow-up*. Paper presented at the meeting of the Canadian Psychological Association, Quebec City, 1979.

Wormith, J. S., & Goldstone, C. *Employing clinical judgment*. Paper presented at the Correctional Services of Canada's 3rd Annual Conference, Ottawa, 1980.

Wormith, J. S., & Hasenpusch, B. Multidimensional measurement of delayed gratification preference with incarcerated offenders. *Journal of Clinical Psychology*, 1979, **35**, 218–225.

Zuckerman, M. Sensation seeking and psychopathy. In R. D. Hare & D. Schalling (Eds.), *Psychopathic behaviour: Approaches to research*. Toronto: Wiley, 1978.

PART THREE

Assessing Outcome in Select Patient Populations

CHAPTER 8

Assessing Outcome in Patients with Sexual Dysfunctions and Sexual Disorders

ROBERT F. SABALIS

A critical review of attempts to measure the effects of treatments for sexual dysfunctions and sexual disorders is presented in this chapter. Recommendations are made regarding future research and outcome measurement in these areas. Since there have been numerous reports previously on the adequacy of this research (Kilmann, 1978; Kilmann & Auerbach, 1979; Munjack & Kanno, 1979; Sotile & Kilmann, 1977), the discussion focuses on attempts to measure change following treatment. For this reason, studies are not differentiated on the basis of methodological considerations or specific dysfunctions or disorders unless such considerations are specifically relevant.

For the purposes of this review, sexual dysfunctions are defined as inhibitions "in the appetitive or psychophysiological changes that characterize the complete sexual response cycle," whereas sexual disorders are defined as sexual activities in which "unusual or bizarre imagery or acts are necessary for sexual excitement" (American Psychiatric Association, 1980). Outcome-related research into treatments for these two different types of sexual difficulty are discussed separately.

SEXUAL DYSFUNCTIONS

Historical Overview

Although the field of sex therapy is of recent origin, its development has paralleled the earlier development of the field of general psychotherapy. To

The author is grateful to Ms. Debra Clark and Ms. Linda Sumter, without whose assistance this project could not have been completed. Preparation of this chapter was supported in part by National Institute of Mental Health Medical Student Education Grant 5T01MH14370-04.

place the clinical practice of sex therapy and research on the treatment of sexual dysfunctions into perspective, it is useful to briefly compare the origins and development of these related fields.

In the field of psychotherapy, Freud was among the first to investigate the role of psychological factors in what had previously been considered problems of exclusively physical etiology. He established the utility of a "talking cure" for some of these difficulties. An orthodoxy of therapeutic techniques developed, based partly on clinical research and partly on the personality of Freud himself. Techniques of dream analysis and free association, as well as attention to developmental history and sexual conflicts, soon came to be seen as necessary components of, and tools for, psychoanalysis. Despite Freud's own conservatism about the practical utility of psychoanalysis, his followers and popularizers were optimistic about the potential of these new techniques for assisting persons with problems of psychic origin.

Disciples of Freud, however, began to alter his theories. On the basis of their new insights and interpretations, old techniques were adapted and revised and new ones developed for the practice of psychoanalysis and, more generally, psychotherapy.

These psychoanalytically derived theories and systems of psychotherapy remained influential for decades after their development; although, in time, their ultimate utility was questioned. Reappraisal became necessary. Competing explanations for human behavior and methods for behavior change increased in influence. This crisis in the fields of psychiatry, psychology, and psychotherapy resulted in an increased emphasis on research; on specification of therapist, patient, and technique variables; and on matching patients, problems, therapies, and psychotherapists in order to maximize the effectiveness of psychotherapeutic interventions. Theorists and researchers in the area are currently involved in attempts to identify relevant variables and hypothesize and test the relationships among them and translate their findings into clinically useful terms (Garfield, 1978; Parloff et al., 1978).

Similarly, the field of sex therapy became popular following the pioneering work of Masters and Johnson (1966, 1970) on human sexual responses and dysfunctions. Previous clinical and research work in the area by Ellis (1958), Semans (1956), Wolpe (1958), and others had not received the same popular or professional response. An orthodox method for treating sexual problems was stressed by Masters and Johnson; it required the participation of both sexual partners, a dual-sex therapy team, a concentrated (usually two-week) period of daily therapy sessions, and an emphasis on current functioning rather than on historical or developmental issues.

Within a short time, others (Hartman & Fithian, 1972; Kaplan, 1974; Lobitz & Lo Piccolo, 1972) developed alternate programs for the treatment of sexual dysfunctions that did not necessarily follow the specifications of the program in St. Louis. The introduction of these various programs generated a great deal of professional interest and optimism. Each program was touted for its brevity, its time-limited nature, its basis in research, and its phenomenal effectiveness.

Although there was some initial skepticism (Vogl, 1970), clinicians have, in general, afforded these sex therapy programs uncritical praise, whereas researchers in the areas of premature ejaculation and erectile dysfunction (Kilmann & Auerbach, 1979), retarded ejaculation (Munjack & Kanno, 1979), orgasmic dysfunction in women (Kilmann, 1978), and psychogenic male and female sexual dysfunctions (Sotile & Kilmann, 1977; Wright et al. 1977) have consistently emphasized the need for more and better defined research. Recently, even clinicians, disappointed because their results do not approximate those reported by Masters and Johnson and others, have begun to question the adequacy of their techniques and theories. Sex therapy research has been criticized for misleading outcome statistics, nonreplicability of research results, and criterion problems (Zilbergeld & Evans, 1980). The very premises that serve as a foundation for sex therapy have been recently questioned and criticized (Szasz, 1980). Sex therapy and sex therapy research have come of age!

Succeeding sections are devoted to discussion of critical issues in sex therapy outcome research, the current status of sex therapy research, and future directions for research in the treatment of sexual dysfunctions.

Critical Issues in Sex Therapy Outcome Measurement

The measurement of outcome in sex therapy requires consideration of several problems. Some problems are imbedded in the nature of therapy in general: choice of assessment techniques; the locus of judgment regarding success or failure; and relationships to outcome of client, therapist, and treatment variables. Other problems derive from the nature of sexual behavior in particular: the process of sexual responding; the definition of sexual dysfunctions; the relationship of psychological and biological variables in sexual functioning; and the fact that sexual behavior usually takes place in the context of an interpersonal relationship.

Levine (1980) asserted that four conceptually separate components of sexual behavior can be identified: desire; arousal; orgasm; and emotional satisfaction. Others have also found it heuristically and clinically valuable to conceptualize sexual behavior as consisting of interrelated components. Masters and Johnson (1966) viewed the human sexual response cycle as consisting of excitement, plateau, orgasm, and resolution phases. Kaplan (1974) divided the human sexual response into two processes based on the portion of the nervous system involved: arousal, based on parasympathetic nervous system functioning; and orgasm, based on sympathetic nervous system functioning. Zilbergeld and Ellison (1980) differentiated between sexual desire and sexual arousal in their discussion of desire and arousal problems. Each author emphasized the fact that sexual dysfunction can occur in any of these component parts of human sexual behavior. Consequently, attention must be paid to each component part in the assessment of sexual problems and in any attempt to evaluate outcome resulting from sex therapy interventions.

Another issue that requires attention is the fact that most theorists in the field of sex therapy, beginning with Kirkendall and Libby (1966), have defined sexual problems as occurring within a relationship and between sexual partners (Nowinski & Lo Piccolo, 1979). Although the psychosexual history of one partner may be more pathological or more restricted than that of the other partner, there is no such thing as an "uninvolved" partner in sexual problems. Neither partner deserves more or less "blame" for the sexual problem. Neither individual is assigned greater or lesser responsibility for its amelioration. The development of such an attitude in the sexually dysfunctional couple is at the core of most sexual treatment programs. It decreases interpersonal hostility, reduces self-consciousness, and results in a cooperative attitude toward the therapeutic tasks and process. However, for the sex therapist and the sex researcher, this attitude creates unique problems for the definition of sexual dysfunctions (Kilmann & Auerbach, 1979), but even more so for the definition of "improvement."

Levine (1980) suggested the concomitant use of three perspectives for determining therapeutic success in outcome reports. Success could be defined as (1) reversal of a previously specified component deficit (e.g., erectile dysfunction), (2) reversal of all an individual's component deficits (e.g., desire, arousal, orgasm, and/or emotional satisfaction), and (3) reversal of all component deficits in both partners. He suggested that the first perspective was the one used most frequently in early research reports. The second perspective was most meaningful in the treatment of only one partner or single individuals. The third perspective was described as most difficult to achieve and thus as yielding the lowest success rates, but as having the greatest significance for the sexual partners. He recommended the use of all three perspectives in outcome reports to encourage more rigorous research and to make outcome data more clinically relevant.

A third issue deserving discussion centers on the locus of judgment of the effectiveness of sex therapy. Is therapeutic success or failure to be judged by the client, by the therapist, or by some societal norm? The absence of reliable data regarding the incidence, prevalence, and spontaneous remission of sexual dysfunctions serves to intensify the complexity of this question and points to the necessity of establishing individualized criteria for outcome measurement. The wide variety in frequency of sexual activity, in types of "normal" sexual behavior, in ease of sexual arousal, in choice of sexual partner, and in ingredients for emotional satisfaction from sexual activity also emphasizes the necessity for individually specified outcome criteria.

A fourth factor of interest is the fact that sexual functioning simultaneously affects and is affected by neuroendocrinologic variables that should be monitored during pretherapy assessment and during outcome evaluation. This is especially true in those cases where chronic illness, alcohol abuse, or drug ingestion are thought to be etiologically related to decreases in libido, lack of sexual arousal, or lack of orgasmic response.

Outcome evaluation in sex therapy shares some problems with outcome measurement in psychotherapy. For example, there is an overall lack of information about the relationship to outcome of client variables, therapist variables, and treatment variables. In a review of the treatment literature for premature ejaculation and impotence, Kilmann and Auerbach (1979) reported that there was little specification in research reports of such basic client variables as age, socioeconomic status, length of sexual relationship, duration of sexual dysfunction, or cooperativeness of sexual partner. Also absent was information about the physical, psychological, and psychiatric status of the client; amount of sexual knowledge; and sexual–social history. Theoretically, all these client variables could be related to outcome measurement in sex therapy in terms of selection of measures and directionality of effects. For example, there have been reports (McGovern et al., 1975; Snyder et al., 1975) that suggest greater incidence of marital discord among women with secondary orgasmic dysfunction than among women with primary orgasmic dysfunction. Also, results of a study by Schneidman and McGuire (1976) suggested that older nonorgasmic women (above age 35) may benefit more from couples therapy than younger women (below age 35), who had significant benefit from a group-oriented approach.

Similarly, the dearth of information about therapist variables that may be relevant to outcome in sex therapy (age, sex, training, experience, therapeutic orientation, professional affiliation, and personality traits) hampers outcome measurement. For example, despite the belief on the part of some sex therapists (Masters & Johnson, 1970) that dual-sex therapy teams are mandatory for effective sex therapy, the question has not yet been subjected to comprehensive investigation. In some studies (Schneidman & McGuire, 1976), the therapist is not specifically identified. In many studies (Zeiss, 1978; Zilbergeld, 1975), the experimenter was also the sex therapist. This injects an element of experimenter bias into the outcome evaluation.

Furthermore, the active, outcome-related process variables in sex therapy have not yet been ascertained. Sex therapy programs vary in terms of length of treatment (two weeks vs. several months) as well as in intensity (daily vs. weekly sessions). The relative merit of massed versus spaced therapeutic tasks has received only minimal attention (Ersner-Hershfield & Kopel, 1979). The effects on transfer of learning resulting from differences in locus of sex therapy (at home vs. away from home) are not known. Such factors may very well have differential impact on specific sexual dysfunctions.

It is not surprising, of course, that these therapist, client, and treatment variables have yet to be systematically addressed by sex therapy researchers. Only recently have psychotherapy researchers begun to seriously investigate them despite the long history of psychotherapy as an organized profession.

Another common problem shared by psychotherapy and sex therapy is the choice of techniques for outcome assessment. There are numerous paper-and-pencil measures of sexual behavior and sexual satisfaction (Schiavi et al.,

1979), but many are of questionable reliability and validity. With some exceptions (Derogatis & Melisaratos, 1979; Lo Piccolo & Steger, 1974), sophisticated test development skills have yet to be brought to bear in this area. It is not yet known how sex therapy procedures affect individual personality functioning, marital functioning, interpersonal and social functioning, or physical functioning. Nevertheless, research studies repeatedly measure such factors in the absence of theoretical rationales and hypothesized relationships for such predictions. For example, the importance of the sexual relationship relative to other aspects of the marital relationship can be expected to differ among couples. Among different couples, therefore, sex therapy may or may not have a significant effect on the marital relationship. In fact, in some marriages where the interpersonal equilibrium has resulted in decreased sexual activities, sex therapy might result in a deterioration of the relationship.

These several issues are among the most critical ones facing sex therapy as the field attempts to provide even more adequate and comprehensive assessment and treatment of sexual dysfunctions to the patient. These are research questions that provide a challenge to sex researchers. Specific recommendations for future research paradigms follow from the discussion above; let us first turn to a discussion of the current status of outcome measurement in sex therapy.

Outcome Measurement in Sex Therapy: Current Status

Tables 8.1 and 8.2 present data regarding outcome criteria from research studies on the treatment of male and female sexual dysfunctions. Table 8.1 summarizes the data from those studies in which the sole outcome measure was subjective self-report by the patient alone. An inspection of Table 8.1 reveals that a majority of studies on the treatment of erectile dysfunction, premature ejaculation, ejaculatory incompetence, orgasmic dysfunction, inhibited sexual excitement, vaginismus, and mixed sexual dysfunctions relied solely on patient self-report for determination of outcome.

Table 8.2 summarizes data from those studies that employed multiple outcome measures. The measures included partner validation of patient reports; behavioral assessment techniques; physiological response measures; paper–pencil tests; and more infrequently, assessment by independent evaluators, hormone level monitoring, and penile plethysmograph measures. The paper–pencil tests included numerous unstandardized adjective checklists, relationship inventories, measures of sexual anxiety and attitudes, symptom checklists, and affect rating scales. The unstandardized nature of these tests made replication difficult. However, the outcome measures also included standardized tests regarding sexual knowledge, sexual behavior, and marital interactions, including the Sex Knowledge and Attitude Test (Lief & Reed, 1972), the Sexual Interaction Inventory (Lo Piccolo & Steger, 1974), and the Locke–Wallace Marital Adjustment Test (Locke & Wallace, 1959).

Inspection of Tables 8.1 and 8.2 also reveals that a majority of research studies included no follow-up measures of treatment effectiveness. Among

Table 8.1.   Studies Using Patient Self-Report as Sole Outcome Measure

Reference	N	Sex	Dysfunction	Follow-Up Period
Alexander, 1974	2	M	Impotence	NS[a]
	2	F	Anorgasmia	
Allison, 1975	1	M	Impotence	NS
Ansari, 1976	65	M	Impotence	NS
Bass, 1974	1	M	Impotence	6 months
Blakeney et al., 1976	38	F	Anorgasmia	2 years
Blight & David, 1978	1	M	Mixed	NS
Brinkley-Birk &	1	F	Vaginismus	NS
Birk, 1975	1	M	Impotence and ejaculatory incompetence	
Cassell, 1977	1	M	Premature ejaculation	NS
Cheek, 1976a	2	F	Frigidity	NS
Cheek, 1976b	1	F	Anorgasmia	NS
Clark, 1976	1	F	Anorgasmia	NS
Deabler, 1976	1	M	Impotence	NS
de Shazer, 1978	1	M	Premature ejaculation	NS
	1	F	Anorgasmia	
Divita & Olsson, 1975	1	M	Impotence	3 months
Duddle, 1977	32	F	Vaginismus	NS
Finkelstein, 1975	1	M	Premature ejaculation	NS
Finkle & Finkle, 1975	62	M	Impotence	NS
Fuchs et al., 1975	1	F	Vaginismus	NS
Gagliardi, 1976	1	M	Ejaculatory incompetence	NS
Gentry, 1978	1	M	Premature ejaculation	12 months
Gottesfeld, 1978	1	F	Vaginismus	NS
Hoch, 1977	8	F	Anorgasmia	NS
Horowitz et al., 1978	1	F	Frigidity	NS
Jacobs, 1977	6	M	Impotence	NS
Jankovich, 1975	23	F	Anorgasmia	NS
Jankovich & Miller, 1978	17	F	Anorgasmia	NS
Jones & Park, 1972	91	C[b]		"Months"
Joseph, 1974	1	F	Anorgasmia	NS
Kelly, 1976	1	M	Ejaculatory incompetence	1 year
Kohlenburg, 1974a	3	C		6 months
Levine, 1975	8	M	Premature ejaculation	NS
Lobitz & LoPiccolo, 1972	8	F	Anorgasmia	6 months
Masters & Johnson, 1970	448	M	Mixed	5 years
	342	F		
McGuire & Wagner, 1978	1	F	Inhibited sexual excitement	NS
McWhirter & Mattison, 1978	22	M	Mixed	NS
Meyer et al., 1975	16	C		NS
Mudd, 1977	1	M	Impotence	NS
Newell, 1976	1	M	Ejaculatory incompetence	1 year
Rathus, 1978	1	M	Ejaculatory incompetence	1 year
Reynolds, 1978	30	M	Erectile dysfunction	NS
Robinson, 1975	23	F	Anorgasmia	NS

(continued)

Table 8.1.   *(continued)*

Reference	N	Sex	Dysfunction	Follow-Up Period
Shahar & Jaffe, 1978	1	F	Vaginismus	8 months
Wijesinghe, 1977	1	F	Inhibited sexual excitement	NS
Yulis, 1976	37	M	Premature ejaculation	6 months
Zilbergeld, 1975	26	M	Premature ejaculation or erectile dysfunctions	4 months

[a]Not specified.
[b]Couples.

those studies containing follow-up data, the mean follow-up period was 9.7 months, with periods varying from six weeks to five years.

Biopsychosocial Model of Human Sexual Response

Although it has been useful for clinicians and researchers engaged in the study of human sexual behavior to identify particular phases of sexual functioning (Kaplan, 1974; Levine, 1980; Masters & Johnson, 1966), it is misleading to conceive of these phases as discrete, independent units. Human sexual behaviors are multidirectional, multidimensional phenomena. For both scientific and clinical purposes, it is useful to apply the biopsychosocial model of Engel (1977, 1980) to human sexual functioning. Such a model serves to remind clinicians and researchers that type of pretherapy assessment and posttherapy assessment and posttherapy evaluation in sex therapy depends on the level of observation of the sexual behavior. The model also reinforces attempts to ensure that assessment and evaluation are multimodal and multidimensional. The dimensions evaluated differ for different patients, different dysfunctions, and different hypothesized etiologies.

In a study of the effects of systematic desensitization on "chronic frigidity," Lazarus (1963) anticipated the need for multimodal outcome evaluation. He specified the following criteria for "successful" treatment: the subject must look forward to sex; she must nearly always experience orgasm; and she should initiate sex at times. The criteria included subjective expectations, physiological response, and initiatory behavior. Others have also attempted multilevel evaluation, but only on a very limited basis. Recently there have been additional requests for this type of evaluation (Derogatis & Melisaratos, 1979; Kilmann & Auerbach, 1979; Wright et al., 1977).

The biopsychosocial model acknowledges that human sexual behavior is affected by individual and interpersonal factors, by psychodynamic and sociocultural factors, and by psychological and biological variables. The model also emphasizes that attention must be paid to both behavioral and phenomenological aspects of sexual behavior.

Table 8.2. Studies Using Multiple Outcome Measures

Reference	N	Sex	Dysfunction	Follow-Up Period	Outcome Measures
Asirdas & Beech, 1975	11 12	M F	Mixed Mixed	NS[a]	Partner interview Attitude scales Self-report
Auerbach & Kilmann, 1977	16	M	Erectile failure	NS	Telephone interview of partner Sexual and nonsexual relationship inventories Self-report Success/experience ratio
Benkert et al., 1975	20	M	Impotence	NS	Sex Behavior Questionnaire Hormone level monitoring
Benkert et al., 1976	12	M	Impotence	NS	Behavior Questionnaire Hormone level monitoring Self-report
Brown et al., 1978	7	M	Parkinson's disease	NS	Sexual Interest Scale Affect Rating Scale Interview
Caird & Wincze, 1974	1	F	Inhibited sexual excitement	NS	Bentler Scale Willoughby Scale Fear Survey Schedule Assertive Questionnaire Spouse report Self-report
Carney et al., 1978	32	F	Inhibited sexual excitement	NS	Weekly diary Anxiety Questionnaire Therapist assessment Assessment by "blind" interviewer

(continued)

213

Table 8.2. *(continued)*

Reference	N	Sex	Dysfunction	Follow-Up Period	Outcome Measures
Ersner-Hershfield & Kopel, 1979	22	F	Orgasmic dysfunction	NS	LWMAT[b] General Information Questionnaire Survey of sexual activities SII[c]
Fisher et al., 1975	8	M	Impotence	NS	Penile response measure EEG EOG EMG
Golden et al., 1978	15	C[d]	Premature ejaculation and orgasmic dysfunction	2 months	SII Background Information Questionnaire Goals for Sex Therapy LWMAT
Herman & Prewitt, 1974	1	M	Impotence	NS	Penile response measure (strain gauge)
Hogan. 1975	?	F	Frigidity	NS	MMPI Self-report
Husted. 1975	1	F	Vaginismus	6 weeks	Sexual Anxiety Questionnaire Sexual Attitude Questionnaire Self-report
Kockott et al., 1975	24	M	Erectile dysfunction	NS	Interview Adjective Rating Scale Anxiety Rating Scale Penile response measure
La Femina, 1977	1	M	Impotence	NS	Self-report Partner report

Study	N	Sex	Dysfunction	Follow-up	Measures
Leiblum & Ersner-Hershfield, 1977	16	F	Mixed	NS	General Information Questionnaire Body Attitude Scale Expectancy Questionnaire SKAT[c] Assertion Inventory LWMAT SII
Leiblum et al., 1976	6	C	Mixed	6 weeks	SII LWMAT Telephone structured interview
Levine & Agle, 1978	16	M	Impotence	12 months	SII Interview by independent evaluator
McGovern et al., 1975	12	F	Anorgasmia	NS	Background Information Questionnaire SII LWMAT
McMullen, 1977	60	F	Orgasmic dysfunction	NS	Card sort SII Battery of unspecified tests Interview by independent rater
McMullen & Rosen, 1979	60	F	Orgasmic dysfunction	NS	Interview SII LWMAT

(continued)

215

Table 8.2. *(continued)*

Reference	N	Sex	Dysfunction	Follow-Up Period	Outcome Measures
Munjack et al., 1976	22	F	Anorgasmia	9 months	Anxiety Scale Symptom Checklist Sexual Adjustment Form MMPI Blind ratings
Nemetz et al., 1978	24	F	Anorgasmia	NS	Card sort Bentler Heterosexual Behavior Hierarchy Rotter Sex Attitude Scale Sexual Semantic Differential Sex Behavior Index by patient and partner Patient interview Partner interview
Obler, 1973	?	F	Anorgasmia	18 months	Sexual Anxiety Scale Taylor Anxiety Scale Heart rate Galvanic skin response Pittsburgh Scale of I/E and Emotionality
O'Gorman, 1978	40	F	Frigidity	NS	Self-report Spouse report Sexual Interest Questionnaire
Perelman, 1977	11	M	Premature ejaculation	NS	SII LWMAT Sexual Attitude and Behavior Questionnaire
Porter, 1978	50	F	Inhibited sexual excitement	NS	Self-report Spouse report

Study	N	Sex	Dysfunction	Follow-up	Measures
Reisinger, 1974	1	F	Orgasmic dysfunction	6 months	Self-report Heart rate monitoring
Reisinger, 1978	6	F	Orgasmic dysfunction	1 year	Heart rate monitoring Self-report Interview
Riley & Riley, 1978	35	F	Orgasmic dysfunction	NS	Self-report Spouse report
Schneidman & McGuire, 1976	20	F	Anorgasmia	6 months	Self-report LWMAT Sexual responsiveness survey
Snyder et al., 1975	1	F	Anorgasmia	3 months	Coital frequency Duration of foreplay Duration of intercourse Percentage of orgasm with masturbation Percentage of orgasm with clitoral stimulation during intercourse
Sotile & Kilmann, 1978	22	F	Anorgasmia	6 weeks	Sexual Behavior and Attitude Questionnaire Sexual Anxiety Scale SII LWMAT
Sotile et al., 1977	6	F	Anorgasmia	6 weeks	Sexual Behavior and Attitude Questionnaire Sexual Anxiety Scale SII LWMAT

(continued)

Table 8.2. *(continued)*

Reference	N	Sex	Dysfunction	Follow-Up Period	Outcome Measures
Spark et al., 1980	105	M	Impotence	NS	Serum testosterone levels Hormone level monitoring
Sue, 1978	1	M	Impotence	NS	Self-report Partner report
Wallace & Barbach, 1974	17	F	Anorgasmia	8 months	Self-Esteem Scale Second Jourard Body Acceptance Scale LWMAT Attitude Toward Women Scale Sexual Acceptance Questionnaire Patient interview Partner interview
Wincze & Caird, 1976	21	F	Inhibited sexual excitement	NS	Self-report Partner report Heterosexual Anxiety Scale Card sort Willoughby Scale Assertiveness Scale Fear Survey Scale
Wincze et al., 1976	6	F	Anorgasmia	NS	Blood Pressure GSR Heart rate Vaginal blood volume Self-report Likert scale rating of sexual responsivity Likert scale rating of awareness of physiological changes Sexual arousability inventory

Study					
Zeiss, 1977	2	M	Premature ejaculation	NS	LWMAT Background Questionnaire Timing by stopwatch of intercourse duration
Zeiss, 1978	18	M	Premature ejaculation	NS	LWMAT Sexual Background Inventory Timing by stopwatch of ejaculatory latency
Zeiss et al., 1978	6	M	Premature ejaculation	8 months	LWMAT Timing by stopwatch of ejaculatory latency
Zeiss et al., 1977	2	F	Anorgasmia	NS	LWMAT SII Self-report Spouse report

[a] Not specified.
[b] Locke-Wallace Marital Adjustment Test.
[c] Sexual Interaction Inventory.
[d] Couples.
[e] Sexual Knowledge and Attitude Test.

A biopsychosocial paradigm of human sexual behavior is presented in Table 8.3. The quality and quantity of sexual behavior is a result of multidirectional interactions among biological, psychological, and interpersonal–societal factors.

Biological determinants of sexual behavior include underlying biochemical and neuroendocrine processes, basic anatomic structures, various components of the nervous system, and the physiological processes of the human sexual response cycle (i.e., excitement, plateau, orgasm, and resolution).

Psychological components include the effects of psychosexual development and sexual history, desire for sexual activity, dynamics of sexual motivation, sexual orientation and sexual knowledge, attitudes, and thoughts. An additional psychological factor is the subjective, internal, individual emotional experience resulting from sexual activities.

Social factors are twofold: interpersonal and societal. Interpersonal elements involve the nature and emotional quality of the relationship with the sexual partner, as well as partners' expectations arising from the specific interpersonal sexual situation. Societal factors refer to partners' expectations about sexual behavior that result from membership in religious, cultural, racial, age, or socioeconomic reference groups. Societal variables also include the prevalence and incidence of specific sexual behaviors and sexual dysfunctions within these various reference groups.

Assessment of specific persons presenting for treatment of specific sexual dysfunctions must take into account all these biopsychosocial variables to establish the best mode of therapy. A model assessment procedure for one form of sexual dysfunction has been described by Lo Piccolo (1980).

Similarly, change resulting from sex therapy programs must be evaluated individually and dyadically, subjectively and objectively, by means of individually specified criteria. This approach has been recommended elsewhere (Bergin & Lambert, 1978) for individual, group, marital, and family therapies. The definition and evaluation of the "success" of a sex therapy program for orgasmic dysfunction given by a 22-year-old, single, agnostic, upper-middle-class woman would probably be different from those given by a 49-year-old woman who is religious, of a lower-middle-class background, and who has been married for 30 years.

The biopsychosocial conceptualization also focuses attention on other important issues that are frequently ignored in outcome measurement in sex therapy. These include definitional problems in sexual dysfunctions, patterns of help seeking for sexual problems, and the inadequacy of current evaluative instruments for measuring changes resulting from sex therapy. The model underscores the current lack of reliable demographic information about the incidence and prevalence of sexual dysfunctions among various societal groups.

Type of outcome measurement in sex therapy programs depends on the level of observation of the scientist. Psychologists, endocrinologists, physicians, physiologists, and marital therapists view sexual phenomena differently.

Table 8.3. A Biopsychosocial Paradigm of Human Sexual Behavior

Biological Factors	Psychological Factors	Social Factors	
		Interpersonal	Societal
Physiology of the human sexual response cycle	Psychosexual development	Expectations of interpersonal sexual situation	Sexual expectations resulting from reference group membership
Anatomy of the human sexual response	Sexual history	Nature of the interpersonal relationship	Incidence of sexual behaviors and dysfunctions
Biochemistry of the human sexual response cycle	Desire for sexual activity	Emotional quality of the interpersonal relationship	Prevalence of sexual behaviors and dysfunctions
Neurological factors	Sexual motivation	Partner's emotional response	
	Sexual thoughts	Partner's sexual response	
	Sexual knowledge		
	Sexual attitudes		
	Sexual orientation		
	Subjective emotion satisfaction		

221

The data derived from their observations may be different, but they are interrelated and complementary. Their frames of reference are not mutually exclusive; they are not "right" or "wrong." This biopsychosocial perspective spans the biological, psychological, and social dimensions. It extends the scientific method to previously neglected areas. It can provide a blueprint for research in sex therapy, a format for teaching, and a plan of action for therapy.

It would not be surprising to find reduced improvement rates from initial research efforts in the treatment of sexual dysfunctions with the biopsychosocial model. As noted by Levine (1980), presentation of outcomes in a multifactorial perspective will reveal both the strengths and weaknesses of sex therapy methodologies. Resolution of one sexual dysfunction in one individual will be less clinically meaningful that the resolution of all sexual deficits in both marital partners. However, the first perspective will yield significantly higher success rate than will the second perspective. Nevertheless, over time, greater specification of relevant variables and more comprehensive evaluation and treatment procedures should result from biopsychosocial research efforts. Gradual increases in improvement rates should follow, with concomitant increases in the clinical utility of these results.

Implications of the Biopsychosocial Model for Outcome Measurement in Sex Therapy

The biopsychosocial model has important implications for outcome measurement in sex therapy research. This section is devoted to a series of conclusions and recommendations about evaluation in future sex therapy programs.

Conclusion and Recommendation 1. Outcome Evaluation Must Reflect the Multidimensionality of Sexual Behavior

Attention must be paid concurrently to biological, psychological, and social variables that affect all sexual behaviors. Table 8.4 presents a preliminary biopsychosocial paradigm for outcome measurement in sex therapy. Multiple, overlapping, and complementary methods of assessing outcome in sex therapy programs are enumerated.

Conclusion and Recommendation 2. Outcome Evaluation in Sex Therapy Should Include Evaluation of Appropriate Biological Variables

Outcome assessment of sex therapy programs should include specific evaluation of the human sexual response cycle (i.e., excitement, plateau, orgasm, and resolution) to evaluate the adequacy of those physiological aspects of sexual behavior and to establish under what conditions they do and do not occur. In the past, because of societal and ethical restrictions on the actual viewing of sexual behavior, this has been accomplished primarily by means of the client's subjective self-report. Future research should seek to supplement self-report measures when possible with physiological measures (e.g., phallometry and heart rate monitoring) in laboratory test situations subject to the limitations of

Table 8.4. A Biopsychosocial Paradigm for Outcome Measurement in Sex Therapy

Biological Factors	Psychological Factors	Social Factors	
		Interpersonal	Societal
Physiological measures	Self-report	Measure of expectancies	Assessment of reference group expectancies about sexual behavior
Behavioral assessment	Behavioral assessment	Measurement of goals for sex therapy	
Hormonal monitoring	Personality assessment	Measures of quality of interpersonal relationship	Comparative incidence and prevalence data
Physical examination	Measures of sexual knowledge and attitudes	Assessment of couple's sexual interaction	Follow-up data
Neurological evaluation	Measures of sexual defensiveness		
	Posttherapy questionnaires		
	Card sort		
	Semantic differential		
	Life history interviews or questionnaires		
	Measures of sexual anxiety		
	Assessment by independent evaluators		

such measures (Freund, 1976). Kockott et al. (1975) reported no differential results in penile response measures in a study of the effectiveness of systematic desensitization procedures for impotence. However, Herman and Prewitt (1974) found that monitoring of penile responses was a useful outcome measure in the biofeedback treatment of erectile dysfunction. Reisinger (1974) found heart rate monitoring to be a reliable and valid measure of sexual response in the treatment of an anorgasmic woman.

Investigations of relationships among hormonal variables, sexual arousal, and sexual behavior (Schiavi, 1976; Schwartz et al., 1980) and among verbal report, overt behavior, and physiological responses (Lang, 1971) have yielded equivocal results. Some studies do suggest a two-way relationship between neuroendocrine factors and sexual functioning (Fox et al., 1972; Pirke et al., 1974; Purvis et al., 1976; Spark et al., 1980), whereas evidence from other studies (Brown et al., 1978; Kraemer et al., 1976; Raboch & Starka, 1972) does not support a reliably predictable relationship. Medications, fatigue, chronic illness, and emotional disorders can have adverse effects on sexual functioning because of decreased levels of sexual hormones in the bloodstream (Kaplan, 1974; Kreuz et al., 1972). Therefore, especially in subjects where hormonal, stress, and/or physical factors are thought to play an etiologic role in sexual difficulties, outcome measures should investigate these variables in evaluating treatment effects.

Attention to hormonal factors can also lead to increased knowledge about the activity or inactivity of specific hormones in primary and secondary sexual dysfunctions. For example, Benkert et al. (1975) found that the application of luteinizing hormone-releasing hormone (LHRH) in a group of 20 endocrinologically normal men with erectile dysfunctions produced significantly greater therapeutic effect than a placebo; however, in another study (Benkert et al., 1976), no beneficial effect over placebo was found with an oral synthetic thyroid-releasing factor (TRF) preparation.

Additionally, behavioral assessment (e.g., stopwatch timing of ejaculatory latency by the client, a success:experience ratio) can be a valuable supplement at the biological level of observation to self-report measures in evaluating the effectiveness of treatments for specific sexual dysfunctions. At the very least, behavioral assessment techniques should assist in the quantification of subjective ratings.

Conclusion and Recommendation 3. Theory Development Is Needed Regarding Relationships Between Psychological Factors and Sexual Behavior

For physiological arousal to take place, the desire for sexual activities must be stimulated in an individual. Psychologically, such motivation is a function of an individual's psychosexual history, personality traits, and situational variables. Such issues of sexual desire have only recently received significant attention from sex therapy researchers (Kaplan, 1979; Kolodny et al., 1979; Lo Piccolo, 1980; Zilbergeld & Ellison, 1980).

Other hypothesized psychological components of the sexual process have received frequent attention from researchers, although more often in the investigation of female sexual dysfunctions. It almost appears, from the comparative amount of research paid to these variables in women and men, that sex researchers adhere to the notion that women are, in general, more psychologically and emotionally involved in their sexual behavior than are men.

Although anxiety has been causally related to sexual dysfunction in men and women, current research on other types of personality variables reflects attempts to empirically determine relationships between specific psychological variables and specific types of sexual dysfunction. It does not yet appear to be based on theoretically derived hypotheses of relationships between them. The literature abounds with contradictory findings in this area. Munjack, et al., (1978) found that premature and retarded ejaculators were significantly depressed and anxious and that they gave evidence of more general psychopathology than did persons in a control group. Their results supported earlier notions of a link between sexual difficulties and various psychiatric problems, including anxiety neuroses (Lidberg, 1972), general level of hostility (Cooper, 1968), and obsessive compulsive personality style (Gagliardi, 1976). The directionality of such effects is, of course, more difficult to ascertain.

No significant changes have been reported as a result of participation in sex therapy programs in measures of attitudes toward women, self-esteem, or body acceptance in women (Wallace & Barbach, 1974), measures of neuroticism or assertiveness (Wincze & Caird, 1976), or on the Eysenck Personality Inventory (Munjack et al., 1976). On the other hand, changes were reported as a function of sex therapy participation on some Minnesota Multiphasic Personality Inventory clinical scales and a symptom checklist (Munjack et al., 1976); on measures of overall sexual anxiety (Sotile & Kilmann, 1978); on the Fear Survey Schedule (Wincze & Caird, 1976); and on a sexual anxiety card sort and semantic differential (Nemetz et al., 1978).

Obviously, greater attention must be devoted to theory development regarding the relationship between personality factors and sexual behavior before significant advances are made in outcome assessment at the psychological level of observation.

Conclusion and Recommendation 4. Development of More Sophisticated Test Instruments Is Necessary

Although there are numerous measures of psychological factors related to sexual functioning in print (Schiavi et al., 1979), many of these have questionable reliability and validity. In many instances, normative data are incomplete or unreported. Few have been subject to methods that are standard in the development of useful psychological tests in other areas (Campbell & Fiske, 1959). Outcome measurement of sex therapy programs in the future is greatly dependent on the drastic improvement of the measures that provide the raw data of experimentation.

The relationship between individual personality factors and individual sexual behavior is not currently well understood theoretically. The relationships among individual attitudes and cognitions, personality, fantasy, and overt behavior are also not yet clearly understood by sex researchers. Therefore, at this point in time, psychological variables can best be tapped (for men and women) by using multiple supplemental sources of information including self-report measures, personality assessment measures, and standardized tests of sexual knowledge and attitudes and sexual functioning (e.g., the Derogatis Sexual Function Inventory and the Sex Knowledge and Attitude Test). In addition, posttherapy questionnaires, including measures of sexual defensiveness such as those suggested by Nowinski and Lo Piccolo (1979), can be valuable as a means of evaluating clients' truthfulness in responding. At this time, "situational" measures may be more promising than measures involving overall personality assessment (Bergin & Lambert, 1978).

Similarly, improvement is needed in assessment techniques for evaluating interpersonal issues in sexual relationships. The interpersonal matrix within which sexual behavior occurs can simultaneously affect and be affected by the adequacy of sexual functioning. The Locke–Wallace Marital Adjustment Scale is one instrument commonly used to measure marital adjustment. Such scales, although extremely useful, do not answer important questions about the directionality of effects between sexual satisfaction and relationship satisfaction. It is impossible to partial out the effects of sexual satisfaction or dissatisfaction on the quality of the interpersonal relationship with existing scales. *The development of relationship questionnaires that partial out sexual satisfaction should be a high priority in future research.*

Conclusion and Recommendation 5. Evaluation of Phenomenological Changes Should Accompany Evaluation of Overt Behavioral Changes

One major psychological variable that is perhaps the most difficult to operationalize is the emotional satisfaction derived by an individual from sexual activities. The level or degree of emotional satisfaction is a function of both the quality and quantity of sexual activities. It arises out of adequate sexual desire and adequate biological and psychological arousal. It is dependent on interpersonal factors. As has been noted elsewhere (Bergin & Lambert, 1978), it is more difficult to assess, although equally important, as changes in overt behavior.

Outcome measurement of this subjective variable must rely, at least in part, on global self-report measures. However, even such simple and commonly used psychological techniques for quantifying subjective data as the semantic differential and the card sort can be useful for purposes of comparison in outcome research. They should be more widely used. In addition, replacement of a global estimate of emotional satisfaction derived from the whole sequence of sexual activities with a more specific, situational approach would probably yield more useful information about the effectiveness of specific aspects of a treatment program for specific clients with specific disorders. The level of emotional satisfaction should also be sampled over time so as to generate a mean measure of satisfaction. This would help to avoid the problems associated with single measures that can be adversely affected by a variety of artifactual issues such as fatigue and stress.

Follow-up measures, therefore, are extremely important. Single measures at the end of treatment programs provide extremely limited data; they are subject to numerous demand characteristics, particularly when the experimenters are also the sex therapists (as is frequently the case in sex therapy research). Measures of emotional satisfaction obtained periodically following the termination of therapy can provide information about long-term effectiveness of sex therapy procedures and also about generalizability of sex therapy results.

Conclusion and Recommendation 6. Interpersonal Factors Must Be Acknowledged in Outcome Evaluation

Most sexual activities take place within an interpersonal matrix. Interpersonal factors affect every sexual relationship. Outcome measures must collect data that focus on the relationship, and more specifically, the sexual relationship between two people.

Sexual relationships arise out of the interaction between persons who bring to the relationship different psychosexual histories, experiences, needs, and goals that can affect the subjective satisfaction derived from them. Sex therapies must consider these expectations for determination of their effect on interpersonal sexual behavior, the definition of sexual dysfunction, and their correlation with the perceived success or failure of sex therapy programs. Confirmation of expectations can be sexually arousing, whereas disconfirmation can have adverse effects. Whereas Leiblum and Ersner-Hershfield (1977) did evaluate expectancies and Golden et al. (1978) inquired about goals for therapy, few other studies did so. Furthermore, in this area as in other areas previously mentioned, sex therapy researchers must develop more sophisticated, reliable, and valid techniques for measuring these variables. Techniques such as those suggested by Kiresuk and Sherman (1968) regarding goal attainment may be useful in this regard. Posttherapy questionnaires may also be helpful.

Changes in the overt sexual behavior of both partners as a function of sex therapy are also legitimate targets for outcome measurement. Because of moral–ethical constraints about actually viewing the sexual behavior of others, reports by the couple about actual sexual behaviors must be relied on. This can be accomplished by means of simple subjective self-reports. However, more useful information for research purposes could probably be transmitted from subject to experimenter by means of behavioral assessment reports (e.g., length of penile intromission, length of foreplay, and types of sexual behavior) and standardized instruments such as the Sexual Interaction Inventory, a behaviorally oriented assessment device that focuses on actual and desired frequency, enjoyment by the respondent, and estimates of the partner's enjoyment for seventeen specific sexual activities. Such an instrument deserves attention as an outcome measure.

Conclusion and Recommendation 7. Societal Factors Affecting Sexual Behavior Must Be Investigated in Future Research Programs

Sexual beliefs, experiences, roles, and expectations, as well as definitions of sexual dysfunctions, have been found to differ for members of different social, socioeconomic, religious, and cultural groups (Kinsey et al., 1948, 1953; Lo Piccolo & Heiman, 1977). Attention must be paid to these variables in future sex therapy research. Little information is currently available with respect to correlation of these variables with successful outcome in sex therapy.

Similarly, persons born into different socioeconomic and sociocultural groups report different expectations regarding sexual behavior and different evaluations of the "normality" of various sexual behaviors (oral–genital sex, foreplay, etc.). Such group differences result in differing definitions of sexual dysfunction; differential rates of presentation to health care practitioners for treatment; and, perhaps most important, differences in their definition of successful outcome. They may also result in differences in expectancies between client and therapist, premature termination of treatment, and other such effects previously noted in psychotherapy (Goldstein, 1962). To some degree, such issues have been so far neglected by sex therapists and researchers. Without greater knowledge of the influence of these societal factors on the perception of human sexual behavior and their implications for sex therapy, the effectiveness of specific programs for members of various reference groups cannot be compared, nor can specific recommendations be made following research programs. Better specification of all of these societal variables is necessary for improved outcome measurement.

Comparative data regarding the incidence and prevalence of specific sexual dysfunctions by age, sociocultural, socioeconomic, religious, and other groupings are currently not available. It is difficult to assess the import of a specific sexual dysfunction and the effectiveness of a specific treatment without knowledge of the relative frequency with which the dysfunction occurs in a specific population, its usual course, its rate of indigenous recovery, and so on. These data must be available if meaningful statements about individualized treatment procedures are to be derived from sex therapy research protocols and if sex therapists are to discover what "nonspecific factors" are operative in the amelioration of sexual difficulties. Further outcome criteria cannot be meaningfully developed in the absence of such data. Research at this level of observation has been neglected; it is necessary for future progress.

Other Methodological Considerations

In addition to the paradigmatic suggestions made above, sex therapy researchers should attempt to improve their experimental procedures and methodologies to improve outcome evaluation.

As addressed specifically by Zilbergeld and Evans (1980), researchers must be explicit in their descriptions of client assessment, screening, and both selection and therapy procedures, including timing of procedures and amount of actual therapist–client contact. They must precisely define individualized, specific criteria for improvement or failure and length of follow-up and post-therapy client contact. They must describe the negative effects of treatment (secondary erectile dysfunction, divorce, etc.). This would allow for greater replicability of sex therapy research, which is the foundation of scientific investigation. Replicability in the area of sex therapy has been difficult to achieve to date. In addition, component analysis studies wherein the individual contributions of the several aspects of a total treatment program were investigated would also be quite valuable (Wright et al., 1977). Reduction of the possibility of experimenter bias by having outcome assessment performed by an independent evaluator who is not knowledgeable about experimental groups or experimental hypotheses would greatly improve the validity of outcome measurement.

SEXUAL DISORDERS

The remainder of this chapter is devoted to a discussion of outcome measurement in the treatment of sexual disorders (paraphilias). Because of the recent controversy about the psychiatric status of homosexual men and women, this review does not consider research on efforts to change the sexual orientation of homosexual persons. Also, since transsexualism is considered a disorder of gender and no longer primarily considered a sexual disorder (American Psychiatric Association, 1980), therapeutic attempts to assist transsexual individuals are not discussed. Outcome related research on the treatment on the following paraphilias are included in this section: exhibitionism, fetishism, masochism, pedophilia, sadism, transvestism, voyeurism, and heterogeneous sexual disorders (e.g., sadistic exhibitionism).

There has not been the same degree of research attention to efforts to alter sexually disordered behavior as there has been in the area of sexual dysfunctions. The majority of the research literature consists of single case reports, with only a small number of studies available that contained group data.

Historical Overview

As compared to the orthodoxy of treatment methods that developed early in the history of the sex therapies, the treatment of sexual disorders has been heterogeneous in nature. Table 8.5 presents data from representative research reports about the treatment of sexual deviations and paraphilias. An inspection of Table 8.5 reveals numerous treatment approaches, including conventional group and insight-oriented psychotherapies, various behavioral therapy methods, marital and sex therapies, drug treatment, biofeedback, sex education,

Table 8.5.   Studies Utilizing Various Treatment Modalities in the Treatment of the Paraphilias

Reference	N	Sex	Paraphilia	Treatment	Length of Treatment
Barlow et al., 1969	1	M	Pedophiliac	Covert sensitization	24 sessions, twice weekly
Bebbington, 1977	1	M	Glove fetishist	Classical conditioning	14 sessions over 8 weeks
Biegel, 1967	3	M	Transvestites	Hypnosis	10–14 sessions, weekly
Bond & Evans, 1967	2	M	Fetishists	Shock avoidance therapy	8 weekly sessions
Brownell & Barlow, 1976	1	M	Exhibitionist	Covert sensitization	16 sessions, twice weekly
				Marital therapy	MT: not specified
Carr, 1974	1	M	Transvestite	Extinction Shaping procedures	13 weeks, FNS[a]
Cooper et al., 1972	1	M	Mixed	Antiandrogen drug therapy	Daily, unspecified period
	1	M	Hypersexual		
Eyres, 1960	2	M	Transvestites	ECT	15 sessions, FNS 29 sessions, biweekly over 3 months
Fensterheim, 1974	1	M	Voyeur	Desensitization Covert sensitization Hypnosis	21 sessions over several months
Floch, 1970	1	M	Exhibitionist	Detailed "autobiographical method"	Not specified
Forgione, 1976	2	M	Pedophiliacs	Aversive training Escape training Avoidance training Overlearning Family therapy Assertion training	12 sessions, FNS
Gelder & Marks, 1970	20	M	Mixed	Faradic aversion therapy	Not specified
Gershman, 1970	2	M	Transvestitic fantasies	Thought stopping Covert sensitization Shock aversion therapy	6 sessions, FNS
Hallam & Rachman, 1972	5	M	Mixed	Shock aversion therapy	12–25 sessions, FNS
Hosford & Rifkin, 1975	1	M	Exhibitionist	Relaxation Self-monitoring Desensitization Contingent reinforcement Thought stopping Therapeutic movie	Not specified
Jackson, 1969	1	M	Voyeur	Counterconditioning	8 sessions, FNS

Reference	N	Sex	Paraphilia	Treatment	Length of Treatment
Johnson, 1977	1	M	Exhibitionist	Insight-oriented therapy	3 years
Joseph, 1971	1	M	Fetishist– sadomasochist	Psychoanalysis	$4\frac{1}{2}$ years
MacDonald, 1961	1	M	Transvestite	Sex education Social skills training	6 sessions
Marshall & Lippens, 1977	1	M	Rapist–fetishist	Aversive therapy Orgasmic reconditioning Boredom induction	Treatments 1, 2: 3 times weekly, 12 weeks Treatment 3: 9 sessions, FNS
Mathis & Collins, 1970		M	Exhibitionists	Group therapy	Weekly, 1 year
Pinta, 1978	1	M	Pedophiliac	Antiandrogen drug therapy Psychotherapy	2 months, FNS
Rosen & Kopel, 1977	1	M	Transvestite– exhibitionist	Biofeedback Shaping procedure Marital therapy Sex therapy	18 sessions over 3 weeks
Serber, 1971	15	M	Mixed	Shame aversion therapy Assertiveness training	SAT: once every 3 days, 1–2 weeks AT: 1–2 times week, 1–3 months
Stevenson & Wolpe, 1960	3	M	Pedophiliacs	Reciprocal inhibition therapy	45 sessions over 18 months
Strzyzewsky & Zierhoffer, 1967	1	M	Fetishist–transvestite	Aversion therapy (drug induced)	15 sessions, 3 times daily over 5 days

[a]Frequency not specified.

social skills training, and even electroshock therapy. The length of treatment varied from five days to three years. Many studies did not contain reports of the length or frequency of treatment.

This tremendous variety in treatment approaches for sexual deviations reflects the uncertainty and disagreement among sexual and personality theorists about the etiology of sexually disordered behavior. Is it an outgrowth of other mental disorders (Brancale et al., 1952; Ward, 1975), a result of developmental immaturity (Witzig, 1968), a consequence of accidental maladaptive learning (McGuire et al., 1965; Rachman, 1966), or a concomitant of hypersexuality (Cooper et al., 1972)? Do sexual disorders result from a lack of satisfaction in marital sexual interactions? Is the sexually variant person symptomatic only in the sexual sphere of personality functioning or in other areas as well? Obviously, the answers to these questions will have significant effects on the choice of treatment modality and techniques for outcome measurement.

In contrast to the optimism that enveloped the field of sex therapy since its inception, there has never been the same degree of hopefulness about the long-term success of treatments for sexual disorders. Some of the paraphilias (e.g., exhibitionism, voyeurism, fetishism) are impulsive and/or solitary activities that do not require the cooperation of a willing partner and that can occur at unpredictable times and in unpredictable places. Also, since the paraphilias are associated with sexual arousal and sexual gratification, they are strongly reinforced behaviors. These factors, in combination, make sexual disorders extremely difficult behaviors to gain initial control over and to permanently modify. Research reports on the treatments of sexual disorders have been difficult to interpret because of methodological inadequacies, a lack of follow-up data, and nonspecific criteria for "success" (Kolodny et al., 1979).

Critical Issues in Outcome Measurement in the Treatment of Sexual Disorders

Sexual disorders differ from sexual dysfunctions and from other psychiatric disorders in that the paraphilias are also criminal acts. They can incur relatively mild to relatively severe penalties, depending on the type of paraphilia and the legal jurisdiction. These facts often create a unique relationship between the therapist and the client. The therapist is frequently an agent of society (e.g., employed in a penal system) as well as a therapist. These facts also create some difficulties for pretherapy assessment and posttherapy outcome assessment of persons treated for sexual disorders.

Pretherapy assessment of persons who engage in paraphiliac behavior but who have never been apprehended by legal authorities (nonoffenders) is made difficult because of the potential for prosecution if these activities were to become known. Expectancy and social desirability factors could thus adversely affect the reliability of these pretherapy assessment data and of any comparisons based on them. For these reasons, outcome evaluation following treatment is difficult for both the offender and the nonoffender. It is especially difficult for the offender because of possible legal ramifications and potential effects on probation, parole, and release. The nonoffender may fear the consequences of reporting a lack of positive changes following therapy. The incarcerated offender wishing to be paroled and/or released may not respond truthfully to outcome evaluation measures if there were any suspicion that the results may not be entirely confidential (as well they might not be in a penal setting). This raises ethical considerations about whom the therapist is primarily responsible to: to the individual or to society as symbolized by the prison system. Motivations for treatment of sexual disorders are also problemmatic, especially in a prison population. In prison, no decision by an inmate is completely voluntary and all decisions are in some way related to release. It is often impossible for the therapist to ascertain whether the apparent reasons for participation in sex offender programs are the "real" reasons. It is probably at times difficult for the prisoner–client as well. Such issues have direct implications for outcome evaluation.

The quality of the sexual disorder also has significance for outcome measurement. An experimenter or therapist may be willing to rely on less robust measures (e.g., self-report) to evaluate the outcome of therapy for a nuisance disorder such as obscene telephone calling or voyeurism. However, more stringent measures would probably be required to evaluate treatments for paraphilias (e.g., sadism or masochism) that are potentially injurious to self or others. Outcome assessment would similarly differ, depending on the object of the variant behavior, whether a child, an unwilling adult, or a consenting adult partner. Another factor in outcome measurement would be the necessity of the behavior for sexual arousal and satisfaction: whether it occurs only occasionally for purposes of variety or whether it is required for arousal and/or orgasm.

Another critical issue in the treatment of paraphilias and in the evaluation of treatment effects is the relationship between fantasy and overt behavior. Issues concerning the role of deviant fantasies in the etiology, maintenance, and cessation of deviant overt sexual behaviors are unresolved. One hypothesis has been proposed (McGuire et al., 1965) and tested (Evans, 1968, 1970) that masturbation to deviant fantasy increases the habit strength of the overt deviant behavior. Some clients may present for treatment because sexually variant fantasies result in personal discomfort and disrupt interpersonal and sexual relationships, even though these fantasies have never been overtly acted out. In some instances, therapeutic attempts are made to reduce the strength of the deviant fantasy only (Gershman, 1970; Mees, 1966). In other cases the focus of therapy is on both fantasy and overt behavior (Evans, 1968). Thus outcome measures must be multimodal to ensure assessment of all levels of the paraphiliac behavior, especially since overt behavioral outcome measures (e.g., rearrest, recidivism) are unreliable. The behavior can continue without arrest (Rosen & Kopel, 1977).

Problems in the definition of sexual variance or deviance can also have effects on outcome measurement. Stoller (1975) has hypothesized that the essence of sexual variance is its motivation. He theorized that sexually variant behavior is motivated primarily by hostility and serves to convert childhood trauma to adult triumph. Money and Wiedeking (1980, p. 272), on the other hand, defined a paraphilia as pathological only when it becomes "too severe, too insistent, and too noxious to the partner, or to the self." Mutuality of consent has also presented as a gauge of the pathology of a paraphilia (Money, 1977). Such conflicting definitions can result in widely varying goals of treatment and in widely divergent means of assessing treatment effectiveness. In some instances, the goals of therapy might include the complete cessation of the deviant act (Wijesinghe, 1977). In other cases treatment might be considered "successful" if only the object of the behavior is changed. For example, in a case of homosexual pedophilia (Kohlenburg, 1974b), the chances of apprehension by police and legal prosecution can be reduced by changing the object of the sexual behavior from a child to a consenting adult.

Finally, the relationship to outcome and outcome evaluation of client variables, therapist variables, and treatment variables is as unclear in the treatment of sexual disorders as it is in the treatment of sexual dysfunctions. The most obvious client variable of interest in the treatment of sexual disorders is the sex of the client. In almost all the studies reviewed, the subjects were male. Either the paraphilias are more common among males in this culture, or women do not present for treatment or come to the attention of legal authorities. The current status of research in this area makes it extremely difficult to make definitive statements about relationships to outcome of subjects' age, previous social and sexual experience and skills, general psychiatric or psychological status, legal status, and duration of the sexual deviation because such information was not routinely collected on subjects. Outcome measures for a person whose sexually variant behavior was the only atypical behavior would differ from those for a person with additional serious psychopathology. Outcome measures for an individual who had extremely poor social and/or heterosexual skills would differ from those for a person with a well-developed social skill repertoire.

Very few studies reported the professional affiliation or extent of professional experience of the therapists. Among those studies that did report therapist sex, most of the therapists were males. Sex may be an important variable in terms of therapeutic outcome in some paraphilias (e.g., transvestism and exhibitionism). Also, the fact that the therapist was also the experimenter in some studies (Maletzsky, 1974) would indicate that the outcome data may have been subject to the effects of experimenter bias.

The heterogeneity of procedures used in the treatment of sexual disorders has already been discussed. The behavioral forms of treatment were usually carefully described in the procedures sections of the research reports so that replication of these procedures could be readily accomplished (Maletzsky, 1974). However, in other studies (Anonymous et al., 1976), experimental procedures were so vaguely described that replication would be impossible. Some behavioral approaches were supplemented by unspecified "supportive" therapy (Wijesinghe, 1977) for periods of time at unknown intervals. Such reports make it difficult to ascertain the active elements in successful treatment or to determine "nonspecific" therapeutic effects. Spacing of treatment was also quite variable, ranging from 400 trials of faradic aversion over six days (Blakemore et al., 1963) to biweekly sessions (Barlow et al., 1969) to weekly sessions (Hughes, 1977). Some studies did not specify frequency of sessions (Jackson, 1969), whereas others did not specify any time format at all (Ball, 1968). In many instances multiple forms of treatment were applied to subjects simultaneously (Miller & Haney, 1976; Stoudenmire, 1973) so that effects of specific treatments on specific disorders could not be evaluated.

Finally, just as with sexual dysfunctions, demographic data are not readily available about the prevalence and incidence of paraphiliac behaviors among different socioeconomic, age, and sociocultural groups in our society (Buckholz, 1972; Kirk, 1975). Outcome evaluation is thus made more difficult since, without such data available, valid predictions cannot be made about indigenous remission, nor can the significance of a specific sexual disorder be appreciated when and if it occurs in a member of a particular age or cultural group.

Outcome Measurement in the Treatment of Sexual Disorders: Current Status

Tables 8.6 and 8.7 present data about outcome criteria from research studies on the treatment of sexual disorders and paraphilias. Table 8.6 summarizes the data from those studies in which the sole outcome measure was the patient's subjective self-report. An inspection of Table 8.6 reveals that approximately half of all studies in this area relied solely on the self-report criterion. This was particularly true in studies investigating the treatment of "nuisance" disorders (i.e., exhibitionism) and disorders performed alone or with a consenting partner (i.e., transvestism and fetishism).

Table 8.7 presents the data from those studies that employed multiple outcome measures. These outcome criteria included interviews with spouses and significant others, physiological measures, self-monitoring of sexual fantasy and activity, response latencies to erotic stimuli and fantasy, penile response measures, review of police arrest records, paper–pencil tests, and less frequently, monitoring of hormone levels. The paper–pencil tests included unspecified measures of sexual attitudes and interest, semantic differential scales, questionnaires, and mood scales. They less frequently included standardized psychological inventories such as the Minnesota Multiphasic Personality Inventory (MMPI) or the Sexual Interaction Inventory.

Multiple methods of outcome evaluation were utilized more often in studies investigating the treatment of pedophilia and other "mixed" sexual disorders (e.g., recidivist offenders, sadomasochists, rapists, voyeurs).

Table 8.6. Studies Using Patient Self-Report as Sole Outcome Measure

Reference	N	Sex	Paraphilia	Follow-Up Period
Anonymous et al., 1976	1	M	Shoe fetishist	NS[a]
Barker et al., 1961	1	M	Transvestite	3 months
Biegel, 1967	3	M	Transvestites	NS
Blakemore et al., 1963	1	M	Transvestite	6 months
Bond & Evans, 1967	2	M	Fetishists	NS
Clark, 1963	1	M	Fetishist	3 months
Cooper, 1963	1	M	Fetishist	9 months
Edmondson, 1972	1	M	Masochist	NS
Eyres, 1960	2	M	Transvestites	2 years
Fensterheim, 1974	1	M	Voyeur	NS
Floch, 1970	1	M	Exhibitionist	18 months
Fookes, 1969	7	M	Exhibitionists	NS
	5	M	Fetishist–transvestites	
Glick, 1972	1	M	Fetishist	9 months
Glynn & Harper, 1961	1	M	Transvestite	7 months
Hosford & Rifkin, 1975	1	M	Exhibitionist	NS
Jackson, 1969	1	M	Voyeur	9 months

(continued)

Table 8.6. *(continued)*

Reference	N	Sex	Paraphilia	Follow-Up Period
Johnson, 1977	1	M	Exhibitionist	NS
Kohlenberg, 1974b	1	M	Pedophiliac	6 months
Lambley, 1974	1	M	Transvestite	6 months
Lavin et al., 1961	1	M	Transvestite	6 months
Lihn, 1971	1	M	Masochist	NS
Lowenstein, 1973	1	M	Exhibitionist	1 year
MacDonald, 1961	1	M	Transvestite	7 weeks
Marquis, 1970	14	M	Mixed	NS
Mathis, 1975	1	M	Exhibitionist	2 years
McSweeney, 1972	1	M	Fetishist	NS
Mees, 1966	1	M	Sadist	NS
Pennington, 1960	1	M	Transvestite	NS
Pinta, 1978	1	M	Pedophiliac	4 months
Quirk, 1974	1	M	Exhibitionist	2 years
Rooth & Marks, 1974	12	M	Exhibitionists	NS
Serber, 1970	8	M	Mixed	NS
Serber, 1972	15	M	Mixed	1 year
Stevenson & Jones, 1972	1	M	Exhibitionist	1 year
Stevenson & Wolpe, 1960	3	M	Pedophiliacs	$6\frac{1}{2}$ years
Strzyzewsky & Zier-hoffer, 1967	1	M	Fetishist–transvestite	NS
Van Moffaert, 1976	1	M	Pedophiliac	NS
	1	M	Fetishist–exhibitionist	

Not specified.

Two innovative measures of outcome deserve specific mention. The first, a "temptation test," was employed by Maletzsky (1974) to assess his covert sensitization treatment of a group of male exhibitionist offenders. The test consisted of an attractive woman approaching each subject in various situations in an attempt to elicit an exhibitionistic response. Whereas this "test" may be measuring factors other than those intended, it does approximate an *in vivo* evaluation of treatment effectiveness.

The second measure, the Sexual Orientation Method (SOM), was originally designed by Feldman et al. (1966) to assess attitudes about various categories of sexual behavior. Previously, Marshall (1973) and Marshall and McKnight (1975) found that it provided useful information about changes in sexual fantasy following treatment of clients with mixed sexual disorders. MacCullough et al. (1971) adapted the SOM and found that it was a valuable means of assessing attitude changes in an adolescent exhibitionist treated with aversion therapy techniques. The SOM, which is presented in questionnaire form, represents a serious attempt to overcome the shortcomings of outcome measures based on subjective self-reports. The results obtained from the SOM were found to be internally consistent, reliable, and valid.

Table 8.7. Studies Using Multiple Outcome Measures

Reference	N	Sex	Pharaphilia	Follow-Up Period	Outcome Measures
Abel et al., 1970	3 2	M M	Exhibitionists Transvestites	18 weeks	Penile response measure MMPI Sexual behavior rating scale
Ball, 1968	1	M	Hair fetishist, transvestite	NS[a]	Temporal lobe tumor discovered after termination
Bancroft et al., 1974	12	M	Mixed	NS	Sexual interest score Sexual activity score Sexual attitude score Penile responses and subjective ratings: response to erotic material
Barlow et al., 1969	1	M	Pedophiliac	NS	Card sort GSR Self-report: diary
Bebbington, 1977	1	M	Glove fetishist	6 months	Diary of sexual fantasy and activity Penile response measure Semantic differential
Brownell & Barlow, 1976	1	M	Exhibitionist	11 weeks	Card sort Behavioral rating scale Self-report
Brownell et at., 1977	5	M	Mixed	NS	Card sort Penile response measure No rearrest Self-report Spouse interview

(continued)

Table 8.7. *(continued)*

Reference	N	Sex	Pharaphilia	Follow-Up Period	Outcome Measures
Callahan & Leitenberg, 1973	6	M	Unspecified	NS	Penile plethysmograph Daily self-report Independent reports
Cooper et al., 1972	1 1	M M	Mixed "Hypersexual"	NS	Plasma testosterone levels Frequency of masturbation
Feldman et al., 1968	5	M	Mixed	NS	Self-report Spouse interview
Forgione, 1976	2	M	Pedophiliacs	3 years	Self-report Interview of significant others
Gaupp et al., 1971	1	M	Voyeur	8 months	GSR EKG Self-report
Gelder & Marks, 1970	20	M	Mixed	6 months	Penile response measure Palmar skin conductance Self-report Semantic differential
Hallam & Rachman, 1972	5	M	Mixed	12 months	HR Skin conductance Mood scores Latency to fantasy
Hayes et al., 1978	1	M	Exhibitionist–sadist	NS	Penile response measure Card sort
Hughes, 1977	1	M	Exhibitionist	3 years	MMPI Self-monitoring

Study	N	Sex	Diagnosis	Follow-up	Measures
Keltner, 1977	2	M	Pedophiliacs	NS	Penile response measure Response latency to erotic stimuli
Levin et al., 1977	1	M	Pedophiliac	10 months	Self-report Penile response measure MMPI Sexual interest rating
MacCullough et al., 1971	1	M	Exhibitionist	5 months	Sexual orientation measure
Maletzky, 1974	10	M	Exhibitionists	NS	Self-monitoring of behavior and fantasy No rearrest "Temptation tests"
Marks & Gelder, 1967	4 1	M M	Transvestites Fetishist	NS	Penile response measure Semantic differential Monitoring of fantasy Patient interview Interview with significant others
Marks et al., 1970	24	Mixed	Transvestites	NS	Self-monitoring of fantasies, feelings, and behavior Semantic differential
Marks et al., 1965	1	M	Fetishist–masochist	3 months	Lever pulling response Semantic differential Latency to obtaining deviant fantasy
Marshall, 1974	1	M	Fetishist	6 months	Penile response measure Self-report

(continued)

Table 8.7. *(continued)*

Reference	N	Sex	Pharaphilia	Follow-Up Period	Outcome Measures
Marshall & Lippens. 1977	1	M	Rapist–fetishist	NS	Penile response measure Self-report Spouse interview
Marshall & McKnight. 1975	3	M	Pedophiliacs	NS	Penile response measure Slide ratings Sexual orientation test Behavioral observation
Mathis & Collins. 1970	45	M	Exhibitionists	NS	Police records
Miller & Haney. 1976	1	M	Pedophiliac–exhibitionist	9 months	Ranking of picture preference Reduction in deviant fantasies No rearrest
Moss et al.. 1970	2	M	Transvestites	8 months	Self-report Spouse interview
Pinard & Lamontague. 1976	1	M	Fetishist–masochist	1 year	Semantic differential Latency to obtaining deviant fantasies
Quinsey et al.. 1976	10	M	Pedophiliacs	NS	Penile response measure Skin conductance Semantic differential Slide sort
Rosen & Kopel. 1977	1	M	Transvestite–exhibitionist	16 months	Penile response measure Self-rating scale
Rosenthal. 1973	1	M	Pedophiliac	32 months	Self-report No rearrest

Study	N	Sex	Disorder	Follow-up	Measures
Stoudenmire, 1973	1	M	Voyeur	6 months	Self-report Spouse interview
Tennent et al., 1974	12	M	Pedophiliacs	NS	Sexual interest self-rating Sexual activity score Sexual attitude score Penile response measure
Van Dewenter & Laws, 1978	2	M	Pedophiliacs	NS	Penile response measures Card sort of fantasies Diary of sex fantasy and activity
Wardlaw & Miller, 1978	3	M	Exhibitionists	4 years	Self-report Police records
Wickramasekera, 1968	1	M	Exhibitionist	10 months	Self-report Fianceé interview
Wickramasekera, 1976	20	M	Exhibitionists	NS	Self-report Interviews with significant others Police records Psychophysiological testing
Woody, 1973	1	M	Transvestite	5 months	Questionnaire Self-report
	1	M	Fetishist		

[a] Not specified.

Inspection of Tables 8.6 and 8.7 also reveals that a majority of research reports did contain follow-up data on treatment effectiveness. The mean follow-up period among these studies was 13.7 months, with time periods varying from 11 weeks to 6½ years.

The Biopsychosocial Model and Sexual Disorders

Engel's (1977, 1980) biopsychosocial model can also be utilized in an attempt to understand sexually disordered behavior. The model again underscores the interaction of biological, psychological, and social variables in the etiology, maintenance, and cessation of paraphiliac behavior. It also emphasizes the need for multimodal, multilevel pre- and posttherapy assessment and outcome evaluation.

Table 8.8 presents an enumeration of biopsychosocial factors that require attention in persons presenting for treatment of sexually variant behavior.

Biological variables include those acute brain injuries or chronic organic brain syndromes that sometimes result in hypersexual or inappropriate sexual behavior. Physiologically, paraphiliac behavior may be necessary to achieve sexual arousal, maintain sexual arousal, and/or attain orgasm. Other biological variables (e.g., estrogen:testosterone ratios, galvanic skin response, heart rate) are also correlated with disordered sexual responses.

Individual psychological factors can be of great significance in the paraphilias. These include personality style, psychopathology, motivation for paraphiliac activities, thought processes and sexual fantasies, and sexual orientation. Additional psychological components are subjective reactions preceding and subsequent to the sexually variant behavior, as well as the presence or absence of other sexual deviations or dysfunctions.

Social factors are also significant. Interpersonal factors include marital adjustment, repertoire of interpersonal social skills, quality of interpersonal relationships, nature of interpersonal relationships, and reactions of significant others. Societal factors involve legal status, dangerousness, and recidivism of the sexually disordered person, as well as the incidence and prevalence of specific sexual disorders among various socioeconomic, racial, cultural, religious, and age groups.

The selection of a treatment modality, the planning of treatment goals, and the choice of evaluative tools depend on familiarity with all these interacting factors. The biopsychosocial model serves the heuristic purpose in this area (as it did previously for sexual dysfunctions) of emphasizing missing incidence and prevalence data, definitional problems, and the complementarity of outcome measures. It underscores the hierarchy of levels of observation and the interrelatedness of the data derived from each level. The concerns and perspective of the legal officer concerning sexual disorders are somewhat different from those of the physician or psychologist. Each, however, must be attended to in outcome evaluation of the treatment of sexual disorders.

Table 8.8. Biopsychosocial Factors in Sexual Disorders

Biological Factors	Psychological Factors	Social Factors	
		Interpersonal	Societal
Physical and organic factors	Personality factors	Interpersonal social skills	Dangerousness of client
Physiological factors	Motivational factors	Marital adjustment	Legal status of client
Hormonal factors	Thought patterns	Reactions of significant others	Recidivism rate
	Sexual orientation	Quality of interpersonal relationship	Incidence of sexual disorders
	Number of deviations	Nature of interpersonal relationships	Prevalence of sexual disorders
	Emotional response to deviant behavior		
	Sexual history		
	Psychopathology		
	Sexual fantasies		
	Presence of sexual dysfunctions		

Implications of Biopsychosocial Model for Outcome Measurement in Treatment of Sexual Disorders

This section is devoted to a series of conclusions and recommendations regarding future research in the treatment of the paraphilias. These conclusions and recommendations result from the application of the biopsychosocial model to sexually disordered behavior.

Conclusion and Recommendation 8. Outcome Assessment Must be Multimodal and Multidmensional

Evaluation procedures must encompass all relevant biological, psychological, and social variables affecting paraphiliac behavior. Table 8.9 contains a biopsychosocial paradigm for outcome assessment in the treatment of the paraphilias. Various complementary means of assessing change are included.

Conclusion and Recommendation 9. Assessment Techniques Must Recognize Biological Factors in Etiology and Maintenance of Paraphiliac Behaviors

Although biological factors rarely occur, they can be etiologically significant in some types of sexual variance. Acute brain injuries or chronic organic brain syndromes (Ball, 1968) can result in hypersexual behavior or inappropriate sexual behaviors. In cases where such involvement is suspected, assessment measures should include neurological and neuropsychological evaluation (e.g., EEG, CAT Scan, Halstead–Reitan neuropsychological test battery) prior to and following medical and/or surgical exploration and intervention.

Pre- and posttreatment evaluation should determine the adequacy of physiological sexual functioning in the absence of paraphiliac behavior and stimuli. This can be accomplished through self-report measures, supplemented by psychophysiological measures and penile response measures of arousability to test stimuli (e.g., fetishistic objects, slides of children chosen previously as sexually attractive) following treatment. Bebbington (1977) found that erectile responses to sexually deviant material decreased significantly following classical conditioning treatment of a glove fetishist. Similarly, auditory biofeedback given to two pedophiliac subjects by Keltner (1977) according to their penile responses to sexually arousing deviant slides resulted in reduced penile arousal to pedophiliac stimuli in the one subject who completed the therapy program. However, Quinsey et al. (1976) reported no significant changes in individual subject penile response data following aversion therapy treatment for pedophilia, although there were mild changes in semantic differential and slide ranking measures. In addition, Hallam and Rachman (1972) reported significant changes in heart rate, although not in skin conductance, as a result of aversion therapy and desensitization therapies for a group of men with mixed sexual variances. Such contradictory findings emphasize the importance of multimodal measurement. Pupillary response data (Hess, 1975) may also supplement self-report data.

Table 8.9. A Biopsychosocial Paradigm for Outcome Measurement of Treatment of Sexual Disorders

Biological Factors	Psychological Factors	Social Factors	
		Interpersonal	Societal
Physical evaluation	Psychodiagnostic assessment (psychological testing)	Behavioral assessment of social skills	Rearrest records
Neurological evaluation	Self-report	Reports from significant others	Slide ratings
Endocrinologic evaluation	Behavioral assessment	Ratings by objective observers	"Temptation test"
Penile response measures	Measures of sexual orientation	Measures of quality of interpersonal relationships	Follow-up measures
Psychophysiological measures	Semantic differential	Measures of sexual interaction	
Pupillographic measures	Card sort		

In those programs that utilize hormonal treatments to reduce sexually deviant behavior (Cooper et al., 1972), neuroendocrine and hormonal factors must be monitored as correlates of treatment effects.

Conclusion and Recommendation 10. Future Research Efforts Should Include an Investigation of Motivational Variables in Paraphiliac Behavior

There is currently no coherent, comprehensive motivational theory to account for the development and maintenance of paraphiliac behavior. It is known that sexual deviations sometimes accompany character disorders such as antisocial personalities and psychoses such as manic-depressive illness (Ward, 1975). Paraphilias can be associated with underlying, unconscious neurotic conflicts (Johnson, 1977). Other motivational explanations have included anxiety reduction (Stevenson & Wolpe, 1960), a need for attention, and expression of hostility (Stoller, 1975). Future research efforts must attempt to remedy these theoretical deficits.

Meanwhile, despite some positive reports (Abel et al., 1970) about the use of standard, global psychological evaluation techniques as outcome measures, more specific criteria for change are necessary. Traditional psychological assessment can reveal additional sources of psychopathology, but it is less useful as a measure of treatment effectiveness.

Conclusion and Recommendation 11. Multiple, Situation-Specific Change Criteria Must be Employed in Outcome Evaluation

Self-report has been a primary means of gaining information about therapeutic change and motivational variables; however, other assessment techniques can be employed to supplement these subjective measures. Biofeedback techniques might be used to measure changes in anxiety levels as a function of treatment. Diary accounts by patients during the course of therapy may be useful.

Therapist evaluations of change and assessment by independent evaluators can be supplemental sources of information about treatment effectiveness. Reports from spouses, sexual partners, family members, and significant others should be sought out when possible.

An individual's thought patterns, and especially sexual fantasies, can play an important role in the origin and maintenance of deviant behavior. They should be attended to in outcome evaluation. Behavioral assessment techniques have proved to be extremely useful in this regard. Such techniques have included daily logs of sexual fantasies (Bebbington, 1977), timing of latencies to sexual fantasies (Hallam & Rachman, 1972), and self-monitoring of sexual fantasy and sexual behavior (Maletzsky, 1974).

An individual's subjective reactions preceding and following the sexually variant activity (e.g., the presence or absence of excitement, anxiety, guilt, disgust) will have direct effects on treatment and outcome. Covert sensitization procedures (Cautela & Wisocki, 1971) and shame aversion therapy (Serber,

1970) both focus on these emotional reactions and attempt to alter them if they appear to reinforce the deviant act. Such reactions can be measured through semantic differential techniques and self-report measures. Changes in emotional reactions to different sexual stimuli can be assessed by means of card sorts and ratings of attractiveness of deviant and nondeviant slides and pictures.

A client's sexual orientation (heterosexual, homosexual, ambisexual, or asexual) will affect the course, type, and goals of therapy provided and the evaluation of therapeutic effectiveness. In some cases sexual orientation may change as a function of treatment. The sexual orientation method (Feldman et al., 1966) provided useful information in studies by Marshall (1973) and Marshall and McKnight (1975) about changes in sexual fantasy following treatment of clients with mixed sexual disorders. The sexual orientation method (SOM) is a technique for assessing attitudes to categories of sexual material and it may be useful in future research to measure changes in these attitudes with treatment. Pupillary reactions (Hess, 1975) and penile response (Freund, 1963; McConaghy, 1967) may also serve as valid and reliable measures of sexual orientation.

The goals of some treatment programs include the development of more appropriate sexual and social skills as means of reducing deviant sexual behaviors. Assessment of the patient's pretreatment and posttreatment sexual and social skills is necessary in such cases to determine treatment effects. Subjective means of evaluating these skills include reports from family members, spouses, and significant others in the environment. More reliable and valid data can be obtained through ratings by objective observers of the client's behavior in standardized role-playing situations designed to measure social and interpersonal functioning, assertiveness, and so on (Goldstein, 1973). For example, MacDonald (1961) successfully treated a male transvestite during six psychotherapy sessions devoted to sex education and social skills training. The author had hypothesized that the cross-dressing behavior was a direct result of the client's social isolation. Similarly, Marshall and McKnight (1975) reported that a comprehensive treatment program for male pedophiliacs that included a social skills training component resulted in a shift away from pedophiliac concerns to attraction to more appropriate sexual objects. In the past, treatment programs have not included adequate pretherapy assessment of social skills.

Sexual skills were evaluated in only one study (Rosen & Kopel, 1977), which included administration of the Sexual Interaction Inventory (SII) before and after treatment. Treatment consisted of biofeedback, shaping procedures, and marital and sex therapy. Other studies (Carr, 1974; Lambley, 1974; Moss et al., 1970) included sex therapy procedures as a part of treatment but failed to evaluate pretherapy sexual functioning. This is crucial to meaningful outcome evaluation. Standardized measures such as the SII and spouse and sexual partner reports should be obtained whenever possible.

Marital adjustment should also be an object of outcome evaluation for those programs that attempt to improve the marital relationship. Such measures as the Locke–Wallace Marital Adjustment Test may be useful for that purpose. Several studies used marital therapy and family counseling procedures (Brownell & Barlow, 1976; Forgione, 1976; Moss et al., 1970), but the lack of systematic pre- and posttreatment evaluation of marital functioning made assessment of effectiveness almost impossible.

Finally, the sexually disordered individual must be evaluated to determine the presence or absence of additional sexual disorders or dysfunctions. A paraphilia that exists in isolation can be treated, to some degree, in isolation. However, if multiple deviations or dysfunctions are present, a hierarchy of treatment objectives must be developed. This has obvious implications for treatment and evaluation (Cooper, 1963; Hosford & Rifkin, 1975; Lambley, 1974). Treatment of paraphilias is most effective when reduction in deviant behavior is accompanied by shaping and reinforcement of more appropriate sexual behaviors (Moss et al., 1970). Whereas treatment goals for potentially dangerous deviations (e.g., pedophilia, sadomasochism) may focus on rapid suppression of those behaviors, treatment goals for more nuisance deviations (e.g., voyeurism, exhibitionism) should include elimination of the variant behavior *and* the concomitant development of more appropriate, nondeviant behaviors. Treatment goals for other types of sexual variance (e.g., transvestism) may focus on assisting the individual to restrict sexual activities to a private setting with a consenting partner. Treatment procedures would thus also vary: from the use of rapid but nonspecific treatments (e.g., injections of female hormones for dangerous male sadomasochists), to sex therapy for the exhibitionist, to impulse control training for the transvestite. The outcome measures would also differ: cessation of deviant sadomasochistic behavior, increase in heterosexual skills, and decrease in impulsivity. Such factors make apparent the need for individually planned treatment programs for persons with sexual deviations. They also underscore the need for situation-specific, individualized outcome criteria.

Conclusion and Recommendation 12. Outcome Evaluation Must Consider Societal Implications of Paraphiliac Behavior

A client's legal status is important for outcome evaluation. Nonoffender subjects who pose a community threat may require a short-term, rapidly effective treatment. Incarcerated offenders are available for participation in longer-term, more comprehensive programs. Similarly, it is reasonable to assume that sexual offenders and nonoffenders may differ in ways other than sexual pathology (e.g., age, intelligence, education, social skills, sociopathy, psychopathology), which would have direct effects on outcome measurement.

Rearrest records and police records can serve as sources of information about recidivism rates, but, used alone, these records are unreliable because of the strong probablity that sexually deviant behaviors occur frequently without coming to the attention of legal and police personnel. One potentially useful outcome measure is an unobtrusive measure, the "temptation test," developed by Maletzsky (1974) and described above. Attempts should be made to develop such nonreactive unobtrusive measures as means of therapy outcome assessment.

Conclusion and Recommendation 13. Epidemiologic Research is Necessary to Determine Incidence and Prevalence Data and Generalizability of Treatment Effects

Societal incidence and prevalence data about sexually variant behavior are needed so that outcome measures can focus more meaningfully on questions of indigenous remission, effects of aging, and progression from one type of deviation to another. Such information would increase understanding of sexual deviancy and variation. It would assist in the planning of more sophisticated research. It would aid in the implementation of more sophisticated and potentially more meaningful outcome evaluation techniques.

Follow-up periods of one to two years or more are necessary in future research programs for determination of long-term effects of treatment and generalizability of treatment effects. Some studies involving subjects with multiple deviations found that effective treatment of one deviation in one subject resulted in reduction of other deviant behaviors (Brownell et al., 1977; Hayes et al., 1978), whereas other studies found that different deviations functioned independently of each other. The relative independence or interdependence of sexual disorders is an empirical question that can be answered only after follow-up evaluations of treatment effects. This question has not yet received adequate research attention.

Other Methodological Considerations

Until recently, sexual disorders research has been almost exclusively limited to single case reports. Groups studies involving subjects who are homogeneous with regard to important client variables (e.g., duration of disorder, sexual and social history, educational level) are needed.

Research attention should be paid also to therapist variables (e.g., sex, employer) that might affect therapeutic outcome. Future studies should require adequate pretherapy assessment of these factors under study so that outcome evaluation can provide comparative data for analysis. Methodological and procedural descriptions should be as specific as possible to ensure replicability. In this regard, studies involving behavioral treatment modes have provided excellent models and examples. Treatment goals should be specifically defined, as should be criteria for "success" or "failure" of treatment.

SUMMARY AND CONCLUSIONS

Research in the areas of sexual dysfunction and sexual disorders has increased in sophistication over the past 20 years. This has resulted from an increased expertise about experimental methodology and a rapidly increasing data base about sexual functioning. Future research should be devoted to the eventual goal of matching clients, therapists, therapy formats, and sexual problems so as to provide the most effective treatment. Such a goal can be reached only with greater attention to specification of variables and individualization of outcome criteria. The biopsychosocial approach is recommended to future researchers in sexual behavior as a comprehensive, useful, realistic, and clinically meaningful model for both research and clinical work.

REFERENCES

Abel, G. G., Levis, D. T., & Clancy, T. Aversion therapy applied to taped sequences of deviant behavior in exhibitionism and other sexual deviations: A preliminary report. *Journal of Behavior Therapy and Experimental Psychiatry*, 1970, **1**, 59–66.

Alexander, L. Treatment of impotency and anorgasmia by psychotherapy aided by hypnosis. *American Journal of Clinical Hypnosis*, 1974, **17**, 33–43.

Allison, J. Choosing a therapeutic system for treating sexual dysfunction: A traditional approach. *Psychotherapy: Theory, Research, and Practice*, 1975, **12**, 320–323.

American Psychiatric Association. *Diagnostic and statistical manual of mental disorders* (3rd ed.). Washington, D.C.: American Psychiatric Association, 1980.

(Anonymous), Chambers, W. M., & Janzen, W. B. The eclectic and multiple therapy of a shoe fetishist. *American Journal of Psychotherapy*, 1976, **30**, 317–326.

Ansari, J. M. Impotence: Prognosis (a controlled study). *British Journal of Psychiatry*, 1976, **128**, 194–198.

Asirdas, S., & Beech, H. R. The behavioral treatment of sexual inadequacy. *Journal of Psychosomatic Research*, 1975, **19**, 345–353.

Auerbach, R., & Kilmann, P. R. The effects of group systematic desensitization on secondary erectile failure. *Behavior Therapy*, 1977, **8**, 330–339.

Ball, J. R. A case of hair fetishism, transvestism, and organic cerebral disorder. *Acta Psychiatrica Scandinavica*, 1968, **44**, 249–254.

Bancroft, J., Tennent, G., Loucas, K., & Cass, J. The control of deviant sexual behavior by drugs: I. Behavioral changes following oestrogens and anti-androgens. *British Journal of Psychiatry*, 1974, **125**, 310–315.

Barker, T. C., Thorpe, J. G., Blakemore, C. G., Lavin, N. I., & Conway, C. G. Behavior therapy in a case of transvestism. *Lancet*, 1961, **1**, 510.

Barlow, D. H., Leitenberg, H., & Agras, W. S. Experimental control of sexual deviation through manipulation of the noxious scene in covert sensitization. *Journal of Abnormal Psychology*, 1969, **74**, 596–601.

Bass, B. A. Sexual arousal as an anxiety inhibitor. *Journal of Behavior Therapy and Experimental Psychiatry*, 1974, **5**, 151–152.

Bebbington, P. E. Treatment of a male sexual deviation by use of a vibrator: Case report. *Archives of Sexual Behavior*, 1977, **6**, 21–34.

Benkert, O., Dahlen, H. G., Jordan, R., Schneider, H. P. G., & Gammel, G. Sexual impotence: A double-blind study of LHRH nasal spray versus placebo. *Neuropsychobiology*, 1975, **1**, 203–210.

Benkert, O., Horn, K., Pickardt, C. R., & Schmid, O. Sexual impotence: Studies of the hypothalamic-pituitary-thyroid axis and the effect of oral thyrotropin-releasing factor. *Archives of Sexual Behavior*, 1976, **5**, 275–281.

Bergin, A. E., & Lambert, M. J. The evaluation of therapeutic outcomes. In S. L. Garfield & A. E. Bergin (Eds.), *Handbook of psychotherapy and behavior change: An empirical analysis* (2nd ed.). New York: Wiley, 1978.

Biegel, H. G. Three transvestites under hypnosis. *Journal of Sex Research*, 1967, **3**, 140–162.

Blakeney, P., Kinder, B. N., Creson, D., Powell, L. C., & Sutton, C. A short-term intensive workshop approach for the treatment of human sexual inadequacy. *Journal of Sex and Marital Therapy*, 1976, **2**, 124–129.

Blakemore, C. B., Thorpe, J. C., Barker, J. C., Conway, C. G., & Lavin, N. I. The application of faradic aversion conditioning in a case of transvestism. *Behaviour Research and Therapy*, 1963, **1**, 29–34.

Blight, E. M., & David, J. R. Treatment of male sexual dysfunction: An interdisciplinary undertaking in a military hospital. *Military Medicine*, 1978, **143**, 322–324.

Bond, I. K., & Evans, D. R. Avoidance therapy: Its use in two cases of underwear fetishism. *Canadian Medical Association Journal*, 1967, **96**, 1160–1162.

Brancale, R., Ellis, A., & Doorbar, R. Psychiatric and psychological investigations of convicted sex offenders: A summary report. *American Journal of Psychiatry*, 1952, **109**, 17–21.

Brinkley-Birk, A., & Birk, L. Sex therapy for vaginismus, primary impotence, and ejaculatory incompetence in an unconsummated marriage. *Psychiatric Opinion*, 1975, **12**, 38–42.

Brown, E., Brown, G. M., Kofman, O., & Quarrington, B. Sexual function and affect in Parkinsonian men treated with L-dopa. *American Journal of Psychiatry*, 1978, **135**, 1552–1555.

Brown, W. A., Monti, P. M., & Corriveau, D. P. Serum testosterone and sexual activity and interest in men. *Archives of Sexual Behavior*, 1978, **7**, 97–103.

Brownell, K. D., & Barlow, D. H. Measurement and treatment of two sexual deviations in one person. *Journal of Behavior Therapy and Experimental Psychiatry*, 1976, **7**, 349–354.

Brownell, K. D., Hayes, S. C., & Barlow, D. H. Patterns of appropriate and deviant sexual arousal: The behavioral treatment of multiple sexual deviations. *Journal of Consulting and Clinical Psychology*, 1977, **45**, 1144–1155.

Buckholz, M. H. Human sexual behavior and social class structure. In H. Gochros & L. Schultz (Eds.), *Human sexuality and social work*. New York: Association Press, 1972.

Caird, W. K., & Wincze, J. P. Videotaped desensitzation of frigidity. *Journal of Behavior Therapy and Experimental Psychiatry*, 1974, **5**, 175–178.

Callahan, E. J., & Leitenberg, H. Aversion therapy for sexual deviation: Contingent shock and covert sensitization. *Journal of Abnormal Psychology*, 1973, **81**, 60–73.

Campbell, D. T., & Fiske, D. W. Convergent and discriminant validation by the multitrait–multimethod matrix. *Psychological Bulletin*, 1959, **56**, 81–105.

Carney, A., Bancroft, J., & Mathews, A. Combination of hormonal and psychological treatment for female unresponsiveness: A comparative study. *British Journal of Psychiatry*, 1978, **133**, 339–346.

Carr, J. E. Behavior therapy in a case of multiple sexual disorders. *Journal of Behavior Therapy and Experimental Psychiatry*, 1974, **5**, 171–174.

Cassell, W. A. Desensitization therapy for body image anxiety. *Canadian Psychiatric Association Journal*, 1977, **22**, 239–242.

Cautela, T. R., & Wisocki, P. A. Covert sensitization for the treatment of sexual deviations. *Psychological Record*, 1971, **21**, 37–48.

Cheek, D. B. Hypnotherapy for secondary frigidity after radical surgery for gynecological cancer: Two case reports. *American Journal of Clinical Hypnosis*, 1976, **19**, 13–19. (a)

Cheek, D. B. Short term hypnotherapy for frigidity using exploration of early life attitudes. *American Journal of Clinical Hypnosis*, 1976, **19**, 20–27. (b)

Clark, D. F. Fetishism treated by negative conditioning. *British Journal of Psychiatry*, 1963, **109**, 404–407.

Clark, M.E. TA and sexual dysfunctions. *Transactional Analysis Journal*, 1976, **6**, 147–150.

Cooper, A. A. A case of fetishism and impotence treated by behavior therapy. *British Journal of Psychiatry*, 1963, **109**, 649–652.

Cooper, A. J. Hostility and male potency disorders. *Comprehensive Psychiatry*, 1968, **9**, 621–626.

Cooper, A. J., Ismail, A. A. A., Phanjoo, A. L., & Love, D. L. Antiandrogen (cyproterone acetate) therapy in deviant hypersexuality. *British Journal of Psychiatry*, 1972, **120**, 58–64.

de Shazer, S. Brief hypnotherapy of two sexual dysfunctions: The crystal ball technique. *Journal of Clinical Hypnosis*, 1978, **20**, 203–208.

Deabler, H. L. Hypnotherapy of impotence. *American Journal of Clinical Hypnosis*, 1976, **19**, 9–12.

Derogatis, L.R., & Melisaratos, N. The DSFI: A multidimensional measure of sexual functioning. *Journal of Sex and Marital Therapy*, 1979, **5**, 244–281.

Divita, E. C., & Olsson, P. S. The use of sex therapy in a patient with a penile prosthesis. *Journal of Sex and Marital Therapy*, 1975, **1**, 305–311.

Duddle, M. Etiological factors in the unconsummated marriage. *Journal of Psychosomatic Research*, 1977, **21**, 157–160.

Edmondson, J. S. A case of sexual asphyxia with fatal termination. *British Journal of Psychiatry*, 1972. **121**, 437–438.

Ellis, A. *Sex without guilt*. New York: Lyle Stuart, 1958.

Engel, G. L. The need for a new medical model: A challenge for biomedicine. *Science*, 1977, **196**, 129–136.

Engel, G. L. The clinical application of the biopsychosocial model. *American Journal of Psychiatry*, 1980, **137**, 535–544.

Ersner-Hershfield, R., & Kopel, S. Group treatment of preorgasmic women: Evaluation of partner involvement and spacing of sessions. *Journal of Consulting and Clinical Psychology*, 1979, **47**, 750-759.

Evans, D. R. Masturbatory fantasy and sexual deviation. *Behaviour Research and Therapy*, 1968, **6**, 17–19.

Evans, D. R. Subjective variables and treatment effects in aversion therapy. *Behaviour Research and Therapy*, 1970, **8**, 147–152.

Eyres, A. E. Transvestism: Employment of somatic therapy with subsequent improvement. *Diseases of the Nervous System*, 1960, **21**, 52–53.

Feldman, M. P., MacCullough, M. J. & MacCullough, M. L. The aversion therapy treatment of a heterogeneous group of five cases of sexual deviation. *Acta Psychiatrica Scandinavica*, 1968, **44**, 113–123.

Feldman, M. P., MacCullough, M. J., Mellor, V., & Pinschoff, J. M. The application of anticipatory avoidance learning to the treatment of homosexuality. III. The sexual orientation method. *Behaviour Research and Therapy*, 1966, **4**, 289–299.

Fensterheim, H. Behavior therapy of the sexual variations. *Journal of Sex and Marital Therapy*, 1974, **1**, 16–28.

Finkelstein, L. Awe and premature ejaculation: A case study. *Psychoanalytic Quarterly*, 1975, **44**, 232–252.

Finkle, A. L., & Finkle, P. S. Urologic counseling can overcome male sexual impotence. *Geriatrics*, 1975, **30**, 119–124.

Fisher, C., Schiavi, R., Lear, H., Edwards, A., Davis, D. M., & Witkin, A. P. The assessment of nocturnal REM erection in the differential diagnosis of sexual impotence. *Journal of Sex and Marital Therapy*, 1975, **1**, 277–289.

Floch, M. The treatment of a chronic case of exhibitionism by means of the autobiographical method of analysis. *Journal of Criminal Law and Criminology*, 1970, **37**, 316–317.

Fookes, B. H. Some experience in the use of aversion therapy in male homosexuality, exhibitionism, and fetishism-transvestism. *British Journal of Psychiatry*, 1969, **115**, 339–341.

Forgione, A. G. The use of mannequins in the behavior assessment of child molesters: Two case reports. *Behavior Therapy*, 1976, **1**, 678–685.

Fox, C. A., Ismail, A. A. A., Love, D. N., Kirkham, K. E., & Loraine, J. A. Studies on the relationship between plasma testosterone levels and human sexual activity. *Journal of Endocrinology*, 1972, **52**, 51–58.

Freund, K. A laboratory method for diagnosing predominance of homo- or hetero-erotic interest in the male. *Behavior Research and Therapy*, 1963, **1**, 85–93.

Freund, K. Assessment of anomalous erotic preferences in situational impotence. *Journal of Sex and Marital Therapy*, 1976, **2**, 173–183.

Fuchs, K., Abramovici, H., Hoch, Z., Timor-Tritsch, I., & Kleinhaus, M. Vaginismus: The hypnotherapeutic approach. *Journal of Sex Research*, 1975, **11**, 39–45.

Gagliardi, F. A. Ejaculatio retardata. *American Journal of Psychotherapy*, 1976, **30**, 85–94.

Garfield, S. L. Research on client variables in psychotherapy. In S. L. Garfield & A. E. Bergin (Eds.), *Handbook of psychotherapy and behavior change: An empirical analysis* (2nd ed.). New York: Wiley, 1978.

Gaupp, L. A., Stern, R. M., & Ratliff, R. G. The use of aversion-relief procedures in the treatment of a case of voyeurism. *Behavior Therapy*, 1971, **2**. 585–588.

Gelder, M. G., & Marks, I. M. Aversion treatment in transvestism and transsexualism. In R. Green & J. Money (Eds.), *Transsexualism and sex reassignment*. Baltimore: Johns Hopkins University Press, 1970.

Gentry, D. L. The treatment of premature ejaculation through brief therapy. *Psychotherapy: Theory, Research and Practice*, 1978, **15**, 32–34.

Gershman, L. Case conference: A transvestite fantasy treated by thought-stopping, covert sensitization and aversive shock. *Journal of Behavior Therapy and Experimental Psychiatry*, 1970, **1**, 153–161.

Glick, B. S. Aversive imagery therapy using hypnosis. *American Journal of Psychotherapy*, 1972, **26**, 432–436.

Glynn, J. D., & Harper, P. Behavior therapy in a case of transvestism. *Lancet*, 1961, **1**, 619–620.

Golden, J. S., Price, S., Heinrich, A. G., & Lobitz, W. C. Group versus couple treatment of sexual dysfunctions. *Archives of Sexual Behavior*, 1978, **7**, 593–600.

Goldstein, A. P. *Therapist-patient expectancies in psychotherapy*. New York: MacMillan, 1962.

Goldstein, A. P. *Structured learning therapy: Toward a psychotherapy for the poor*. New York: Academic Press, 1973.

Gottesfeld, M. L. Treatment of vaginismus by psychotherapy with adjunctive hypnosis. *American Journal of Clinical Hypnosis*, 1978, **20**, 272–277.

Hallam, R. S., & Rachman, S. Some effects of aversion therapy on patients with sexual disorders. *Behaviour Research and Therapy*, 1972, **10**, 171–180.

Hartman, W., & Fithian M. *Treatment of sexual dysfunction: A bio-psycho-social approach*. Long Beach, Calif.: Center for Marital and Sexual Studies, 1972.

Hayes, S. C., Brownell, K. D., & Barlow, D.H. The use of self-administered sensitization in the treatment of exhibitionism and sadism. *Behavior Therapy*, 1978, **9**, 283–289.

Herman, S. H., & Prewitt, M. An experimental analysis of feedback to increase sexual arousal in a case of homo- and heterosexual impotence: A preliminary report. *Journal of Behavior Therapy and Experimental Psychiatry*, 1974, **5**, 271–274.

Hess, E. H. *The tell-tale eye*. New York: Van Nostrand Reinhold, 1975.

Hoch, Z. Orgasmic dysfunction in the female: A marital and family problem. *International Journal of Family Counseling*, 1977, **5**, 66–71.

Hogan, R. A. Frigidity and implosive therapy. *Psychology*, 1975, **12**, 39–45.

Horowitz, L. M., Sampson, H., Siegelman, E. Y., Weiss, J., & Goodfriend, S. Cohesive and dispersal behaviors: Two classes of concomitant change in psychotherapy. *Journal of Consulting and Clinical Psychology*, 1978, **46**, 556–564.

Hosford, R. E., & Rifkin, H. B. Application of behavior therapy to compulsive exhibitionism and homosexuality. In R. E. Hosford & C. S. Moss (Eds.), *The crumbling walls: Treatment and counseling of prisoners*. Urbana: University of Illinois Press, 1975.

Hughes, R. C. Covert sensitization treatment of exhibitionism. *Journal of Behavior Therapy and Experimental Psychiatry*, 1977, **8**, 177–179.

Husted, J. R. Desensitization procedures in dealing with female sexual dysfunction. *Counseling Psychologist*, 1975, **5**, 30–37.

Jackson, B. T. A case of voyeurism treated by counter-conditioning. *Behaviour Research and Therapy*, 1969, **7**, 133–134.

Jacobs, L. I. The impotent king: Secondary impotence refractory to brief sex therapy. *American Journal of Psychotherapy*, 1977, **31**, 97–104.

Jankovich, R. A. Treatment of orgasmic dysfunction using women's groups. *Dissertation Abstracts International*, 1975, **36** (2–B), 912.

Jankovich, R., & Miller, P. R. Response of women with primary orgasmic dysfunction to audiovisual education. *Journal of Sex and Marital Therapy*, 1978, **4**, 16–19.

Johnson, T. F. Couple therapy as a method for treating male exhibitionism: "Flashing." *Journal of Marriage and Family Counseling*, 1977, **25**, 33–38.

Jones, W. J., & Park, P. M. Treatment of single partner sexual dysfunction by systematic desensitization. *Obstetrics and Gynecology*, 1972, **39**, 411–417.

Joseph, B. A clinical contribution to the analysis of perversion. *International Journal of Psycho-Analysis*, 1971, **52**, 441–449.

Joseph E. D. An aspect of female frigidity. *Journal of the American Psychoanalytic Association*, 1974, **22**, 116–122.

Kaplan, H. S. *The new sex therapy*. New York: Brunner/Mazel, 1974.

Kaplan, H. S. *Disorders of sexual desire and other new concepts and techniques in sex therapy*. New York: Brunner/Mazel, 1979.

Kelly, G. F. Multiphasic therapy for a severe sexual dysfunction. *Psychotherapy: Theory, Research, and Practice*, 1976, **13**, 40–43.

Keltner, A. A. The control of penile tumescence with biofeedback in two cases of pedophilia. *Correctional and Social Psychiatry and Journal of Behavior Technological Methods and Therapy*, 1977, **23**, 117–121.

Kilmann, P. R. The treatment of primary and secondary orgasmic dysfunction: A methodological review of the literature since 1970. *Journal of Sex and Marital Therapy*, 1978, **4**, 155–175.

Kilmann, P. R., & Auerbach, R. Treatment of premature ejaculation and psychogenic impotence: A critical review of the literature. *Archives of Sexual Behavior*, 1979, **8**, 81–100.

Kinsey, A. C., Pomeroy, W. B., & Martin, C. E. *Sexual behavior in the human male*. Philadelphia: Saunders, 1948.

Kinsey, A. C., Pomeroy, W. B., Martin, C. E., & Gebhard, P. H. *Sexual behavior in the human female*. Philadelphia: Saunders, 1953.

Kiresuk, T. J., & Sherman, R. E. Goal attainment scaling: A general method for evaluating comprehensive community mental health programs. *Community Mental Health Journal*, 1968, **4**, 443–453.

Kirk, S. A. The sex offenses of whites and blacks. *Archives of Sexual Behavior*, 1975, **4**, 295–302.

Kirkendall, L. A. , & Libby, R. W. Interpersonal relationships: Crux of the sexual renaissance. *Journal of Social Issues*, 1966, **22**, 45–59.

Kockott, G., Dittmar, F., & Nusselt, L. Systematic desensitization for erectile impotence: A controlled study. *Archives of Sexual Behavior*, 1975, **4**, 493–500.

Kohlenberg, R. J. Directed masturbation and the treatment of primary orgasmic dysfunction. *Archives of Sexual Behavior*, 1974, **3**, 349–356.

Kohlenberg, R. J. Treatment of a homosexual pedophiliac using *in vivo* desensitization: A case study. *Journal of Abnormal Psychology*, 1974, **83**, 192–195.

Kolodny, R. C., Masters, W. H., & Johnson, V. E. *Textbook of sexual medicine*. Boston: Little, Brown, 1979.

Kraemer, H. C., Becker, H. B., Brodie, H. K. H., Doering, C. H., Moos, R. H., & Hamburg, D. A. Orgasmic frequency and plasma testosterone levels in normal human males. *Archives of Sexual Behavior*, 1976, **5**, 125–132.

Kreuz, L. E., Rose, R. M., & Jennings, J. R. Suppresssion of plasma testosterone levels and psychological stress. *Archives of General Psychiatry*, 1972, **26**, 479–482.

La Femina, R. The use of an auditory stimulus to arouse masturbatory fantasy in an impotent male. *Journal of Behavior Therapy and Experimental Psychiatry*, 1977, **8**, 433–435.

Lambley, P. Treatment of transvestism and subsequent coital problems. *Journal of Behavior Therapy and Experimental Psychiatry*, 1974, **5**, 101–102.

Lang, P. J. The application of psychophysiological methods to the study of psychotherapy and behavior modification. In A. E. Bergin & S. L. Garfield (Eds.), *Handbook of psychotherapy and behavior change*. New York: Wiley, 1971.

Lavin, N. I., Thorpe, J. G., Barker, J. C., Blakemore, C. B., & Conway, C. G. Behavior therapy in a case of transvestism. *Journal of Nervous and Mental Disease*, 1961, **133**, 346–353.

Lazarus, A. The treatment of chronic frigidity by systematic desensitization. *Journal of Nervous and Mental Disease*, 1963, **136**, 272–278.

Leiblum. S. R., & Ersner-Hershfield, R. Sexual enhancement groups for dysfunctional women: An evaluation. *Journal of Sex and Marital Therapy*, 1977, **3**, 139–152.

Leiblum, S. R., Rosen, R. C., & Pierce, D. Group treatment format: Mixed sexual dysfunction. *Archives of Sexual Behavior*, 1976, **5**, 313–322.

Levin, S. L., Barry, S. M., Gambaro, S., Wolfinsohn, L., & Smith, A. Variations of covert sensitization in the treatment of pedophiliac behavior: A case study. *Journal of Consulting and Clinical Psychology*, 1977, **45**, 896–907.

Levine, S. B. Premature ejaculation: Some thoughts about its pathogenesis. *Journal of Sex and Marital Therapy*, 1975, **1**, 326–334.

Levine, S. B. Conceptual suggestions for outcome research in sex therapy. *Journal of Sex and Marital Therapy*, 1980, **6**, 102–108.

Levine, S. B., & Agle, D. The effectiveness of sex therapy for chronic secondary psychological impotence. *Journal of Sex and Marital Therapy*, 1978, **4**, 235–258.

Lidberg, L. Social and psychiatric aspects of impotence and premature ejaculation. *Archives of Sexual Behavior*, 1972, **2**, 135–146.

Lief, H., & Reed, D. *Sex Knowledge and Attitude Test*. Philadelphia: Division of Family Study, Department of Psychiatry, University of Pennsylvania, School of Medicine, 1972.

Lihn, H. Sexual masochism: A case report. *International Journal of Psycho-Analysis*, 1971, **52**, 469–478.

Lobitz, W., & Lo Piccolo, J. New methods in the behavioral treatment of sexual dysfunction. *Journal of Behavior Therapy and Experimental Psychiatry*, 1972, **3**, 265–271.

Locke, H. J., & Wallace, K. M. Short marital adjustment and prediction tests: Their reliability and validity. *Marriage and Family Living*, 1959, **21**, 251–255.

Lo Piccolo, L. Low sexual desire. In S. R. Leiblum & L. A. Pervin (Eds.), *Principles and practices of sex therapy*. New York: Guilford Press, 1980.

Lo Piccolo, J., & Heiman, J. Cultural values and the therapeutic definition of sexual function and dysfunction. *Journal of Social Issues*, 1977, **33**, 166–183.

Lo Piccolo, J., & Steger, J. C. The Sexual Interaction Inventory: A new instrument for assessment of sexual dysfunction. *Archives of Sexual Behavior*, 1974, **3**, 585–595.

Lowenstein, L. F. A case of exhibitionism treated by counter-conditioning. *Adolescence*, 1973, **8**, 213–218.

MacCullough, M. J., Williams, C., & Birtles, C. J. The successful application of aversion therapy to an adolescent exhibitionist. *Journal of Behavior Therapy and Experimental Psychiatry*, 1971, **2**, 61–66.

MacDonald, I. J. Behavior therapy in a case of transvestism. *Lancet*, 1961, **1**, 889–890.

Maconaghy, N. Penile volume responses to moving and still pictures of male and female nudes in heterosexual and homosexual males. *Behaviour Research and Therapy*, 1967, **5**, 43–48.

Maletsky, B. M. "Assisted" covert sensitization in the treatment of exhibitionism. *Journal of Clinical and Consulting Psychology*, 1974, **42**, 34–40.

Marks, I. M., & Gelder, M. G. Transvestism and fetishism: Clinical and psychological changes during faradic aversion. *British Journal of Psychiatry*, 1967, **113**, 711–729.

Marks, I. M., Gelder, A. M., & Bancroft, J. H. J. Sexual deviants two years after electric aversion. *British Journal of Psychiatry*, 1970, **117**, 173–185.

Marks, I. M., Rachman, S., & Gelder, M. G. Methods for assessment of aversion treatment in fetishism with masochism. *Behaviour Research and Therapy*, 1965, **3**, 253–258

Marquis, J. N. Orgasmic reconditioning: Changing sexual object choice through controlling masturbation fantasies. *Journal of Behavior Therapy and Experimental Psychiatry*, 1970, **1**, 263–271.

Marshall, W. L. The modification of sexual fantasies: A combined treatment approach to the reduction of deviant sexual behavior. *Behaviour Research and Therapy*, 1973, **11**, 557–564.

Marshall, W. L. A combined treatment approach to the reduction of multiple fetish-related behaviors. *Journal of Consulting and Clinical Psychology*, 1974, **42**, 613–616.

Marshall, W. L., & Lippens, K. The clinical value of boredom: A procedure for reducing inappropriate sexual interest. *Journal of Nervous and Mental Disease*, 177, **165**, 283–287.

Marshall, W. L., & McKnight, R. D. An integrated treatment program for sexual offenders. *Canadian Psychiatric Association Journal*, 1975, **20**, 133–138.

Masters, W. H., & Johnson, V. E. *Human sexual response*. Boston: Little, Brown, 1966.

Masters, W. H., & Johnson, V. E. *Human sexual inadequacy*. Boston: Little, Brown, 1970.

Mathis, H. I. Instating sexual adequacy in a disabled exhibitionist. *Psychotherapy: Theory, Research, and Practice*, 1975, **12**, 97–100.

Mathis, J. L., & Collins, M. Mandatory group therapy for exhibitionists. *American Journal of Psychiatry*, 1970, **26**, 1162–1167.

McGovern, K. B., Stewart, R. C., & Lo Piccolo, J. Secondary orgasmic dysfunction I. Analysis and strategies for treatment. *Archives of Sexual Behavior*, 1975, **4**, 265–275.

McGuire, L. S., & Wagner, N. N. Sexual dysfunctions in women who were molested as children: One response pattern and suggestions for treatment. *Journal of Sex and Marital Therapy*, 1978, **4**, 11–15.

McGuire, R. J., Carlisle, J. M., & Young, B. G. Sexual deviations as conditioned behavior: A hypothesis. *Behaviour Research and Therapy*, 1965, **2**, 185–190.

McMullen, S. J. Automated procedures for treatment of primary orgasmic dysfunction. *Dissertation Abstracts International*, 1977, **37** (10-B), 5364–5365.

McMullen, S. J., & Rosen, R. C. Self-administered masturbation training in the treatment of primary orgasmic dysfunction. *Journal of Consulting and Clinical Psychology*, 1979, **47**, 912–918.

McSweeney, A. J. Fingernail fetishism: Report of a case treated with hypnosis. *American Journal of Clinical Hypnosis*, 1972, **15**, 139–143.

McWhirter, D. P., & Mattison, A. M. The treatment of sexual dysfunction in gay male couples. *Journal of Sex and Marital Therapy*, 1978, ˙ 213–218.

Mees, H. L. Sadistic fantasies modified by aversive conditioning and substitution: A case report. *Behavior Research and Therapy*, 1966, **4**, 317–320.

Meyer, J. K., Schmidt, C. W., Lucas, M. J., & Smith, R. N. Short-term treatment of sexual problems: Interim report. *American Journal of Psychiatry*, 1975, **132**, 172–176.

Miller, H. L., & Haney, J. R. Behavior and traditional therapy applied to pedophiliac exhibitionism: A case study. *Psychological Reports*, 1976, **39**, 119–124.

Money, J. Paraphilias. In J. Money & H. Musaph (Eds.), *Handbook of sexology*. New York: Elsevier/North Holland Biomedical Press, 1977.

Money, J., & Wiedeking, C. Gender identity/role and normal differentiation and its transpositions. In B. B. Wolman & J. Money (Eds.), *Handbook of human sexuality*. Englewood Cliffs, N. J.: Prentice-Hall, 1980.

Moss, G. R., Rada, R. T., & Appel, J. B. Positive control as an alternative to aversion therapy. *Journal of Behavior Therapy and Experimental Psychiatry*, 1970, **1**, 291–294.

Mudd, J. W. Impotence responsive to glyceryl trinitrate. *American Journal of Psychiatry*, 1977, **134**, 922–925.

Munjack, D. J., Cristol, A., Goldstein, A., Phillips, D., Goldberg, A., Whipple, K., Staples, F., & Kanno, P. Behavioural treatment of orgasmic dysfunction: A controlled study. *British Journal of Psychiatry*, 1976, **129**, 497–502.

Munjack, D. J., & Kanno, P. H. Retarded ejaculation: A review. *Archives of Sexual Behavior*, 1979, **8**, 139–150.

Munjack, D. J., Kanno, P. H., & Oziel, L. J. Ejaculatory disorders: Some psychometric data. *Psychological Reports*, 1978, **43**, 738–787.

Nemetz, G. H., Craig, K. D., & Reith, G. Treatment of female sexual dysfunction through symbolic modeling. *Journal of Consulting and Clinical Psychology*, 1978, **46**, 62–73.

Newell, A. G. A case of ejaculatory incompetence treated with a mechanical aid. *Journal of Behavior Therapy and Experimental Psychiatry*, 1976, **7**, 193–194.

Nowinski, J. K., & Lo Piccolo, J. Assessing sexual behavior in couples. *Journal of Sex and Marital Therapy*, 1979, **5**, 225–243.

Obler, M. Systematic desensitization in sexual disorders. *Journal of Behavior Therapy and Experimental Psychiatry*, 1973, **4**, 93–101.

O'Gorman, E. C. The treatment of frigidity: A comparative study of group and individual desensitization. *British Journal of Psychiatry*, 1978, **132**, 580–584.

Parloff, M. B., Waskow, I. E., & Wolfe, B. E. Research on therapist variables in relation to process and outcome. In S. L., Garfield & A. E. Bergin (Eds.), *Handbook of psychotherapy and behavior change* (2nd ed). New York: Wiley, 1978.

Pennington, V. M. Treatment in transvestism. *American Journal of Psychiatry*, 1960, **117**, 250–251.

Perelman, M. A. The treatment of premature ejaculation by time-limited group sex therapy. *Dissertation Abstracts International*, 1977, **37** (10-B), 5369.

Pinard, G., & Lamontague, Y. Electric aversion, aversion relief, and sexual retraining in treatment of fetishism with masochism. *Journal of Behavior Therapy and Experimental Psychiatry*, 1976, **7**, 71–74.

Pinta, E. R. Treatment of obsessive homosexual pedophilic fantasies with medroxy-progesterone acetate. *Biological Psychiatry*, 1978, **13**, 369–373.

Pirke, K. M., Kockott, G., & Dittmar, F. Psychosexual stimulation and plasma testosterone in man. *Archives of Sexual Behavior*, 1974, **3**, 577–584.

Porter, J. Pleasuring enhanced by suggestive therapy for frigidity. *Psychotherapy and Psychosomatics*, 1978, **30**, 37–46.

Purvis, K., Landgren, B. M., Cekan, Z., & Diczfalusy, E. Endocrine effects of masturbation in men. *Journal of Endocrinology*, 1976, **70**, 439–444.

Quinsey, V. L., Bergerson, S. G., & Steinman, C. M. Changes in physiological and verbal responses of child molesters during aversion therapy. *Canadian Journal of Behavioral Science*, 1976, **8**, 202–212.

Quirk, D. A. A follow-up on the Bond-Hutchison case of systematic desensitization with an exhibitionist. *Behavior Therapy*, 1974, **5**, 428–431.

Raboch, J., & Starka, L. Coital activity of men and the levels of plasmatic testosterone. *Journal of Sex Research*, 1972, **8**, 219–224.

Rachman, S. Sexual fetishism: An experimental analogue. *Psychological Record*, 1966, **16**, 293–296.

Rathus, S. A. Treatment of recalcitrant ejaculatory incompetence. *Behavior Therapy*, 1978, **9**, 962.

Reisinger, J. J. Masturbatory training in the treatment of primary orgasmic dysfunction. *Journal of Behavioral Therapy and Experimental Psychiatry*, 1974, **5**. 179–183.

Reisinger, J. J. Effects of erotic stimulation and masturbatory training upon situational orgasmic dysfunction. *Journal of Sex and Marital Therapy*, 1978, **4**, 177–185.

Reynolds, B. S. Voluntary facilitation of erection in men with erectile dysfunction: Effects of continuous tumescence feedback and contingent erotic film. *Dissertation Abstracts International*, 1978, **39** (1-B), 395–396.

Riley, A. J., & Riley, E. J. A controlled study to evaluate directed masturbation in the management of primary orgasmic failure in women. *British Journal of Psychiatry*, 1978, **133**, 404–409.

Robinson, C. H. The effects of observational learning on sexual behaviors and attitudes in orgasmic dysfunctional women. *Dissertation Abstracts International*, 1975, **35** (9-B), 4662.

Rooth, F. G., & Marks, I. M. Persistent exhibitionism: Short-term response to aversion, self-regulation and relaxation treatments. *Archives of Sexual Behavior*, 1974, **3**, 227–248.

Rosen, R. C., & Kopel, S. A. Penile plethysmography and biofeedback in the treatment of a transvestite-exhibitionist. *Journal of Consulting and Clinical Psychology*, 1977, **45**, 908–916.

Rosenthal, T. L. Response-contingent versus fixed punishment in aversion conditioning of pedophilia: A case study. *Journal of Nervous and Mental Disease*, 1973, **156**, 440–443.

Schiavi, R. C. Sex therapy and psychophysiological research. *American Journal of Psychiatry*, 1976, **133**, 562–565.

Schiavi, R. C., Derogatis, L. R., Kuriansky, J., O'Connor, D., & Sharpe, L. The assessment of sexual function and marital interaction. *Journal of Sex and Marital Therapy*, 1979, **5**, 169–224.

Schneidman, B., & McGuire, L. Group therapy for nonorgasmic women: Two age levels. *Archives of Sexual Behavior*, 1976, **5**, 239–247.

Schwartz, M. F., Kolodny, R. C., & Masters, W. H. Plasma testosterone levels of sexually functional and dysfunctional men. *Archives of Sexual Behavior*, 1980, **9**, 355–366.

Semans, J. H. Premature ejaculation. *Southern Medical Journal*, 1956, **49**, 353–357.

Serber, M. Shame aversion therapy. *Journal of Behavior Therapy and Experimental Psychiatry*, 1970, **1**, 213–215.

Serber, M. Shame aversion therapy with and without heterosexual training. In R. D. Rubin, H. Fensterheim, T. D. Henderson, & L. P. Ullman (Eds.), *Advances in behavior therapy: Proceedings of the Fourth Conference of the Association of Advancement of Behavior Therapy*. New York: Academic Press, 1972.

Shahar, A., & Jaffe, J. Behavior and cognitive therapy in the treatment of vaginismus: A case study. *Cognitive Therapy and Research*, 1978, **2**, 57–60.

Snyder, A., Lo Piccolo, L., & Lo Piccolo, J. Secondary orgasmic dysfunction II. Case study. *Archives of Sexual Behavior*, 1975, **4**, 277–283.

Sotile, W. M., & Kilmann, P. R. Treatments of psychogenic female sexual dysfunctions. *Psychological Bulletin* 1977, **84**, 619–633.

Sotile, W. M., & Kilmann, P. R. The effects of group systematic desensitization on orgasmic dysfunction. *Archives of Sexual Behavior*, 1978, **7**, 477–491.

Sotile, W. M., Kilmann, P., & Follingstad, D. R. A sexual-enhancement workshop: Beyond group systematic desensitization for women's sexual anxiety. *Journal of Sex and Marital Therapy*, 1977, **3**, 249–255.

Spark, R. F., White, R. A., & Connolly, P. B. Impotence is not always psychogenic. *Journal of the American Medical Association*, 1980, **243**, 750–755.

Stevenson, J., & Jones, I. H. Behavior therapy technique for exhibitionism: A preliminary report. *Archives of General Psychiatry*, 1972, **27**, 839–841.

Stevenson, J., & Wolpe, J. Recovery from sexual deviations through overcoming non-sexual neurotic responses. *American Journal of Psychiatry*, 1960, **116**, 733–742.

Stoller, R. J. *Perversion: The erotic form of hatred*. New York: Pantheon Books, 1975.

Stoudemire, J. Behavioral treatment of voyeurism and possible symptom substitution. *Psychotherapy: Theory, Research, and Practice*, 1973, **10**, 328–330.

Strzysewsky, J., & Zierhoffer, M. Aversion therapy in a case fetishism and transvestitic component. *Journal of Sex Research*, 1967, **3**, 163–167.

Sue, D. Masturbation in the *in vivo* treatment of impotence. *Journal of Behavior Therapy and Experimental Psychiatry*, 1978, **9**, 75–76.

Szasz, T. *Sex by prescription*. New York: Doubleday, 1980.

Tennent, G., Bancroft, J., & Cass, J. The control of deviant sexual behavior by drugs: A double-blind controlled study of benperidol, chlorpromazine, and placebo. *Archives of Sexual Behavior*, 1974, **3**, 261–271.

Van Dewenter, A. D., & Laws, D. R. Orgasmic reconditioning to redirect sexual arousal in pedophilias. *Behavior Therapy*, 1978, **9**, 748–765.

Van Moffaert, M. Social reintegration of sexual delinquents by a combination of psychotherapy and anti-androgen treatment. *Acta Psychiatrica Scandanavica*, 1976, **53**, 29–34.

Vogl, A. J. Are Masters and Johnson really infallible? *Hospital Physician*, 1970, **6**, 105–112.

Wallace, D. H., & Barbach, L. G. Preorgasmic group treatment. *Journal of Sex and Marital Therapy*, 1974, **1**, 146–154.

Ward, N. G. Successful lithium treatment of transvestism associated with manic-depression. *Journal of Nervous and Mental Disease*, 1975, **161**, 204–206.

Wardlaw, G. R., & Miller, P. J. A controlled exposure technique in the elimination of exhibitionism. *Behavior Therapy and Experimental Psychiatry*, 1978, **9**, 27–32.

Wickramasekera, I. The application of learning theory to the treatment of a case of sexual exhibitionism. *Psychotherapy: Theory, Research, and Practice*, 1968, **5**, 108–112.

Wickramasekera, I. Aversive behavior rehearsal for sexual exhibitionism. *Behavior Therapy*, 1976, **7**, 167–176.

Wijesinghe, B. A case of frigidity treated by short-term hypnotherapy. *International Journal of Clinical and Experimental Hypnosis*, 1977, **25**, 63–67.

Wincze, J. P., & Caird, W. K. The effects of systematic desensitization and video desensitization in the treatment of essential sexual dysfunction in women. *Behavior Therapy*, 1976,**7**, 335–342.

Wincze, J. P., Hoon, E. F., & Hoon, P. W. Physiological responsivity of normal and sexually dysfunctional women during erotic stimulus exposure. *Journal of Psychosomatic Research*, 1976, **20**, 445–451.

Witzig, J. S. The group treatment of male exhibitionists. *American Journal of Psychiatry*, 1968, **125**, 75–81.

Wolpe, J. *Psychotherapy by reciprocal inhibition*. Stanford: Stanford University Press, 1958.

Woody, R. H. Integrated aversion therapy and psychotherapy: Two sexual deviation case studies. *Journal of Sex Research*, 1973, **9**, 313–324.

Wright, J., Perreault, R., & Mathieu, M. The treatment of sexual dysfunction. *Archives of General Psychiatry*, 1977, **34**, 881–890.

Yulis, S. Generalization of therapeutic gain in the treatment of premature ejaculation. *Behavior Therapy*, 1976, **7**, 355–358.

Zeiss, R. A. Self-directed treatment for premature ejaculation: Preliminary case reports. *Journal of Behavior Therapy and Experimental Psychiatry*, 1977, **8**, 87–91.

Zeiss, R. A. Self-directed treatment for premature ejaculation. *Journal of Consulting and Clinical Psychology*, 1978, **46**, 1234–1241.

Zeiss, R. A., Christensen, A., & Levine, A. G. Treatment for premature ejaculation through male-only groups. *Journal of Sex and Marital Therapy*, 1978, **4**, 139–143.

Zeiss, A. M., Rosen, G. M., & Zeiss, R. A. Orgasm during intercourse: A treatment strategy for women. *Journal of Consulting and Clinical Psychology*, 1977, **45**, 891–895.

Zilbergeld, B. Group treatment of sexual dysfunction in men without partners. *Journal of Sex and Marital Therapy*, 1975, **1**, 204–214.

Zilbergeld, B., & Ellison, C. R. Desire discrepancies and arousal problems in sex therapy. In S. R. Leiblum & L. A. Pervin (Eds.), *Principles and practices of sex therapy*. New York: Guilford Press, 1980.

Zilbergeld, B., & Evans, M. The inadequacy of Masters and Johnson. *Psychology Today*, 1980, **14**, 28–43.

CHAPTER 9

A Review of Current Assessment Tools for Monitoring Changes in Depression

PETER W. MORAN AND MICHAEL J. LAMBERT

Depression is one of the most popular labels used today, both inside and outside the mental health profession. Although widely used, the term "depression" is not well understood. It is difficult to comprehend this malady when so many theoreticians of various backgrounds and schools disagree about its nature. Descriptively, the phenomenon of depression has involved various affective, cognitive, behavioral, and physiological symptomatology. In fact, many symptoms used by mental health professionals have, at one time, been considered inherent in the depression picture. An illustrative case concerns a study by Watts (1966), who recorded 71 different symptoms in a sample of 590 depressed individuals. A quick review of the depression literature reveals that symptom lists have varied as widely as have theoretical descriptions (Ayd, 1961).

Factor analytic studies of depression have also failed to achieve any unitary consensus. In reviewing such studies, Costello (1970) concluded that no one factor, other than psychomotor retardation, was common to research findings. Costello surmised that such factorial conclusions often reflected the personal biases of the investigators rather than objective and precise data analysis. Furthermore, even if biases did not have a confounding effect, our stinted knowledge of depressive symptoms simply precludes any sophisticated mathematical data analysis at this time.

The numerous symptomatic theories and factor analytic studies referred to here are indicative of the need for continued research in the depression area. The increasing prevalence and consequent dangerous ramifications of this disorder demonstrate the current need for adequate intervention (Johnson & Weitzman, 1980; Lester et al., 1979). A major factor in effective intervention is the accurate identification and assessment of depressive disorders. To reach this goal of accuracy in depression assessment, current diagnostic strategies of depression and their philosophical foundation must be understood. In addition, we must be familiar with the assessment instruments available and, of these tools, which ones provide the most reliable and valid measures of depressive symptomatology. Let us begin examining these important dimensions of depression assessment in hopes of acquiring a basic understanding of why we choose to diagnose and assess the way we do and how we might change assessment techniques so that assessment accuracy is attained. Following this a review of specific instruments will be provided.

PHILOSOPHY, DEPRESSION, AND DSM-III

Before reviewing current assessment techniques of depression, it is crucial to explore the philosophical approaches used in diagnosing and assessing depressive illness.

When clinicians in the United States are trained today in the areas of diagnosis and assessment, the philosophy followed is usually that mirrored in the Diagnostic and Statistical Manual (DSM). Since its inception in 1952, the DSM has developed into one of the most popular of diagnostic references. This development is reflected in the rapid sell-out of the DSM-III's first printing just weeks after it was available to U.S. mental health professionals. Philosophically, the DSM-III can be described as approaching mental illness from a symptomatological perspective. Because the manual is generally neutral with regard to etiology (an exemplary exception would be Organic Mental Disorders), the DSM-III attempts to comprehensively describe the manifestations of mental disorders; rarely does it attempt to account for how the disturbances come about. This approach is considered "descriptive" in that definitions of the disorders are comprised of descriptions of the clinical features or symptoms of the disorders (DSM-III, 1980).

Although we are familiar with the philosophical limitations of DSM-III's symptomatologic approach as well as the difficulties of the etiologic perspective, we must determine whether we have a better philosophy to offer. The purpose of this chapter is not to develop or discuss any innovative philosophies to diagnosis and assessment. Our goal here is to describe and evaluate the present state of depression assessment. Although we recognize that many philosophical issues remain unresolved and that alternative approaches are possible, we evaluate the methods currently in use within the philosophical orientation that dominates the symptomatically oriented DSM-III.

From a symptomatologic approach, depression can be considered from two viewpoints. First, depression can be viewed as a simple, unanalyzable, first-order state that cannot be described or broken down into simpler components. This is how DSM-I (1952) and DSM-II (1968) dealt with depressive reaction and depressive neurosis, respectively. Second, depression can be viewed as a complex, made up of simpler primary symptoms. The DSM-III (1980) deals with major depression, single episode, and recurrent as a secondary symptom where primary symptoms such as dysphoric mood (an affective–behavioral symptom) and fatigue (a motor symptom) are noted as symptoms that, together with other primary symptoms, describe depressed affect.

Before evaluating current assessment tools for monitoring changes in depression, let us review the criteria for depression as defined by the DSM-III. Through a content analysis of DSM-III depressive symptomatology, the following criteria were established:

1. Dysphoric mood
   a. Affective symptoms—depressed, sad, "blue," hopeless, low, "down in the dumps," irritable
   b. Behavioral symptoms—loss of interest or pleasure in usual activities
2. Feelings of worthlessness or guilt
3. Thoughts of death and suicide; suicidal attempts
4. Inability to think or concentrate
5. Increase or decrease in appetite and/or weight
6. Increase (agitation) or decrease (retardation) in psychomotor activity
7. Increase or decrease in sleeping behavior
8. Decrease in energy (i.e., fatigue)
9. Decrease in sexual drive

Are DSM-III criteria adequate for assessing depression? Although there has been little study analyzing the factorial make-up of DSM-III depressive criteria, examination of the depressive symptomatology involved reveals inherent coverage of affective, cognitive, behavioral, and physiological features of depression. One distinct advantage of the DSM-III approach is that it is indeed comprehensive, atheoretical, and relatively concrete in its presentation of inclusive and exclusive criteria. This facilitates an accurate, differential mode of diagnostic decision making. However, since it is based on fixed clinical description, DSM-III depressive criteria lack clear-cut indicators of the severity of that depressed symptomatology.

The reliability and validity of DSM-III depressive criteria will be determined as future research explores the DSM-III approach to depression. Presently, in our examination of the DSM-III system, we speculate that problems will arise involving diagnostic reliability. Since a fixed number (four of eight) of a variety of depressive symptoms are required for a diagnosis of a major depressive episode, consequent decision making among diagnosticians may also vary. Nevertheless, in the following analysis we evaluate, among other factors, the degree to which current assessment tools assess depression as defined by DSM-III criteria.

ASSESSMENT OF DEPRESSION

A review of the literature on depression assessment reveals numerous instruments designed to measure depressed affect (see Table 9.1). Symptoms assumed central to assessment have been classified into two major diagnostic areas (Rehm, 1976): the verbal–cognitive area and the motor area. Verbal–cognitive assessment is accomplished in two ways. The first involves direct reporting by the client requiring tools described as self-rated inventories. The second approach involves participation by a skilled clinician or trained paraprofessional for scoring or recording purposes; these tools are described as interviewer-rated scales.

Behavior of depressive typography has also been evaluated in attempts to diagnose depression from a motoric perspective. Depressed motor behavior is often assessed from two general modes: overt–verbal behavior and overt–motor behavior (Rehm, 1976). Like the verbal–cognitive area, motoric assessment involves self as well as interviewer rating tools.

As is the case when several alternatives are available, advantages and disadvantages must be considered. An informed decision to choose either or both verbal–cognitive and/or motor assessment devices requires not only the consideration of inherent strengths and weaknesses of those devices, but also the primary purpose of that particular assessment. With their purpose in mind, assessors should be aware of what their chosen assessment methodology involves.

The self-rating approach does not require a skilled administrator. Thus this approach is time-saving and economical. Because such data are independent of a clinician's theoretical bias, eclectic interpretation among interdisciplinary staff is possible. On the other hand, the self-rating method assumes that accurate information will be reported by the patient. The weakness of such an assumption is that the depressed patient may be unaware of subjective feelings or be unable or even unwilling to reveal them (Levitt & Lubin, 1975). The accuracy of self-report assessment information is thus a function of the patient's awareness, literacy, and motivation.

Although the self-report method is most vulnerable to a "patient-masking" effect, both the interviewer method of verbal–cognitive assessment and the overt behavioral methods have problems as well. With interviewer scales and behavior ratings, the clinician is the ultimate data source. Although the clinician receives data from the patient, the data are "processed" through the clinician before it is reported. The assumption is that accurate information will be reported by the clinician. Various problems can occur involving the confounding differences among clinicians:

1. Differences in training, education, experience, and competency of the rating clinician. For example, what is "severe" pathology to the psychology intern may be "moderate" to the experienced clinician.

2. Differences in theoretical bias of rater. What is "obviously" manifested and reported by the behaviorist may go unchecked by the analyst.

3. Differences in role of the rater. The consulting physician may evaluate symptomatology in terms of medication needed; the psychiatric nurse may focus on symptoms that predict the problems this patient may bring to her ward (Zung, 1974).

Assessment of overt behavior, whether verbal or motor, requires not only skilled observers, but also well-equipped facilities. Although data collection on speech rate may not be vulnerable to theoretical bias, it does require a valid and reliable rater resource. Family members, although ideal in some ways for collecting speech rate or interpersonal conversation time, are not always willing, or if so, skilled enough for the task. Unobtrusiveness and consistency can be assumed only on the word of a loving mother or coerced sibling. Because of such control problems, behavioral assessment is often limited to institutional settings that require appropriate facilities. Many clinic settings do not have two-way mirrors or large rooms and grounds where unobtrusive measurement is possible. Often, behavioral assessment procedures are considered advantageous because mental health professionals are not required for data gathering; yet paraprofessionals that may be involved are often not a part of a community clinic's staff. Such personnel resources are usually limited to university settings.

It is of paramount importance that the clinician realize the advantages and disadvantages of varying assessment procedures. Often, individual assessment needs can best be satisfied by individualized assessment methodology. Familiarization with assessment strengths and weaknesses will aid the clinician in choosing that approach that best fits the client's needs as well as the particular work setting.

INDIVIDUAL ANALYSIS OF THE MAJOR TOOLS

As indicated in Table 9.1, there is a variety of depression assessment tools available. With such a large number to choose from, clinicians need to know what specific instruments have been studied most and more importantly, what the resulting research has to offer in terms of demonstrating test utility as well as identifying test limitations. We review those scales that in our judgment have been researched most consistently and extensively in hopes of providing the clinician with a pragmatic guide to the assessment of depression.

Self-Rated Tools

Beck Depression Inventory

DESCRIPTION. The Beck Depression Inventory (BDI) (Beck et al., 1961) is a 21-item, multiple-choice questionnaire that provides an objectively derived

Table 9.1. Measures of Depression[a,b]

Name of Scale	Primary Reference	Source of Data	Type of Measure
Beck Depression Inventory	Beck et al., 1961	Self (client)	Paper–pencil; multiple choice (increasing severity)
Center for Epidemiologic Studies— Depression Scale (CES-D)	Radloff, 1977	Self	Paper–pencil; multiple choice (increasing frequency)
Depression Adjective Checklists	Lubin, 1965	Self	Paper–pencil; checklist
Feelings and Concerns Checklist	Grinker et al., 1961	Interviewer	Paper–pencil; multiple choice (increasing severity)
Hamilton Rating Scale for Depression	Hamilton, 1960,1967	Interviewer	Paper–pencil; multiple choice (increasing severity)
Index of Depression	Popoff, 1969	Self	Paper–pencil; multiple choice
Kupfer Detre Scale (KDS-3A)	Kupfer et al., 1975	Self	Paper–pencil, Nos. 1–36 yes–no, three items: longevity inquiry; Nos. 37–39 multiple choice (increasing frequency)
Levine–Pilowsky Depression Questionnaire	Pilowsky et al., 1969	Self	Paper–pencil; yes–no
Middlesex Hospital Questionnaire (MHQ)	Crown & Crisp, 1966	Self	Paper–pencil; mixed: yes–no, increasing frequency, and level of agree-ment with item
MMPI-D Scale	Hathaway & McKinley, 1942	Self	Paper–pencil; true–false
Montgomery— Asberg Depression Rating Scale	Montgomery & Asberg, 1979	Interviewer (parapro-fessional)	Paper–pencil; multiple choice (increasing severity)
Multiscore Depression Inventory	Berndt et al., 1980	Self	Paper–pencil; true–false

Name of Scale	Primary Reference	Source of Data	Type of Measure
Pleasant Events Schedule	MacPhillamy & Lewinsohn, 1976	Self	Pencil–paper; multiple choice (increasing frequency and increasing pleasantness)
Self-Rating Questionnaire for Depression	Rockliff, 1969	Self	Paper–pencil; multiple choice (increasing frequency)
Visual Analogue Scales	Lewinsohn, et al., 1978 1978	Self	Paper–pencil; continuum line (very depressed –very happy)
Wakefield Self-Assessment Depression Inventory	Snaith et al., 1971	Self	Paper–pencil; multiple choice (increasing frequency)
Wechsler Depression Scale	Wechsler et al. 1963	Interviewer	Paper–pencil; multiple choice
Zung Self-Rating Depression Scale	Zung, 1965	Self	Paper–pencile; multiple choice (increasing frequency)

[a]Additional measures reviewed by Levitt and Lubin (1975):

Depression–Elation Scale

Pessimism: Depression–Optimism: Elation Scale

Factor D^2

Paired Adjective Checklist

Depression Rating Scale

Clinical Quantification of Depressive Reactions

British Hospital Progress Test

Behavioral and Subjective Depression Questionnaire

Current Behavior Checklist

Psychiatric Judgment Depression Scale

Depression Reaction Scale

Anxiety–Depression Scale

Self–Other Mood Inventory

D_{30} Scale of Depression

PPC Depression Progress Test

Depression Rating Scale

Patient's Depression Scale

Depression Evaluation Scale

Sad–Glad Scale

Test of Liability to Depressive Illness

(continued)

Table 9.1. *(continued)*

Trait Depression Scale
Depression Scale
Self-Rating Inventory
Behavioral Depression Scale
Physician Depression Scale
Depressive Rating Scale
KAS–Hogarty Depression Scale
Mania–Depression Scale
[b]Non-English Scales:
FKD Scale (Vinar, 1966)
Von Zerssen Scale (Zerssen et al., 1970)

score indicating the severity of depressive symptomatology. This tool is a state measuring device that attempts to tap recent (up to one-week old) symptoms. Although Beck (1978) states that there is no arbitrary cut-off score that can be used for all purposes, he does provide scoring guidelines to be utilized when interpreting the single score:

BDI Score	Severity of Depressive Symptomatology
0–9	Normal range
10–15	Mild depression
16–19	Mild–moderate depression
20–29	Moderate–severe depression
30–63	Severe depression

This instrument takes less than 30 minutes to complete. The only materials needed are a pencil and the single-sheet protocol. No training is necessary to either administer or score the inventory.

NORMATIVE DATA–DEMOGRAPHIC EFFECTS.   The BDI was normed on 409 inpatients and outpatients from Pennsylvania. This population was predominately white with a higher frequency of lower socioeconomic status (SES) groups in the sample. Although research reports that race is a negligible factor concerning the reliability of this instrument, there are negative correlations reported between the educational and SES levels of individuals tested and their resulting BDI scores (Beck & Beamesderfer, 1974; Dorus & Sensay, 1980; Schwab et al., 1967). Most studies examining the effects of sex on BDI scores suggest no significant relationship (Hackney & Ribordy, 1980; Oliver & Burkham, 1979; Schwab et al., 1967b), whereas one study (Dorus & Senay, 1980) found females to have significantly higher scores.

FACTORIAL MAKEUP.   The items in the BDI were clinically derived through Beck's and his associates' "systematic observations and records of the characteristic attitudes and symptoms of depressed patients" (Beck et al., 1961). From these data, this research group also selected a specified number of symptoms and attitudes that he felt was most consistent with both empirical data and the then-current psychiatric literature.

Several studies have attempted to identify what type of depressive symptomatology is measured by the BDI. As early as 1967, Schwab et al. compared the BDI to the Hamilton Rating Scale and concluded that the BDI had several categories alluding to pessimism, failure, and self-punitive wishes. These researchers estimated that somatic symptomatology accounted for just 29% of the maximal BDI score. In 1974, Beck and Beamesderfer, utilizing a Varimax rotation, reported three major factors: (1) negative view of self and future; (2) physiological symptomatology; and (3) physical withdrawal. Giambra (1977) identified four major variables in the BDI along with several minor ones. He reported that 12 of the 21 items measured a stable depressive dimension that he labeled "Depression: Affective Malaise." The three remaining major variables were identified as suicidal ambivalence, appetite–weight loss, and fatigability. Together, these studies suggest that the BDI is tapping the affective dimension of depression. Along with that, the BDI appears to also measure cognitive and physiological symptomatology. Incidentally, Giambra observed that all the minor variables he identified, measured depression best from a severity approach (e.g., crying spells) that strengthens the validity of Beck's proposed cut-off score interpretations.

RELIABILITY.   The reliability of the BDI is somewhat difficult to measure. Since the tool is a self-report measure, interrater reliability is not possible. Because of the questionnaire's brevity, the effects of memory may confound test–retest correlations. Yet even if a long interval were provided between administrations, fluctuations in severity of depressive symptomatology confound these same measures of reliability. As a result, we look toward split-half measures for an estimate of the BDI's reliability. Although there seems to be few such studies, Beck and Beamesderfer (1974) reported a split-half Pearson r of .86, which suggests that certain depressive symptomatology are reliably measured by the 21-item questionnaire. However, more research is needed before any definitive conclusions on the reliability of the BDI can be made.

Depression Adjective Checklists

DESCRIPTION.   The Depression Adjective Checklists (DACL) (Lubin, 1967) are a collection of seven separate lists of affective adjectives that provide the clinician with a state measure ("how you feel now—today") of self-reported depressive mood. The seven lists are separated into two sets. Set I consists of Forms A to D; each form is made up of 32 items. Set II includes Forms E, F, and G; each form is made up of 34 items.

The author reports that each DACL list can usually be completed by normal subjects in about 2.5 minutes. Test materials include the seven checklists, a pencil, and one cardboard stencil for scoring. The subject is required to simply "check all the words that describe your feelings" (Lubin, 1967). These words include both depressive, "plus" (e.g., unhappy) as well as positive, "minus" (e.g., active) adjectives. The score for *each* list is the number of "plus" adjectives checked and the number of "minus" adjectives not checked. In his review of the DACL, Goodstein (1972) reports possible confusion over the scoring of minus adjectives by clinical personnel, advising careful training of scorers.

NORMATIVE DATA AND DEMOGRAPHIC EFFECTS. Normative study on the DACL is extensive, particularly with Form E. Previous reviewers (Lewinsohn & Lee, 1981; Rehm, 1976) rate the DACL's psychometric qualities as excellent. Goodstein (1972) describes the DACL as "clearly the most psychometrically sophisticated and potentially useful instrument of this type currently available." Original normative data were collected for Sets I and II separately. Adjectives for Set I were chosen because they successfully discriminated (.001 level) between 179 normal females and 48 female neuropsychiatric patients rated by clinicians as "marked" or "severely" depressed. Items for Set II were selected because of comparable discriminating results obtained from 100 male normals and a sample of 47 male psychiatric patients (Lubin, 1967). Since these original groups were tested, numerous populations of both sexes, including high school, college and graduate students, senior citizens (females), adolescent delinquents (females), and several psychiatric groups, have provided normative data in the form of means and standard deviations for each individual list (Lubin, 1967). With this information, it is possible to compare any client falling into any of the above-mentioned populations on any of the seven lists. Specifically, normative data on Form E of the DACL is excellent (Levitt & Lubin, 1975; Lubin & Levitt, 1979).

Studies on the effects of demographic variables are limited. Virtually all such work has been done by Lubin and his associates. Lubin (1967) reported correlative data between the DACL and age and education. He concluded, "It appears that there is no important systematic tendency for DACL scores to be correlated with age or education." Goodstein (1972, p. 133) observed the effects of sex on the seven lists:

> The normal males were, however, significantly lower than the nondepressed male patients only on lists E through G, the lists originally developed with male subjects. Also, there is clear evidence that females . . . obtain higher DACL scores than do the equivalent male groups, suggesting that lists A through D might be more discriminating with females and lists E through G might be more effective with males, a caution not directly suggested by the author.

Thus the effects of demographic variables on resulting DACL scores has not been well documented. Further work needs to focus on Lubin's dismissal of the effects of age and education; SES effects have apparently not been explored. Clinicians should be aware that sex does affect scores between Sets 1 and 2.

FACTORIAL MAKEUP. The factors of depressive symptomatology inherent in the DACL are not discussed by Lubin (1967) in the test manual.

Although Lubin has studied correlates of depressed mood (Lubin et al., 1978) and factor structure of psychological assessment (Lubin et al., 1974b), there appears to be little factor analytic research done by Lubin or his associates. McNair (1972), in his review of the DACL, criticized Lubin for ignoring factor analytic studies of mood and affective states. McNair cited research (Borgatta, 1961; McNair & Maurice, 1964; Nowlis & Nowlis, 1956) indicating that many of the adjectives utilized in the DACL measure affective states other than depression. Giambra (1977), however, performed factor analysis on the Zung SDS, the Beck DI, and Lubin's DACL. His findings revealed the DACL to load on one factor alone described as "Depression: Affective Malaise." Correlating highly with this depressed mood was a sense of failure, lack of satisfaction, sense of emptiness, pessimism, guilt feelings, work inhibition, mental confusion, social withdrawal, personal devaluation, hopelessness, self-hate, suicidal wishes, and indecisiveness (Giambra, 1977). It appears from Giambra's work that the DACL focuses specifically on the affective dimension of depression (the illness' major factor) and does not attempt to tap other aspects of depressive symptomatology such as physiological features. Although such straightforward emphasis on depressive mood will reliably detect depressed affect, the DACL seems, by its factorial nature, to be limited in its ability to measure the multiple dimensions of depression.

RELIABILITY. Unlike many self-report measures, the development of alternate forms of the DACL lends itself well to extensive reliability data. Lubin (1967) and Lubin and Himelstein (1976) took advantage of this characteristic and provided varied analysis that demonstrated the DACL to be a reliable assessment tool. Internal consistency of the DACL varied from .79 to .90 as a function of list (A to E) and subject sex. Split-half reliabilities of the seven lists are based on correlational data between the two item-balanced (positive vs. negative) columns that make up each list. Overall, the reliabilities range between .82 and .93 for normals and .86 and .93 for patients. Intercorrelations between lists (parallel form reliability) is one of the DACL's strongest features. Lubin (1967) reports that for a new group of male and female normals given the seven lists in scrambled order, interlist correlations ranged from .80 to .93, suggesting that the lists are indeed comparable. Similar findings utilizing Forms E, F, and G were gathered almost a decade later by Lubin and Himelstein (1976).

MMPI-D Scale

DESCRIPTION. The MMPI-D Scale (MMPI-D) (Hathaway & McKinley, 1942) is comprised of 60 true-false items that provide a raw score (usually converted to a standard score) measuring "symptomatic" depression. This one scale can be completed by most patients in less than fifteen minutes. Hathaway and McKinley (1980) described such depression as a clinically recognizable, present state of mind characterized by poor morale, lack of hope in the future, and dissatisfaction with one's current status. The raw score represents the number of items answered in the depressed direction. Items answered "cannot say" are disregarded since there are so few such responses.

The MMPI-D Scale is one of the many scales making up the well-known MMPI. The scale is usually given in the context of the complete MMPI, and the resulting D-Scale score is utilized in relation to the total MMPI profile. The inventory's administration is straightforward; the test-taking task is easily understood by a variety of patient and nonpatient populations taking approximately 1½ hours.

NORMATIVE DATA/DEMOGRAPHIC EFFECTS. The D-Scale normative group (Hathaway & McKinley, 1942) consisted of (1) 139 normal, married males and 200 normal, married females, between the ages of 26 and 43 (referred to as the normal group), (2) 265 college students who served as a check for the effects of age on item selection, (3) 40 normals having a high depression score on a preliminary depression scale (depressed normal group), (4) 50 patients without observable depression but with a tendency to score high on the preliminary depression scale (the nondepressed group), and (5) 50 clinically diagnosed depressed patients (the criterion group). Of the 504 items given to this diverse population, the chosen 60 met the following requirements: a progressive increase in item frequency from the normal to depressed normal to criterion group; a difference in item percentage between the normal and the criterion groups of 2.5 or more times the item's standard error; nondepressed group percentage for any item approached that for normals (Hathaway & McKinley, 1980). Eleven of the 60 items are considered "correction items" (i.e., items that hold the scores down on cases that are not truly depressed) and are not especially indicative of depression. Normative data gathered by Hathaway and McKinley (1942) provide mean raw scores for varying populations:

Group	Mean Raw Score
Clinically depressed	36.68
Pretested depressed	32.49
Nondepressed	28.86
Symptomatically depressed	28.20
Random psychiatric cases	24.44
Physically ill	21.70
Normals	18.14

The differing mean scores among the groups appear reasonable except for the nondepressed individuals. In their review of these norms, Hathaway and McKinley (1980) provide some explanation. They reason that since the correction items control for false positives, the group may really have been depressed but hid their symptomatology prior to testing.

For clinical use, all raw scores are transformed to standard scores in which the means of each of the whole normal groups of males and females between the ages of 16 and 45 are given the value of 50. All other raw scores are assigned standard scores where the standard deviation is 10, with larger scores denoting more depression (Hathaway & McKinley, 1980).

Demographic variables appear to influence D-Scale outcome, particularly with normals (Hathaway & McKinley, 1980). Among normals, there is a clear tendency for higher scores to occur with older subjects. This age effect is supported by Salzman et al. (1972) with geriatric patients. Sex differences are more constant where females tend to score significantly higher than males. The college and precollege students have the lowest scores of any subgroup within the normal population; this suggests that the higher a person's educational level, the lower the resulting D score. Thus clinicians should be aware that the sex of the client significantly affects MMPI-D Scale scoring where females score higher. The lesser effects of age and education should also be considered before scores are interpreted.

FACTORIAL MAKEUP.   Factorial studies by numerous researchers (Comrey, 1957; Harris & Lingoes, 1955; O'Connor et al., 1957; Tuthill et al., 1967) as reviewed by Dahlstrom et al. (1972) reveal that the D-Scale taps the depressive dimensions of affect, cognition, behavior, and physiology. Common factors identified among these studies include subjective depression, physical complaints, and attitudinal characteristics such as cynicism, apathy, brooding, and hostility. Thus the D-Scale is not a unidimensional measure of depressive symptomatology. Although depressive affect is well covered, the clinician is assured that several other depressive dimensions will also be tapped.

RELIABILITY.   The D-Scale of the MMPI is a state measuring device, and thus it is somewhat difficult to measure its reliability. It appears that the majority of reliability studies were conducted in the 1940s and 1950s. Dahlstrom and Welsh (1960) provide tables listing both test–retest and split–half research. Split–half coefficients seem to be the most appropriate reliability measure. In several studies reported by Dahlstrom and Welsh, all but two of the six resulting split-half correlations were above .70, suggesting that the MMPI-D Scale is a modestly reliable measure.

Zung Self-Rating Depression Scale

DESCRIPTION.   The Zung Self-Rating Depression Scale (SDS) (Zung, 1965) is a 20-item, multiple-choice, assessment tool that provides an objective measure quantifying the frequency of depressive symptoms. The final score is an index expressed as a decimal. This index was derived by Zung (1965) by dividing the total raw score by the maximum possible score:

$$\text{SDS index} = \frac{\text{raw score total}}{\text{maximum score of } 80} \times 100$$

The SDS is constructed so that the higher the resulting index, the more severe is the depressive symptomatology. Hedlung and Vieweg (1979) provided interpretive guidelines for SDS indices:

SDS Index	Equivalent Clinical Global Impression
< 50	Within normal range, no psychopathology
50–59	Presence of minimal to mild depression
60–69	Presence of moderate to marked depression
≥ 70	Presence of severe to most extreme depression

The SDS can usually be completed within 30 minutes. Test materials include the scale's protocol and a pencil. Clinicians should be aware that the nature of the test-taking task may be confusing for some patients. The confusion lies in the wording of the items. In completing the SDS, a patient assigns a value of 1, 2, 3, or 4 to a response based on the length of time (from "a little of the time" to "most of the time") a certain symptom has been experienced. But the value 1 to 4 is assigned to an item depending on whether that item is worded positively or negatively (Zung, 1965). For example, for Item 1 (a positively worded item), "I feel down-hearted and blue," a response of "a little of the time" is scored 1. For Item 2 (a negatively worded item), "Morning is when I feel best," a response of "a little of the time," would be scored 4. It is the patient's responsibility to correctly identify which items are positively worded and negatively worded and score accordingly. Item 11, "My mind is as clear as it used to be," suggests that such a task can lead to scoring errors with depressed individuals.

NORMATIVE DATA AND DEMOGRAPHIC EFFECTS.   The SDS was normed on only 31 patients who were diagnosed as suffering from a depressive disorder upon admission to the psychiatric service of a hospital during a five-month period. In addition, the SDS was given to a normal control group of 100 people. This control population was made up of an approximately equal number of staff and patients who were hospitalized in the same hospital as the depressed subjects. These individuals manifested no symptoms of depression and had no history of recent depressive illnesses (Zung, 1965). The results of this 1965 study provided Zung with his original SDS normative indices. Depressed patient indices ranged from .63 to .90, with a mean of .74 (corresponding to a raw score of 59), which were significantly different from control indices, which ranged from .25 to .43, with a mean of .33 (corresponding to a raw score of 26).

Since the 1965 study provides no information concerning the demographic makeup of the original SDS normative population, additional research was necessary to determine the effects that various demographic variables would have on the scale. Zung (1967) provided such information utilizing 157 outpatients from the Duke Psychiatric Outpatient Clinic. He reported that for this outpatient population, the outcome of the SDS taken as a whole was not affected by the patient's age, sex, marital status, educational level, financial status, or intelligence level. In 1974 Zung qualified his position concerning the effects of the age variable on the SDS, reporting that depressive symptomatology as measured by this tool is age related in a nonpatient ("normal") population where normal subjects 19 years of age or younger and 65 years of age or older had higher baseline values than those individuals in between these ages. There has been no clear relationship demonstrated between age and SDS scores for patient populations (Hedlund & Vieweg, 1979). Thus it appears that SDS indices are affected by the age variable as a function of the population tested (patient vs. nonpatient). The effects of sex on SDS scoring have revealed that females tend to score higher than males in both patient and nonpatient populations (Byrne et al., 1977; Selzer et al., 1978), but this tendency is relatively small and unstable (Hedlund & Vieweg, 1979). Finally, in their comprehensive review of the SDS, Hedlund and Vieweg also found that education correlated negatively with SDS scores, ranging from −.08 to −.28. Thus clinicians should be aware that although the effects of SES levels are unknown, less educated subjects tend to score higher on the SDS as do some age groups.

FACTORIAL MAKEUP.   The factorial roots of SDS can be traced back to Zung's initial efforts in formulating the scale. Zung (1965) reported utilizing depressive criteria from Overall (1962) and Friedman (1963) in devising the instrument. These criteria were identified as pervasive affect, physiological equivalents or concomitants, and psychological concomitants. Once Zung established these depressive variables, he collected verbatim interview material from depressed patients and, from a content validity approach, chose those statements which in his own judgment were most representative of a particular depressive variable (Zung, 1965). An example would be the pervasive-affect factor; the subtype would be depressed, sad, and blue, and Item 1 would be "I feel down-hearted and blue."

Since 1965 there have been numerous studies attempting to identify and analyze the factorial components of the SDS. These studies have utilized both patient and nonpatient populations and have extracted from two to seven factors, accounting for 33 to 75% of the variance of SDS indices (Hedlund & Vieweg, 1979). Hedlung and Vieweg's review of these studies revealed four major factors in the SDS. Factor A has been referred to as "emptiness, retarded depression, self-satisfaction, loss of self-esteem, depressive feeling: outlook for future, and well-being index." Factor B has been identified as "anxiety depression, agitation, biologic symptom complex, general depression and agitation and somatic symptoms, as well as depressed mood index and somatic symptoms." Factor C has been described with less consistency among the researchers but is generally referred to as "appetite disturbance or biologic symptom disturbance." Factor D was referred to as "performance disturbance" and was associated particularly with the patient population. Thus it appears that the tool's theoretical approach to depression involves affective, cognitive, behavioral, and physiological components. Carroll et al. (1973) estimated that the physiological and general behavioral features contributed to a full 50% of the total score (Items 2 through 10 and Item 13).

RELIABILITY. Like other mood-rating devices, the reliability of the Zung index is somewhat challenging to measure. Because it is a self-report scale of only 20 items, accurate split-half reliability measures are difficult to collect. Split-half measures by Zung (1972) reveal a .73 correlation for a psychiatric population. Such split-half reliability data appear to be sparse, and additional data for determination of SDS reliability is recommended. Hedlung and Vieweg (1979) suggest that further test–retest information is desirable, yet because of the fluctuating nature of depression, such measures would be of questionable worth. Specifically, test–retest reliability measures for only a two- or three-day period may be desirable.

In recent years, other self-rating scales have been developed that have demonstrated psychometric worth and deserve mention. The Center for Epidemiologic Studies Depression Scale (CED-D) (Radloff, 1977), which has 20 items selected from previous scales (e.g., MMPI-D Scale, SDS, BDI), shows promise as a reliable and valid measure of depressive symptomatology, especially when used as a screening device. The Visual Analogue Scales (Lewinsohn et al., 1978) also shows promise as a reliable assessment tool (Davies et al., 1975). Its strength lies in its simplicity. Nevertheless, these scales cannot be considered to be based on sufficient evidence to recommend their use at this time.

Interviewer-Rated Tools

Of the interviewer-rated tools reviewed in Table 9.1, the Hamilton Rating Scale (HRS) stands alone as a well received and researched instrument. Other tools such as the Feelings and Concerns Checklist (Grinker et al., 1961) have not met with the same success as the HRS [see Rehm (1976) for a review of the The Feelings and Concerns Checklist].

Hamilton Rating Scale

DESCRIPTION. The Hamilton Rating Scale (HRS) [Hamilton, 1960; 1967 (revised)] is a 17-item assessment tool designed to measure the severity of depressive symptomatology in patients already diagnosed as depressed. This instrument is a state-measuring device ("from a few days to a week") and must be administered by trained clinicians only.

The HRS is usually given in the course of a clinical interview, taking into account all available information from significant sources. The value of this tool is thus totally dependent on the skill and experience of the rater and the adequacy of the information available (Hamilton, 1967). Test materials include the scale's protocol and a pencil. The 17 items have either five (absent, 0; mild or trivial, 1; moderate, 2 or 3; severe, 4) or three (absent, 0; slight or doubtful, 1; clearly present, 2) grades of severity (depending on the difficulty that had been found in practice to determine five item-severity discriminations). Hamilton (1967) provides rating guidelines for each item according to client sex. Hamilton suggests that a discrepancy of two or more points between independent clinicians on any item is suggestive of a reliability problem. Similarly, a difference of five or more points on the total score suggests the need for reexamination of assigned scores. The final objective score is derived by simply adding up the ratings; this sum expresses the severity of the depressive symptomatology. Mowbray (1972) provides a guide for interpreting final HRS scores:

HRS Score	Severity of Depressive Symptomatology
0–10	Normal mood
15–20	Mild depression
20–25	Moderate depression
25–35	Severe depression
≥35	Very severe depression

To increase rater reliability, Hamilton (1967) suggests that two skilled clinicians be utilized for every administration. If one assessor is used, the resulting score should be doubled for purposes of numerical consistency.

NORMATIVE DATA AND DEMOGRAPHIC EFFECTS. Although originated on 49 male patients in 1960, the HRS was revised and renormed on 152 male and 120 female patients in 1967. The male population consisted of four groups: the original 49 cases tested in 1960; an additional 39 cases collected in a manner similar to the first group; a group of 15 cases seen in an acute admissions ward of a mental hospital, rated by different personnel from the first two groups; and a group of 49 cases containing both outpatients and inpatients. Since groups were collected at different times, rated by different staff, and consisted of different diagnostic categories of varying depressive severity, this male population can be considered quite diverse. Unfortunately, we could find no information concerning the age range, SES levels, or educational status of the male population. Demographic information on the 120 females who made up the norm group is even more sparse. All we know of the female population is that they were "patients."

Due to the lack of descriptive information concerning the initial normed populations, we have turned to later research to determine whether any demographic variables have been observed to affect scoring. Although numerous outcome studies involving the HRS mention no effects, there are some studies providing conflicting information. Schwab et al. (1967a) found age, race, and financial level to significantly effect HRS scores. Of the 15 blacks tested, 57% scored in the depressed category whereas only 19% of the Caucasions tested had such scores. Schwab et al. explained that this observed racial effect was probably due to the fact that the blacks tested came from lower SES groups. Age was inversely related to HRS scoring, as was financial level. Conversely, Schnurr et al. (1976), in their outcome comparison of five depression inventories, found HRS scores to be unrelated to age, sex, or educational level. Thus it seems that there is no conclusive evidence demonstrating the HRS to be significantly affected by demographic variables.

FACTORIAL MAKEUP.   The factorial makeup of the HRS emphasizes classical melancholy. Factor I is described as a "general factor of depressive illness" that clearly taps the severity of depressive symptomology. Factor I has been found to correlate almost completely (.93 to .96) with the total HRS score (Hamilton, 1967; Mowbray, 1972). Factor II is bipolar and reflects the pattern of depressive symptoms. Low scores indicate a retarded depression (loadings of depression, suicide, psychomotor retardation, and loss of insight); high scores indicate an anxious or agitated depression (loadings of somatic and psychic anxiety, agitation, and loss of interest) (Hamilton, 1974). Research has found that Factor II correlates .06 to .3 with the total HRS score (Hamilton, 1967; Mowbray, 1972). Mowbray (1972) also found factor II to be bipolar but anxiety rather than agitation to emerge opposite retardation. Factor III was difficult for Hamilton (1967, 1974) to interpret in clinical terms but can be described, for male patients, as involving insomnia, loss of appetite, and fatigability at one pole and guilt, suicide, and loss of insight at the other. For females, Factor III contrasts loss of libido, and fatigability with insomnia, agitation, and hypochondriasis at the other. Factor IV was defined by Hamilton (1974) to include hypochondriasis, loss of insight, and loss of weight at one pole; the other pole shows no dominating symptoms. Although newer studies have failed to replicate Hamilton's findings (Weckowicz et al., 1971) whereas others have agreed with the nature of some but not all factors (Mowbray, 1972), it is clear that the HRS does measure a variety of depressive dimensions involving affective, cognitive, behavioral, and physiological features of depressive symptomatology in terms of severity. Emphasis is placed on behavioral and physiological (somatic) components that make up between 50 and 80% of the total score (Carroll et al., 1973). Rehm (1976) criticizes the HRS for mixing different depressive features within the same depressive dimension. For example, she illustrates how the suicide dimension is anchored by cognitive ("feels life is worth living") as well as behavioral ("attempts at suicide") components, concluding that unidimensionality is questionable. On the other hand, we applaud the multidimensionality of the HRS in its attempts to tap the severity of the multidimensional symptomatology of depression, although it would be ideal if the scale were made up of many easily-identifiable unidimensional scales.

RELIABILITY.   Because of the brevity of the HRS as well as the fluctuating nature of depressive symptomatology, accurate split–half and test–retest reliability data are difficult to gather. However, because the HRS is completed by skilled clinicians, this depressive assessment scale lends itself well to interrater reliability studies. Since its inception, the HRS has consistently demonstrated high interrater reliability. Hamilton (1960) reported interrater reliabilities ranging from .84 for 10 patients to .90 for a total of 70 patients (as raters compared successive 10-member patient groups). Hamilton (1974) in his review of the scale, states that previous investigators have reported interrater reliabilities ranging from .80 to .90. An innovative approach by Ziegler et al. (1978) also supported the scale's high interrater reliability. These researchers utilized videotapes to demonstrate such reliability. Agreement between trained physicians (personal raters) who rated 22 depressed patients on 39 occasions and raters observing these same patients on videotape was .95. Correlation between the two personal raters was .96. Correlation between the 39 scores of the two videotape raters was .97. Such findings give merit to the HRS as a highly reliable assessment tool when applied by trained raters who have considerable clinical experience and expertise.

Overt Behavior Tools

The Pleasant Events Schedule

DESCRIPTION.   The Pleasant Events Schedule (PES) (MacPhillamy & Lewinsohn, 1976) is a 320-item self-rating scale that provides measures of the frequency and subjective enjoyability of "pleasant" events for the past 30 days. In addition to detecting depressive actions, the PES is also described as a useful tool for developing individually tailored activity programs for the monitoring of daily reinforcing events in behavior therapy.

Administration materials include only the schedule's protocol and a pencil. The testing task, which can be completed in about 1 to 1½ hours, requires that the client go through the 320 items twice. Initially, the client rates events according to their frequency of occurrence during the past month, utilizing the following scale:

1.   This has not happened in the past 30 days.
2.   This has happened a few times (1 to 6) in the past 30 days.
3.   This has happened often (7 or more) in the past 30 days.

The client then repeats all items once again, this time rating how enjoyable or rewarding each event was during the past month:

1.   This was not pleasant.
2.   This was somewhat pleasant.
3.   This was very pleasant.

In addition to the frequency and enjoyability ratings, a third score called a *product score* (the frequency times enjoyability rating) is computed for each item. Thus there are three derived scores:

1.   *Activity level.*   The sum of all frequency ratings that is assumed to reflect the rate at which events occurred during the past 30 days.

2. *Reinforcement potential.* The sum of the enjoyability ratings that is assumed to reflect the potential reinforcement value of the client's events.

3. *Obtained reinforcement.* The sum of the products for each item that is assumed to provide an approximate measure of response—contingent positive reinforcement experienced by the client during the past 30 days (Lewinsohn & Lee, 1981; Rehm, 1976). The PES was designed to be read, scored, and converted by computer. Advice on programming may be obtained from its authors.

NORMATIVE DATA AND DEMOGRAPHIC EFFECTS.   The PES was initially normed on 641 university and junior college students. Additional items were generated by a "wide variety of people of diverse educational and social backgrounds, and ranging in age from 35 to 76 years" (MacPhillamy & Lewinsohn, 1976). The effects of age and sex on test results are dealt with in a unique fashion. In the manual, there is a table of norms based on a sample of 464 normal individuals that provides age–sex means for frequency, enjoyability, and product scores according to the schedule's individual scales. Resulting Z scores furnish a standard deviation measure for a client's performance on each scale. The manual cautions that these norms are only approximate and a clinician's own normative data (if it indeed exists) should be used whenever possible. Thus the effects of various demographic variables such as age, sex, educational, and SES levels require additional study before any definitive conclusions can be documented.

FACTORIAL MAKEUP.   Factorial studies reported in the PES manual demonstrate that the schedule is measuring the type of activity the client has been engaged in as well as the tendency to report such activity. For example, the scale identified as "SN" differentiates between socially and nonsocially reinforcing activities. In addition, these activities are described, such as being female-role versus masculine-role related (Scale MF–bipolar) or related to outdoorsmanship (Scale RB). Not surprisingly, the PES also measures reported mood (Scale MR and its subscales). The PES's emphasis on behavior makes it a unique measure of depressive symptomatology. As a result of its unique factorial makeup, the small number of concurrent validity studies (with other scales reviewed here) reveal moderate correlations at best (Burkhart et al., 1980). Although the manual reports comprehensive data on PES factors, additional research sources are recommended to support this information.

RELIABILITY.   Test–retest reliability figures are reported by MacPhillamy and Lewinsohn (1976). These measures represent correlational averages of the frequency, enjoyability, and product data for each scale. They range from .25 to .88, demonstrating, as a whole, satisfactory stability from one to three months in all but two scales. Since mood, with the potential to fluctuate, is apparently being measured, such data are of questionable worth. Measures of item stability given for a six-week interval are expressed as the frequency of ratings agreement and the resulting correlational coefficient. Complete rating agreement occurred on 76% of the occasions for frequency ratings ($r = .53$) and 63% for enjoyability ratings ($r = .55$). Like the factorial research on this scale, it appears that additional forms of reliability data from sources other than the PES manual would aid in substantiating current findings.

Other Overt Behavior Scales

As reviewed by Rehm (1976, 1978), depressed behavior can be assessed by observing overt verbal behavior and overt motor behavior. Verbal behavior assessment often involves paralinguistic (e.g., speech rate) or verbal content (e.g., number of expressed feelings per unit of time) measures. Overt motor behavior approaches have included such measures as frequency counts of smiles, eye-contact latencies and dimensions of posture and also involve mechanical instrumentation such as electronic wristband activity counters. In addition to these and self-rating schedules such as the PES, paraprofessionally rated behavioral checklists combining overt–verbal and motor behaviors have been developed (Williams et al., 1972).

The research on depressed overt behavior appears to be as diversified as the studies undertaken. Behavioral measurement seems to be fitted to research objectives, and, as a result, no standard assessment format has taken shape. We suggest that overt behavior methodology involve the measurement of DSM-III behavioral symptomatology in hopes of developing an assessment approach that focuses on depressive variables seen most often and deemed most valid in the behavior of depressed individuals.

COMPARATIVE VALIDITIES OF THE MAJOR TOOLS

Concurrent Validity

Table 9.2 lists correlational data between the various depression instruments. Examination of such data, for each individual tool, reveals unique instrument characteristics.

The Beck Depression Inventory correlates best with the SDS. In their review of four affective measures, Meites et al. (1980) support these findings with their report on the factorial similarities between the BDI and SDS, particularly in the areas of cognitive and physiological manifestations. Like the SDS, the BDI correlates well with clinician ratings.

The majority of DACL correlations are moderate at best. Such low correlations may be the result of DACL's factorial emphasis on the affective dimension of depression.

The D-Scale of the Minnesota Multiphasic Personality Inventory correlates well with the SDS and BDI. Like these two scales, the MMPI-D taps affective, cognitive, and physiological symptomatology. The few studies examining the D-Scale with the HRS provide low correlational figures. This seems somewhat

Table 9.2.　Correlation Between Rating Measures of Depression

Measure	BDI	DACL	MMPI-D	SDS	Clinical Ratings
HRS	$.56-.72^a$		$.27^e$(ns)	$.25^e$(ns)	$.69^j$
	$.68^b$		$.34^f$	$.41^g$	$.84-.91^a$
	$.75^c$			$.76^i$	$.89^k$
	$.80^d$			$.79^h$	
BDI		$.38-.50^l$	$.49^n$	$.60^o$	$.77^q$
		$.41^m$	$.55^f$	$.69^i$	$.77-.82^a$
				$.70^f$	
				$.83^p$	
DACL			$.32-.47^l$	$.27$(ns)	$.32-.38^l$
			$.54-.57^r$	$.38^l$	$.34^m$
				$.44^m$	$.59+.71^t$
				$.51-.64^s$	
MMPI-D				$.56^e$	$.51^v$
				$.58^g$	$.59^v$
				$.71^u$	
SDS					$.69^j$
					$.74^w$

[a] Bech et al., (1975).
[b] Bailey & Coppen (1976).
[c] Schwab et al. (1967).
[d] Hammen (1980).
[e] Keeler et al. (1979).
[f] Schnurr et al. (1976).
[g] Carroll et al. (1973).
[h] Brown & Zung (1972).
[i] Davies et al. (1975).
[j] Biggs et al. (1978).
[k] Knesevich et al. (1977).
[l] Lubin (1967). Forms A to D.
[m] Christenfield et al. (1978). Form E.
[n] Burkhart et al. (1980).
[o] Meites et al. (1980).
[p] Seitz (1970).
[q] Bumberry et al. (1978).
[r] Lubin (1967). Forms E to G.
[s] Marone & Lubin (1968). Forms E to G.
[t] Lubin (1967). Form A.
[u] Equi & Jabara (1976).
[v] Dahlstrom et al. (1972).
[w] Master & Zung (1977).

unexpected since both tools attempt to measure multiple factors of depression. Such data do suggest that together these tools broadly tap depressive symptomatology and would be useful to administer concurrently in outcome studies.

　　Although the HRS is a clinician's rating instrument, research reveals that it correlates as well or better with self-report measures as these self-rating tools correlate with each other. Table 9.2 indicates that the HRS correlates best with the BDI. Such high correlations may be due to the fact that both measures tap severity of depressive symptomatology. Davies et al. (1975) report higher HRS–BDI correlations in cases with less severe symptomatology. As might be expected, the HRS correlates highest with subjective clinician rating procedures since both require a trained clinician as the data source.

Construct Validity

The validity of any instrument can be measured in a variety of ways; every alternative has its strengths and weaknesses. Although the concurrent validity approach is a popular method for examining an instrument's validity, its value is limited by the very nature of those instruments providing such data. If these validating instruments are of questionable validity, the resulting correlational data is of limited worth. Construct validity (in this case, how well the instrument correlates with theoretical constructs of depression) is a valued validity measure. If an assessment tool relates highly with other depression phenomena, clinicians and researchers can utilize the tool in outcome assessment with greater confidence.

Concordance with DSM III Criteria

BECK DEPRESSION INVENTORY.   In reference to our content analysis of DSM-III depressive symptomatology, the BDI taps six of the nine identified depressive variables. The patient's dysphoric mood is assessed well in five different items (Nos. 1, 2, 4, 10, 11, and 12). Inquiry concerning feelings of guilt is observed directly in Item 5 as well as implied in Items 7 and 8. The characteristic loss of energy or fatigue is investigated in Items 15 and 17. Suicidal thoughts, a decreased sex drive, and an inability to think or concentrate are covered in Items 9, 21, and 13 respectively.

Two depressive variables that are part of the DSM-III criteria for depression are only partially covered in the Beck Depression Inventory. The DSM-III regards increases as well as decreases in eating behavior to be symptomatic of depression. The BDI contains two items (18 and 19) that assess decreased appetite and weight, but no items for possible increases in food consumption. Similarly, both an increase and a decrease in sleeping are now considered depressive criteria in the DSM-III. A decrease in sleep is tapped (Item 16), but an increase in sleeping behavior is not.

Although the DSM-III refers to increases (agitation) as well as decreases (retardation) in psychomotor activity as being symptomatic of depression, the Beck Depression Inventory includes neither. There is a real difference between a loss of energy (Items 15 and 17) and motor retardation (DSM-III, 1980, pp. 210) that is not included in the BDI. We suggest that the above-mentioned items be added to the BDI in an effort to increase its similarity to depression as defined by DSM-III.

DEPRESSION ADJECTIVE CHECKLISTS.   In reference to DSM-III criteria, the DACL taps two variables well and one indirectly. The remaining six

DSM-III depressive factors are never assessed. Similar to Giambra's (1977) findings, these authors agree that the dysphoric mood of the depressed state is well covered, involving a large majority of the 230 items contained in the seven lists. In addition, the factor, "decrease in energy" is assessed by at least one item and often several items of every form. For example, Form A covers this variable with positive adjectives such as Item 19, "listless," and Item 31, "weary"; Form E taps this factor with negative adjectives such as Item 16, "vigorous," and Item 2, "active."

A third factor—worthlessness and guilt—is assessed, with items that could be classified as implying worthlessness. A sense of worthlessness is implied: for example, in Form A, Item 14, "failure," and Form D, Item 12, "rejected." However, only one item, Item 30, on Form F, "unworthy," directly measures this variable.

Depressive factors missing throughout the seven lists include inability to think or concentrate; thoughts pertaining to death, suicide, and attempts of suicide; increases or decreases in appetite and/or weight, sleeping, and psychomotor activity; and a decrease in sexual drive. Obviously, if the DACL is to measure depressive symptomatology as described by the DSM-III adequately, major adjective additions, as noted, will be necessary.

MMPI-D SCALE. Although the MMPI-D Scale is a multidimensional measure of depression, DSM-III symptomatology is not completely covered. Five variables are tapped directly; two are measured partially. Two other variables are not covered. The MMPI-D Scale taps dysphoric mood best (e.g., Items 36, 38, 49). Other variables covered include worthlessness (Item 57), an inability to think or concentrate (Items 10 and 55), an increase and decrease in appetite and/or weight (a decrease emphasized; Items 4 and 18), and a loss of energy (Items 12 and 46). Investigation of psychomotor agitation is limited to questions involving nervousness and tension (Items 6 and 56, respectively); psychomotor retardation is not considered. A decrease in sleeping behavior is questioned (Item 20); there are no items for detection of possible increases. The MMPI-D Scale fails to measure thoughts of death or suicide and suicidal attempts and possible decreases in sexual drive. For complete DSM-III concordance, item additions for these missing variables are recommended.

SELF-RATING DEPRESSION SCALE. The Zung SDS covers five DSM-III depressive variables completely and four partially. There is one variable that is overlooked. Symptomatology covered well includes dysphoria (Items 1, 12, 14, 15, and 20 directly; Item 18 implied), suicidal ideation (Item 19), a decrease in sexual drive (Item 6), and a decrease in energy level (Item 10).

A measure of worthlessness is implied in Item 17, but no direct statement about "feelings of worthlessness," is included. Items 5 and 7 involve decreases in appetite and/or weight; no item refers to possible increases. Item 4 involves a decrease in sleeping behavior; no item inquires about an increase. Although an increase in psychomotor activity is implied in Item 9, there is no mention of a decrease. Items 2 and 8 are of questionable use in reference to DSM-III criteria. Zung (1965) suggested Item 12: "I find it easy to do the things I used to do" measures psychomotor retardation. Utilizing current DSM-III criteria, this item implies loss of energy (i.e., fatigue) but does not describe psychomotor retardation as defined by DSM-III. Item ideas for direct investigation of increases and decreases of psychomotor behavior (agitation and retardation) are provided in the DSM-III (1980, pp. 210).

HAMILTON RATING SCALE.   In relation to DSM-III depressive factors, the HRS covers seven completely and two partially. Symptomatology covered well includes dysphoric mood (Items 1 and 7), worthlessness or guilt (Item 2), inability to think or concentrate (Item 10); thoughts of suicide and suicide attempts (Item 3); both an increase (agitation) and a decrease (retardation) in psychomotor activity (Items 9 and 8, respectively); a decrease in sexual drive (Item 14); and a loss of energy (Item 13). A decrease in sleeping behavior is well covered (Items 4, 5, and 6), but there is no item involving possible increases in sleeping. Similarly, a decrease in appetite and/or weight is measured by Items 12 and 17, but no increase in such behavior is tapped. We deem Items 11 (anxiety–somatic symptoms) and 15 (hypochondriasis) to be related to associated features of DSM-III depressive symptomatology. Since the HRS is utilized to measure severity of symptoms and not as a diagnostic tool, these two items will broaden the descriptive scope of symptom severity for the clinician. Item 16 (loss of insight) is certainly not specific to depression, and perhaps it is not necessary in reference to DSM-III criteria.

PLEASANT EVENTS SCHEDULE.   Since the PES is behaviorally oriented, focusing on the frequency and enjoyability of certain activities, six of the nine DSM-III variables of depressive symptomatology are measured only indirectly. For example, Item 28 in Part 2 of the schedule is "crying." The frequency and subjective enjoyability ratings of this item imply a sense of dysphoric mood, but certainly do not measure it directly. Similarly, Item 138 in Part 2, "thinking about an interesting question," implies the ability or inability to think or concentrate. Only two DSM-III factors are measured directly. An increase or decrease in sleeping behavior is assessed well in Item 73, "taking a nap" in Part 1 and Items 41, "getting up early in the morning"; 85, "sleeping late"; and 134, "staying up late" in Part 2. In addition, a decrease in sexual drive is measured in Part 2 of the PES with Items 78, "petting, necking"; 80, "talking about sex"; 88, "having sexual relations with a partner of the opposite sex"; and 89, "having other sexual satisfactions." Thoughts of death or suicide and suicide attempts are never assessed. The PES indirectly covers a variety of DSM-III depressive symptomatology, but such implied measurement does not result in very high DSM-III concordance.

On the basis of the degree of each measure's concordance with DSM-III criteria, the devices were ranked from most to least comprehensive: (1) Hamilton Rating Scale; (2) Beck Depression Inventory; (3) Self-Rating Depression Scale; (4) MMPI-D Scale; (5) Depression Adjective Checklist; and (6) Pleasant Events Schedule.

Sensitivity to Differentiate Among Different Types or Levels of Psychopathology

One method of evaluating the criterion validity of depression assessment tools is to examine their ability to be sensitive to various kinds or degrees of mental illness. Several studies were found where the relative ability of two or more instruments was tested. Simultaneously, these studies involved either the test's ability to discriminate between different psychiatric populations or between varying levels of depressive symptomatology. It was possible to determine the comparative ability of these instruments to make these discriminations by observing the frequency with which they discriminated between groups at a level of statistical significance (.05 or greater). These data are presented in Table 9.3.

It is apparent from Table 9.3 that although the instruments were involved in an approximately equal number of comparisons, the HRS appeared to be superior to the other measures in discriminating pathology. It should be

Table 9.3.   Relative Sensitivity of Depression Measures to Differentiate Among Different Psychiatric Populations or Levels of Depressive Symptomatology[a]

	Tools			
	BDI	MMPI-D	SDS	HRS
Number of studies in which the tool is involved	5	3	3	5
Number of comparisons in which the tool was involved	7	7	9	8
Number of comparisons in which the tool was significantly sensitive	2	2	0	5
Percentage of comparisons in which the tool was significantly sensitive	29%	29%	0%	63%

[a]The data were based on tool comparisons from the following studies: Biggs et al. (1978); Carroll et al. (1973); Hackney and Ribordy (1980); Langevin and Stancer (1979); and Schnurr et al. (1976).

realized that since five of the eight HRS comparisons involved two studies, the reliability of these data is limited. The BDI and MMPI-D Scale appear to be equally sensitive although a distant second to the HRS. The SDS was unable to detect significant differences of depressive symptomatology among psychiatric or depressed groups in any of the nine comparisons in which it was involved.

Studies utilizing the BDI suggest that this tool is a more valid measure of depression severity for mild and moderate levels, but not severe. A study by Schwab et al. (1967b) revealed that BDI high scores of medical inpatients were not indicative of more severe depressive symptomatology whereas scores below 10 usually indicated psychiatric disorders other than depression. Gong and Hammen (1980) supported the validity of BDI at lower levels of depressive symptomatology in nonclinical and outpatient samples.

In conclusion, if clinicians are interested in choosing a device that is most likely to accurately discriminate between different psychiatric populations or varying levels of depressive symptomatology, the HRS would appear to be the preferred instrument. Although the BDI and MMPI-D Scale seem to be equally sensitive, the BDI appears to be more valid for mild and moderate levels of depressive symptomatology as opposed to severe. The SDS is not a sensitive measure of depressive symptomatology. The DACL's evidence as a sensitive depression measure is too sparse to be conclusive, as is the research on the PES.

Sensitivity to Treatment Effects in Drug and Psychotherapy Outcome Studies

It is important to have some idea of the degree to which an outcome measure will provide a conservative versus liberal estimate of improvement. Will a measure be highly sensitive to a variety of treatments and perhaps even placebo effects? Or is it possible that it will fail to reflect significant changes in the patient's pathology that have actually taken place? An ideal assessment tool will be reflective of real changes in the patient's condition without detecting insignificant changes or experimental demand characteristics.

One method of reflecting the conservative versus liberal sensitivity of a test is to examine the results of past outcome studies. Is there a tendency for a specific depression tool to be more conservative or liberal in comparison to other tools in past outcome studies? Eighteen drug and psychotherapy treatment studies that used two or more depression devices simultaneously to measure outcome were reviewed. From these 18 studies, 65 two-tool comparisons were examined. An analysis of the frequency with which one or another of these devices showed changes in depression to be statistically significant (.05 level of confidence or greater) versus nonsignificant or to reach a higher level of confidence is presented in Table 9.4.

It is apparent from Table 9.4 that the BDI and HRS are the most popular tools used alone or concurrently with other measures in treatment outcome studies. Note that only these tools were involved in multiple tool comparisons involving both drug and psychotherapy treatment. Although the MMPI-D Scale was compared extensively to other tools as an outcome measure of psychotherapy treatments, it was found to be used in only one drug study involving no tool comparisons. Not surprisingly, the PES and various overt behavior scales were used exclusively in psychotherapy treatment studies. Although the DACL and SDS were found to be involved in both drug and psychotherapy studies, their performances in relation to other measures are found only in drug studies.

In comparing the BDI and HRS as general outcome measures [see "Ttl (total) Average %" columns], the BDI was classified as sensitive more often; the BDI specifically was more sensitive in drug versus therapy research. The

Table 9.4. Relative Sensitivity of Depression Instruments in Measuring Treatment Effects in Drug and Psychotherapy Outcome Studies[a,b]

	BDI			MMPI-D	SDS	DACL	HRS			PES	OBS
	Dg	Thy	Av%	Ttl Dg/Thy/Av%	Ttl Dg/Thy/Av%	Ttl Dg/Thy/Av%	Dg	Thy	Av	Ttl Dg/Thy/Av%	Ttl Dg/Thy/Av%
Number of studies in which the tool is involved	8	6	14	5	5	2	11	2	13	3	2
Number of comparisons in which the tool is involved	14	30	44	27	7	4	17	4	21	17	8
Number of comparisons in which the tool is more sensitive	9	12	21	14	0	1	4	1	5	1	3
Type of Comparison: Significance vs. nonsignificance	6	4	10	3	0	1	3	0	3	0	2
More significant level	3	8	11	11	0	0	1	1	2	1	1
Percentage of comparisons in which the involved tool is more sensitive	64%	40%	48%	52%	0%	25%	24%	25%	24%	6%	38%

Ratio of number of comparisons in which the tool is more sensitive for that specific population[a] to number of comparisons involving that specific population

Inpatient (IP):	3/6 0/1		0/5	1/2	2/9 1/1	
resulting percentage	50% 0% 43%		0%	50%	22% 100% 33%	
Outpatient (OP):	6/8 1/6	2/4	0/2	0/2	2/8 0/3	0/3
resulting percentage	75% 17% 50%	50%	0%	0%	25% 0% 18%	0%
Volunteer (VLN):	11/23	12/23			1/14	3/8
resulting percentage	48% 48%	52%			7%	38%
Population in which tool is more sensitive	OP/VLN —[f]	—[g]	—[g]	IP[e]	—[f] IP[e] IP	—[c,g]

[a]The drug studies (both double blind and not) involved outcome comparisons of one or more drugs on one or more treatment groups as measured by two or more outcome tools. The therapy studies involved outcome comparisons of one or more therapy treatments as measured by two or more outcome tools.

[b]Twenty-one tool comparisons were reviewed in 11 drug studies (Bowen, 1978; Burrows et al., 1972; Dorus & Senay, 1980; Hague et al., 1976; Kay et al., 1970, 1973; Lapierre & Butter, 1978; Rickels et al., 1981; White et al., 1980; Woody et al., 1975; Wright & Denber, 1978). Forty-four tool comparisons were reviewed in seven psychotherapy studies (Davidson et al., 1978; Fuchs & Rehm, 1977; Grosscup & Lewinsohn, 1980; Rehm et al., 1979, Rush et al., 1977; Sanchez et al., 1980; Zeiss et al., 1979).

[c]Other overt behavior scales.

[d]Includes both types of comparisons: significant versus nonsignificant and more significant level.

[e]Based on one study only.

[f]Too close to call.

[g]Unable to determine.

relatively conservative HRS was more consistent in its outcome measurements across drug and psychotherapy studies. When considering all studies, the BDI was most liberal with outpatients, yet the volunteer and inpatient population percentages are so close behind that reliable conclusions about specific uses are difficult to draw. The HRS appears to be most sensitive with inpatients.

Concerning drug outcome measurement, the HRS was the most popular depression instrument used. However, the BDI was classified as sensitive more often than any of the tools. The HRS came in a distant second with the DACL, but it should be realized that the DACL was found in only two drug studies, as it was the more sensitive in just one of four comparisons. Although the SDS was involved in seven tool comparisons from five studies, it was never the more sensitive tool. As noted, the popular MMPI-D Scale was found in only one drug study (Donnelly et al., 1979) and the PES and overt behavior scales, in none. It is interesting to note the trend between type of study and choice of instrument. The HRS and BDI were formulated by psychiatrists and are now used most often in drug studies. The MMPI, one of the most popular instruments used by psychologists today, is involved in little drug research. Similarly, the behaviorally oriented PES was not involved in any drug-related work. Although a limited number of comparisons among patient categories make it difficult to draw reliable conclusions, certain relationships between depression instruments and sample populations were derived. In drug research, the BDI was more sensitive with outpatients than inpatients. The HRS was relatively consistent between these two populations.

A review by McNair (1974) evaluated the sensitivity of self-report (thus not including the HRS) depression measures on antidepressant drug treatment covering studies from 1955 to 1972. Comparison of McNair's findings with our current work reveals some interesting trends and developments. McNair found the MMPI-D Scale to be the most popular tool, with the SDS a close second. Up until 1972, the BDI had been involved in just five studies. Of the tools reviewed in this chapter, McNair reported the BDI to be most sensitive to drug treatment, with the SDS next. Although most popular, the MMPI-D Scale's performance was disappointing, particularly in drug-comparison studies, as it ranked last of the three measures. Concerning these three instruments, the SDS and BDI were recommended for drug research; however, McNair concluded that the BDI be used only as an alternative to the SDS since BDI research was then so sparse. Apparently, researchers took McNair's advice because since the 1960s the popularity of the MMPI-D Scale as a drug-research tool has decreased dramatically. Although McNair found the SDS to be a sensitive measure in drug treatment, in our review we found it to be less sensitive than the BDI or HRS. Similarly, Carroll et al. (1973) criticized the SDS, concluding that it was inadequate as a measure for comparing depressed patients in studies calling for matched groups such as drug trials. In addition, Hedlund and Vieweg (1979), in their review of the SDS, favored trained observer ratings, like the HRS, for measurement of drug-induced changes in depression.

In conclusion, if clinicians prefer a sensitive measure of drug treatment, the BDI is the instrument of choice. It is more sensitive with outpatients versus inpatients. The HRS is a more conservative measure of drug treatment and measures consistently across inpatients and outpatients. The SDS is not sensitive to drug treatments in comparison to other depression measures and, therefore, cannot be recommended in this type of outcome research.

As psychotherapy outcome measures, the BDI and MMPI-D Scale were the most popular. However, the MMPI-D Scale was classified as the most reactive tool in measuring psychotherapy treatment effects. The Beck came in second with overt behavior scales closely behind. Although it should be noted that these overt scales were found in just two studies, they were the more liberal measure in three of eight tool comparisons, thus demonstrating some promise as sensitive measures of psychotherapy treatment. The behaviorally oriented PES did not show similar promise. Surprisingly, the well-known HRS was found in only two psychotherapy treatment studies. Apparently, as a psychotherapy outcome measure, the MMPI-D Scale seems equally sensitive to inpatients and outpatients while the BDI appears most liberal with volunteers. (Volunteer data were taken from two studies.)

Although neither the DACL nor the SDS was involved in any tool comparison research measuring the effects of psychotherapy treatment, both were utilized in several psychotherapy outcome studies alone. The DACL reflected significant improvement in all the studies where it was a dependent measure (Lubin et al., 1967, 1974a; Turner, et al., 1979), yet a patient population was involved in only one of these. It appears the DACL has proved its effectiveness as an outcome measure best with volunteers. More work is needed exploring the sensitivity of the DACL to psychotherapy treatment involving inpatients and outpatients. Although the SDS has demonstrated sensitivity to psychotherapeutic treatment (Equi & Jabara, 1976; Wadsworth & Barker, 1976; Zung, 1968), it is unfortunate that there are no comparative studies for the acquisition of a better understanding of its sensitivity in relation to other depression assessment tools. It is interesting to note that in two separate studies, the BDI applied to outpatients and the DACL applied to depressed volunteers both reflected the significant improvement in control as well as treatment groups.

In conclusion, the most sensitive measure of psychotherapy treatment effects is the MMPI-D Scale, which seems to be equally liberal with outpatient and volunteer populations. The BDI is a more conservative measure of psychotherapy treatment as it is the most sensitive with volunteers. Considering behavioral measures, various overt behavior scales showed promising sensitivity whereas the PES did not.

SUMMARY AND CONCLUSIONS

The need for reliable and valid tools for assessing depressive symptomatology is reflected in the ever-increasing number of individuals suffering from depression. Although this affective disorder is often approached philosophically from a symptomatologic perspective, philosophical alternatives, such as the etiologic approach, encourage the view that more accurate philosophical viewpoints may exist; the possibility that new assessment procedures could be based on an undiscovered alternative should not be overlooked. Currently, one of the most popular references mirroring the symptomatologic approach to the assessment of depression is the DSM-III. However, because of its recent development, and as a result of numerous other factors (e.g. tools based on theoretical preferences), no assessment devices have been derived from this classificatory system. Consequently, the assessment of changes in depression does not rest on a systematic philosophy.

Forty or more methods that have been used to rate depression can be evaluated in terms of their agreement with DSM-III symptoms, thus providing some additional order or position from which to evaluate their adequacy (albeit one that is based on the questionable assumptions of the symtomatologic perspective). Instruments used to assess depression fall into three general categories: (1) self-rated tools; (2) interviewer-rated tools; and (3) overt behavior tools. In reviewing specific instruments that represent these categories, we conclude the following:

Self-Rated Tools

Beck Depression Inventory

The BDI provides a measure of the severity of depressive symptomatology. This inventory appears to be negatively correlated with educational and SES levels. The BDI seems to measure the affective dimension of depression, along with cognitive and physiological features. The reliability of the BDI is not well researched. In regard to concordance with DSM-III depressive criteria, the BDI measures six of the nine variables directly, two partially, and one is overlooked. In light of these findings, we rank the BDI second of the six tools reviewed as far as DSM-III concordance is concerned. The BDI seems to be more accurate in assessing mild and moderate levels of depression as opposed to severe. When considering drug and psychotherapy outcome research together, the BDI is the most sensitive, that is, most likely to show statistically significant results. When drug outcome research alone is considered, the BDI is again the most sensitive measure, as it is even more liberal with outpatients than inpatients. For consideration of psychotherapy outcome research, the BDI is less liberal, ranking second behind the MMPI-D Scale in reflecting significant improvement. In psychotherapy studies, the BDI is the most sensitive with a volunteer population.

Therefore, one cannot make a simple statement about the BDI on the dimension of whether it presents a liberal versus conservative estimate of improvement (or treatment effects). Its sensitivity may depend on both the type of treatment offered and the patient populations studied. Taking the most extreme case, one could say that if drugs are used for treatment with an outpatient population, then, of the measures studied, a most liberal estimate of improvement would be provided by the BDI. One implication of such a conclusion is that if a study were undertaken contrasting drugs with psychotherapy, with only the BDI used as an outcome measure, the study may be biased in favor of the drug treatment.

Depression Adjective Checklists

The DACL is a collection of seven adjective checklists that provide a state measure of self-reported depressed mood. Although normative data have been extensive, the effects of such demographic variables as age, education, and SES level are not well researched; the variable of sex does affect scores between sets 1 and 2. Ample research indicates that the DACL is a reliable measure. The DACL seems to be overly focused on the affective dimension of depression. Referring to DSM-III depressive factors, the DACL seems to tap, at most, three of nine directly, and it ranks fifth of the six tools reviewed on this dimension. The DACL has not been well researched in its role as a sensitive indicator of depression or as an outcome measure, particularly with psychotherapy treatment. It cannot be recommended, at this time, as an outcome measure with patient populations, although its use in analogue studies with normals may be appropriate.

MMPI-D Scale

This scale is a 60-item (true–false) assessment device that measures present-state depressive symptomatology. Clinicians should be aware that, among normals, the sex of the client significantly effects scoring, with females scoring higher. Split-half research conducted in the 1940s and 1950s indicates that the MMPI-D Scale is a reliable measure. The MMPI-D Scale is a multidimensional measure of depression, tapping affective, cognitive, behavioral, and physiological features. The MMPI-D Scale measures five DSM-III variables completely; two are measured partially, and two are not covered. According to these criteria, we rank it fourth of the six tools reviewed. This tool was less sensitive to differing types or levels of pathology than the top-ranked HRS but was as sensitive as the BDI. As an outcome measure, the MMPI-D Scale is the most liberal of the scales with psychotherapy treatment; it seems equally liberal in measuring psychotherapy effects with both outpatients and volunteers. Research on this scale is too sparse for drawing any firm conclusions about the role of this scale as a drug treatment measure.

Self-Rating Depression Scale

The SDS provides an objective measure quantifying the frequency of depressive illness. Because of the effects of the age variable, the SDS is not the instrument of choice for normal subjects 19 years of age or younger and 65 years of age or older. This assessment tool is a multidimensional depression measure as it seems to tap affective, cognitive, behavioral, and physiological components. Reliability research for the SDS is sparse. The SDS covers five DSM-III depressive variables completely and four partially; one variable is overlooked. According to these criteria, it ranks third of the six tools reviewed. Relative to other measures reviewed, it appears that the SDS is not successful in differentiating different psychiatric groups or levels of depressive symptomology. As an outcome device, it is not well researched as a psychotherapy measure; as a drug measure, it was found to be least sensitive to treatment effects when compared to the other instruments. On the basis of this analysis, it is difficult to defend the use of the SDS as an outcome tool in treatment outcome studies.

Interviewer-Rated Tool

Hamilton Rating Scale

The HRS is designed to measure the severity of depressive symptomatology in patients already diagnosed as depressed. Scoring appears to be unaffected by any demographic variables. The HRS seems to measure the affective, cognitive, behavioral, and physiological features of depression. There are moderate differences noted in the factorial design of the HRS as a function of sex, but since total HRS scores appear to be unaffected by the sex variable, clinicians should simply be cautious of generalizing HRS scores between the sexes. Because the HRS is a clinician-rating scale, interrater studies are an appropriate source of reliability status. Such data reveal the HRS to be a highly reliable assessment tool when used by trained clinicians. In relation to DSM-III depressive factors, the HRS covers seven completely and two partially and thus ranks first of the six tools examined.

Of the instruments reviewed, the HRS is the instrument of choice for accurate discrimination between different psychiatric populations or varying levels of depressive symptomatology. Short of a comprehensive diagnostic examination, the HRS is the instrument of choice for identifying a depressed population. For instance, it could be used for screening patients who are research volunteers in depression treatment studies. As a general outcome measure, the HRS is consistent in its degree of sensitivity across psychotherapy and drug studies. As a well-researched drug treatment measure, the HRS appears to be more conservative than the BDI and yet, unlike the BDI, is consistent across inpatient and outpatient populations. As a psychotherapy treatment measure, research on the HRS is too sparse to draw any firm conclusions. Future research should employ the HRS (in combination with the BDI) in psychotherapy outcome studies, so that we can assess its relative sensitivity to these treatment modalities. Moreover, because of its consistency across in- and outpatient populations in drug outcome research, it is ideal for studies that include both patient types (i.e., a broad range of severity).

Overt Behavior Tools

Pleasant Events Schedule and Other Overt Behavior Scales

The PES is a behavioral self-rating tool that provides measures of the frequency and subjective enjoyability of "pleasant" events. The effects of demographic variables require additional study. The PES focuses on the behavioral symptomatology inherent in the depressed individual. Reliability research on the PES is limited; additional study is recommended. Referring to DSM-III depressive criteria, two of the nine variables are measured directly, six are measured indirectly, and one is overlooked. It ranks last of the six tools reviewed on this dimension. The PES has not been well researched in its role as a sensitive indicator of depression or as an outcome measure. It should be noted that the PES is a self-report scale and, therefore, differs from ideal overt behavior rating scales. The PES cannot be recommended as a depression outcome rating scale. Other ratings of overt depressive behavior are not well researched and must be considered highly experimental at this time.

Final Recommendations

Overall, clinicians are advised to choose either the BDI or MMPI-D Scale as a self-rating assessment tool. For those interested in close concordance with DSM-III depressive criteria, the BDI would be the instrument of choice between the two. It would be best to use either the BDI or MMPI-D Scale with outpatients versus inpatients. One or the other of these scales should be administered in conjunction with an interviewer-rated instrument. The HRS is the tool to use for this purpose, particularly if inpatients are the target population. The PES, as well as other individualized overt behavior scales, are available to assess depressed behavior. Presently, no one behavioral tool or assessment format can be recommended.

Even though there are over 40 depression assessment tools to choose from, we found only six that were based on a substantial body of empirical research. Although research quantity does not guarantee research quality, the intergration of past research results may be used to guide future research efforts. It is clear to us from past studies that the variety of available depression outcome measures are not equal in their ability to reflect treatment effects. This review strongly supports the notion that multiple outcome measures are needed in depression research. For this purpose, we recommend that the HRS be used concurrently with the BDI or MMPI-D Scale, depending on the patient population and treatment type.

New experimental scales for measuring depression (e.g., overt behavior scales) may be added to this minimal core battery for experimental purposes. However, new self-report scales of the sort already developed are not needed and will probably only delay the development and assessment of effective therapies. New assessment procedures would be most valuable if they had some resemblance to DSM-III criteria by giving comprehensive coverage to the variety of symptoms that constitute depression. Our ability to effectively evaluate patient improvement will eventually lead to great benefits for the patients to whom these treatments are directed by fostering the use of the most efficient and powerful treatments.

REFERENCES

Ayd, F. J. *Recognizing the depressed patient*. New York: Grune & Stratton, 1961.

Bailey, J., & Coppen, A. A comparison between the Hamilton Rating Scale and the Beck Inventory in the measurement of depression. *British Journal of Psychiatry*, 1976, **128**, 486–489.

Bech, P., Gram, L. F., Dein, E., Jacobsen, O., Vitger, J., & Bolwig, T. G. Quantitative rating of depressive states. *Acta Psychiatrica Scandinavia*, 1975, **51**, 161–170.

Beck, A. T. Beck Depression Inventory. Unpublished manuscript, 1978. (Available from Center for Cognitive Therapy, Room 602, 133 South 36th Street, Philadelphia, PA 19104.)

Beck, A. T., & Beamesderfer, A. Assessment of depression: The depression inventory. In P. Pichot (Ed.), *Modern problems in pharmacopsychiatry*. Basel, Switzerland: Karger, 1974.

Beck, A. T., Ward, C. H., Mendelson, M., Mock, J., & Erbaugh, J. An inventory for measuring depression. *Arhives of General Psychiatry*, 1961, **4**, 561–571.

Berndt, D. J., Petzel, T. D., & Berndt, S. M. Development and initial evaluation of a multiscore depression inventory. *Journal of Personality Assessment*, 1980, **44**, 396–403.

Biggs, J. T., Wylie, L. T., & Ziegler, V. E. Validity of the Zung Self-rating Depression Scale. *British Journal of Psychiatry*, 1978, **132**, 381–385.

Borgatta, E. F. Mood, personality, and interaction. *Journal of General Psychology*, 1961, **64**, 105–137.

Bowen, R. C. The effect of diazepam on the recovery of endogenously depressed patients. *The Journal of Clinical Pharmacology*, 1978, **18**, 280–283.

Brown, G. L., & Zung, W. W. Depression scales: Self-or physician-rating? A validation of certain clinically observable phenomena. *Comprehensive Psychiatry*, 1972, **13**, 361–367.

Bumberry, W., Oliver, J. M., & McClure, J. N. Validation of the Beck Depression Inventory in a university population using psychiatric estimate as the criterion. *Journal of Consulting and Clinical Psychology*, 1978, **46**, 150–155.

Burkhart, B. R., Gynther, M. D., & Fromuth, M. E. The relative predictive validity of subtle versus obvious items on the MMPI Depression Scale. *Journal of Clinical Psychology*, 1980, **36**, 748–751.

Burrows, G. D., Davies, B., & Scoggins, B. A. Plasma concentration of nortriptyline and clinical response in depressive illness. *The Lancet*, 1972, **2**, 619–623.

Byrne, D. G., Boyle, D., & Prichard, D. W. Sex differences in response to a self-rating depression scale. *British Journal of Social and Clinical Psychology*, 1977, **16**, 269–273.

Carroll, B. J. Fielding, J. M., & Blashki, T. G. Depression rating scales: A critical review. *Archives of General Psychiatry*, 1973, **28**, 361–366.

Christenfield, R., Lubin, B., & Satin, M. Concurrent validity of the Depression Adjective Checklists (DACL) in a normal population. *American Journal of Psychiatry*, 1978, **135**, 582–584.

Comrey, A. L. A factor analysis of items on the MMPI depression scale. *Educational and Psychological Measurement*, 1957, **17**, 578–585.

Costello, C. G. Classification and psychopathology. In C. G. Costello (Ed.), *Symptoms of psychopathology: A handbook*. New York: Wiley, 1970.

Crown, S., & Crisp, A. H. A short clinical diagnostic self-rating scale for psychoneurotic patients: The Middlesex Hospital Questionnaire (MHQ). *British Journal of Psychiatry*, 1966, **112**, 917–923.

Dahlstrom, W. G., & Welsh, G. S. *An MMPI handbook*. Minneapolis: University of Minnesota Press, 1960.

Dahlstrom, W. G., Welsh, G. S., & Dahlstrom, L. E. *An MMPI handbook*. (Vol. 1) Minneapolis: University of Minnesota Press, 1972.

Davidson, J., McLeod, M., Law-Yone, B., & Linnoila, M. A comparison of electroconvulsive therapy and combined phenelzine-ametriptyline in refractory depression. *Archives of General Psychiatry*, 1978, **35**, 639–642.

Davies, B., Burrows, G., & Poynton, C. A comparative study of four depression rating scales. *Australian and New Zealand Journal of Psychiatry*, 1975, **9**, 21–24.

Diagnostic and statistical manual of mental disorders (1st ed.). Washington D.C.: American Psychiatric Association, 1952.

Diagnostic and statistical manual of mental disorders (2nd ed.). Washington, D.C.: American Psychiatric Association, 1968.

Diagnostic and statistical manual of mental disorders (3rd ed.). Washington, D.C.: American Psychiatric Association, 1980.

Donnelly, E. F., Murphy, D. L., Waldman, I. N., & Goodwin, F. K. Prediction of antidepressant responses to imipramine. *Neuropsychobiology*, 1979, **5**, 94–101.

Dorus, W., & Senay, E. C. Depression, demographic dimensions, and drug abuse. *American Journal of Psychiatry*, 1980, **137**, 699–704.

Equi, P. J., & Jabara, R. F. Validation of the self-rating depression scale in an alcoholic population. *Journal of Clinical Psychology*, 1976, **32**, 504–507.

Friedman, A. S. Syndromes and themes of psychotic depression. *Archives of General Psychiatry*, 1963, **9**, 504–509.

Fuchs, C. Z., & Rehm, L. P. A self-control behavior therapy program for depression. *Journal of Consulting and Clinical Psychology*, 1977, **45**, 206–215.

Giambra, L. M. Independent dimensions of depression: A factor analysis of three self-report depression measures. *Journal of Clinical Psychology*, 1977, **33**, 928–935.

Gong, G. E., & Hammen, C. Causal perceptions of stressful events in depressed and nondepressed outpatients. *Journal of Abnormal Psychology*, 1980, **89**, 662–669.

Goodstein, L. D. In O. K. Buros (Ed.), *Seventh mental measurements yearbook* (Vol. 1). Highland Park, N.J.: Gryphone Press, 1972.

Grinker, R. R., Miller, J., Sabshin, M., Nunn, J., & Nunally, J. D. *The phenomena of depression.* New York: Harper, 1961.

Grosscup, S. J., & Lewinsohn, P. M. Unpleasant and pleasant events, and mood. *Journal of Clinical Psychology*, 1980, **36**, 252–259.

Hackney, G. R., & Ribordy, S. C. An empirical investigation of emotional reactions to divorce. *Journal of Clinical Psychology*, 1980, **36**, 103–110.

Hague, W. H., Wilson, L. G., Dudley, D. L., & Cannon, D. S. Post-detoxification drug treatment of anxiety and depression in alcohol addicts. *The Journal of Nervous and Mental Disease*, 1976, **162**, 354–359.

Hamilton, M. A rating scale for depression. *Journal of Neurology, Neurosurgery, and Psychiatry*, 1960, **23**, 56–62.

Hamilton, M. Development of a rating scale for primary depressive illness. *British Journal of Social and Clinical Psychology*, 1967, **6**, 278–296.

Hamilton, M. General problems of psychiatric rating scales. In P. Pichot & R. Olivier-Martin (Eds.), *Psychological measurements in psychopharmocology*. Basel, Switzerland: Karger, 1974.

Hammen, C. L. Depression in college students: Beyond the Beck Depression Inventory. *Journal of Consulting and Clinical Psychology*, 1980, **48**, 126–128.

Harris, R. E., & Lingoes, J. C. *Subscales for the MMPI: An aid to profile interpretation.* Mimeographed materials. Department of Psychiatry, University of California, 1955. (Revised edition, 1968)

Hathaway, S. R., & McKinley, J. C. A multiphasic personality schedule (Minnesota): III. The measurement of symptomatic depression. *Journal of Psychology*, 1942, **14**, 73–84.

Hathaway, S. R., & McKinley, J. C. Scale 2 (depression). In W. G. Dahlstrom & L. Dahlstrom (Eds.), *Basic readings on the MMPI*. Minneapolis: University of Minnesota Press, 1980.

Hedlund, J. L., & Vieweg, B. W. The Zung Self-Rating Depression Scale: A comprehensive review. *Journal of Operational Psychiatry*, 1979, **10**, 51–64.

Johnson, D. F., & Weitzman, M. S. *Social indicators III: Selected data on social conditions and trends in the United States* (Federal Statistical System, Publication No. 328-848). Washington, D.C.: U.S. Government Printing Office, 1980.

Kay, D. W. K., Fahy, T. J., & Garside, R. F. A seven-month double-blind trial of amitriptyline and diazepam in ECT-treated depressed patients. *British Journal of Psychiatry*, 1970, **117**, 667–671.

Kay, D. W. K., Garside, R. F., & Fahy, T. J. A double-blind trial of phenelyine and amitriptyline in depressed outpatients: A possible differential effect of the drugs on symptoms. *British Journal of Psychiatry*, 1973, **123**, 63–67.

Keeler, M. H., Taylor, C. I., & Miller, W. C. Are all recently detoxified alcoholics depressed? *American Journal of Psychiatry*, 1979, **136**, 586–588.

Knesevich, J. W., Biggs, J. T., Clayton, P. J., & Ziegler, V. E. Validity of the Hamilton Rating Scale for depression. *British Journal of Psychiatry*, 1977, **131**, 49–52.

Kupfer, D., Pickar, D., Himmelhoch, & Detre, T. D. Two types of unipolar depression. *Archives of General Psychiatry*, 1975, **32**, 866–871.

Langevin, R., & Stancer, H. Evidence that depression rating scales primarily measure a social undesirability response set. *Acta Psychiatrica Scandinavica*, 1979, **59**, 70–79.

Lapierre, Y. D., & Butter, H. J. Imipramine and maprotiline in agitated and retarded depression: A controlled psychiatric and psychophysical assessment. *Progressive Neuropsychopharmacology*, 1978, **2**, 207–216.

Lester, D., Beck, A. T., & Mitchell, B. Extrapolation from attempted suicides to completed suicides: A test. *Journal of Abnormal Psychology*, 1979, **88**, 78–80.

Levitt, E. E., & Lubin, B. *Depression: Concepts, controversies, and some new facts.* New York: Springer, 1975.

Lewinsohn, P. M., & Lee, W. M. Assessment of affective disorders. In D.H. Barlow (Ed.), *Behavioral assessment of adult disorders*. New York: Guilford Press, 1981.

Lewinsohn, P. M., Munoz, R. F., Youngren, M. A., & Ziess, A. M. *Control your depression*. Englewood Cliffs, N.J.: Prentice-Hall, 1978.

Lubin, B. Adjective checklists for the measurement of depression. *Archives of General Psychiatry*, 1965, **12**, 57–62.

Lubin, B. *Manual for the Depression Adjective Check Lists*. San Diego: Educational and Industrial Testing Service, 1967.

Lubin, B., Bangert, C. J., & Hornstra, R. K. Factor structures of psychological assessment at a community mental health center. *Psychological Reports*, 1974, **35**, 455–460.(b)

Lubin, B., Dupre, V. A., & Lubin, A. W. Comparability and sensitivity of set 2 (lists e, f, & g) of the Depressive Adjective Check Lists. *Psychological Reports*, 1967, **20**, 756–758.

Lubin, B., & Himelstein, P. Reliability of the Depression Adjective Checklists. *Perceptual and Motor Skills*, 1976, **43**, 1037–1038.

Lubin, B., Hornstra, R. K., & Love, A. Course of depressive mood in a psychiatric population upon application for service and at 3- and 12 mo. reinterview. *Psychological Reports*, 1974, **34**, 424–426.(a)

Lubin, B., & Levitt, E. E. Norms for the Depression Adjective Check Lists: Age group and sex. *Journal of Consulting and Clinical Psychology*, 1979, **47**, 192.

Lubin, B., Roth, A. V., Dean, L. M., & Hornstra, R. K. Correlates of depressed mood among normals. *Journal of Clinical Psychology*, 1978, **34**, 650–653.

MacPhillamy, D., & Lewinsohn, P. M. *Manual for the Pleasant Events Schedule*. Eugene: University of Oregon, 1976.

Marone, J., & Lubin, B. Relationship between set two of the Depression Adjective Check Lists (DACL) and the Zung Self-rating Depression Scale (SDS). *Psychological Reports*, 1968, **22**, 333–334.

Master, R. S., & Zung, W. W. Depressed symptoms in patients and normal subjects in India. *Archives of General Psychiatry*, 1977, **34**, 972–974.

McNair, D. M. In O. K. Buros (Ed.), *Seventh mental measurements yearbook* (Vol. 1). High Park, N.J.: Gryphone Press, 1972.

McNair, D. M. Self-evaluations of antidepressants. *Psychopharmacologia*, 1974, **37**, 281–302.

McNair, D. M., & Maurice, L. An analysis of mood in neurotics. *Journal of Abnormal and Social Psychology*, 1964, **69**, 620–627.

Meites, M., Lovallo, W., & Pishkin, V. *Journal of Clinical Psychology*, 1980, **36**, 427–432.

Montgomery, S. A., & Asberg, M. C. A new depression scale designed to be sensitive to change. *British Journal of Psychiatry*, 1979, **134**, 382–389.

Mowbray, R. M. The Hamilton Rating Scale for Depression: A factor analysis. *Psychological Medicine*, 1972, **2**, 272–280.

Nowlis, V., & Nowlis, H. H. The description and analysis of mood. *Annals of the New York Academy of Sciences*, 1956, **65**, 345–355.

O'Connor, J. P., Stefic, E. C., & Gresock, C. J. Some patterns of depression. *Journal of Clinical Psychology*, 1957, **13**, 122–125.

Oliver, J. M., & Burkham, R. Depression in university students. Duration, relation to calendar time, prevalence, and demographic correlates. *Journal of Abnormal Psychology*, 1979, **88**, 667–670.

Overall, J. E. Dimensions of manifest depression. *Psychiatric Research*, 1962, **1**, 329–345.

Pilowsky, I., Levine, S., & Boulton, D. M. The classification of depression by numerical taxonomy. *British Journal of Psychiatry*, 1969, **115**, 937–945.

Popoff, L. M. A simple method for diagnosis of depression by the family physician. *Clinical Medicine*, 1969, **76**, 24–29.

Radloff, L. S. The CED-D Scale: A self-report depression scale for research in the general population. *Applied Psychological Measurement*, 1977, **1**, 305–401.

Rehm, L. P. Assessment of depression. In M. Hersen & A. S. Bellach (Eds.), *Behavioral assessment: A practical handbook*. Oxford: Pergamon Press, 1976.

Rehm, L. P. *The assessment of depression in therapy outcome research. A review of instruments and recommendations for an assessment battery*. Report presented to the Psychotherapy and Behavioral Intervention Section, Clinical Research Branch, NIMH, November 1978.

Rehm, L. P., Fuchs, C. Z., Roth, D. M., Kornblith, S. J., & Romano, J. M. A comparison of self-control and assertion skills treatment of depression. *Behavior Therapy*, 1979, **10**, 429–442.

Rickels, K., Case, W. G., Werblowsky, J., Csanalosi, I., Schless, H., & Weise, C. C. Amoxapine and imipramine in the treatment of depressed outpatients: A controlled study. *American Journal of Psychiatry*, 1981, **138**, 20–24.

Rockliff, B. W. A brief self-rating questionnaire for depression (SRQ-D). *Psychosomatics*, 1969, **10**, 236–243.

Rush, A. J., Beck, A. T., Kovacs, M., & Hollon, S. Comparative efficacy of cognitive therapy and pharmacotherapy in the treatment of depressed outpatients. *Cognitive Therapy and Research*, 1977, **1**, 17–37.

Salzman, C., Kochansky, G. E., Shader, R. I., & Cronin, D. M. Rating scales for psychotropic drug research with geriatric patients. II. Mood ratings. *Journal of the American Geriatric Society*, 1972, **20**, 215–221.

Sanchez, V. C., Lewinsohn, P. M., & Larson, D. W. Assertion training: Effectiveness in the treatment of depression. *Journal of Clinical Psychology*, 1980, **36**, 527–529.

Schnurr, R., Hoaken, P. C. S., & Jarrett, F. J. A comparison of depression inventories in a clinical population. *Canadian Psychiatric Association Journal*, 1976, **21**, 473–476.

Schwab, J. J., Bialow, M. R., Clemmons, R. S., & Holzer, C. E. Hamilton Rating Scale for depression with medical in-patients. British Journal of Psychiatry, 1967, **113**, 83–88.(a)

Schwab, J. J., Bialow, M. R., Clemmons, R. S., Martin, P., & Holzer, C. E. The Beck Depression Inventory with medical inpatients. *Acta Psychiatrica Scandinavica*, 1967, **43**, 255–266.(b)

Seitz, F. C. Five psychological measures of neurotic depression: A correlational study. *Journal of Clinical Psychology*, 1970, **26**, 504–505.

Selzer, M. L., Paluszny, M., & Carroll, R. A comparison of depression and physical illness in men and women. *American Journal of Psychiatry*, 1978, **135**, 1368–1370.

Snaith, R. P., Ahmed, S. N., Mehta, S., & Hamilton, M. Assessment of the severity of primary depressive illness: Wakefield self-assessment depression inventory. *Psychological Medicine*, 1971, **1**, 143–149.

Turner, R. W., Ward, M. F., & Turner, D. J. Behavioral treatment for depression: An evaluation of therapeutic components. *Journal of Clinical Psychology*, 1979, **35**, 166–175.

Tuthill, E. W., Overall, J. E., & Hollister, L. E. Subjective correlates of clinically manifested anxiety and depression. *Psychological Reports*, 1967, **20**, 535–542.

Vinar, O. Methods to evaluate a patient's mental condition during drug therapy. *Abhandlunger der deutschen Akademie der Wissenshaften zu Berlin*, 1966, **2**, 293–295.

Wadsworth, A. P., & Barker, H. R. Comparison of two treatments for depression: The antidepressive program versus traditional therapy. *Journal of Clinical Psychology*, 1976, **32**, 445–449.

Watts, C. A. *Depressive disorders in the community*. Bristol, U.K.: Wright, 1966.

Wechsler, H., Grosser, G. H., & Busfield, B. L. The Depression Rating Scale. *Archives of General Psychiatry*, 1963, **9**, 334–343.

Weckowicz, T. E., Cropley, A. J., & Mair, W. An attempt to replicate the results of a factor analytic study in depressed patients. *Journal of Clinical Psychology*, 1971, **27**, 30–31.

White, K., Pistole, T., & Boyd, J. L. Combined monoamine oxidase inhibitor-trycyclic antidepressant treatment: A pilot study. *American Journal of Psychiatry*, 1980, **137**, 1422–1425.

Williams, J. G., Barlow, D. H., & Agras, W. S. Behavioral measurement of severe depression. *Archives of General Psychiatry*, 1972, **27**, 330–333.

Woody, G. E., O'Brien, C. P., & Rickels, K. Depression and anxiety in heroin addicts: A placebo-controlled study of doxepin in combination with methadone. *American Journal of Psychiatry*, 1975, **132**, 447–450.

Wright, J. H., & Denber, H. C. B. Clinical trial of fluvoxamine: A new serotonergic antidepressant. *Current Therapeutic Research*, 1978, **23**, 83–89.

Zeiss, A. M., Lewinsohn, P. M., & Munoz, R. F. Nonspecific improvement effects in depression using interpersonal skills training, pleasant activity schedules, or cognitive training. *Journal of Consulting and Clinical Psychology*, 1979, **47**, 427–439.

Zerssen, D. V., Koeller, D. M., & Rey, E. R. Die Befindlichkeits (B-S) Skalaein enfaches instrument zur objektivierung von befindlichkeitsstorunger, insbesondere. *Rachmen von Langsschaittuntersuchungen Arzneimittelforsch*, 1970, **20**, 915–918.

Ziegler, V. E., Meyer, D. A., Rosen, S. H., & Biggs, J. T. Reliability of videotaped Hamilton ratings. *Biological Psychiatry*, 1978, **13**, 119–122.

Zung, W. W. A self-rating depression scale. *Archives of General Psychiatry*, 1965, **12**, 63–70.

Zung, W. W. Factors influencing the Self-Rating Depression Scale. *Archives of General Psychiatry*, 1967, **16**, 543–547.

Zung, W. W. Evaluating treatment methods for depressive disorders. *American Journal of Psychiatry*, 1968, **124**, 40–47.

Zung, W. W. The depression status inventory: An adjunct to the Self-Rating Depression Scale. *Journal of Clinical Psychology*, 1972, **28**, 539–543.

Zung, W. W. The measurement of affects: Depression and anxiety. In P. Pichot & R. Oliver-Martin (Eds.), *Psychological measurements in psychopharmocology*. Basel, Switzerland: Karger, 1974.

Chapter 10

Measurement of Outcome in Anxiety Disorders

S. ROBERTS, J. ARONOFF, J. JENSEN, AND M. J. LAMBERT

This chapter deals with the assessment of improvement in patients diagnosed as having an anxiety disorder. The *Diagnostic and Statistical Manual* (DSM-III) of the American Psychiatric Association (1980) served as the definition for the patient problems considered in the present review. Thus we concern ourselves here with methods and instruments that have been employed to measure improvement in anxiety and related symptoms associated with this broad diagnostic category. More specifically, we review assessment tools and make recommendations for future assessment of patients who have either a panic disorder; generalized anxiety disorder; obsessive–compulsive disorder; or phobic disorder including agoraphobia (with and without panic attacks), social phobia, or simple phobia.

To the extent possible we have not covered material that has been reviewed extensively elsewhere. We emphasize measurement tools that are highly specific to the disorders under consideration. The interested reader may wish to also consider reviews of tools to measure anxiety published by Barlow (1981) or Ciminero et al. (1978). These volumes differ from the current one in that they are aimed at practitioners subscribing to the behavioral schools whereas this chapter is atheoretical in its approach.

Anxiety disorders show dysfunctions in cognition, affect, physiological arousal, and behavior. Despite the fact that physiological arousal is a main component in the conceptualization of anxiety disorders, we do not elaborate on the different physiological measures for the following reasons: (1) these instruments are not specific to a single anxiety disorder; and (2) the results of the studies conducted to date do not enable one to conclude that measures of physiological responding will consistently add reliable information to the assessment of anxiety disorders. For a more elaborate discussion of the general use of different physiological measures, we refer the reader to Lick and Katkin (1976) and Kallman and Freuerstein, (1977). Our interest is in a complex of interrelated patterns of responding. It is not our assumption that these interacting components are equally important. It is clear that their interrelationship is a complex one that may even be individualistic.

It is our hope that a review of instruments and methods used to evaluate changes in patients with anxiety disorders will facilitate future research and the discovery of potent treatment methods.

ASSESSMENT OF CHANGE IN PANIC DISORDER AND GENERALIZED ANXIETY DISORDER

Research on the efficacy and modes of action of treatments used to ameliorate anxiety states as currently classified in the DSM-III reflects the diversity of the anxiety phenomenon. Clearly, no single therapeutic approach or assessment procedure has adequately conceptualized nor sufficiently defined all the components and characteristics of anxiety. Our contention is that specific therapeutic treatments for anxiety states (or anxiety neuroses) each propose a specific set of ameliorative changes that are considered ideal. These, in turn, direct the process and outcome of therapy as well as define those aspects of anxiety that are to be addressed in therapy. Each therapeutic approach defines anxiety according to the dominant component it seeks to modify. For example, Gatchel (1979) states that heart rate biofeedback may only be effective for those clients who are capable of learning voluntary heart rate control and for whom heart rate is a dominant component of their anxiety response. He maintains that the expectation of an overall reduction in general anxiety through learning to control physiological response may be unrealistic and that the principal advantage of such training may be in helping a person to more effectively cope with a specific situational stress.

Optimally, the standard criteria used for diagnosing anxiety disorders should *also* function as a foundation for the conceptualization and measurement of therapy. The diagnostic criteria of the DSM-III delineates the following as the defining characteristics of the anxiety states (or anxiety neuroses).

Diagnostic Criteria for Panic Disorder

A. At least three panic attacks within a three-week period in circumstances other than during marked physical exertion or in a life-threatening situation. The attacks are not precipitated only by exposure to a circumscribed phobic stimulus.

B. Panic attacks are manifested by discrete periods of apprehension or fear, and at least four of the following symptoms appear during each attack:

  (1) dyspnea
  (2) palpitations
  (3) chest pain or discomfort
  (4) choking or smothering sensations
  (5) dizziness, vertigo, or unsteady feelings

(6) feelings of unreality

(7) paresthesias (tingling in hands or feet)

(8) hot and cold flashes

(9) sweating

(10) faintness

(11) trembling or shaking

(12) fear of dying, going crazy, or doing something uncontrolled during an attack

C. Not due to a physical disorder or another mental disorder, such as Major Depression, Somatization Disorder, or Schizophrenia.

D. The disorder is not associated with Agoraphobia (P. 231–232).

Diagnostic Criteria for Generalized Anxiety Disorder

A. Generalized, persistent anxiety is manifested by symptoms from three of the following four categories:

(1) motor tension: shakiness, jitteriness, jumpiness, trembling, tension, muscle aches, fatigability, inability to relax, eyelid twitch, furrowed brow, strained face, fidgeting, restlessness, easy startle

(2) autonomic hyperactivity: sweating, heart pounding or racing, cold, clammy hands, dry mouth, dizziness, light-headedness, paresthesias (tingling in hands or feet), upset stomach, hot or cold spells, frequent urination, diarrhea, discomfort in the pit of the stomach, lump in the throat, flushing, pallor, high resting pulse, and respiration rate

(3) apprehensive expectation: anxiety, worry, fear, rumination, and anticipation of misfortune to self or others

(4) vigilance and scanning: hyperattentiveness resulting in distractibility, difficulty in concentrating, insomnia, feeling "on edge," irritability, impatience

B. The anxious mood has been continuous for at least one month.

C. Not due to another mental disorder, such as a Depressive Disorder or Schizophrenia.

D. At least 18 years of age (P. 233).

The DSM II was developed atheoretically so that it might prove to be useful to the many professionals espousing different theoretical approaches. The emphasis given to the symptomatic aspects of anxiety states, even to the parenthetic inclusion of the term "anxiety neurosis," evidences the APA committee's efforts toward producing a more atheoretical manual than the DSM-II. The DSM-III provides a specific rather than general definition of anxiety states and is well suited to those treatments that can be translated best into specific symptomatic terms. Thus the DSM-III criteria may be most appropriate for treatments based on behavioral therapy and a cognitive–behavioral therapy paradigm or through psychopharmacological methods. Therapies whose modes of action are defined by the more enduring structural aspects of anxiety or by anxiety determinants whose roots extend into the past and are linked with the present through the progressive impact of anxiety over time, are not as well represented by these defining criteria.

The use of psychopharmacological treatment of the mentally ill marked the end of an era when the focus of psychometric test design on the whole had been toward the diagnostic aspects of personality. Symptomatology during this period had been given only cursory consideration in the construction of tests, perhaps in part, as a result of the test–retest reliability requirement then emphasized. Now, sensitivity to changes in symptomatology has become the *sine qua non* of an instrument's virtue. In the measurement of psychopharmacological treatment effects, precisely the opposite of the traditional psychometric tests is requisite, since now it is "instability" that is required of them (Pichot, 1974).

Instruments appropriate to the exigencies of psychopharmocological therapies may also serve to measure outcome for the treatment of anxiety states with the use of behavioral or cognitive–behavioral therapies in which the treatment goals are specified in terms of specific symptomatic relief. The following will lead into the description of some of the major scales developed for these purposes. The specific conditions and symptoms that serve as the basis for the operational definition of anxiety in each measure are outlined. Reference is made to historical groundings, undergirding theoretical foundations, and suggested principal uses of the scales where they have been reported by their originators. Reference to pertinent reported criticism is also made.

Anxiety Specific Symptoms

The Symptom Checklist 90.

The Symptom Checklist 90 (SCL-90) was developed in the United States and has been used primarily as a criterion measure for the study of the efficacy of psychopharmacological agents in clinical treatment (Derogatis et al., 1973). It is a 90-item expanded revision of the Hopkins Symptom Checklist (HSCL), a self-report inventory that had evolved through several major and numerous minor revisions and was developed from earlier scales extending back to the more general item pool of the Cornell Medical Index. The HSCL was devised to measure primary psychiatric symptom dimensions and these were determined by means of clinical–rational clustering and empirical–analytic factor analysis. Five factor scales were labeled, one of which measures anxiety. The principal use of the HSCL has been as a measure of symptoms of outpatients, a large portion of whom were classified as suffering anxiety states and depressive neuroses. One of the major normative samples was developed with neurotic patients manifesting primary symptoms of anxiety. Although the symptom dimensions have shown factorial invariance, the anxiety and depressive dimensions have demonstrated the greatest variation among groups (Derogatis et al., 1974).

In contrast to the HSCL, the SCL-90 is made up of nine primary symptom dimensions. The anxiety factor dimension is comprised of items that index symptoms of manifest anxiety, including general indicators and cognitive signs of anxiety, plus items indicating symptoms of free-floating anxiety and panic attacks. Examples of items to be checked for the anxiety dimension are: nervousness or shakiness inside; trembling; suddenly becoming scared for no reason or feeling fearful; heart pounding or racing; having to avoid certain things, places, or activities because they are frightening; and being tense and keyed up. The items are measured on a five-point scale format that allows the patient to respond to an item by marking the degree of distress within a range from "not at all" to "extremely" (Derogatis et al., 1973).

Motivated by concern that the majority of the previous factor analyses of the HSCL and the SCL-90 were focused primarily on patients manifesting symptoms of anxiety and/or depression, Hoffman and Overall (1978) conducted a study of the factor structure of the SCL-90 in a general psychiatric outpatient population to determine whether the scale could be effectively used for the assessment of psychopathology in this more heterogeneous population. Their results showed that the unselected outpatient group responded similarly to the anxious and/or depressed outpatient populations of previous psychopharmacological studies. Consequently, they have expressed reservation in using the factor score profiles for differentiating different aspects of pathology or for use in making specialized interpretations such as distinguishing between anxiety and depression. They recommend, however, the scales' promise as a global index of psychopathology or psychological distress. Another group of researchers who attempted to verify the hypothesized factor structure of the SCL-90 found a noticeable absence of an independent anxiety dimension (Evanson et al., 1980). They concluded that "The resiliency of anxiety as a stable factor remains in our opinion, problematic." They also questioned how much information the individual scales reveal beyond the distress level measured by the total score.

Despite the growing popularity of the SCL-90 for assessing symptomatic improvement this scale does not appear to be especially adept at identifying and reflecting changes in anxiety per se. The anxiety factor score cannot be said to be an especially effective means of rating changes in patients with an anxiety disorder.

The Middlesex Hospital Questionnaire

The Middlesex Hospital Questionnaire (MHQ) (Crown & Crisp, 1966) was developed in Great Britain to fulfill the need for an instrument capable of quick quantification of the prevalent symptoms and traits pertinent to the conventional diagnostic categories of psychoneurotic illness. The most widely used British scale at the time, the Maudsley Personality Inventory (MPI), was developed by H. J. Eysenck on the broad scientifically based dimensions of neuroticism and extraversion and used for the measurement of hysteria and dysthymia. The authors of the MHQ, Sydney Crown and A. H. Crisp, found

the MPI inadequate in describing the wide variety of psychoneurotic disturbances they encountered. Although they acknowledged that aspects of the
neurotic personality could be classified through factor analytic methods, they
asserted the need for a clinically derived scale that could approximate a clinical
psychiatric diagnostic interview. From their studies the authors concede, however, that the subtests of the MHQ only measure the general factor of
neuroticism and that a score on this factor dimension says very little that is
useful diagnostically except in terms of the overall degree of a patient's illness.

The MHQ is a self-rating scale of psychoneurotic symptoms and traits. The
items were formulated and categorized by the authors and then independently
categorized by one clinical psychologist and two psychiatrists and validated
against conventional clinical diagnostic categories. It is comprised of six subtests measuring free-floating anxiety (A), phobic anxiety (P), obsessive–compulsive traits and symptoms (O), somatic symptoms (S), depressive symptoms
(D), and hysterical traits and symptoms (H) (Crown & Crisp, 1966). The
Free-floating Anxiety Scale includes such items as (Crisp et al., 1978a):

"Do you often feel upset for no obvious reason?"
"Have you felt as though you might faint?"
"Do you sometimes feel panicky?"
"Would you say you were a worrying person?"
"Do you feel 'strung-up' inside?"
"Have you ever had the feeling you are 'going to pieces'?"

Crisp et al. (1978b) report that the anxiety scale correlates highly with the
Taylor Manifest Anxiety Scale, with the Neuroticism Scale of Eysenck's EPI,
and with the anxiety scale of Cattell's Neuroticism Scale Questionnaire. The
fact that these reference scales are associated more with trait anxiety than
state anxiety raises questions about the MHQ's sensitivity to symptomatic
improvement.

The general reliability and validity of the MHQ has been confirmed in a
series of studies (Bagley, 1980); Crisp et al., 1978a,b; Crown & Crisp, 1966;
Crown, et al., 1970). However, the authors' stated purposes for constructing
the scale are confronted by the following reports. Crisp et al. (1978a) reveal
that a clear distinction could not be made between subjects diagnosed with
anxiety states and those diagnosed with depressive illness on the A, P, O, and
D scales even though a previous study (Crisp et al., 1978b) determined these
conditions to be relatively distinct as measured by the MHQ. Williamson et al.
(1976), in their search for a psychiatric screening instrument that would differentiate abnormal and potentially abnormal patients, found neither the subtests
nor the total score of the MHQ to be of sufficient specificity or sensitivity to be
used as a screening instrument in routine psychiatric practice. Bagley (1980), in
a factorial reliability study, discussed an overlap between the subscales of the
MHQ due to an underlying factor of general neuroticism. These findings are

ironic in view of the purposes for developing the scale, that is, to provide an alternative measure to Eysenck's Neuroticism and Extraversion Scales—a measure that would better discriminate between the wide range of neurotic symptoms. The MHQ, although constructed within a clinical context, does not seem to adequately distinguish different psychiatric symptoms and anxiety states. Its use cannot be recommended for profile analysis of symptomatic disorders. Although the total score may be useful as an index of psychoneuroticism, one might be better advised to use the more established and widely researched Eysenck Personality Inventory to be discussed subsequently.

The Anxiety Status Inventory and the Self-Rating Anxiety Scale

Responding to the need for an instrument to assess anxiety as a clinical disorder, Zung (1971) constructed the Anxiety Status Inventory (ASI) and the Self-rating Anxiety Scale (SAS). Zung designed his instrument to fulfill the following: comprehensive inclusion of the psychiatric symptoms of anxiety as a disorder; quantification of the symptoms; simplicity and brevity; and availability of the measure in two formats, a self-report scale and a clinician-rated scale, each with the same set of criteria. Symptoms of anxiety measured by the scales were selected on the basis of psychiatric definitions and classification as presented in the DSM-II where "anxiety disorder" is defined as a neurosis characterized by anxiety, overconcern, panic, and as frequently being accompanied by somatic symptoms. Other definitions and descriptions of anxiety as given by major psychiatric texts were also used.

The clinician-rated scale, ASI, comprises the diagnostic criteria for anxiety, 5 affective and 15 somatic symptoms, plus an interview guide for eliciting the symptoms. Both clinical observations and patient reports are used to quantify the items on a four-point scale ranging from "none" to "severe." The self-report scale, SAS, is based on the same 20 diagnostic criteria as the ASI. To avoid a response set, some of the symptoms are referenced in positive terms and others in negative terms. The patient is asked to respond within the time frame of the past week. The items are scaled in four quantitative terms ranging from "none" or "a little of the time" to "all of the time." The less anxious a person, the lower the score.

The 20 diagnostic criteria used for both the ASI and the SAS are (1) anxiousness, (2) fear, (3) panic, (4) mental disintegration, (5) apprehension, (6) tremors, (7) body aches and pains, (8) easy fatigabiltiy, weakness, (9) restlessness, (10) palpitation, (11) dizziness, (12) faintness, (13) dyspnea, (14) paresthesias, (15) nausea and vomiting, (16) urinary frequency, (17) sweating, (18) face flushing, (19) insomnia, and (20) nightmares. These affective and somatic symptom terms have then been formulated into questions. Examples of some of the questions from the ASI are: "Have you ever felt uneasy? Or that something terrible was going to happen?" (apprehension), or "Have you ever felt that your heart was running away?" (palpitations). Examples of some of the statements from the SAS are: "I feel that everything is all right and nothing bad will happen" (apprehension) or "I even feel my heart beating fast" (palpitations).

The Zung anxiety scales recommend themselves for the measurement of the effects of therapy with anxiety states (or anxiety neuroses) and were constructed to fulfill this requirement. The comparable clinician-rated and client-rated scales allow for greater cross-validation of measurement within individual therapeutic cases. However, very little additional data on the ASI or SAS has become available to insure credible results with their use.

The Hamilton Anxiety Rating Scale

A clinician-rated scale for the assessment of the symptoms of anxiety states was developed by Hamilton (1959). The instrument was designed to be used with patients diagnosed with neurotic anxiety states and not for use in the assessment of anxiety in patients of other disorders. The scale was intended to focus on the subjective experience of anxiety. Symptoms considered to be descriptive of these states were assigned to 12 groups on the basis of clinical experience together with the patient's behavior in the interview. These formed the 13 variables of the scale: (1) anxious mood; (2) tension; (3) fears; (4) insomnia; (5) intellect; (6) depressed mood; (7) somatic general (muscular and sensory); (8) cardiovascular system; (9) respiratory system; (10) gastrointestinal system; (11) genitourinary system; (12) autonomic nervous system; and (13) behavior at interview (general and physiological). Each variable is defined by a series of brief statements to be asked by the clinician during the interview with the patient and are quantified on a five-point scale ranging from "none" to "very severe or grossly disabling." Examples of the brief statements given by the interviewer to elicit patient responses concerning each anxiety variable are worries, anticipation of the worst, apprehension, and irritability (anxious mood); and dry mouth, flushing, pallor, tendency to sweat, giddiness, tension headache, and raising of hair (autonomic symptoms). Ratings made on the last grade of the scale are to be rarely used for outpatients with the maximum score not being recommended with patients who obviously could be much worse.

The reliability of the scale was determined by the correlation of scores between pairs of raters: a principal interviewer who conducted the interview and observed and recorded the patients' symptoms and a second interviewer who made independent ratings on the same interview. The correlation between the raters was positive and statistically significant. Factor analysis of the variables was also done. One general anxiety factor and a bipolar factor divided into psychic and somatic symptoms were discovered. Psychic symptoms include tension, fears, insomnia, anxiety, intellectual (cognitive) changes, depression , and behavior at interview. Somatic symptoms include gastrointestinal, genitourinary, respiratory, cardiovascular, somatic general, and autonomic symptoms. The matrix of correlations can also be resolved into two orthogonal group factors of psychic anxiety and somatic anxiety. On the basis of experience with the scale, Hamilton (1969) separated the "somatic general" dimension of the scale into somatic sensory and somatic muscular divisions extending the original scale from 13 to 14 items.

The Hamilton Anxiety Rating Scale is used frequently to measure outcome of psychopharmacological treatment of anxiety states and warrants further research as to its effectiveness in this domain as well as in assessing psychological treatments. The author reports that his scale has received surprisingly little practical criticism and that those who have used it seem to be satisfied with their data (Hamilton, 1969). Other estimations of the scales' capabilities are needed.

The measures described that have developed from the psychopharmacological and psychiatric treatment of anxiety specific symptoms have emphasized the medical orientation of treating the patient's subjective state as the first priority for both the criterion of illness and the criterion of improvement. Assessment of changes in particular symptoms requires the use of scales specific to those symptoms, whereas symptom-specific scales seem particularly vulnerable to factor variance and to the capricious nature of symptoms themselves. These measures also seem too susceptible to the patient's defensive structures against admission to the obvious signs of their illnesses.

Assessment of Anxiety in the Context of the Total Personality

Usually, symptomatic clinical phenomena are not significant in and of themselves (Kolb, 1977). Symptom disorders are extensions of the patient's basic personality pattern manifest under exaggerated or special conditions. The meaning and significance of symptoms become clear only in view of the patient's personality and should be explained in respect to that pattern (Millon, 1969).

Anxiety measures that have developed out of the personality research tradition provide assessment criteria for therapeutic change as the more stable and permanent aspects of the anxiety neuroses. The following discussion presents ideas and major anxiety scales developed from this research tradition.

Sixteen Personality Factor Questionnaire and the IPAT Anxiety Scale Questionnaire

In 1930 Cattell began his systematic multivariate research to delineate the universe of all personality traits that could conceivably consist in what he called the "personality sphere." Krug et al., (1976) and Pawlik and Cattell (1964) chronicle this research. From a collection of more than 4000 trait names, he planned to identify primary source traits and construct precise operational definitions of each itemized, reproducible pattern that would then be outlined into a nucleus of assessment devices. From this research he developed the Sixteen Personality Factor Questionnaire (16-PF).

Although Cattell's research delineated 16 primary source traits for the measurement of the total personality, practicality pointed to the need for a means of assessing clinical anxiety in a rapid, objective, and standard way.

Consequently, Cattell, who worked in conjunction with the Institute for Personality and Ability Testing (IPAT) to develop the 16-PF and other IPAT measures, constructed the shorter Anxiety Scale Questionnaire (ASQ). First published in 1957, the test was composed of the 40 "best" anxiety items from among the several thousand that had been investigated up to that time. Overt and covert anxiety measures were also built into the test. In 1976 the test items were updated to adjust for language changes since the first publication. Experimental comparisons were made between the old and new formats, and changes were not evidenced between them. The scale is purported to provide an accurate assessment of free-floating anxiety level to supplement clinical diagnosis and to facilitate research or screening where diagnostic assessment time is limited. Examples of items are: "My interests in people and ways to have fun, seem to change quite fast," "Even if people think poorly of me I still go on feeling O.K. about myself," and "I like to be sure that what I'm saying is right, before I join in on an argument."

The IPAT suggests that, time permitting, the most productive procedure for anxiety assessment may be within the total context of the personality. When assuming this approach, they recommend that the 16-PF Questionnaire be used. The 16-PF measures sixteen source traits and anxiety as a derived composite of these primaries. Measures for extraversion and other criteria can concurrently be calculated from this data base (Krug et al., 1976).

Levonian (1961) presented the results of a statistical analysis of Cattell's 16-PF. He used a sample that was similar to the one used in the original construction of the questionnaire. In general, his results did not support Cattell's factors. In fact, the extreme item heterogeneity substantiated in this study summons a judicious appraisal of the 16-PF Questionnaire. Another opponent, Becker (1961), performed a comparative analysis of the factor structure of the 16-PF and Guilford–Martin Personality Inventory. His study confirmed the major importance of the Anxiety and Extraversion factors in both inventories and that the 16-PF was revealing at most eight factors, only two or three of which were sufficiently reliable for individual prediction. Becker concluded, "Cattell would be well advised to try to measure half as many independent factors reliably instead of persisting with his scheme of 12 to 16 questionnaire factors which he is presently recommending for use at three levels."

In a further analysis of Cattell's work, Eysenck and Eysenck (1969) performed a joint factorial study of the Guilford, Cattell, and Eysenck scales. They concluded that Guilford's primary factors were superior to Cattell's and that in their analysis extraversion (E) and neuroticism (N) were clearly seen at the super factor level. Eysenck was unable to replicate Cattell's main factors and stated that at only the third-order factor level were replicable factors found, and these were not Cattell's but Eysenck's E and N. "In other words," states Eysenck, "Cattell's questionnaires may be used to measure these two type factors [extraversion and neuroticism] and do so probably with the same degree of accuracy as do the Eysenck and Guilford questionnaires, but they should not be used to measure the Cattell primary factors, whose existence receives no support from this investigation" (Eysenck & Eysenck, 1969, p. 402).

In response to the criticism of his 16 factors, Cattell (1972a) carried out a 184-item factor analysis of the 16-PF on a population of 780 adults. He concluded that when technical standards required of all sound factor analyses are met, there are no less than 16 factors present in the data and that these correspond with the factors found in research to support the 16-PF.

The depth and breadth of Cattell's contribution to research in this area cannot be matched nor can the significance of its repercussions be appraised. Nonetheless, the strength of the criticism launched against the 16-PF and the Cattellian factors advises discretion and knowledge in their use.

The Eysenck Personality Inventory

H. J. Eysenck (1975) asserted that anxiety is not a unidimensional variable, as is assumed in the construction of such measures as the Taylor Manifest Anxiety Scale (TMAS). Rather, he conceptualizes anxiety as conditioned fear reactions that arise contingent on two independent variables: (1) the strength of the unconditioned stimulus that determines the extent of emotionality or fearfulness; and (2) the conditionability of the person which influences the degree to which the conditioned stimulus and unconditioned stimulus will be paired. Emotionality or fearfulness is measured on the dimension neuroticism (N), and conditionability is measured on the dimension extraversion–introversion (E).

Eysenck (1970a) conceives of anxiety as a conditioned pain response and expects people who are constitutionally high in introversion and high in emotionality to have especially low thresholds for the arousal of anxiety. This compound nature of anxiety has made much published work difficult to rationally integrate into a theoretical framework. For example, high scores or low scores on the TMAS are ambiguous because they could be due to differences in extraversion–introversion or in emotionality–stability. According to Eysenck, measures of these two dimensions are needed to understand human behavior. He further claims that all discussions of the personality literature on anxiety are vitiated by this fault.

Eysenck and Eysenck (1969) have suggested that neurotic behavior can be defined in terms of four quadrants: neuroticism (or emotionality) as opposed to stability and extraversion as opposed to introversion. His interest in N and E typologies and the fact that there were no instruments available that sufficiently measured them led him to construct his own inventories to fulfill this purpose. The first such inventory was the Maudsley Medical Questionnaire (MMQ), which was constructed to measure neuroticism. When he decided on its revision, he constructed a new scale the Maudsley Personality Inventory (MPI) to measure extraversion as well as neuroticism. He prepared a questionnaire including the items of Guilford's R scale as an index of extraversion and Guilford's C scale as an index of neuroticism. These two scales had previously proven to be valid and reliable measures of the two dimensions. Items from the MMQ were also incorporated in the scale. The scale was administered to 200 men and 200 women, British born, white, and over 18 years of age. Items were analyzed by use of the X^2 Factor. On the basis of these results, two new scales were devised; 24 items in a neuroticism scale and 24 items in an extraversion–introversion scale. Factor analysis of the items was then performed and the two scales were found to be independent.

Eysenck's next progressive step in the measurement of neuroticism and extraversion–introversion was the development of the Eysenck Personality Inventory (EPI) in 1964—a revision of the MPI. The test consists of 108 questions regarding neuroticism (N) and extraversion–introversion (E). It also incorporates a lie scale.

Cattell (1966), criticizing Eysenck's E and N factors, calls them pseudo-second orders because they resemble the second-order pattern but are rather the first and second primaries rotated in inadequate space. "The overlap of these space-deformed factors with the true second orders is due to the fact that both explain variance in say, three to four factors, where perhaps fifteen may be necessary." This pseudo-second-order approach is scientifically indefensible, states Cattell, because of "the guess work involved in deciding on how many orders exist before one has taken out the primaries and the inelegance of seeking a solution in short, deformed space." He further states that precise separation of such concepts as anxiety, introversion, and neuroticism are prevented with this approach and that "the illegitimate manner of reaching such resolutions should suffice to warn factorists to avoid such mongrel concepts which are neither one thing nor the other." (Cattell, 1966, p. 260).

Unlike Cattell, whose primary theoretical approach to the analysis of personality has been in the factorial discovery and identification of independent traits, Eysenck has been concerned with the correlations actually observed between these traits that resolve themselves into a typology of personality based on the very broad factor dimensions of E and N. Rychlak (1981) explained the distinction between types and traits in the description of personality. "A therotype is a global description of the total personality in the light of a generally accepted personality theory" (Rychlak, 1981, p. 22), in other words, an effort to perceive the total person at once. Whereas a trait theory accounts for behavior in sets of traits, appropriating more or less of the same general characteristics to all personalities. Because of the dimensional rather than categorical nature of Eysenck's typologies, the continuity of the E and N factors threads itself into the entirety of the proposed classification system, and as Eysenck (1970b) describes, any position along the two continua is assumed as the composite of quantitative variations of E and N. The question is then raised as to whether E and N are simply secondary trait constructs abstracted from the primary trait level and not typologies at all. Rychlak (1981) notes that in the course of history, typologies move to trait theories and that those often classify people along a scale according to the relative degree that a person possesses a given trait. Certainly, in one sense Eysenck's E and N have followed this historical trend in classifying people along a measurement scale according to the relative degree that they can be described in terms of these two factors. Nonetheless, research has repeatedly shown that these factors do correlate and resolve into more encompassing elements that describe the more total personality.

Whether Eysenck's system measures types or traits seems to be more a theoretical matter than one that can be determined by reliance on mathematical techniques.

The Taylor Manifest Anxiety Scale

The core role given anxiety in many personality theories and the interest shown by psychologists in anxiety as a phenomenon of personality are no better displayed than in the extensive research using the Taylor Manifest Anxiety Scale (TMAS). However, Taylor-Spence and Spence (1966) affirm that their central interest in developing the scale was not with the assessment of anxious persons, nor in anxiety as a personality characteristic. Taylor (1953, p. 289) states that "The anxiety scale was developed for and has been used exclusively as a device for selecting experimental subjects without regard to the relationship of the scores to more common clinical definitions." Rather, the author's interests have been in understanding the function of aversive motivational or drive factors in learning situations, principally of a classical conditioning format as structured within the Hull-Spence behavior theory.

Taylor (1953) claimed construction of the manifest anxiety scale and outlined the two following assumptions on which the TMAS was initially implemented: (1) variance in individual drive levels is related to the intensity of internal anxiety or emotionality of subjects; and (2) the strength of this anxiety can be discovered by a test composed of items descriptive of overt or manifest symptoms of this condition. She submitted approximately 200 items from the Minnesota Multiphasic Personality Inventory (MMPI) to five clinicians and an accompanying definition of manifest anxiety derived from Cameron's descriptions of chronic anxiety reactions. The clinicians then served as judges in designating those items most indicative of manifest anxiety according to the ascribed definition. Sixty-five items with 80% or greater agreement were selected. These and 135 items identified as nonanxiety items were administered to 352 college students. Through statistical analysis, the original scale was narrowed to the 50 most discriminating items. These were supplemented by 175 statements nonindicative of anxiety. A further revision is reported in which certain items in the scale were simplified as to vocabulary and sentence structure for purposes of better use with noncollege norms.

Despite the fact that it was not intended as a clinical device nor a personality test when it was developed, the TMAS achieved widespread use. Sarason (1960) has suggested that this was caused by the need for measures of personality that were relevant to issues of intellectual performance, reaction to stress, and the ability to learn. In view of the absence of such measures, psychologists "seized upon" this easily administered objective test.

Eysenck (1971, p. 85) defined the TMAS as "an *a priori* collection of items from the MMPI supposedly measuring anxiety" and further added that it never has convincingly demonstrated its correlation with outside criteria. He claims that its factorial virtue is doubtful in that it simultaneously measures the two orthogonal dimensions of neuroticism and extraversion–introversion, making for difficult and ambiguous interpretation of results because they cannot simply be associated to any one dimension.

Cattell (1972a) did not disagree with Eysenck's criticism regarding certain obvious defects of the TMAS. However, Cattell (1972b) discussed this issue further by explaining that when the ASQ was designed in 1960 the finished scale was analyzed with the TMAS and the EPI. Results showed that the TMAS followed the course that was expected from items derived from clinical data diverging from the factor axis in the direction of neuroticism. At the same time, Eysenck's scale deviated in another direction from the same axis. Consequently, they demonstrated a better correlation with the ASQ than they did with each other. "But now, to make a masterpiece of confusion for students," Cattell complains, "Eysenck has insisted on calling his anxiety scale a neuroticism (N) scale. So that we have on the one hand something explicitly called an 'anxiety scale,' which proves to have marked neurotic intrusions, and something called a 'neuroticism scale' which measures anxiety more than it does anything else" (Cattell, 1972a, p. 155).

A separate factor analysis of the TMAS has been reported by O'Connor et al., (1956) to determine by factorial method whether the TMAS is in fact unitary and to discover whether there are more factors than one, and if so, to determine their identities. The authors concluded that the TMAS is evidently as multidimensional as general intelligence tests. They identified five factors: chronic anxiety or worry; increased physiological activity; sleep disturbances associated with inner strain; sense of personal inadequacy; and motor tension. However, a single common factor was not found.

The TMAS has, by its widespread use in concurrent validity studies, become a standard of manifest anxiety. Nevertheless, it does not provide the best benchmark device for a symptom specific or personality relevant measure of anxiety. It seems to tap some kind of anxiety relevant emotionality factor that has physiological implications. It covers less well state-related or specific symptoms of anxiety and thus cannot be recommended for use in therapies that aim to change limited, specific symptoms.

Conceptualizing and operationally defining anxiety symptom disorders within the context of the personality characterizes the work of Cattell and Eysenck in the anxiety research area and also is reflected in the origination and personality research tradition of the TMAS. Those investigating therapeutic process and outcome for the long-term treatment of neurotic personalities diagnosed with anxiety states or the chronic anxiety neuroses will find the measures described in this section very useful and important. Also, those concerned with directly treating the symptoms of anxiety states will benefit from the assessment of the personality conditions of their patients.

Anxiety Assessment in the Context of Research Hypotheses

Other theoretical assumptions about the nature of anxiety and anxiety assessment have led to the development of anxiety measures to test these research hypotheses. The State–Trait Anxiety Inventory is one such device. It was developed to test the state–trait theory of anxiety advanced by Charles Spielberger and originally postulated by R. B. Cattell. Cattell (1973) has suggested that moods, states, and temporary roles are perhaps as important in understanding and predicting behavior as are traits. "People stand, at a given moment of measurement at different levels on, for instance, their anxiety state response, and the immediate statistical analysis is quite incapable of distinguishing between a trait structure and this instantaneously frozen state, just as a person who had never seen the sea might interpret a photo of the big waves as mountains" (Cattell,1973, p. 123). Cattell (1972b) contends that we can remove trait variance altogether through the use of statistical procedures that isolate scores varying across occasions from those that are highly stable. Thus stable individual characteristics can be blocked from the measurements leaving a representation of the flow of mood in response to the changing situation.

Charles Spielberger has constructed an inventory for the assessment of A-State and A-Trait anxiety that is perhaps the most widely used anxiety measure and perhaps the most widely used measure in the entirety of outcome research (Lambert, Chapter 1, this volume). The State–Trait Anxiety Inventory (STAI) is composed of two separate self-report scales for measuring state anxiety (A-State) and trait anxiety (A-Trait) and was originally constructed for the study of anxiety in normals. It has since been successfully used with neuropsychiatric, medical, and surgical patients, as well as junior and senior high-school students. Spielberger et al., (1970) recommend the STAI for experimental research where an index of drive level (D) as defined by Hull and Spence is needed or for clinical work where a sensitive instrument for the measurement of the levels of transitory anxiety or changes in A-State experienced by clients in counseling, psychotherapy, behavior therapy, or on a psychiatric ward is required.

The A-Trait scale comprises 20 items that investigate how people generally feel. Individual items are expected to be unaffected by situational stress and to be relatively stable. Examples of A-Trait items are: "I feel pleasant," "I tire quickly," and "I try to avoid facing a crisis or difficulty." Correlations between scores on the A-Trait scale, the TMAS, and the ASQ are between .75 and .80 for college students and above .80 for neuropsychiatric patients. The A-State scale (also 20 items) asks people to relate their feelings at a specified moment in time. The A-State scale delineates a continuum of anxiety intensity ranging from states of calmness to panic. Examples of A-State items are: "I feel calm," "I feel secure," and "I am presently worrying over possible misfortunes" (Spielberger et al., 1970). Correlations between the A-State scale and other anxiety state measures such as Zuckermann's Affect Adjective Checklist–Today Form give evidence of its concurrent validity (Spielberger, 1972c).

Spielberger (1976) has encouraged the adoption of terminological conventions in anxiety research to allow for accurate exchange in the description of anxiety among investigators. Terms must be descriptive of physiological, behavioral, and phenomenological aspects of anxiety. He also calls for a distinction in the terminology used by the experimenter and the subject in describing subjective experience. He suggests that the term "threat" be used to refer to the phenomenological experiences of the subject and that the term "stress" be reserved for reference to the real dangers associated with objective stimulus events. Finally, he proposes that the term "A-States" be used to refer to emotional reactions consisting of the feelings of tension, apprehension, and heightened activity of the autonomic nervous system.

Spielberger (1972a) used the term "anxiety-as-process" to describe the sequence of cognitive, affective, and behavioral responses created in reaction to stress. Stress is the external or internal cue that is perceived or interpreted as dangerous or threatening. The cognition of danger initiates the anxiety state reaction or increases the intensity of A-states, placing the anxiety state at the core of the anxiety process. The temporally ordered sequence of anxiety-as-process events is as follows:

$$\text{stress} \rightarrow \text{perception of danger} \rightarrow \text{A- state reaction}$$

This process can be elaborated into further steps: as the A-State is experienced as painful, the individual will engage in cognitions and behaviors or responses for its minimization. Thus stress may be reappraised, which may proffer appropriate coping mechanisms causing relief, or avoidance behavior may be enacted to permit escape. If coping or avoiding the stress are not feasible, psychological defenses may be executed to reduce stress through perceptual distortions of the anxiety provoking stimuli. A-State reactions may precipitate the following sequence:

$$\begin{array}{ccc} \text{A-state} & \text{cognition} & \text{coping, avoidance behaviors,} \\ \text{reaction} \rightarrow & \text{reappraisal} \rightarrow & \text{or psychological defenses} \end{array}$$

Elucidating Freud's concept, Spielberger (1972b) defines neurotic "anxiety-as-process." He distinguished neurotic anxiety from more objective anxiety in that the source of danger is internal instead of external. Repressed sexual and aggressive impulses in childhood due to the strong and consistent punishment the child experienced in the face of their expression creates the complex process resulting in the following sequence of events:

$$\begin{array}{cccc} \text{Internal} & \text{external danger} & \text{objective} & \\ \text{impulses} \rightarrow & \text{(punishment)} \rightarrow & \text{anxiety} & \rightarrow \text{repression} \end{array}$$

$$\begin{array}{cccc} \text{partial breakdown} & \text{derivatives of} & \text{perception} & \text{neurotic} \\ \text{of repression} \rightarrow & \text{internal impulses} \rightarrow & \text{of danger} \rightarrow & \text{anxiety} \end{array}$$

Reflecting the sequence of events in the anxiety-as-process models, Spielberger et al., (1971) summarized variables in addition to the A-State and A-Trait constructs that they consider most important in anxiety research: the qualities of the internal and external stimuli invoking anxiety states; the cognitive processes involved in the appraisal of stimuli as threatening; and the defense mechanisms employed to avoid or reduce these states once they occur.

Two types of significant stressor situations are also noted by Spielberger (1972c) to have differing implications for invoking A-State in persons who vary in A-Trait: (1) persons high in A-Trait appear to interpret situations where their individual adequacy is challenged as more threatening than do low A-Trait persons; and (2) settings conveying physical danger do not carry the same difference in threat for high- and low-A-Trait persons. Correspondingly, differential elevations in A-State should follow the same pattern in the two types of stressor situations as is the described pattern for A-Trait.

Measurement of state anxiety in relation to trait anxiety is reflective of measuring symptom disorders in the context of the personality. An advantage of the STAI is that both can be measured in a very short period of time with similar formats and comparable norms. The body of research using the STAI is growing, and most evaluative studies of the instruments' performance are favorable. The criticisms that have been leveled at the STAI are those that are typically leveled at all self-report measures, although some authors question the actual existence of the state–trait anxiety distinction.

Of greatest contemporary concern would be the failure of the STAI to provide a measure for Spielberger's anxiety-as-process model, particularly the effective measurement of cognitions, coping strategies, and psychological defenses.

A faction of behavioristic clinicians are dissatisfied with the traditional trait approach to psychometrics and champion the assessment of states rather than traits. Typical of this orientation is Marvin Zuckerman, who asserts that trait measures are of diminutive advantage, except to the extent that they can predict responses, whereas state measures are responses in themselves.

Most trait measures are but a sampling of the labels people ascribe to themselves or their remembrances of collective accounts of past states. The very nature of a trait test is its inflexibility over time, making it an insensitive index of behavioral change (Zuckerman, 1976). The Multiple Affect Adjective Checklist was designed as a state measure on which the symptoms of anxiety as a mood state may be assessed.

The Multiple Affect Adjective Checklist

Zuckerman (1960) reported the development of the Affect Adjective Checklist (AACL) for the assessment of anxiety. He chose an empirical rather than factor analytic method of item selection. Affective adjectives from Gough's and Nowlis's checklist and from a thesaurus were collected. A scoring key was then constructed from words found to be often used by anxious patients and by normals hypnotically induced into anxiety states. Examples of anxiety-plus words are: afraid, desperate, frightened, nervous and panicky. Examples of anxiety-minus words are: calm, cheerful, contented, happy and joyful. Anxiety-plus items are scored 1 if checked, and anxiety-minus items are scored 1 if not checked. Two forms of the tests, which may be changed by a simple adjustment of the instructions, reflecting the different time sets, "General" and "Today," were also devised— the former as a general version of the test, and the latter as a version where repeated anxiety assessments could be made with the results sensitive to changes in anxiety level within a relatively limited interval of time. Both use the same list of items, but the General form instructs the subject to check adjectives descriptive of how he generally feels, and the Today form asks subjects to check adjectives descriptive of how they are feeling now or today.

Zuckerman and Lubin (1965) outlined the details of the construction of the Multiple Affect Adjective Checklist (MAACL), which was designed to provide measures of three clinically significant negative affects: anxiety, depression, and hostility. Positive affects are not considered, although there is evidence that the scales are bipolar. The anxiety scale is composed of the same items that make up the AACL. Administration of the MAACL takes approximately five minutes, and the time set in the instructions, again, can be changed without any necessary change in the items.

Zuckerman and Biase (1962), in a study designed to replicate and gather further data on the validity of the AACL, found support for the hypothesized relationship between the AACL score fluctuations and the degree of expectation of failure on exams. Also, they reported that the AACL correlated significantly with the MMPI-based measures of anxiety: D, Pt, TMAS, Welsh A−I, and Rosen ARS. In another validation study of the MAACL, Zuckerman et al., (1965) showed that it correlated positively and significantly with the MMPI scales: D, Pa, Sc, and Hs. In addition, all the MAACL scales correlated highly with each other.

On a more cautious note, Herron (1969), in a critical analysis of the MAACL, concluded that it should be used with caution. The results of his study showed that any student who had turned in a completely blank MAACL-Today in the "low-anxious" test sections scored considerably above the mean on all three scales. This resulted from the fact that anxiety has 10 adjectives scored when left blank and hostility has 12 adjectives scored when left blank. Herron concluded that the MAACL−Today scale score is due to the effect of response sets.

Research on the whole has shown the MAACL to be an effective measure of state anxiety; however, more research on its effectiveness as a measure of anxiety disorders is needed before the scale can be used with confidence in the assessment of therapy with the anxiety states (or neuroses). Certainly this device best lends itself to behavioral and pharmacological approaches.

The S−R Inventory of Anxiousness

According to Endler (1975), Spielberger's state−trait anxiety theory is a theoretically correct conceptualization of the relationship between A-Trait, A-State, and type of threat. Nonetheless, the STAI is limited to measuring only interpersonal trait anxiety and overlooks other aspects of anxiety. He suggests that in investigation of the relationship between trait and state, it is essential to assess anxiety multidimensionally. Neither trait nor state anxiety scores yield enough information on which to base accurate behavioral predictions. Information as to the evocative situations must also be integrated by assessing the person-(trait)-by-situation interaction. The Endler–Hunt interaction model directly confronts these questions through the theory and research that has evolved from the development of the S–R Inventory of Anxiousness (Endler, 1975).

From the "logical analysis" of the meaning of trait ratings, Endler et al., (1962) suggested a new format for trait inventories (as exemplified in the S–R Inventory of Anxiousness) that separately samples situations, responses, and individual differences and that makes possible an analysis of variance attributable to subjects, situations, and modes of response and to the various interactions among these. The analyses of the factor structure of both situations and responses is also made possible.

This new format employs a sampling of 11 situations and 14 modes of response. Examples of situations are: "You are just starting off on a long automobile trip," "You are going to meet a new date," and "You are crawling along a ledge high on a mountain side." Examples of response modes are: "Heart beats faster," "Get an uneasy feeling," and "Feel exhilarated and thrilled." A five-step scale ranging from "none" to "very much" is utilized to allow subjects to register the intensity of their own responses to the situation.

Endler et al., (1962) reported the results of an analysis of their samplings of situations and modes of response suggesting the possibility of forming the following categories in each: three situational factors (interpersonal, inanimate, and ambiguous) and three modes-of-response factors (distress, exhilaration, and autonomic). Nine possible situation modes-of-response combinations are also suggested with which to describe and predict individuals' behavior.

The S–R Inventory of Anxiousness has been shown to be widely used in the literature as a therapy outcome measure (Lambert, chapter 1, this volume). The format of the test shows versatility for the measurement of different dimensions and components of the anxiety response. Tailoring of treatment according to the individual nature of the patient's anxiety seems possible given the adaptability of the modes of response factors and the situational factors of the test. However, further research will be needed to bear out these assumptions and to test for the instrument's effectiveness in measuring the anxiety states (or neuroses).

OUTCOME MEASURES OF OBSESSIVE–COMPULSIVE DISORDER

Although obsessive or compulsive tendencies are frequently found in various pathological conditions, it is rare that they are sufficiently extreme to be representative of the obsessive–compulsive disorder as defined by DSM-III criteria. The common age of onset for persistent obsessional symptoms occurs in the early 20s. On the average, the patient will wait another two years before seeking professional help. It is likely that the patient will be of high intelligence and a member of the middle to upper socioeconomic class. Most patients report that their symptoms began between the ages of 10 and 15 and that the disorder had a fluctuating course, often marked by an exacerbation of symptoms (Mavissakalian & Barlow, 1981).

Research and clinical observations have contributed to a generally agreed-on description of symptomatology present in the obsessive–compulsive condition:

A. Either obsessions or compulsions:

Obsessions: recurrent, persistent ideas, thoughts, images, or impulses that are ego-dystonic, i.e., they are not experienced as voluntarily produced, but rather as thoughts that invade consciousness and are experienced as senseless or repugnant. Attempts are made to ignore or suppress them.

Compulsions: repetitive and seemingly purposeful behaviors that are performed according to certain rules or in a stereotyped fashion. The behavior is not an end in itself, but is designed to produce or prevent some future event or situation. However, either the activity is not connected in a realistic way with what it is designed to produce or prevent, or may be clearly excessive. The act is performed with a sense of subjective compulsion coupled with a desire to resist the compulsion (at least initially). The individual generally recognizes the senselessness of the behavior (this may not be true for young children) and does not derive pleasure from carrying out the activity, although it provides a release of tension.

B. The obsessions or compulsions are a significant source of distress to the individual or interfere with social or role functioning.

C. Not due to another mental disorder, such as, Tourettes Disorder, Schizophrenia, Major Depression, or Organic Mental Disorder. (American Psychiatric Association, 1980, p. 235)

Despite the tremendous uncertainty as to whether the obsessional personality is a valid construct, a few measures sensitive to changes in obsessive–compulsive traits are examined. For a more elaborate discussion of these trait measures, the reader is referred to Rachman and Hodgson (1980).

The measures primary to the study of the obsessive–compulsive disorder can be subdivided into two major categories: self-report and behavioral. The use of a clinician-rated scale is also reviewed. A discussion of individual measures ensues, followed by a summary of the problems encountered in the assessment of obsessional illness as well as recommendations for future outcome research.

Self-Report Measures

Symptom Checklists

Symptom checklists can be divided into two groups on the basis of their relative emphases: those whose purpose is to measure obsessive–compulsive traits and those designed to assess obsessive–compulsive symptomatology.

To date, the greatest amount of research has been concerned with discovering the more permanent characteristics of the obsessive–compulsive personality. One of the earliest attempts to create a measure specific to obsessional illness was that due to Sandler and Hazari (1960). The authors studied 100 neurotics on the basis of their responses to 40 items from the Tavistock Self-Assessment Inventory (TSAI) and identified two distinct and independent personality types. The first was a reactive, somewhat narcissistic character type, and the second type was described as being represented on a continuum from obsessional personality to obsessional state.

Critics of these findings have suggested that (1) the two factors may not be significantly different (Reed, 1969); (2) patients with obsessional symptoms do not have higher scores than patients without (Snaith et al., 1971), and (3) it does not differentiate phobics from obsessionals (Orme, 1965). As a dependent measure, this derivative of the TSAI does not appear to be sensitive to changes in symptomatology (a task for which it was not designed), nor does it appear to be useful in measuring obsessional traits.

Another trait measure, the Hysteroid–Obsessional Questionnaire (HOQ), was developed by Caine and Hawkins (1963) and modified by Foulds (1965). The development of the HOQ was based on Jung's theory of two polar types of personality—"hysteroid" and "obsessional." Hysteroid types were characterized by hysterical symptoms, whereas obsessional types were characterized by obsessional symptoms. The HOQ is a 48-item checklist intended as a measure of *ego–syntonic* obsessionality. Unfortunately, the scale contains very few items whose content is obsessional in the clinical sense of the word. The scale was cross-validated with Eysenck's Personality Inventory and was found to correlate .84 with this measure of introversion. Thus the result of efforts to find a measure of the obsessional personality ended with a measure that added little beyond Eysenck's E factor (Rachman & Hodgson, 1980). As with Sandler and Hazari's scale, the HOQ lacks sensitivity to obsessional symptomatology. As a dependent measure of change in the obsessive–compulsive disorder, it can be concluded that the HOQ has limited utility.

The most widely used of all the symptom checklists is the Leyton Obsessional Inventory (LOI) developed by Cooper (1970). It taps both trait and state dimensions. The inventory appears to have test–retest reliability with most *t*-test comparisons, yielding at least a .01 level of significance on each subscale of the instrument. The inventory also appears to have good face validity. Its standardization was achieved on both normals and obsessional neurotics and discriminates well between the two groups (Cooper, 1970; Marks et al., 1975; Murray et al., 1979).

The administration of the LOI consists of giving the subject 69 cards, on which is printed 46 symptom-related and 23 trait-related questions. The subject responds to each of these questions by dropping the card into a box labeled "yes" or a box labeled "no," thus giving symptom and trait scores. Further, 35 of the 69 questions provide a resistance score (which measures the severity of the symptoms) and an interference score (which measures the disability caused by the symptoms). In all, four scores are obtained from the LOI—one from each of the symptom, trait, resistance, and interference scales.

The apparent purpose of the LOI was to differentiate between personality traits and obsessional symptoms. Because personality traits have not been shown to have any clear bearing on obsessional symptomatology, one must conclude that the LOI has not yet fulfilled its purpose. However, this conclusion does not question the efficacy of this measure as being sensitive to changes in symptomatology. In fact, numerous researchers have demonstrated the sensitivity of the LOI to changes in their patient's symptoms when employed as a pre- and postmeasure (Allen & Rack, 1975; Boersma et al., 1976; Emmelkamp & Kraanen, 1977; Foa & Goldstein, 1978; Hackman & McLean, 1975; Kendell & Discipio, 1970).

Not only is the LOI sensitive to symptomatic changes, but it also appears to measure symptoms as they are outlined by DSM-III. The resistance and interference scales measure the degree of impairment, an important part of DSM-III criteria. An item analysis indicates that of the 46 symptom questions, 17 reflect obsessional symptoms directly and 15 are direct indicators of compulsions. The remaining 14 items are indirect questions related to obsessions or compulsions but do not elicit responses based on the repetitive, persistent, or recurrent nature of the disorder. These 14 items were dominated by the themes of meticulousness, order, and cleanliness.

Critics of the LOI have suggested that the inventory lacks items that represent the total range of obsessional and compulsive symptoms (Philpott, 1975). This criticism, however, seems unrealistically harsh since no questionnaire could possibly encompass the complete range of intensity and comprehensively consider all the possible symptoms. This criticism seems even more unrealistic when contrasted with an even more frequently mentioned limitation of the LOI—that it is too lengthy. Several authors have mentioned this problem (Allen & Tune, 1975; Murray et al., 1979; Rachman & Hodgson, 1980). Such criticism appears to be merited, and steps are being taken to shorten the inventory. Presently the scale takes 30 minutes to 2 hours to administer. It also has the disadvantage of requiring individualized administration. In addition, Philpott (1975) has suggested that the results are contaminated by the effects of depression. The validity of the trait scale as a valid measure of obsessional personality has also been questioned (Murray et al., 1979).

There are also a number of advantages to using the LOI. One such advantage is that it has some power in discriminating between types of obsessionality (Cooper, 1970; Murray, et al., 1979). It is sensitive to the degree of obsessionality in psychiatric conditions other than obsessive–compulsive disorder and gives information as to the severity of the disorder.

The Lynfield Obsessional/Compulsive Questionnaire (Allen & Tune, 1975) was one of the initial attempts to shorten the LOI. It is a 20-question, pencil–paper version of its precurser, the LOI. The questionnaire is short, can be administered to groups, and is easily interpreted. It also taps ruminations that were neglected in the LOI. As with the LOI, one obtains interference and resistance scores but no symptom score. The absence of a symptom score appears to affect the accuracy with which the Lynfield would be sensitive to changes in symptomatology. Inspection of the items indicates that the questionnaire could be sensitive to changes in compulsive rituals and the impairment related thereto. The scale also appears to be potentially sensitive to changes in obsessionality. A measure of the severity of ego–dystonic feelings related to the obsessions is absent, however. At this time, it has only been cross/validated against the LOI. No data have been collected that would establish the test–retest reliability of the questionnaire. The author did, however, achieve a split-half reliability coefficient of .78. The absence of a symptom score, its limited use, and its lack of test–retest reliability are clear disadvantages.

Hodgson and Rachman (1977) attempted to develop a questionnaire that would be sensitive to changes in obsessional symptomatology. Their interest was to develop an inventory that would assess obsessional complaints and not obsessional personality traits. Thus the authors set out to choose items that had the ability to differentiate obsessionals from equally neurotic introverts with no obsessional complaints. They developed what is known as the Maudsley Obsessional–Compulsive Inventory (MOC).

The MOC is a 30-item, true–false inventory that covers four major types of obsessional complaint: checking, cleaning, slowness, and doubting. A score is obtained from each of these complaint categories as well as a total score. Concurrent validity for the MOC was computed by determining the correlation between factor scores and therapists' symptomatic ratings. The inventory showed moderate correlations with therapist ratings on the cleaning and checking subscales. Unfortunately, ratings on obsessional slowness and doubting could not be adequately studied because therapists were unable to make retrospective ratings of slowness and doubting. Most important for this discussion, however, is that the MOC was studied as a pre- and postmeasure and was found to be sensitive to changes in obsessional–compulsive complaints. This was determined by correlating MOC change scores with subjective (but reliable) ratings of improvement. Correlations ranged from .42 to .81. The reliability of the MOC was established over a one-month period on a test–retest basis. The coefficient of correlation obtained was .80.

With regard to coverage of the DSM-III diagnostic criteria, the MOC is an excellent measure. Of its 30 items, 14 are accounted for by compulsion related questions and 11 reflect obsessional symptoms. The five remaining items are difficult to classify as either obsessional or compulsive. In spite of these five items, the MOC does appear to be an efficient measure of obsessional–compulsive symptomatology. Unfortunately, however, there is no measure of the degree of impairment caused by obsessional or compulsive symptoms. Such an addition to the inventory would improve it substantially. The MOC suffers in its ability to tap ruminations and is lacking in ascertaining the degree of ego–dystonia associated with the disorder. It has also had limited use in clinical settings.

The MOC has some very clear assets that make it an extremely useful tool. It takes little time to administer, is easy to interpret, and differentiates normals from obsessionals, as well as nonobsessional neurotics from obsessionals. Because it has been shown to be a valid and reliable measure and because of its ease of administration, greater use of the MOC should be encouraged in related psychotherapy outcome studies.

Rating Scales

Clinical rating scales are the most commonly used dependent measure in psychotherapy outcome studies of the obsessive–compulsive disorder. Their ease of construction and administration, as well as their proven sensitivity to changes in symptomatology, accounts for their widespread use. Another factor that enhances the utility of clinical rating scales is their versatility. The fact that they can be constructed to measure a wide variety of dimensions render them invaluable dependent measures. Examples of dimensions measured in association with obsessional symptoms are the extent and severity of depression, amount of distress felt by the patient, degree to which symptoms interfere with daily functioning, degree and disability caused by anxiety, and amount of time consumed by obsessing or by performing compulsive rituals.

Those rating scales that can be used by patients and by clinical judges provide several advantages. Such a rating scale provides not only an estimate of interjudge reliability, but also a measure of reliability between patient and expert ratings. An example of such a scale is discussed and presented by Philpott (1975). The rating scale consists of two complimentary measures of the time and discomfort associated with two obsessions or compulsions as they are rated by the patients and expert judges. Because the rater selects the obsessions or compulsions that are primary to the patient's illness, the rating scale has the advantage of modifiability to the individual needs of patients.

However, since this scale does not provide direct comparability between patients of different research projects, a second behavioral assessment was devised, the obsessive–compulsive checklist. This checklist is an interview schedule consisting of 64 items often found in obsessive–compulsive patients. Each item is scored by the interviewer on a four-point scale ranging from 0 (nil) to 3 (complete impairment). The scale provides a total impairment score, offers the possibility of intertrial comparisons, and is a good interviewing aid. Although the scale has not had extensive use clinically, the author reports that "preliminary results indicate good agreement between different raters and patient's self-ratings." The author also contends that interrater reliability can be established with minimal training of the raters. No estimates of reliability accompanied the author's preliminary results.

With regard to DSM-III diagnostic criteria, the scale does very well in assessing the degree of impairment associated with the illness. Unfortunately, however, it offers little differentiation between obsessions and compulsions. This is an obvious liability because of its potential to confuse what is obsessional with what is ritual.

Aside from the fact that the reliability and validity of clinical rating scales have not been adequately tested, there is the general lack of cross-trial comparisons by use of rating scales. This deficiency appears to be the result of general dissatisfaction with existing scales, as well as the fact that the majority of the scales are not published nor are available for easy access. Hence most researchers create a new rating scale or modify one made for the study of phobic disorders. To rectify this problem, it seems imperative that future investigators make their rating scales more accessible.

Diaries

The use of diaries as dependent measures in psychotherapy outcome studies is less frequent than either clinical rating scales or symptom checklists. Nevertheless, record-keeping methods have assets not shared by other assessment techniques. One such asset is the accumulation of information regarding the patient's subjective experience of symptoms on a day-to-day basis. Often the effect of psychotherapeutic intervention is demonstrated in the changes in occurrence of various behaviors outside the treatment situation. The capacity of record-keeping techniques to measure such changes is their greatest asset. Perhaps another asset that is often overlooked is the therapeutic value of monitoring one's behavior on a regular basis.

Researchers using diaries have been primarily concerned with the frequency and duration of targeted symptoms (Boersma et al., 1976; Emmelkamp & Kraaenen, 1977; Foa et al., 1980). In each case the investigators required the subjects to record the frequency and duration of targeted symptoms on a precoded observation form. Thus the subject would note the occurrence of the targeted symptoms at specific times of the day, and a diary for the duration of a week was collected. In some cases a counting device or stopwatch was used. Unfortunately, most of these studies did not require the patient to monitor and report the degree of impairment caused by their symptoms.

Marks (1978) describes a record-keeping tool that requires the patients to monitor and record their successes or failures at assigned tasks during specific periods of time throughout the week. Although this tool was created for use as a homework assignment for phobic patients, it could be modified easily for use as a dependent measure with obsessional patients. The tool is not significantly different from those of other researchers, but it does have a built-in rating scale to assign the level of felt anxiety associated with the experiencing of the symptom. Thus the tool could be modified to measure the frequency, duration, and degree of impairment of obsessional symptoms.

Because the use of diaries as an assessment tool for measuring obsessive compulsive disorders follows a similar format for the measurement of phobic disorders, there is no further discussion of their use in the subsequent sections of this chapter.

Other Self-Report Measures

The use of two other self-report measures has been reported infrequently in the literature. The following two instruments have their greatest value in idiographic rather than nomothetic investigations. The first to be discussed is the repertory grid technique. To date this technique has had limited use in the study of obsessive–compulsive disorders. In fact, at the time of this writing, research using the repertory grid technique as a psychotherapy outcome measure is either unavailable or nonexistent. Perhaps the difficulty of administration and interpretation and the time-consuming nature of the technique account for its limited use. With the recent creation of new software, one might expect greater use of the repertory grid technique in the near future (Edwards & Johnson, 1981).

The Shapiro Cards Scale has also had limited use as a nomothetically oriented research tool. Nevertheless, it has been employed to measure changes due to psychotherapeutic intervention with obsessive–compulsive patients. An example of such use comes from Capstick (1975). In this investigation the Shapiro method was used to assess changes in two patients after psychopharmacological intervention. The patients' symptoms are discussed and written down on cards. For each symptom, there is a card with three statements. The three statements are then arranged in pairs so that each symptom is compared with every other. The pairs are then administered to the patient, whereupon the patient chooses which of the two statements represents the "truth" at the time of administration.

The cards can be constructed to represent all the DSM-III criteria effectively. Thus one could obtain a measure of obsessional or compulsive symptomatology as well as a measure of the degree of impairment caused by those symptoms. This could be done by simply manipulating the statements of the scale. The advantages of the Shapiro card method is that it is simple to use, gives valuable and subjective information on any number of dimensions, and it is sufficiently versatile to be sensitive to changes in symptomatology as defined by the DSM-III.

The apparent liabilities of the Shapiro cards are that it requires individualized administration, it takes one hour to administer, and it may not be sensitive to minor changes in symptoms. Moreover, patients may become fatigued and give inaccurate responses, and it is practical only in small-numbers studies. As pointed out by Pinkava (1975), both the Shapiro Card and the grid techniques are limited because of the fact that individual results cannot be grouped for further evaluation, as they would not comply with the respective methodological requirements. Because of their construction, they lack utility in nomothetic research.

Behavioral Measures

Behavioral measures as methods of assessing outcome in psychotherapy are rarely reported in the literature with regard to the obsessive–compulsive disorder. Rachman and his colleagues have demonstrated greater interest in this area than any other group of researchers. Their involvement has been demonstrated by the use of performance tests, which they seem to have adopted from their research with phobic disorders. These behavioral measures are very nearly identical to the avoidance tests used for phobias.

Through the use of behavioral measures, a patient's compulsions or rituals will be available for observation and assessment. The degree of impairment, the time consumed in repetitive behavior, and the avoidance of stimuli that evoke compulsive behavior are all available for observation and measurement. The value of such information is that the therapist can chart from direct observations the extent and severity of the patient's compulsive symptoms. If one assumes that compulsions are an attempt to reduce the patient's subjective distress, the reduction compulsive symptomatology may signify a reduction in obsessive–compulsive symptomatology.

Behavioral measures give clearer information concerning compulsions than do any other measurement tool. They are therapeutically oriented and thus have the advantage of leading one directly into intervention. Unfortunately, direct observation requires a good deal of time, and this has direct implications for the number of subjects used in a study when behavioral measures are employed. Certainly the greatest drawback of behavioral measures in the measurement of obsessive–compulsive disorders is that obsessions go unmeasured. Consequently, researchers will not gain an understanding of the patients' subjective experience of their symptoms from behavioral measures alone.

ASSESSMENT METHODS FOR PHOBIC DISORDERS

In the most recent version of the DSM, phobias have been subdivided into four categories based on their different clinical pictures, ages of onset, and treatment approaches. These categories include *agoraphobia with panic attacks*, *agoraphobia without panic attacks*, *social phobia*, and *simple phobia*. Unfortunately, no distinction has been made between agoraphobic subjects with and without panic attacks in the outcome studies reviewed. Therefore, these two DSM-III categories of agoraphobia have been collapsed and are treated as a single category in this chapter. However, it should be noted that it is desirable to include indices of panic attack in assessments of the symptomatology of agoraphobics. This topic is discussed further later on.

Outcome Measures of Agoraphobia

Agoraphobia has been the most extensively studied phobic disorder among clinical populations. A multitude of outcome measures have been employed in these studies. To give the reader a feel for the diversity of measures employed and the variety of procedures used in current outcome research on agoraphobia, data on this topic were tabulated. A list of the different measures that were used in a sample of 45 recent controlled outcome studies are displayed in Table 10.1. These measures were subdivided into five major categories: self-report, independent-assessor report, therapist report, behavioral measures, and physiological measures. The frequency with which outcome measures from each of these categories were used in these 45 studies are also shown in Table 10.1.

Several trends can be noted from these data. First, the use of self-report measures is common. Fifty-eight percent of all dependent measures were self-report. Their variety far exceeds the variety of methods used to assess outcome from other points of view. In addition, an average of three self-report measures were used per study. In contrast, physiological measures were used in approximately every third study. The self-report measures that were used showed considerable diversity in focus. They include general personality measures, symptom-rating schedules, measures of social role performance, mood scales, marital satisfaction, and measures of daily activities. Very few measures seemed to be uniquely appropriate for the complex of symptoms associated with agoraphobia. This may help to explain the large number of diverse devices used in the sample of studies investigated.

Table 10.1. Frequency of Outcome Measures Employed in a Representative Sample of 45 Studies of Agoraphobia

Name of Measure and Primary Reference	Number of Times Used
SELF-REPORT MEASURES	
Fear Questionnaire (Watson & Marks, 1971)	15
Fear Survey Schedule (FSS III) (Wolpe & Lang, 1964)	10
Fear Questionnaire (Gelder & Marks, 1966)	8
Internal-External Locus of Control Scale (Rotter, 1966)	7
Self-Rating Depression Scale (SDS) (Zung, 1965)	7
Eysenck Personality Inventory (EPI) Eysenck, 1971)	7
Fear Survey Schedule (FSS) (Marks & Herst, 1970)	5
Social Anxiety Scale (SAS) Willems et al., 1972)	5
The Middlesex Hospital Questionnaire (MHQ) (Crown & Crisp, 1966)	5
Diary (Marks, 1978)	5
Semantic Differential Scale (Osgood et al., 1957)	4
Symptom Checklist 90 (Derogatis et al., 1973)	4
Taylor Manifest Anxiety Scale (Taylor, 1953)	3
The Hostility & Direction of Hostility Questionnaire (HDHQ) (Caine & Hope, 1967)	3
Tavistock Self-Assessment Inventory (Dixon et al., 1957)	3
Global Phobic Severity Scale (Gelder et al., 1973)	2
Fear Questionnaire (Marks & Herst, 1970)	1
Self-Adjustment Scale (Rogers & Dymond, 1954)	1
Personalized Scale of Phobic Anxiety (Munby & Johnston, 1980)	1
Total Phobic Anxiety (Mathews, 1977)	1
Symptom Checklist (Arrindell & Ettema, 1978)	1

(continued)

Table 10.1. *(continued)*

Name of Measure and Primary Reference	Number of Times Used
McNair and Lorr Mood Scale (McNair & Lorr, 1964)	1
Delftse Vragenlijst (Appels, 1975)	1
Leidse Lizst Voor Sociale Situaties (Groot & Walburg, 1977)	1
Agoraphobia Inventory (Zitrin et al., 1980)	1
Acute Panic Inventory (Zitrin et al., 1980)	1
Social Cohesion Questionnaire (Liberman, 1972)	1
Avoidance and Anxiety Scales (Lipsedge et al., 1973)	1
Hysteroid and Obsessoid Questionnaire (HOQ) (Caine & Hawkins, 1963)	1
Marital Questionnaire (Crowe, 1976)	1
Adult Self-Expression Scale (Gay et al., 1975)	1
Expectancy Scales (Stern & Marks, 1973)	1
Beck Depression Inventory (Beck et al., 1961)	1
Willoughby Personality Schedule (Willoughby, 1934)	1
Fear Thermometer (Rachman, 1965)	1
Spielberger State Trait Anxiety Inventory A-Trait (Spielberger et al., 1970)	1
Fear Questionnaire (Marks & Mathews, 1979)	1
Level of Anxiety Assessment Scale (Jannoun et al., 1980)	1
Other Scales[a]	13
Total	128
INDEPENDENT ASSESSOR-REPORT MEASURES	
Fear Questionnaire (Watson & Marks, 1971)	9
Fear Questionnaire (Gelder & Marks, 1966)	8
Fear Questionnaire (Marks et al., 1977)	2
Brief Psychiatric Rating Scale (Spitzer & Endicott, 1975)	1
Clinical Global Impression Scale (Spitzer & Endicott, 1975)	1
Anxiety Symptom Rating Scale (Hamilton, 1959)	1
Avoidance and Anxiety Scales (Lipsedge et al., 1973)	1
The Middlesex Hospital Questionnaire (MHW) (Crown & Crisp, 1966)	1
Hysteroid and Obsessoid Questionnaire (HOQ) (Caine & Hawkins, 1963)	1
Marital Questionnaire (Crowe, 1976)	1
Ratings of Social Adjustment (Tyrer et al., 1973)	1
Global Ratings of Severity of Illness (Tyrer et al., 1973)	1
Severity of Phobia and Level of Anxiety Scales (Mawson, 1970)	1
Severity of Anxiety Scale (Yorkston, Sergeant & Rachman, 1968)	1
Level of Anxiety Assessment Scale (Jannoun et al., 1980)	1
Other Scales[a]	7
Total	38
THERAPIST REPORT MEASURES	
Fear Questionnaire (Watson & Marks, 1971)	6
Fear Questionnaire (Gelder & Marks, 1966)	4
Therapists' Marital Rating Scale (Hafner & Marks, 1976)	1
Severity of Anxiety Scale (Yorkston et al., 1968)	1
Severity of Phobia and Level of Anxiety Scales (Mawson, 1970)	1
Global Improvement Form (Spitzer & Endicott, 1975)	1
Other Scales	5
Total	19

Table 10.1.

Name of Measure and Primary Reference	Number of Times Used
BEHAVIORAL MEASURES	
Distance	10
Time	9
Flicker fusion	1
Eyelid blinks	1
Total	21
PHYSIOLOGICAL MEASURES	
Galvanic skin response	6
Electrocardiogram	5
Pulse rate	2
Phenocardiography	1
Echocardiography	1
Total	15

[a]Scales without names.

More than half of these measures, however, do not obtain an adequate assessment of agoraphobia; that is, many of these self-report methods of assessment [e.g., I–E Locus of Control Scale (Rotter, 1966), Self-Rating Depression Scale (Zung, 1965), Social Anxiety Scale (Willems et al., 1972), Taylor Manifest Anxiety Scale (Taylor, 1953), and the Hostility and Direction of Hostility Questionnaire (Cain et al., 1967)] measure general and secondary features of the agoraphobic disorder such as trait anxiety, depression, and anger. Furthermore, these self-report measures assess few and, in some cases, none of the major attributes of agoraphobia as defined by the DSM-III. Thus it is recommended that these methods of measurement not be used as the main method for evaluating agoraphobia prior to and subsequent to treatment.

In accordance with the need to broadly sample phobias, our review of current assessment of agoraphobia shows the healthy tendency to measure outcome from a variety of patient systems (physiological, behavioral, and cognitive–affective). It appears that researchers are trying to capture the variety of dysfunctions associated with agoraphobia, although the use of a wide variety of specific measures leaves the general impression that measurement in this area is chaotic. We now attempt to bring more order into the assessment of agoraphobia by further evaluating assessment practices. Before we begin this evaluation, it is necessary to specify the DSM-III criteria of agoraphobia. According to the DSM-III, an agoraphobia has the following symptoms (American Psychiatric Association, 1980):

1. A marked fear and avoidance of being alone or being in public places from which it would be difficult to escape or to obtain help in an incapacitated state of fear, such as in crowds, tunnels, bridges, elevators, and public transportation.

2. Normal activities are constricted and the fear dominates the individual's life.
3. The disturbance is not due to a major depressive episode, obsessive–compulsive disorder, paranoid personality disorder or schizophrenia.
4. A history of panic attacks may or may not be evident.

The reader can refer to these criteria as we discuss the different methods of measurement for agoraphobia.

Self-Report Measures

The 10 most frequently used self-report measures (Table 10.1) were examined independently of the rest of the self-report measures reported in Table 10.1. These 10 methods of assessment account for 34% of the total measures ($N = 221$) used in the sample of 45 studies. Five of these self-report measures are inadequate methods of assessing agoraphobia (I–E Scale, SDS, EPI, SAS, and MHQ) because they fail to provide a specific measure of this disorder. As stated above, these self-report measures assess general and secondary features of agoraphobia, such as trait anxiety, depression, anger, many of which are not included in the DSM-III definition of this disorder. Of the remaining five self-report measures, four are fear questionnaires (Gelder & Marks, 1966; Marks & Herst, 1970; Watson & Marks, 1971; Wolpe & Lang, 1964), and one involves keeping a diary. Each of these measures directly assess some of the symptoms of agoraphobia.

The fear questionnaire (no official title yet) devised by Marks and Mathews (1979) provides the best self-report measure of agoraphobia at this time. This self-rating scale is a synthesis of the other fear questionnaires cited previously (Gelder & Marks, 1966; Marks & Herst, 1970; Watson & Marks, 1971). A detailed description of this synthesis can be found in the study by Marks and Mathews (1979). The questionnaire calls for individuals to rate, on a nine-point scale, their avoidance of a main phobia, specified by them, and of 15 phobic situations listed in the questionnaire. This list of 15 situations was derived from Hallam and Hafner's 1978) factor-analytic study of fear questionnaires. Individuals also indicate their overall disability due to their phobia(s) and reveal their current state of anxiety depression based on their responses to five items. The list of 15 common phobias were divided into three categories: agoraphobia, social phobia, and blood–injury phobia. A score, ranging from zero to 40 can be determined for each category. The sum of these scores provides a total phobia score (range = 0 to 120).

Marks and Mathews (1979) found that the questionnaire had a test–retest reliability of at least .80. Item and subscore correlations were ascertained, yielding reliability coefficients from .79 (global phobic rating) and .96 (blood–injury score) to .89 for the agoraphobia score.

The validity of the questionnaire is supported by a limited but growing body of evidence. First, all five agoraphobia items in the questionnaire are reflective of the DSM-III criteria for agoraphobic disorder. Marks and Mathews (1979) demonstrated a correlation of .87 between questionnaire scores on the agoraphobia items and a research worker's blind ratings of patient (N = 63) disability. Second, agoraphobics exhibited a lower agoraphobia score than did social phobias following treatment, whereas the converse was true for the social phobics who showed reductions on the social phobia scale. Thus there is some evidence that this questionnaire may be specifically sensitive to agoraphobia and social phobia.

Similar fear survey schedules (Greer, 1965; Lang and Lazovick, 1963; Marks and Herst, 1970; Wolpe and Lang, 1964) have been commonly used as self-report measures. Wolpe and Lang's fear survey schedule (FSS-III) was the second most frequently used self-report measure in the 45 studies we reviewed. However, it does not provide as much information for agoraphobia outcome research as the questionnaire by Marks and Mathews (1979). Furthermore, Cooke (1966) points out that the reliability of the fear surveys varies greatly from one study to another. The utility of using the FSS to assess specific fears can also be questioned as they may be best for assessing general fear.

The FSS-III consists of a large number of infrequently encountered items, and there is a paucity of agoraphobia specific items. Wolpe and Lang's survey assesses specific fearful situations and objects on five-point scales. The amount of information one can obtain from this fear survey is minimal. In contrast, Marks and Mathew's (1979) survey is multidimensional and should provide a more in-depth self-report assessment of agoraphobia that is more sensitive to treatment effects than any of the other commonly used self-report measures.

Behavioral Measures

Behavioral measurement is an important method for assessing agoraphobia as defined by the DSM-III. Avoidance behavior, including fear of being alone or in public places, is frequently measured by either the amount of time or the distance the subject is away from home (Emmelkamp & Wessels, 1975; Emmelkamp et al., 1978; Lipsedge et al., 1973; Yorkston et al., 1968). There are two main behavioral methods for assessing agoraphobia outcome: the Behavioral Avoidance Test (BAT) and the amount of time the public individual spends away from a place of safety. Even though neither is entirely satisfactory, it is still worthwhile to discuss them because they deal directly with the target behavior of many treatments.

The BAT method for assessment of agoraphobia involves recording the amount of avoidance behavior exhibited by the phobic individual as that individual attempts to successfully approach various fearful situations involving increased intimate contact (Hafner, 1976, 1977). There are several problems with this method. First, the fears of the agoraphobic cannot typically be ranked hierarchically. Not all agoraphobics fear the same situations; even if there are common fears, subjects do not typically agree on the order of these situations based on the degree of fearfulness. Furthermore, many of these fearful situations are complex and cannot be easily controlled.

The amount of time that the patient spends away from a place of safety is a behavioral measure that has been the second most frequently used measure of fear reduction for agoraphobics (Emmelkamp & Emmelkamp-Benner, 1975; Emmelkamp & Wessels, 1975; Emmelkamp, et al., 1978). There are two-major problems with times as indices of change. Time spent away from a place of safety, such as the home, does not necessarily mean that the phobic individual is free of anxiety. Furthermore, time as a variable by itself may not accurately reflect the level of anxiety that the phobic individual is experiencing. For example, two agoraphobics may have spent the same amount of time away from a safe place, but one of them may have been able to travel much further away and thereby enter a relatively more fearful situation than the other. A second problem with time as a measure is that the subject may be responding to the demand characteristics of the situation. Thus the amount of tension that subjects are willing to tolerate may be to a great extent a function of their assumption of the experimenter's expectations. Consequently, outcome results may not accurately reflect the patient's actual anxiety level.

A less problematic method involves allowing each subject to devise his or her own 15-item hierarchy of fearful situations, ranging from a situation in which she or he feels totally relaxed to one in which she or he feels most anxious (Gelder et al., 1973; Mathews et al., 1976, 1977). Subjects rate, on a 1 to 10-point scale, the anxiety that they experience following each situation to which they are exposed. These ratings can be compared to posttreatment ratings for exposure to the same situations. The advantage of this method for measuring behavior is that it more realistically evaluates each subject's agoraphobic symptoms rather than a correlate of this psychopathology. The major limitation of this method is that individual measurements (idiographics) are difficult to compare between individuals and to evaluate in terms of standards of ideal mental health.

Physiological Measures

A third component of the interactive model of agoraphobia includes the physiological reactions that are correlated with a fearful stimulus or situation. The results of the few agoraphobia studies employing physiological responses in assessing outcome have not been very satisfactory. Only one study (Marks et al., 1971) has demonstrated that changes in physiological responses are sensitive to different treatment effects. Flooding, in contrast to desensitization, resulted in a reduction in heart rate, skin conductance fluctuation, and skin conductance deflections. Gelder et al., (1973) conducted a study using heart rate as a dependent measure to compare two behavior therapies and a control treatment. The results indicated that there was no difference between the therapeutic modalities based on heart rate, whereas the behavioral methods appeared more effective based on the nonphysiological measures. In a study by Mathews et al., (1976), a similar finding was obtained. There was no differential effectiveness of various behavioral treatments on heart rate responses even though the treatments had approximately the same effect for several nonphysiological measures.

Most of the studies examining the effects of treatment on physiological responses have used phobic imagery to induce anxiety. For example, it has been demonstrated that phobic imagery leads to an increase in skin conductance fluctuations (Marks et al., 1971; Watson & Marks, 1971), increased skin conductance level (Gelder et al., 1973; Mathews et al., 1976), larger skin conductance deflections (Gelder et al., 1973; Marks et al., 1971), and an increase in heart rate (Marks et al., 1971). These studies provide consistent evidence that phobic imagery is associated with increased physiological arousal for agoraphobic subjects. However, these studies may not reflect the same findings that one would obtain if these studies were conducted in the patient's home environment. Furthermore, it is not possible to determine whether the decrease in the physiological responses to the phobic imagery following treatment is the result of treatment, repeated testing, or time. The results of the studies conducted to date do not lead to the conclusion that measures of physiological responding will add reliable information to the assessment outcome of agoraphobics. Their use at this time must be considered experimental.

Outcome Measures of Social Phobia

The term "social phobia" refers to individuals who are afraid of and avoid specific social stimuli. The DSM-III definition of social phobia states that an individual with this anxiety disorder has "a persistent, irrational fear of and compelling desire to avoid, a situation in which the individual is exposed to possible scrutiny by others and fears that he or she may act in a way that will be humiliating or embarrassing" (APA, 1980, p. 227). Anxiety is heightened by the individual's awareness that his or her fear is excessive and unreasonable. Because social stimuli are complex, vary in each situation, and are perceived differently by each individual, it has been difficult to develop methods for assessing this phobia. In general, assessment has tended to focus primarily on an individual's social skills rather than social fears per se. For a review of techniques for assessing changes in social skills, the reader is directed to Barlow (1981). We do not address assessment techniques that focus on social skill deficits, but rather changes in the levels of fear or anxiety that are thought to result from increased social skills.

The results of researching using physiological and behavioral measures to assess social phobia are similar to research on the assessment of agoraphobia and simple phobias. Therefore, they are not discussed further in this section of the chapter. We turn our attention instead to the use of self-report measures.

Self-report measures that have been devised to assess social phobia are similar in concept to other fear inventories. Watson and Friend (1969) developed two frequently used scales: the Social Avoidance Distress Scale (SAD) as a measure of the level of discomfort an individual experiences in various social situations and the Fear of Negative Evaluation (FNE) as a measure of the degree to which an individual fears negative social evaluation. If used together, these scales assess many aspects of social phobia as defined by the DSM-III.

The psychometric properties for both scales are fairly good. Tests for homogeneity revealed average biscrial correlation values of .72 for the FNE items and .77 for the SAD items. A second test of homogeniety, such as the KR-20 reliability statistic, revealed correlations of .94 for both FNE and SAD items. Watson and Friend (1969) concluded, after conducting three validity studies, that individuals with high scores on the SAD "tended to avoid social interactions, preferred to work alone, reported that they talked less, and were more worried and less confident about social relationships . . ." (Watson & Friend, 1969, p. 448). Individuals with high scores on the FNE "tended to become nervous in evaluative situations, and worked hard either to avoid disapproval or gain approval" (Watson & Friend, 1969, p. 448).

Richardson and Tasto (1976) developed a self-report measure of social anxiety (Social Anxiety Inventory) that consists of 166 items identifying different situations that elicit anxiety. A factor analysis was conducted from which the following seven factors associated with social anxiety were identified: (1) disapproval or criticism; (2) social assertiveness and visibility; (3) confrontation and anger expression; (4) heterosexual contact; (5) intimacy and interpersonal warmth; (6) conflict with or rejection by parents; and (7) interpersonal loss. This inventory and several other self-report measures that have been used to assess social phobia have a common weakness in that they do not enable the evaluator to determine whether an individual's social avoidance and fear reflects someone with anxiety-suppressed behavior or behavioral deficits which lead to anxiety. It is important to be able to make this distinction to treat the problem specifically as well as to clearly specify the unique effects of treatments.

Marks and Mathews's (1979) fear survey questionnaire enables the evaluator to calculate a subscore for social phobia based on five items that are each rated on a scale of 0 to 8. The advantage of this self-report measure is that it enables the evaluator to extensively assess the individual's anxiety in relation to social situations as well as other situations and objects. Unfortunately, this self-report measure of social phobia consists of only five items specific to social phobia. It is recommended that the relationship between the social phobia subscale on Marks and Mathews's questionnaire and the SAD and FNE questionnaires be ascertained. It may be that these questionnaires are not measuring the same variables.

Other self-report measures that have been used in the assessment of social phobia include the fear survey schedules (Geer, 1966), the Social Situations Questionnaire (Bryant & Trower, 1974), the Fear Thermometer (Walk, 1956), and a method for recording and scoring an individual's frequency of social activities and social contacts (Marzillier et al., 1976). The most promising of these appears to be the Social Situations Questionnaire. In contrast to the fear survey schedules but similar to Watson and Friend's questionnaires, Bryant and Trower's questionnaire provides an in-depth assessment of an individual's fear of social situations. There are two sections of the questionnaire: the first section consists of 30 items that the individual rates on a five-point scale for difficulty (i.e., anxiety); the second section consists of 22 items that the client rates on a seven-point scale indicating the amount of time spent in the same situation during the past three months. In spite of the depth of assessment that this questionnaire allows, it focuses primarily on the individual's degree of difficulty in avoidance of different social situations. In contrast to Watson and Friend's questionnaires, Bryant and Trower's questionnaire fails to include important features of social phobia; namely, the individual's anticipation of scrutiny and fear of acting in a way that will be humiliating and embarrassing. In addition, reliability and validity scores have yet to be calculated for Bryant and Trower's questionnaire.

Outcome Measures of Simple Phobia

The DSM-III defines a simple phobia as any persistent, irrational fear of an object or situation that compels the individual to avoid it; causes significant distress; is recognized by the subject as being an excessive and unreasonable fear; does not meet the criteria for agoraphobia or social phobia; and is not due to schizophrenia or to an obsessive–compulsive disorder (American Psychiatric Association, 1980). This definition is too broad and general for the purpose of determining ideal outcome measures for assessing the therapeutic treatment of various simple phobias. It fails to provide criteria specific to any given simple phobia and implies that all individuals who manifest the symptoms for a simple phobia are similar. Unfortunately, there is little evidence to support this assumption. Whereas the DSM-III guidelines for diagnosing simple phobias are not ideal for assessing outcome, standards for assessing simple phobias can still be determined.

Ninety different simple phobias were identified from a sample of 648 studies on phobias conducted from 1970 (inclusive) to the present (1981). The 24 most common simple phobias from the list of ninety are shown in Table 10.2. From these 24 simple phobias, seven were selected for more intensive analysis. These include ophidiophobia (snake phobia), school phobia, rat phobia, flight phobia, acrophobia, claustrophobia, and blood phobia. These seven phobias were selected because they represent either the most commonly studied phobias or a broad range of fears, from simple animal phobias to somewhat more debilitating phobias, such as fear of school or flight.

An evaluation of the outcome measures employed for the aforementioned seven simple phobias (425 studies) indicated that 59% of the change measures were derived from self-report instruments, whereas behavioral and physiological measures made up 31.7% and 9.3% of these dependent measures, respectively. Clearly, self-report measures form the core of assessing outcome in simple phobias. In the discussion to follow, we identify the best self-report, behavioral, and physiological measures for the assessment of the seven simple phobias.

Table 10.2.   Frequency and Percentage of 24 Phobia Types[a]

Type of Phobia	Number of Studies, 1970–1981	Percentage of all Studies (N = 648)	Type of Phobia	Number of Studies, 1970–1981	Percentage of all Studies (N = 648)
Ophidiophobia	242	37.3	Blood and injury	7	1.1
School	98	15.1	Animal	7	1.1
Spider	35	5.4	Dog	7	1.1
Rat	28	4.3	Homophobia	6	.9
Flight	25	3.9	Aquaphobia	5	.8
Public speaking	17	2.6	Anthropophobia	4	.6
Acrophobia	15	2.3	Thunderstorm	3	.5
Dysmorphophobia	14	2.2	Darkness	3	.5
Claustrophobia	10	1.5	Cockroach	3	.5
Injections	10	1.5	Buildings	3	.5
Insect	8	1.2	Sex	3	.5
Dentist	8	1.2	Travel	3	.5

[a]The phobias were abstracted from a list of 90 different phobia types found in psychological abstracts from 1970 to 1981.

Self-Report Measures

There was a total of 69 different self-report measures used in the studies of the seven phobias we are examining! The same criticisms that were made for the self-report measures of agoraphobia can be made for approximately three-fourths of the 69 self-report measures of simple phobias—mainly, that they did not specifically deal with the symptoms of phobia. A significant majority of studies used standard rating scales that were considered to have possibilities for widespread use in the study of simple phobias. These measures are considered in the following paragraphs because they attempt to directly assess specific criteria of the seven phobias.

Several fear inventories have been devised and employed to measure simple phobias. These can be divided into three categories: general fear surveys, specific fear surveys, and multidimensional fear hierarchies.

GENERAL FEAR SURVEYS.   The general fear surveys used in our sample of simple phobias include the FSS-II (Geer, 1965), the FSS-III (Wolpe & Lang, 1964), and the Temple Fear Survey Inventory (Braun and Reynolds, 1969). These fear surveys are similar in that they consist of a list of common fears to be rated by the individual on a Likert-type scale. Geer designed his FSS primarily for research purposes, whereas Wolpe and Lang devised their FSS to be used as an adjunct to behavior therapy. Braun and Reynolds developed their fear survey by compiling all the items (avoiding duplication of items) from all the previously published fear surveys (Geer, 1965; Lang and Lazovick, 1963; Manosevitz and Lanyon, 1965; Wolpe and Lang, 1964).

The psychometric properties and the correlations of these fear schedules with other measures have been discussed elsewhere (Agras and Jacob, 1981;

Hersen, 1973; Tasto, 1979; Taylor and Agras, 1980) and thus are not elaborated on here. Instead, we would like to emphasize that these general fear surveys have been used extensively for clinical and research purposes even though they yield limited information about the individual's fear. At most, the clinician or researcher using these self-report measures obtains a list of fears, each rated by the patient on a five- or seven-point scale (depending on the fear survey). Unfortunately, there is no compelling evidence that a change of these ratings for individual fear items on the survey following treatment is correlated with a change in fear as measured by avoidance. (Cooke, 1966; Fazio, 1969; Hersen, 1973; Lang, 1968). It is also impossible to determine from these fear surveys the extent to which a rating on a specific item affects the individual's overall level of anxiety and avoidance behavior in real life.

The fear survey schedules are useful for quick screening purposes for determining the specific situation or objects that the individual fears. A psychologist might use the FSS in a psychological evaluation of a patient to expediently ascertain whether that patient has a specific phobia. For research purposes, the FSS could be used as a screening device for the selection of subjects for a study examining specific fears. Their use for measuring changes in specific phobias cannot be recommended.

SPECIFIC FEAR SURVEYS.   Specific fear schedules have been devised for several of the more common simple phobias. Unlike the general fear surveys, which are best suited for screening and treatment planning, these specific fear surveys are commonly used and are well-suited for measuring treatment effectiveness, for example. Several of these surveys measure a number of dimensions of the specific fear that they are designed to assess, such as cognitive, behavioral, and/or physiological dimensions. Surveys designed to measure ophidiophobia (fear of snakes) include Lang et al., (1970) Snake Anxiety Questionnaire (SNAQ) and Murray and Foote's (1979) Snake Fear Questionnaire. The former questionnaire has the advantage of having a body of research dealing with its psychometric properties (Klorman et al., 1974). The results of this research indicate that the questionnaire has high internal consistency, test–retest reliability, and external validity.

To date, there is only one specific fear questionnaire that evaluates changes in blood phobias. Hastings (1971) developed the Mutilation Questionnaire (MQ) for this purpose. An evaluation of the psychometric properties of the MQ was also conducted by Klorman et al., (1974), who reported similar findings regarding questionnaire reliability and validity to those obtained for the Lang et al., (1970) Snake Anxiety Questionnaire.

Specific fear surveys also have been devised for acrophobia, claustrophobia, rat phobia, and flight phobia. The Acrophobic Questionnaire (AQ) designed by Baker et al., (1973) and the Fear of Heights Survey developed by Cohen (1977) are the two best specific measures for the fear of heights. Both questionnaires consist of 20 situations relating to the phobia, which the individual rates on a Likert-type scale. The AQ has been tested for reliability (split-half, test–retest) and validity by Baker et al., (1973) and is recognized as being a good measure of acrophobia. Specific fear surveys for flight phobia have been devised by Goorney (1970)—Flight Anxiety Scale—and by Scrignar et al., (1973)—Airplane Fear Survey. There is no evidence that the psychometric properties of these scales have been assessed, nor are the specifics of the surveys revealed in the literature. Recommendations, therefore, cannot be given at this time for specific surveys measuring flight phobia.

Most recently, Ost et al., (1981a, 1981b) have designed a specific fear survey to measure rat phobia and claustrophobia. Both surveys are described in articles that were not published at the time of this review. The Rat Questionnaire consists of 30 items that are answered true or false, whereas the Claustrophobia Scale contains 20 items that are rated on a scale of 0 to 4 for the degree of anxiety the subject usually experiences in the depicted situations.

The Fear Thermometer (Rimm et al., 1975; Walk, 1956) is another self-report measure that is frequently employed in studies of simple phobia. This instrument can be used for the assessment of any specific phobia. It is most useful as a self-report measure of an individual's fear at different levels of a behavior avoidance test (BAT). The individual indicates the level of fear on a scale at each BAT level, which can be summed as a total Fear Thermometer score at the end of treatment. The Fear Thermometer Scale can be administered easily, quickly, and several times during the treatment of any phobia. It is limited as a self-report measure, however, in that at most the relative change of self-reported fear can be assessed during treatment.

MULTIDIMENSIONAL FEAR HIERARCHIES.   Although specific fear surveys have been more useful in outcome research than general fear surveys, both may be inferior to the multidimensional fear hierarchies that have recently been devised. The best illustration of this type of fear hierarchy has been designed by Marks and Mathews (1979). Their fear hierarchy includes items that pertain to cognitive, behavioral, and affective characteristics of persons in relation to the fearful object or situation. This method of assessing fear provides a more accurate report of the complex and multidimensional nature of fear than those provided by the general and specific fear surveys. A second value of this method of measurement is that it enables one to assess the effectiveness of treatment for a specific fear separate from the subject's overall fear. Since the overall fear may consist of the specific phobia plus several other fears, a decrease in the target phobia as a result of treatment may occur whereas no sign of a decrease will be evident in the overall fear. A third advantage of this survey is that it allows the subject to indicate the main phobia and to rate it on scales of 0 to 8 for the degree of anxiety and avoidance behavior. Fourth, several questions regarding secondary features of the phobia (e.g., depression, anger, upsetting thoughts, and panic) are rated on scales of 0 to 8 for the degrees to which they are troublesome. Finally, 15 specific phobias are rated on scales of 0 to 8 for avoidance behavior. Three subscores can be derived from the 15 specific phobias by summing the scores for the five items designated as an agoraphobic subcategory, with five items designated as a social phobia subcategory and five items designated as a blood–injury phobia subcategory. It is possible, therefore, to compare the specific and main phobias in a hierarchical fashion at pre- and posttreatment. In addition, the composite scores of the three phobia subcategories can be compared with each other, and the degree to which the subject is experiencing secondary features can be examined. The reliability and validity for this measurement is adequate, although further research is needed (Marks and Mathews, 1979).

Ost and Hugdall (1981) recently developed a fear questionnaire that also assesses fear as a multidimensional system. There are four sections of the questionnaire, each evaluating a main feature of fear: behavior, affect, cognition, and physiology. The individual specifies in his or her own words the phobic situation experienced as the most anxiety producing. In the first section of the questionnaire the individual answers nine questions regarding the criteria of the phobia; two questions inquire about conditioning experiences, three questions inquire about instructional learning, and four questions inquire about different vicarious experiences with the fearful stimulus. The physiological reactions of the individual are assessed in the second section of the questionnaire. The individual rates (on a 0 to 4-point scale) the extent to which these reactions are experienced in the presence of the phobic situation. Anticipatory anxiety of the individual is assessed in the third section with five questions. The final section of the questionnaire examines the individual's negative thoughts in the phobic situations. For 10 situations, the individual rates (0 to 4-point scale) how often the different thoughts appear. This questionnaire is valuable for an initial clinical assessment of a fear, the outcome of treatment for the fear, and for other research. However, the psychometric properties of this questionnaire require further investigation as its reliability, validity, and sensitivity to change are unknown.

Self-report measures have been developed for six of the seven simple phobias considered in this review. At present, there are no self-report inventories, questionnaires, or scales that are commonly used in the research of school phobia. This paucity of self-report measures may be a function of the inherent problems in the conceptualization of school phobia. There is a lack of agreement about the operational definition and the associated symptoms of school phobia. Furthermore, many of the school phobia studies have been cases in which intrafamilial and interpersonal dynamics are strongly emphasized. It can be argued that school phobia is a complex rather than simple phobia or that school phobia symptoms are the premorbid features of an agoraphobic disorder. The presumed etiology of the individual's school phobia seems to vary from one study to another. It is difficult, therefore, to agree on the causes as well as the symptoms of school phobia. It is not surprising that specific self-report measures for school phobia are basically nonexistant.

Behavioral Measures

Behavior measures were the second most frequently used method of assessing therapy outcome in the sample of seven simple phobias we examined. As indicated, 31.7% of all the measures used to assess therapy outcome in these studies were behavioral measures. Seventy-eight percent of these studies ($N = 96$) included at least one behavioral measure. The BAT was the behavioral method most frequently employed in this sample of simple phobias. It was used in the assessment of ophidiophobia (Arrick et al., 1981) acrophobia (Bourque & Ladouceur, 1980), rat phobia (Engum et al., 1980), claustrophobia (Speltz & Bernstein, 1979), and flight phobia (Timm, 1977).

The behavioral measure for school phobia has usually been the amount of school attendance (McDonald & Sheperd, 1976; Pront et al., 1978). Behavioral measures were not commonly used in blood phobia studies. Although the general principle of the BAT has remained the same in all these studies, the format has varied. Most studies have involved the subject approaching a feared situation (Lang and Lazovik, 1963), whereas other studies have tried to replicate a feared situation, such as placing a subject in a closed room to measure claustrophobia or seeing how high an acrophobic subject is able to climb a ladder.

Behavioral methods, despite their popularity, for measuring fear have been criticized (Tasto, 1979; Taylor & Agras, 1980). Several authors found that subjects who received instructions emphasizing the critical importance of maximum approach produced more approach behavior on the BAT than did subjects who received less demanding instructions (Bernstein, 1973; Bernstein & Nietzel, 1973, 1974; Miller & Bernstein, 1972; Smith et al., 1974).It is also argued that patients are not as afraid in the testing situation as they are in a real situation. This may be because the subject believes that the experimenter will not place him or her in danger in the testing situation. In general, it appears that improved performance on the BAT may not reflect the subject's performance in real phobic situations (Lick & Unger, 1975; Lick et al., 1975). The interpretation of improved real-life behavior measured on the traditional laboratory BAT is thus questionable. These findings emphasize the importance of developing natural *(in vivo)* observations of phobic behaviors.

Physiological Measures

Physiological measures accounted for 9.3% of all the outcome measures employed in our sample of simple phobic studies. Galvanic skin response (GSR) and heart rate (HR) were the two most common physiological measures used and were employed in studies of ophidiophobia, rate phobia, claustrophobia, and blood phobia. Other infrequently used physiological measures included respiration ($N = 2$), and blood pressures ($N = 1$). Evaluation of this method for assessment of treatment outcome can be found in the section on agoraphobia and in other writings (Garfield & Bergin, 1978; Lick & Katkin, 1976; Taylor & Agras, 1980). The research generally supports the use of heart rate and electrodermal measures of fear even though there are some limitations and inconsistencies with both these variables. It is recommended that simultaneous measurement of both cardiac and electrodermal systems be conducted to maximize the sensitivity of the physiological assessment.

SUMMARY

A range of measures for assessing therapy process and outcome in the treatment of anxiety disorders has been presented for the provision of specificity in
measuring the treatment of individual cases. The instruments suggested for use
in measuring the panic disorder and the generalized anxiety disorder have not
been devised explicitly for this purpose, except perhaps in the Zung and
Hamilton scales. This appears to reflect the lack of development in the specific
treatments devised for these disorders. Measurement of anxiety as a core
component of variable symptom complexes, rather than as a singular phenomenon, appears to be emerging with greater emphasis in current anxiety research. The measures described show potential for adaptation toward various
treatment approaches. What is needed is an understanding of the underlying
principles and governing characteristics on which these devices operate so that
intelligent application can be achieved. Hopefully, the latitude and potential
responsivity of these scales will be further researched and evaluated while their
use increases the possibilities in the treatment of anxiety disorders themselves.
Our general recommendation would be that the assessment of panic and
generalized anxiety disorders include symptomatic measures as well as measures of the more stable and lasting personality dimensions associated with
anxiety.

In reviewing the literature concerning the measurement of the effects of
psychotherapeutic intervention on obsessive–compulsive disorders, a common theme of dissatisfaction is apparent. Research results are frequently
inconsistent and conflicting because the relationship between obsessions and
compulsions and their accompanying symptoms is not clearly understood.
Researchers might benefit by a more comprehensive and thorough use of the
DSM-III diagnostic categories to achieve a more unified and practical approach to research. These criteria dictate that the most sensitive measure to
changes in patients due to psychotherapeutic intervention will include three
components: (1) a measure of obsessions; (2) a measure of compulsions; and
(3) the degree of impairment due to the obsession or compulsion.

Our review of research on measuring change in the obsessive–compulsive
disorder suggests the following battery: the Maudsley Obsessional Checklist;
the Rating Scales of Philpott (1975); a modification of Marks's (1978) diary;
and, when possible, a performance test that would be accompanied by a
measure of heart rate fluctuations. The assessment battery would provide a
great deal of information concerning the disorder without sacrificing any
diagnostically important data. The battery could be administered quickly and
would not require arduous interpretation. The self-report measures could be
administered to a group. The behavioral and physiological measures would
require more extensive involvement from the researchers.

A multitude of measures have been devised for assessing phobic disorders.
Most of these measures are self-report. To date, no single measure can be

employed to assess each phobic disorder discussed in this chapter. Some of these measures are clearly better than others in that they are more reliable and valid, evaluate specific as well as secondary features of a phobia, and can be employed in the assessment of several specific phobias. Most of the measures that meet the aforementioned criteria are self-report.

It has been difficult for researchers to develop a single method for assessing the entire spectrum of phobic disorders, because some phobias are "complex" whereas others are "simple." Assessment of a complex phobia necessitates a multidimensional evaluation procedure consisting of cognitive-affective, behavioral, and physiological measures. Agoraphobia and social phobia are both complex. We recommend that the inventory devised by Marks and Mathews (1979) be used as a self-report measure of psychotherapy outcome for these phobic disorders. This inventory enables the therapist or researcher to obtain cognitive and affective measures, meets all the criteria of a good measure, and has been devised particularly to measure agoraphobia and social phobia. Additional measures using the behavioral avoidance test and physiology (heart rate or galvanic skin responses) are also recommended. Therapist and independent-assessor evaluations are seldom necessary, although more information on this conclusion is needed.

Therapy outcome measures of simple phobias do not necessitate such a large-scale multidimensional procedure. Self-report and behavioral measures are sufficient as methods for evaluating the phobic individual's level of fear. The behavioral avoidance test is a particularly good method for assessing changes in individuals with simple phobias. Specific inventories have been devised for most of the simple phobias discussed in this chapter. Further research is needed, however, to determine the validity and reliability for most of these inventories.

REFERENCES

Agras, W. S., & Jacob, R. Phobia: Nature and measurement. In M. Mavissakalian & D. H. Barlow (Eds.), *Phobia: psychological and pharmacological treatment.* New York: Guilford Press, 1980.

Allen, J. J., & Rack, P. H. Changes in obsessive-compulsive patients as measured by the Leyton Inventory before and after treatment with clomipramine. *Scottish Medical Journal Supplement*, 1975, **20**, 41–42.

Allen, J. J., & Tune, G. S. The Lynfield Obsessional-Compulsive Questionnaires. *Scottish Medical Journal Supplement*, 1975, **20**, 21–24.

American Psychiatric Association. *Diagnostic and statistical manual of mental disorders* (3rd ed.). Washington, D.C.: American Psychiatric Association, 1980.

Appels, A. *Screenen als methode voor preventice in de geestelizke gezohdheidszorg.* Amsterdam: Swets en Zeitlinger B.V., 1975.

Arrick, M. C., Voss, J., & Rimm, D. C. The relative efficacy of thought-stopping and covert assertion. *Behavior Research and Therapy*, 1981, **19**, 17–24.

Arrindell, W. A., & Ettema, H. De symptom checklist (SCL-90): Dimensionele structuur, betrouw-baarheid en validiteit van een klachtenlijst in een "normale" populatie. *Heymans Bulletin*, 1978, **HB-78-368-EX**, Groningen.

Bagley, C. The factorial reliability of the Middlesex Hospital Questionnaire in normal subjects. *British Journal of Medical Psychology*, 1980, **53**, 53–58.

Baker, B. L., Cohen, D. C., & Saunders, J. T. Self-directed desensitization for acrophobia. *Behavior Research and Therapy*, 1973, **11**, 79–89.

Barlow, D. H. (Ed.). *Behavioral assessment of adult disorders*. New York: Guilford Press, 1981.

Beck, A. T., Ward, C. H., Mendelson, M., Mock, J. E., & Ekbaugh, J. K. An inventory for measuring depression. *Archives of General Psychiatry*, 1961, **4**, 561–571.

Becker, W. C. A comparison of the factor structure and other properties of the 16 PF and the Guilford-Martin Personality Inventories. *Educational and Psychological Measurement*, 1961, **21**, 393–404.

Bernstein, D. A. Situational factors in behavioral fear assessment: A progress report. *Behavior Therapy*, 1973, **4**, 41–48.

Bernstein, D. A., & Neitzel, M. T. Procedural variation in behavior avoidance tests. *Journal of Consulting and Clinical Psychology*, 1973, **41**, 165–174.

Bernstein, D. A., & Neitzel, M. T. Behavioral avoidance tests: The effects of demand characteristics and repeated measures on two types of subjects. *Behavior Therapy*, 1974, **5**, 183–192.

Boersma, K., Den Hengst, S., Dekker, J., & Emmelkamp, P. M. G. Exposure and response prevention in the natural environment: A comparison with obsessive/compulsive patients. *Behavior Research and Therapy*, 1976, **14**, 19–24.

Bourque, P., & Ladouceur, R. An investigation of various performance-based treatments with acrophobics. *Behavior Research and Therapy*, 1980, **18**, 161–170.

Braun, P. R., & Reynolds, D. N. A factor analysis of a 100-item fear survey inventory. *Behavior Research and Therapy*, 1969, **7**, 399–402.

Bryant, B. & Trower, P. E. Social difficulty in a student sample. *British Journal of Educational Psychology*, 1974, **44**, 13–21.

Caine, T. M., & Hawkins, L. G. Questionnaire measure of the hysteroid/obsessoid component of personality: The HOQ. *Journal of Consulting Psychology*, 1963, **27**, 206–209.

Caine, T. M., & Hope, K. *Manual of the Hysteroid-Obsessoid Questionnaire*. London: University of London Press, 1967.

Capstick, N. The Shapiro cards scale as a method of assessment of obsessional symptoms in clomipramine therapy. *Scottish Medical Journal Supplement*, 1975, **20**, 17–20.

Cattell, R. B. Higher order factor structures and reticular-vs-hierarchical formulae for their interpretation. In C. Banks & P. L. Broadhurst (Eds.), *Studies in psychology*. New York: Barnes & Noble, 1966.

Cattell, R. B. The 16 PF and basic personality structure: A reply to Eysenck. *Journal of Behavioural Science*, 1972, **1**, 169–187. (a)

Cattell, R. B. The nature and genesis of mood states: A theoretical model with experimental measurements concerning anxiety, depression, arousal, and other mood states. In C. D. Spielberger (Ed.), *Anxiety, current trends and research*. New York: Academic Press, 1972. (b)

Cattell, R. B. *Personality and mood by questionnaire*. San Francisco: Jossey-Bass, 1973.

Ciminero, A. R., Calhoun, K. S., & Adams, H. E. *Handbook of behavioral assessment*. New York: Wiley, 1977.

Cohen, J. *Statistical power analysis for the behavioral sciences*. New York: Academic Press, 1977.

Cooke, G. The efficacy of two desensitization procedures: An analogue study. *Behavior Research and Therapy*, 1966, **4**, 17–24.

Cooper, J. The Leyton Obsessional Inventory. *Psychological Medicine*, 1970, **1**, 48–64.

Crisp, A. H., Jones, M. G., & Slater, P. The Middlesex Hospital Questionnaire: A validity study. *British Journal of Medical Psychology*, 1978, **51**, 269–280. (a)

Crisp, A. H., Ralph, P. C., McGuinness, B., & Harris, G. Psychoneurotic profiles in the adult population. *British Journal of Medical Psychology*, 1978, **51**, 293–301. (b)

Crowe, M. J. Evaluation of Conjoint Marital Therapy. Unpublished doctoral dissertation, University of Oxford, 1976.

Crown, S., & Crisp, A. H. A short clinical diagnostic self-rating scale for psychoneurotic patients: The Middlesex Hospital Questionnaire (M.H.Q.). *British Journal of Psychiatry*, 1966, **112**, 917–923.

Crown, S., Duncan, K. P., & Howell, R. W. Further evaluation of the Middlesex Hospital Questionnaire (M.H.Q.). *British Journal of Psychiatry*, 1970, **116**, 33–37.

Derogatis, L. R., Lipman, R. S., Rickels, K., Uhlenhuth, E. H., & Covi, L. The Hopkins Symptom Checklist (HSCL): A measure of primary symptom dimensions. In P. Pichot & R. Olivier-Martin (Ed.), *Psychological measurements in psychopharmacology*. In T. Ban, F. A. Freyhan, P. Pichot, & W. Poldinger (Eds.), *Modern problems of pharmacopsychiatry*, Vol. 7. Basel, Switzerland: Karger, 1974.

Derogatis, L. R., Lipman, R. S., & Covi, L. SCL-90: an outpatient psychiatric rating scale—preliminary report. *Psychopharmacological Bulletin*, 1973, **9**, 13–28.

Dixon, J. J, de Monchaux, C., & Sandler, J. Patterns of anxiety: The phobia. *British Journal of Medical Psychology*, 1957, **30**, 34–40.

Edwards, D., & Johnson, S. *The DXTX (JM) Program©*. San Diego: Grid Limited, 1981.

Emmelkamp, P. M. G., & Emmelkamp-Benner, A. Effects of historically portrayed modeling and group treatment on self-observation: A comparison with agoraphobics. *Behavior Research and Therapy*, 1975, **13**, 135–139.

Emmelkamp, P. M. G., & Kraanen, J. Therapist controlled exposure in vivo: A comparison with obsessive-compulsive patients. *Behavior Research and Therapy*, 1977, **15**, 491–495.

Emmelkamp, P. M. G., Kuipers, A. C. M., & Eggeraat, J. B. Cognitive modification versus prolonged exposure in vivo: A comparison with agoraphobics as subjects. *Behavior Research and Therapy*, 1978, **16**, 33–41.

Emmelkamp, P. M. G., & Wessels, H. Flooding in imagination vs. flooding in vivo: A comparison with agoraphobics. *Behavior Research and Therapy*, 1975, **13**, 7–15.

Endler, N. S., Hunt, J., McV., & Rosentein, A. J. An S-R inventory of anxiousness. *Psychological Monographs: General and Applied*, 1962, **76**, 1–31.

Endler, N. S., A person-situation interaction model for anxiety. In C. D. Spielberger & I. G. Sarason (Eds.), *Stress and anxiety*. New York: Hemisphere, 1975.

Engum, E. S., Miller, F. D. & Meredith, R. L. An analysis of three parameters of covert positive reinforcement. *Journal of Clinical Psychology*, 1980, **36**, 301–309.

Evanson, R. C., Holland, R. A., Mehta, S., & Yasin, F. Factor analysis of the Symptom Checklist-90. *Psychological Reports*, 1980, **46**, 695–699.

Eysenck H. J. Psychological aspects of anxiety. *British Journal of Psychiatry, Special Publication No. 3*, 1970, 7–20.(a)

Eysenck, H. J. *Theoretical and methodological issues*. New York: Wiley, 1970.(b)

Eysenck, H. J. On the choice of personality tests for research and prediction. *Journal of Behavioural Science*, 1971, **1**, 85–89.

Eysenck, H. J. A genetic model of anxiety. In C. D. Spielberger & I. G. Sarason, (Eds.), *Stress and anxiety*, Vol. 2. New York: Hemisphere, 1975.

Eysenck, H. J., & Eysenck, S. B. G. *Personality structure and measurement*. San Diego: Knapp, 1969.

Fazio, A. F. Verbal and overt-behavioral assessment of a specific fear. *Journal of Consulting and Clinical Psychology*, 1969, **33**, 705–709.

Foa, E. B., & Goldstein, A. Continuous exposure and complete response prevention in the treatment of obsessive/compulsive neurosis. *Behavior Therapy*, 1978, **9**, 821–829.

Foa, E. B., Stekeete, G., & Milby, J. B. Differential effects of exposure and response prevention in obsessive/compulsive washers. *Journal of Consulting and Clinical Psychology*, 1980, **48**, 71–79.

Foulds, G. A. *Personality and personal illness*. London: Tavistock Publications, 1965.

Garfield, S. L., & Bergin, A. E. *Handbook of psychotherapy and behavior change: An empirical analysis* (3rd ed.) New York: Wiley, 1978.

Gatchel, R. J. Biofeedback and the treatment of fear and anxiety. In R. J. Gatchel & K. P. Price (Eds.), *Clinical applications of biofeedback: appraisal and status*. New York: Pergamon Press, 1979.

Gay, M. L., Hollandworth, J. G., & Galassi, J. P. An assertiveness inventory. *Journal of Counseling Psychology*, 1975, **22**, 340–344.

Geer, J. H. The development of a scale to measure fear. *Behavior Research and Therapy*, 1965, **3**, 45–53.

Gelder, M. G., Bancroft, J. H. J., Gath, D. H., Johnston, D. W. Mathews, A. M., & Shaw, P. M. Specific and non-specific factors in behavior therapy. *British Journal of Psychiatry*, 1973, **123**, 445–462.

Gelder, M. G., & Marks, I. M. Severe agoraphobia: A controlled prospective trial of behavior therapy. *British Journal of Psychiatry*, 1966, **112**, 309 –319.

Goorney, A. B. Treatment of aviation phobias by behavior therapy. *British Journal of Psychiatry*, 1970, **117**, 535–544.

Groot, P. de, & Walbert, J. Konstruklie van een assertiviteitsschaal. *Vakgroep Klinische Psychologie*, Unpublished manuscript, 1977.

Hackman, A., & McLean, C. A comparison of flooding and thought stopping in the treatment of obsessional neurosis. *Behavior Research and Therapy*, 1975, **13**, 164–169.

Hafner, R. J. Fresh symptom emergence after intensive behavior therapy. *British Journal of Psychiatry*, 1976, **129**, 378–383.

Hafner, R. J. The husbands of agoraphobic women: Assertive mating or pathogenic interactions? *British Journal of Psychiatry*, 1977, **130**, 233–239.

Hafner, R. J., & Marks, I. Exposure in vivo of agoraphobics: Contributions of diazepam, group exposure and anxiety evocation. *Psychological Medicine*, 1976, **6**, 71–88.

Hallam, R. S., & Hafner, R. J. Fears of phobic patients: Factor analysis of self-report data. *Behaviour Research and Therapy*, 1978, **16**, 1–6.

Hamilton, M. The assessment of anxiety states by rating. *British Journal of Medical Psychology*, 1959, **32**, 50–55.

Hamilton, M. Diagnosis and rating of anxiety. In M. H. Lader (Ed.), *Studies in anxiety*, Ashford, England: Headley Brothers, 1969.

Hastings, J. E. *Cardiac and Cortical Responses to Affective Stimuli in a Reaction Time Task.* Unpublished doctoral dissertation, University of Wisconsin, 1971.

Herron, E. W. The multiple affect adjective checklist: A critical analysis. *Journal of Clinical Psychology*, 1969, **25**, 46–53.

Hersen, M. Fear scale norms for an inpatient population. *Journal of Clinical Psychology*, 1971, **27**, 375–378.

Hersen, M. Self assessment of fear. *Behavior Therapy*, 1973, **4**, 241–257.

Hodgson, R. J., & Rachman, S. J. Obsessional-compulsive complaints. *Behavior Research and Therapy*, 1977, **15**, 389–395.

Hoffman, N. G., & Overall, P. B. Factor structure of the SCL-90 in a psychiatric population. *Journal of Consulting and Clinical Psychology*, 1978, **46**, 1187–1191.

Jannoun, L., Munby, M., Catalan, J., & Gelder, M. A. A home-based treatment programme for agoraphobia: Replication and controlled evaluation. *Behavior Therapy*, 1980, **11**, 294–305.

Kallman, W. M., & Freuerstein, M. Psychophysiological procedures. In A. Ciminero, K. Calhoun, & H. Adams (Eds.) *Handbook of behavioral assessment*. New York: Wiley, 1977.

Kendell, R. E., & Discipio, W. J. Obsessional symptoms and obsessional personality traits in patients with depressive illnesses. *Psychological Medicine*, 1970, **1**, 65–72.

Klorman, R., Weerts, T. C., Hastings, J. E., Melamed, B. G., & Lang, P. J. Psychometric description of some specific fear questionnaires. *Behavior Therapy*, 1974, **5**, 401–409.

Kolb, L. C. *Modern clinical psychiatry*. Philadelphia: Saunders, 1977.

Krug, S. E., Scheier, I. H., & Cattell, R. B. *Handbook for IPAT Anxiety Scale*. Champaign, Ill.: Institute for Personality and Ability Testing, 1976.

Lambert, M. J. Introduction to assessment of psychotherapy outcome: Historical perspective and current issues. In M. J. Lambert, E. R. Christensen, & S. S. De-Julio (Eds.) *The assessment of psychotherapy outcome*. New York: Wiley, this volume.

Lang, P. J. Fear reduction and fear behavior: Problems in treating a construct. In J. M. Shlien (Ed.) *Research in psychotherapy*, Vol. 3. Washington, D.C.: American Psychological Association, 1968.

Lang, P. J., & Lazovik, A. D. Experimental desensitization of a phobia. *Journal of Abnormal and Social Psychology*, 1963, **66**, 519–525.

Lang, P. J., Melamed, B. G., & Hart, J. A psychophysiological analysis of fear-modification using an automated desensitization procedure. *Journal of Abnormal Psychology*, 1970, **76**, 220–234.

Levonian, E. A statistical analysis of the 16 personality factor questionnaire. *Educational and Psychological Measurement*, 1961, **21**, 589–596.

Liberman, R. P. *A guide to behavioral analysis and therapy*. New York: Pergamon Press, 1972.

Lick, J. R., Condiotte, M., and Unger, T. *Habituation to repeated presentations of a phobic stimulus as a function of uncertainty about phobic stimulus behavior*. Unpublished manuscript, State University of New York at Buffalo, 1975.

Lick, J. R., & Katkin, E. S. Assessment of anxiety and fear. In M. Hersen & A. Bellack (Eds.), *Behavioral assessment: A practical handbook*. New York: Pergamon Press, 1976.

Lick, J. R., & Unger, T. External validity of laboratory fear assessment: Implications from two case studies. *Journal of Consulting and Clinical Psychology*, 1975, **43**, 864–866.

Lipsedge, M., Hajioff, J., Hoggins, P., Napier, L., Pearce, J., Pike, D. J., & Rich, M. The management of severe agoraphobia: A comparison of ipronizaid and systematic desensitization. *Psychopharmacologia*, 1973, **32**, 67–80.

McDonald, J. E., & Sheperd, G. School phobia: An overview. *Journal of School Psychology*, 1976, **14**, 291–306.

McNair, D. M., & Lorr, M. An analysis of mood in neurotics. *Journal of Abnormal and Social Psychology*, 1964, **69**, 620–627.

Manosevitz, M., & Lanyon, R. I. Fear survey schedule, a normative study. *Psychological Reports*, 1965, **17**, 699–703.

Marks, I. M. *Living in fear*. New York: McGraw-Hill, 1978.

Marks, I. M., Boulougouris, J., & Marset, P. Flooding versus desensitization in the treatment of phobic patients: A cross-over study. *British Journal of Psychiatry*, 1971, **119**, 353–376.

Marks, I. M., Hallam, R., & Conolly, J. *Nursing in behavioral psychotherapy*. London: Royal College of Nursing, 1977.

Marks, I. M., & Herst, E. R. A survey of 1,200 agoraphobics in Britain. *Social Psychiatry*, 1970, **5**, 16–24.

Marks, I. M., Hodgson, R. J., & Rachman, S. J. Treatment of chronic obsessive-compulsive neurosis by in-vivo exposure. *British Journal of Psychiatry*, 1975, **127**, 349–364.

Marks, I. M., Marset, P., Boulougouris, S., & Husen, J. Physiological accompaniments of neutral and phobic imagery. *Psychological Medicine*, 1971, **1**, 299–307.

Marks, I. M., & Mathews, A. M. Brief standard self-rating for phobic patients. *Behavior Research and Therapy*, 1979, **17**, 263–267.

Marzillier, J. S., Lambert, C., & Kellet, J. A controlled evaluation of systematic descnsitization and social skills training for socially inadequate psychiatric patients. *Behavior Research Therapy*, 1976, **14**, 225–238.

Mathews, A. M. Recent developments in the treatment of agoraphobia. *Behavior Analysis and Modification*, 1977, **2**, 64–75.

Mathews, A. M., Johnston, D. W., Lancashire, M., Munby, M., Shaw, P. M., & Gelder, M. G. Imaginal flooding and exposure to real phobic situations: Treatment outcome with agoraphobic patients. *British Journal of Psychiatry*, 1976, **129**, 362–371.

Mathews, A. M., Teasdale, J., Munby, M., Johnston, D. W., & Shaw, P. M. A home-based treatment program for agoraphobia. *Behavior Therapy*, 1977, **8**, 915–924.

Mavissakalian, M. R., & Barlow, D. H. Assessment of obsessive-compulsive disorders. In D. H. Barlow (Ed.), *Behavioral assessment of adult disorders*. New York: Guilford Press, 1981.

Mawson, A. B. Methohexitone-assisted desensitization in treatment of phobias. *Lancet*, 1970, **1**, 1084–1086.

Miller, B. V., & Bernstein, D. A. Instructional demand in a behavioral avoidance test for claustrophobic fears. *Journal of Abnormal Psychology*, 1972, **80**, 206–210.

Millon, T. *Modern psychopathology: A biosocial approach to maladaptive learning and functioning*. Philadelphia: Saunders, 1969.

Munby, M., & Johnston, D. W. Agoraphobia: The long term follow-up of behavioral treatment. *British Journal of Psychiatry*, 1980, **127**, 418–427.

Murray, E. J., & Foote, F. The origins of fear of snakes. *Behavior Research and Therapy*, 1979, **17**, 1979.

Murray, R. M., Copper, J. E., & Smith, A. The Leyton Obsessional Inventory: An analysis of the responses of 73 obsessional patients. *Psychological Medicine*, 1979, **9**, 305–317.

O'Connor, J. P., Loor, M., & Stafford, J. W. Some patterns of manifest anxiety. *Journal of Clinical Psychology*, 1956, **12**, 160–163.

Orme, J. E. The relationship of obsessional traits to general emotional instability. *British Journal of Medical Psychology*, 1965, **38**, 269–270.

Osgood, C. E., Suci, G. J., & Tannenbaum, P. H. *Measurement of meaning*. Urbana: University of Illinois Press, 1957.

Ost, L. G., & Hugdahl, K. Acquisition of phobias and anxiety response patterns in clinical patients. *Behavior Research and Therapy*, 1981, **19**, 439–447.

Ost, L. G., Jerremalm, A., & Johansson, J. Individual response patterns and the effects of different behavioral methods in the treatment of social phobia. *Behavior Research Therapy*, 1981, **19**, 1–16. (a)

Ost, L. G., Jerremalm, A., & Johansson, J. *Fading versus exposure in the treatment of snake and rat phobia*. Unpublished manuscript, 1981.(b)

Pawlik, K., & Cattell, R. B. Third-order factors in objective personality tests. *British Journal of Psychology*, 1964, **55**, 1–18.

Philpott, R. Recent advances in the behavioral measurement of obsessional illness, difficulties common to these and other measure. *Scottish Medical Journal Supplement*, 1975, **20**, 33–39.

Pichot, P. Psychological measurements in psychopharmacology. In T. Ban, F. A. Freyhan, P. Pichot, & W. Poldinger (Eds.), *Modern problems of pharmacopsychiatry*, Vol. 7. Basel, Switzerland: Karger, 1974.

Pinkava, V. Psychometric assessment of phobias and obsessions. *Scottish Medical Journal Supplement*, 1975, **20**, 13–15.

Pront, H., Thompson, H. & Harvey, J. R. Applications of desensitization procedures for school-related problems: A review. *Psychology in the Schools*, 1978, **15**, 533–541.

Rachman, S. Studies in desensitization—1: The separate effects of relaxation and desensitization. *Behavior Research and Therapy*, 1965, **3**, 245–251.

Rachman, S. J., & Hodgson, R. J. *Obsessions and compulsions*. Englewood Cliffs, N.J.: Prentice-Hall, 1980.

Reed, G. F. Obsessionality and self-appraisal questionnaires. *British Journal of Psychiatry*, 1969, **115**, 205–209.

Richardson, R. C., & Tasto, D. C. Development and factor analysis of a social anxiety inventory. *Behavior Therapy*, 1976, **7**, 453–462.

Rimm, D. C., Saunders, W. D., & Westel, W. Thought stopping and covert assertion in the treatment of snake phobics. *Journal of Consulting and Clinical Psychology*, 1975, **43**, 92–93.

Rogers, C., & Dymond, R. *Psychotherapy and personality change*. Chicago: University of Chicago Press, 1954.

Rotter, J. B. Generalized expectancies for internal versus external control of reinforcement. *Psychological Monographs*, 1966, **80**, (1, Whole No. 609).

Rychlak, J. F. *Introduction to personality and psychotherapy: A theory-construction approach*. Boston: Houghton Mifflin, 1981.

Sandler, J., & Hazari, A. The "Obsessional": On the psychological classification of obsessional character traits and symptoms. *British Journal of Medical Psychology*, 1960, **33**, 113–122.

Sarason, I. G. Empirical findings and theoretical problems in the use of anxiety scales. *Psychological Reports*, 1960, **57**, 403–415.

Scrignar, C. B., Swanson, W. C., & Bloom, W. A. Use of systematic desensitization in the treatment of airplane phobic patients. *Behavior Research and Therapy*, 1973, **11**, 129–131.

Smith, R. E., Diener, E., & Beaman, A. L. Demand characteristics and the behavioral avoidance measure of fear in behavior therapy analogue research. *Behavior Therapy*, 1974, **5**, 172–182.

Snaith, R., McGuire, R., & Fox, K. Aspects of personality and depression. *Psychological Medicine*, 1971, **1**, 239–246.

Speltz, M. L., & Bernstein, D. A. The use of participant modeling for claustrophobia. *Journal of Behavior Therapy and Experimental Psychiatry*, 1979, **10**, 251–255.

Spielberger, C. D. Anxiety as an emotional state. In C. D. Spielberger (Ed.), *Anxiety: Current trends in theory and research*, (Vol. 1). New York: Academic Press, 1972.(c)

Spielberger, C. D. Theory and research on anxiety. In C. D. Spielberger (Ed.), *Anxiety: Current trends in theory and research*, (Vol. 1). New York: Academic Press, 1972.(b)

Spielberger, C. D. Conceptual and methodological issues in anxiety research. In C. D. Spielberger (Ed.), *Anxiety: Current trends in theory and research*, (Vol. 2). New York: Academic Press, 1972.(a)

Spielberger, C. D. The nature and measurement of anxiety. In C. D. Spielberger & E. Diaz-Cuerrero (Eds.), *Cross-cultural anxiety*. New York: Hemisphere, 1976.

Spielberger, C. D., Gorsuch, R. L., & Luchene, R. E. *Manual for the Stait-Trait Anxiety Inventory*. Palo Alto, Calif.: Consulting Psychologists Press, 1970.

Spielberger, C. D., Luchene, R. E., & MeAdoo, W. G. Theory and measurement of anxiety states. In R. B. Cattell (Ed.), *Handbook of modern personality theory*. Chicago: Aldine, 1971.

Spitzer, R. L., Endicott, J. Psychiatric rating scales. In A. M. Freedman, H. I. Kaplan, & B. J. Sadock (Eds.), *Modern synopsis of comprehensive textbook of psychiatry*. Baltimore: Waverly Press, 1975.

Stern, R., & Marks, I. Brief and prolonged flooding. *Archives of General Psychiatry*, 1973, **28**, 270–276.

Tasto, D. L. Self-report schedules and inventories. In A. Ciminero, K. Calhoun, & H. Adams (Eds.), *Handbook of behavioral assessment*. New York: Wiley, 1979.

Taylor, J. A. A personality scale of manifest anxiety. *The Journal of Abnormal and Social Psychology*, 1953, **48**, 285–290.

Taylor, C. B., & Agras, S. Assessment of phobia. In D. Barlow (Ed.), *Behavioral Assessment of adult disorders*. New York: Guilford Press, 1981.

Taylor-Spence J. A., & Spence, K. W. The motivational components of manifest anxiety: Drive and drive stimuli. In C. D. Spielberger (Ed.), *Anxiety and behavior*. New York: Academic Press, 1966.

Timm, S. A. Systematic desensitization of a phobia for flying with the use of suggestion. *Aviation, Space and Environmental Medicine*, 1977, **48**, 370–372.

Tyrer, P., Candy, J., & Kelly, D. A study of the clinical effects of phenelzine and placebo in the treatment of phobic anxiety. *Psychopharmacologia (Berlin)*, 1973, **32**, 237–254.

Walk, R. D. Self-ratings of fear in a fear-invoking situation. *Journal of Abnormal and Social Psychology*, 1956, **52**, 171–178.

Watson, D., & Friend, R. Measurement of social-evaluative anxiety. *Journal of Consulting and Clinical Psychology*, 1969, **33**, 448–457.

Watson, J. P., & Marks, I. M. Relevant and irrelevant fear in flooding—a crossover study of phobic patients. *Behavior Therapy*, 1971, **2**, 275–293.

Willems, L. F. M., Tuender, H., de Haan, H. A., & Defares, P. B. *Een nieuw instrument om sociale angst te meten*. Psychologisch Laboratorium, University of Amsterdam, 1972.

Williamson, J. D., Robinson, D., & Rowson, S. Psychiatric screening and the Middlesex Hospital Questionnaire (M.H.Q.). *International Journal of Social Psychiatry*, 1976, **22**, 167–188.

Willoughby, R. R. Norms for the Clark-Thurstone Inventory. *Journal of Social Psychology*, 1934, **5**, 91–97.

Wolpe, J., & Lang, P. S. A fear survey schedule for use in behavior therapy. *Behavior Research and Therapy*, 1964, **2**, 27–30.

Yorkston, N. J., Sergeant, H. G. S., & Rachman, S. Methohexitone relaxation for desensitizing agoraphobic patients. *Lancet*, 1968, **2**, 651–655.

Zitrin, C. M., Klein, D. F., & Woerner, M. G. Treatment of agoraphobia with group exposure in vivo and imipramine. *Archives of General Psychiatry*, 1980, **37**, 63–72.

Zuckerman, M. The development of an affect adjective checklist for the measurement of anxiety. *Journal of Consulting Psychology*, 1960, **24**, 457–462.

Zuckerman, M. General and situation-specific traits and states: New approaches to assessment of anxiety and other constructs. In M. Zuckerman & C. D. Spielberger (Eds.), *Emotions and anxiety: New concepts, methods and applications*. Hillsdale, N. J.: Lawrence Erlbaum Associates, 1976.

Zuckerman, M., & Biase, D. V. Replication and further data on the validity of the affect adjective checklist measure of anxiety. *Journal of Consulting Psychology*, 1962, **26**, 291.

Zuckerman, M., & Lubin, B. Normative data for the multiple affect adjective checklist. *Psychological Reports*, 1965, **16**, 438.

Zuckerman, M., Lubin, B., & Robins, S. Validation of the multiple affect adjective checklist in clinical situations. *Journal of Consulting Psychology*, 1965, **29**, 594.

Zung, W. W. K. A self-rating depression scale. *Archives of General Psychiatry*, 1965, **12**, 63–70.

Zung, W. W. K. A rating instrument for anxiety disorders. *Psychosomatics*, 1971, **12**, 371–379.

CHAPTER 11

Assessment of Habit Disorders: A Tripartite Perspective in Measuring Change

MICHAEL G. EPPINGER AND MICHAEL J. LAMBERT

Within the last 15 years there has been a virtual explosion of treatment outcome studies for problems that have been loosely classified under a habit-disorder rubric. These studies demonstrate a typical pattern in the assessment of change: posttreatment measures show impressive support for a particular treatment procedure but then lose significance on long-term follow-up or replication. Although this trend is most characteristic of habit disorders, it occurs with many other disorders as well (Bergin & Lambert, 1978; Garfield et al., 1971; Strupp, 1978). From our perspective, psychotherapy outcome patterns of this type, when they are not the result of weak treatment methods, can be traced directly to a lack of philosophical direction, an unclear conception of the disorder, and an unyielding reliance on traditional measures.

In a trial and error fashion, subtle, but important changes have evolved in strategies of habit disorder treatment. Researchers are beginning to recognize the inadequate procedure of treating habit disorders from a single dimension: most often, a dimension of behavioral–external focus. For example, Lazarus (1973, 1976) has parted from traditional behavior therapy by rejecting the notion that complex disorders can be treated from a unidimensional strategy of intervention. As an alternative, he proposed that greater endurance of change can be achieved through the pragmatic application of techniques from behavioral, cognitional, emotional, and social realities. In a similar thrust, Mahoney (1974a) has championed the idea that "private events" (thoughts, feelings, and memories) are a viable and necessary dimension of treatment. The denial or exclusion of such phenomena is a serious drawback to treatment success. From a more general perspective, Walter Mischel has recognized the inadequacies of a unidimensional assumption to reality and repeatedly emphasized the need for a broadening of philosophical and professional outlook:

> For me, one of the most impressive—and obvious—lessons from the history of personality measurement is the recognition that complex human behavior tends to be influenced by many determinants and reflects the almost inseparable and continuous interaction of a host of variables both in the person and in the situation. (Mischel, 1977, p. 246)

Although treatment planners are now employing multidimensional treatment procedures, outcome research has failed to keep pace in providing valid, multidimensional measures of change (Garfield, 1978; Goldstein et al., 1966; Kiesler, 1966; 1971; Strupp, 1964; Urban & Ford, 1971). Nowhere is this trend more evident than in habit disorder research. To illustrate, Wilson (1978) points out that a large number of outcome studies and dissertations on obesity treatment are rejected each year as a result of the reliance on a single measure of change (weight reduction) to account for a multifaceted treatment success. Thus the intricacies in treating the problem of obesity cannot be known through this simplistic and unrealistic approach to measurement. Nonetheless, a great many researchers continue to rely on a single dependent measure or a "stock" package of dependent measures without questioning such fundamentals as reliability, validity, comparability, and dimensionality of focus.

This general tendency continues, although there have been several attempts to help organize and improve research methodology for various habit or impulse control disorders: alcoholism and drug abuse (Miller, 1977, 1981; Sobell & Sobell, 1976; Sobell, et al., 1980), eating disorders (Brownell, 1981; Wilson, 1978), and tobacco smoking (McFall, 1978). Each review contains a "state-of-the-art" examination of research methodology for their respective topic. Although some of these reviews contain a detailed summary of dependent measures (Brownell, 1981; Sobell et al., 1980), the majority focus on a large variety of methodological issues; as a result, generalities are fostered rather than useful specifics. Moreover, each is concerned primarily with assessment from a single dimension of measurement: behavior. Those researchers who look to these reviews as a source for dependent measure selection come away with a hazy notion as to which assessment strategies are necessary, appropriate, valid, and economical. Thus a review of outcome methodology with habit disorders that focuses on evaluation, dimensionality of measures, and recommendations for dependent measure selection is needed.

THE HABIT-DISORDER CONCEPT

The label of habit disorder has been a catchall term for a variety of loosely related symptoms of external as well as internal etiology. Unlike other diagnostic categories, the habit disorder lacks a clear consensus of symptoms and processes of the disorder. As a consequence, it has been difficult to place disorders of this type within an independent category of a classification system. Diagnosticians, for the lack of a better approach, have deemed it more efficient to categorize habit disorders from the major symptom exhibited. The recent publication of the Diagnostic and Statistical Manual of Mental Disorders III reflects this trend. Traditional habit- or impulse-related disorders are widely dispersed under such categories as eating disorders, stereotyped movement disorders, substance use disorders, other disorders with physical manifestations, and disorders of impulse control not elsewhere classified (American Psychiatric Association, 1980).

Traditional attempts to define a habit disorder have focused largely on a behavioristic or psychoanalytic explanation. For example, the behaviorists emphasize the acquisition of habits; that is, a stimulus and response must be spatially and temporally associated, and the response must be followed by a positive consequence. Thus one may find a lecturer who is just about to deliver an important speech (stimulus)—the lecturer lights up a cigarette (response)— and tension is released (positive consequence). From an analytic perspective, habit disorders are thought to reflect unconscious conflict from the developmental past. The performance of the habit sequence can temporarily reduce the level of conscious anxiety. Both explanations are very general in scope, leaving a vague impression of origins and processes.

Without a clear conceptual framework, it is not surprising to find considerable variability between sources in determining habit disorder symptomatology. Regardless of theoretical orientation, the symptoms most commonly cited are repetitious behavior, heightened tension, sudden tension release, high anxiety, psychological dependency, unrealistic thoughts, irresistible impulse, self-destructive tendencies, loss of personal control, and low self-worth (American Psychiatric Association, 1980; Freedman, 1975; Kolb, 1977). There is a tendency in the compilation of symptoms to bifurcate these manifestations into external and internal realities, emphasizing one reality over the other. Furthermore, one side of the external–internal dichotomy is often considered to be incompatible or irrelevant, depending on one's theoretical orientation. However, it is our contention that each reality is an essential aspect of the total habit disorder syndrome and that the interrelationships of these symptoms can be better conceptualized within three primary dimensions of human functioning: conation; cognition; and affection. This tripartite paradigm contains three independent dimensions that combine to form a complex, interactional system of human functioning. To give the reader a fuller understanding of this process, we briefly explored its philosophical underpinnings and then applied them to a conceptualization of the disorder.

A TRIPARTITE FOUNDATION

Empirical materialism was a dominant force in early Greek philosophy (Sahakian, 1975). It was believed that the proper study of the universe was through observation and experience; moreover, reality can be understood only by reducing phenomenon to a basic, indivisible essence. In response to these ideas, Socrates (470 B.C.) rejected the prevailing notion of reducing reality to a single dimension. He believed that ultimate truth comes not from the senses, but from within the individual through examination of the promptings of a universal unconsciousness, the repository of all knowledge. Thus, refusing a materialistic basis for knowledge, Socrates chose the soul as the key to understanding.

A tripartite system of functioning is best known through the work of Plato (427 to 347 B.C.), a student of Socrates. Plato accepted his mentor's precept that truth can be understood through the rational processes of the soul. With this idea in mind, Plato proposed that the soul is composed of three separate realities, all of which function in a complex interaction. In addition, these three dimensions permeate both the mind and body (Allport, 1954). Figure 11.1 illustrates the influence configuration of the tripartite model. Plato proposed that the soul functions in unity when harmony exists between each of the three dimensions. However, an imbalance or lack of harmony between dimensions results in maladjusted or abnormal manifestations (Sahakian, 1975). Thus the "normal" individual is one who can integrate and maintain a positive balance between each dimension of functioning.

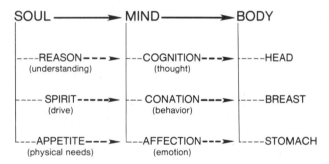

Figure 11.1. Influence configuration of the tripartite model.

Plato's views had a lasting effect on another influential philosopher of the time. Aristotle (384 to 322 B.C.) advanced a tripartite reality very similar to Plato's. This theme is most evident in his conceptualization of an increasing dimensionality of existence as organisms become more complex. Aristotle believed that: plants grow (physical dimension); animals grow and sense (physical and affective dimensions); and humans grow, sense, and know (physical, affective, and cognitive dimensions). Although Aristotle accepted the view that only the physical dimension could be known, he did not deny the influence of nonphysical dimensions.

The basic elements of Plato's tripartite reality provide a useful orientation in conceptualizing habit disorder symptoms and process. In terms of symptomatology, the manifestations of habit disorders can be roughly placed within one or more of the three dimensions; however, it is important to realize that this is an artificial categorization and does not represent the complex interaction of dimensions that is always present. Table 11.1 specifies the dimension or dimensions most characteristic of each habit-disorder symptom based on the descriptions of symptom components from varied diagnostic sources (American Psychiatric Association, 1980; Freedman, 1975; Kolb, 1977). Conceptualization of the habit disorder process in one or two dimensions is thoroughly inadequate. The actual sequence of a disruptive habit follows a circular type of pattern: impulse→ tension→ release→ impulse→, and so on (American Psychiatric Association, 1980). Within this circularity, the individual can be operating in one or all dimensions at the same time, such as negative self-statements (cognition), feelings of guilt (affection), and uncontrolled behavior (conation). Therefore, according to this model, effective intervention should be undertaken within each realm of functioning. Treatment from a single dimension could result in a temporary reduction in the habit-disorder cycle; however, long-term change is less of a possibility, and, as alluded to before, this is exactly what treatment planners are discovering.

TABLE 11.1.   Habit-Disorder Symptoms Classified in the Tripartite Model

Symptom	Functioning Dimensions		
	Cognition	Conation	Affection
Anxiety			X
Tension	X		X
Tension release (gratification)	X		X
Repetitious behavior		X	
Unrealistic thoughts	X		
Irresistible impulse	X		X
Loss of self-control	X	X	X
Self-destructive tendencies		X	
Psychological dependence	X		
Low self-worth	X	X	X

Although the tripartite orientation provides a theoretical direction for the treatment and evaluation of habit disorders, there are a number of issues that must be ultimately understood: (1) whether the reduction of human functioning into three realms of existence can accurately reflect the complex interaction of the whole; (2) whether the three dimensions exhaustive in their coverage; (3) whether the three conceptual dimensions related directly to empirical dimensions; and (4) whether one dimension is more influential than the others. Future research must help to expand and clarify these important issues.

With or without the emergence of a multidimensionality in treatment, there must be a corresponding alteration in the dimensionality of outcome measures used to assess change. It is the purpose of this chapter to thoroughly investigate the specifics of dependent measure selection for habit disorder research. Within the tripartite dimension of functioning, devices are described, classified, and evaluated in terms of (1) ease of administration, (2) dimension of measurement, (3) reliability and validity, and (4) cost efficiency. On the basis of these criteria, recommendations for the selection of dependent measures are made at the conclusion of this chapter. Instruments are placed in rank order of preference in terms of their overall quality. If measures are deficient in one or more areas of the tripartite model, proposals are made for future research.

It is beyond the scope of this chapter to investigate all manifestations that may fall within the parameters of a habit-disorder label. In response to this dilemma, we have selected two disorders that are receiving considerable research attention of late: obesity and tobacco smoking. Each is a prime example of the problems encountered when measuring changes in habit disorders.

OUTCOME MEASURES OF OBESITY RESEARCH

One negative by-product of the American affluent society is the ever-increasing prevalence of obesity. The National Center for Health Statistics has completed a lengthy survey of obesity prevalence rates for men and women in the United States. Their findings indicate an alarming increase in the percentage of overweight citizens in the 20- to 74-year-old age bracket (U.S. Department of Health, Education, and Welfare, 1979a). It was estimated that 18.4 million men were 10% above the desirable weights established by the Health and Nutrition Examination Survey (HANES). In addition, 8 million men were classified as 20% or more overweight. The statistical picture is even more bleak for women. Approximately 23.4 million women are considered 10% or more above the desirable weight, and 23.8 million are categorized as 20% or more above the desirable weight. In accordance with these estimates, approximately 73.6 million people or 29% of the U.S. population can be considered as overweight or more importantly, a serious health risk. Perhaps the increasing concern for the consequences of this disorder (e.g., U.S. Senate, 1977) has contributed to the recent surge of fad diets and the establishment of a multi-million dollar weight loss industry. With the increase in methods and practices for losing weight, researchers have the formidable task of accurately measuring outcome and specifying the necessary components of treatment packages.

The obese person is often ridiculed and burdened with labels such as "weak-willed," "lazy," and "overindulgent." In reality, however, the phenomenon is much more intricate than this simple stereotype portrays. Obesity has been determined to be a product of genes, physical conditions, psychological problems (cognitions, emotions, and behaviors), and social pressures (Bray, 1976; Stunkard & Mahoney, 1976; Wolley et al., 1979). Under normal conditions, the body will maintain an optimum weight range; that is, the amount of calories consumed per day is equivalent to the energy-producing value needed to maintain bodily functions, exert activity, and so on. However, it is an illusion to consider that a precise static condition for the weight of the human body exists. The so-called ideal weights proposed by insurance companies (Metropolitan Life Insurance Company, 1960) and the U.S. Government (U.S. Department of Health, Education, and Welfare, 1979a) are gross, average estimates to account for internal as well as external fluctuations. For these agencies, this is an efficient means to gather data for their statistical purposes. However, a more precise concept of "normal" and "obese" is needed for methodological assessment.

Although body weight is the typical measure used to define the obese person, it is only an indirect measure of a body fat content. If body weight and the body fat percentage were perfectly correlated, this measure would be an acceptable assessment device; however, this is not the case. Muscle density, bone structure, and water weight fluctuations are all factors that can influence body weight. Nevertheless, body weights are easy to obtain and remain the standard measure in weight reduction studies. The concept of obesity is more than a statistical cutoff level established by comprehensive surveys. It is a disorder that is composed of a complex interaction of internal and external variables, all of which must be considered to formulate a complete understanding. Since the epoch work of Stuart (1967), the literature has been inundated with weight reduction treatment packages that are largely behavioral in orientation. Several of these studies have been cited consistently to show impressive support for a particular treatment procedure but most often contain serious methodological problems or lack clinical relevance (Wilson, 1978). The most frequent methodological violations are unidimensional dependent measures, invalid dependent measures, inadequate short-term follow-ups, and the lack of comparable control groups (Abrahams & Allen, 1974; Balch & Ross, 1975; Mahoney, 1974b; Manno & Marston, 1972). Perhaps as a consequence, obesity studies typically fail to hold up under replication. Bellack and Rozensky (1975) have specified three problem areas in the selection of dependent measure that may contribute to nonreplication: measures that are incompatible with data analysis; a lack of multiple criteria for measuring all important effects of treatment; and a lack of standardization of dependent measures across studies. The last two problems are of paramount importance to improve the accuracy and quality of obesity outcome research; to remediate these, the following evaluation is directed.

The measurement devices in the forthcoming sections are classified and reviewed within the three dimensions of the tripartite orientation. The conation dimension will include all measures that focus on assessment of external phenomena, including behavior and physiological reactions. The cognitive dimension contains those measures of subjective thought processes. Within the affective dimension category, devices are reviewed that attempt to measure change in subjective feeling states. The cognitive and affective dimensions have been combined in a single section because of the limited number of measurement devices currently available. This section is presented following reviews of the conation dimension in obesity and tobacco smoking research.

Measures of Obesity: Conation Dimension: Body Fat Determination

The single most popular measure in obesity research is the calculation of weight reduction. This procedure is based on the assumption that a reduction in body weight signifies a corresponding change in the level of body fat. In most cases this is true, but not always. As elaborated previously, other metabolic factors significantly influence fluctuations in weight. Therefore, weight reduction calculations are not totally sufficient to measure body fat levels. However, this device is helpful in providing general change data and in providing feedback about the subject's progress.

The least acceptable, but most common, of any weight measure is the recording of absolute pounds lost. Without a comparison of pretest weight levels, the magnitude of change is lost; for instance, a 10-pound weight loss is more significant for a person weighing 140 pounds than for a person weighing 300 pounds. Another popular method is the change in percent overweight. This dependent variable is a percentage derived from the actual weight exceeding the ideal weight from pretest to posttest. Although this measure is more meaningful than absolute pounds lost, it possesses two major difficulties: body weight is assumed to be an accurate measure of body fat; and ideal weights are based on national normative statistics listed in insurance companies or government weight–height tables. LeBow (1977) has been a critic of these weight-loss-based dependent measures. For example, a gross body mass measure cannot differentiate the subtle influences of water weight, muscle mass, bone structure, and body fat. Such factors can produce misleading results. In addition, reliance on a standard weight–height chart for establishing an ideal weight is laden with difficulties. Typically, such charts use a frame-size criterion (small, medium, and large) without specifying precise guidelines for determination. Furthermore, there is indication that insurance companies are economically biased to underestimate national norms (Mayer, 1968; Simms, 1977) and thus propose, as normal, lower ranges of normative body weights.

The use of relative weight indices has shown promise as an indirect measure of body fat. These indices are usually expressed in a weight:height ratio. Keys et al. (1972), for example, conducted a concurrent validity study to compare the weight:height ratio, body mass index (weight:height squared), and the ponderal index (cube root of weight divided by height) to more precise measures of body density and skinfold thickness. The body mass index proved to be slightly more accurate in estimating body fat, whereas the ponderal index was least accurate. Although correlations were strong between the body mass index and measures of skinfold thickness (r_s = .7 to .8 range for all groups), it is not sufficiently accurate to use as a single measure of body fat content.

Feinstein (1959) has formulated a weight reduction index to avoid the typical weight measure pitfalls. In this formula, a variety of important factors, pounds overweight, target weight, initial weight, and absolute pounds lost are taken into account:

$$\text{Weight reduction index: } \frac{\text{pounds lost}}{\text{overweight}} \times \frac{\text{initial weight}}{\text{target weight}} \times 100 \text{ pounds}$$

This formula is quite useful because it takes into consideration the great variability of body weight among obese subjects (Wilson, 1978). A heavier subject must lose more pounds to reach the same percentage of the target weight goal. Thus the formula provides a more conservative but meaningful estimate of treatment effects. However, as with the change in percent over-weight strategy, part of this formula must rely on the nebulous concept of ideal or target weight. Originally, Feinstein (1959) suggested that target weights should be determined by either a national norm chart or by the participants' subjective view of an ideal body weight. From the above discussion on weight–height tables, we suggest caution in their selection as an ideal level of weight until some of the major flaws are corrected. The use of the participant's subjective view appears to be a possible alternative. With the use of a sub-jective estimate of target weight, the resulting weight reduction index will have greater meaning and relevance to the subject rather than artificially contrived norms. Without considering the subject's point of view, the investigator may assume a weight reduction success, when in fact the subject views the results as dismal failure. Unfortunately, clients may be far too "arbitrary" in setting ideal weights. From the researcher's point of view, ideal weight set by the patient may not be a good conative measure. Perhaps an acceptable compromise would be to compare the results of both subjective and ideal target weights.

In summary, body weight measures are easy to calculate, economical, convenient, and provide general measures of weight change that are easy to comprehend. Nevertheless, body weight measures are only moderately accu-rate in predicting body fat percentage (Rogers et al., 1980). In addition, these measures lose much of their accuracy with grossly obese subjects or when special groups are the focus of study, such as children and the elderly (Wilson, 1978). The logical solution is to include a more precise measure of body fat percentage.

The most common method of deriving a body fat percentage is through the use of a skinfold caliper. This method is considered by many sources to be a reliable and accurate instrument (Bray, 1976; Durnin & Rahaman, 1967; Franzini & Grimes, 1976; Grimes & Franzini, 1977; Haisman, 1970; Sims, 1977). There are three calipers that are widely used for this type of measure-ment: the Best caliper (Best, 1954); the Harpenden caliper (Edwards et al., 1955; Tanner & Whitehouse, 1955); and the Lange caliper (Lange & Brozek, 1961). In a comparison study of these instruments, Sloan and Shapiro (1972) found no significant difference between caliper readings; however, the Harpenden was the most consistent. After a careful review, Grimes and Franzini (1977) recommend the Lange Skinfold Caliper (Cambridge Scientific Industry, Cambridge, Maryland) as a measure of body fat. This model has easy accessibility in the United States, has a greater measuring range capacity, is smaller, and is less expensive (approximately $150); hence these qualities earmark the Lange caliper as the best instrument of choice. A recent study by Franzini and Grimes (1980) illustrates the use of a Lange caliper assessment in addition to gross body fat measures.

The major problem with skinfold measures of fat percentage is their reliability (Burkinshaw et al., 1973; Womersley & Durnin, 1973). Nonetheless, consistency can be achieved through careful implementation of measurement procedure (Durnin & Rahaman, 1967; Johnson & Stalonas, 1977; Weiner & Lourie, 1969). The simplest and most economical way of selecting and measuring body fat was proposed by Durnin and Rahaman (1967). Use of the following procedures will increase the value of skinfold measurements: (1) measurements should be read from the right side of the body; however, Womersley and Durnin (1973) found no significant variations between either side; (2) to ensure accuracy, all measurement readings should be taken from the tricep, bicep, suprailiac, and subscapular regions (Burkinshaw et al., 1973; Durnin & Rahaman, 1967; Durnin & Womersley, 1974; Weiner & Lourie, 1969; Womersley & Durnin, 1973); and (3) the final measurement is composed of repeated readings until two are within 5% agreement. The average of these two measurements is recorded as the final reading for that particular site. Womersley and Durnin (1973) found that the greatest reproducibility of measurement is from the total areas of skinfold thickness.

A second important drawback to the skinfold caliper technique is difficulty in measuring morbidly obese people. With these subjects, it is exceptionally difficult to reliably locate, isolate, and measure fat tissue; however, for the majority of subjects, this will not be a problem. Although obesity criteria with the use of a body fat percentage varies, it is generally thought that obesity in men ranges from 20 to 25% body fat and for women, 25 to 30% body fat (Human Performance Center, 1980).

The most accurate measure of body fat is by far the most expensive and cumbersome to administer. On the basis of Archimedes' (287 to 212 B.C.) principle of hydrostatic displacement, this method measures body density that is converted to a body fat percentage by use of a simple formula. Katch et al., (1967) describe a practical and very reliable (test–retest, $r = .87$) method for accomplishing this measurement. After a reading is obtained for both dry and submerged body weights, body density can be calculated from the following formula:

M/V (mass per unit volume) $= M_a$ (weight of the body in the air) $- M_w$ (weight of the body submerged)

With the use of a regression formula derived by Brozek et al. (1963), body density can be converted to a more useful body fat percentage:

$$F\% = 100 \left(\frac{4.570}{\text{density}} - 4.142 \right)$$

As one may deduce from the brief description of this measurement, the necessary equipment (e.g., water vat or pool, scale, carriage, and snorkel) is very expensive. In addition, the inconvenience and embarrassment of being stripped, hoisted, and dipped is not conducive for happy subjects and may increase the bias in samples and attrition rates. Therefore, this method is more properly used with experimental studies that require highly precise body fat percentages.

Observations—Measures of Eating Behavior

The observation of eating style can provide twofold information on the components of eating behavior as well as measures of change in outcome research (Brownell, 1981). Although important data are derived from a component analysis of eating behavior in obese and nonobese subjects, this section focuses attention on the use of these measures in determining outcome. Objective measures of eating behavior can be roughly viewed in two category types: experimental analogue and naturalistic or quasinaturalistic observation.

The laboratory traditionally has been considered an ideal place to provide the necessary experimental control in evaluating behavior; however, certain drawbacks exist with this approach. These problems are specified later. The most frequently used measures of eating behavior are the taste-rating task and the food-presentation machine.

In a widely cited study, Schachter et al. (1968) developed a taste-rating task measurement that has proved to have wide applicability for the measurement of ingestive habit disorders in laboratory settings, such as tobacco smoking (Briddell et al., 1979) and alcoholism (Conners et al., 1978; Cooper et al., 1979). Schachter has used this method repeatedly in investigating the influence of environmental factors on eating behavior (Goldman et al., 1968; Schachter & Gross, 1968; Schachter & Rodin, 1974). The taste-rating method has been further modified to help identify eating topography (Diament & Wilson, 1975); (Mahoney, 1975). There have been a few attempts to measure eating behavior through the use of machine dispersal systems; however, the practicality and expense of such procedures has been prohibitive. Jordan et al. (1966) attempted to measure subject consumption levels by passing liquid meals through a glass straw. By the use of this device, precise ingestion levels can be monitored. Recently, a "universal eating monitor" was developed to assess amounts of food consumption by subjects (Kissileff et al., 1980). The weights of food presented to subjects can be secretly monitored through scales placed within the eating table. This machine can precisely monitor liquid as well as solid foods. The major problem with the experimental analogue methods described above is the artificiality of the situation. It is difficult to imagine that eating behavior in laboratory experiments will closely approximate real life. Moreover, the demand characteristics of the situation will greatly influence behavior unless it is specified and controlled.

Because of the concern for laboratory findings generalization, investigators have moved into such natural settings as cafeterias (Dodd et al., 1976; Krantz, 1979; Krassner et al., 1979), luncheons (Adams et al., 1978), and snack bars (Coll et al., 1979; Gaul et al., 1975; O'Brien et al., 1978). These studies are designed to investigate the topography of eating habits rather than for measuring outcome change per se (social influences, type of food eaten, number of calories, number of chews, latency between bites, bite size, length of meal time, etc). Typically, precise time samples are taken to establish an estimate of a specific behavior per unit of time (Brownell, 1981). Effective observational studies require precise definitions of target behaviors to ensure an acceptable level of agreement between judges. In addition, training sessions and *in vivo* practice runs are mandatory to establish a high level of interjudge reliability (usually $r = .85$ or greater). In some studies it may be more advantageous to use a quasi-naturalistic environment to improve observational accuracies. To illustrate, if a study endeavors to investigate food selection and calorie levels of obese and nonobese subjects, a university cafeteria or any other eating establishment that meticulously measures food proportions would be more accurate than training observers to estimate food quantity (Dodd et al., 1976). The difference between the known weight of the food portion and the weight of the food fragments left would provide an accurate estimate of calorie intake.

The use of naturalistic or quasi-naturalistic observational settings has strong possibilities for the experimental investigation of eating styles. Nevertheless, this approach is not ideally suited for testing the efficacy of a treatment program. The complexity of establishing adequate controls is time consuming and somewhat costly. Other approaches are much more cost-efficient.

Energy Expenditure Measurement

In recent years, energy expenditure rates have become an important but unclear component in weight reduction treatment strategies. Contrary to popular biases, obesity is not solely a product of an inability to control calorie consumption. The level of weight maintained by an individual is the result of a complex process of energy consumption and expenditure interaction. Although this relationship is not completely clear, some researchers speculate that the level of energy expenditure is a major factor in obesity (Bloom & Eidex, 1967; Epstein et al., 1979; Harris & Hallbauer, 1973; Mann, 1974; Wooley et al., 1979). Indeed, an energy expenditure treatment component is viewed as essential for the continued maintenance of weight reduction (Dahlkoetter et al., 1979, Stunkard & Mahoney, 1976).

The measurement of energy levels is more complicated than one might guess. Energy expenditure is not only related to overt activity, but to the basic metabolism rate of the body (Bray, 1976). The basic metabolism rate (total minimal activity of body tissue under steady-state conditions) is influenced by a variety of factors, all of which remain unclear as to their specific contribution to the total level of energy expenditure (Brownell, 1981). Nevertheless, until energy levels are understood more clearly, researchers must attempt to investigate the influence of physical exercise on outcome data.

Calorie expenditure has been the target of assessment for researchers. The most popular method of measurement, but possibly least accurate, involves the use of self-report records. Despite their popularity, prior attempts at self-monitoring physical activity have been discouraging. Jeffery and Wing (1979) found that self-reported exercise was not a good predictor of weight loss. These investigators point out that an accurate measure of caloric expenditure requires precise evaluation of intensity and duration that is difficult to achieve. For example, it is irrelevant to assign an expenditure value of 2 kilocalories per minute for a specific task. Each person will vary in the amount of effort put into the activity. Moreover, activity levels rarely stay within the confines of the task, thus further confounding the intensity of the activity. If an average kilocalorie expenditure per activity is utilized, the resulting measurements are subject to wide variations. Another problem with self-report energy measures is the lack of convenience for the subject. It is beyond practical boundaries for subjects to compartmentalize, temporalize, and measure the intensity of their own behavior. Clearly, a self-measurement of activity is not a precise method of assessment for this parameter of obesity research. It can only provide general information about the activity level of the subject during treatment.

Indirect physiological measurement provides a more precise assessment of energy expenditure. Previous attempts to estimate these levels have focused on total energy expenditure through carbon dioxide production, oxygen uptake, and nitrogen excretion (Brownell, 1981). As with most physiological measures, equipment is very expensive and difficult to collect. Furthermore, the artificial insertion of such devices in a weight-reduction program may produce biased effects on the energy expenditure activity.

Before accurate measurement of energy expenditure is achieved, future research will be necessary to (1) delineate the contributions of the basic metabolism rate and physical activity and (2) establish accurate, nonobtrusive devices. One possible direction for research is to set aside the notion of measuring total energy expenditure for a given activity and focus on complete measures of body conditioning such as heart rates, muscle tone and strength, and aerobic capacity. In the meantime, self-report estimates of activity can provide a less costly measure of energy expenditure influence.

Self-Monitoring Records

A subject's self-report has the potential for revealing a wealth of data that is virtually unretrievable by any other method. Conversely, the accuracy of such reports may be subject to conscious or unconscious distortions. Often, a subject will be influenced by the need to present a socially desirable front, thus biasing the recorded data. Another problem with this source of data is reactive effects. For example, the obtrusive measurement of data by the subject will not accurately reflect data gathered by unobtrusive means. As a consequence, self-report data must act as a supplement to other measurement sources.

Many obesity treatment programs incorporate the use of a self-monitoring log to isolate the factors involved in the subject's eating pattern. Such logs most often contain a daily record of body weight. Although this is a simple task to perform for the subject, there are a number of factors that render these data inaccurate. Subjects tend to be less than honest in reporting weights, especially if a hefty deposit hangs in the balance. Also, Wilson (1978) points out that spring-operated home scales are grossly inaccurate and tend to vary a great deal.

Nutritional quality has been another self-report source of data. Subjects record the types of food eaten per meal period. This information is essential for studies that utilize nutritional education as part of the total treatment package (Beneke et al., 1978; McReynolds et al., 1976). The self-monitoring of caloric intake is a very important source of data. For a minimal purchase, subjects can obtain a small food scale and any currently published booklet on food–calorie conversions. A total caloric intake can be simply recorded each day. Several studies of obesity treatment research are including this measure as a matter of course (Green, 1978; Jeffery & Wing, 1979). Other sources of data in a self-monitoring log can include a means of recording pre- and postactivities of eating, pre- and postmeal mood checklists, eating durations, and social factors (e.g., people present and activities during the meal), all of which provide useful data in the overall day-to-day eating style of the subject. From these data, potentially destructive events can be identified and included in the treatment focus. However, it must be pointed out that the value of monitoring intervening behaviors (e.g., chewing behavior, calorie intake, exercise) for the purpose of specifying outcome is less certain. It would appear that in general they do not correlate highly with weight loss and thus may be of no or only limited value as outcome measures.

COMMENTS

The final selection of obesity-dependent measures from the conation dimension should reflect an overlap strategy; that is, each measure should provide a clarification of results and cover the blind spots of other devices. Moreover, some less technical measures can be used to give a general level of progress feedback to the subject. For example, absolute pounds lost would be more meaningful to the subject whereas a weight index, paired with a skin caliper body fat percentage, would provide a more accurate assessment of body fat level for the experimenter.

On the basis of the previous review, dependent measures for the conation dimension have been rank ordcrcd in Table 11.2. These orderings are based on overall quality from the criteria specified in the first part of section of this chapter. Nevertheless, these recommendations are made with caution. Future work is needed to ascertain the interrelatedness of these measures and to establish their relative contribution in predicting outcome.

OUTCOME MEASURES OF TOBACCO SMOKING RESEARCH

Giving up smoking is the easiest thing in the world. I've done it a hundred times.

MARK TWAIN

Since the U.S. Surgeon General raised serious health questions about tobacco smoking, the prevalence rate of smokers in the United States has been steadily declining (U.S. Department of Health, Education, and Welfare, 1979b). Data from a recent survey indicate, however, that one of every three adults in the United States (33.7%) is still a cigarette smoker. Nevertheless, these statistics do not reflect the contribution of other forms of tobacco consumption, such as pipes and cigars. Although the prevalence rates for male smokers have been on a steady decline since 1950, female smoker rates have remained remarkably constant (U.S. Department of Health, Education, and Welfare, 1979b). With the heightened awareness of the potential health risk in tobacco smoking, the public is increasingly seeking professional help to overcome this most persistent and satisfying habit. As a result, the recent upsurge in tobacco research has focused primarily on studies of treatment outcome effectiveness (McFall, 1978).

Outcome studies on tobacco smoking cessation suffer from similar measurement problems as presented in the previous section on obesity: target behaviors are ill defined; the conation dimension dominates outcome measurement; measures have questionable reliability and validity; and measures lack comparability across studies. Without a clear, comprehensive evaluation of measures, treatment outcome will remain contestable, leaving most treatment strategies without demonstrable utility.

Contrary to popular notions, tobacco smoking is not a simple progression of habit-forming behaviors. Smoking is best conceptualized as a complex phenomenon of physiological, social, and environmental stimuli (Bernstein, 1969; Hunt & Matarazzo, 1973) as well as mental constructs (Ferraro, 1973; Mausner, 1973) and affective states (Ikard & Tomkins, 1973; Tomkins, 1968). Consequently, treatment interventions are beginning to support and develop multicomponent strategies to accommodate the dimensional expansion of the tobacco smoking concept (Bernstein & McAlister, 1976). Before any certainty of intervention success can be achieved, each dimension must be assessed and compared in relation to the other dimensions of functioning.

The most difficult problem facing researchers of tobacco smoking outcome

TABLE 11.2. Rank-Order Recommendations for Dependent Measure Selection in Obesity Outcome Research

Measurement[a] Source	Measurement Device	Order of Preference	Measurement Dimension		
			Conation	Cognition	Affection
Body weight	Weight reduction index	1	✔		
	Body mass index	2	✔		
	Weight:height ratio	3	✔		
	Ponderal index	4	✔		
	Percent weight loss	5	✔		
	Absolute pounds lost[b]	6	✔		
Body fat	Skinfold caliper[c]	1	✔		
	(Lange)	(1)			
	(Harpenden)[d]	(2)			
	(Best)	(3)			
	Hydrostatic displacement[e]	2	✔		
Observations	Natural observations	1	✔		
	(Quasi-natural)	(1)			
	(Natural)	(2)			
	Analogue	2	✔		
	(Taste-rating task)	(1)			
	(Food machines)	(2)			
Energy expenditure	Self-report estimates	1	✔		
	Body Condition[f]	2	✔		
Self-report	Monitoring logs	1	✔	✔	✔
Cognitions	Construct grid[g]	1		✔	✔
	Dialogue recording	2		✔	
	Self-perception scales	3		✔	✔
	(Tennessee)	(1)			
	(IAV)	(2)			
	(Janis)	(3)			
	(Coopersmith)	(4)			
	(SES)	(5)			
Emotions	Depression rating scales[h]	1		✔	✔
	(Beck)	(1)			
	(MMPI-D)	(2)			
	(Zung)	(3)			
	(DACL)	(4)			
	Mood self-reports	2			✔
	(PMS)	(1)			
	(MACL)	(2)			
	(MAACL)	(3)			
	(EPI)	(4)			
General adjustment	SCL-90-R	1	✔	✔	✔
	MMPI	2	✔	✔	✔

[a]Devices should be selected so that a multidimensional overlap of measurement sources is achieved (e.g., body weight, body fat, energy expenditure, self-report, cognitions, affections, and general adjustment levels).
[b]This measure can be used as a general source of feedback to the subject.
[c]The four-site body determination illustrated by Durnin & Rahaman (1967) should be used.
[d]This caliper is manufactured in Great Britain.
[e]This is appropriate for precise measurements.
[f]Extensive research is needed in this area to establish its utility.
[g]Grids have the potential for measurement within both cognitive and affective dimensions.
[h]Since depression rating scales and mood self-reports are easy to administer, both should be given to subjects.

is the precise specification of target goals to ensure reliability of measurement across studies. Too often these loosely formulated goals prevent an accurate comparison of treatment success. Each researcher must ultimately confront and resolve certain issues that are poignantly related to the success or failure of the study: whether there is such a thing as a basic unit of measurement for smoking and whether it can be assessed directly or indirectly; what types of change can be deemed a success; who is responsible for setting the target goal; who is responsible for determining the outcome as a success or failure; and when the treatment outcome is considered a success. Hopefully, the following review will present directions so that the researcher can make a more informed decision on specifying and measuring target goals.

Measures of Tobacco Smoking, Conation Dimension: Tobacco Consumption Measures

A logical candidate for tobacco consumption measurement is the simple procedure of recording the number of cigarettes consumed per day. Indeed, the typical outcome study uses this calculation as the main device for consumption assessment. However, this measure is grossly misleading because it does not reflect the influence of important factors, such as the subject's style of smoking (number of puffs, amount inhaled, length of time inhaled, etc.), nicotine concentration levels (filter vs. nonfilter), and cigarette length (Frederiksen et al., 1977; McFall, 1978). To help control for some of these problems, Rapp et al. (1959) suggested a weight measurement of tobacco smoked. This procedure involves the preweighing of the cigarette and a postweighing of the discarded remnant. The difference can be readily calculated to provide a percentage measure of tobacco consumed. Although this method is more accurate than counting cigarettes, it falls short in accounting for the influence of the subject's style of smoking. As it stands, this strategy of measurement is suitable only as a general indication of tobacco consumption. It must be supplemented with other measurements.

A more precise measure, albeit indirect, is the assessment of chemical components and/or physiological metabolites of tobacco products. More specifically, four areas of measurement have shown promise as a biochemical index of tobacco consumption: carbon dioxide levels; nicotine–cotinine levels; thiocyanate levels; and carbon monoxide levels. Each receives an in-depth examination in this chapter.

The least accurate physiological measure is the level of carbon dioxide (CO_2) in the blood. Cahoon (1971) first proposed that chronic smokers have higher than normal CO_2 levels as a result of the irregular breathing patterns of smoking. In conjunction with these unusual breathing habits, cigarettes contain chemicals that increase the metabolation of carbon dioxide. Furthermore, CO_2 is maintained at higher levels in smokers because of its psychologically addicting qualities, such as the reduction of tension and anxiety. Thus blood samples of smokers usually possess inordinately high CO_2 levels; however, a high CO_2 level is not exclusive in a smoking population. This index can be influenced by environmental factors, physical activity, and other variables. Another problem with this method is the expense of the chemical analyzing equipment. Unless an experimental setting contains such sophisticated analyzers, the cost:benefit ratios of CO_2 measurement devices are prohibitive.

The ingestion of nicotine is another addicting quality of tobacco consumption. Because this stimulant is a major component of tobacco products and is less likely to be found in extraneous sources, it has the possibility of providing a reliable and valid index of tobacco consumption. Nicotine levels can be determined from two sources: the tobacco product and body concentration levels.

Estimates of tobacco smoking behavior can be readily accessible through the determination of nicotine level in tobacco products. By measuring the percentage of tobacco consumed, for example, and knowing the nicotine concentration levels of that cigarette (this information is provided for all consumers on the side of each pack of cigarettes in the United States), one can calculate a rough estimate of the nicotine consumption level; however, this measurement cannot account for the influence of the subject's smoking style. A more precise technique, and one that can account for certain aspects of the smoker's style, is the determination of a nicotine "mouth level exposure" from discarded cigarette butts. This procedure has been used in the successful delineation of a smoker's topography (Ague, 1972; Ashton & Watson, 1970; Forbes et al., 1976; Robinson & Young, 1980). Subjects are instructed to collect their cigarette butts in a plastic bag during a prescribed period of time. Each cigarette butt is dismantled to the filter wadding substance. Nicotine concentration levels in the wadding are determined by chemical analysis. Once this level is known, a mouth level exposure can be calculated from the following formula:

(known filter efficiency)

$$\text{Mouth level exposure} = \frac{1-e}{e} \times \text{(nicotine levels in cigarette butt)}$$
(known filter efficiency)

The drawbacks to this method are obvious: subject collection of cigarette butts may have a reactive effect on data; analysis equipment is expensive and complex; only filtered tobacco products can be used; and the validity of measurement has yet to be determined. More accurate estimates of nicotine consumption levels can be achieved through the measurement of chemical presence in the body.

Concentration levels of nicotine in the body can be assessed by either blood or urine analysis. Each method requires the use of sophisticated gas–liquid chromotography (GLC) equipment to assay levels of nicotine. However, the urinary analysis sampling procedure is a more convenient method for the experimenter and less painful for the subject. Some sources suggest that urinary nicotine detection has many more advantages than the more common method of assaying blood carbon monoxide levels discussed below (Paxton &

Bernacca, 1979; Russell & Feyerabend, 1975). The advantages to the urinary nicotine assay are that skin puncture is not required, specimens can be frozen and tested in groups, values in smokers and nonsmokers do not overlap a great deal, and reliable measures can be assayed up to 15 hours after tobacco consumption. Nonetheless, a serious drawback to this method involves the contamination of readings by extraneous tobacco smoke in a room. In fact, the presence of only one or two smokers in a room can produce significant levels of nicotine in the blood or urine (Russell & Feyerabend, 1975).

Zeidenberg et al. (1977) have proposed the measurement of the nicotine metabolite, cotinine, as an indirect measure of nicotine in the bloodstream. These researchers found that cotinine has a much longer half-life (30 hours) in the blood than does nicotine (30 minutes). Also, greater quantities of cotinine can be found in the blood. The assessment procedure requires a blood sample and a sensitive radioimmunoassay technique. Gas–liquid chromotography is the most widely used method (Langone et al., 1975). In the preparation of samples, blood is distilled and assayed. As with all blood sampling techniques, equipment is expensive, procedures are complicated, and subjects are required to experience skin puncture.

One of the most promising biochemical assays in differentiating levels of tobacco consumption is thiocyanate determination. Thiocyanate (SCN) is the end product of the body's chemical detoxification of cyanide compounds. Although the body contains normal levels of SCN to perform certain biological functions, elevated levels of this metabolite indicate an abnormal consumption of products that contain cyanide compounds, such as hydrogen cyanide gases in tobacco smoke. However, certain ingestive products (e.g., yams, broccoli, cabbage, turnips, horseradish, garlic, and some over-the-counter drugs) contain amounts of SCN that may contaminate results. Several studies have shown SCN determination to be an accurate method for differentiating smokers and nonsmokers (Butts et al., 1974; Dacre & Tabershaw, 1970; Densen et al., 1967; Dogon et al., 1971; Tenovuo & Makinen, 1976) and as a measure of cigarette consumption (Brockway, 1978; Butts et al., 1974; Tenovuo & Makinen, 1976).

In a recent review, Prue et al. (1980) comprehensively explored the various parameters of four potential sources of measuring SCN in the body: saliva, urine, blood, and sweat. These authors found saliva SCN sampling to be the most sensitive test source; moreover, this method is much easier to implement and evaluate. Of the methods currently available for determining SCN levels in saliva, the colorimetric assays are the most accurate and cost-efficient (Bark & Higson, 1963; Prue et al., 1980). Levinson and MacFate (1969) provide a detailed description of the necessary spectrophotometer procedures.

The final method of measuring tobacco consumption focuses on abnormal levels of carbon monoxide (CO) in the body: another negative by-product of tobacco smoke. Carbon monoxide can be detected by two methods: the amount of CO absorbed in the alveoli of the lungs (alveolar CO) and CO absorbed in the bloodstream (carboxyhemoglobin). Because of the inconvenience and expense of direct carboxyhemoglobin assessment, the alveolar CO breath sample has received greater research attention. Expired air CO values have shown a direct correlation with carboxyhemoglobin levels (Jones et al., 1958; Stewart & Stewart, 1975).

Obtaining a reliable sample of expired CO is a persistent problem with this method. Jones et al. (1958) found the end-expiratory alveolar sample procedure to be the most consistent. The breath is inhaled for 20 seconds and then exhaled, all from the resting state. A small portion of the exhaled breath is discarded; the remainder is blown into a polyvinyl bag. It is important to note that the use of any other type of collection bag increases the risk of sample contamination because of the possible presence of extraneous CO molecules (Horan et al., 1978; Ringold et al., 1962). Breath samples typically are estimated by a portable, nondispersive infrared analyzer. In determining the CO level in the breath sample, the polyvinyl bag is attached to the analyzer, where a metering pump extracts a measured flow of air. This air is passed over a sensor that oxidizes the sample into carbon dioxide. In this process, each molecule loses two electrons, producing a minute current flow that is amplified by the meter. The measurement is displayed on a meter in parts per million (ppm). Carbon monoxide analyzers are made by a number of companies in the United States; however, the Ecolyzer 2000 Series monitor (Energetics Science Inc., Elmsford, New York) has consistently demonstrated accurate estimates of carboxyhemoglobin levels (Blurton & Bay, 1974; Henningfield et al., 1980; Hughes et al., 1978; Stewart & Stewart, 1975; Stewart et al., 1976).

A recent review by Frederiksen and Martin (1979) proposes that carbon monoxide measurement is an essential device for determining the general risk of smoking as well as smoking behavior. Nevertheless, there are serious problems with this method that will require precise experimental control. Horan et al. (1978) specify a number of factors that may contribute to the contamination of CO measurements. First, ambient CO (e.g., smog) has the potential to affect both subject CO body level and the calibration of the machine. Indeed, even the congregation of a few smokers in relatively tight quarters can influence CO levels. Second, the individual's activity level can greatly bias measures of CO. Increased breathing rates will cause a corresponding decrease in CO levels. Third, CO monitoring has a short half-life (2 to 4 hours). As time progresses, CO sensitivity becomes less accurate, thus limiting its versatility as a measure (Pechacek, 1979). Fourth, arbitrary environmental restrictions can confound measurement results. For instance, subjects may not be allowed to smoke in particular areas or under certain circumstances during the day. To help overcome some of these problems, the above authors suggest the following: readings of ambient CO levels should be checked during the assessment periods; assessment periods should be conducted in the evening, hopefully when ambient CO levels have diminished from peak hours; and each assessment period should be held at the same time. It also has been recommended that experimenters screen for alcohol consumption (Hughes et al., 1978). Not only alcohol, but certain drugs can produce artificial elevations in the subject's CO level. Filters can be purchased from the manufacturer of the

Ecolyzer to screen for alcohol; furthermore, drugs can be screened (albeit with questionable accuracy) through subject interview.

One may deduce from the following review that a universal measure of tobacco consumption does not exist. In our estimation, this is true. As such, measures of tobacco consumption must be complementary to one another; that is, each must provide verification and clarification of other indices to help cover blind spots. For example, not only can physiological measures help support the amount of tobacco consumed, but also provide a verification of other measures, especially self-reports (Frederiksen & Martin, 1979; Henningfield et al., 1980; Lando, 1975; Prue et al., 1980). In the final recommendations (see Table 11.3), the selection of instruments will reflect this interdependence of measures.

Observations—Measures of Smoking Behavior

Although the laboratory analogue provides strict control from many influencing variables of tobacco abuse, one must settle for a certain lack of real life representation (McFall, 1978). However, the decision of whether to use the laboratory in lieu of a more realistic situation is dependent on the type of experimental focus. For example, a study designed to investigate particular components of smoking behavior is better suited for a tightly controlled environment. Conversely, if treatment effectiveness is the experimental question, a more real life circumstance is warranted.

Understanding the elements of smoking behavior has spawned a number of studies on the specification of smoking topography. By understanding the subject's specific smoking behavior, the experimenter can control for differences that affect level of consumption. Moreover, some sources suggest that smoking topography can be used as a dependent measure for subjects who cannot or will not quit smoking entirely (Frederiksen & Martin, 1979; Frederiksen et al., 1977). Within this type of treatment strategy, it is important to isolate those smoking behaviors that are deemed a potential health risk. Frederiksen et al. (1977) propose five types of smoking behavior that can be included as part of a multiple measurement approach: interpuff interval; cigarette duration; puff time length; puff frequency; and percentage of tobacco burned. An illustration of this measurement method is provided by Miller et al. (1979). These investigators used the above five topography measures, plus time of cigarette in the mouth, and time of cigarette in the hand, to examine the influence of social interaction in "light" and "heavy" smokers. It was found that more frequent and longer puffs were characteristic of light smokers when alone. Conversely, the total amount of smoke inhaled for light smokers was reduced in the social interaction condition. Heavy smokers were not influenced in either social condition.

Another frequently used analogue method is one that is modeled after Schachter et al.'s (1968) food taste test described in the previous section on obesity measures. A description of the smoking taste test is outlined by Levenberg and Wagner (1976). Subjects were told that they had been chosen to give opinions on several cigarette brands. To differentiate smoking topography, judges behind a one-way mirror rated such behaviors as number of puffs, the length of puffs, and interpuff intervals. In addition, cigarette remnants were weighed after the subjects left to accurately determine the amount of tobacco consumed per person. Briddell et al. (1979) have criticized the smoking taste test as a potentially nonobtrusive, nonreactive assessment device. Although this measurement strategy helps to isolate expectancy and attitudinal factors, there are certain validity problems that need to be resolved, such as the constricted nature of the laboratory and the lack of social interaction. Before one can depend on the smoking taste-test measurement with any degree of certainty, the resolution of these validity problems is essential (Briddell et al., 1979).

Although analogue methods lack generalizability to real-life circumstance, natural observation typically fails to maintain controls that would alleviate data contamination. As a consequence, researchers must be very creative in devising measures that are nonobtrusive. The most common naturalistic measure is the employment of trained judges to accurately observe target behaviors. As with all measures of individual judgment, a reliability index is a must to establish levels of agreement. Measures of observed behavior must be precisely defined and accurately measured in terms of time and/or frequency. A supplement to this observational data would be the measurement of the remaining smoking debris. For example, cigarette butts can be collected from an ashtray. This data can provide direct support for other observations.

McFall (1978) has specified a number of problems with the naturalistic observation method: (1) the monitoring of a subject's behavior without consent poses important legal and ethical questions; (2) smoking data will vary among subjects depending on the location that a subject will frequent (i.e., some environments will be more conducive for smoking behavior, e.g., a bar), and consequently group data will be difficult to compare; and (3) this type of study is difficult to conduct and rather expensive. Nevertheless, a naturalistic observation study, if carefully implemented, has the potential to provide a real-life data supplement on smoking behavior.

Self-Monitoring Reports

Self-report monitoring contains a wealth of information about the subject's smoking habits in a day-to-day existence. Although no other source can know more about a person than the subject in question, there are inherent problems with any self-report method. One of the major difficulties is the denial or distortion of data (McFall, 1978). Delarue (1973) found that 20% of the subjects who complete a smoking treatment program were guilty of inaccurate abstinence reports; a higher rate (48%) also has been noted (Ohlin et al., 1976). Measurement reactivity is another potential problem of self-reports. McFall (1970) compared the self-recorded data of two groups: one recorded the number of cigarettes smoked; the other recorded frequencies of resisted temptation. The results indicate that consumption rates and smoking frequency was significantly influenced by self-monitoring. From these data it was concluded that self-reports are reactive to what the subject is asked to monitor; however, the results of this study have been criticized on the grounds that certain demand characteristics limited the generalizability of findings (Orne, 1970).

There is general consensus that if a self-monitoring record is used, other measuring devices must be employed as a verification source (Briddell et al., 1979; McFall & Hammen, 1971), e.g., physiological assessment or collaborative reports.

Studies by Marston and McFall (1971) and McFall and Hammen (1971) have used a convenient self-monitoring method to gather mean daily smoking rates in the natural environment. Each subject maintained a 2 × 3-inch booklet that could be carried in the cellophane wrapper of their cigarette packages. The data sheets contained spaces for name and date, including 24 blank squares to represent the hours in a day. With this record blank, subjects can record the number of cigarettes smoked per hour. In the McFall and Hammen study, subjects were instructed to purchase all cigarettes from the smoking clinic, thus providing partial independent verification of self-reported smoking consumption.

The recording booklets in these studies supply only a small portion of potential subject data. For example, self-recorded data also can include time of day cigarette smoked, time taken to consume the cigarette, social situation (alone or in a group), environment (home, office, etc.), and mood. Although a log of this scope contains very important data, convenience and time are sacrificed. Furthermore, the chances of inaccurate recording become greater when a cumbersome amount of information is demanded of the subject. Nevertheless, a monetary contract system, where subjects are paid money from a deposit, can greatly improve accuracy by making payoffs contingent on properly filled-in reports (although this procedure may also cause subjects to distort data).

Research has focused attention recently on the use of a self-report, indirect measure of the tobacco smoking habit. Schachter (1977) proposed that the assessment of nicotine addiction is an important component in outcome treatment effectiveness. In response to Schachter's study, Fagerstrom (1978) composed a face validity questionnaire to assess the degree of nicotine dependence. These questions were compared to the following withdrawal responses: body temperature change; increase in a regular smoker's heart rate while smoking a cigarette; and increase in an ex-smoker's heart rate while smoking a cigarette. Modest correlations were found between the questions and withdrawal responses. Albeit superficial, Fagerstrom's questionnaire has definite possibilities as a self-report measurement of nicotine addiction. For example, this device would have less contaminating influence on treatment gains. A subject of long-term cigarette abstinence may be tempted to return to the habit if given a cigarette on follow-up to assess addiction levels. Further research is needed, however, to expand related questions and to establish validity in this type of measurement device. One problem to overcome is the clarification of the addiction concept. Not all smokers, even heavy smokers, are physically addicted to nicotine (Schachter, 1977). Of course, other psychological or social factors can maintain the smoking habit as well.

Informant Reports

The use of relatives and friends as observers can provide a valuable supplement to the subject's self-monitoring data. These people have direct access to the subject's undisturbed behavior in the natural setting. Unless collaborators are trained to make precise observations, however, this type of data only provides general information. To illustrate, Lichtenstein et al. (1973) used informants who *verified* smoking behavior of friends or relatives on follow-up to smoking treatment. This measurement strategy helped to validate self-reported estimates. Collaborator reports can never be relied on as a major source of data in assessing smoking behavior until more is known about their reliability. Observer bias and reactive effects can seriously influence the data (McFall, 1978).

COMMENTS

The selection of dependent measures for tobacco smoking outcome research will require a similar overlap of measures as described in the previous section on obesity assessment. This overlap of measures is a necessity because each focus of measurement has weak points that must be covered by other devices. In terms of expense, physiological measures of tobacco consumption have limited application unless analytic equipment is available or funds have been allocated for their purchase. Nevertheless, this thrust of measurement is an important adjunct to the overall measurement of tobacco consumption and should be included as a matter of course.

On the basis of the previous review, dependent measures for the conation dimension have been rank ordered in Table 11.3.

MEASURES OF THE COGNITION DIMENSION: OBESITY AND TO-BACCO SMOKING

From our review of the literature, it is interesting to note the overwhelming imbalance between measures of the conation and cognition dimensions in habit disorder research. Cognitive measurement strategies are virtually nonexistent in these areas, despite the general acceptance of a cognitive influence operating in disorders of this type (Freedman et al., 1975). This imbalance is still further indication of the strong unidimensional influence present in behavior change research with these disorders.

TABLE 11.3. Rank-Order Recommendations for Dependent Measure Selection in Tobacco Outcome Research

Measurement[a] Source	Measurement Device	Order of Preference	Measurement Dimension		
			Conation	Cognition	Affection
Tobacco consumption	Percent tobacco consumed	1	✔		
	Number of products consumed	2	✔		
Biochemical analysis	Thiocyanate	1	✔		
	Carbon monoxide[b]	2	✔		
	Nicotine–cotinine	3	✔		
	Carbon dioxide	4	✔		
	MLE tobacco assay	5	✔		
Observations	Natural observations	1	✔		
	Analogue	2	✔		
	(topography)	(1)			
	(taste test)	(2)			
Self-report	Monitoring logs	1	✔	✔	✔
	Addiction measurement	2	✔	✔	✔
Informant reports		1	✔		
Cognitions	Construct grid	1		✔	✔
	Dialogue recording	2		✔	
	Self-perception scales	3		✔	✔
	(Tennessee)	(1)			
	(IAV)	(2)			
	(Janis)	(3)			
	(Coopersmith)	(4)			
	(SES)	(5)			
Emotions	Depression rating scales[c]	1		✔	✔
	(Beck)	(1)			
	(MMPI-D)	(2)			
	(Zung)	(3)			
	(DACL)	(4)			
	Mood self-reports	2			✔
	(PMS)	(1)			
	(MACL)	(2)			
	(MAACL)	(3)			
	(EPI)	(4)			
General adjustment	SCL-90-R	1	✔	✔	✔
	MMPI	2	✔	✔	✔

[a]Devices should be selected so that a multidimensional overlap of measurement sources is achieved (e.g., tobacco consumption, biochemical analysis, self-reports, informant reports, cognitions emotions, and general adjustment levels).
[b]The Ecolyzer 2000 Series monitor and polyvinyl collection bags should be used.
[c]Since depression rating scales and mood self-reports are easy to administer, both should be given to subjects.

Without a precedence set for cognitive measurement of obesity and tobacco smoking research, this section explores the current methods of cognitive assessment and relates them to the potential measurement of cognitive change in these treatment areas. Three general topics are considered: mental dialogue measures; mental construct measures; and measures of self-perception.

Mental Dialogue Measures

One potentially rich source of cognitive data lies within the continuous stream of thoughts ever present in the conscious person. The basic assumptions behind this source of measurement are: (1) all people have distinguishable thoughts; (2) there are distinct differences in what and how people think; (3) there is a direct or indirect link between thoughts and actions; and (4) there is a qualitative difference in thoughts between those who are most adaptive and those who are least adaptive. It is these assumptions that are the cornerstone to the new strategies emerging in cognitive treatment. One area of particular note is the use of internal dialogue to acquire new skills or remove maladaptive ones such as thought stopping (Wolpe, 1958, 1969), self-instructional training (Meichenbaum, 1977), and stress-inoculation (Meichenbaum, 1975, 1977). Even though these treatment procedures have demonstrated success with a variety of problems (Meichenbaum, 1977; Meichenbaum & Cameron, 1973; Novaco, 1976; Turk, 1978; Wish, 1975), there has been little attempt to customize cognitive measurement to aid in the confirmation of these results. However, Genest and Turk (1981) have recently initiated the difficult task of differentiating the possible sources of measurement for subvocal dialogue, or what they refer to as "think aloud." Although several internal dialogue measures are considered in their chapter, we believe that the continuous monologue techniques (private speech) have good measurement potential in obesity and tobacco smoking research.

The basic continuous monologue strategy is a very straightforward procedure. While the subject is involved in the performance of a prearranged activity, the experimenter invites that subject to verbalize all mental content as it becomes conscious. Once the subject is alone, engaging in the prescribed activity, the free-flow of speech is assumed to reflect the individual's "private speech," or those sequences of events available only to the subject. It is important that the monologue be recorded as unobtrusively as possible; thus, a concealed audio or video recording instrument would be the instrument of choice, although certain ethical problems must be considered.

Because of the overwhelming abundance of verbal material produced in even a short period of time, the experimenter has a formidable task of analyzing the data. Genest and Turk have proposed three possible methods to do so: formulate overall indices through the global ratings of the monologue by judges; select blocked time segments whereby judges can rate dimensions of experimental interest; and select segments based on a naturally occurring unit, such as sentence structure, changes in content, pauses, content change, or ideational change. However, none of these analytic procedures are devoid of problems. For instance, global ratings are more prone to distortion effects (demand characteristics) than are ratings of smaller unit segments. Moreover, the reliability and validity of global ratings are reduced substantially unless precise specification of targets can be attained. With blocked time segment analysis, important data are lost in the artificial selection of time periods, such as the overall thought sequence. The third method of analysis is a very complex rating procedure, using "natural" units that rely on paralinguistic cues (pauses, tone, speed, etc.) that are difficult to reliably rate. Whereas each analysis method has positive and negative features, the ultimate selection of analytic procedure is dependent on what the experimenter is interested in knowing.

Although cognitive dialogue measures have not been used in habit disorder research as yet, a direct application can be made to both obesity and tobacco smoking disorders. For example, an obesity researcher may be interested in the changes of private speech over the course of a subject's treatment. Recording pre- and posttest measurements during an actual meal, the subject is instructed to think about the foods eaten and verbalize these thoughts as they occur. Once recorded and transcribed, judges can select time segments and rate the subject on predetermined dimensions such as positive or negative self-statements, time devoted to food dialogue, and statements reflecting self-control or impulse. A similar procedure can be used with the tobacco smoking subjects. The researcher may be interested in the progression of thoughts over the entire sequence of smoking behavior. Therefore, samples of thoughts can be taken from three distinct periods (1) preparations to smoke; (2) smoking; and (3) termination of tobacco product. The dialogue can be rated from similar dimensional terms of experimental interest such as cigarette-related content.

As with any new measurement strategy, further research is needed to expand and refine its assessment potential. Nevertheless, this device suffers from the inherent deficiencies of all self-report devices: distortion of data; omission of data; and reactive effects. Moreover, Genest and Turk specify that the continuous monologue verbalization techniques also can be influenced by (1) a subject's inability to verbalize a thought, (2) the artificiality of the imposed task, (3) subject self-consciousness, and (4) subject selection bias. (Simultaneously occurring thoughts are under the selecting discretion of the thinker.) An overlearned, trite, or easily defined thought has a greater chance of being verbalized than those more related to experimental interests). With these limitations, the continuous monologue technique is not an independent measurement source; rather, it is a possible adjunct to other cognitive measures to help clarify the totality of change within cognitive processes.

Mental Construct Measures

Along with the myriad of external changes occurring from therapeutic intervention, there are corresponding changes in the way a person will perceive, organize, integrate, understand, and predict his or her world. Old beliefs or constructs, such as "I am a popular person when I am fat and jolly," "I am more confident when I have a cigarette in my hand," or "I have the right or need to indulge myself," can be influenced by events that invalidate the maintenance of these constructs, therefore necessitating a change in the way these events are anticipated. As such, it is of great research importance to systematically observe changes in the way subjects will construe themselves in relation to their changing perceptions of food, cigarettes, tension, depression, people, body image, and life in general.

Mental construct theory is largely attributed to the prolific work of George Kelly and his students at Ohio State University. In this theory, Kelly rejected the notion that humans are passive recipients of incoming data. Rather, humans are much like scientists, who make observations, form predictions, and test hypotheses. By using these helpful capacities, humans can formulate constructs that remove contradictions and confusion and restore regularity to life. Constructs are the controls of order. They lock the individual into a fixed action course. If individuals have the ability to continually incorporate new elements into their own construct systems, the capacity to anticipate the replication of events is enhanced. However, psychological difficulty begins to surface when the person repeatedly uses constructions that are consistently invalidated. Erroneously, individuals believe that problems stem from the elements of life rather than their construction of them, for example, "The comfort I feel when I am full of food is as satisfactory as feeling loved."

Constructs are not isolated entities; rather, they form a system wherein each is related on various levels to form a complex hierarchy. Each successive level of this hierarchy becomes more cognitively abstract than the previous one; for instance, the lower-order construct of "unselfishness" can be incorporated or subsumed under the more abstract construct of "loyalty." Kelly believed that all construct systems are composed of a finite number of dichotomous beliefs, for this is the basis of determining all elements as similar or different; thus constructs acquire meaning when two elements are viewed as similar when contrasted to a third. This construct proposition is the very essence of Kelly's methodological procedure for measuring construct systems. A more detailed understanding of Kellian theory can be found in a two-volume book entitled *The Psychology of Personal Constructs* (Kelly, 1955).

The Role Construct Repertory Test (REP Test) is a device that systematically examines an individual's construct system through the use of a matrix technique. The most outstanding feature of the REP Test is its versatility in design and application (Easterby-Smith, 1980). Although the REP Test was originally designed and applied in individual therapy situations, matrix grids have been modified and applied to other settings such as business management, education, and communications (Collett, 1979; Edwards, 1980; Shaw & Thomas, 1978; Slater, 1980).

Even though most repertory grids are rather formidable looking, these devices are easily understood when broken down into basic components:

elements (located on the matrix columns); constructs (located on the matrix rows); and a system connection (located in the squares that comprise the grid). Figure 11.2 is an example of a 10 × 10 basic grid.

The elements of a grid are defined as those entities that represent the parameters of the material sought after, such as roles, statements, and concepts. The number of eliciting elements is only as limited as the creativity of the grid designer. However, Easterby-Smith (1980) has suggested two important rules that govern the selection of elements: (1) all elements must be homogeneous; that is, categories of elements should not be mixed; and (2) the elements should represent all facets of the investigative area; both good and bad qualities should be evenly represented to reduce the possibility of a biased grid. As to the number of elements in a grid, no set number is mandatory. Whereas one source indicates that an eight-element, eight-construct grid is the minimum size for statistical evaluation purposes (Collett, 1979), others suggest that grids can provide high-quality data with a 40-element, 40-construct grid (Bennion, 1981; Edwards & Johnson, 1981).

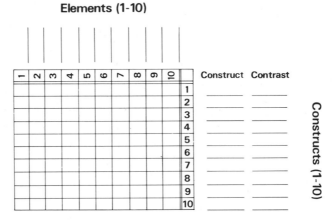

Figure 11.2.   A basic 10 × 10 repertory grid.

The constructs of the grid are defined as the stylized way the subject discriminates and groups elements to form a belief. In the typical process of eliciting constructs, the subject is requested to attach a cognitive label to the generated belief. This is accomplished by using Kelly's triad elicitation of meaning: compare the similarity of two elements as contrasted to a third. One drawback to this approach involves the time length in establishing constructs. Some people have difficulty in communicating a construct, often preferring to settle for a superficial or stereotyped one, for example, construct: "man"; contrast: "woman." One strategy to overcome this problem is for the experimenter to *supply* the constructs or evenly split them between elicited and supplied ones (Easterby-Smith, 1980). The experimenter must take great pains, however, to ensure that the supplied constructs are representative of the experimental parameters.

The system connection component is defined as a strategy used to show how elements and constructs are connected. There are three procedures for achieving this purpose: dichotomizing; ranking; and rating. In the *dichotomizing method*, three elements are selected whereby two elements are determined by the subject as similar as contrasted with the third. Once the construct and contrast have been communicated, all other elements are categorically split into being more like the construct or more like the contrast. Traditionally, circles are made in the grid squares to specify the three comparison elements; Xs through two of the circles designate similarity, whereas a blank circle indicates a contrasting pole. Check marks are used to specify all other elements that are more similar to the construct; blanks denote contrast similarity. This type of system connection was first proposed by Kelly (1955) and is most widely used in therapy. The *ranking method* involves the rank ordering of elements as they pertain to each construct; thus, for example, a lower number indicates similarity to the construct whereas a higher number indicates similarity to the contrast. The *rating method* is the most popular of all the system connection techniques. Shaw (1980) points out that about 70% of all grid studies use a rating method. A rating grid is derived by specifying a set number in a rating scale with the assumption that each number has equal gradation between the construct and contrast poles. Slater (1980) is an excellent example of a study that utilizes a rating system. In this experiment, statements by pro-IRA (Irish Republican Army) factions were compared with the statements by anti-IRA advocates. Statements (elements) were compared and rated on a scale where +3 indicated that the statements meant exactly the same and −3 indicated that the statements were exactly opposite. Intervening numbers in this range signified graded level of agreement or disagreement. Through this manner of analysis, data can be supplied to both factions that helps them to better negotiate their position.

Once the grid has been completed, the matrix is now ready for statistical analysis. Originally, Kelly and his students spent many arduous hours scoring the grid by hand. With the advent of sophisticated computer procedures, however, computer analysis of the grid provides more information, greater accuracy, and cost-efficiency; several grid analysis programs are now available, including ARGUS (Shaw & McKnight, 1980), CORE (Shaw, 1979), DXTX (TM) (Edwards & Johnson, 1981), DYAD (Keen & Bell, 1980), FOCUS and PEGASUS (Shaw & Thomas,1978), and INGRID (Slater, 1977). There are two types of statistical analysis used by the computer to extract information from the grids: *principal components* (Slater, 1977), and *cluster analysis* (Atkins, 1974). Each presents a unique and useful way of reviewing data. The principal component analysis delineates the greatest variations within the grid and plots these variations on imposed mathematical axes. In a cluster analysis, high correlations within the grid are grouped together to form hierarchial trees. Although the computer analysis selection depends on the type of information desired, it is our opinion that the cluster analysis closely approximates Kelly's original view of hierarchial construct systems. An in-depth discussion of these measurement systems can be found in Easterby-Smith (1980). For those investigators who desire a cluster analysis computer scoring of any grid type, or who desire consultation on the construction of grids, a service is now available for these purposes (TRI Community Service Systems, 5402 Ruffin Road, Suite 100, San Diego, California 92123).

Traditional methods for establishing reliability and validity for the repertory grid have not been especially helpful. Reliability is most difficult to determine because of the very nature of constructs; that is, constructs are subject to change or replacement when they are consistently invalidated. Nevertheless, some constructs (core constructs) are highly resistant to change and thus relatively consistent over time. Fjeld and Landfield (1961) conducted a test–retest study of repertory grids over a two-week period. Reliability correlations were found within the .7 to .8 range. From these data, these authors suggest that REP grids remain relatively consistent because people use the same axes of meaning, even though the objects of these conceptual axes may change. Using a modified form of the REP Test to measure cognitive complexity (Bieri et al., 1966), Schneier (1979) conducted an investigation of the reliability and convergent– discriminant validities of this grid. The test–retest reliability results yielded a correlation coefficient of .82. When the grid was compared with other measurement devices of cognitive complexity and used to discriminate cognitively complex individuals, the results showed significant support ($p < .05$) for the grid as a valid measure. Among the limited studies conducted to investigate the REP Test grid as a measurement device, there is tentative support for its reliability and validity.

The versatility of the REP Test grid suggests that it may have useful application in the measurement of outcome change in obesity treatment and cigarette smoking. Subjects can be given several different types of grid to investigate important construct changes over the course of treatment. For example, to understand construct changes in obesity treatment, a grid can be designed to investigate the relationships of perceived roles to life constructs. The elements could contain such roles as self, mother, father, ideal self (the ideal self can be one person or a conglomerate of positive attributes from others), someone (known to the subject) who is ideally trim, someone who is quite obese, someone who is impulsive, someone respected, someone who is self-assured, someone who appears to have complete control over his or her life, and so on. The subject will mark the names of these people in each of the lines provided for elements (see Figure 11.2). As for constructs, the subject can generate these by the dichotomizing method or the experimenter can supply important constructs related to obesity (success, happiness, satisfaction, critical, etc.). Constructs are listed on the lines provided (see Figure 11.2). Subjects then place a check mark under the roles they feel are most closely associated to that construct. Each successive construct is connected to the elements in a like manner.

In cigarette smoking research, another example of grid construction is the rating of smoking-related statements as they pertain to a specific goal, such as the elimination or reduction of tobacco consumption. The elements would contain an even split of both positive and negative statements about the smoking habit, such as "smoking is relaxing for me," "smoking may give me lung cancer," "I look sophisticated with a cigarette in my hand," or "I'm going broke due to the price of cigarettes." Constructs can be generated by the subject or provided by the examiner as illustrated in the obesity example. A seven-point scale $(-3, -2, -1, 0, 1, 2, 3)$ can be supplied to rate the level at which an element and construct reflects (3) or does not reflect (-3) the reduction or elimination of tobacco consumption. A pre- and posttest measurement could provide a cognitive sketch as to how the subject's statements or perceptions have changed.

The number and type of grids are limited only by the scope of the investigation and the confines of the experiment. However, we do not wish to give the impression that the REP Test grid is a problem measurement device; this is not the case. Further research is needed to firmly establish its utility in cognitive assessment and outcome research. Another limitation of this device is its overwhelming adherence to a single theory of personality. A rejection of the basic postulate and correlates of Kellian theory may render this procedure only minimally useful.

Measures of Self-Perception

Past outcome treatment studies have demonstrated that obesity and tobacco smoking habit disorders are highly resistant to current treatment techniques, instilling feelings of frustration in the treatment planner, and especially in the troubled person. In many cases the habit disorder person feels helpless, unable to control or understand emotions, thoughts, and behaviors. Actions, such as "the midnight binge from the refrigerator" or the "desperate smoke in the bathroom," leave people feeling confused, ashamed, and lacking confidence. A lifetime of these typical scenarios can greatly affect one's self-perception and whether this perception is positive. Negative self-perception has been especially problematic in obesity research where changes in body image do not always reflect a corresponding change in self-esteem (Berblinger, 1969; Stunkard, 1976; Stunkard & Mendleson, 1967). Unless the treatment planner is aware of the subject's self-perceptions, there is the risk of possible relapse due to factors such as a self-defeat expectancy. These possibilities suggest the need for accurate measures of self-perception.

Measures of self-perception are usually described within three popular terms: self-concept; self-esteem; and self-acceptance. Although these terms are often used interchangeably, subtle differences do exist in measurement definitions (Crandall, 1973). Self-esteem is typically defined as a personal evaluation of oneself that reflects approval or disapproval (Coopersmith, 1967). "Self-acceptance" usually means the ability to accept oneself (Crandall,

1973). "Self-concept" is a term that generally describes many cognitive elements related to self-perception. It is this general overlap in terms that contributes to the confusion surrounding the utility of self-perception devices. Validity studies have provided ambiguous and often conflicting results. Nevertheless, Crandall (1973) has compiled a thorough review of 30 measurements that fall within a self-perception classification. After considering the available data on test construction factors (e.g., sample size, available data on test construction factors, reliability, and validity), Crandall rank ordered these devices in terms of overall quality. It is beyond the scope of this section to present all these measures. Therefore, five self-perception devices are selected on the basis of high quality and are briefly described below.

The *Tennessee Self-Concept Scale* (Fitts, 1964) is a 90-item, self-report questionnaire that provides a global self-esteem score and a complex self-concept profile. The test items reflect five general self-perception categories: physical self; moral–ethical self; personal self; family self; and social self. Responses to the test statements are selected from a five-point scale; (5) are completely true and (1) is completely false. Its *advantages* are: (1) it uses global and individual subtest scores; (2) lie controls are provided; (3) reliability is good (r_s = .7 to .9); (4) validity is fair to good (r_s = .61 to .70); (5) it is commercially available (Counselor Recordings and Tests, Nashville, Tennesse); and (6) it can be computer scored. Its *disadvantages* are: (1) there is no control for social desirability; (2) there is nonindependence of subscores; and (3) it is not specific to perceptions of self-control.

The revised *Janis-Field Feelings of Inadequacy Scale* (Eagly, 1967) is a 20-question test aimed at direct inquiry of positive and negative self-perception feelings. The subject responds by selecting one answer on a five-point, Likert-type scale, such as very often—practically never. The majority of test questions are oriented toward self-esteem in social situations. Its *advantages* are: (1) it is easy to administer; and (2) it has good reliability (r_s = .72 to .88). Its *disadvantages* are: (1) it lacks a systematic scoring system; (2) it has conflicting validity (r_s = .35 to .84); (3) it lacks social desirability and lie controls; and (4) it is commercially unavailable.

The Coopersmith (1967) *Self-Esteem Inventory* contains 46 declarative sentences wherein the subject responds with either "like me" or "unlike me." Although this test was originally formulated for children, Coopersmith has produced an adult version. Self-derogation, leadership–popularity, family–parents, and assertiveness–anxiety have been identified as the four main factors of this test. Its *advantages* are: (1) it is easy to administer; (2) it has the potential to measure subcomponents of self-esteem (e.g., family and social); and (3) it has good reliability (r_s = .90). Its *disadvantages* are: (1) it has fair validity (r_s = .60); (2) it has no systematic scoring system; (3) it lacks social desirability and lie controls; (4) it lacks an adequate normative sample; and (4) it is commercially unavailable.

Rosenberg's (1965) *Self-Esteem Scale* is a 10-declarative statement questionnaire designed to measure self-acceptance. The subject responds by selecting from a four-point scale that ranges from strongly agree to strongly disagree. The 10 test statements are all directed at liking or admitting approval of the self. Its *advantages* are: (1) it is very brief; (2) it is easy to administer; (3) it has good reliability ($r = .85$); and (4) it has a large normative sample. Its *disadvantages* are: (1) it is unidimensional (measures only self-acceptance); (2) it has conflicting validity ($r_s = .56$ to $.83$); (3) it has no social desirability or lie controls; and (4) it is commercially unavailable.

The *Index of Adjustment and Values* (Bills et al., 1951) provides a twofold measurement: acceptance of self and self-ideal discrepancy. The subject is presented with 49 adjectives and is asked to rate these words along three dimensions: (a) "I am a(n)————person." (b) "How do you accept yourself as described by the first rating?" (c) "I would like to be a(n)————person." The subject rates how descriptive each sentence is from a five-point Likert scale; (5) very much to (1) very little. Its *advantages* are: (1) it has good to excellent reliability ($r_s = .88$ to $.91$); and (2) it provides comparisons between self and ideal self. Its *disadvantages* are: (1) it has fair validity ($r_s = .47$ to $.60$); (2) it is somewhat lengthy; (3) it can be a complex task for some subjects; and (4) the majority of adjectives are positive, therefore suggesting possible bias.

From the previous descriptions of the higher-quality self-perception devices, many unresolved problems limit their usefulness as an outcome measure. Nevertheless, they still can provide *general* indications of self-perception changes. All other problems aside, self-perception measures are rather simple, easily administered measurements—all desirable qualities in a multidimensional approach to assessment. Clearly, a more specific measure of self-perception related to impulse (self) control is badly needed.

COMMENTS

Many problems remain to be solved before cognitive measurement becomes an integral part of habit disorder assessment. Ultimately, measurement devices must be formulated around the specific parameters of each disorder. This project will require an in-depth investigation of cognitions that are characteristic of the disorder, the influence of cognitions in the maintenance of the disorder, and the interactive influences of cognitions with behaviors and emotions.

On the basis of the previous review, dependent measures for the cognition dimension have been rank ordered in Tables 11.2 and 11.3.

MEASURES OF THE AFFECTION DIMENSION: OBESITY AND TOBACCO SMOKING

The role of emotions in the overall assessment of human functioning has not been entirely clear. Some researchers suggest that emotions are the central motivating force in human existence, permeating the characteristics of thoughts and behaviors (Messick, 1965; Tomkins, 1962). According to this assumption, change cannot occur then until relevant affect is altered (Tomkins, 1962). Indeed, affect is an important dimension in the overall context of human function; nevertheless, we are not certain whether any dimensions of the tripartite model exert precedence over others. As a tentative observation, it appears that each dimension is intricately woven into a complex totality, exerting complimentary and antagonistic forces in a manner that is not as yet fully understood. Thus it is important to remember that the tripartite model is an artificial dissection of a "whole process" for the purpose of understanding change on a more concrete level, hopefully to provide a useful construct in the treatment and evaluation of habit or other disorders.

Research has identified several emotions characteristic of obesity or tobacco smoking and several common to both. In obesity research, Stunkard (1957) has investigated the manifestations of "dieting depression" during treatment and at follow-up. Several of his subjects experienced short periods of intense anxiety that progressed into prolonged periods of depression. Stunkard concluded that dieting subjects may be vulnerable to emotional upheaval as the result of a significant life change. Thus it appears that the actual processes of dieting and related issues can facilitate negative feelings, most noticeably of a depressive nature (Stunkard & Rush, 1974). Another fruitful area of investigation has been the specification of emotional response to food deprivation. Glucksman and Hirsch (1968) noted that food-deprived subjects manifest a variety of unpleasant responses such as preoccupation with food, decreased sexual drive, irritability, anxiety, and affective lability. With these results in mind, Glucksman et al. (1968) compared the emotional responses of people on a dieting program who were experiencing a similar form of food deprivation. Many of the same symptoms were present: anxiety; fantasies of food or eating; depression; diet breaking; sexual problems; and overestimation of body size. These results suggest that a variety of negative emotions as well as unrealistic cognitions are a natural consequence to this major change in life-style and thus should be carefully monitored to reduce the risk of relapse.

Similar signs of unpleasant emotional reaction have been noticed in tobacco smoking research. For example, brief periods of abstinence in people have evoked signs of anxiousness, inability to concentrate, tension, irritability, mild depression, and general feelings of being out of control (Clark, 1977; Social Research, Inc., 1952). In addition, symptoms become more pronounced with greater degrees of prior tobacco consumption. Thomas (1973) found that heavy smokers experience higher levels of depression and tiredness than do light smokers or nonsmokers. With increased levels of these negative emotions present, researchers have noticed a corresponding boost in levels of tobacco consumption or, in many cases, a "falling off the wagon" (Heimstra, 1973; Thomas, 1973).

This section of the chapter explores the various experimental avenues available for the measurement of the affective dimension. Special emphasis is placed on the assessment devices of depression, moods, and global indicators of psychological adjustment, although many of these measures overlap to some degree.

Measures of Depression

Since a number of depressive symptoms have been found among obese and tobacco smoking patients, some type of depression assessment might be included in the measurement package. Lewinsohn and Lee (1981) have identified several assessment orientations to accomplish this goal, such as behavioral observations, self-report depression scales, and rating of symptoms. In consideration of convenience, time, and expense, the authors evaluated four self-report depression scales: the *Beck Depression Inventory* (Center for Cognitive Therapy, Philadelphia, Pennsylvania); the *Depression Adjective Checklist* (EdITS/Educational and Industrial Testing Service, San Diego, California); the *MMPI-Depression Scale* (The Psychological Corporation, New York, New York); and the *Zung Self-Depression Scale* (Merrell-National Laboratories, Cincinnati, Ohio). A further elaboration of these measures is not warranted in this section because of the in-depth coverage of these devices in a chapter of this volume (Moran & Lambert, in press).

Measures of Mood

For the most part, references to mood in everyday conversation are usually of two types: transient emotions that are dependent on current circumstances and emotions that are a pervasive and permanent coloration of the individual's personality. This state–trait bifurcation of moods has presented certain difficulties in the development of emotional measures, such as which criteria differentiates an emotional state from an emotional trait. Those researchers who adhere to a state–trait concept of moods have largely failed to clearly specify the parameters of each. Nowlis (1965, p. 353) has attempted to define the process of moods, choosing to reduce the significance of a bifurcated assumption:

> Mood is the effect on a person of his own configuration of activity. These configurations may be conceptualized as fundamental patterns of general functioning and orientation, such as level of activation, level of control, level of concentration, direction of social orientation, and positive (pleasant) or negative (unpleasant) general appraisal. The effect of these general patterns on the person may be mediated by cues associated with them in the life history and involves affective, cognitive, motivational, and motor responses to the cues; such responses may in turn become functionally related to the general patterns, and may modify, maintain, or even instigate them.

Nowlis regards the concept of mood as rather multidimensional in nature, reflecting not only general circumstances, but the functional dimensionality of the past as well. Therefore, an ideal measure of mood must be broad enough to provide a representation of the emotions brought forth by the major variables affecting the person, without regard to state–trait assumption. Several attempts have been initiated to systematically develop global measures of mood, and with some success. However, an assessment procedure of this type is not the most desirable measure of obesity or tobacco smoking research. The ideal mood measure is one that is tailor-made for the specific parameters of emotion identified in these disorders. Unfortunately, much research is needed to further delineate problematic emotions within the disorder as well as the emotional and psychological characteristics of a general life-style that indirectly contributes to the overall problem.

Although some negative emotions have been identified in the obesity and tobacco smoking disorders, the total picture is still rather vague and sketchy. Nevertheless, the following evaluations attempt to describe and evaluate the best available measures of mood as they pertain to the specified emotional problems of these habit disorders.

The *Multiple Affect Adjective Checklist* (Zuckerman, 1960) is composed of 132 adjectives that describe a variety of feeling states. Two forms, "In general," and "Today," provide a state and trait measurement along three affective dimensions: anxiety; depression; and hostility. The subject reads each of the 132 adjectives and places an "X" by the word that describes his or her feeling state of the day (Today form) or how she or he feels generally (General form). The *advantages* of this measure are: (1) it is an uncomplicated assessment task; (2) it is commercially available (EdITS/Educational and Industrial Testing Service, San Diego, California); (3) it has fair reliability ($r = .72$); and (4) it has conflicting validity results (fair for anxiety scores, $r_s = .33$ to $.67$). Its *disadvantages* are: (1) it is subject to response sets; (2) it has a small normative sample; (3) the concurrent validity of hostility and depression scales is poor; (4) it makes a state–trait assumption about moods.

The *Emotions Profile Index* (Kellerman & Plutchik, 1968) is based on the assumptions that (1) personality traits are a mixture of primary emotions, (2) emotions are dialectrical in nature, and (3) that eight scales accurately represent the relationships of emotions to traits. The eight scales are reproduction, incorporation, orientation, protection, deprivation, rejection, exploration, and destruction. The respondent is instructed to select one element of a trait pair from 12 trait names. Results are plotted on a circular grid. The *advantages* of this index are: (1) it is an uncomplicated assessment task; (2) it is relatively brief; (3) it has forced-choice answers to reduce response bias; (4) its reliability is fair ($r = .78$); and (4) it is commercially available (Western Psychological Services, Los Angeles, California). Its *disadvantages* are: (1) it lacks validity data; (2) it has no data reported on scale intercorrelations; (3) its philosophical assumptions are fairly weak; (4) it lacks a systematic rationale for normative sample selection; and (5) it makes a state–trait assumption about moods.

The *Profile of Mood States* (McNair et al., 1971) consists of 65, five-point adjective rating scales that have been factor analyzed into six mood scores:

tension–anxiety; depression–dejection; anger–hostility; vigor–activity; fatigue–inertia; and confusion–bewilderment. Respondents are to choose the rating that best reflects their emotional state. The *advantages* of this scale are: (1) it is an uncomplicated assessment task; (2) it is relatively brief; (3) computer scoring is available; (4) it is commercially available (EdITS/Educational and Industrial Testing Service, San Diego, California); (5) its reliability is fair ($r = .74$); (6) it has a large and varied normative sample; and (7) it has been used as an outcome measure in psychiatric populations. Its *disadvantages* are: (1) the few validity studies conducted have been disappointing; and (2) scales overlap considerably.

The *Mood Adjective Checklist* (Nowlis, 1965) contains 49 adjectives that are used to describe the feelings of the subject at that moment. Four responses are possible on each adjective: definitely feel relaxed; slightly relaxed; not sure of being relaxed; and definitely not relaxed. After considerable analysis, Nowlis selected 12 factors that best represent mood states: aggression; anxiety; surgency; elation; concentration; fatigue; social affection; sadness; skepticism; egotism; vigor; and nonchalance. Its *advantages* are: (1) it is an uncomplicated assessment task; (2) it is brief; and (3) it has less indication of social desirability response bias. Its *disadvantages* are: (1) it has conflicting reliability results ($r_s = .52$ to $.80$); (2) it needs comprehensive validity studies; and (3) it is commercially unavailable.

There are a number of single-dimension measurement devices, such as the State–Trait Anxiety Inventory, the Cattell Anxiety Questionnaire, and the Taylor Manifest Anxiety Scale for the assessment of a particular mood. However, these measures lack a comprehensive application and thus are less desirable for the affective dimension.

General Indicators of Psychological Adjustment

Measures of overall personality adjustment can provide data on potential problems outside the limited realm of a particular habit disorder. In addition, a certain amount of overlap does occur between these measures and other affective devices, thus providing a measurement supplement to aid in the clarification of results. Two popular measures are briefly considered: the Minnesota Multiphasic Personality Inventory (MMPI) and the Symptom Checklist 90-R (SCL-90-R).

Perhaps the most widely employed test of personality and psychopathology is the MMPI (Hathaway & McKinley, 1967). The original intent of this self-report inventory was the identification of certain disorders in a psychiatric population. The instrument consists of 550 true–false statements that cover a broad range of difficulties, including physical problems to social activity. The scoring system of the MMPI produces three validity scales and ten scales of measurement: lie; K; F; hypochondriasis; depression; hysteria; psychopathic deviate; masculinity–femininity; paranoia; psychoasthenia; schizophrenia; hypomania; and social introversion. As stated above, the Depression Scale has been evaluated as one of the better measures of depressive symptoms. In addition, research has generated a plethora of supplementary scales to increase its measurement scope (anxiety, ego strength, suicide risk, etc.). Its *advantages* are: (1) it is an uncomplicated assessment task; (2) it has a systematic scoring procedure; (3) it has a large selection of computer scoring programs; (4) it is commercially available (The Psychological Corporation, New York, New York); and (5) it has scales to measure protocol validity. Its *disadvantages* are: (1) there are biases in the selection of the normative sample (2) it has structural redundancies to increase interscale reliabilities; (3) it is heavily oriented toward serious psychopathological disorders; (4) its long and short forms are both very lengthy; (5) it is dependent on intuition of personality traits by scale configurations; (6) it has conflicting reliability and validity (the overwhelming studies in these areas are inconclusive, reflecting more of a bipartisan trend than solid evidence).

A recently revised measure of psychological adjustment is the SCL-90-R (Derogatis, 1977). This device is a 90-item rating list of symptoms. The respondent is asked to describe on a five-point scale (0—"not at all" to 5—"extremely") how much they are distressed by a particular symptom (headaches, trembling, crying easily, etc.). Raw scores are tallied, converted into t scores, and plotted along 12 factors: somatization; obsessive–compulsive; interpersonal sensitivity; depression; anxiety; hostility; phobic anxiety; paranoid ideation; and psychoticism. The remaining three factors (global severity index, positive symptom distress index, and positive symptom total) provide a measure of validity. Several of these measures reflect the important affectional symptoms characteristic of obesity and tobacco smoking research. Its *advantages* are: (1) it is an uncomplicated assessment task; (2) it is brief; (3) it has a systematic scoring system (including a method to calculate sources when items are avoided); (4) it has good reliability (r_s = .81 to .90); (5) it has excellent levels of invariance for all nine factors (Derogatis & Cleary, 1977a); (6) it has strong construct validity (Derogatis & Cleary, 1977b); and (7) it has scales for measurement of protocol validity. Its *disadvantages* are: (1) it is heavily oriented toward the psychopathological dimension; and (2) it is commercially unavailable (test material must be directly purchased from the author).

COMMENTS

Recommendations for measures in the affective dimension are tentative at best. Many of the same problems in the cognition area of this chapter apply equally here. Much preliminary groundwork is needed to fully delineate the influences of affection in obesity and tobacco smoking research. This early experimental groundwork is essential before tailor-made measurement devices can be formulated.

On the basis of the previous review, dependent measures for the affective dimension have been rank ordered in Tables 11.2 and 11.3.

CONCLUSIONS

As a conclusion to this chapter, recommendations are made for dependent measure selection within the three dimensions of human functioning.These recommendations have been rank ordered in terms of overall quality (ease of administration, reliability, validity, and cost-efficiency) and relevancy to the particular habit disorder.

Throughout this chapter, tailor-made assessment devices have been repeatedly called for as the ideal measurement strategy direction. Both obesity and tobacco smoking measures are largely deficient in this orientation, especially in the cognitive and affective realms of functioning.

To better illustrate this movement toward customizing measures, a recent attempt has been made to formulate a questionnaire exclusively for use as an adjunct measure in obesity outcome research (Straw et al., 1980). The master questionnaire (MQ) is a 302-item, true–false self-report that is constructed to measure four areas: spouse support; energy balance habits; cognitive factors; and energy balance knowledge. This device was not only developed as an outcome measure, but as a predictor of success in treatment as well. Although further refinement of the scales is needed at this time, this measure has promise as a standard measure in obesity research; and more importantly, it establishes a positive direction in the development of customized measures within obesity research. Hopefully, this trend will continue.

In retrospect, habit disorder evaluations have progressed quite impressively over the last decade. Researchers are beginning to realize the vast complexities that are characteristic of general habit disorders, and most specifically in obesity and tobacco smoking research. Nevertheless, a disturbing tendency in measurement is very apparent from the preceding review: the conation dimension dominates the measurement emphasis in both these habit disorders. As eluded to earlier, this trend is perhaps a product of behavioral theory, tradition, convenience, and a lack of a broad philosophical direction. Be that as it may, we as researchers are faced with the difficult project of reformulating outmoded research opinions and practices to keep pace with new clinical innovations. Hopefully, this review has provided some experimental direction to meet this challenge.

REFERENCES

Abrahams, J. I.., & Allen, G. J. Comparative effectiveness of situational programming, financial pay-offs and group pressure in weight reduction. *Behavior Therapy*, 1974, **5**, 391–400.

Adams, N., Ferguson, J., Stunkard, A. J., & Agras, S. The eating behavior of obese and non-obese women. *Behaviour Research and Therapy*, 1978, **16**, 225–232.

Ague, C. Nicotine content of cigarettes and the smoking habit: Their relevance to subjective ratings of preferences in smokers. *Psychopharmacologia*, 1972, **24**, 326–330.

Allport, G. W. The historical background of modern social psychology. In G. Lindzey (Ed.), *Handbook of Social Psychology*. Massachusetts: Addison-Wesley Publishing, 1954, pp. 3–56.

American Psychiatric Association. *Diagnostic and statistical manual of mental disorders* (3rd ed.). Washington, D.C.: American Psychiatric Association, 1980.

Ashton, H., & Watson, D. W. Puffing frequency and nicotine intake in cigarette smokers. *British Medical Journal*, 1970, **3**, 679–681.

Atkins, R. H. *Mathematical structure in human affairs*. London: Heinemann, 1974.

Balch, P., & Ross, W. A. A behaviorally oriented didactic-group treatment of obesity: An exploratory study. *Journal of Behavior Therapy and Experimental Psychiatry*, 1975, **5**, 239–243.

Bark, L. S., & Higson, H. G. A review of the methods available for the detection and determination of small amounts of cyanide. *Analyst*, 1963, **88**, 751–760.

Bellack, A. S., & Rozensky, R. H. The selection of dependent variables for weight reduction studies. *Journal of Behavior Therapy and Experimental Psychiatry*, 1975, **6**, 83–84.

Beneke, W. M., Paulsen, B., McReynolds, W. T., Lutz, R. N., & Kohrs, M. B. Long-term results of two behavior modification weight loss programs using nutritionists as therapists. *Behavior Therapy*, 1978, **9**, 501–507.

Bennion, R. C. Personal communication. Brigham Young University, Provo, Utah, 1981.

Berblinger, K. W. Obesity and psychologic stress. In N. L. Wilson (Ed.), *Obesity*. Philadelphia: F. A. Davis Company, 1969.

Bergin, A. E., & Lambert, M. J. The evaluation of therapeutic outcomes. In S. L. Garfield & A. E. Bergin (Eds.), *Handbook of psychotherapy and behavior change* (2nd ed.). New York: Wiley, 1978.

Bernstein, D. A. Modification of smoking behavior: An evaluative review. *Psychological Bulletin*, 1969, **71**, 418–440.

Berstein, D. A., & McAlister, A. The modification of smoking behavior: Progress and problems. *Addictive Behaviors*, 1976, **1**, 89–102.

Best, W. R. An improved caliper for measurement of skinfold thickness. *Journal of Laboratory Clinical Medicine*, 1954, **43**, 967–970.

Bieri, J., Atkins, A. L., Briar, S., Leaman, R. L., Miller, H., & Tripodi, T. *Clinical and social judgment: The discrimination of behavior information*. New York: Wiley, 1966.

Bills, R., Vance, E., & McLean, O. An index of adjustment and values. *Journal of Consulting Psychology*, 1951, **15**, 257–261.

Bloom, W. L., & Eidex, M. F. Inactivity as a major factor in adult obesity. *Metabolism, Clinical and Experimental*, 1967, **16**, 679–684.

Blurton, F. K., & Bay, H. W. Controlled-potential electro-chemical analysis of carbon monoxide. *American Laboratory*, 1974, **6**, 50–54.

Bray, G. A. *The obese patient*. Philadelphia: Saunders, 1976.

Briddell, D. W., Rimm, D. C., Caddy, G. R., & Dunn, N. J. Analogue assessment, affective arousal, and the smoking taste test. *Addictive Behaviors*, 1979, **4**, 287–295.

Brockway, B. S. Chemical validation of self-reported smoking rates. *Behavior Therapy*, 1978, **9**, 685–686.

Brownell, K. D. Assessment of eating disorders. In D. H. Barlow (Ed.), *Behavioral assessment of adult disorders*. New York: Guilford Press, 1981.

Brozek, J. F., Grande, F., Anderson, J. T., & Keys, A. Densitometric analysis of body composition: Revision of some quantitative assumptions. *Annals of New York Academy of Science*, 1963, **110**, 113–140.

Burkinshaw, L., Jones, P. R. M., & Krupowicz, D. W. Observer error in skinfold thickness measurements. *Human Biology*, 1973, **45**, 273–279.

Butts, W. C., Kuehneman, M., & Widdowson, G. M. Automated method for determining serum thiocyanate to distinguish smokers from non-smokers. *Clinical Chemistry*, 1974, **20**, 1344–1348.

Cahoon, D. D. Cigarette addiction and carbon dioxide inhalation: An hypothesis. Psychological Record, 1971, **21**, 247–249.

Clark, R. R. Smoking. *A social interaction theory of cigarette smoking and quitting*. New York: Dabor Science Publications, 1977.

Coll, M., Meyer, A., & Stunkard, A. J. Obesity and food choices in public places. *Archives of General Psychiatry*, 1979, **36**, 795–797.

Collett, P. The repertory grid in psychological research. In G. P. Ginsburg (Ed.), *Emerging strategies in social psychological research*. New York: Wiley, 1979.

Connors, G. J., Maisto, S. A., & Sobell, M. B. Extension of the taste-test analogue as an unobtrusive measure of preference for alcohol. *Behavior Research and Therapy*, 1978, **16**, 289–291.

Cooper, A. M., Waterhouse, G. J., & Sobell, M. B. Influence of gender on drinking in a modeling situation. *Journal of Studies on Alcohol*, 1979, **40**, 562–570.

Coopersmith, S. *The antecedents of self-esteem*. San Francisco: Freeman, 1967.

Crandall, R. The measurement of self-esteem and related constructs. In J. P. Robinson & P. R. Shaver (Eds.), *Measures of social psychological attitudes*. Ann Arbor: Institute for Social Research, University of Michigan, 1973.

Dacre, J. C., & Tabershaw, I. R. Thiocyanate in saliva and sputum. *Archives of Environmental Health*, 1970, **21**, 47–49.

Dahlkoetter, J., Callahan, E. J., & Linton, J. Obesity and the balanced energy equation: Exercise versus eating habit change. *Journal of Consulting and Clinical Psychology*, 1979, **47**, 898–905.

Delarue, N. C. The anti-smoking clinic: Is it a potential community service? *Canadian Medical Association Journal*, 1973, **108**, 1164–1165.

Densen, P. M., Davidow, B., Bass, H. E., & Jones, E. W. A chemical test for smoking exposure. *Archives of Environmental Health*, 1967, **14**, 865–874.

Derogatis, L. R. *SCL-90-R Manual*. Clinical Psychometrics Research Unit, Johns Hopkins University School of Medicine, 1977.

Derogatis, L. R., & Clearly, P. A. Factorial invariance across gender for the primary symptom dimensions of the SCL-90. *British Journal of Social and Clinical Psychology*, 1977, **16**, 347–356. (a)

Derogatis, L. R., & Cleary, P. A. Confirmation of the dimensional structure of the SCL-90: A study in construct validation. *Journal of Clinical Psychology*, 1977, **33**, 981–989. (b)

Diament, C., & Wilson, G. T. An experimental investigation of the effects of covert sensitization in an analogue eating situation. *Behavior Therapy*, 1975, **6**, 499–509.

Dodd, D. K., Birky, H. J., & Stalling, R. B. Eating behavior of obese and normal weight females in a natural setting. *Addictive Behaviors*, 1976, **1**, 321–325.

Dogon, I. L., Amdur, B. H., & Bell, K. Observations on the diurnal variation of some inorganic constituents of human parotid saliva in smokers and non-smokers. *Archives of Oral Biology*, 1971, **16**, 95–105.

Durnin, J. V. G. A., & Rahaman, M. M. The assessment of the amount of fat in the human body from measurements of skinfold thickness. *British Journal of Nutrition*, 1967, **21**, 681–689.

Durnin, J. V. G. A., & Womersley, J. Body fat assessed from total body density and its estimation from skinfold thickness: Measurements on 481 men and women aged from 16 to 72 years. *British Journal of Nutrition*, 1974, **32**, 77–97.

Eagly, A. H. Involvement as a determinant of response to favorable and unfavorable information. *Journal of Personality and Social Psychology Monographs*, 1967, **7**(3, Whole No. 643).

Easterby-Smith, M. The design, analysis, and interpretations of repertory grids. *International Journal of Man-Machine Studies*, 1980, **13**, 3–24.

Edwards, D. A. W., Hammond, W. H., Healey, M. J. R., Tanner, J. M., & Whitehouse, R. H. Design and accuracy of calipers for measuring subcutaneous tissue thickness. *British Journal of Nutrition*, 1955, **9**, 133–143.

Edwards, D. *Conceptual grid*. Paper presented at the conference on Personal Construct Theory, San Diego, California, May 1980.

Edwards, D., & Johnson, S. *The DXTX (TM) Program©*. San Diego: Grid Limited, 1981.

Epstein, L. H., Wing, R. R., & Thompson, K. J. The relationship between exercise intensity, caloric intake, and weight. *Addictive Behaviors*, 1979, **3**, 185–190.

Fagerstrom, K. Measuring degree of physical dependence to tobacco smoking with reference to individualization of treatment. *Addictive Behaviors*, 1978, **3**, 235–241.

Feinstein, A. R. The measurement of success in weight reduction: An analysis of methods and a new index. *Journal of Chronic Diseases*, 1959, **10**, 439–456.

Ferraro, D. P. Self-control of smoking: The amotivational syndrome. *Journal of Abnormal Psychology*, 1973, **81**, 152–157.

Fitts, W. Manual: Tennessee Self-Concept Scale. Nashville: Counselor Recordings and Tests, 1964.

Fjeld, S. P., & Landfield, A. W. Personal construct consistency. *Psychological Reports*, 1961, **8**, 127–129.

Forbes, W. F., Robinson, J. C., Hanley, J. A., & Colburn, H. N. Studies on the nicotine exposure of individual smokers I. Changes in mouth-level exposure to nicotine on switching to lower nicotine cigarettes. *The International Journal of the Addictions*, 1976, **11**, 933–950.

Franzini, L. R., & Grimes, W.B. Skinfold measures as the criterion of change in weight control studies. *Behavior Therapy*, 1976, **7**, 256–260.

Franzini, L. R., & Grimes, W. B. Contracting and Stuart's three-dimensional program in behavior modification of the obese. *Psychotherapy: Theory, Research, and Practice*, 1980, **17**, 44–51.

Freedman, A. M., Kaplan, H. I., & Sadock, B. J. *Comprehensive textbook of psychiatry—II* (2nd ed). Baltimore: Williams & Wilkins, 1975.

Frederiksen, L. W., & Martin, J. E. Carbon monoxide and smoking behavior. *Addictive Behaviors*, 1979, **4**, 21–30.

Frederiksen, L. W., Miller, P. M., & Peterson, G. L. Topographical components of smoking behavior. *Addictive Behaviors*, 1977, **2**, 55–61.

Gaul, D. J., Craighead, W. E., & Mahoney, M. J. Relationship between eating rates and obesity. *Journal of Consulting and Clinical Psychology*, 1975, **43**, 123–125.

Garfield, S. L. Research on client variables in psychotherapy. In S. L. Garfield & A. E. Bergin (Eds.), *Handbook of psychotherapy and behavior change* (2nd ed.). New York: Wiley, 1978.

Garfield, S. L., Prager, R. A., & Bergin, A. E. Evaluating outcome in psychotherapy: A hardy perennial. *Journal of Consulting and Clinical Psychology*, 1971, **37**, 320–322.

Genest, M., & Turk, D. C. Think-aloud approaches to cognitive assessment. In T. Merluzzi, C. Glass, & M. Genest (Eds.), *Cognitive assessment*. New York: Guilford Press, 1981.

Glucksman, M. L., & Hirsch, J. The response of obese patients to weight reduction: A clinical evaluation of behavior. *Psychosomatic Medicine*, 1968, **30**, 1–11.

Glucksman, M. L., Hirsch, J., McCully, R. S., Barron, B. A., & Knittle, J. L. The response of obese patients to weight reduction II. A quantitative evaluation of behavior. *Psychosomatic Medicine*, 1968, **30**, 359–373.

Goldman, D., Jaffe, M., & Schachter, S. Yom Kippur, Air France, dormitory food, and eating behavior of obese and normal persons. *Journal of Personality and Social Psychology*, 1968, **10**, 117–123.

Goldstein, A. P., Heller, K., & Sechrest, L. B. *Psychotherapy and the psychology of behavior change*. New York: Wiley, 1966.

Green, L. Temporal and stimulus factors in self-monitoring by obese persons. *Behavior Therapy*, 1978, **9**, 328–341.

Grimes, W. B., & Franzini, L. R. Skinfold measurement techniques for estimating percentage body fat. *Journal of Behavior Therapy and Experimental Psychiatry*, 1977, **8**, 65–69.

Haisman, M. F. The assessment of body fat content in young men from measurements of body density and skinfold thickness. *Human Biology*, 1970, **42**, 679–688.

Harris, M. B., & Hallbauer, E. S. Self-directed weight control through eating and exercise. *Behaviour Research and Therapy*, 1973, **11**, 523–529.

Hathaway, S. R., & McKinley, J. C. *Minnesota Multiphasic Personality Inventory Manual-Revised*. New York: The Psychological Corporation, 1967.

Heimstra, N. W. The effects of smoking on mood change. In W. L. Dunn, Jr. (Ed.), *Smoking behavior: Motives and incentives*. Washington, D.C.: Winston, 1973.

Henningfield, J. E., Sitzer, J. L., & Griffiths, R. R. Expired air carbon monoxide accumulation and elimination as a function of number of cigarettes smoked. *Addictive Behaviors*, 1980, **5**, 265–272.

Horan, J. J., Hackett, G., & Linberg, S. E. Factors to consider when using expired air carbon monoxide in smoking assessment. *Addictive Behaviors*, 1978, **3**, 25–28.

Hughes, J. R., Frederiksen, L. W., & Frazier, M. A carbon monoxide analyzer for measurement of smoking behavior. *Behavior Therapy*, 1978, **9**, 293–296.

Human Performance Center. Personal Communication. Brigham Young University, Provo, Utah, 1980.

Hunt, W. A., & Matarazzo, J. D. Three years later: Recent developments in the experimental modification of smoking behavior. *Journal of Abnormal Psychology*, 1973, **81**, 107–114.

Ikard, F. F., & Tomkins, S. The experience of affect as a determinant of smoking behavior: A series of validity studies. *Journal of Abnormal Psychology*, 1973, **81**, 172–181.

Jeffery, R. W., & Wing, R. R. Frequency of therapist contact in the treatment of obesity. *Behavior Therapy*, 1979, **10**, 186–192.

Johnson, W. G., & Stalonas, P. Measuring skinfold thickness—a cautionary note. *Addictive Behaviors*, 1977, **2**, 105–108.

Jones, R. H., Ellicott, M. F., Cadigan, J. B., & Gaensler, E. A. The relationship between alveolar and blood carbon monoxide concentrations during breathholding: Simple estimation of COHb saturation. *Journal of Laboratory and Clinical Medicine*, 1958, **51**, 533–564.

Jordan, H. A., Wieland, W. F., Zebley, S. P., Stellar, E., & Stunkard, A. J. Direct measurement of food intake in man: A method for the objective study of eating behavior in man. *Psychosomatic Medicine*, 1966, **28**, 836–842.

Katch, F., Michael, E. D., & Horvath, S. M. Estimation of body volume by underwater weighing: Description of a simple method. *Journal of Applied Physiology*, 1967, **23**, 811–813.

Keen, T. R., & Bell, R. C. One thing leads to another: A new approach to elicitation in the repertory grid technique. *International Journal of Man-Machine Studies*, 1980, **13**, 25–38.

Kellerman, H., & Plutchik, R. Emotio-Trail interrelations and the measurement of personality. *Psychological Reports*, 1968, **23**, 1107–1114.

Kelly, G. A. *The psychology of personal constructs* (Vols. 1 & 2). New York: Norton, 1955.

Keys, A., Fidanza, F., Karvonen, M. J., Kimura, N., & Taylor, H. L. Indices of relative weight and obesity. *Journal of Chronic Disease*, 1972, **25**, 329–343.

Kiesler, D. J. Some myths of psychotherapy research and the search for a paradigm. *Psychological Bulletin*, 1966, **65**, 110–136.

Kiesler, D. J. Experimental designs in psychotherapy research. In S. L. Garfield & A. E. Bergin (Eds.), *Handbook of psychotherapy and behavior change*. New York: Wiley, 1971.

Kissileff, H., Klingsberg, H. R., & Van Itallie, T. B. A universal eating monitor for measuring solid-liquid consumption in man. *American Journal of Physiology*, 1980, **238**, 14–22.

Kolb, L. C. *Modern clinical psychiatry* (9th ed.). Philadelphia: Saunders, 1977.

Krantz, D. S. A naturalistic study of social influences on meal size among moderately obese and non-obese subjects. *Psychosomatic Medicine*, 1979, **41**, 19–27.

Krassner, H. A., Brownell, K. D., & Stunkard, A. J. Cleaning the plate: Food left over by over-weight and normal weight persons. *Behaviour Research and Therapy*, 1979, **17**, 155–156.

Lando, H. A. An objective check upon self-reported smoking levels: A preliminary report. *Behavior Therapy*, 1975, **6**, 547–549.

Lange, K. O., & Brozek, J. A. A new model of skinfold caliper. *American Journal of Physical* Anthropology, 1961, **19**, 98–99.

Langone, J. J., Van Vunakis, H., & Levine, L. Antibodies: Analytical tools to study pharmacologically active compounds. *Accounts of Chemical Research*, 1975, **8**, 335–342.

Lazarus, A. A. Multimodal behavior therapy: Treating the basic id. *Journal of Nervous and Mental Disease*, 1973, **156**, 404–411.

Lazarus, A. A. *Multi-modal behavior therapy*. New York: Springer, 1976.

LeBow, M. Can lighter become thinner? *Addictive Behaviors*, 1977, **2**, 87–94.

Levenberg, S. B., & Wagner, M. K. Smoking cessation: Long-term irrelevance of mode of treatment. *Journal of Behavior Therapy and Experimental Psychiatry*, 1976, **7**, 93–95.

Levinson, S. A., & MacFate, R. P. *Clinical laboratory procedures*. Philadelphia: Lea & Febiger, 1969.

Lewinsohn, P. M., & Lee, W. M. L. Assessment of affective disorders. In D. H. Barlow (Ed.), *Behavioral assessment of adult disorders*. New York: Guilford Press, 1981.

Lichtenstein, E., Harris, D. E., Birchler, G. R., Wahl, J. J., & Schmahl, D. P. Comparison of rapid smoking, warm, smoky air, and attention placebo in the modification of smoking behavior. *Journal of Consulting and Clinical Psychology*, 1973, **40**, 92–98.

Mahoney, M. J. *Cognition and behavior modification*. Massachusetts: Balinger, 1974. (a)

Mahoney, M. J. Self-reward and self-monitoring techniques for weight control. *Behavior Therapy*, 1974, **5**, 48–57. (b)

Mahoney, M. J. The obese eating style: Bites, beliefs, and behavior modification. *Addictive Behaviors*, 1975, **1**, 47–53.

Mann, G. V. The influence of obesity on health. *New England Journal Medicine*, 1974, **291**, 178–185, 226–232.

Manno, B., & Marston, A. R. Weight reduction as a function of negative covert reinforcement (sensitization) versus positive covert reinforcement. *Behaviour Research and Therapy*, 1972, **10**, 201–207.

Marston, A. R., & McFall, R. M. Comparison of behavior modification approaches to smoking reduction. *Journal of Consulting and Clinical Psychology*, 1971, **36**, 153–162.

Mausner, B. An ecological view of cigarette smoking. *Journal of Abnormal Psychology*, 1973, **81**, 115–126.

Mayer, J. *Overweight: Causes, cost, and control*. Englewood Cliffs, N. J.: Prentice-Hall, 1968.

McFall, R. M. Effects of self-monitoring on normal smoking behavior. *Journal of Consulting and Clinical Psychology*, 1970, **35**, 135–142.

McFall, R. M. Smoking-cessation research. *Journal of Consulting and Clinical Psychology*, 1978, **46**, 703–712.

McFall, R. M., & Hammen, C. L. Motivation, structure, and self-monitoring: Role of non-specific factors in smoking reduction. *Journal of Consulting and Clinical Psychology*, 1971, **37**, 80–86.

McNair, D. M., Lorr, M., & Doppleman, L. F. *Profile of Mood states* (POMS). San Diego, Calif.: Educational and Industrial Testing Service, 1971.

McReynolds, W. T., Lutz, R. N., Kennedy-Paulsen, B., & Kohrs, M. B. Weight loss resulting from two behavior modification procedures with nutritionists as therapists. *Behavior Therapy*, 1976, **7**, 283–291.

Meichenbaum, D. A self-instructional approach to stress management: A proposal for stress inoculation training. In I. Sarason & C. D. Spielberger (Eds.), *Stress and anxiety* (Vol. 2). New York: Wiley, 1975.

Meichenbaum, D. *Cognitive-behavior modification: An integrative approach.* New York: Plenum Press, 1977.

Meichenbaum, D., & Cameron, R. Training schizophrenics to talk to themselves: A means of developing attentional controls. *Behavior Therapy*, 1973, **4**, 515–534.

Messick, S. The impact of negative affect on cognition and personality. In S. S. Tomkins & C. E. Izard (Eds.), *Affect, cognition, and personality*. New York: Springer, 1965.

Metropolitan Life Insurance Company. Frequency of overweight and underweight. *Statistical Bulletin*, 1960, **41**, 4–7.

Miller, P. M. Assessment of addictive behaviors. In A. R. Ciminero, K. S. Calhoun, & H. E. Adams (Eds.), *Handbook of behavioral assessment*. New York: Wiley, 1977.

Miller, P. M. Assessment of alcohol abuse. In D. H. Barlow (Ed.), *Behavioral assessment of adult disorders*. New York: Guilford Press, 1981.

Miller, P. M., Frederiksen, L.W., & Hosford, R. L. Social inter-action and smoking topography in heavy and light smokers. *Addictive Behaviors*, 1979, **4**, 147–153.

Mischel, W. On the future of personality measurement. *American Psychologist*, 177, **32**, 246–254.

Moran, P. W., & Lambert, M. J. Assessing outcome in affective disorders. In M. J. Lambert, E. R. Christensen, & S. S. DeJulio (Eds.), *The assessment of psychotherapy outcome*. New York: Wiley, 1983.

Novaco, R. W. Treatment of chronic anger through cognitive and relaxation controls. *Journal of Consulting and Clinical Psychology*, 1976, **44**, 681.

Nowlis, V. Research with the mood adjective checklist. In S. S. Tomkins & C. E. Izard (Eds.), *Affect, cognition, and personality*. New York: Springer, 1965.

O'Brien, T., Kelley, J. E., Rosenthal, T. L., & Theobald, D. E. Snack bar seduction and obesity. *Behavior Therapy*, 1978, **9**, 968.

Ohlin, P., Lundh, B., & Westling, H. Carbon monoxide blood levels and reported cessation of smoking. *Psychopharmacology*, 1976, **49**, 263–265.

Orne, M. T. From the subject's point of view, when is behavior private and when is it public: Problems of inference. *Journal of Consulting and Clinical Psychology*, 1970, **35**, 143–147.

Paxton, R., & Bernacca, G. Urinary nicotine concentration as a function of time since last cigarette: Implications for detecting faking in smoking clinics. *Behavior Therapy*, 1979, **10**, 523–528.

Pechacek, T. F. Modification of smoking behavior. *USPHS, Surgeon General's Report on Smoking and Health*. Washington, D.C.: U.S. Government Printing Office, 1979.

Prue, D. M., Martin, J. E., & Hume, A. S. A critical evaluation of thiocyanate as a biochemical of smoking exposure. *Behavior Therapy*, 1980, **11**, 368–379.

Rapp, G. W., Dusza, B. T., & Blanchet, L. Absorption and utility of lobeline as a smoking deterrent. *American Journal of the Medical Sciences*, 1959, **237**, 287–292.

Ringold, A., Goldsmith, J. R., Helwing, H. I., Finn, R., & Schuette, F. Estimating recent carbon monoxide exposures. *Archives of Environmental Health*, 1962, **5**, 308–318.

Robinson, J. C., & Young, J. C. Temporal patterns in smoking rate and mouth-level nicotine exposure. *Addictive Behaviors*, 1980, **5**, 91–95.

Rogers, T., Mahoney, M. J., Mahoney, B. K., Straw, M. K., & Kenigsberg, M. I. Clinical assessment of obesity: An empirical evaluation of diverse techniques. *Behavioral Assessment*, 1980, **2**, 161–181.

Rosenberg, M. *Society and the adolescent self-image*. Princeton, N. J.: Princeton University Press, 1965.

Russell, M. A., & Feyerabend, C. Blood and urinary nicotine in non-smokers. *Lancet*, 1975, **1**, 179–181.

Sahakian, W. S. *History and systems of psychology*. New York: Schenkman, 1975.

Schachter, S. Nicotine regulation in heavy and light smokers. *Journal of Experimental Psychology: General*, 1977, **106**, 5–12.

Schachter, S., Goldman, R., & Gordon, A. Effects of fear, food deprivation, and obesity on eating. *Journal of Personality and Social Psychology*, 1968, **10**, 91–97.

Schachter, S., & Gross, L. Manipulated time and eating behavior. *Journal of Personality and Social Psychology*, 1968, **10**, 98–106.

Schachter, S., & Rodin, J. (Eds.). *Obese humans and rats*. Washington, D.C.: Erlbaum/Halsted, 1974.

Schneier, C. E. Measuring cognitive complexity: Developing reliability, validity, and norm tables for a personality instrument. *Educational and Psychological Measurement*, 1979, **39**, 599–612.

Shaw, M. L. G. Conversational heuristics for eliciting shared understanding. *International Journal of Man-Machine Studies*, 1979, **11**, 621–634.

Shaw, M. L. G. The analysis of a Kelly repertory grid. *British Journal of Medical Psychology*, 1980, **53**, 117–126.

Shaw, M. L. G., & McKnight, C. ARGUS: A program to explore intrapersonal personalities. *International Journal of Man-Machine Studies*, 1980, **13**, 59–68.

Shaw, M. L. G., & Thomas, L. F. FOCUS on education—An interactive computer system for the development and analysis of repertory grids. *International Journal of Man-Machine Studies*, 1978, **10**, 139–173.

Sims, E. A. H. *The types of obesity: Definitions, criteria, and prevalence*. Paper presented at the Fogarty Conference on Obesity, Washington, D.C., 1977.

Slater, P. *The measurement of intrapersonal space by grid technique* (Vol. 2). *Dimensions of Intrapersonal Space*. London: Wiley, 1977.

Slater, P. Construct systems in conflict. *International Journal of Man-Machine Studies*, 1980, **13**, 49–57.

Sloan, A. W., & Shapiro, M. A comparison of skinfold measurements with three standard calipers. *Human Biology*, 1972, **44**, 29–36.

Sobell, M. B., & Sobell, L. C. Assessment of addictive behaviors. In M. Hersen & A. S. Bellack (Eds.), *Behavioral assessment: A practical handbook*. New York: Pergamon Press, 1976.

Sobell, L. C., Sobell, M. B., & Ward, E. *Evaluating alcohol and drug abuse treatment effectiveness: Recent advances*. New York: Pergamon Press, 1980.

Social Research Incorporated. *Cigarettes: Their role and function*. Chicago: Chicago Tribune, 1952.

Stewart, R. D., & Stewart, R. S. Breath analyzer used to test CO levels in fireman's blood. *Fire Engineering*, 1975, Aug., 92–94.

Stewart, R. D., Stewart, R. S., Stamm, W., & Seelan, R. P. Rapid estimation of carboxyhemoglobin level in fire fighters. *Journal of the American Medical Association*, 1976, **235**, 390–392.

Straw, M. K., Mahoney, M. J., Straw, R.B., Rogers, T., Mahoney, B. K., Craighead, L. W., & Stunkard, A. J. *The Master Questionnaire: A self-report measure of variables relevant to obesity treatment*. Unpublished manuscript, 1980. (Available from Dr. Margret K. Straw, Section on Medical Psychology, Bowman Gray School of Medicine, Winston-Salem, NC 27103).

Strupp, H. H. The outcome problem in psychotherapy revisited. *Psychotherapy: Theory, Research, and Practice*, 1964, **1**, 1–13.

Strupp, H. H. Psychotherapy research and practice: An overview. In S. L. Garfield & A. E. Bergin (Eds.), *Handbook of psychotherapy and behavior change: An empirical evaluation* (2nd ed.). New York: Wiley, 1978.

Stuart, R. B. Behavioral control of overeating. *Behavior Research and Therapy*, 1967, **5**, 357–365.

Stunkard, A. J. The dieting depression: Untoward responses to weight reduction. *American Journal of Medicine*, 1957, **23**, 77–86.

Stunkard, A. J. *The pain of obesity*. Palo Alto, Calif.: Bull Publishing, 1976.

Stunkard, A. J., & Mahoney, M. J. Behavioral treatment of the eating disorders. In H. Leitenberg (Ed.), *Handbook of behavior modification and behavior therapy*. Englewood Cliffs, N.J.: Prentice-Hall, 1976.

Stunkard, A. J., & Mendleson, M. Obesity and the body image: I. Characteristics of disturbances in the body image of some obese persons. *American Journal of Psychiatry*, 1967, **123**, 1296–1300.

Stunkard, A. J., & Rush, J. Dieting and depression reexamined: A critical review of reports of untoward responses during weight reduction for obesity. *Annals of Internal Medicine*, 1974, **81**, 521–533.

Tanner, J. M., & Whitehouse, R. H. The Harpenden skinfold caliper. *American Journal of Physical Anthropology*,1955, **13**, 743–746.

Tenovuo, J., & Makinen, K. K. Concentration of thiocyanate and ionizable iodine in saliva of smokers and nonsmokers. *Journal of Dental Research*, 1976, **55**, 661–663.

Thomas, C. B. The relationship of smoking and habits of nervous tension. In W. L. Dunn, Jr. (Ed.), *Smoking behavior: Motives and incentives*. Washington, D.C.: Winston, 1973.

Tomkins, S. S. *Affect, imagery, consciousness* (Vol. 1). *The positive affects*. New York: Springer, 1962.

Tomkins, S. S. A modified model of smoking behavior. In E. Borgatto & R. Evans (Eds.), *Smoking, health, and behavior*. Chicago: Aldine, 1968.

Turk, D. C. An expanded skills training approach for the treatment of experimentally induced pain. (Doctoral dissertation, University of Waterloo, 1977). *Dissertation Abstracts*, 1978, **39**, No. 1972.

Urban, H. B., & Ford, D. H. Some historical and conceptual perspectives on psychotherapy and behavior change. In S. L. Garfield & A. E. Bergin (Eds.), *Handbook of psychotherapy and behavior change*. New York: Wiley, 1971.

U.S. Department of Health, Education, and Welfare. *Overweight adults in the United States*. Washington, D.C.: U.S. Government Printing Office, 1979.(a)

U.S. Department of Health, Education, and Welfare. *Changes in cigarette smoking and current smoking practices among adults: United States, 1978*. Washington, D.C.: U.S. Government Printing Office, 1979.(b)

United States Senate Select Subcommittee on Nutrition and Human Needs. Proceedings from hearings. Washington, D.C.: U.S. Government Printing Office, 1977.

Weiner, J. S., & Lourie, J. H. *Human biology: A guide to field methods*. Oxford: Blackwell Scientific Publications, 1969.

Wilson, G. T. Methodological considerations in treatment outcome research on obesity. *Journal of Consulting and Clinical Psychology*, 1978, **46**, 687–702.

Wish, P. The use of imagery-based techniques in the treatment of sexual dysfunction. *The Counseling Psychologist*, 1975, **5**, 52–55.

Wolpe, J. *Psychotherapy by reciprocal inhibition*. Palo Alto, Calif.: Stanford University Press, 1958.

Wolpe, J. *The practice of behavior therapy*. New York: Pergamon Press, 1969.

Womersley, J., & Durnin, J. V. G. A. An experimental study on variability of measurement of skinfold thickness on young adults. *Human Biology*, 1973, **45**, 281–292.

Wooley, S. C., Wooley, O. W., & Dyrenforth, S. R. Theoretical, practical, and social issues in behavioral treatments of obesity. *Journal of Applied Behavior Analysis*, 1979, **12**, 3–26.

Zeidenberg, P., Jaffe, J. H., Kanzler, M., Levitt, M. D., Langone, J. J., & Van Vunakis, H., Nicotine: Cotinine levels in blood during cessation of smoking. *Comprehensive Psychiatry*, 1977, **18**, 93–101.

Zuckerman, M. The development of an affect adjective check list for the measurement of anxiety. *Journal of Consulting Psychology*, 1960, **24**, 457–462.

CHAPTER 12

Assessing Outcome in Disorders of Childhood and Adolescence

MICHAEL G. TRAMONTANA AND STEVEN D. SHERRETS

Tramontana (1980) has provided a critical review of the research on psychotherapy outcome with adolescents, and both Levitt (1971) and Barrett et al. (1978) have reviewed the research on children. In each case, relevant substantive findings were summarized and particular methodological issues discussed in relation to the evaluation of psychotherapy outcome in disturbances of youth. Although there were differences in the studies included for review and in some of the conclusions reached, there was clear unanimity among the different reviewers on at least one observation: there have been far fewer outcome studies on children and adolescents than on adults.

Of the possible reasons for this, none seems greater than the simple fact that outcome studies with children and adolescents are difficult to design and implement, far more so than with adults. This is because of the greater number of potentially confounding factors that can obscure and complicate the appraisal of therapeutic change in childhood or adolescence. Factors such as maturation, developmental changes in personality and symptom manifestation, the often profound influence of family and other environmental factors, and age-specific constraints on how personality and psychopathology are assessed—especially for the very young—all contribute to the relatively greater complexity involved in studying the child or adolescent. Obviously, these are factors that complicate many kinds of study involving youngsters but appear to have produced particularly difficult obstacles in research on therapeutic outcome.

These obstacles are not insurmountable, however. Worthwhile studies have been done, despite the complexities involved. No single study can ever fully control the many relevant variables that may jeopardize or limit the validity and generalizability of its findings, especially in outcome studies with youngsters. To expect this is to set an unrealistic standard that would only serve to perpetuate the already evident shortage of research in this area and to intensify the seemingly unremitting schism between clinical research and clinical practice (Barlow, 1981). What is needed is a clearer recognition of the relevant issues involved in assessing child and adolescent outcome—not to deter investigators from undertaking the challenge of research in this complex area, but to help assure greater comparability and utility in the research performed.

This chapter focuses on the general topic of assessing psychotherapy outcome in disorders of childhood and adolescence. The measurement of therapist and process variables—although obviously relevant to the assessment of therapeutic change—is not addressed, as this would take us beyond the scope of the chapter. Likewise, methodological problems that have been elucidated in the adult psychotherapy literature—although applicable here—are not discussed in depth, as the focus is on concepts and issues more specific to the evaluation of therapeutic change in youngsters. As will be seen, this largely entails the addition of a developmental perspective to the many methodological considerations inherent in the evaluation of therapy outcome more generally. A framework for conceptualizing outcome in childhood and adolescence is proposed, and criteria for evaluating therapeutic change are discussed. An overview of methods and instruments used in research assessing outcome with youngsters is provided, their limitations are discussed, and examples of particularly promising approaches are highlighted. The review is selective, however, as the emphasis is more on the development of conceptual and practical guidelines for future investigations in this area.

PROBLEMS AND ISSUES

Confounding Variables

Collateral Interventions

Psychotherapeutic intervention with the child or adolescent is often accompanied by some kind of joint intervention with the parents, the school, or other significant agents in the life of the youngster. Because of this, isolating the effects of psychotherapy per se becomes a particular problem. Collateral intervention with significant others is also provided in the treatment of adults, of course, but it appears to be a less common practice and is perhaps not always viewed as quite so critical in its impact on the identified patient. Practitioners often see the provision of collateral services such as parent education and collaboration with the school as necessary in maximizing the impact of therapy on the youngster and in helping to assure that its effects will endure. Critics might even argue that these services, not direct therapy with the child or adolescent, are largely responsible for whatever positive outcome occurs (Donofrio, 1976).

Although it may be clinically and ethically indefensible to withhold collateral services from some youngsters receiving psychotherapy for the sake of studying their specific effects, *metacontrol*, so to speak, could be achieved if investigators would at least give a detailed description of what collateral interventions are being provided, so that their effects could be estimated across studies through an accumulation of findings. However, as indicated in the review by Tramontana (1980), most of the outcome studies on adolescents failed to give more than minimal specification of what interventions, besides psychotherapy, were concurrently provided. Many gave no specification at all.

Maturation

Children in treatment may become better able to recognize and regulate their emotions and behavior and to take another person's point of view; younger adolescents may be observed as becoming less impulsive and more inclined to engage in foresight and to apply appropriate principles of conduct. However, such changes may have nothing to do with the therapy itself but instead may reflect developmental changes that have naturally occurred.

Development can bring about profound changes in the abilities and behavior of the child or adolescent, changes that can become confounded with the effects of treatment unless controlled. Moreover, it is certainly reasonable to expect that an intervention would tend to have different effects, depending on the youngster's level of maturity on specific developmental dimensions. An intervention that may produce only minimal impact, or perhaps even negative effects, at one stage of development may show clearly positive effects at a later stage, once the youngster has achieved a level of development that enables him or her to profit from it. Likewise, comparative treatment effects, or the superiority of one form of therapy over another on assorted outcome variables, may depend greatly on the point in development at which the different treatments are applied. Thus whether the issue is to distinguish the main effects of therapy versus maturation or to assess their interaction, particular attention must be given to individual differences in maturational level as an important factor affecting outcome.

The lack of control over maturation effects is obviously a major factor jeopardizing validity in any pretest–posttest, single–group study of outcome (Campbell & Stanley, 1963), especially when there is an extended period of time over which therapeutic change is assessed. Control in this case requires that outcome be assessed across appropriate comparison groups in which maturational level is either equalized or its effects are statistically removed on selected dependent measures. Better yet, as already implied, maturational level can be deliberately incorporated into the research design as a separate independent variable so that its main effects and interaction with treatment effects can be directly assessed. This was done, for example, in a large-scale study by Jesness (1975) in which the effects of two treatment programs for institutionalized delinquent boys were compared. The superiority of one program over the other depended not only on the particular outcome measure involved, but also on the rated interpersonal maturity level of the subjects.

To speak of maturity level, however, is not quite the same as simply considering the age of the youngster. Concepts such as maturity level or level of development refer more specifically to the youngster's successive attainment of skills and abilities, which, although age related, show considerable variation in terms of actual age of acquisition. Moreover, maturation itself is not a unitary process that proceeds uniformly across all aspects of the youngster's functioning. It is instead a multidimensional process in which the rate of development varies according to the particular aspect of development involved. In some cases the pattern of development can be highly variable, producing a pronounced unevenness in the youngster's preparedness to meet different age-expected tasks. So, whereas physical and cognitive development may be within normal limits, a youngster nonetheless may show striking delays in emotional or social maturity in comparison to chronologic peers. These differences—both between and within individual youngsters—are likely to comprise important sources of variance in outcome as well as in differential responsiveness to therapeutic efforts. Besides maturity *level*, therefore, individual differences in developmental *profile* (i.e., the pattern of development across specific developmental dimensions) should be considered in assessing the effects of maturation on therapeutic outcome.

Variability in "Target" Symptoms

A child or adolescent is typically brought to a mental health professional for treatment because someone (parent, teacher, or other societal agent) has identified a set of problems that are judged to require therapeutic attention. These problems become earmarked as presenting symptoms, which then tend to serve as targets toward which subsequent diagnostic and therapeutic efforts are aimed and against which therapeutic progress may be entirely gauged. Although an appraisal of target symptoms must certainly be included in any comprehensive assessment of therapeutic change, to focus exclusively on them can lead to a myopic view of the youngster's evolving adjustment and may ultimately lead to errors of either a false-positive or false-negative variety in judging therapy effectiveness. An example will help to illustrate the point.

Weiss and Burke (1970) conducted a clinical follow-up study of children and adolescents who had been hospitalized 5 to 10 years earlier for school phobia. At follow-up, most had graduated from high school and, in relation to IQ, most had demonstrated expected or better-than-expected academic achievement. Just knowing this, one might have concluded that treatment had been quite successful in that in almost all cases there was a complete remission in the target symptom. On closer inspection, however, it was found that the mental status profiles of most cases did not differ essentially from what they had been initially and that only about half of the cases were judged as having made an adequate social adjustment. Moreover, few subjects conceptualized their earlier problems in terms of a fear of school per se. What, then, was the significance of the initial target symptom, namely, the observed fear of school? The results of this study would suggest that for many it was only a specific manifestation—at a particular point in their lives—of larger adjustment difficulties, the onward form of which changed as adjustment demands themselves changed over time.

Development can bring about alterations in the outward form of underlying problems. Whereas we dealt with the issue of confounding effects or interactions involving maturation and treatment in the previous section, the discussion here is concerned with the confounding effects of development on manifest psychopathology. Different life experiences and adjustment demands encountered at particular points in development may provide specific form or color to manifest symptoms, changing their outward appearance as the youngster progresses from childhood through adolescence, although not necessarily altering the underlying problems themselves. So the symptoms of the socially avoidant individual may be expressed initially as school adjustment difficulties for the school-aged child, as peer relationship difficulties for the adolescent, and perhaps as work adjustment problems for the young adult.

Thus the specific form that symptoms may take depends in part on the point in development at which they are assessed. This variability in symptom expression poses a formidable problem for the researcher investigating outcome, for it is unclear as to precisely which criteria should be used in making the appraisal, especially in studies of long-range outcome (Levitt, 1971; Tramontana, 1980). Focusing only on target symptoms will not produce findings of much substance because these may represent only transitory or fluctuating phenomena at particular points in the youngster's development. A more comprehensive and multidimensional assessment is necessary, one that is preferably grounded in a developmental psychopathology of childhood and adolescence, to gain a clearer and more valid picture of the youngster's adjustment over time and across different situational demands. An excellent review of past empirical efforts in measuring and classifying deviant behavior in children and adolescents can be found elsewhere (Achenbach & Edelbrock, 1978). Suffice it to say that little progress in the evaluation of treatments can be achieved, and generalizability will be quite limited, without a clear taxonomy of developmentally-relevant symptom characteristics in child and adolescent disorders.

We mention one final point concerning symptom variability: specifically, that apparent changes may occur over time, as a result of changes not in the symptoms themselves, but in the methods or criteria by which they are assessed. The confounding effects of method variance are a particular problem in the case of the younger child, for whom there are a number of age-dependent constraints on how personality and psychopathology can be assessed. Measures in early years that must rely almost entirely on observations or inferences by others may later be replaced by a variety of self-report devices, once the child has become more verbal or at least is able to read and write. Although perhaps intended to tap similar psychological domains, these differences in method of assessment would constitute systematic sources of variance that could become confounded with appraisals of change in longitudinal studies of outcome. This further underscores the need for multidimensional, multimethod appraisals of outcome as the best safeguard against the kinds of spurious result that can occur when any single, unidimensional focus is applied in evaluating therapeutic change.

Spontaneous Remission

A related matter pertaining to the natural history of manifest symptomatology concerns the concept of spontaneous remission—that is, the rate of recovery or improvement for untreated disturbances. Much attention (some would say too much) has been devoted to this concept within the psychotherapy literature in an effort to answer the general question as to whether psychotherapy works.

The reasoning was quite simple. If psychotherapy is to be judged effective, it must be shown that it produces a greater rate of improvement—whether expressed in terms of percentage of cases improved, amount of improvement, or how quickly improvement is achieved—when compared with the rate of change that occurs naturally, without the benefit of psychotherapy. Put differently, there is a risk of a false–positive appraisal in judging therapy effectiveness, as a result of a confounding of spontaneous or natural recovery processes with therapeutic change. By knowing the rate of spontaneous remission, however, one can estimate how much the recovery process is improved on through the provision of therapy per se. This sort of thinking held for many years, beginning with the controversial claim first made by Eysenck (1952), who argued that whereas two-thirds of adult neurotics improve with psychotherapy, the rate is no better than the rate of improvement over a two-year period for untreated cases. The two-thirds spontaneous remission rate introduced by Eysenck led to much debate, with many investigators taking issue with this figure and the evidence on which it was based (Bergin, 1971; Lambert, 1976).

The details of this debate are not recounted here, as excellent general discussions on the topic can be found elsewhere (Bergin & Lambert, 1978; Gottman & Markman, 1978). Hopefully, the search for *the* rate of spontaneous recovery has been put to rest. The best available evidence indicates that rates of improvement without treatment vary widely, depending on a variety of factors such as the criteria on which improvement is evaluated, the time at which it is assessed, the kinds of subject and types of disturbance investigated, the availability of environmental supports, and so forth. An overall spontaneous remission rate, regardless how it is computed, masks a great deal of this variability and thus cannot be used as a reliable baseline against which therapy effectiveness can be compared (Bergin & Lambert, 1978; Tramontana, 1980). Moreover, disturbances with low rates of spontaneous recovery are not necessarily associated with low rates of success with treatment, nor do disturbances with high rates of spontaneous recovery always respond well to treatment (Bergin & Lambert, 1978).

Even if one were concerned with having an overall estimate of the spontaneous recovery rate, indications are that Eysenck's figure was inflated. The median recovery rate for untreated adult neuroses is more like 43%, whereas the overall rate of improvement with psychotherapy is about 67% and is achieved within a period of roughly six months or less (Bergin & Lambert, 1978). Similar rates of positive outcome have been reported on the basis of variously composed groups of adolescents, with a median rate of 75% with psychotherapy versus a rate of 39% without psychotherapy (Tramontana, 1980). For children, however, the overall rate of improvement with psychotherapy is between 67 and 78%, but the rate of spontaneous recovery has been estimated to be as high as 60 to 70% (Barrett et al., 1978; Levitt, 1971). Granted that these different figures across age groups are not directly comparable because of differences in the data on which they were based, the pattern does suggest that by adolescence, psychological problems tend to become more severe and chronic than in childhood and thus are less likely to improve without formal treatment. This returns us to an issue previously discussed, namely, what changes occur in manifest psychopathology from childhood through adolescence.

We know, for example, that diagnosis can be particularly unreliable during the early stages of a serious disturbance such as schizophrenia. Follow-up studies of adolescent-onset schizophrenia indicate that it is often misinterpreted as either withdrawal or antisocial behavior during early adolescence (the latter is more common among boys), before the more distinctive features associated with the disorder become more clearly manifested (Weiner, 1980). A history of childhood disturbance is a poor prognostic sign for the symptomatic adolescent (Pichel, 1974), as is a gradual as opposed to a more sudden or reactive onset of symptoms (Gossett et al., 1973). The symptomatic adolescent tends not "to grow out of it"—as has sometimes been held—when there is a history of earlier disturbance or a gradual onset of symptoms (Masterson, 1967). In these cases the youngster's symptoms appear to signify larger, underlying difficulties, problems that have been developing for some time and that will likely persist despite symptom remission, albeit perhaps in somewhat different outward form. It is possible, therefore, at least for younger patients, that much of what is designated as spontaneous remission may instead be tied to the problem discussed earlier regarding developmentally based variation in target symptoms. That is, changes may occur in manifest symptoms, not because of "spontaneous recovery," but because of developmental changes in the outward form of ongoing difficulties. This may at least partly account for the rather high spontaneous recovery rate that both Levitt and Barrett et al. reported for children (i.e., 60 to 70%), in that during childhood—more so than in later years—developmental changes are so rapidly occurring. Hence their estimate of spontaneous recovery is perhaps inflated and does not provide a realistic baseline in judging therapy effectiveness.

The concept of spontaneous remission lacks heuristic value, for it implies that the change process without treatment is random and thus not specifiable, when in reality there probably are complex but systematic factors operating to produce change in the absence of formal psychotherapy. So much of the emphasis has been on the *amount* of change that occurs without treatment. More attention should be given to the *kinds* of change that occur at different points in development and how these might differ between therapy and no-therapy conditions.

Who–What–When: A Framework for Evaluating Outcome

In their review of research on psychotherapy outcome with adults, Bergin and Lambert (1978) emphasized the distinction between *internal* and *external* criteria in evaluating therapeutic change. "Internal criteria" refer to psychological states and dynamic processes within the individual, such as level of distress, coping operations, and so forth, whereas "external criteria" pertain to behavior and symptoms manifested overtly. They argued that the distinction between internal and external criteria has proved valuable in the interpretation of change data, that a number of apparent contradictions in outcome studies can be resolved by distinguishing between these two types of criteria, and that factor analytic studies on assorted outcome measures have generally supported the dichotomy. The judged value of a particular therapeutic intervention or technique may depend on the *kind* of change desired. Each dimension addresses a different domain of human functioning and adjustment; both are significant and both are subject to change in therapy, although perhaps at different rates and in different ways. With respect to spontaneous recovery, for example, Malan (1976) found that rates of improvement without treatment ranged from 33 to 50% on dynamic criteria as opposed to 60 to 70% on symptomatic criteria. This finding bears some relevance to our earlier discussion regarding symptom variability and developmental changes in manifest psychopathology, namely, that the external form of inner difficulties are relatively more likely to show change over time.

Thus it is important to consider *what* is being assessed, whether it is in terms of internal criteria or external criteria that therapeutic change is judged. A comprehensive appraisal should include assessments on both sets of criteria to gain an integrated perspective on what are divergent dimensions of outcome.

Besides the question of what is assessed, it is important to consider *who* is evaluating therapeutic outcome. In addressing precisely this issue, Strupp and Hadley (1977) proposed a tripartite model of mental health and therapeutic outcomes. They regard the term "mental health" as having a multiplicity of meanings, depending on one's perspective or vantage point. According to the model, there are three major parties concerned with definitions of mental health: the individual client; the mental health professional; and society and its representatives (including significant persons in the patient's life). Each of these interested parties operates from a different vantage point in judging mental health and therapeutic outcomes and is guided by different aims or values in making these judgments. The client wishes to be happy and to have his or her needs gratified and to feel content. Mental health is thus defined in terms of highly subjective perceptions of self-esteem, acceptance, and well-being. The mental health professional, although not indifferent to the client's sense of well-being, is more uniquely concerned with the individual's psychological functioning as viewed within the framework of some theory of personality structure and mental health. Accordingly, mental health is defined in terms of sound personality structure characterized by balance, mastery, growth, and other psychological constructs. Society, however, is more concerned with maintaining orderly social relations in which individuals assume responsibility for their assigned social roles, conform to prevailing standards of sanctioned conduct, and adapt to situational requirements appropriately. Thus societal agents (including significant others) tend to define mental health in terms of behavioral stability, predictability, and conformity to social expectations. Strupp and Hadley further proposed that only by considering these multiple perspectives *simultaneously* is it possible to derive a truly comprehensive definition of mental health and meaningful evaluations of therapeutic outcomes. Reflecting independent definitions of mental health, however, these divergent vantage points may yield discrepant evaluations of an individual's functioning and performance, with different profile configurations having different implications for evaluating therapeutic change.

Distinguishing outcome appraisals according to the source of observation (i.e., client, therapist, or significant others) corresponds closely to factors derived from various analyses of multiple change criteria (Bergin & Lambert, 1978). This "who" factor, together with the "what" factor outlined before, appear to provide two meaningful and valid schemes for organizing or classifying different outcome data. Strupp and Hadley have done an admirable job of articulating differences according to the "who" that is involved in evaluating change but have nested within it differences having to do with *what* is assessed. So, according to their model, the client's perspective is concerned mainly with internal criteria of change, the societal perspective focuses on external criteria, whereas the perspective of the mental health professional falls somewhere in between, drawing on both internal and external events in making inferences regarding change in psychological attributes and processes. However, as is acknowledged by Strupp and Hadley, the individual client may also be concerned with his or her behavioral and social adaptation. Under conditions in which persons are asked to provide specific as opposed to global self-ratings, self-report measures can in fact yield highly valid information on external behavior that corresponds closely with direct observation (Gottman & Markman, 1978). On the other hand, parents and other significant persons in the life of the child are not necessarily insensitive to the psychological needs and emotional state of the youngster and may place considerable value on seeing the child become happy and content. At least for the younger child, such persons may provide the only meaningful source of information regarding changes on internal criteria that are manifested within the natural environment.

It seems preferable, therefore, to distinguish the source of observation and its object, by considering the "who" and "what" of evaluation to be independent factors. The different levels of these two factors when treated independently can be completely crossed, resulting in six different categories of outcome appraisal. Thus outcome may be assessed on either internal criteria or external criteria as reported by the client, as observed or inferred by the therapist or other mental health professional (including trained observers), or as observed or inferred by societal representatives and significant or relevant others (including parents, teachers, or peers). Internal criteria may be based on thinking, perception and emotional states, attitudes, beliefs, and motives, as well as other aspects of psychological functioning and behavioral disposition reported by the client or inferred by others. External criteria, in contrast, may be based on overt behavioral manifestations, including observable symptoms, as well as school, home, and community adjustment as reported by the client or observed by others. Some assessment measures may yield a dual focus with respect to these broadly defined categories, as in the case of self-report inventories that survey the client's responses regarding overt behavior as well as subjective experiences, or as in the case of parents' ratings of children that focus on both affect and behavior. Inasmuch as these still may reflect divergent dimensions of change despite their common source, they should be examined separately in evaluating therapeutic change.

The configuration among these six outcome foci can depend on *when* outcome is assessed. This is true with respect to both the stage of development at which the youngster's status is evaluated and the point in treatment or follow-up that therapeutic change is assessed. For example, a child seldom is motivated to seek treatment by a feeling that something is wrong. More often there is likely to be a subjective sense of well-being on the part of the child but agreement between professional and societal observers that something is indeed wrong and that therapeutic change is desired. As treatment progresses, however, the child may come to experience subjective discomfort in the form of anxiety or depression on becoming better able to recognize his or her emotion and behavior and to take another person's point of view. Should such affective changes be regarded as deterioration effects induced by therapy? No, not necessarily, not when viewed as reflecting the child's convergence on a more objective point of view. There can also be varying patterns of convergence or divergence between professional and societal observers, depending on the youngster's stage of development. So, whereas the mental health professional and parents may agree on the value of the child's socialization and conformity to parental rules in appraising outcome, divergence may occur regarding the value of the adolescent's increasing independence and sense of separate identity. Changes may also occur over time in the convergence or divergence of outcome appraisals based on internal and external criteria. For example, the meanings attached to specific behavioral problems are likely to differ considerably between the early and later stages of a serious mental or emotional disturbance. As time passes, these may come to be viewed as outward expressions of broader, underlying difficulties (Masterson, 1967; Weiner, 1980).

Taken together, therefore, a who–what–when framework for evaluating outcome is proposed. It encompasses questions as to what is evaluated and from whose perspective and at what point in time. It focuses on the kinds of change that may occur from different vantage points for the purpose of judging their developmental and therapeutic significance. No specific measures nor battery of measures is implied. Rather, any of a variety of measures can be classified according to outcome focus as defined by the model, although it can broadly guide the selection and organization of various measures across different categories of content, method, or source. Ideally, a comprehensive evaluation of outcome in childhood or adolescence would consider all the components of the model *simultaneously*, through assessments of change on multiple criteria obtained from multiple sources at multiple points in time. This follows from our previous discussions regarding the multidimensionality of therapeutic change as it pertains to multiple dimensions of development and psychopathology in childhood and adolescence.

REVIEW OF STUDIES ASSESSING PSYCHOTHERAPY OUTCOME

Having considered the relevant problems and issues that pertain to evaluating psychotherapy outcome for children and adolescents, we now examine some of the actual methods and instruments that have been used. In simplifying this task, however, we have chosen to focus on studies of adolescents, both because of the more extensive attention that already has been given to outcome assessment on children (Barrett et al., 1978; Levitt, 1971) and because of the similar conclusions that we believe can be drawn regarding the state of the art in research on either age group. Our purpose is to provide—by way of a selective but representative sample of studies—an overview of outcome research on adolescents as it relates to the various aspects of child and adolescent assessment that have been discussed and to highlight some of the more worthwhile studies that have been performed.

Adolescent Outcome Assessment: 1967 to 1979

The present survey reanalyzes the studies included in the Tramontana (1980) review, with special emphasis on their design, instrumentation, and methodology. The earlier review was based on a search through *Psychological Abstracts* for journal articles published from 1967 to 1977 in which there was a quantifiable description of outcome for adolescents receiving individual, group, or family therapy. Case studies were excluded. For inclusion, a study either had to have focused exclusively on adolescents (i.e., with most subjects falling roughly between the ages of 12 and 18 at the outset of therapy) or had to be reported in a way that permitted the determination of outcome specifically for adolescent subjects. The initial search located 35 reports that met the stated criteria. Because three of these (Persons, 1967; Shore & Massimo, 1969, 1973) were follow-up studies of investigations reported prior to 1967, the earlier reports in these cases were also included in the Tramontana (1980) review (Massimo & Shore, 1963; Persons, 1966; Shore & Massimo, 1966). Since then, two more studies were located covering the period up to 1979 and are included in the present review (Fiedler et al., 1979; Rosenstock & Vincent, 1979). Altogether, therefore, there are 40 reports based on 35 independent investigations of psychotherapy outcome with adolescents.

Table 12.1 provides a descriptive overview of each of these studies arranged in chronological sequence. Where specified, it indicates the particular population of adolescents and type of disturbance investigated, the type and duration of therapy provided, and the type of study performed and its formal features in terms of design, sample size, and temporal arrangements. The particular measures and instruments used in assessing outcome are noted, along with whether in each case there was a therapeutic effect or difference demonstrated on it (+), whether the results were equivocal or inconclusive (?), or whether no therapeutic effect or difference was found (−). In the case of a comparative treatment study, however, these designations signify whether a superiority of one treatment over another on the particular criterion measure was obtained. The various measures and instruments used in each study are listed according to when outcome was assessed—that is, at therapy termination and/or at some point in follow-up. Also in keeping with the who–what–when framework for evaluating outcome, the composite assessment of outcome in each study is classified according to six possible categories of outcome focus, depending on the source(s) of observation that were used (i.e., client, professional, and/or societal perspective) and the general dimension(s) on which change was assessed (i.e., internal and/or external criteria). This helps to reduce the variety of specific measures and instruments used into more homogeneous groupings based on the who and what of assessment that were discussed before.

There was rather wide variation among the different studies in terms of design and methodological adequacy. Studies ranged from various single-sample, clinical investigations—which were largely uncontrolled but included some quantified description of outcome—to more complex experimental studies in which psychotherapy was an independent variable that was directly manipulated between appropriate comparison groups. Most of the clinical studies reported positive psychotherapy outcome, but because of their general lack of control, their findings did not constitute convincing evidence of effectiveness. This is why in most cases there is a question mark entered in Table 12.1 next to the outcome assessments performed in these studies. In terms of assessment, outcome was typically evaluated at only a single point in time and usually was based on only a single dependent measure. Reliance was placed solely on self-report or clinical judgment in about half of these studies. However, nearly all the clinical studies on delinquents included some objective index of community adjustment. With the experimental studies, in contrast, there was greater use of multiple measures of outcome, with only about a third of these studies evaluating outcome through a single type of assessment proce-

Table 12.1. Studies of Psychotherapy Outcome with Adolescents

Study (Reference)	Subjects	Type of Therapy	Type of Study	Outcome Assessment[a]		Focus[b]
				Termination	Follow-up	Who–What
Massimo & Shore, 1963; Shore & Massimo, 1966, 1969, 1973	Delinquent boys, expelled or dropped out of school	Informal individual psychotherapy within a vocationally-oriented program, including remedial education and job placement (40 weeks)	Randomized therapy ($n = 10$) vs. no-therapy ($n = 10$) groups; pretest, posttest, and 10-year follow-up	Achievement test scores (+); clinically judged improvement in attitudes toward self (+), control of aggression (+), and authority (−) inferred from thematic stories; rate of employment or return to school (+); legal status (+)	Employment histories (+) and legal records (+)	Soc/Ext Pro/Int
Persons, 1966, 1967	Institutionalized delinquent boys	Individual and group psychotherapy aimed at improving interpersonal relationships (20 weeks)	Matched cohorts, randomized therapy ($n = 41$) vs. no-therapy ($n = 41$) groups; pretest, posttest, and 1-year follow-up	Reduced scores on the Taylor Manifest Anxiety Scale (+), a delinquency scale (+), and selected MMPI scales (+); clinically judged improvement in MMPI profiles (+);[c] indices of institutional adjustment (+)[d]	Rates of recidivism (+) and employment (+)	Clt/Int, Ext Pro/Int Soc/Ext

418

Study	Sample	Treatment	Design			
Kaufmann & Deutsch, 1967	Unwed pregnant girls	Group therapy and counseling, combined with prenatal care and collateral counseling of patient's mother (72 weeks)	Randomized therapy (n = 8) vs. no-therapy (n = 12) groups;[e] follow-up at 1 year after termination	—	Rate of repeated pregnancy (+)	Soc/Ext
Masterson, 1967	Mixed psychiatric outpatient sample judged to be moderately to severely impaired	Unspecified psychotherapy	Clinical follow-up at 5 years after initial evaluation (N = 30)	—	Clinically judged improvement in level of impairment (?)	Pro/Int, Ext
Miezio, 1967	Institutionalized retardates with IQs of 50 to 70	Group therapy aimed at better institutional adjustment (72 weeks)	Single sample, therapy outcome (N = 15)	Staff judgment of improvement in appearance, expressions of well-being, and in school and work performance (?)	—	Pro/Ext
Taylor, 1967	Institutionalized delinquent girls	Psychoanalytically oriented group psychotherapy (40 weeks)	Therapy (n = 11) vs. counseling (n = 11) vs. no-therapy (n = 11) groups;[f] pretest, posttest, and follow-up at 26 weeks after release	Changes on various personality scales, including the MMPI and 16 PF (?); attitudinal change on specially constructed questionnaires (?); behavior ratings by institutional officials (?); discharge rate (−)	Behavior ratings by assorted community informants (?); recidivism rate (−)[g]	Clt/Int, Ext Soc/Ext
Coughlin & Wimberger, 1968	Boys having conflicts with parents	Group family therapy focusing on communication patterns (18 weeks)	Single sample, therapy outcome (N = 9)	Global self-appraisal of improved family relationships (?)	—	Clt/Ext

(continued)

Table 12.1. (continued)

| Study (Reference) | Subjects | Type of Therapy | Type of Study | Outcome Assessment[a] | | Focus[b] |
				Termination	Follow-up	Who–What
Hilgard, et al., 1969	Boys with poor peer relationships	Group therapy with better-adjusted peers in a program to improve social skills (8 weeks)	Single sample, therapy outcome; pretest, posttest, and 1-month follow-up (N = 6)	Observer ratings of social skills (?)[h]	Self-reported changes in attitudes toward self and in social behavior (?); global appraisal by parents of behavioral improvement (?)	Pro/Ext Clt/Int, Ext Soc/Ext
Mordock et al., 1969	Institutionalized boys with emotional disturbance and learning difficulties	Group psychotherapy or individual psychotherapy (32 weeks)	Comparative treatment: group (n = 40) vs. individual (n = 19) psychotherapy;[i] pretest, posttest	Increases on measures of sociometric choice (?)	—	Soc/Ext
Bauman, 1970	Middle-class drug abusers	Hypnotic substitution combined with short-term psychotherapy	Clinical follow-up over an unspecified period (N = 179)	—	Rate and type of drug abuse known to the therapist (?)	Pro/Ext
Ostrom et al., 1971	Delinquent boys on probation	Group therapy based on application of various social psychology principles (7 weeks)	Matched cohorts, randomized therapy (n = 19) vs. no-therapy (n = 19) groups; follow-up at 5 months and at 10 months after therapy began	Arrest records for first 5-month period (?)[j]	Arrest records for second 5-month period (–); number of "external" responses on an oral version of the Rotter Internal–External Locus of Control Scale (+)[k]	Soc/Ext Clt/Int

420

Perkins, 1971	Hospitalized drug abusers on probation	Group–individual relaxation training and hypnotherapy to enhance self-control (24 weeks)	Clinical follow-up at 1 year after discharge (N = 25)	—	Rate of drug abstinence (?); rate of employment or return to school (?)	Soc/Ext
Marvit, 1972	Institutionalized delinquent volunteers	Group therapy with a psychoeducational emphasis within a behavior modification program (24 weeks)	Single sample, therapy outcome; pretest, posttest, and follow-up at 6 months after release (N = 10)	Change on social attitudes questionnaire (+)	Recidivism rate (?)	Clt/Int Soc/Ext
Redfering, 1972, 1973	Institutionalized delinquent girls	Client-centered group counseling (11 weeks)	Randomized therapy (n = 18) vs. no-therapy (n = 18) groups; posttest and 1 year follow-up	Attitudes toward self (+), parents (+), and peers (+) on semantic differential	Attitudes toward self (+), parents (+), and peers (–) on semantic differential; rate of release (+);[a] rates of recidivism (–) and employment (–)	Clt/Int Soc/Ext
Endler & North, 1973	Unspecified outpatients	Unspecified psychotherapy (12 weeks)	Ex post facto comparison of treated patients with a sample of nonpatients; pretest, posttest	Changes in anxiety on various self-report measures (?)	—	Clt/Int

(continued)

Table 12.1. *(continued)*

Study (Reference)	Subjects	Type of Therapy	Type of Study	Outcome Assessment[a]		Focus[b]
				Termination	Follow-up	Who–What
Felton & Davidson, 1973	High-school low achievers	Gestalt-oriented group counseling, part of a special academic program including contracting and emphasis on individual responsibility (20 weeks)	Therapy ($n = 61$) vs. no-therapy ($n = 18$) groups;[i] pretest, posttest	Increased internality on the Rotter Internal–External Locus of Control Scale (+)	—	Clt/Int
Homer, 1973	Court-referred runaway girls	Combination of individual therapy, group counseling, family therapy, and client advocacy	Follow-up over an unspecified period for those classified as "running to" or "running from'"[m] ($N = 20$)	—	Recidivism rate (?)	Soc/Ext
Kahn et al., 1974	Native American delinquent boys paid for attendance	Group therapy, using topical discussions initially to stimulate interaction (44 weeks)	Single sample, therapy outcome; subjects as own controls for 1 year preceding and following beginning of treatment ($N = 15$)	Arrest rate (+); rate of school attendance (?)[h]	—	Soc/Ext
Marvit et al., 1974	Mixed delinquent sample	Group therapy, with or without videotape feedback (4 sessions)	Randomized, comparative treatment: videotape ($n = 23$) vs. no videotape ($n = 21$) groups; pretest, posttest	Changes in questionnaire responses intended to measure attitudes and perceptions of self and others (+ for videotape condition)	—	Clt/Int

422

Miran et al., 1974	Junior high school boys referred for behavior problems and poor school performance	Group therapy combined with a period of contingent rewards for positive school performance (32 weeks)	Randomized therapy ($n = 14$) vs. no-therapy ($n = 6$) groups;[n] pretest, posttest	Teacher ratings on behavior and academic performance (+); rates of detention (−) and suspension (?)[o]	—	Soc/Ext
Pichel, 1974	Mixed psychiatric outpatient sample	Unspecified psychotherapy	Clinical follow-up at least 10 years after initial evaluation ($N = 37$)[p]	—	Rate of self-reported positive adjustment on questionnaire (?)	Clt/Int, Ext
Rachman, 1974	Delinquent boys for whom participation was a condition of parole	Group therapy with therapist explicitly adopting a fathering role	Single sample, therapy outcome ($N = 25$)	Legal status (?)	—	Soc/Ext
Rosenstock & Hansen, 1974	Students referred because of poor academic performance, disruptive behavior, and poor social skills	Group therapy to improve school adjustment, with separate groups for boys and girls (28 weeks)	Therapy ($n = 8$) vs. no-therapy ($n = 8$) groups;[a] pretest, posttest	Changes on teacher-reported inventory of problem behaviors (?)[d]	—	Soc/Ext
Wunderlich et al., 1974	Court-referred drug offenders	Group therapy, with separate groups for offenders and parents to improve their relationships (at least 12 weeks)	Follow-up at 1 year after termination ($N = 100$)	—	Arrest rate (?)	Soc/Ext
Brown & Kingsley, 1975	Students referred for behavior problems who completed at least 5 sessions	Group therapy, including guided group interaction and reality therapy, combined with contracting on educational goals (7 weeks)	Single sample, therapy outcome; pretest, posttest ($N = 30$)	Congruence between real and ideal self-perception (+)	—	Clt/Int

(continued)

Table 12.1. *(continued)*

Study (Reference)	Subjects	Type of Therapy	Type of Study	Outcome Assessment[a]		Focus[b]
				Termination	Follow-up	Who–What
Jesness, 1975	Institutionalized delinquent boys	Group therapy within a program based on transactional analysis principles, with contracting on treatment goals (30 weeks) or behavior modification program, including a token economy, a parole-contingent point system, and behavioral contracts (35 weeks)	Randomized, comparative treatment: transactional analysis (TA) vs. behavior modification (BM) programs; pretest, posttest, and follow-up for 2 yr. after release (N = 904)	Self-reported attitudes toward program and staff (+ for TA); achievement test scores (?); subscales of the Jesness Inventory, a self-report measure of personality and delinquency (+ for TA); subscales of the Jesness Behavior Checklist: self-rated (+ for TA) observer-rated (+ for BM); clinically judged level of ego development on test of moral judgment (?)	Parole violation rates (–)[r]	Clt/Int, Ext Pro/Int, Ext Soc/Ext
Meyer & Zegans, 1975	Mixed psychiatric outpatient sample	Individual psychotherapy (at least 4 sessions)	Single sample, therapy outcome (N = 25)[s]	Client perceptions of therapy effects in a semistructured posttherapy interview (?)	—	Clt/Int

Study	Sample	Treatment	Design			Code
Moser, 1975	Institutionalized delinquent boys scoring as "externals" on the Rotter Internal–External Locus of Control Scale	Group therapy aimed at increasing belief in internal locus of control (8 weeks)	Matched cohorts, randomized therapy ($n = 8$) vs. discussion ($n = 8$) vs. no-therapy ($n = 8$) groups;[f] pretest, posttest	Increased internality on the Rotter Internal–External Locus of Control Scale (+)	—	Clt/Int
Fine et al., 1976	Mixed psychiatric outpatient sample	Group therapy, with or without better-adjusted peers (15 weeks)	Randomized, comparative treatment: group therapy with ($n = 8$) vs. without ($n = 8$) better-adjusted peers; pretest, posttest	Improvement on the Piers-Harris Self Concept Scale (−); Parent ratings on the Devereux Adolescent Behavior Rating Scale (−)	—	Clt/Int Soc/Ext
Lessing et al., 1976	Clients with emotional or educational problems seen at a guidance clinic	Unspecified psychotherapy (at least 10 sessions)	Single sample, multivariate prediction of outcome; pretest, posttest ($N = 54$)	Arbitrary classification as improved, based on pre–post factor scores from parent ratings on the Institute for Juvenile Research Behavior Checklist (?)	—	Soc/Ext
Gossett et al., 1977	Discharged psychiatric inpatients who continued in posthospital psychotherapy	Posthospital, psychodynamic psychotherapy	Single sample, multivariate prediction of hospital outcome, with follow-up at 20 to 48 months after discharge and using continuation in therapy as a predictor ($N = 40$)	—	Clinical consensus on overall level of functioning, based on findings in a semistructured interview (?)[a]	Pro/Int, Ext

(continued)

425

Table 12.1. (continued)

Study (Reference)	Subjects	Type of Therapy	Type of Study	Outcome Assessment[a]		Focus[b]
				Termination	Follow-up	Who–What
Hayes, 1977	Mildly to moderately retarded psychiatric outpatients	Individual, psychoanalytically oriented psychotherapy, combined with parent counseling (at least 32 weeks)	*Ex post facto* comparison of therapy outcome for retarded patients (n = 10) vs. a matched group of nonretarded patients (n = 4)[v]	Therapists' ratings of overall change in presenting problems (?)[w]	—	Pro/Int, Ext
Ro-Trock et al., 1977	Mixed sample of psychiatric inpatients who had been living with both parents	Family therapy, eclectic in orientation (10 sessions) or individual therapy, focusing on patient-therapist relationship (10 sessions)	Randomized, comparative treatment: family (n = 14) vs. individual (n = 14) therapy;[x] pretest, posttest, and follow-up at 3 months after discharge	Improvement on self-report inventories of parent–adolescent communication (+ for family therapy), marital communication (−), and interpersonal behavior (−); observer codings of verbal and nonverbal family interaction on the Revealed Differences Test, a questionnaire requiring *in vivo* problem solving and agreement (?)	Readmission rate and rates of return to school or work (+ for family therapy)	Clt/Ext Pro/Ext Soc/Ext

Fiedler et al., 1979	Mixed sample of psychiatric inpatients with excessive passivity or aggressiveness	Structured assertiveness-training group, including videotape feedback and suppression of hostility or process-oriented group therapy to promote insight and reality testing (4 sessions)	Randomized, comparative treatment: assertiveness trainirg ($n = 14$) vs. process-oriented ($n = 11$) groups; pretest, posttest	Improvement on the Tennessee Self Concept Scale ($-$); positive change in observer ratings of hostility ($-$) and assertiveness ($+$) in a contrived roleplaying situation	—	Clt/Int Pro/Int, Ext
Rosenstock & Vincent, 1979	Moderately impaired psychiatric outpatients	Posthospital group psychotherapy, with or without voluntary participation of parents in collateral therapy (24 weeks)	*Ex post facto* comparison of outcome at 8 to 12 months follow-up: with ($n = 42$) vs. without ($n = 21$) paren:al involvement	—	Clinically judged success based on reported absence of presenting problems ($+$ for parental involvement)[y]	Pro/Ext

[a]In parentheses: $+$ = positive effect, ? = equivocal or inconclusive, $-$ = no effect demonstrated.

[b]Abbreviations: Clt = outcome according to client; Pro = mental health professional (or trained observer); Soc = society (including relevant others); Int = on internal criteria; Ext = on external criteria.

[c]There was 97% agreement between judges, but it is not stated whether the profiles were rated blindly.

[d]It was not stated whether officials knew which subjects were treated.

[e]It was not stated whether control subjects had the same opportunity for birth-control counseling as did the therapy subjects.

[f]Subjects in the counseling condition were not randomly assigned, but were similar to subjects in the other conditions in most respects.

[g]Apart from the negative findings on discharge and recidivism rates, the lack of clarity in the report largely precludes a determination of outcome on the other measures used.

[h]No test of significance was reported.

[i]There was probable selection bias in the assignment of subjects to conditions. There was a problem with differential dropout, and it seems that new enrollees were mostly assigned to the individual therapy condition. There was also the possibility of experimenter bias in the execution of the different conditions, in that the same therapists served under both therapy conditions.

(continued)

427

Table 12.1. (continued)

[j] A significant difference in arrest rate between the two conditions was obtained only when the data on therapy subjects with poor attendance and their matched controls were excluded.

[k] Demand characteristics may have been introduced, in that the interviews were conducted by project personnel.

[l] Possible selection bias, in that it is unclear whether controls had refused to be in the special program. However, there was no significant difference between groups on the criterion measure at pretest.

[m] This classification was largely made post hoc and seems to have been confounded with the actual process and outcome of therapy.

[n] Although subjects were randomly assigned, subjects in the therapy condition initially had significantly lower grades, more frequent academic problems, and more suspensions than the controls.

[o] The frequency of suspensions for the therapy subjects significantly decreased only during the period of contingent reinforcement.

[p] Of the 83 patients contacted for follow-up, 60 replied; of these, 37 had continued in treatment after the initial evaluation.

[q] Ten of 32 students were initially invited into therapy; 8 actually participated. Control subjects were drawn from the remaining students and reportedly were matched with therapy subjects on selected variables.

[r] No difference was observed between the TA and BM programs, but the combined recidivism rate at 12 months after release was significantly less than the rates during a baseline period and the rates of two other institutions.

[s] Fifty percent of the patients solicited for posttherapy interviews responded.

[t] There was a possibility of experimenter bias in that the investigator served as group leader under both the group therapy and group discussion conditions.

[u] Although there was a higher rate of positive outcome among these patients than for a group who had not continued in posthospital therapy, this was probably as much an indication of differential prognosis for continuers and terminators as it was a reflection of therapy outcome.

[v] These group sizes refer only to the adolescent subjects in the study.

[w] Ratings of change for the retarded patients were no less than for the nonretarded patients, but the two groups were drawn from separate clinics where different standards of improvement may have been applied. Also, a possible bias was introduced in obtaining therapists' ratings through interviews by the investigator.

[x] There was a possibility of bias in the execution of the two conditions, in that the therapists for individual therapy also served in the family therapy condition.

[y] There was possible confounding of group membership with one aspect of determining outcome, in that uninvolved parents may have been unreliable or negatively biased informants.

428

dure. There was much greater use of standardized psychological tests and greater use of observations by others, but no reliance was placed solely on patient or therapist appraisals of change. Outcome assessments were performed both at termination and at follow-up in almost half of the experimental studies, but the methods of assessment tended to differ between termination and the time of follow-up.

Of the six possible types of outcome focus, there was an overall average of 1.71 categories used per study. Only 43% of the studies had more than one type of focus, and whereas 40% assessed outcome on both internal and external criteria, only 11% included assessments through a complete combination of client, professional, and societal sources. Although it was not a clear-cut relationship, the better designed and executed studies were the ones that generally tended to evaluate change across multiple categories of outcome focus.

Table 12.2 shows the frequency distribution across each of these assessment categories for the entire sample of studies. It also indicates the overall rate of positive effects yielded with each type of outcome focus. In general, it appears that greater emphasis was given to assessing change on external as opposed to internal criteria, and whereas the societal–external and client–internal categories were most often used, no study evaluated change on internal criteria as viewed by parents, teachers, or other societal agents. Further analysis shows that the societal–external focus was represented mainly by various dichotomous indices of follow-up community adjustment, such as rates of recidivism, employment, or return to school, especially in the studies on delinquents. Only one study (Mordock et al., 1969), however, used sociometric measures in evaluating therapeutic change. The client–internal focus, in contrast, consisted largely of assorted attitudinal assessments, particularly measures of self-concept and locus of control. It was evidently within this general category of assessment that therapeutic change or differences were most often achieved, but these did not necessarily correspond to changes in other categories that were simultaneously assessed. For example, in those studies that assessed both client–internal and societal–external indications of change, there was only about a 50% correspondence in overall outcomes. Moreover, whereas Fielder et al. (1979) found that an assertiveness-training group in four sessions produced greater changes in observer ratings of behavioral assertiveness than did a process-oriented insight group, there were no differences between the treatments by the end of this brief period in either self-concept or observer ratings of underlying mood. All these observations tend to support the conclusion that the different categories of outcome focus do indeed represent independent dimensions of therapeutic change.

Taken together, the research on psychotherapy outcome with adolescents has not adequately addressed the various assessment issues that are especially relevant with this age group. In many respects, it has not even come to grips with the very basic methodological considerations inherent in the study of outcome that were articulated some time ago within the literature on adults.

Table 12.2.   Assessment Frequencies According to Outcome Focus and Percentage[a] with Positive Effects[b]

Source	Criteria		Totals
	Internal	External	
Client	16(.56)	7(.43)	23(.52)
Professional	7(.29)	10(.30)	17(.29)
Society	0 (—)	20(.35)	20(.35)
Totals	23(.48)	37(.35)	60(.40)

[a]Shown in parentheses.
[b]Based on 35 independent investigations of psychotherapy outcome with adolescents.

Similar conclusions have been made regarding the research on children (Barrett et al., 1978). So, whereas one might argue that the various complexities involved in studying the child or adolescent require that—by comparison—*greater* assessment sophistication is necessary than in studies on adults, this certainly has not been the norm. If there has been a single, overriding limitation among the existing studies on adolescents, it has been that the focus in assessing outcome has tended to be rather narrow in scope. Heavy use has been made of various objective and convincing indices of therapeutic impact, such as reduced recidivism, return to school, and so forth. The problem with relying on such measures alone is that outcome is evaluated as if it were simply an all-or-none affair. Gross measures such as these are too insensitive to capture subtle internal or external changes that therapy might produce. Likewise, to base an appraisal of outcome solely on attitudinal changes in self-concept or locus of control is very limited in value. In some cases the dice may be loaded—so to speak—in favor of finding a positive effect, when the therapeutic intervention is specifically aimed at changing the particular attitudes or beliefs being measured (Moser, 1975). This can lead the skeptic to conclude that the only demonstrated value of the therapy was its apparent effectiveness in educating subjects on how to improve their responses on the particular assessment device that was used. In general, the studies on adolescents have tended to fall quite short of the assessment ideals so far discussed—that is, the need for assessments of change on multiple criteria obtained from multiple sources at multiple points in time.

Although much can be learned from the assessment shortcomings of existing research, more important lessons can be gleaned from those studies that serve to exemplify the kinds of outcome investigation that are much needed in this area. There were a number of exemplary studies among the ones included in this review that are now highlighted in terms of the assessment approaches that were used.

Exemplary Studies

Many of the studies on psychotherapy outcome with adolescents focused exclusively on delinquents. The best of these, in terms of methodological scope and rigor, were the series of investigations on therapy effectiveness by Persons (1966, 1967) and the large-scale comparative treatment study by Jesness (1975).

In the initial study by Persons (1966), 82 institutionalized delinquent boys were selected in matched pairs and then randomly assigned to therapy and no-therapy conditions. The variables on which subjects had been matched included age, IQ, race, socioeconomic background, type of offense, number of previous offenses, total time incarcerated, and present institutional adjustment. The therapy condition consisted of a total of 80 hours, over a 20-week period, of combined individual and group psychotherapeutic methods aimed at improving interpersonal relationships and self-appraisal. Five therapists of varied experience were used, with each subject having the same therapist for both individual and group therapy. Subjects in the therapy and no-therapy conditions continued to participate in the same institutional programs outside therapy. All subjects were pretested and tested again at therapy termination on the Minnesota Multiphasic Personality Inventory (MMPI), the Taylor Manifest Anxiety Scale, and a delinquency scale derived from a self-report inventory (Peterson et al., 1959).

At termination, therapy subjects showed significantly greater reductions on the measures of anxiety, delinquency, and on all but the L, K, Mf, and Si scales of the MMPI. Minnesota Multiphasic Personality Inventory profiles of 73% of the treated subjects, compared with only 29% of the controls, were judged as reflecting improvement. Presumably these were done blindly, although it was not explicitly stated—only that there was 97% interrater agreement between the two clinical psychologists making the judgments. Treated subjects received passes significantly sooner, had fewer disciplinary reports, and more often made the school's honor roll, but, here again, one can only assume that these decisions by institution officials were not biased by a knowledge of which subjects participated in therapy. Furthermore, with respect to outcome at termination, no differences were found as a function of experience level across the five therapists that were used. In a follow-up investigation on all 82 boys, Persons (1967) was also able to show that the therapeutic intervention made a positive difference in terms of subsequent community adjustment. On the basis of the report of each boy's parole officer at 1 year after therapy termination and at an average of 9.5 months after release, the therapy subjects had a significantly lower rate of recidivism (32 vs. 61% for the controls), fewer parole violations, and a higher rate of employment.

Taken together, the two studies by Persons provide a convincing case for the effectiveness of therapy over no-therapy conditions with delinquent adolescents. The exemplary aspects of the overall investigation were its sound experimental design and the varied array of measures on which the appraisal of outcome was based. No innovative assessment instruments or methods were introduced, but the broad scope of the data base served to compensate for what otherwise would have been limitations or interpretive problems with some of the individual criterion measures used.

In the Jesness (1975) study, the product of a four-year demonstration project performed in cooperation with the California Youth Authority, the effects of two separate treatment programs in the rehabilitation of institu-tionalized delinquents were compared. Over 1100 delinquent boys—most of whom were prior offenders with offenses ranging from murder to incorrigibil-ity—were randomly assigned to one of two newly opened correctional institu-tions that were alike in most respects, except that one program was based entirely on transactional analysis principles and included group psychotherapy, whereas the other was based strictly on behavior modification principles. Exceptional training and continuing education were provided to staff in both programs, but whereas the average duration of treatment in the transactional analysis (TA) program and the behavior modification (BM) program was 30 and 35 weeks, respectively, more time reportedly was spent by staff with subjects in the TA program. Complete pretest, posttest, and follow-up data were available on 904 subjects.

The assessment of outcome was based on multiple change criteria as viewed by multiple sources. These included the Gates-MacGinitie Reading Survey and the arithmetic subtest of the Comprehensive Test of Basic Skills for tapping academic achievement; the Jesness Inventory (Jesness, 1966), an 11-scale self-report measure of personality and delinquency that was supplemented with a drug-use scale; self-ratings and observer-ratings on the Jesness Behavior Checklist (Jesness, 1971), an 80-item instrument yielding scores on 14 factor-analytically derived scales; Loevinger's level of ego development (Loevinger, 1966; Loevinger & Wessler, 1970), scored blindly, and based on a shortened, 15-item form on which each subject provided written responses to open-ended sentences requiring moral judgments; and parole follow-up based on records of arrests, reconviction, and other disposition data. Additional assessments in-cluded the rating of each subject at entry with respect to level of interpersonal maturity (three levels with a total of nine subtypes, based on data from the Jesness Inventory, a sentence-completion test, and a brief interview), and a survey of all subjects just prior to release on the Postopinion Poll—a 45-item questionnaire aimed at eliciting attitudes toward program experiences and program staff.

Sophisticated statistical analyses such as multivariate analysis of variance (ANOVA) and multiple covariance analysis were used in comparing program effects. However, no overall superiority of one program over the other was found. Whereas the BM program tended to do better on observer ratings of behavioral change, the TA program was viewed more positively by subjects and tended to do better on internal criteria and self-reported behavioral change. Aside from these qualitative differences at termination, the two programs did not differ with respect to parole outcome at follow-up periods ranging from 3 to 24 months after release. The recidivism rate at 12 months for both programs was 32%, which was significantly lower than the rates during a baseline period ($M = 45\%$) and the rates of two other institutions ($M = 43\%$). Therapeutic decay was becoming apparent by 24 months, however, in that the recidivism rate for both programs had risen to 48%. Additional findings showed that program differences depended not only on the particular outcome measure involved, but also on the rated interpersonal maturity level of the subjects. Moreover, whereas differences in the type of therapy between the two programs accounted for 19% of the total variance in outcome, the positive opinion or regard expressed by subjects toward their therapists and the program on the Postopinion Poll accounted for an additional 13% of the variance on the dependent measures, including parole outcome.

Few investigators would have the opportunity to match the large-scale features of the Jesness study, but it was not its size per se that made the study so worthwhile. Rather, it was its broad-based and multifaceted assessment of outcome; its emphasis on examining qualitative aspects of change; and its attempt to evaluate the relative contributions of client characteristics, treatment variables, and therapist–milieu variables in treatment outcomes that distinguished the study as truly exemplary.

Very few studies within the adolescent literature have examined the effects of family therapy, despite the claims that are often heard regarding the presumed superiority of this mode of therapy over individual treatment. One notable exception, however, was the well-conducted study by Ro-Trock et al. (1977) that compared the effects of family therapy and individual therapy on a mixed sample of psychiatrically hospitalized adolescents.

Subjects were randomly drawn from patients referred to a psychiatric inpatient service, provided the youngster came from an intact family with both parents present. They were then randomly assigned to either family therapy or individual therapy, with 14 subjects receiving each condition. Family therapy was reportedly eclectic in orientation, and cases were divided between two male–female cotherapist teams. Individual therapy focused mainly on the interpersonal aspects of the patient–therapist relationship, and cases were divided between the two male therapists who also served in the family therapy condition. The parents of the subjects receiving individual therapy were seen only during pretesting and posttesting sessions. Both therapy conditions were offered in 10 sessions.

Assessment included three self-report measures and one observational measure administered at both pretest and posttest, along with telephone follow-up on community adjustment at three months after discharge. The Parent–Adolescent Communication Inventory (Bienvenu, 1959) and the Marital Communication Inventory (Bienvenu, 1970) were used to assess aspects of communication patterns and styles between parents and adolescents and between marital pairs. The Interpersonal Checklist (LaForge & Suczek, 1955), which was intended to assess interpersonal aspects of personality, was also completed by all patients and parents. The observational measure was based on actual family interaction while taking the Revealed Differences Test (Strodtbeck, 1951, 1954), a 47-item questionnaire requiring *in vivo* problem solving and three-way agreement among father, mother, and adolescent on family issues. These interactions were videotaped and coded blindly by eight trained observers according to an explicit coding system that incorporated seven categories of verbal and nonverbal behavior. Interrater reliability was reportedly maintained at a minimum of .70.

The only difference found on the self-report measures was the significantly greater improvement in family communication reported by subjects in the family therapy condition on the Parent–Adolescent Communication Inventory. The results on the observational measures of family interaction were mixed and generally did not confirm the expected superiority of the family therapy condition. However, at three months after discharge, significantly fewer adolescents in the family therapy condition had been rehospitalized (0 vs. 43%), and they had taken significantly fewer days to return to school or work.

The latter was an important finding, but generalization from it should await a replication of the study. The sample size was small, the youngsters in the two conditions differed in mean age—with subjects receiving individual treatment being somewhat older, and there was a possibility of experimenter bias in the execution of the two therapy conditions because of the overlap of therapists serving in both. Outcome was found to vary according to therapist, but the investigators were unable to ascertain the precise factors that accounted for the obtained differences. Also, as Ro-Track et al. pointed out, it is still to be demonstrated that differences in family interaction actually precede and mediate the better adolescent adjustment that may result from family therapy. Perhaps because of the assessment of family process at termination of therapy, rather than at follow-up, it was too early for changes in parent– adolescent communication to be observed in overt behavior (although it was suggested on the self-report inventory). This relates to our earlier discussion regarding *when* change is assessed and underscores the importance of obtaining repeated measures at multiple points in time.

Two more studies merit special consideration. Although neither was a controlled investigation of psychotherapeutic effects, at least not in the sense of the previous studies considered here, they each represent a kind of investigation that is much needed in this area. These were the studies by Lessing et al. (1976) and Gossett et al. (1977).

Lessing et al. used multivariate statistical methods to test the validity of selected demographic and behavior-descriptive variables in predicting therapy continuation–defection and improvement–nonimprovement for adolescents seen at a guidance clinic. Mothers of 87 consecutive male and female adolescent applicants accepted for therapy completed the Institute for Juvenile Research Behavior Checklist (Lessing et al., 1973), a 229-item inventory with yes–no-response options and with separate subscores for mild, moderate, and severe deviant behaviors. This was done at the end of the intake interview and again either after one year or at the final therapy interview, whichever came first. The total sample was divided into 54 continuers (i.e., those seen for at least 10 sessions) and 22 early defectors. Eleven subjects were deleted whose therapy was terminated prematurely by parent or therapist. The continuers were further subdivided into those who were classified as improved ($n = 18$) or unimproved ($n = 16$), based on arbitrary cutoffs with pre–post differences on their two sets of checklist scores. The 74 most frequently endorsed items on the checklist were factor analyzed to identify the major dimensions of psychopathology within the sample. Two separate discriminant function analyses were then used to predict continuation–defection and improvement–nonimprovement with 13 predictor variables: nine behavior checklist factor scores, sex, race, age, and occupational level of the principal family wage earner.

Continuers were found to be less tense and less disorganized or impulsive than defectors, whereas those who improved in comparison with those who did not were more likely to be 15 years of age or older and were also more likely to act out rather than withdraw when stressed. Thus, although an inclination to act out placed the youngster at greater risk to discontinue therapy, it ultimately indicated a more active coping stance for those who managed to remain. This finding should be viewed with caution, however, as there was a restricted range of psychopathology within the subject sample, with no subjects diagnosed as having a conduct disorder or hyperactivity and only a few who were described as severely disturbed. Moreover, the criteria for evaluating improvement were too lenient and narrow in scope, and the sample size was too small for some of the analyses performed. Despite these limitations, the Lessing et al. study represents an excellent attempt to examine an array of client variables—including age as an estimate of maturity level—as they relate not only to therapy outcome, but also to therapy continuance, a matter that is of particular importance with adolescents. The study was also noteworthy in its examination of the predictive power of selected demographic variables—an area that has received very little systematic investigation within the child and adolescent literature. Needless to say, factors such as the socioeconomic level and cultural–ethnic background of the youngster's family, as well as the "match" between patient and therapist on these factors, may constitute important sources of variance in both the process and outcome of therapy.

In the first of a series of follow-up studies from the Timberlawn Adolescent Treatment Assessment Project, Gossett and his colleagues (Gossett et al., 1977) examined the power of selected patient variables and treatment variables, including psychotherapy, in predicting the long-range outcome of adolescents treated in a psychiatric hospital. The treatment program incorporated a variety of therapeutic modalities and was specialized in the intermediate to long-term reconstructive treatment of youngsters who had failed to benefit from one or more previous outpatient or short-term inpatient treatment attempts. Follow-up was based on 55 male and female adolescents who had been treated between 1966 and 1968 and was performed at 20 to 48 months after hospital discharge. Outcome was assessed through semistructured interviews, with both the former patient and parents and/or spouse, that elicited information as to the patient's status and functioning in a variety of areas after discharge. The interviews were performed either face-to-face or by way of telephone contact and were preferably assigned to the one of five follow-up investigators with whom the former patient was most familiar. The follow-up information on each subject was then reviewed in a staff conference, wherein a consensual judgment was reached as to overall current level of functioning (good, fair, or poor).

Outcome was found to be better for those adolescents who had less severe symptoms on admission (.62), who completed the full course of hospital treatment (.62), who had a more reactive onset of symptoms (.58), who continued in psychotherapy after discharge until a mutually agreed termination (.40), and who had a higher energy level (.35) but little physically threatening behavior prior to hospitalization (.24). A multiple regression analysis showed that diagnostic severity accounted for the largest portion of predictive power, with prognosis ranging from good to poor depending on whether the adolescent carried the diagnosis of neurosis, behavior disorder, or psychosis at the outset. With respect to continuation in recommended outpatient psychotherapy after discharge, 68% of those who continued, compared with 47% of those who prematurely terminated, were judged as functioning at a good level at follow-up. Continuation appeared to make a positive difference only for those adolescents with the diagnosis of psychosis or behavior disorder, especially if there had been a gradual onset of symptoms (i.e., process disorders). For these more severely and chronically disturbed youngsters, the better prognosis associated with therapy continuation was perhaps as much as or more of an indication of differential motivation for change between continuers and terminators as it was a reflection of therapy effects per se. It also suggested that an important skill on the part of the therapist working with such youngsters may have involved the conversion of the "terminator" into a "continuer" until something positive took place (Gossett, 1980, Reference Note at end of chapter 1).

There have been a number of further developments and refinements that have developed as a result of the Timberlawn Project since its inception, including improved procedures for follow-up assessment (Gossett et al., 1976a, 1980). In their 1973 review of follow-up studies on hospitalized adolescents, the Timberlawn group (Gossett et al., 1973) had identified six variables having a demonstrated relationship to long-term outcome: (1) severity of patient psychopathology; (2) process versus reactive onset of symptomatology; (3) intelligence; (4) the provision of a specialized adolescent treatment program; (5) completion of recommended hospital treatment; and (6) continuation in recommended outpatient psychotherapy after discharge. Their subsequent work, which is based on a follow-up of 120 patients at an average of five years after discharge (summarized in Gossett, 1981, Reference Note 2), has continued to confirm the predictive power of those six variables and has identified two more: (1) family level of competence or psychopathology at the time of the adolescent's hospital admission as assessed on the Beavers–Timberlawn Family Evaluation Scale (Lewis et al., 1976) and (2) locus of control, which they have found to be, in fact, one of the most powerful predictors of long-term outcome. Process versus reactive onset continues to be assessed with the Onset of Symptomatology Scale (Gossett et al., 1976b), but the Gossett-Timberlawn Adolescent Psychopathology Scale (Barnhart & Gossett, 1973) has since been introduced as a more sensitive measure of symptom severity than the initial measure, which simply used the gross, three-level classification of neurotic, behavior disordered, or psychotic diagnosis.

The Timberlawn Adolescent Treatment Assessment Project represents a commendable effort in the appraisal of the relative contributions of patient, family, and treatment variables to the long-term outcome of treatment-resistive youngsters. A similar project by Blotcky is currently in progress with preadolescent children treated on the Timberlawn Children's Unit (Gossett, 1981, Reference Note 2). Although not a laboratory-elegant approach to the study of outcome, the Timberlawn effort is a practical and clinically meaningful approach to assessment that can be relatively easily incorporated into real-life clinical settings, most of which are sorely in need of empirical data on which to base predictions and treatment decisions for the youngsters that they serve. The reader would be well advised to consider the evolving approach to the Timberlawn group.

SPECIFIC MEASURES AND INSTRUMENTS

The quality of research on child and adolescent outcome can be no better than the quality of instruments and measures available for tapping important aspects of the child or adolescent's adjustment. Although innovations are much needed, progress could be achieved if there were greater use of the more reliable and valid assessment procedures presently available. In our review of the research literature on adolescent therapy outcome, we already identified particular problems and prospects with respect to the actual assessment methods used in those studies. Here, we more generally outline a variety of measures and instruments that are suitable for use with both children and adolescents. This is not intended to be an exhaustive compilation of available assessment methods, but rather is aimed at providing a representative sampling of those measures and instruments that appear to be especially worth incorporating in future studies of outcome.

A newly devised, general-purpose instrument that appears to be particularly promising is the Personality Inventory for Children (PIC), developed by Wirt and his colleagues and students at the University of Minnesota (Wirt et al., 1977). The PIC was designed for both children and adolescents and consists of 3 validity scales, 1 screening scale, and 12 clinical scales that were constructed either empirically with contrasting groups or by using a content-oriented and/or internal consistency strategy. The resemblance to its older cousin, the MMPI, is quite striking, with the major exception that the PIC is based on the item responses of a parent or guardian rather than the self-report of the patient. The individual scales provide an assessment of general adjustment (adjustment) and informant response style (lie, F, defensiveness); cognitive development (intellectual screening, development) and academic performance (achievement); personality (somatic concern, depression, delinquency, withdrawal, anxiety, psychosis, hyperactivity, social skills) and family cohesion (family relations). There has been a rapidly accumulating body of validation research on the PIC in only the short time since its introduction. An overview of this work can be found in the interpretive guide prepared by Lachar and Gdowski (1979).

Another particularly promising instrument is the newly developed Child Behavior Profile (Achenbach, 1978; Achenbach & Edelbrock, 1979, 1981). There are separate standardized editions of the profile for each sex at ages 4 to 5, 6 to 11, and 12 to 16 years that are designed to record the behavioral problems and social competencies of youngsters as reported by their parents, parent-surrogates, or other adults who have had the opportunity to observe the youngster closely for at least six months. The behavior problem scales were derived through factor analysis of checklist responses by parents of children referred for mental health services. Norms for both the behavior problem and social competence scales of each edition are based on responses of randomly selected parents of normal (nonreferred) children. Behavioral symptomatology is further distinguished with respect to elevations on internalizing and externalizing scales. These are two second-order scales, derived through factor analysis of symptoms on the individual behavior problem scales, that provide an empirical basis for classifying youngsters according to internalizing and externalizing symptomatology.

Other available instruments for measuring deviant behavior in youngsters are the Louisville Behavior Checklist (Miller, 1967; Miller et al., 1971), which is based on parent report, and the School Behavior Checklist (Miller, 1972), which instead uses teachers as informants. Miller and his colleagues (Miller et al., 1972) have also developed the Louisville Fear Survey for Children—an 81-item inventory administered to parents that taps children's fears in three empirically derived categories: fear of physical injury, fear of natural events, and fear of psychic stress. Similar instruments have been developed by Conners. The Parent Symptom Questionnaire (Conners, 1970) is a checklist of items, grouped into 24 general categories of behavioral symptoms commonly associated with childhood disorders that are each rated by parents on a four-point scale of severity. Ten of the items overlap with the Teacher Questionnaire (Conners, 1969), a checklist that was initially designed for use in drug studies of children with learning and/or behavior disorders. Other instruments within this category are the Institute for Juvenile Research Behavior Checklist, which was already described in our review of the Lessing et al. (1976) study, and the child and adolescent versions of the Devereux Behavior Rating Scale that can be obtained through the Devereux Foundation Institute for Research and Training.

There are a number of self-report measures of special symptoms and personality constructs that are available for use with children. However, these share the same limitations that apply to self-report measures more generally (Gottman & Markman, 1978). For assessment of anxiety, there is the Children's Manifest Anxiety Scale (Reynolds & Richmond, 1978), and for depression there are both the Kovacs–Beck Depression Scale (Kovacs, 1980; Kovacs & Beck, 1977) and the Poznanski Depression Scale (Poznanski et al., 1979). Each of these should be accompanied by both behavioral and physiological measures of change, as divergent processes are likely involved even in such seemingly specific symptoms. A great deal of emphasis has been given to the assessment of attitudes and beliefs such as self-concept and locus of control, as was quite apparent in our review of outcome studies on adolescents. The Piers-Harris Children's Self Concept Scale (Piers & Harris, 1964) and the Nowicki–Strickland Locus of Control Scale for Children (Nowicki & Strickland, 1973) are among the more effective instruments available for measuring these particular constructs. With respect to locus of control, it was noted before that there is growing evidence indicating that this variable may indeed be a powerful predictor of long-range outcome (Gossett, 1981, Reference Note 2).

Studies on delinquents will continue to be limited in value as long as investigators are not more precise in defining relevant behavioral and psychological characteristics of their delinquent subjects. Delinquency is a sociolegal term, not a diagnosis. Youngsters who are called "delinquent" comprise a heterogeneous population in which personality factors and psychopathology can vary widely (Quay, 1979). A self-report measure of personality and psychopathology that is well suited for this population is the Jesness Inventory (Jesness, 1966), which consists of 11 empirically derived scales, including social maladjustment, value orientation, immaturity, autism, alienation, manifest aggression, withdrawal–depression, social anxiety, repression, denial, and an asocial index. This instrument was discussed before in our review of the exemplary study by Jesness (1975) and has since received more extensive empirical application (Graham, 1981).

There has been some progress in the standardization of diagnostic interviews and rating schedules for use with children, but the present status of these generally lags behind the procedures available for use with adults. Recent developments include the Children's Mental Health Assessment Form (Kestenbaum & Bird, 1978) and the Schedule for Affective Disorders and Schizophrenia for School Aged Children (Kiddie–SADS) introduced by Puig-Antich et al. (1980), based on an earlier version of the SADS that had been developed for adults by Spitzer and Endicott (1978). Another instrument, the Children's Psychiatric Rating Scale (Werry, 1976), is a 63-item checklist completed by the clinician on the basis of direct observations of the child's behavior and verbalizations in a face-to-face interview. Each symptom is explicitly defined and rated on a seven-point scale of severity. Because much of the work in this area has grown out of drug evaluation studies, the reader is referred to Guy (1976), *ECDEU Assessment Manual for Psychopharmacology*, for a sourcebook on the subject.

The Rorschach method is an approach to assessment that has been around for quite some time but seldom receives consideration in discussions of this kind. (Some may experience a conditioned aversion to even the mention of its name.) Whereas it once seemed to enjoy the status of an indispensable tool in psychological assessment, it suffered a near fatal loss of credibility and popularity in the 1960s and early 1970s as a result of both the disconfirming results that had accumulated in validational studies and the corresponding emergence of applied behavioral assessment. Although some undoubtedly would applaud its decline and only wish that it were complete, there has since been a renewed interest in the Rorschach method on the part of clinicians and researchers alike. Much of this is due to the extensive work of Exner and his colleagues (Exner, 1974, 1978) in developing a comprehensive system for standardized Rorschach administration and scoring and empirically based interpretation. Although it is not a "royal road to the unconscious," as was once held, nor is it able to assess everything from brain dysfunction to oedipal urges, it does provide a sampling of certain aspects of cognitive and perceptual style, reality testing, and other formal elements of thinking and reaction that otherwise would not always be as readily apparent, especially with children. It can provide a relatively unique perspective on the youngster's functioning—a professional–internal focus in terms of the framework proposed earlier—and is commonly used in many child treatment settings. Objective consideration should be given to its incorporation within a diversified but well-rounded appraisal of outcome.

Direct behavioral sampling and rating by trained observers will undoubtedly continue to grow as an important component in assessing change in child and adolescent disorders. The merits of the approach are obvious, and the potential applications of the technology are virtually limitless. However, several points must be emphasized. First, like all forms of psychological assessment, the reliability and validity of a particular behavioral assessment procedure must be demonstrated and not simply assumed. Dealing with observable phenomena per se does not exempt such procedures from meeting the same psychometric standards that apply to assessment procedures more generally. Second, investigators must be careful not to focus exclusively on target symptoms, such as specific fears, social withdrawal, and excessive attention-seeking, without also attempting to assess the youngster's more general psychological adjustment. The problems that this would pose were addressed earlier in our discussion of variability in manifest symptoms. Third, because generalizability requires behavioral sampling in multiple settings, this form of assessment can sometimes be rather costly. Where the costs are not outweighed by the benefits of obtaining a direct behavioral assessment of the child in the home or school, consideration should be given to obtaining an indirect appraisal through use of one of the available behavioral checklists with parents and/or teachers as informants.

The direct assessment of parent–child communication or interaction is an aspect of evaluating outcome that must be given greater attention—both as a dependent measure in appraising treatment effects and as a predictor of treatment outcomes. Good examples of how this can be approached were seen before in our review of the study by Ro-Trock et al. (1977) and in the more recent work of the Timberlawn group (Gossett, 1981, Reference Note 2) using the Beavers–Timberlawn Family Evaluation Scale (Lewis et al., 1976). Both approaches use trained observers in obtaining reliable ratings of videotaped family interactions in standardized tasks. Another example of how parent–child interactions can be objectively assessed is provided by Peed et al. (1977).

We have already noted the problems involved in relying too heavily on various dichotomous indices of school, home, and community adjustment—including recidivism rates—in evaluating therapeutic effects. The continued use of such measures is recommended provided it is within a more broad-based assessment of outcome (Jesness, 1975; Persons, 1966, 1967). It is surprising, however, that so little use has been made of sociometric measures of outcome, especially when one considers that a frequent goal of therapy is to improve the youngster's relations with peers. Sociometric measures have had a superb record with respect to formal psychometric features, ranking near the top in their indices of reliability and validity (Gottman & Markman, 1978). Moreover, findings from longitudinal studies suggest that sociometric measures of peer acceptance are among the best predictors of the child's later social functioning (Cowen et al., 1973; Roff et al., 1972).

Consideration should also be given to the incorporation of life history methodology (Ricks et al., 1974) in research on therapeutic outcomes, both in the idiographic investigation of the natural course of childhood disturbances and in the study of long-term therapy effects. This was done, for example, by Ricks (1974) in his report on "Supershrink," the therapist whose methods and personality seemed to be positively related to the eventual adult adjustment of severely disturbed adolescent boys. Goal attainment scaling (Kiresuk & Sherman, 1968) is another general framework for organizing idiographic data. It offers a sound means of individualizing outcome evaluation without sacrificing the power of group statistical methods.

There is a wide variety of measures and standardized tests of achievement and ability from which investigators may choose in assessing changes in cognitive functioning when these are judged to comprise relevant dimensions of therapeutic outcome. Performance measures of skill and ability may also be used in identifying and controlling pretreatment variation in cognitive and developmental capabilities that may interact with treatment effects. In this regard, much emphasis was given earlier to the appraisal of individual differences in both level and pattern of development, as these likely comprise important sources of variance in therapeutic outcome. A particularly useful instrument for this is the newly revised Developmental Profile (Alpern et al., 1980). This was designed for children from birth through age 9 and uses the yes–no responses of parents (or other knowledgeable informants) to a series of developmentally sequenced items that tap the youngster's skills and abilities on each of five scales: physical, self-help, social, academic, and communication.

A developmental age is obtained on each scale, expressed in six-month intervals from birth to age 3½ years and in one-year intervals thereafter. The inventory need not be administered by a trained professional and can provide a relatively quick, inexpensive, but accurate multidimensional description of the child's development. As with any indirect assessment procedure, however, its reliability is as good as the reliability of its informants.

Another source of variance that can interact with treatment effects has to do with the classification of psychopathology in child and adolescent subjects. Rather than specific diagnosis, however, severity and chronicity of disturbance are the patient variables that thus far have received the greatest attention and around which there apparently is greatest agreement regarding the relationship to outcome. A major advance in assessing chronicity—or type of onset—has accompanied the development of the Onset of Symptomatology Scale (Gossett et al., 1976b), as was noted before in our review of the Timberlawn Project. Severity appears to be a more complex concept—certainly more complex than reflected in past efforts to measure it through simply the three-level classification of neurotic, behavior disordered, or psychotic diagnosis. A more complex and multidimensional definition of severity has been proposed by Barrett et al. (1978) that takes into account (1) the intensity of subjective distress, (2) the extensiveness of this stress, or the number of areas of the person's life that are invaded by the disorder, (3) community tolerance for the problem, and (4) the probability for successful treatment. Although their fourth factor may be difficult to quantify, the Barrett et al. definition of severity makes clinical sense and seems to incorporate the perspectives of the three "interested parties" involved in defining mental health that were discussed before—namely, the client, the professional, and society (Strupp & Hadley, 1977). Besides the severity and chronicity of the youngster's disturbance, another dimension on which outcome can vary concerns the availability of supportive environmental resources, including the level of parental or family psychopathology (Gossett, 1981, Reference Note 2). In some cases it may be this latter variable, rather than the degree of disturbance in the youngster per se, that is the more critical determinant of the child's or adolescent's outcome. Lastly, in a somewhat different fashion, Sherrets and Tramontana (1979, Reference Note 3) have proposed a bipartite classification of psychopathology in youngsters that may prove to have predictive validity. This consists of a qualitative classification of the youngster according to the type of symptoms manifested (acting in vs. acting out) and the nature of interpersonal object relations (attached vs. detached).

The foregoing should give the reader some idea of the kinds of measures and instruments presently available for tapping various aspects of the child's or adolescent's adjustment. It should also be clear as to where innovation and refinement in assessment procedures are especially needed. As was emphasized at the outset, outcome assessment with children and adolescents is inherently more complex than with adults. Hopefully, we have been able to clarify what those complexities are so that future investigations will be guided by a clearer recognition of the particular problems and issues involved in assessing child and adolescent outcome. Future assessments of therapeutic outcome must be more comprehensively based and provide a better reflection of the multidimensionality of development and psychopathology in childhood and adolescence. Despite the difficulties involved and the need for innovation, we believe that worthwhile studies can be performed with the instrumentation and methodology presently available. What is most needed at this time is a clear commitment to a more intensive investigative effort.

REFERENCE NOTES

1. Gossett, J.T. Personal communication, October 28, 1980.
2. Gossett, J.T. Personal communication, January 26, 1981.
3. Sherrets, S.D., & Tramontana, M.G. *Developmental and diagnostic considerations in selecting psychological interventions with adolescents.* Paper presented at the 87th Annual Convention of the American Psychological Association, New York, September 1979.

REFERENCES

Achenbach, T. M. The Child Behavior Profile: I. Boys aged 6–11. *Journal of Consulting and Clinical Psychology*, 1978, **46**, 478–488.

Achenbach, T. M., & Edelbrock, C. S. The classification of child psychopathology: A review and analysis of empirical efforts. *Psychological Bulletin*, 1978, **85**, 1275–1301.

Achenbach, T. M., & Edelbrock, C. S. The Child Behavior Profile: II. Boys aged 12–16 and girls aged 6–11 and 12–16. *Journal of Consulting and Clinical Psychology*, 1979, **47**, 223–233.

Achenbach, T. M., & Edelbrock, C. S. Behavioral problems and competencies reported by parents of normal and disturbed children aged 4 through 16. *Monographs of the Society for Research in Child Development*, 1981, **46** (Serial No. 188).

Alpern, G. D., Boll, T. J., & Shearer, M. S. *Developmental Profile II: Manual.* Aspen, Colo.: Psychological Development Publications, 1980.

Barlow, D. H. On the relation of clinical research to clinical practice: Current issues, new directions. *Journal of Consulting and Clinical Psychology*, 1981, **49**, 147–155.

Barnhart, F. D., & Gossett, J. T. Preliminary analysis of psychopathology scale data. *Timberlawn Foundation Report*, 1973, (No. 73).

Barrett, C. L., Hampe, I. E., & Miller, L. C. Research on child psychotherapy. In S. L. Garfield & A. E. Bergin (Eds.), *Handbook of psychotherapy and behavior change: An empirical evaluation* (2nd. ed.). New York: Wiley, 1978.

Bauman, F. Hypnosis and the adolescent drug abuser. *American Journal of Clinical Hypnosis*, 1970, **13**, 17–21.

Bergin, A. E. The evaluation of therapeutic outcomes. In A. E. Bergin & S. L. Garfield (Eds.), *Handbook of psychotherapy and behavior change*. New York: Wiley, 1971.

Bergin, A. E., & Lambert, M. J. The evaluation of therapeutic outcomes. In S. L. Garfield & A. E. Bergin (Eds.), *Handbook of psychotherapy and behavior change: An empirical evaluation* (2nd ed.). New York: Wiley, 1978.

Bienvenu, M. Measurement of parent-adolescent communication. *Family Coordinator*, 1959, **18**, 117–121.

Bienvenu, M. Measurement of marital communication. *Family Coordinator*, 1970, **1**, 26–31.

Brown, W., & Kingsley, R. The effect of individual contracting and guided group interaction upon behavior-disordered youths' self-concept. *Journal of School Health*, 1975, **45**, 399–401.

Campbell, D. T., & Stanley, J. C. *Experimental and quasi-experimental designs for research*. Chicago: Rand McNally, 1963.

Conners, C. K. A teacher rating scale for use in drug studies with children. *American Journal of Psychiatry*, 1969, **126**, 884–888.

Conners, C. K. Symptom patterns in hyperkinetic, neurotic, and normal children. *Child Development*, 1970, **41**, 667–682.

Coughlin, F., & Wimberger, H. Group family therapy. *Family Process*, 1968, **7**, 37–50.

Cowen, E. L., Pederson, A., Babigian, H., Izzo, L. D., & Trost, M. A. Long-term followup of early detected vulnerable children. *Journal of Consulting and Clinical Psychology*, 1973, **41**, 438–446.

Donofrio, A. F. Parent education vs. child psychotherapy. *Psychology in the Schools*, 1976, **13**, 176–180.

Endler, N., & North, C. Changes in adolescents' self-report anxiety during psychotherapy. *Psychotherapy: Theory, Research and Practice*, 1973, **10**, 251–252.

Exner, J. E. *The Rorschach: A comprehensive system*. New York: Wiley, 1974.

Exner, J. E. *The Rorschach: A comprehensive system (Vol. 2): Current research and advanced interpretation*. New York: Wiley, 1978.

Eysenck, H. J. The effects of psychotherapy: An evaluation. *Journal of Consulting Psychology*, 1952, **16**, 319–324.

Felton, G., & Davidson, H. Group counseling can work in the classroom. *Academic Therapy*, 1973, **8**, 461–468.

Fiedler, P. E., Orenstein, H., Chiles, J., Fritz, G., & Breitt, S. Effects of assertive training on hospitalized adolescents and young adults. *Adolescence*, 1979, **14**, 523–528.

Fine, S., Knight-Webb, G., & Breau, K. Volunteer adolescents in adolescent group therapy: Effects on patients and volunteers. *British Journal of Psychiatry*, 1976, **129**, 407–413.

Gossett, J., Barnhart, D., Lewis, J., & Phillips, V. Follow-up of adolescents treated in a psychiatric hospital: Predictors of outcome. *Archives of General Psychiatry*, 1977, **34**, 1037–1042.

Gossett, J. T., Barnhart, D., Lewis, J. M., & Phillips, V. A. Follow-up of adolescents treated in a psychiatric hospital: Measurement of outcome. *Southern Medical Journal*, 1980, **73**, 459–466.

Gossett, J. T., Lewis, J. M., Barnhart, F. D., & Phillips, V. A. The adolescent treatment assessment project: Lessons learned in process. *Journal of the National Association of Private Psychiatric Hospitals*, 1976, **8**, 26–30.

Gossett, J. T., Lewis, S. B., Lewis, J. M., & Phillips, V. Follow-up of adolescents treated in a psychiatric hospital: I. A review of studies. *American Journal of Orthopsychiatry*, 1973, **43**, 602–610.

Gossett, J. T., Meeks, J. E., Barnhart, F. D., & Phillips, V. A. Follow-up of adolescents treated in a psychiatric hospital: Onset of Symptomatology Scale. *Adolescence*, 1976, **11**, 195–211.

Gottman, J., & Markman, H. J. Experimental designs in psychotherapy research. In S. L. Garfield & A. E. Bergin (Eds.), *Handbook of psychotherapy and behavior change: An empirical evaluation* (2nd ed.). New York: Wiley, 1978.

Graham, S. A. Predictive and concurrent validity of the Jesness Inventory Asocial Index: When does a delinquent become a delinquent? *Journal of Consulting and Clinical Psychology*, 1981, **49**, 740–742.

Guy, W. *ECDEU assessment manual for psychopharmacology*. Washington, D.C.: DHEW, No. 76-338, 1976.

Hayes, M. The responsiveness of mentally retarded children to psychotherapy. *Smith College Studies in Social Work*, 1977, **47**, 112–153.

Hilgard, J., Straight, D., & Moore, U. Better-adjusted peers as resources in group therapy with adolescents. *Journal of Psychology*, 1969, **73**, 75–100.

Homer, L. Community-based resource for runaway girls. *Social Casework*, 1973, **54**, 473–479.

Jesness, C. F. *The Jesness Inventory*. Palo Alto, Calif.: Consulting Psychologists Press, 1966.

Jesness, C. F. *The Jesness Behavior Checklist*. Palo Alto, Calif.: Consulting Psychologists Press, 1971.

Jesness, C. F. Comparative effectiveness of behavior modification and transactional analysis programs for delinquents. *Journal of Consulting and Clinical Psychology*, 1975, **43**, 758–779.

Kahn, M., Lewis, J., & Galvez, E. An evaluation study of a group therapy procedure with reservation adolescent Indians. *Psychotherapy: Theory, Research and Practice*, 1974, **11**, 239–242.

Kaufmann, P., & Deutsch, A. Group therapy for pregnant unwed adolescents in the prenatal clinic of a general hospital. *International Journal of Group Psychotherapy*, 1967, **17**, 309–320.

Kestenbaum, C. J., & Bird, H. R. A reliability study of the Mental Health Assessment Form for School-Aged Children. *Journal of the American Academy of Child Psychiatry*, 1978, **17**, 338–347.

Kiresuk, T. J., & Sherman, R. E. Goal attainment scaling: A general method for evaluating comprehensive community mental health programs. *Community Mental Health Journal*, 1968, **4**, 443–453.

Kovacs, M. Rating scales to assess depression in school-aged children. *Acta Paedopsychiatry*, 1980, **46**, 305–315.

Kovacs, M., & Beck, A. T. An empirical-clinical approach toward a definition of childhood depression. In J.G. Schulterbrandt & A. Raskin (Eds.), *Depression in childhood: Diagnosis, treatment and conceptual models*. New York: Raven Press, 1977.

Lachar, D., & Gdowski, C. L. *Actuarial assessment of child and adolescent personality: An interpretive guide for the Personality Inventory for Children Profile.* Los Angeles: Western Psychological Services, 1979.

LaForge, R., & Suczek, R. The interpersonal dimension of personality: III. An interpersonal checklist. *Journal of Personality*, 1955, **25**, 94–112.

Lambert, M. J. Spontaneous remission in adult neurotic disorders: A revision and summary. *Psychological Bulletin*, 1976, **83**, 107–119.

Lessing, E. E., Beiser, H., Krause, M. S., Dolinko, P., & Zagorin, S. W. Differentiating children's symptom checklist items on the basis of judged severity of psychopathology. *Genetic Psychology Monographs*, 1973, **88**, 329–350.

Lessing, E., Black, M., Barbera, L., & Seibert, F. Dimensions of adolescent psychopathology and their prognostic significance for treatment outcome. *Genetic Psychology Monographs*, 1976, **93**, 155–168.

Levitt, E. E. Research on psychotherapy with children. In A. E. Bergin & S. L. Garfield (Eds.), *Handbook of psychotherapy and behavior change.* New York: Wiley, 1971.

Lewis, J. M., Beavers, W. R., Gossett, J. T., & Phillips, V. A. *No single thread: Psychological health in family systems.* New York: Brunner/Mazel, 1976.

Loevinger, J. The meaning and measurement of ego development. *American Psychologist*, 1966, **21**, 195–206.

Loevinger, J., & Wessler, R. *Measuring ego development I & II.* San Francisco: Jossey-Bass, 1970.

Malan, D. H. *Toward the validation of dynamic psychotherapy: A replication.* New York: Plenum Press, 1976.

Marvit, R. Improving behavior of delinquent adolescents through group therapy. *Hospital and Community Psychiatry*, 1972, **23**, 239–241.

Marvit, R., Lind, J., & McLaughlin, D. Use of videotape to induce attitude change in delinquent adolescents. *American Journal of Psychiatry*, 1974, **131**, 996–999.

Massimo, J., & Shore, M. The effectiveness of a comprehensive vocationally oriented psychotherapeutic program for adolescent delinquent boys. *American Journal of Orthopsychiatry*, 1963, **33**, 634–642.

Masterson, J. The symptomatic adolescent five years later: He didn't grow out of it. *American Journal of Psychiatry*, 1967, **123**, 1338–1348.

Meyer, J., & Zegans, L. Adolescents perceive their psychotherapy. *Psychiatry*, 1975, **38**, 11–22.

Miezio, S. Group therapy with mentally retarded adolescents in institutional settings. *International Journal of Group Psychotherapy*, 1967, **17**, 321–327.

Miller, L. C. Louisville Behavior Check List for males, 6–12 years of age. *Psychological Reports*, 1967, **21**, 885–896.

Miller, L. C. School Behavior Check List: An inventory of deviant behavior for elementary school children. *Journal of Consulting and Clinical Psychology*, 1972, **38**, 134–144.

Miller, L. C., Barrett, C. L., Hampe, E., & Noble, H. Comparison of reciprocal inhibition, psychotherapy and waiting list control for phobic children. *Journal of Abnormal Psychology*, 1972, **79**, 269–279.

Miller, L. C., Hampe, E., Barrett, C., & Noble, H. Children's deviant behavior within the general population. *Journal of Consulting and Clinical Psychology*, 1971, **37**, 16–22.

Miran, M., Lehrer, P., Koehler, R., & Miran, E. What happens when deviant behavior begins to change? The relevance of a social systems approach for behavioral programs with adolescents. *Journal of Community Psychology*, 1974, **2**, 370–375.

Mordock, J., Ellis, M., & Greenstone, J. The effects of group and individual therapy on sociometric choice of disturbed, institutionalized adolescents. *International Journal of Group Psychotherapy*, 1969, **19**, 510–517.

Moser, A. Structured group interaction: A psychotherapeutic technique for modifying locus of control. *Journal of Contemporary Psychotherapy*, 1975, **7**, 23–28.

Nowicki, S., & Strickland, B. R. A locus of control scale for children. *Journal of Consulting and Clinical Psychology*, 1973, **40**, 153–158.

Ostrom, T., Steele, C., Rosenblood, L., & Mirels, H. Modification of delinquent behavior. *Journal of Applied Social Psychology*, 1971, **1**, 118–136.

Peed, S., Roberts, M., & Forehand, R. Evaluation of the effectiveness of a standardized parent training program in altering the interaction of mothers and their concompliant children. *Behavior Modification*, 1977, **1**, 323–350.

Perkins, I. Use of hypnotherapy in drug abuse. *Journal of the American Institute of Hypnosis*, 1971, **12**, 83–84.

Persons, R. Psychological and behavioral change in delinquents following psychotherapy. *Journal of Clinical Psychology*, 1966, **22**, 337–340.

Persons, R. Relationship between psychotherapy with institutionalized delinquent boys and subsequent community adjustment. *Journal of Consulting Psychology*, 1967, **31**, 137–141.

Peterson, D. R., Quay, H. C., & Cameron, G. R. Personality and background factors in juvenile delinquency as inferred from questionnaire responses. *Journal of Consulting Psychology*, 1959, **23**, 395–399.

Pichel, J. A long-term follow-up of 60 adolescent psychiatric outpatients. *American Journal of Psychiatry*, 1974, **131**, 140–144.

Piers, E. V., & Harris, D. B. The Piers-Harris Children's Self-Concept Scale. *Journal of Educational Psychology*, 1964, **55**, 91–95.

Poznanski, E. D., Cook, S. C., & Carroll, B. J. A depression rating scale for children. *Pediatrics*, 1979, **64**, 442–450.

Puig–Antich, J., Oryashel, H., Tabrizi, M., & Chambers, W. *Schedule for Affective Disorders and Schizophrenia for School Age Children*. Biometrics Research, New York State Psychiatric Institute, 1980.

Quay, H. C. Classification. In H. C. Quay & J. S. Werry (Eds.), *Psychopathological disorders of childhood* (2nd ed.). New York: Wiley, 1979.

Rachman, A. The role of "fathering" in group psychotherapy with adolescent delinquent males. *Corrective and Social Psychiatry and Journal of Behavior Technology, Methods and Therapy*, 1974, **20**, 11–22.

Redfering, D. L. Group counseling with institutionalized delinquent females. *American Corrective Therapy Journal*, 1972, **26**, 160–163.

Redfering, D. L. Durability of effects of group counseling with institutionalized delinquent females. *Journal of Abnormal Psychology*, 1973, **82**, 85–86.

Reynolds, C. R., & Richmond, B. O. What I think and feel: A revised measure of children's manifest anxiety. *Journal of Abnormal Child Psychology*, 1978, **6**, 271–280.

Ricks, D. F. Supershrink: Methods of a therapist judged successful on the basis of adult outcomes of adolescent patients. In D.F. Ricks, A. Thomas, & M. Roff (Eds.), *Life history research in psychopathology* (Vol. 3). Minneapolis: University of Minnesota Press, 1974.

Ricks, D. F., Thomas, A., & Roff, M. *Life history research in psychopathology* (Vol. 3). Minneapolis: University of Minnesota Press, 1974.

Roff, M., Sells, B., & Golden, M. M. *Social adjustment and personality development in children*. Minneapolis: University of Minnesota Press, 1972.

Rosenstock, H., & Hansen, D. Toward better school adaptability: An early adolescent group therapy experiment. *American Journal of Psychiatry*, 1974, **131**, 1397–1399.

Rosenstock, H. A., & Vincent, K. R. Parental involvement as a requisite for successful adolescent therapy. *Journal of Clinical Psychiatry*, 1979, **40**, 132–134.

Ro-Trock, G. K., Wellisch, D., & Schoolar, J. A family therapy outcome study in an inpatient setting. *American Journal of Orthopsychiatry*, 1977, **47**, 514–522.

Shore, M., & Massimo, J. Comprehensive vocationally oriented psychotherapy for adolescent delinquent boys: A follow-up study. *American Journal of Orthopsychiatry*, 1966, **36**, 609–615.

Shore, M., & Massimo, J. Five years later: A follow-up study of comprehensive vocationally oriented psychotherapy. *American Journal of Orthopsychiatry*, 1969, **39**, 769–773.

Shore, M., & Massimo, J. After ten years: A follow-up study of comprehensive vocationally oriented psychotherapy. *American Journal of Orthopsychiatry*, 1973, **43**, 128–132.

Spitzer, R. L., & Endicott, J. *Schedule for Affective Disorders and Schizophrenia: Lifetime version*. Biometrics Research, New York State Psychiatric Institute, 1978.

Strodtbeck, F. Husband-wife interaction over revealed differences. *American Sociological Review*, 1951, **16**, 468–473.

Strodtbeck, F. The family as a three-person group. *American Sociological Review*, 1954, **19**, 23–29.

Strupp, H. H., & Hadley, S. W. A tripartite model of mental health and therapeutic outcomes: With special reference to negative effects in psychotherapy. *American Psychologist*, 1977, **32**, 187–196.

Taylor, A. An evaluation of group psychotherapy in a girls' borstal. *International Journal of Group Psychotherapy*, 1967, **17**, 168–177.

Tramontana, M. G. Critical review of research on psychotherapy outcome with adolescents: 1967–1977. *Psychological Bulletin*, 1980, **88**, 429–450.

Weiner, I. B. Psychopathology in adolescence. In J. Adelson (Ed.), *Handbook of adolescent psychology*. New York: Wiley, 1980.

Weiss, M., & Burke, A. A 5- to 10-year follow-up of hospitalized school phobic children and adolescents. *American Journal of Orthopsychiatry*, 1970, **40**, 672–676.

Werry, J. S. Diagnosis for psychopharmacological studies in children. In W. Guy (Ed.), *ECDEU assessment manual for psychopharmacology*. Washington, D.C.: DHEW, No. 76-338, 1976.

Wirt, R. D., Lachar, D., Klinedinst, J. K., & Seat, P. D. *Multidimensional description of child personality: A manual for the Personality Inventory for Children.* Los Angeles: Western Psychological Services, 1977.

Wunderlich, R., Lozes, J., & Lewis, J. Recidivism rates of group therapy participants and other adolescents processed by a juvenile court. *Psychotherapy: Theory, Research and Practice*, 1974, **11**, 243–245.

PART FOUR

Assessing Outcome from the Viewpoint of Different Data Sources

CHAPTER 13

Self-Report Measures
of Psychotherapy Outcome

L. E. BEUTLER, AND MARJORIE CRAGO

In assessing the value of self-report measures of psychotherapy outcome, one must also consider in some detail what constitutes a dependable outcome measure in a more general sense. Some of the issues inherent in assessing therapy outcome have been addressed in a previous chapter (Mintz, 1981). It is also suggested that the reader review the discussions by Meltzoff and Kornreich (1970) and by Cronbach et al. (1972) relative to the special problems inherent in self-report measures. Certain of these problems bear underscoring in the current context. Accordingly, in the following pages we explore patient-based measures within the context of problems encountered with any measure of change or improvement. Among these problems are the tendency for "improvement" ratings to be confounded with *posttherapy status* and for pre- to posttherapy "change" scores to be confounded with *initial levels* of disturbance. In addition, we revisit the frequently observed inconsistent relationship between target and global change measures, the difficulty in selecting criteria of change that are sensitive to the types of therapy studied, and the chronically low correspondence between patients' reports and other sources of outcome ratings. These issues are, of necessity, addressed somewhat redundantly throughout the following pages as we attempt to evaluate the usefulness of selecting various self-report measures of psychotherapy gain.

METHODS OF ASSESSING OUTCOME

In selecting measures that will be applicable to determining reliable treatment-induced effects, one must be sensitive both to the breadth and the specificity of the measurement undertaken. Broad measures of psychological functioning, including measures of personality and psychological disturbance, have been suggested (Cartwright, 1975) as well as those that attend to the individual needs of each patient. To this, we add the observation that there are occasions when measurements may be desired that are sensitive to the particular gains or changes anticipated to be effected by particular types of treatment. It is our intent to consider these concerns at some length.

Any serious consideration of patient-based outcome ratings for psychotherapy must consider the conclusions and recommendations of the NIMH Outcome Measures Project (Waskow & Parloff, 1975). This project arose out of a concern with the accumulation of nonreplicable results among psychotherapy researchers. The National Insitute of Mental Health (NIMH), in an effort to respond to this concern, developed a study group in 1969, charged with the responsibility of developing a core battery of assessment devices to introduce some consistency to the measurement of psychotherapy outcome. In the resulting volume, four chapters were devoted to self-report measures of psychotherapy outcome.

In his contribution to the NIMH Project, Dahlstrom (1975) suggests that change should be evaluated in three areas: values, common personality characteristics; and overall impairment or disturbance. He recommends using the Ways to Live Test (Morris et al., 1960), the California Psychological Inventory (CPI) (Megargee, 1972a), and the Minnesota Multiphasic Personality Inventory (MMPI) (Dahlstrom et al., 1972) to measure these three conceptual areas. It is noteworthy that Gleser (1975) also reviews the potential utility of the MMPI and CPI along with a variety of other measures. In contrast to Dahlstrom, however, Gleser concludes both that the test–retest reliabilities of many of the MMPI scales are too low to be of value and that the scales of the CPI are not sufficiently independent to warrant inclusion of either instrument in a battery designed to assess treatment-induced change. Instead, Gleser recommends the use of the S–R Inventory of Anxiousness (Endler et al., 1962), the Sixteen Personality Factor Questionnaire (Cattell et al., 1970), and the Hopkins Symptom Checklist (Derogatis et al., 1974). Although Imber (1975), in the same volume, concurs with the selection of the Hopkins Symptom Checklist, he further recommends only the Profile of Mood States (McNair et al., 1971) as a "core" assessment device.

Finally, Cartwright (1975) considers some of the methodological concerns one must address in selecting instruments for assessing change and concurs with the selection of the Hopkins Symptom Checklist. Beyond this, however, she departs from the previous recommendations and promotes the use of the Butler–Haigh Q-Sort (Dymond, 1954), the Behavioral Adequacy Scales (Cartwright et al., 1963), and the Client Posttherapy Questionnaire (Strupp et al, 1964).

The variety of contradictary offerings by Dahlstrom, Gleser, Imber, and Cartwright underscores the improbability of obtaining consensual agreement regarding the use of self-report assessment procedures even among respected researchers. It is notable that three of the four writers suggested the use of instruments to which they had personally contributed. The importance of personal investment in selecting research procedures is clearly seen both in this fact and in the discrepant recommendations within the current volume. It is apparent that the usefulness of any given assessment procedure will be determined largely by the perspective and viewpoint of the psychotherapy researcher who applies it. Even the conference participants who compiled the conclusions for the NIMH outcome measures project had to arbitrate among the discrepant preferences of their consultants. Whereas the NIMH conference group concurred with their contributor–consultants in selecting The Hopkins Symptom Checklist for the recommended core battery, for example, they were not persuaded to abandon the use of the MMPI even though it generated the support of only one of the four consultants who addressed the use of self-report measures.

One way of discovering what instruments for assessment of psychotherapy change might be responsive to the needs of most researchers is to determine the instruments most commonly used in this type of research. Although one might argue that including instruments and procedures on the basis of popularity does not compensate for their possible lack of validity, it may at least provide a starting point from which we can determine what concepts and methods are valued by most researchers and for what purposes.

In trying to define an appropriate battery, we have referred to a wide range of psychotherapy research projects that represent both a variety of viewpoints and a heterogeneous group of patients. A sample pool of 150 outcome research studies (see Appendix A) was surveyed, drawn from the citations in three recent review articles by the senior author (Beutler, 1979a, 1979b, 1981) coupled with a library search of more recent studies. In each case the studies were selected on the basis of methodological adequacy and scope. An inspection of procedures in these studies suggests two major methodologies by which patients rated their treatment gains. For convenience we refer, hereafter, to the first as an *improvement* rating and to the second as a measurement of *change*. The former method asks patients to rate the amount of "improvement" or "benefit" incurred on a scale or series of scales ranging between two extremes. This methodology is designed to determine the degree to which the patients perceive their benefits as deriving from treatment itself, rather than simply being incurred over the course of time. This direct form of assessing *improvement* contrasts with the method of assessing *change*. This second method subtracts initial "current status" evaluations from similar, posttreatment ratings as obtained from either established psychological assessment devices (e.g., objective tests) or devices specifically designed for a given study. Each of these two methodologies have their unique problems, however, and we address these as they arise in the following pages.

Assessing Improvement

One observes in Table 13.1 that 59 (40%) of the studies reviewed employed a direct assessment of patient felt *improvement*. Typically, patients were asked

Table 13.1.   Frequency of Use of Specific Tests in 150 Outcome Studies

Type and Title of Measure	Frequency
Posttherapy improvement ratings	59
Personality and psychopathology measures	
Butler–Haigh Q-Sort	10
California Psychological Inventory	1
Cornell Medical Index	6
Draw-A-Person	1
Edwards Personal Preference Schedule	1
Eysenck Personality Inventory	5
Holland Vocational Personality Inventory	1
Inventory of Social and Psychological Functioning	1
Jesness Inventory	1
MMPI	24
Personal Orientation Inventory	8
Q-Sort	5
Rorschach	2
Rotter Incomplete Sentence Blank	2
Semantic Differential	5
Sixteen PF	3
TAT	7
Tavistock Self-Assessment Inventory	2
Total usage	85
Number of studies	58
Symptom checklists	
Adjective Checklist	2
Becker Bipolar Adjective Checklist	1
Depression Adjective Checklist	1
Interpersonal Checklist	1
Jesness Behavior Checklist	1
Life Changes Checklist	1
Multiple Affect Adjective Checklist	6
Mooney Problem Checklist	2
Profile of Mood States	5
Psychosomatic Checklist	1
SCL-90 and HSCL	5
Symptom Disability Checklist	2
Total usage	28
Number of studies	25
Single symptoms or traits measures	
Achievement Anxiety Test	5
Alienation Scale	1
Allport–Vernon–Lindzey Scale of Values	1
Anxiety Differential	2
Anxiety Reaction Scale	1
Barron Ego Strength Scale	5
Beck Depression Inventory	3
California E Scale	1
Fear Inventory	3
Fear Survey Schedule	4
Freeman Manifest Anxiety Scale	1
Husek–Alexander Anxiety Differential	1

Type and Title of Measure	Frequency
IPAT Anxiety Scale	3
Liebert–Morris Worry Scale	1
Loevinger Ego Development Scale	1
Marlowe–Crowne Social Desirability Scale	2
Marlowe Security–Insecurity Inventory	1
Michigan Alcoholism Screening Test	2
Nowicki–Strickland Locus of Control Scale	2
Rathus Assertiveness Scale	3
Rokeach Dogmatism Scale	1
Rotter's I–E Scale	3
Social Fear Scale	1
S–R Inventory of Anxiousness	3
S–R Inventory of Hostility	1
State–Trait Anxiety Inventory	11
Suinn Test Anxiety Behavior Scale	2
Taylor Manifest Anxiety Scale	4
Test Anxiety Questionnaire	2
Tolerance–Intolerance of Cognitive Ambiguity	1
Willoughby E–M Scale	1
Wolpe–Lazarus Assertiveness Scale	1
Worry–Emotionality Scale	1
Total usage	75
Number of studies	45
Specific Measures	
Specific Behavioral Measures	
Alcoholic Involvement Scale	1
Alcoholism Questionnaire	1
Alpert–Haber Test Anxiety Questionnaire	1
Assertion Difficulty Quesitonnaire	1
Attitude Toward Snakes	2
Behavioral Inhibition Questionnaire	1
Behavioral Target Complaints	1
Eating Patterns Questionnaire	1
Fear Thermometer	5
Iowa Scale of Attitudes Toward Stuttering	1
Personal Report of Confidence as a Speaker	3
Problems Due to Drinking Scale	1
Sarason Test Anxiety Scale	1
Sleep Disturbance Questionnaire	7
Snake Questionnaire	1
Spider Anxiety Scale	1
Total usage (F1)	29
Number of studies	20
Other measures	
Acceptance of Others Scale	1
Assumptions About Groups Questionnaire	1
Avowed Turmoil Questionnaire	1
Barrett–Lennard Relationship Inventory	3

(continued)

Table 13.1.   *(continued)*

Type and Title of Measure	Frequency
Client Personal Reaction Questionnaire	1
Cognitive Events Schedule	1
College Self-Expression Scale	1
Conflict Resolution Inventory	2
Correctional Institution Environment Scale	1
Dependency Scale	1
Discontentment Scale	2
Embedded Figures Test	1
Experiences Questionnaire	1
Fear of Negative Evaluation	2
Goal Attainment Scale	2
Health Locus of Control Scale	1
Human Relations Inventory	1
Idea Inventory	2
Index of Indiscrimination	1
Interpersonal Behavior Scale	2
Interpersonal Events Schedule	1
Irrational Beliefs Test	1
Management of Differences Exercises	1
Personal Beliefs Inventory	1
Personal Goals Rating Form	1
Pleasant Events Schedule	1
Reaction to Pictures Questionnaire	1
Resistance to Analyzing Problems	1
Rod and Frame Test	1
Shipley IQ Scale	1
Situational Attitude Test	1
Social Attitude Scale	1
Social Memory Scale	1
Social Openness Questionnaire	1
Social Reaction Inventory	1
Social Stability Index	1
Stroop Color–Word Test	1
Student Life Events Inventory	1
Subjective Probability Questionnaire	1
Symbolic–Literal Meaning Test	1
Test of Emotional Styles	2
Therapy Attitude Inventory	1
Therapy Session Report	1
WAIS	1
Wechsler Memory Scale	1
Word Association Test	1
Total usage (F2)	55
Number of studies	42
Total usage of specific measures (F1 + F2)	84
Number of studies (F1 + F2)	62

to judge their improvement on some type of rating scale, frequently assessing specific areas of gain as well as global benefit.

It appears that psychotherapy researchers value this type of subjective, after-the-fact impression of *improvement*. It has been suggested (Cartwright, 1975; Wilson, 1971, Reference Note 4 at end of chapter) that such ratings include global estimates of satisfaction with and change in therapy as well as specific areas in which patients note the greatest change. Cartwright (1975) presents evidence that some specific client posttreatment rating questionnaires correspond with other assessments of change at a sufficiently high level to conclude that they are reliable and valid. It is noteworthy, however, that this conclusion stands at some contrast to that of others who have evaluated the general method of obtaining posttreatment *improvement* ratings. Several recent writers have suggested that *improvement* ratings are inordinately influenced by the patient's condition at the time of discharge and do not represent accurate reflections of the patient's response to therapy. For example, Garfield et al. (1971) have thoughtfully assessed the relationship among client initial and postdischarge status on the one hand and subjective ratings of *improvement* on the other. In what has proved to be a reliable finding, they observe little relationship between measures of initial disturbance, difference scores on objective pre- and posttreatment measures, and the foregoing subjective, posttreatment ratings of *improvement*. Others (Green et al., 1975) have also found that such direct *improvement* ratings are virtually identical with "current status" ratings obtained at the end of treatment and that there appears to be an inordinately high degree of correspondence between patient's *global* and *target* ratings made in this manner (Cartwright et al., 1963).

These findings suggest that *improvement* ratings do not take into account either the amount of disturbance present when the patient began treatment or the amount of actual change incurred on specific symptoms. They tend to be predominantly influenced by the degree of overall psychological adjustment observed or felt at the end of treatment.

Because of their lack of sensitivity to initial levels of disturbance, it is unlikely that direct ratings of *improvement* are very sensitive to psychotherapy effects. Nonetheless, judging by their widespread use, some type of subjective, posttreatment rating from the patient's point of view is considered desirable by most researchers. Therefore, we offer some suggestions for assessing treatment effects post hoc through subjective ratings. Drawing in part from the NIMH project (Waskow & Parloff, 1975), we propose that patients be asked to first rate their status on each of a variety of identified dimensions as they remember it to have been at the time they entered treatment and then to rate their status as they feel it now, at the end of treatment. The mean difference between these two ratings, then, represents a measure of treatment related change. The targeted dimensions might be selected both in accordance with each study's unique requirements and with the biases and interests of the research team in mind (e.g., depression, anxiety, cognition). We are *not* recommending that these individual dimensions be treated separately as "target" measures unless preliminary statistical analysis reveals them to be sufficiently independent from other measures to justify their being treated as specific dimensions of change. The means for making such decisions are discussed later. Suffice it to say here that the issue of target versus global measures of change is very complex, and we do not consider it to be adequately solved by any single measurement method currently available. The most reasonable course currently available is to suggest that the identified dimensions of change both remain constant for all subjects and that the individual ratings normally be combined with other self-report measures (averaged or weighted) to yield statistically defined dimensions of patient-felt *improvement*. It is anticipated that the mean difference between the pre- and posttreatment levels obtained in this way will more clearly reflect treatment induced *change* than will direct ratings of *improvement*.

Figure 13.1 represents a sample instrument for assessing areas of change in psychotherapy, utilizing this procedure. As indicated in the foregoing, the particular dimensions on which a given treatment might be assessed will be a function of the project aims and the type of treatment employed. Before going on to other topics, it must be observed that after having translated direct *improvement* ratings into assessments of *change*, other problems are incurred. Indeed, since the results obtained in the manner suggested in Figure 13.1 are treated like difference scores, the problems inherent in such scores are relevant to these methods of assessment as well. Let us keep this point in mind as we now consider formal assessment devices used to derive difference or *change* scores.

Methods of Change Assessment

The second dominant method by which patients are asked to evaluate treatment outcome is by comparing current status ratings taken at two points in time (e.g., contrasting the patient's status at the time of entry into treatment with that rated at the time of discharge and/or follow-up). Eighty-five percent of the studies we surveyed included some such ratings. This form of evaluation is amenable to the application of formal psychological tests and thus has an advantage over the previous, subjective method of obtaining patient ratings.

In our attempt to determine the types of measures most likely to meet the particular needs of individual researchers, we refer back to Table 13.1 An inspection of our pool of research studies suggests that pre- to posttreatment difference measures can be grouped into four categories: personality tests; multiple-symptom measures; single-symptom or single-trait measures; and specific behavior or personality instruments.

Personality Tests

Thirty-nine percent* of the research studies surveyed relied on scores obtained from so-called objective personality tests to assess change, most notably the MMPI and the Butler–Haigh Q-Sort. This observation tends to confirm our

PERSONAL EVALUATION

Instructions to rater:

Below are seven lines on which we would like you to rate how helpful you think psychotherapy has been. On each of these lines, *put one mark to indicate how you think you were at the time you first came into the clinic. Place another mark on the line to indicate how you are doing now.* Indicate the direction you think you've changed by placing an arrow between the two marks. Only if there has been absolutely no change should you put only one vertical mark on any of the seven lines.

EXAMPLE

	Severe problems	(Before) / (Now)	No problems
Relationships with other people		/ → /	

(The direction of the arrow indicates improvement after coming to the clinic.)

	Severe problems		No problems
1. Overall problems			
2. Relationships with other people (including sexual partners)			
3. Work and social activities			
4. Ability to control your feelings			
5. Relationships with authorities			

	Strongly dislike		Strongly like
6. Liking for your therapist?			

	Totally unhelpful		Extremely helpful
7. How helpful do you think psychotherapy is? (before and after)			

Figure 13.1 Sample instrument for assessment of areas of change in psychotherapy.

own impression and that of Dahlstrom (1975) that a measure of general psychopathology and personality integration is important to the needs of many researchers. Accordingly, we recommend that such a measure be included in any core battery of assessment instruments.

*The total usage sums reported in Table 13.1 include considerable redundancy since most studies that used objective measures used more than one such instrument. For example, objective personality tests were used 85 times in the 150 studies reviewed, but they were employed in only 58 actual studies.

The MMPI is clearly the most popular such instrument, with 29 of the 58 studies that utilized general personality or psychopathology measures, assessing some or all of the MMPI dimensions. The Barron Ego Strength Scale (Barron, 1953), certain scales of the neurotic triad, and global estimates derived from combining the MMPI scales are frequently incorporated into psychotherapy studies. This is true in spite of the suggestion (Cartwright, 1975) that the individual scales do not have sufficient reliability or sensitivity to highlight treatment-induced change.

The next most popular general personality instruments for assessing *change* are the Butler–Haigh Q-Sort (BHQS) (Dymond, 1954) and the Personal Orientation Inventory (POI) (Shostrom, 1966).

The Butler–Haigh Q-Sort consists of 100 empirically derived statements referring to general aspects of personality. Each statement is printed on a card and is sorted by the subject into nine piles ranging from "least like me" to "most like me." The two scores that are usually derived from the BHQS are the self-ideal correlation (QSI) and an adjustment score (QAS). Test–retest reliability has been reported to be .76 for the QSI and .86 for the QAS (Cartwright, 1975). Both the QSI and and QAS have been used to demonstrate change during psychotherapy. Estimates of poor adjustment obtained from the QAS have been found to be positively correlated with indices of disturbance obtained from the MMPI Depression Scale, the Taylor Manifest Anxiety Scale, and the Barron Ego Strength Scale. As with the MMPI, a major drawback to using the BHQS is the amount of time it takes to complete. An average of 40 minutes per sort is a significant problem since multiple sorts are required for assessment of the relevant dimensions.

The test–retest reliability of the POI, in turn, has been reported to range from .55 to .85 (Tosi & Lindamood, 1975). Its validity has been demonstrated in a variety of studies where it has been used to successfully discriminate between high and low scorers on the Eysenck neuroticism scale (Knapp, 1965), well-adjusted and poorly adjusted individuals (Shostrom, 1964), and patients at different stages in therapy (Shostrom & Knapp, 1966).

Although both the BHQS and POI have established psychometric qualities (Bergin & Strupp, 1972; Cartwright, 1975), they were developed with a specific philosophy of psychotherapy in mind. Hence, in our opinion, their value as theory-independent measures of change is suspect.

Multiple-Symptom Measures

A second variety of objective devices for assessment of personality change are those that measure multiple-symptom dimensions. Only 17% of the studies surveyed utilized this type of assessment, however. Most studies did not attempt to identify specific symptom categories or entities relevant to their particular project by standardized multisymptom procedures. The most usual of those that were employed included the Hopkins Symptom Checklist or its derivative, the SCL-90-R (Derogatis et al., 1974), the Multiple Affect Adjective Checklist (MAACL) (Zuckerman, 1960), and the Mooney problem Checklist (Mooney, 1942).

The SCL-90-R is a 90-item self-report symptom checklist originally developed by Derogatis et al. (1973). The present revised form (Derogatis et al., 1976) consists of nine symptom dimensions and three global indices of distress. Among the symptom dimensions included are somatization, obsessive–compulsiveness, depression, anxiety, and hostility. Internal consistency coefficients for the nine symptom dimensions range from .77 to .90 with test–retest reliability measures falling within approximately the same range (Derogatis et al., 1976). Validity studies have indicated moderate correlations between the SCL-90-R scales and both the MMPI scales (Derogatis et al. 1976) and the Middlesex Hospital Questionnaire scales (Bolelouchy & Hornath, 1974).

The MAACL (Zuckerman, 1960) is somewhat longer than the SCL-90-R and consists of 132 adjectives aimed at assessing three negative affects: anxiety; depression; and hostility. Depending on the instructions, the MAACL is purported to reflect either a trait or state measure of these three affects. Test–retest reliabilities have been reported to be .70, .65, and .54 for the anxiety, depression, and hostility scales, respectively (Megargee, 1972b). Correlations with clinical ratings for these dimensions have indicated that the MAACL provides a significantly more valid measure of anxiety than of depression or hostility. Unfortunately, the MAACL is also subject to deviant response sets. For example, the number of adjectives checked contributes significantly to the variance of scores (Herron, 1969).

Single-Symptom or Single-Trait Measures

A more often used method of assessing symptom change has employed specific, standard measures of single symptoms or traits such as the Beck Depression Inventory (BDI) (Beck et al., 1961), the State–Trait Anxiety Inventory (STAI) (Spielberger et al., 1970), and the Achievement Anxiety test (Alpert & Haber, 1960). Thirty percent of the studies reviewed assessed outcome in this way. Frequently, these specific affect or symptom measures were utilized in studies designed to treat a group of patients that were characterized dominantly by the targeted affect (e.g., depression or anxiety) or trait. When more general populations are utilized, a multiple affect rating scale (e.g., the SCL-90-R) or personality measure (e.g., the MMPI) is probably more useful.

The most used single measure of general anxiety in our survey was the STAI (Spielberger et al., 1970). It consists of 40 items aimed at assessing both state anxiety (a temporary anxiety reaction) and trait anxiety (a more enduring characteristic of anxiety proneness). Test–retest reliabilities of trait scores are reported to be in the .70s and .80s (Dreger, 1978). The test–retest reliability of state anxiety scores are considerably lower, which is to be expected since these scores are designed to reflect a temporary state rather than an enduring condition. Trait anxiety scores are highly correlated with other anxiety measures such as the IPAT Anxiety Scale and the Taylor Manifest Anxiety Scale (Dreger, 1978). The major weakness of the STAI is its obvious content, which may make it subject to faking. Nonetheless, we consider the STAI to be one of the best standardized measures of anxiety currently available.

The Beck Depression Inventory (BDI), used to assess general depressive symptoms, is composed of 21 categories of attitudes related to depression. Each item is answered on a four-point scale reflecting degree of severity. Some of the symptom–attitude categories are mood, sense of failure, sleep disturbance, social withdrawal, and somatic preoccupation. A measure of the internal consistency of the BDI yields a reliability coefficient of .93 (Beck et al., 1961). Comparisons between scores on the BDI and independent clinical evaluations of depth of depression indicate a high degree of validity (Beck et al., 1961).

Specific Behavior or Personality Instruments

In addition to the foregoing, there were, in our survey, a wide variety of specific behavior or personality instruments used or developed for specific needs. These were usually nonstandardized instruments and were often so specific to a given study and so idiosyncratic to the treatment used that their value is questionable. Sixty-two (41%) of our surveyed studies utilized such measures, and yet no single scale was used in more than three studies in the entire sample.*Apparently many researchers either do not have faith in or are not able to obtain standardized instruments by which to measure the particular and often very specific constructs valued by them. A wide variety of self-assessment devices, including measures of self-concept, social and interpersonal relationships, and assertiveness have also been utilized.

The Problem of Target Versus Global Changes

As noted in the foregoing paragraphs, intersource variability among measures of psychotherapy outcome is much larger than intrasource variability. Green et al. (1975), for example, suggest that correspondence among estimates of outcome is more a function of either the scaling methods employed or the source of the rating (patient, therapist, etc.) than of the object being rated (anxiety, target complaint, etc.). Averaging *across* raters as well as across instruments has been touted as a way of increasing measurement reliability while reducing the number of separate outcome variables (Strahan, 1980). Ratings made on similar scales and at similar points in time usually result in highly correlated measures that seem to reflect global rather than "target" symptom, regardless of how specific the item content may have been. In all probability, therefore, one or two composite scores can usually be derived that will adequately represent the patient's change (Cartwright et al., 1963).

These conclusions are supported by Cartwright et al. (1963), who maintain that the specific methods of measurement rather than the content of the measurement devices dictate the degree of interrelationship that will be observed among the outcome variables. That is, the more similar the methods of

---

* As indicated in Table 13.1, specific behavioral measures were utilized 29 times. Although there was replication across studies in the target or *content* of some of these measures (e.g., sleep disturbance), there was no replication of specific instruments.

measurement, the more closely two sources of rating will correspond regardless of their breadth of focus. Nonetheless, there is a strong tendency for intrasource (either the patient, the therapist, or an outside observer) correlations to be higher than intersource correlations (Berzins et al., 1975; Cartwright et al., 1963; Green et al., 1975), even when the former represent ratings of different outcome criteria (e.g., target vs. global change) and the latter represent the same criteria (e.g., both are global ratings). In other words, regardless of differences in the content specificity (e.g., target versus global symptoms) of two measurement devices, a given rater (i.e., source), whether patient, therapist, or outside observer, is likely to produce more similar scores than will two different raters using the same device.

This general observation has led some to conclude (Kraemer, 1981) that only a limited number of outcome variables should be selected but that the *method* of measuring these should vary. Indeed, the method of measurement within any given source should probably be of a somewhat greater concern than the object or specificity of that measurement. Rather than looking for agreement on the amount of *change* occurring on either a supposed "target" or global symptom across sources, for example, the primary concern should be for obtaining a variety of measurements (varying in specificity of targeted behavior) within any given source, collecting a relatively few critical variables from each and reducing all measurements to as few common denominators as possible.

Strupp and Hadley (1977) were sensitive to the foregoing concerns when they proposed a tripartite model of therapy outcome. Assessment of psychotherapy from three different vantage points or sources, as opposed to assessment of multiple aspects of change, seems to be a more statistically sound procedure, given the interrelationships noted above.

Typically, authors have suggested that one must focus on both target and global changes in psychotherapy. Although this may still be a useful suggestion (Bergin & Lambert, 1978), we believe that it must be considered secondary to the concern of assessing outcome from a variety both of viewpoints and scaling methods. Indeed, global estimates, compiled from a number of sources, may produce more stable and sensitive measures than do even specific and *individually tailored* targets of change (Garfield et al., 1971; Green et al., 1975).

Currently, any effort to comply with the recommendation (Waskow & Parloff, 1975) to devise individually tailored target change measures (including goal attainment scaling) for each patient is fraught with problems. Numerous researchers (Cartwright et al., 1963; Green et al., 1975), for example, have observed that patients might optimistically rate positive global change on appropriately designed instruments but that when they are asked more specifically about areas of change, their estimates may be more pessimistic. Indeed, sums (or averages) of individual areas of improvement are frequently lower than global ratings. The meaning of these discrepancies is unknown. Moreover, it is unlikely that the units of change derived from individually tailored measures will be comparable. It is also likely that there will be wide variations in the susceptibility of these targets to the same treatment influences. More specifically, whenever individualized target symptoms are being identified for each patient, one never knows whether the units of change will either be influenced by the same process or are equal in the two different measures. Although the idea of such individuality is important, it is our belief that these problems argue against the utility of individually tailored target measures at this time.

If target change is assessed, we believe it should represent a common target for application to a homogeneous group of subjects and be measured on the same scaling device for all. Indeed, measurement of several commonly held "targets" on all subjects may be helpful, but rather than treating each outcome variable (target or global) separately, they should be reduced to more reliable clusters or factors.

Reliable reduction of numbers of outcome variables (from whatever source) to common denominators can be accomplished through factor analytic techniques. Such procedures effectively combine variables with high interrelationship into composite scores. If target measures represent sources of variance that are characteristically distinct from global measures, a principal components analysis should reveal these differences. Such a finding would provide an empirical rationale for separating target from global *change* measurements for purposes of analysis. On the other hand, if most or all variables load on a single, global *change* cluster, the analysis will allow weights to be derived for reducing the measures into a composite score with maximal reliability. It is our belief that in spite of such problems as lack of comparability among computer programs and the potential for the construction of artifactual clusters (Blashfield, 1980), the ability of statistically derived composites to eliminate overly redundant data analyses makes it a useful procedure (Beutler & Mitchell, 1981; McLean & Hakstian, 1979).

Conclusions

Collectively, the foregoing findings suggest that some measure of global personality functioning and psychopathology will be useful for a variety of research purposes. A smaller but still significant number of studies might find it valuable to employ measures of multiple symptoms or affects as well. Indeed, 83% of studies surveyed utilized some combination of a posttreatment rating by the patient, along with either a measure of general psychopathology (e.g. MMPI, 16-PF, Eysenck Personality Inventory) or a measure of multiple symptoms (e.g. Hopkins Symptom Checklist, Profile of Mood States, Multiple Affect Adjective Checklist).

We tend to concur with the NIMH Committee in selecting the Hopkins Symptom Checklist (Derogatis et al., 1974), or better yet its derivative—the SCL-90-R—for inclusion in a "core battery." We depart from the committee's recommendations by virtue of our belief that the MMPI is still too cumbersome and insensitive to serve as a measure of *change*. The MMPI might be useful for the initial identification of suitable patient samples; however, an instrument with a more reliable factorial structure and one that is more easily administered like the Eysenck Personality Inventory (Eysenck & Eysenck, 1969) may better serve as a general measure of change in personality and psychopathology. This latter instrument has been shown to be useful in predicting psychophysiological changes as well as psychotherapy change and contains good measures of both defensive style and coping adequacy that are highly correlated with independent measures of repression–sensitization, internalization–externalization, ego strength, and intensity of symptomatic behavior (Roessler, 1973).

The NIMH Committee also suggested the development of individually tailored target scales for evaluating the impact of treatment on specific complaints. Although we believe the latter suggestion to be premature, we do add the suggestion (agreeing with Cartwright in doing so) that each patient be allowed the opportunity to evaluate how effective she believes treatment to have been, assessing her perception of the treatment process itself rather than just differences between pre- and posttreatment status. We refer the reader back to the example given in Figure 13.1.

On one hand, we are impressed by the lack of consistency in the use and selection of specific measures in our survey. This observation underscores how strongly individual researchers' biases and dispositions might influence their choice of instruments. The significance of this observation is further seen when we observe that the *method* of measurement and the *source* of report rather than the concept being measured are more important determinants of the intercorrelation among outcome criteria (Green et al., 1975). With this understanding, it is our position that psychotherapy researchers should pay more attention to the way in which the format is varied when obtaining patient reports and ultimately should choose as few reliable instruments as possible to get the job done. A true–false method, a rating scale or checklist method, and a posttreatment rating method might, aggregately, provide the variety needed to assess a breadth of dimensions of self-reported change. For the most part, we agree with Cartwright et al. (1963) and Kraemer (1981), who maintain that the scaling methods for evaluating outcome should be kept quite diverse but that the final outcome should be reduced to as few scores as possible. One or two composite change measures, statistically drawn both from a variety of viewpoints (e.g., patient, therapist, and other) and from a variety of scaling procedures probably will result in stable measures of treatment gain. Indeed, empirically derived composite measures compiled from individual measures may introduce a degree of statistical stability into psychotherapy outcome research that will not appreciably sacrifice sensitivity. This point of view is further reflected in the writings of both Green et al. (1975) and Garfield et al. (1971).

ASSESSMENT DEVICES FOR PARTICULAR THEORETICAL APPROACHES

With the burgeoning number of psychotherapy theories that have developed, it is virtually impossible to identify assessment devices that may be specific to the particular needs of each. Moreover, it should now be abundantly clear that most self-report measures of psychotherapy gain are intercorrelated and are dependent on the similarity of the scaling procedures utilized and the source of these ratings. Even more important, selecting assessment devices for the purpose of validating specific theories limits the utility and generalizability of any finding. If two different theoretical approaches are being compared, we again face the problems encountered in discussing target versus global *change*. One must ensure that both theory sensitive measures are equally reliable and sensitive and that their units of measurement are comparable. "Experiencing," for example, might be more easily altered than "insight" by *any* treatment or vice versa. Likewise, one of these concepts might be more closely related to more general measures of change than the other.

Transformations of the scores into standard units might reduce but would not eliminate these problems. For example, one given treatment might be determined to have greater impact than another on altering either the construct specific to it or a specific target measure, one must not lose sight of the possibility that these changes are largely independent of more general estimates of improvement.

Nonetheless, in situations where a clinical trial of a given psychotherapy theory rather than a comparison of two or more theories is being undertaken, it may be justifiable to include a measurement that highlights a specific characteristic or theoretical formulation of the theory being investigated. Inclusion of these theory-specific scales, however, should not transcend the value of more theory independent measures of change.

In the following pages we review some of the procedures that have been utilized to study the specific needs of given theories. However, there are now over 250 different psychotherapy theories in vogue. To study each theory with an instrument specific to its needs would both necessitate an exponential increase in the number of instruments available and, in turn, further increase the improbability that any two studies would utilize the same instrument of measurement. It is useful, therefore, to reduce the variety of psychotherapy theories into smaller clusters representing similar ingredients or dimensions. Accordingly, we have collapsed the various theories into five categories: (1) experiential and humansitic therapies; (2) analytic and insight therapies; (3) cognitive change therapies; (4) response or behavior elimination therapies; and (5) behavioral enhancement therapies. In investigating the various instruments, preparatory to making recommendations, however, we turn back to our review of the 150 studies described in the foregoing pages. One hundred of these studies are of special concern since they represented efforts either to compare one type or "brand" of psychotherapy against another or to investigate certain theoretical premises of a given theory. The remaining studies were designed to investigate certain therapist, patient, or therapy process variables as related to therapy outcome.

In reviewing the 100 studies that investigated specific psychotherapy theories, it is noteworthy that most have followed our suggestions in selecting a general measure of psychological disturbance or personality as a major dependent variable. As reflected in Table 13.2, studies under all of the five categories, with the exception of the cognitive change therapies (only 19%, compared to 40, 62, 24, and 36%), have tended to rely quite heavily on direct ratings of *improvement*. They also appear to be nearly equally reliant on measures of *change* such as those obtained through pre- and posttreatment administrations of the MMPI. Measures for assessment of specific theoretical constructs occupy a lower priority. This observation reinforces our own reservations about the utility of such theory-specific measures. Nonetheless, with the consideration that some situations may arise in which such theory-specific measurement is valuable, we turn our attention to a consideration of some of the available possibilities.

Experiential and Humanistic Therapies

Whereas 68% of the 25 studies investigating experiential and humanistic theories relied either on direct *improvement* ratings or on *changes* in broad ranging measures of psychopathology and personality, two instruments emerged as being used repeatedly to investigate changes in specific constructs deemed valuable in these types of therapies. One, the Butler–Haigh Q-Sort, was earlier recommended by Cartwright (1975) for inclusion in the core battery during the course of the NIMH psychotherapy outcome project (Waskow & Parloff, 1975). Cartwright observed that the instrument has demonstrated reliability and utility across treatment approaches. Nonetheless, it was originally constructed to evaluate congruity between self and ideal self-concepts. As such, it may have its greatest value in demonstrating the significance of client-centered and other experiential or "self theories" for altering these constructs. This limitation is especially true since the instrument has little data to support its correspondence with other measures of change.

A second instrument whose application may be even more broad ranging has also been utilized on numerous occasions in investigations of experiential and humanistic therapies. The Personal Orientation Inventory (Shostrom, 1966) is a questionnaire designed to evaluate a variety of constructs related to self-actualization and personal awareness. In the current context, 44% of the studies employed one or the other of these latter two instruments in assessing the constructs relevant to treatment outcome from an experiential and humanistic standpoint. The remaining studies utilized a wide diversity of instruments, with little overlap or redundancy across studies. On reviewing the available evidence, we tend to concur with Bergin and Strupp (1972), who suggest that the Personal Orientation Inventory is a suitable instrument for assessing per-

Table 13.2. Number of Studies in Which Five Types of Outcome Measure Were Used with Five Types of Psychotherapy

	Type of Psychotherapy				
Type of Measure	Experiential and Humanistic (N = 25)	Analytic and Insight (N = 29)	Cognitive (N = 16)	Extinction (N = 38)	Behavioral Enhancement (N = 14)
Posttherapy improvement ratings	10	18	3	9	5
Personality and psychopathology					
Eysenck Personality Inventory	0	0	3	2	0
MMPI	5	9	2	4	0
Personal Orientation Inventory	6	1	0	0	1
BHQS	5	1	0	1	0
TAT	3	0	0	0	0
Other	4	6	2	4	0
Symptom checklists					
Depression Adjective Checklist	0	0	1	0	0
Multiple Affect Adjective Checklist	1	0	3	2	0
Profile of Mood States	0	1	0	3	1
SCL-90 and HSCL	0	4	0	0	0
Mooney Problem Checklist	1	1	0	0	0
Other	3	0	0	2	2
Single target measures					
Barron Ego Strength Scale	1	2	0	0	0
Beck Depression Inventory	0	0	2	0	0
Fear Survey Schedule	0	0	1	3	1
State–Trait Anxiety Inventory	1	0	4	6	0
Taylor Manifest Anxiety Scale	0	1	0	1	1
Rotter's I–E Scale	0	0	0	2	1
Other	3	8	6	8	3
Specific measures					
Behavioral Inhibition Questionnaire	0	0	0	1	0
Fear Thermometer	0	0	1	3	0
Personal Report of Confidence as a Speaker	0	0	2	1	0
Rathus Assertiveness Questionnaire	1	0	0	0	2
Sleep Questionnaire	0	0	0	6	0
Other	0	1	7	12	4

sonal values. However, we believe that its values are best representative of experiential therapy and that, like any theory-specific instrument, it has less value for assessing outcome than for evaluating the construct validity of the theory itself. Nonetheless, the instrument has significant value for indicating changes that accrue across time and that are related to experiential concepts of emotional health. Its broader application, when contrasted to the Butler–Haigh Q-Sort, is also significant since it assesses not only isolated concepts of "ideal" versus "perceived" self but presents more refined discriminations of subconcepts within these categories as well.

The Personal Orientation Inventory yields twelve scores associated with self-actualization. These scores include inner directedness, self-actualizing values, feeling reactivity, spontaneity, self-regard, and capacity for intimate contact. The variety of scores as well as the reliability of the individual scales make it a potentially valuable instrument for assessing the impact of experientially oriented therapy in increasing an individual's sensitivity to private experience.

In addition, the FIRO Scales developed by Schutz (1958) bear mentioning. They have been utilized successfully in a variety of studies designed to evaluate treatment outcome and change (Beutler et al., 1979; Sapolsky, 1965). the FIRO-B was designed to assess three aspects of interpersonal relationships: inclusion (desire to associate with others), affection (need for close relationships), and control (desire for responsibility and control in relationships). The test–retest correlations that have been reported are all over .70 (Bloxom, 1972). Validity studies have demonstrated a relationship between FIRO-B scores and behavioral measures of interpersonal relations as well as correlations with other personality measures. Unfortunately, we believe that the scales are somewhat limited in scope and are too susceptible to patient response sets. In spite of some contrary opinion (Bloxom, 1972), we do not believe that there is sufficient evidence of the validity of the FIRO-B to recommend its use in psychotherapy research.

Analytic and Insight Treatments

As reflected in Table 13.2, the most frequently utilized patient reported outcome measure for investigations of analytic therapy is a direct estimate of *improvement*. These ratings are followed by broad measures of *change* in general psychological functioning, most notably utilizing the MMPI. Of the 29 studies investigating analytic and insight therapy, 27 utilized one, the other, or both of these kinds of rating.

Patient-tailored target symptoms (not shown in Table 13.2) were the most used assessment procedures for generating patient ratings of concepts valued by analytic or insight therapy. Since these latter were individually created for both the study and the patient involved, it is difficult to generalize the value of the scales used to the point of making recommendations. Nonetheless, the interest in such individually tailored ratings has increased in recent years as emphasis has been placed on identifying core or nuclear conflicts. Although such conflicts are ordinarily defined by external raters such that outcome can be assessed on them in an objective fashion (Armstrong et al., 1979, Reference Note 1; Malan, 1975), the issue of common units of measurement still remains a critical problem.

It is also noteworthy that analytically oriented researchers rely relatively little on change in objective personality measures of concepts specific to these theories when assessing outcome. This pattern probably reflects a general skepticism toward assessment devices designed to evaluate dynamically relevant concepts and also the difficulty inherent in measuring these constructs. Among the most accepted instruments is the Barron Ego Strength Scale (Barron, 1953), which purports to measure adequacy of cognitive defenses. This scale has enjoyed wide utility for a variety of purposes and has often been considered to be both predictive of response to psychotherapy and representative of adequate psychological adjustment (Barron, 1953; Roessler, 1973). There is increasing concern, however, that the early promise of the scale will not be realized (Garfield, 1978).

In addition, although not used widely in the studies surveyed, the Loevinger Ego Development Scale (Loevinger, 1966) may have some applications to studies of analytic and insight-oriented therapies. This scale purports to assess level of ego functioning in terms of developmental stages extrapolated from analytic thought. Although the research is relatively primitive to this point, there are some data to suggest that it is sensitive to certain types of therapy-induced changes and may provide a valuable adjunct to other measures in assessing these forms of treatment (Jesness, 1975).

Cognitive Change Therapies

A wide variety of instruments have been designed to evaluate cognitive changes that may occur in psychotherapy. Among the more widely applied instruments, the various methods of assessing internal versus external attribution may have promise. It is noteworthy, however, that the studies evaluating cognitive change therapies reviewed in Table 13.2 have not relied on such attribution scales as heavily as has research with noncognitive psychotherapies. This pattern attests to the viability of the concept, across a variety of theoretical approaches. Studies relating to process, outcome, and the psychotherapy relationship as well as specific techniques have employed this type of measure as both an independent and a dependent variable (Beutler, 1978, 1979a).

The most popular measures for assessing cognitive change in the 16 studies reviewed in Table 13.2 are either individual symptom or especially tailored assessments of patient *improvement*. Indeed, of the five categories of psychotherapy considered in the current context, there is less consensus in the studies investigating cognitive change therapies than in any of the others. Even the MMPI was utilized in only two of the 16 studies, and ratings of patient *improvement* were utilized in only three studies. Hence we must turn to other sources to find useable measures of cognitive change.

In evaluating cognitive change, much attention has been given in the literature to the utility of such approaches with specific symptoms, most notably depression (Beck et al. 1979). Hence it is not surprising that the BDI is frequently utilized in studying cognitive change (LaPointe & Rimm, 1980). Like other instruments mentioned, however, the BDI is not specific to cognitive change and may have applications at a much broader level.

Of more pertinence to assessing cognitive changes are the Attribution Questionnaire developed by Gong-Guy and Hammen (1980), the Cognitive Bias Questionnaire developed by Krantz and Hammen (1979), and a scale of attributional style developed by Seligman et al. (1979). A scale that is similar to the latter one has also been developed by Doyne et al. (1981). To date, however, none of these instruments have shown persuasive construct validity with reference to the concept of depression for which they were designed. An exploration of the Cognitive Bias Questionnaire and the Scale of Attributional Style (Blaney et al., 1980), for example, failed to reveal correlations beyond the moderate range with independent estimates of depression. Similarly, the Doyne et al. scale failed on a number of tests designed to demonstrate discriminative and convergent validity. Because of these difficulties, we cannot, at this point, recommend a specific scale for assessing depressive attribution. In spite of its conceptual shortcomings [e.g., the discussions of attribution by Abramson et al. (1979) and Doyne et al. (1981)], the Locus of Control Scale (Rotter, 1966) and its various derivatives might still be the most useful. The value of this scale, however, still rests on the weakness of the other available attribution scales rather than on its own demonstrated strengths.

Among attempts to assess cognitive change along a broader range of psychological disturbance and disrupted affect, several authors have designed attitude scales commensurate with certain cognitive theories. For example, the Irrational Beliefs Scale (Jones, 1969), the Idea Inventory (Kasinove et al., 1977), and the Personality Data Form (Friedenheit, 1969, Reference Note 2) were developed in accordance with the constructs of Rational–Emotive Psychotherapy (Ellis & Harper, 1961). Although the latter instrument appears to have some promise on a construct validity level (Fox & Davies, 1971; LaPointe & Crandall, 1978, Reference Note 3), it still lacks much in the way of reliability and empirically demonstrated utility.

With the foregoing in mind, one must conclude that in most instances, the literature is weak in providing a method for assessing cognitive change in a reliable and consistent fashion.

Response or Behavior Elimination Methods

The most used outcome measure for any behavioral symptom still remains frequency of symptomatic behavior; however, theorists appear to be increasingly incorporating both individually tailored and standardized assessment devices into their research. Direct ratings of patient *improvement*, for example, are frequently employed in the assessment of both extinction and behavioral enhancement therapies. Table 13.2 reveals that 24 and 36% of the studies in the two categories included such ratings. Moreover, broad-ranging measures of psychological disturbance are frequently employed for assessment of extinction procedures. Eleven percent of the studies investigating response elimination approaches utilized the MMPI, for example, and 55% incorporated some objective measure of single or multiple affective or personality characteristics.

Most studies, however, aside from directly assessing patient ratings of *improvement*, utilized assessments of *change* in specific target symptoms and individually tailored questionnaires. Hence a wide variety of instruments were employed with little overlap across studies. In reducing specific fears, however, the use of the Fear Survey Schedule (FSS) (Wolpe & Lang, 1964) is particularly noteworthy. This instrument has been widely touted in the behavioral literature and is frequently employed in behavioral research. The FSS consists of 73 items classified into six categories of fear-provoking stimuli: animal; illness or death; classical phobias; social stimuli; noises; and miscellaneous. Each item is answered on a five-point scale of severity.

Using a modification of the FSS, Geer (1965) reported internal consistency reliability to be .93. Moreover, validity studies by Geer yielded significant correlations between FSS scores and behavioral measures of fear responses.

Behavioral Enhancement Therapies

Most behavioral enhancement procedures are designed to facilitate the development of social skills. Although direct *improvement* ratings of specific skills targeted by the patient prior to treatment are still the most used patient rated outcome measure, there are also a variety of social effectiveness scales that primarily attend to *changes* in self-assertion. For example, Wolpe and Lazarus (1966) have advocated the use of such a scale in conjunction with homework assignments. This scale has been partially validated and modified on psychiatric patients (Hersen et al., 1979). Numerous other instruments have been advocated as well. For example, in a recent review, Andrasik et al. (1981) viewed the readability and utility of eleven such instruments, determining that there are frequently large discrepancies between the level of skill needed to read the directions and that required to read the inventory items themselves. Whereas inventory items may be comprehended by individuals of limited education, the directions require at least a high-school reading level in most instances. Nonetheless, such assertion scales as the revised version of the Wolpe–Lazarus scale (Hersen et al., 1979) and the Conflict Resolution Inventory (McFall & Lillesand, 1971) may have utility for targeted areas of change.

Conclusions

In summary, there is little to support the utility of specific instruments for evaluation of the outcome attendant on specific theoretical approaches. In most instances the instruments utilized or developed to highlight the needs of specific theories are weak in the availability of reliability and validity data.

Most have been applied in a very limited context and frequently to nonclinical populations. The instruments on which the best data exist are the BDI, which is perhaps best suited for (but not limited to) studies of cognitive therapy; both the Personal Orientation Inventory and the Butler–Haigh Q-Sort, especially suited to studies of experiential and humanistically oriented treatments; and the Fear Survey Schedule for assessing behavior elimination therapies. Although we suggest that such instruments may be useful for limited purposes, it is difficult to generalize the utility of many of these scales to other types of treatment. Hence we believe that it is premature to advocate the use of specific devices for particular theoretical approaches, especially if two or more divergent approaches are being studied.

Additional data and information are required to develop scales that are sensitive to psychodynamic and behavioral enhancement concepts. Treatments that emphasize desensitization might benefit from the use of the Fear Survey Schedule, but again, the assumptions on which the device is built may not be as appropriate to alternative treatments. Although the scale itself has value and validity to recommend it, it is still unassessed as to its utility in other than particular behavioral treatments. The same is true for the various social skills surveys. Too few instruments are available that assess skills other than social assertiveness. Indeed, the latter area is the only one that has received significant attention in the literature and in which there has resulted the development of numerous instruments. All these scales are virtually unassessed in other than behavioral treatments, and their value remains limited.

ISSUES IN ASSESSMENT OF CHANGE*

To this point we have uncritically discussed the method of deriving raw difference scores to reflect *change*. However, such uncritical acceptance is not warranted. Before drawing final conclusions, therefore, we must turn to some important issues relating to this method of measuring change.

Just as direct ratings of *improvement* taken at the end of treatment are inordinately influenced by posttreatment status, direct assessments of *change* (i.e., pre- to poststatus differences) are confounded by other sources of error. One such confound accrues because patients who initially have high levels of psychopathology or emotional stress on pretreatment measures have more room for change than those who have little initial psychological disturbance. That is, in contrast to direct ratings of *improvement*, *change* measures attribute the greatest benefit to those who are initially the most disturbed (Green et al., 1975; Mintz, 1972).

Parenthetically, if one understands that *pretreatment* status inordinately affects pre- to posttreatment *change* scores while *posttreatment* status alone

*The authors wish to thank Cole Thies, Ph.D. and Darrell Sabers, Ph.D. for their review and comments on the statistical arguments presented in this session.

inordinately affects ratings of *improvement*, it might become clear why psychotherapy outcome measures have shown so little correspondence with one
another. Suddenly it is not surprising that an evaluation of the interrelationships among eight measures of psychotherapy outcome (Garfield et al., 1971)
produced only four that were significant. The effects of self-perceived posttreatment status on direct *improvement* ratings and the inordinate effects of
pretreatment status on *change* scores may have suppressed the emergence of a
common change factor.

   The artifactual change inherent in pre- to posttreatment difference scores
may accrue in part as a function of regression toward the mean and in part
because of the errors inherent in the process of deriving differences between
any two measures. A frequently used correction for regression toward the
mean has been suggested by Fiske et al. (1964), who maintain that raw
difference scores should be corrected for the correlation between initial and
end point ratings. This "residual change score" (Luborsky, 1971; Mintz, 1972)
is thought to provide a more reliable and stable method of assessing outcome.
The formula for this transformation is represented by the following:

$$\text{Residual change} = Z_t - r_{it}Z_i$$

Where Z_i is the patient's standard score on a composite estimate of initial
psychological disturbance, Z_t is the patient's standard score on a composite
estimate of posttreatment status; and r_{it} represents the correlation between
pretreatment and posttreatment status measures. The effect of applying this
correction is observed in Figure 13.2. Line *A* represents the point of "equality"
in which temination status equals pretreatment status, and line *B* represents a
"best-fit" line of regression (the pre–post correlation). The formula is designed to compensate for the general tendency for intial disturbance scores to
be higher than posttreatment status scores. To the degree that there is a
constant decline (as in Figure 13.2) in scores (e.g., a regression toward the
mean), the subtraction of a value corrected for the influence of pretreatment
scores on final outcome scores compensates for this effect. When such a
subtraction is performed, the resulting scores vary about the line of "best fit"
(the regression or correlation line).

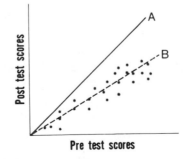

Pre test scores

Figure 13.2   Hypothetical regression lines based on residual gain scores to correct for initial
status when the assumption of uniform movement is met: A = point of "equality"; B = "best-fit"
line of regression.

Unfortunately, the adequacy of this formula for correcting the influence of initial status can be severely compromised when not all scores change in the same direction from pre- to posttreatment assessments. The formula assumes that the relationship between initial and posttreatment levels is both linear and consistent. It also assumes that a uniform regression or movement of extreme scores toward the mean reflects a statistical phenomenon rather than real change. Both sets of assumptions may be questionable in the case of psychotherapy, however. For example, some apparent regression tendencies reflect real change of status (Nesselroade et al., 1980) and alternatively, some patients do not manifest regression toward the mean at all, becoming even worse with treatment (Bergin & Lambert, 1978). Even a single deviation from a general pattern of regression can potentially produce a distortion in the linear relationship sufficient to lower or raise the correlation inordinately, thus compromising the residual gain score. This characteristic is illustrated in Figure 13.3, wherein a single case shows an actual "deterioration effect" (i.e., has worsened, as indicated by scores that increase) during the course of treatment. This "outlier" lowers the linear correlation coefficient.

If there is a significant deterioration effect induced in some patients by psychotherapy as has been suggested (Bergin & Lambert, 1978), the validity of the residual gain score may be questionable. Hence, before applying residual change measures to raw difference scores, a scatter plot should be inspected. In the event that any deterioration effect accrues in which posttherapy status does not deviate from pretherapy status in a uniform direction, the method of assessing residual gain must be modified. One might consider dropping the outliers from the analysis, for example, and inspecting it more intensively and individually. Outliers may represent a different population than the other subjects.

Although the foregoing discussion might appear to resolve the issue of difference scores, there is also a second, potential source of confounding influence that is independent of statistical regression effects. Namely, raw difference scores obtained between two measures of current status may be highly influenced by compounded sources of "error" variance. Since any score obtained from a rating or assessment instrument is composed of both a "true score" and an "error score," subtraction of the pre- and posttreatment scores

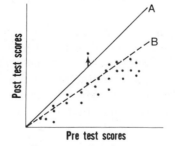

Figure 13.3 Hypothetical regression lines demonstrating a lower correlation resulting from a failure to meet the assumption of uniform movement: A = point of "equality"; B = "best-fit" line of regression.

essentially extracts from the remainder, the proportion of "true" score that is common to both administrations (i.e., the reliability). The resulting difference score will be composed both of that portion of the obtained posttreatment score that was contributed by treatment and the "error scores" present in *both* measures of status. One argument holds that this means that any direct change score derived by substracting may be more heavily influenced by the un-reliability of the instrument than will be either of the raw scores themselves (Cronback & Furby, 1970).

This relationship can be illustrated more specifically by representing an obtained score (X_{01}) on any reliable assessment of *pretreatment* status with the following formula:

$$X_{01} = X_t + E_1 \tag{1}$$

Where X_t is that portion of the obtained score that accurately reflects the scale's test–retest reliability (it will be the same from occasion to occasion), and E_1 represents the contribution to the total score from various sources of random error.

To refresh the reader's memory there are three pertinent assumptions about the "error score." Namely, error scores are (1) uncorrelated with true scores, (2) uncorrelated with other error scores obtained on different occasions, and (3) average to zero on repeated administrations of the instrument. That is, error factors are assumed to be independent of one another and are as likely to make the obtained score higher than the "true score" as they are to lower it.

In the usual event, X_t contributes more to any given obtained score than does the error score, making for a reliable assessment device. Assume, for example, that in the above formula $X_{01} = 14$ and the $X_t = 12$. The contributors to the total score from sources of error have made the obtained score higher than the true score by two points ($E_1 = 2$).

Now, assume that an obtained score reflecting *end* of treatment status (X_{02}) can be represented thus:

$$X_{02} = X_t + X_g + E_2 \tag{2}$$

Where X_g represents the portion of the obtained score influenced or caused by treatment.

Since the error scores are assumed to eventually average out, in the interest of simplicity let us assign an arbitrary value of minus two (-2) to the error value in this equation.* Therefore, if our obtained score (X_{02}) on this occasion is 20 and X_t remains the same as on the pretreatment occasion (as it should since it reflects the stability of measure from occasion to occasion), the *true* gain is 10 ($X_g = 10$). In this event the observed difference underestimates the

---

*In actuality, numerous readministrations would probably be necessary before error scores averaged to zero.

effectiveness of treatment because of the influence of error variance. When the pre- and posttreatment scores are subtracted, the obtained difference score (X_d) looks like this:

$$X_d = (X_t + X_g + E_2) - (X_t \pm E_1) \tag{3}$$

This formula can be further reduced to become

$$X_d = X_g + E_2 - E_1 \tag{4}$$

However, when we substitute our hypothetical numbers in the foregoing equation, we must observe that E_2 is a negative number; hence both error scores work to suppress the obtained score. Therefore, the observed difference (X_d) of six units is largely influenced by error variance. In this case four units (40%) of the true change are suppressed as a result of compounding the error variance through subtraction. Theoretically, the errors could have just as easily overestimated change as well. In our example, error variables forced a 40% suppression effect on difference scores, whereas they comprised only 14% of the initial score and 9% of the posttreament score.

After reviewing the foregoing argument and various procedures designed to compensate for the encumbrances of error variance in difference scores, Cronbach and Furby (1970) advocate the abandonment of change scores whenever feasible. They conclude that when subjects (i.e., patients) are initially selected to be homogeneous in level and type of initial status, posttreatment evaluations alone are more sensitive than any difference formula. However, clinical research rarely allows for this degree of initial homogeneity.

It should also be noted that the foregoing argument holds only in cases where the assumption of uncorrelated error variances are met. Numerous authors (Labouvie, 1980; Williams & Zimmerman, 1977) have argued that the mere repetitious use of a measuring instrument introduces correlated error variances; therefore, the reliability of raw *change* scores may actually be higher than either the pre- or posttreatment measures alone. Observe, for example, what happens in Equation (4) if E_2 is a positive rather than a negative number, as would be the case if it happened to be directly and positively correlated with E_1. Error variances* would be canceled and the resulting difference (i.e., *change*) score would be a "pure" reflection of true gain. In these events a reasonable estimate of change can be obtained by applying Cronbach and Gleser's (1953) D^2 transformation to assess similarity of profiles across time. As the D^2 transformation sums several differences (e.g., the various scales of a test), it capitalizes on correlated error variances to increase reliability of raw *change* scores.

---

*Strictly speaking, the use of the term "error variance" in this context is correct only if one considers error apportionment from a validity model. From a reliability viewpoint, the proportion of "error variances" that are correlated become part of the true score since they enhance the reliability of the measure.

For performance of this D^2 transformation, several areas of status must be measured on both pre- and posttreatment occasions. Each difference between the initial and posttreatment level is squared and then summed with every other difference, yielding a single assessment of change or pre- to posttreatment similarity. By squaring the differences, we effectively exaggerate the importance of large as opposed to small gains. This strategy is employed on the assumption that large changes are more likely to reflect true gain than are small differences. Hence, by capitalizing on these more robust reflections of change and minimizing small gains that might only reflect rater or test bias, we can anticipate that the D^2 estimate will be relatively unclouded by error variance. The difficulty with D^2 as a means of assessment, however, is that it does not reflect the direction of change and thus should be implemented without modification only when direction of change is uniform across dimensions. In the case wherein the direction of change is not uniform, one must apply a correction factor (i.e., an algebraic rather than absolute sum of squared differences, retaining the signs). This type of procedure has been utilized in psychotherapy research to some advantage (Beutler et al., 1975).

It should be obvious that neither the D^2 transformation nor the residual gain score accounts for both sources of bias in direct measures of change. Unless there is some reason to believe that one source of error is of greater concern than the other in a particular research project, a psychotherapy researcher might be best advised to apply and compare both corrections. Since both transformations are designed to measure unbiased *change*, seriously discrepant findings should be carefully inspected for outliers, recording errors, and the like. Ideally, a homogeneous group of patients (in terms of initial disturbance) would be studied, however, eliminating the need for change scores altogether. In this case posttreatment status scores would suffice (Cronbach & Furby, 1970; Green et al., 1975).

SUMMARY

The foregoing pages have described some of the concerns and considerations that a researcher must have when using self-report outcome measures. With due consideration to the influence of initial and final status levels on patient ratings and to the format and structure of the assessment devices, we come to a number of conclusions. We believe that a comprehensive assessment battery for evaluating patient estimates of treatment effects should include (1) a general personality or psychopathology measure, (2) either a multiple- or single-symptom checklist, depending on the specificity of one's focus within a given population, and (3) a measure of direct change made by the patient at the end of treatment.

1.   Although the MMPI has many failings (Cartwright, 1975), it may still be a very useful device because of its clinical utility in assessing general personality

and psychopathology *before treatment*. However, it is our belief that a more factorially pure and statistically sound instrument such as the Eysenck Personality Inventory might better serve the purpose of evaluating *change*. We recommend the use of the MMPI as an independent measure for assessing patient personality characteristics or personality styles, but not as a treatment outcome measure. Hence it might be used in initial selection and homogenation of samples, as Strupp and Hadley (1979) and Beutler and Mitchell (1981)have attempted to do. The Eysenck Personality Inventory (EPI), however, provides a better estimate of a variety of combinations of both stable versus unstable and introverted versus extroverted patients and is not faced with the problems of reliability seen with the MMPI. The EPI (Eysenck & Eysenck, 1969) is a revision of the Maudsley Personality Inventory and was developed as a measure of extraversion—introversion and neuroticism—stability. It is considered one of the best measures of these two factors (Cline, 1972). Moreover, the extroversion–introversion dimension correlates highly with measures of repressive defensive style from the MMPI, and the neuroticism scale is highly correlative with the Barron Ego Strength Scale (Roessler, 1973). These correlations approach the test–retest reliabilities, which, in turn, range from .80 to .97. Correlations between the two forms of the EPI range from .75 to .91 (Cline, 1972).

2.   In regard to a symptom-specific measure, we concur with Waskow and Parloff (1975) in suggesting the utility of the revised form of the Hopkins Symptom Checklist. The SCL-90-R has been widely used in a variety of contexts, including psychiatric and nonpsychiatric populations (Hoffman & Overall, 1978; Snyder et al., 1980). Its sensitivity to a variety of symptoms is consistent with our general admonition that outcome be assessed along a broad range of dimensions rather than being restricted to target change. If single-symptom dimensions are of focus, however, we recommend that other measures to assess such symptoms be applied in addition to or instead of the SCL-90-R. When applied, the single-target measures should fit the special requirements of any given study and population. At this point we can make recommendations only on targets relating to depression and anxiety. In regard to the former, we recommend the Beck Depression Inventory, whereas the State–Trait Anxiety Inventory is recommended for the assessment of anxiety symptoms.

3.   We also recommend the use of direct, posttherapy patient measures of *improvement*, commensurate with the suggestion presented in Figure 13.1. We do not recommend, however, that these scales call for ratings of *improvement*, but that they be constructed in a format that allows the development of *change* since these are easier to handle statistically by the application of residual gain and/or D^2 transformations.

4.   At this point we are unable and unwilling to make recommendations for specific, individualized target measures of change. Our concerns in this regard have been detailed in the foregoing paragraphs but include our belief that

individually tailored target symptoms are not comparable across patients. Since different patients may target different symptoms and since it is difficult to determine the degree to which the units of change in each are equivalent, we depart from the NIMH recommendation that such measures are appropriate. Although we still consider them desirable, from an idealistic perspective, we believe that much work is needed before a suitable measurement device is available.

5.   Likewise, we favor combining all outcome measures into as few dimensions as possible. We propose the use of a principal components analysis to reduce dependent variables along statistical rather than rational lines. For most purposes, moreover each dependent measure should first be transformed to residual gain scores. We do not deem it justifiable, in view of the literature, to assess individualized target measures at this time, and advocate, instead, the use both of uniform target and global measures of change wherever feasible. We recommend that these several measures, each derived from multiple viewpoints, then be subjected to a principal components analysis and combined appropriately to reflect a relatively few target and/or global *change* scores. We anticipate that this procedure will result in stable, source-specific (i.e. patient, therapist, or observer) ratings of rather global changes. It is our belief that most so-called target ratings are, in fact, more reflective of a general, source-specific change than of change in specific symptoms. If target changes are indeed distinct from global changes, however, it should become apparent in the performance of the suggested analysis.

6.   Finally, we do not feel in a position to recommend the use of specific measures that are sensitive to specific theoretical orientations. We have highlighted the difficulties in contrasting treatments utilizing instruments that are more sensitive to one therapy than another. In those instances where a single theory is being evaluated, however, the use of such theory-specific measures would probably enhance the value of the study. Unfortunately, only in a few instances are instruments available that meet the requirements of validity and reliability at a sufficiently high level to recommend them. In our judgment, these latter instruments include the Personal Orientation Inventory and the Butler–Haigh Q-Sort for assessment of changes accruing in experiential and humanistic treatments, the Beck Depression Inventory for evaluation of cognitive treatments of depression, and the Fear Survey Schedule for assessment of change accruing as a function of extinction treatments. We do not find evidence to support the value of any specific self-report instruments designed to assess psychodynamic and analytically oriented treatments or behavioral enhancement treatments.

REFERENCE NOTES

1.   Armstrong, S., Yasuna, A., & Hartley, D. Brief psychodynamic psychotherapy: Interrater agreement and reliability of individually specified outcomes. Paper

presented at the 10th Annual Meeting of the Society for Psychotherapy Research, Oxford, England, July 1979.

2. Friedenheit, A. R. Statistical analysis and norms for an adjustment inventory. Unpublished master's degree thesis, Hunter College, New York, New York, 1969.

3. LaPointe, K. A., & Crandall, C. Measures of irrational thinking: Their intercorrelations and relationship to neuroticism and depression. Unpublished manuscript, University of Georgia, Athens, Georgia, 1978.

4. Wilson, N. C., Morton, W. D., & Swanson, R. M. Development and validation of a scale to measure treatment effectiveness in psychotherapy. Paper presented at the meeting of the Rocky Mountain Psychological Association, Denver, May 1971.

REFERENCES

Alpert, R., & Haber, R. N. Anxiety in academic achievement situations. *Journal of Abnormal and Social Psychology*, 1960, **61**, 207–215.

Andrasik, F., Heimberg, R. G., Edlund, S. R., & Blankenberg, R. Assessing the readibility levels of self-report assertion inventories. *Journal of Consulting and Clinical Psychology*, 1981, **49**, 142–144.

Barron, F. An ego-strength scale which predicts response to psychotherapy. *Journal of Consulting Psychology*, 1953, **17**, 327–333.

Beck, A. T., Rush, A. J., Shaw, B. V., & Emery, G. *Cognitive therapy of depression*. New York: Guilford Press, 1979.

Beck, A. T., Ward, C. H., Mendelson, M., Mock, J., & Erbaugh, J. An inventory for measuring depression. *Archives of General Psychiatry*, 1961, **4**, 561–569.

Bergin, A. E., & Lambert, M. J. The evaluation of therapeutic outcomes. In S. L. Garfield & A. E. Bergin (Eds.), *Handbook of psychotherapy and behavior change: An empirical evaluation* (2nd ed.). New York: Wiley, 1978.

Bergin, A. E., & Strupp, H. H. *Changing frontiers in the science of psychotherapy*. New York: Aldine-Atherton, 1972.

Berzins, J. I., Bednar, R. L., & Severy, L. J. The problem of intersource consensus in measuring therapeutic outcomes: New data and multivariate perspectives. *Journal of Abnormal Psychology*, 1975, **84**, 10–19.

Beutler, L. E. Interpersonal persuasion in psychotherapy. In L. E. Beutler & R. Greene (Eds.), *Special problems in child and adolescent behavior*. Westport, Conn.: Technomic Publishing Co., 1978.

Beutler, L. E. Toward specific psychological therapies for specific conditions. *Journal of Consulting and Clinical Psychology*, 1979, **47**, 882–897.(a)

Beutler, L. E. Values, beliefs, religion and the persuasive influences of psychotherapy. *Psychotherapy: Theory, Research and Practice*, 1979, **16**, 432–440.(b)

Beutler, L. E. Convergence in counseling and psychotherapy: A current look. *Clinical Psychology Review*, 1981, **1**, 79–101.

Beutler, L. E., Johnson, D. T., Neville, C. W., Jr., Elkins, D., & Jobe, A. M. Attitude similarity and therapist credibility as predictors of attitude change and improvement in psychotherapy. *Journal of Consulting and Clinical Psychology*, 1975, **43**, 90–91.

Beutler, L. E., & Mitchell, R. Psychotherapy outcome in depressed and impulsive patients as a function of analytic and experiential treatment procedures. *Psychiatry*, 1981, **44**, 297–306.

Beutler, L. E., Oro-Beutler, M. E., & Mitchell, R. A systematic comparison of two-parent training programs in child management. *Journal of Counseling Psychology*, 1979, **26**, 531–533.

Blaney, P. H., Beahr, V., & Head, R. Two measures of depressive cognitions: Their association with depression and with each other. *Journal of Abnormal Psychology*, 1980, **89**, 678–682.

Blashfield, R. K. Propositions regarding the use of cluster analysis in clinical research. *Journal of Consulting and Clinical Psychology*, 1980, **48**, 456–459.

Bloxom, B. The FIRO scales. In O. K. Buros (Ed.), *The seventh mental measurements yearbook*. Highland Park, N.J.: Gryphon Press, 1972.

Bolelouchy, Z., & Hornath, M. The SCL-90 rating scale: First experience with the Czech version in healthy male scientific workers. *Activitas Nervosa Superior*, 1974, **16**, 115–116.

Cartwright, D. S. Patient self-report measures. In I.E. Waskow & M. B. Parloff (Eds.), *Psychotherapy change measures*. Rockville, Md.: National Institute of Mental Health, No. 74-120, 1975.

Cartwright, D. S., Kirtner, W., & Fiske, D. W. Method factors in changes associated with psychotherapy. *Journal of Abnormal and Social Psychology*, 1963, **66**, 164–175.

Cattell, R. B., Eber, H. W., & Tatsuoka, M. M. *Handbook for the 16 Personality Factor Questionnaire* Champaign, Ill.: Institute for Personality and Ability Testing, 1970.

Cline, V. B. Eysenck Personality Inventory. In O. K. Buros (Ed.), *The seventh mental measurements yearbook*. Highland Park, N.J.: Gryphon Press, 1972.

Cronbach, L. J., & Furby, L. How we should measure "change"—or should we? *Psychological Bulletin*, 1970, **74**, 68–80.

Cronbach, L. J., & Gleser, G. C. Assessing similarity between profiles. *Psychological Bulletin*, 1953, **50**, 456–473.

Cronbach, L. J., Gleser, G. C., Nanda, H., & Rajaratnam, N. *The dependability of behavioral measurements*. Palo Alto, Calif.: Wiley, 1972.

Dahlstrom, W. G. Recommendations for patient measures in evaluating psychotherapy: Test batteries and inventories. In I. E. Waskow & M. B. Parloff (Eds.), *Psychotherapy Change Measures*. Rockville, Md.: National Institute of Mental Health, No. 74–120, 1975.

Dahlstrom, W. G., Welsh, G. S., & Dahlstrom, L. E. *An MMPI handbook: Volume 1: Clinical Interpretation*. Minneapolis: University of Minnesota Press, 1972.

Derogatis, L. R., Lipman, R. S., & Covi, L. The SCL-90: An outpatient psychiatric rating scale—preliminary report. *Psychopharmacology Bulletin*, 1973, **9**, 13–27.

Derogatis, L. R., Lipman, R. S., Rickels, K., Uhlenhuth, E. H., & Covi, L. The Hopkins Symptom Checklist (HSCL): A measure of primary symptom dimensions. In P. Pichot & R. Olivier-Martin (Eds.), *Psychological measurements in psychopharmacology: Modern problems in pharmacopsychiatry*. Basel, Switzerland: Karger, 1974.

Derogatis, L. R., Rickels, K., & Rock, A. F. The SCL-90 and the MMPI: A step in the validation of a new self-report scale. *British Journal of Psychiatry*, 1976, **128**, 280–289.

Doyne, E., Beutler, L. E., & Calhoun, J. The Personal Reactions Inventory: A scale to measure depressive attributions. *Journal of Clinical Psychology*, 1981, **37**, 299–308.

Dreger, R. M. State-Trait Anxiety Inventory. In O. K. Buros (Ed.), *The eighth mental measurements yearbook*. Highland Park, N.J.: Gryphon Press, 1978.

Dymond, R. F. Adjustment changes over therapy from self-sorts. In C. R. Rogers, & R. F. Dymond (Eds.), *Psychotherapy and personality change*. Chicago: University of Chicago Press, 1954.

Ellis, A., & Harper, R. A. *A guide to rational living*. Englewood Cliffs, N.J.: Prentice-Hall, 1961.

Endler, N. S., Hunt, J. McV., & Rosenstein, A. J. An SR inventory of anxiousness. *Psychological Monographs*, 1962, **76** (17, Whole No. 536).

Eysenck, H. G., & Eysenck, S. B. G. *Personality structure and measurement*. San Diego: R. R. Knapp, 1969.

Fiske, D. W, Cartwright, D. S., & Kirtner, W. L. Are psychotherapeutic changes predictable? *Journal of Abnormal and Social Psychology*, 1964, **69**, 418–426.

Fox, E. E., & Davies, R. L. Test your rationality. *Rational Living*, 1971, **5**, 23–25.

Garfield, S. L. Research on client variables in psychotherapy. In S. L. Garfield & A. E. Bergin (Eds.), *Handbook of psychotherapy and behavior change: An empirical evaluation*. (2nd ed.). New York: Wiley, 1978.

Garfield, S. L., Prager, R. A., & Bergin, A. E. Evaluation of outcome in psychotherapy. *Journal of Consulting and Clinical Psychology*, 1971, **37**, 307–313.

Geer, J. H. The development of a scale to measure fear. *Behaviour Research and Therapy*, 1965, **3**, 45–53.

Gleser, G. C. Evaluation of psychotherapy outcome by psychological tests. In I. E. Waskow & M. B. Parloff (Eds.), *Psychotherapy change measures*. Rockville, Md: National Institute of Mental Health, No. 74-120, 1975.

Gong-Guy, E., & Hammen, C. Causal perceptions of stressful events in depressed and nondepressed outpatients. *Journal of Abnormal Psychology*, 1980, **89**, 662–699.

Green, B. L, Gleser, G. C., Stone, W. N., & Siefert, R. F. Relationships among diverse measures of psychotherapy outcome. *Journal of Consulting and Clinical Psychology*, 1975, **43**, 689–699.

Herron, E. W. The Multiple Affect Adjective Check List: A critical analysis. *Journal of Clinical Psychology*, 1969, **25**, 46–53.

Hersen, M., Bellack, A. S., Turner, S. M., Martin, M. T., Harper, K., & Watts, J. G. Psychometric properties of the Wolpe-Lazarus Assertiveness Scale. *Behaviour Research and Therapy*, 1979, **17**, 63–69.

Hoffman, N. G., & Overall, P. B. Factorial structure of the SCL-90 in a psychiatric population. *Journal of Consulting and Clinical Psychology*, 1978, **46**, 1187–1191.

Imber, S. D. Patient direct self-report techniques. In I. E. Waskow & M. B. Parloff (Eds.), *Psychotherapy change measures*. Rockville, Md.: National Institute of Mental Health, No. 74-120, 1975.

Jesness, C. F. Comparative effectiveness of behavior modification and transactional analysis programs for delinquents. *Journal of Consulting and Clinical Psychology*, 1975, **43**, 758–779.

Jones, R. G. A factored measure of Ellis' irrational belief system, with personality and maladjustment correlates (Doctoral dissertation, Texas Technological College, 1968). *Dissertation Abstracts International*, 1969, **29**, 4379B–4380B. (University Microfilms No. 6-6443)

Kasinove, H., Crisci, R., & Tiegerman, S. Developmental trends in rational thinking: Implications for rational-emotive school mental health programs. *Journal of Community Psychology*, 1977, **5** 266–274.

Knapp, R. R. Relationship of a measure of self-actualization to neuroticism and extraversion. *Journal of Consulting Psychology*, 1965, **29**, 168–172.

Kraemer, H. Statistical coping strategies for clinical research. *Journal of Consulting and Clinical Psychology*. 1981, **49**, 390–319.

Krantz, S., & Hammen, C. Assessment of cognitive bias in depression. *Journal of Abnormal Psychology*, 1979, **88**, 611–619.

LaBouvie, E. W. Measurement of individual differences in intraindividual changes. *Psychological Bulletin*, 1980, **88**, 54–59.

LaPointe, K. A., & Rimm, D. C. Cognitive, assertive, and insight-oriented group therapies in the treatment of reactive depression in women. *Psychotherapy: Theory, Research and Practice*, 1980, **17**, 312–321.

Loevinger, J. The meaning and measurement of ego development. *American Psychologist*, 1966, **21**, 195–206.

Luborsky, L. Perennial mystery of poor agreement among criteria for psychotherapy outcome. *Journal of Consulting and Clinical Psychology*, 1971, **37**, 316–319.

Malan, D. H. *A study of brief psychotherapy*. New York: Plenum Press, 1975.

McFall, R. M., & Lillesand, D. B. Behavioral rehearsal, modeling and coaching in assertion training. *Journal of Abnormal Psychology*, 1971, **77**, 313–323.

McLean, P. D., & Hakstian, A. R. Clinical depression: Comparative efficacy of outpatient treatments. *Journal of Consulting and Clinical Psychology*, 1979, **74** 818–836.

McNair, D. M., Lorr, M., & Droppleman, L. F. *EITS Manual for the profile of mood states*. San Diego, Calif.: Educational and Industrial Testing Service, 1971.

Megargee, E. I. *The California psychological inventory handbook*. San Francisco: Jossey-Bass, 1972.

Megargee, E. I. Multiple Affect Adjective Check List. In O. K. Buros (Ed.), *The seventh mental measurements yearbook*. Highland Park, N.J.: Gryphon Press, 1972.

Meltzoff, J., & Kornreich, M. *Research in psychotherapy*. New York: Atherton, 1970.

Mintz, J. What is "success" in psychotherapy? *Journal of Abnormal Psychology*, 1972, **80**, 11–19.

Mintz, J. special issues in outcome assessment: Agreement among sources of ratings. In M. J. Lambert, E. R. Christensen, & S. S. DeJulio (Eds.), *The measurement of psychotherapy outcome in research and evaluation*. New York: Wiley, 1981.

Mooney, R. L.. Surveying high school students' problems by means of a problem check list. *Education Research Bulletin*, 1942, **21**, 57–69.

Morris, C., Eiduson, B. D., & O'Donovan, D. Values of psychiatric patients. *Behavioral Sciences*, 1960, **5**, 297–312.

Nesselroade, J. R., Stigler, S. M., & Baltes, P. B. Regression toward the mean and the study of change. *Psychological Bulletin*, 1980, **88**, 622–637.

Roessler, R. Personality, psychophysiology and performance. *Psychophysiology*, 1973, **10**, 315–327.

Rotter, J. B. Generalized expectancies for internal vs external control of reinforcement. *Psychological Monographs*, 1966, **80**, (1, Whole No. 609).

Sapolsky, A. Relationship between patient-doctor compatibility, mutual perception, and outcome of treatment. *Journal of Abnormal Psychology*, 965, **70**, 70–76.

Schutz, W. C. *FIRO: A three-dimensional theory of interpersonal behavior*. New York: Holt, Rinehart & Winston, 1958.

Seligman, M. E. P., Abramson, L. Y., Semmel, A., & VonBaeyer, C. Depressive attributional style. *Journal of Abnormal Psychology*, 1979, **88**, 242–248.

Shostrom, E. L. An inventory for the measure of self-actualization. *Educational and Psychological Measurements*, 1964, **24**, 207–218.

Shostrom E. L. *Manual: Personal Orientation Inventory*. San Diego: Educational and Industrial Testing Service, 1966.

Shostrom, E. L., & Knapp, R. R. The relationship of a measure of self-actualization (POI) to a measure of pathology (MMPI) and to therapeutic growth. *American Journal of Psychotherapy*, 1966, **20**, 193–202.

Snyder, D., Lynch, J. J., Derogatis, L., & Gruss, L. Psychopathology and communication problems in a family practice. *Psychosomatics*, 1980, **21**, 661–670.

Spielberger, C. D., Gorsuch, R. L., & Lushene, R. E. *The State-Trait Anxiety Inventory (STAI) test manual for form X*. Palo Alto: Consulting Psychologists Press, 1970.

Strahan, R. F. More on averaging judges' ratings: Determining the most reliable composite. *Journal of Consulting and Clinical Psychology*, 1980, **48**, 587–589.

Strupp, H. H., & Hadley, S. W. Specific versus non-specific factors in psychotherapy. *Archives of General Psychiatry*, 1979, **36**, 1125–1136.

Strupp, H. H., and Hadley, S. W. A tripartite model of mental health and therapeutic outcomes. *American Psychologist*, 1977, **32**, 187–196.

Strupp, H. H., Wallach, M. S., & Wogan, M. Psychotherapy experience in retrospect: Questionnaire survey of former patients and their therapists. *Psychological Monographs*, 1964, **78** (11, Whole No. 588).

Tosi, D. J., & Lindamood, C. A. The measurement of self-actualization: A critical review of the Personal Orientation Inventory. *Journal of Personality Assessment*, 1975, **39**, 215–224.

Waskow, I. E., & Parloff, M. B. *Psychotherapy Change Measures*. (Publication No. 74-120) Rockville, Md.: National Institute of Mental Health, 1975.

Williams, R. H., & Zimmerman, D. W. The reliability of difference scores when errors are correlated. *Educational and Psychological Measurement*, 1977, **37**, 679–689.

Wolpe, J., & Lang, P. J. A fear survey schedule for behavior therapy. *Behaviour Research and Therapy*, 1964, **2**, 27–30.

Wolpe, J., & Lazarus, A. A. *Behavior Therapy Techniques*. Oxford: Pergamon Press, 1966.

Zuckerman, M. The development of an Affect Adjective Check List for the measurement of anxiety. *Journal of Consulting Psychology*, 1960, **24**, 457–462.

APPENDIX A. REFERENCES OF 150 OUTCOME STUDIES

1. Abramowitz, C. V., Abramowitz, S. I., Roback, H. B., & Jackson, C. Differential effectiveness of directive and nondirective group therapies as a function of client internal-external control. *Journal of Consulting and Clinical Psychology*, 1974, **42**, 849–853.

2. Allen, D. A., & Janowitz, J. F. A study of the outcome of psychotherapy in a university mental health service. *American College Health Association Journal*, 1965, **13**, 361–378.

3. Andrasik, F., & Holroyd, K. A. A test of specific and nonspecific effects in the biofeedback treatment of tension headache. *Journal of Consulting and Clinical Psychology*, 1980, **48**, 575–586.

4. Ashby, J. D., Ford, D. H., Guerney, B. G., Jr., & Guerney, L. F. Effects on clients of a reflective and a leading type of psychotherapy. *Psychological Monographs*, 1957, **71**, (24, Whole No. 453).

5. Baehr, S. O. The comparative effectiveness of individual psychotherapy, group psychotherapy, and a combination of these methods. *Journal of Consulting Psychology*, 1954, **18**, 179–183.

6. Baker, E. The differential effects of two psychotherapeutic approaches on client perceptions. *Journal of Counseling Psychology*, 1960, **1**, 46–50.

7. Bandura, A., Blanchard, E. G., & Ritter, B. Relative efficacy of desensitization and modeling approaches for inducing behavioral, affective, and attitudinal changes. *Journal of Personality and Social Psychology*, 1969, **13**, 173–199.

8. Bare, C. E. Relationship of counselor personality and counselor-client personality similarity to selected counseling success criteria. *Journal of Counseling Psychology*, 1967, **14**, 419–425.

9. Barrera, M., Jr. An evaluation of a brief group therapy for depression. *Journal of Consulting and Clinical Psychology*, 1979, **47**, 413–415

10. Barron, F., & Leary, T. Changes in psychoneurotic patients with and without psychotherapy. *Journal of Consulting Psychology*, 1955, **19**, 239–245

11. Berzins, J. I., Ross, W. F., & Friedman, W. H. A-B therapist distinction, patient diagnosis, and outcome of brief psychotherapy in a college clinic. *Journal of Consulting and Clinical Psychology*, 1972, **38**, 231–237

12. Beutler, L. E., Jobe, A. M., & Elkins, D. Outcomes in group psychotherapy: Using persuasion theory to increase treatment efficiency. *Journal of Consulting and Clinical Psychology*, 1974, **42**, 547–553.

13. Beutler, L. E., Johnson, D. T., Neville, C. W., Jr., Elkins, D., & Jobe, A. M. Attitude similarity and therapist credibility as predictors of attitude change and

improvement in psychotherapy. *Journal of Consulting and Clinical Psychology*, 1975, **43**, 90–91.

14. Beutler, L. E., Pollack, S., & Jobe, A. M. "Acceptance," values, and therapeutic change. *Journal of Consulting and Clinical Psychology*, 1978, **46**, 198–199.

15. Bierenbaum, H., Nichols, M. P., & Schwartz, A. J. Effects of varying session length and frequency in brief emotive psychotherapy. *Journal of Consulting and Clinical Psychology*, 1976, **44**, 790–798

16. Blanchard, E. B. Relative contributions of modeling, informational influences, and physical contact in extinction of phobic behavior. *Journal of Abnormal Psychology*, 1970, **76**, 55–61.

17. Board, F. A. Patients' and physicians' judgements of outcome of psychotherapy in an outpatient clinic. *Archives of General Psychiatry*, 1959, **1**, 185–196.

18. Boe, E. E., Gocka, E. F., & Kogan, W. S. The effect of group psychotherapy on interpersonal perceptions of psychiatric patients. *Multivariate Behavior Research*, 1966, **1**, 177–187.

19. Borkovec, T. D., & Fowles, D. C. Controlled investigation of the effects of progressive and hypnotic relaxation of insomnia. *Journal of Abnormal Psychology*, 1973, **82**, 153–158.

20. Cappon, D. Results of psychotherapy. *British Journal of Psychiatry*, 1964, **110**, 35–45.

21. Carr, J. E. Differentiation similarity of patient and therapist and the outcome of psychotherapy. *Journal of Abnormal Psychology*, 1970, **76**, 361–369.

22. Carr-Kaffachan, L., & Woolfolk, R. L. Active and placebo effects in treatment of moderate and severe insomnia. *Journal of Consulting and Clinical Psychology*, 1979, **47**, 1072–1080.

23. Cartwright, D. S. The effects of psychotherapy on self-consistency: A replication and extension. *Journal of Consulting Psychology*, 1961, **25**, 376–382.

24. Cartwright, D. S., Kirtner, W. L., & Ficke, D. W. Method factors in changes associated with psychotherapy. *Journal of Abnormal and Social Psychology*, 1963, **66**, 164–175.

25. Cartwright, D. S., & Roth, I. Success and satisfaction in psychotherapy. *Journal of Clinical Psychology*, 1957, **13**, 20–26.

26. Cook, T. E. The influence of client-counselor value similarity on change in meaning during brief counseling. *Journal of Counseling Psychology*, 1966, **13**, 77–81.

27. Covi, L., Lipman, R. S., Derogatis, L. R., Smith, G. E., & Pattison, J. H. Drugs and group psychotherapy in neurotic depression. *American Journal of Psychiatry*, 1974, **131**, 191–198.

28. Cox, D. J., Freundlich, A., & Meyer, R. G. Differential effectiveness of electromyograph feedback, verbal relaxation instructions, and medication placebo with tension headaches. *Journal of Consulting and Clinical Psychology*, 1975, **43**, 892–899.

29. Crighton, J., & Jehu, D. Treatment of examination anxiety by systematic desensitization or psychotherapy in groups, *Behaviour Research and Therapy*, 1969, **7**, 245–248.

30. Denney, D. R., & Sullivan, B. J. Desensitization and modeling treatments of spider fear using two types of scenes. *Journal of Consulting and Clinical Psychology*, 1976, **44**, 573–579.

31. Dietzel, C. S., & Abeles, N. Client-therapist complementarity and therapeutic outcome. *Journal of Counseling Psychology*, 1975, **22**, 264–272.

32. D'Zurilla, T. J., Wilson, G. T., & Nelson, R. A preliminary study of the effectiveness of graduated prolonged exposure in the treatment of irrational fear. *Behavior Therapy*, 1973, **4**, 672–685.

33. Edwards, B. C., & Edgerly, J. W. Effects of counselor-client cognitive congruence on counseling outcome in brief counseling. *Journal of Counseling Psychology*, 1970, **17**, 313–318.

34. Elkins, D., Beutler, L. E., Jones, R. L., & Ray, C. Anxiety reduction in group process experience as a function of nonverbal vs. role-playing exercises. *Group Process*, 1977, **7**, 213–220.

35. Ends, E. J., & Page, C. W. A study of functional relationships among measures of anxiety, ego strength and adjustment. *Journal of Clinical Psychology*, 1957, **13**, 148–150.

36. Epstein, N., & Jackson, E. An outcome study of short-term communication training with married couples. *Journal of Consulting and Clinical Psychology*, 1978, **46**, 207–212.

37. Eyberg, S. M., & Johnson, S. M. Multiple assessment of behavior modification with families: Effects of contingency contracting and order of treated problems. *Journal of Consulting and Clinical Psychology*, 1974, **42**, 594–606.

38. Farson, R. E. Introjection in the psychotherapeutic relationship. *Journal of Counseling Psychology*, 1961, **8**, 337–342.

39. Feifel, H., & Eells, J. Patients and therapists assess the same psychotherapy. *Journal of Consulting Psychology*, 1963, **27**, 310–318.

40. Forsyth, R. P., & Fairweather, G. W. Psychotherapeutic and other hospital treatment criteria: The dilemma. *Journal of Abnormal and Social Psychology*, 1961, **62**, 598–604.

41. Frank, J. D., Gliedman, L. H., Imber, S. D., Stone, A. R., & Nash, E. H. Patients expectancies and relearning as factors determining improvement in psychotherapy. *American Journal of Psychiatry*, 1959, **115**, 961–968.

42. Friedman, M. L., & Dies, R. R. Reactions of internal and external test anxious students to counseling and behavior therapies. *Journal of Consulting and Clinical Psychology*, 1974, **42**, 921.

43. Garfield, S. L., Prager, R. A., & Bergin, A. E. Evaluation of outcome in psychotherapy. *Journal of Consulting and Clinical Psychology*, 1971, **37**, 307–313.

44. Gatchel, R. J., Hatch, J. P., Maynard, A., Turns, R., & Taunton-Blackwood, A. Comparison of heart rate biofeedback, false biofeedback, and systematic desensitization in reducing speech anxiety: Short- and long-term effectiveness. *Journal of Consulting and Clinical Psychology*, 1979, **47**, 620–622.

45. Gelder, M. G., & Marks I. M. Severe agoraphobia: A controlled prospective trial of behavior therapy. *British Journal of Psychiatry,* 1966, **112**, 309–319.

46. Gelder, M. G., Marks, I. M., Wolff, H. H., & Clarke, M. Desensitization and psychotherapy in the treatment of phobic states: A controlled inquiry. *British Journal of Psychiatry*, 1967, **113**, 53–73.

47. Goldfried, M. R., Linehan, M. M., & Smith, J. L. Reduction of test anxiety through cognitive restructuring. *Journal of Consulting and Clinical Psychology*, 1978, **46**, 32–39.

48. Gomes-Schwartz, B. Effective ingredients in psychotherapy: Prediction of outcome from process variables. *Journal of Consulting and Clinical Psychology*, 1978, **46**, 1023–1035.

49. Gould, E., & Glock, I. D. The effects of family presence and brief family intervention on global outcome for hospitalized schizophrenic patients. *Family Process*, 1977, **16**, 503–510.

50. Green, B. L., Gleser, G. C., Stone, W. N., & Seifert, R. F. Relationships among diverse measures of psychotherapy outcome. *Journal of Consulting and Clinical Psychology*, 1975, **43**, 689–699.

51. Grigg, A. E., & Goodstein, L. D. The use of clients as judges of the counselor's performance. *Journal of Counseling Psychology*, 1957, **4**, 31–36.

52. Gurman, A. S. Attitude change in marital cotherapy. *Journal of Family Counseling*, 1974, **2**, 50–54.

53. Halperin, K. M., & Snyder, C. R. Effects of enhanced psychological test feedback on treatment outcome: Therapeutic implications of the Barnum effect. *Journal of Consulting and Clinical Psychology*, 1979, **47**, 140–146.

54. Hammen, C. L., Jacobs, M., Mayol, A., & Cochran, S. D. Dysfunctional cognitions and the effectiveness of skills and cognitive-behavioral assertion training. *Journal of Consulting and Clinical Psychology*, 1980, **48**, 685–695.

55. Harris, C., & Johnson, S. B. Comparison of individualized covert modeling, self-control desensitization, and study skills training for alleviation of test anxiety. *Journal of Consulting and Clinical Psychology*, 1980, **48**, 186–194.

56. Heine, R. W. A comparison of patients' reports on psychotherapeutic experience with psychoanalytic, nondirective and Adlerian therapists. *American Journal of Psychotherapy*, 1953, **7**, 16–23.

57. Henry, W. E., & Shlien, J. M. Affective complexity and psychotherapy: Some comparisons of time-limited and unlimited treatment. *Journal of Projective Techniques*, 1958, **22**, 153–163.

58. Hill, J. A. Therapist goals, patient aims and patient satisfaction in psychotherapy. *Journal of Clinical Psychology*, 1969, **25**, 455–459.

59. Hirt, M., & Greenfield, H. Implosive therapy treatment of heroin addicts during methadone detoxification. *Journal of Consulting and Clinical Psychology*, 1979, **47**, 982–983.

60. Holroyd, K. A. Cognition and desensitization in the group treatment of test anxiety. *Journal of Consulting and Clinical Psychology*, 1976, **44**, 991–1001.

61. Jesness, C. F. Comparative effectiveness of behavior modification and transactional analysis programs for delinquents. *Journal of Consulting and Clinical Psychology*, 1975, **43**, 758–779.

62. Johnson, R. K., & Meyer, R. G. The locus of control construct in EEG alpha rhythm feedback. *Journal of Consulting and Clinical Psychology*, 1974, **42**, 913.

63. Jones, D. S., & Medmene, A. M. Self-actualization effects of a marathon growth group. *Journal of Counseling Psychology*, 1975, **22**, 39–43.

64. Kahn, M., Baker, B. L., & Weiss, J. M. Treatment of insomnia by relaxation training. *Journal of Abnormal Psychology*, 1968, **73**, 556–558.

65. Kapp, F. T., Gleser, G. C., Brissenden, A., Emerson, R., Winget, J. A., & Kashdan, B. Group participation and self-perceived personality change. *Journal of Nervous and Mental Disease*, 1964, **139**, 255–265.

66. Karst, T. O., & Trexler, L. D. Initial study using fixed-role and rational-emotive therapy in treating public-speaking anxiety. *Journal of Consulting and Clinical Psychology*, 1970, **34**, 360–366.

67. Kelly, A. H., & Curran, J. P. Comparison of a self-control approach and an emotional coping approach to the treatment of obesity. *Journal of Consulting and Clinical Psychology*, 1976, **44**, 683.

68. Keniston, K., Boltax, S., & Almond, R. Multiple criteria of treatment outcome. *Journal of Psychiatric Research*, 1971, **8**, 107–118.

69. Kilmann, P. R., & Howell, R. J. Effects of structure of marathon group therapy and locus of control on therapeutic outcome. *Journal of Consulting and Clinical Psychology*, 1974, **42**, 912.

70. Kilmann, P. R., Pilbert, B. M., & Sotile, W. M. Relationship between locus of control, structure of therapy, and outcome. *Journal of Consulting and Clinical Psychology*, 1975, **43**, 588.

71. Kirsch, I., & Henry, D. Self-desensitization and meditation in reduction of public speaking anxiety. *Journal of Consulting and Clinical Psychology*, 1979, **47**, 536–541.

72. Koren, P., Carlton, K., & Shaw, D. Marital conflict: Relations among behaviors, outcomes, and distress. *Journal of Consulting and Clinical Psychology*, 1980, **48**, 460–468.

73. LaCrosse, M. B. Perceived counselor social influence and counseling outcomes: Validity of the Counselor Rating Form. *Journal of Counseling Psychology*, 1980, **27**, 320–327.

74. Lazarus, A. A. Group therapy of phobic disorders by systematic desensitization. *Journal of Abnormal and Social Psychology*, 961, **63**, 504–510.

75. Lerner, B. Democratic values and therapeutic efficacy: A construct validity study. *Journal of Abnormal Psychology*, 1973, **82**, 491–498.

76. Lesser, W. M. The relationship between counseling progress and empathic understanding. *Journal of Counseling Psychology*, 1961, **8**, 330–336.

77. Levis, D. J., & Carrera, R. Effects of ten hours of implosive therapy in the treatment of outpatients. *Journal of Abnormal Psychology*, 1967, **72**, 504–508.

78. Lewinsohn, P. M., & Nichols, R. C. Dimensions of change in mental hospital patients. *Journal of Clinical Psychology*, 1967, **23**, 498–503.

79. Lick, J. Expectancy, false galvanic skin response feedback, and systematic desensitization in the modification of phobic behavior. *Journal of Consulting and Clinical Psychology*, 1975, **43**, 557–567.

80. Lick, J. R., & Heffler, D. Relaxation training and attention placebo in the treatment of severe insomnia. *Journal of Consulting and Clinical Psychology*, 1977, **45**, 153–161.

81. Linehan, M. M., Walker, R. O., Bronheim, S., Haynes, K. F., & Yenzeroff, H. Group versus individual assertion training. *Journal of Consulting and Clinical Psychology*, 1979, **47**, 1000–1002.

82. Lipkin, S. The client evaluates non-directive psychotherapy. *Journal of Consulting Psychology*, 1948, **12**, 137–146.

83. Lipsky, M. J., Kassinove, H., & Miller, N. J. Effects of rational-emotive therapy, rational role reversal, and rational-emotive imagery on the emotional adjustment of community mental health center patients. *Journal of Consulting and Clinical Psychology*, 1980, **48**, 366–374.

84. Lira, F. T., Nay, W. R., McCullough, J. P. & Etkin, M. W. Relative effects of modeling and role playing in the treatment of avoidance behaviors. *Journal of Consulting and Clinical Psychology*, 1975, **43**, 608–618.

85. Luborsky, L., Mintz, J., Auerbach, A., Christoph, P., Bachrach, H., Todd, T., Johnson, M., Cohen, M., & O'Brien, C. P. Predicting the outcome of psychotherapy: Findings of the Penn psychotherapy project. *Archives of General Psychiatry*, 1980, **37**, 471–481.

86. Marks, J., Sonoda, B., & Schalock, R. Reinforcement versus relationship therapy for schizophrenics. *Journal of Abnormal Psychology*, 1968, **73**, 397–402.

87. Marmen, J. S. Group therapy as viewed by hospitalized patients. *Archives of General Psychiatry*, 1973, **28**, 404–408.

88. Martini, J. L. Patient-therapist value congruence, interpersonal attraction, and outcome in marathon group therapy with alcoholics. A paper presented at the annual meeting of the Canadian Federation of Alcohol & Drug Addiction, Toronto, June, 1976.

89. McCardel, J., & Murray, E. J. Nonspecific factors in weekend encounter groups. *Journal of Consulting and Clinical Psychology*, 1974, **42**, 337–345.

90. McCordick, S. M., Kaplan, R. M., Finn, M. E., & Smith, S. H. Cognitive behavior modification and modeling for test anxiety. *Journal of Consulting and Clinical Psychology*, 1979, **47**, 419–420.

91. McFall, R. M., & Lillesand, D. B. Behavior rehearsal with modeling and coaching in assertion training. *Journal of Abnormal Psychology*, 1971, **77**, 313–323.

92. McFall, R. M., & Marston, A. R. An experimental investigation of behavior rehearsal in assertive training. *Journal of Abnormal Psychology*, 1970, **76**, 295–303.

93. McFall, R. M., & Twentyman, C. T. Four experiments on the relative contributions of rehearsal, modeling, and coaching to assertion training. *Journal of Abnormal Psychology*, 1973, **81**, 199–218.

94. McLean, P. D., & Hakstian, A. R. Clinical depression: Comparative efficacy of outpatient treatments. *Journal of Consulting and Clinical Psychology*, 1979, **47**, 818–836.

95. McNair, D. M., Callahan, D. M., & Lorr, M. Therapist "type" and patient response to psychotherapy. *Journal of Consulting Psychology*, 1962, **26**, 425–429.

96. McReynolds, W. T. *Systematic desensitization, insight-oriented psychotherapy and relaxation therapy in a psychiatric population.* (Doctoral dissertation, Univer-

sity of Texas, 1969). *Dissertation Abstracts International*, 1970, **30**, 5694B. (University Microfilms No. 70-10, 834)

97.   Meichenbaum, D. H. Cognitive modification of test anxious college students. *Journal of Consulting and Clinical Psychology*, 1972, **39**, 370–380.

98.   Melnick, B. Patient-therapist identification in relation to both patient and therapist variables and therapy outcome. *Journal of Consulting and Clinical Psychology*, 1972, **38**, 97–104.

99.   Miller, W. R. Behavioral treatment of problem drinkers: A comparative outcome study of three controlled drinking therapies. *Journal of Consulting and Clinical Psychology*, 1978, **46**, 74–86.

100.   Miller, W. R., Taylor, C. A., & West, J. C. Focused versus broad-spectrum behavior therapy for problem drinkers. *Journal of Consulting and Clinical Psychology*, 1980, **48**, 590–601.

101.   Moleski, R., & Tosi, D. J. Comparative psychotherapy: Rational-emotive therapy versus systematic desensitization in the treatment of stuttering. *Journal of Consulting and Clinical Psychology*, 1976, **44**, 309–311.

102.   Monti, P. M., Curran, J. P., Corrineau, D. P., DeLancey, A. L., & Hagerman, S. M. Effects of social skills training groups and sensitivity training groups with psychiatric patients. *Journal of Consulting and Clinical Psychology*, 1980, **48**, 241–248.

103.   Muench, G. A. An investigation of the efficacy of time-limited psychotherapy. *Journal of Counseling Psychology*, 1965, **12**, 294–299.

104.   Munro, J. N., & Bach, T. R. Effect of time-limited counseling on client change. *Journal of Counseling Psychology*, 1975, **22**, 395–398

105.   Nicassio, P., & Bootzin, R. A comparison of progressive relaxation and autogenic training as treatments for insomnia. *Journal of Abnormal Psychology*, 1974, **83** 253–260.

106.   Nichols, M. P. Outcome of brief cathartic psychotherapy. *Journal of Consulting and Clinical Psychology*, 1974, **42**, 403–410.

107.   Nichols, M. P., & Refler, C. B. The study of brief psychotherapy in a college health setting. *American College Health Association Journal*, 1973, **22**, 128–133.

108.   Nichols, R. C., & Beck, K. W. Factors in psychotherapy change. *Journal of Consulting Psychology*, 1960, **24**, 388–399.

109.   Orlinsky, D. E., and Howard, K. I. *Varieties of psychotherapeutic experience: Multivariate analyses of patients' and therapists' reports.* New York: Columbia University, 1975.

110.   Parloff, M. B. Therapist-patient relationships and outcome of psychotherapy. *Journal of Consulting Psychology*, 1961, **25**, 29–38.

111.   Parrino, J. J. Effects of pretherapy information on learning in psychotherapy. *Journal of Abnormal Psychology*, 1971, **77**, 17–24.

112.   Parsons, B. V., Jr., & Alexander, J. F. Short-term family intervention: A therapy outcome study. *Journal of Consulting and Clinical Psychology*, 1973, **41** 195–201.

113.   Patterson, V., Levene, H., & Breger, L. Treatment and training outcomes with two time-limited therapies. *Archives of General Psychiatry*, 1971, **25**, 161–167.

114. Piper, W. E., Debbane, E. G., & Garant, J. An outcome study of group therapy. *Archives of General Psychiatry*, 1977, **34**, 1027–1032.

115. Piper, W. E, Doan, B. D., Edwards, E. M., & Jones, B. D. Cotherapy behavior, group therapy process, and treatment outcome. *Journal of Consulting and Clinical Psychology*, 1979, **47**, 1081–1089.

116. Prager, R. A., & Garfield, S. L. Client initial disturbance and outcome in psychotherapy. *Journal of Consulting and Clinical Psychology*, 1972, **38**, 112–117.

117. Rosenthal, D. Changes in some moral values following psychotherapy. *Journal of Consulting Psychology*, 1955, **19**, 431–436.

118. Saltzman, C., Luetgert, M. J., Roth, C. H., Creaser, J., & Howard, L. Formation of a therapeutic relationship: Experiences during the initial phase of psychotherapy as predictors of treatment duration and outcome. *Journal of Consulting and Clinical Psychology*, 1976, **44**, 546–555.

119. Scher, M. Verbal activity, sex, counselor experience, and success in counseling. *Journal of Counseling Psychology*, 1975, **22**, 97–101.

120. Schwartz, R. D., & Higgins, R. L. Differential outcome from automated assertion training as a function of locus of control. *Journal of Consulting and Clinical Psychology*, 1979, **47**, 686–694.

121. Shaw, B. F. *A systematic investigation of two psychological treatments of depression.* (University of Western Ontario, Canada, 1975). *Dissertation Abstracts International*, 1976, **36**, 4179B–4180B.

122. Shaw, B. F. Comparison of cognitive therapy and behavior therapy in the treatment of depression. *Journal of Consulting and Clinical Psychology*, 1977, **45** 543–551.

123. Shealy, R. C., Lowe, J. D., & Ritzler, B. A. Sleep onset insomnia: Personality characteristics and treatment outcome. *Journal of Consulting and Clinical Psychology*, 1980, **48**, 659–661.

124. Shlien, J. M., Mosak, H. H., & Dreikurs, R. Effect of time limits: A comparison of two psychotherapies. *Journal of Counseling Psychology*, 1962, **9**, 31–34.

125. Sloane, R. B., Staples, F. R., Cristol, A. H., Yorkston, J. G., & Whipple K. Short-term analytically oriented psychotherapy versus behavior therapy. *American Journal of Psychiatry*, 1975, **132**, 373–377.

126. Smith, A. B., Bassin, A., & Froehlich, A. Change in attitudes and degree of verbal participation in group therapy with adult offenders. *Journal of Consulting Psychology*, 1960, **24**, 247–249.

127. Smith, R. E., & Nye, S. L. A comparison of implosive therapy and systematic desensitization in the treatment of test anxiety. *Journal of Consulting and Clinical Psychology*, 1973, **41**, 37–42.

128. Snyder, A. L., & Deffenbacher, J. L. Comparison of relaxation as self-control and systematic desensitization in the treatment of test anxiety. *Journal of Consulting and Clinical Psychology*, 1977, **45**, 1202–1203.

129. Steinmark, S. W., & Borkovec, T. D. Active and placebo treatment effects on moderate insomnia under counterdemand and positive demand instructions. *Journal of Abnormal Psychology*, 1974, **83**, 157–163.

130. Storrow, H. A. The measurement of outcome in psychotherapy: A study in method. *Archives of General Psychiatry*, 1960, **2**, 142–146.

131. Strupp, H. H., Fox, R. E., & Lessler, K. *Patients view their psychotherapy.* Baltimore: Johns Hopkins University Press, 1969.

132. Strupp, H. H., & Hadley, S. W. Specific vs. nonspecific factors in psychotherapy: A controlled study of outcome. *Archives of General Psychiatry*, 1979, **36**, 1125–1136.

133. Strupp, H. H., Wallach, M. S., & Wogan, M. Psychotherapy experience in retrospect: Questionnaire survey of former patients and their therapists. *Psychological Monographs*, 1964, **78**, (11, Whole No. 588).

134. Suarez, Y., Adams, H. E., & McCutcheon, B. A. Flooding and systematic desensitization: Efficacy in subclinical phobics as a function of arousal. *Journal of Consulting and Clinical Psychology*, 1976, **44**, 872.

135. Targow, J. G., & Zweber, R. V. Participants' reactions to treatment in a married couples' group. *International Journal of Group Psychotherapy*, 1969, **19**, 221–225.

136. Thorley, A. S., & Craske, N. Comparison and estimate of group and individual methods of treatment. *British Medical Journal*, 1950, **1**, 97–100.

137. Townsend, R. E., House, J. F., & Addario, D. A comparison of biofeedback-mediated relaxation and group therapy in the treatment of chronic anxiety. *American Journal of Psychiatry*, 1975, **132**, 598–601.

138. Trexler, L. D., & Karst, T. O. Rational-emotive therapy, placebo and no-treatment effects on public-speaking anxiety. *Journal of Abnormal Psychology*, 1972, **79**, 60–67.

139. Truax, C. B. Therapist empathy, warmth, and genuiness and patient personality change in group psychotherapy: A comparison between interaction unit measures, time sample measures, patient perception measures. *Journal of Clinical Psychology*, 1966, **22**, 225–229.

140. Truax, C. B., Carkhuff, R. R., & Kodman, F. Relationships between therapist-offered conditions and patient change in group psychotherapy. *Journal of Clinical Psychology*, 1965, **21**, 327–329.

141. Truax, C. B., Wargo, D. G., Frank, J. D., Imber, S. D., Battle, C. C., Hoehn-Saric, R., Nash, E. H., & Stone, A. R. Therapist empathy, genuiness, and warmth and patient therapeutic outcome. *Journal of Consulting Psychology*, 1966, **30**, 395–401.

142. Turner, R. M., & Ascher, L. M. Controlled comparison of progressive relaxation, stimulus control and paradoxical intention therapies for insomnia. *Journal of Consulting and Clinical Psychology*, 1979, **47**, 500–508.

143. Ukeritis, M. D. *A study of value convergence in a group psychotherapy setting.* (Doctoral dissertation, University of Pittsburgh, 1977). *Dissertation Abstracts International*, 1978, **38**, 4488B. (University Microfilms No. 7801842)

144. Vansteenwegen, A. *Residential couple-therapy: A controlled outcome study.* A paper presented at the 10th annual meeting of the Society for Psychotherapy Research, Oxford, England, July, 1979.

145. Vogler, R. E., Compton, J. V., & Weissbach, T. A. Integrated behavior change techniques for alcoholics. *Journal of Consulting and Clinical Psychology*, 1975, **43**, 233–243.

146. Weitz, L. J., Abramowitz, S. I., Steger, J. A., Calabria, F. M., Conable, M., & Yarus, G. Number of sessions and client-judged outcome: The more the better? *Psychotherapy: Theory, Research and Practice*, 1975, **12**, 337–340.

147. Wiener, M. The effects of two experimental counseling techniques on performances impaired by induced stress. *Journal of Abnormal and Social Psychology*, 1955, **51**, 565–572.

148. Wogan, M. Effect of therapist-patient personality variables on therapeutic outcome. *Journal of Consulting and Clinical Psychology*, 1970, **35**, 356–361.

149. Yalon, I. D., Houts, P. S., Zimerberg, S. M., & Rand, K. Prediction of improvement in group psychotherapy: An exploratory study. *Archives of General Psychiatry*, 1967, **17**, 159–168.

150. Zeiss, A. M., Lewinsohn, P. M., & Munoz, R. F. Nonspecific improvement effects in depression using interpersonal skills training, pleasant activity schedules, or cognitive training. *Journal of Consulting and Clinical Psychology*, 1979, **47**, 427–429.

CHAPTER 14

Therapist's Evaluation of Psychotherapy

FREDERICK L. NEWMAN

CHAPTER THEME

Consider an interesting paradox about the therapist. On the one hand, the therapist is given primary responsibility for the conduct of therapy (even if there is supervision, or peer review). On the other hand, an extensive body of literature suggests that the therapist's evaluations of a client (patient) are often unreliable, biased, and/or inaccurate (Arkes, 1981; Dawes, 1979; Eisenberg, 1979; Meehl, 1954). If the latter negative view of the therapist is true, a logical line would follow that the therapist might not be properly trusted with either the task of therapy, the task of evaluating the process and outcome of therapy, or both.

Fortunately, the logical line is interrupted, although not completely dispelled, by three arguments. First, reviews of controlled studies within the outcome literature show that these so-called "unreliable" observers do have successful therapeutic outcomes (Bergin & Lambert, 1978; Shapiro & Shapiro, 1981; Smith et al., 1980; VandenBos & Pino, 1980). One could rhetorically ask, "How could such unreliable observers of human behavior be expected to achieve such successful results?" Although the evidence of successful outcome is still not overwhelming, there has been a steady line of well-controlled studies suggesting that psychotherapy, when properly applied, can successfully improve or maintain functional behavior patterns.

The second argument is that the therapist's view of the therapeutic processes and outcomes represents a unique view that cannot be reported by any other observer. Whereas there has been ample reason to question whether the view of the therapist is an "unbiased" view, the therapist is, nevertheless, a rich source of information and insight about the facets that comprise the therapeutic experience (Orlinsky & Howard, 1975) and outcome (Green et al., 1975; Mintz et al., 1973). Moreover, an analysis of the bias can in itself offer an insight into the therapeutic process (Arkes, 1981; Newman & Rinkus, 1978; Orlinsky & Howard, 1975).

Another line of evidence for the second argument is offered by Mintz et al. (1973). These investigators addressed the issue of whether the therapist's report of a therapy session ought to be considered any better or worse than that offered by the client or by trained observers. In their study, each of the three classes of observers reported on 12 successive therapy sessions using the Orlinsky and Howard Therapy Session Report. The objectively "trained" observers, one a psychiatrist and one a psychiatric technician, both had six years of experience in psychotherapy research, including experience in rating psychotherapy processes and outcomes. The findings suggested that there were areas of reliability and unreliability for all three groups (i.e., the clients, therapists, and observers). Each group had its own unique reliable contribution to offer, and it would be a mistake not to take all three perspectives into account. Mintz and his colleagues also found that the degree of unreliability in observations among clients, therapists, and "trained" observers was surprisingly similar. That is, there was a high degree of consensus and similar degrees of judgment variance within the three groups regarding the description of the client's emotional state. These data, therefore, suggest that the data derived from therapists may be no better or no worse than data derived from other sources. The data simply represent different perspectives, each of which carries its own contribution to the unreliability of the data.

Shrauger and Osberg (1981) reviewed the literature that contrasted the relative accuracy of self-assessment with the judgments of others. In spite of a long-standing assumption that self-assessment and self-prediction would be biased (Dawes, 1979; Mischel, 1968), their review of the literature suggests the opposite conclusion. They found 29 studies that favored self-assessment, 10 studies that favored other types of assessment, and four studies that they called a "tie." When considering multiple comparisons both within and between studies, the differences were even more impressive, with 84 favoring self-assessment versus 26 unfavorable and nine ties. Thus the Shrauger and Osberg analysis supports the conclusions of Mintz et al. (1973). Each observer–participant of therapy has a unique contribution to make, and each is blessed or plagued with comparable degrees of reliability or, conversely, unreliability. This leads into the next argument.

The third argument is that for many varieties of the therapist's evaluation, areas of reliability or unreliability and bias can be identified (Arkes, 1981; Newman & Rinkus, 1978; Orlinsky & Howard, 1975) and potentially controlled in a study of psychotherapy process or outcome. As is detailed later in the chapter, these investigators have described methods for identifying major facets that influence the reliability of therapists' observations in both analogue and *in vivo* studies. Thus it appears possible, in any one outcome study conducted in a carefully supervised clinical setting, to either attenuate the biasing influences in clinical communication or data collection or at least to statistically control for their influence in an analysis of the data.

Integrating the data offered by Mintz et al. (1973), with the reviews of the literature and data offered by Shrauger and Osberg (1981) and Arkes (1981), the therapist's evaluation can represent a valid perspective of the therapeutic processes and outcomes, but with some potentially identifiable sources of unreliability and bias.

Together, the three arguments suggest that therapist observations and evaluations not only can, but should, be considered as a valuable source of data about the processes and outcomes of psychotherapy. In this light, the goal of the present chapter is to describe what is known about factors influencing therapist evaluations so that researchers and evaluators can make better use of therapist-derived data in the research and evaluation endeavor. Specifically, the present chapter undertakes to accomplish three things: (1) to describe the perspective of therapist evaluations in terms of the demand characteristics placed on the therapist during the course of treatment (the literature review here focuses on what factors appear to influence therapists' evaluations at different points in the therapeutic process); (2) to provide a review of the major techniques and instruments used to obtain therapist evaluations; and (3) to describe some techniques that can be used to detect when and how extraneous facets influence therapists' evaluations.

There are four issues, or concerns, that will guide the theme of discussion through each of the three chapter sections: (1) how a therapist evaluation technique is useful for research and clinical care; (2) what facets negatively detract from the reliability, accuracy, and generalizability of the therapist's evaluation; (3) what facets can positively influence the reliability, accuracy, and generalizability of these evaluations; and (4) how one might arrange to better control studies so that more positive than negative influencing facets occur—or how one might at least provide some degree of statistical, if not experimental, control over influencing facets. The end product ought to be some guidelines for the better use of therapist evaluation data in research and evaluation studies.

The Therapist's Perspective and the Demand Characteristics of Therapy

The therapist is a participating observer in the therapeutic process. As such, the therapist represents an important source of information about the client, about him or herself, and about the therapeutic encounter. The therapist is actively involved in the process and outcome of therapy and thus has information that others cannot offer. No other observer can capture and systematically record these observations from the same perspective. Simply stated, only the therapist's observations can represent the therapist's observations. Of course, the same can be said of the importance of the observations systematically and dependably collected from the client, a "significant other," or a trained independent observer. Data collected from each perspective can, if properly collected, be representative of a unique and valid perspective of what occurs during and after therapy. But the focus of this chapter is on the evaluations, judgments, and decisions of the therapist.

The most important consideration is that the therapist is an active participant in the therapeutic process. Verbal and nonverbal behavior provided by
the client and information about the client offered by family, friends, referral
agents, schools, or employers must be processed and used (or disregarded) in
the pursuit of therapeutic assessment and goals. Although similar information
processing and synthesis is required of other observers, the role of the therapist
has demand characteristics and outcome contingencies that are sufficiently
different to warrant a review of the demands.

The review of the demand characteristics on the therapist follows a sequen-
tial "six-stage" outline representing a "prototypical therapeutic process." The
outline, although useful for an exposition of demand characteristics on the
therapist, should not be considered as the outline followed by all therapies and
therapists. It is simply a convenient outline for describing demand characteristics gleaned from a review of standard texts (Brown & Brown, 1977; Fromm-
Reichmann, 1950; Krumboltz & Thoresen, 1969; Rogers, 1961), professional
standards (e.g., CHAMPUS, JCAH), and the research literature.

With this preamble of caution, let us next identify the six stages of the
prototypical therapeutic process and then describe the major demand characteristics at each stage:

1. *Referral and triage.* This stage includes the referral procedures and
   environmental factors influencing which clients are presented to the
   therapist for assessment, diagnosis, and treatment.

2. *Assessment and diagnosis.* The sorting of information about the
   client's symptoms, life situation, social supports, and so on for purposes
   of initial labeling "the problem" or "the diagnosis" included in this
   stage.

3. *Therapeutic plan.* Given the unique characteristics of the problem
   diagnosed, therapeutic goals and a set of therapeutic procedures for
   achieving those goals must be selected.

4. *Provision of therapy.* This phase appears to have two interacting
   parts: (a) the ongoing interaction of client, therapist, and auxiliary
   services to impact problems and achieve goals and (b) the reassessment
   (and possible reformulation) of client problems, situation, supports,
   therapeutic goals, and therapeutic strategy.

5. *Termination.* This stage involves the cessation of therapy, which may
   be initiated by the therapist, the client, the client and therapist together,
   or by an outside agent (e.g., third-party payer such as an insurance
   carrier or a clinical supervisor).

6. *Follow-up.* This phase involves review of outcome with either the
   client, significant other, or simply a review of the documentation of the
   first five phases to decide where modifications could benefit future
   therapeutic efforts.

Referral and Triage

This stage is extremely potent and seldom under the complete control of the therapist. The issues center around the circumstances that set the occasion for the client to come to the therapist: (1) whether the referral was voluntary, socially coerced by a significant other (parent, spouse, co-worker), or involuntary (courts, employer, school authorities); (2) what expectations have been set by the referral agents or by general reputation of the therapist or the clinical setting in which the therapist practices; and (3) what the influences of such incidental factors as geographic distance and means of travel to reach the therapist, the neighborhood, and "looks" of the therapeutic setting are.

A major issue in the success of psychotherapy is expectancy of the client (Wilkins, 1979). What if the perceptions and expectations of the agents of referral and triage (sometimes called "gatekeepers") are different from those of the therapist? Wilkins's review does offer strong support for the hypothesis that congruent expectations between client and therapist do lead to better outcomes, particularly in terms of agreed-on goals. Thus it would appear to be important to understand what the general reputation and expectations are of the overall community and how these might relate to the demands placed on the therapist. Miller (1981) performed an interesting survey on samples of people from the general public, personnel at health and social service agencies, and public officials (commissioners and board members) in two rural North Carolina counties, asking which of a list of mental health services provided by the community mental program were "most important." Importance was rated on a scale of 1 to 4, with 4 as the most important. Ratings with an average of 3.75 and above were considered as "most important." The lists of "most important" services for these outsiders were contrasted with the lists rated by clients, clinical staff, clerical staff, and administrators of the mental health program. The clinical staff listed only "individual psychotherapy" and "family psychotherapy" as most important. The range of most important services rated by all the other groups was much broader. The most striking result was that neither the general public nor the public officials listed individual or family psychotherapy as "most important." Thus these data suggest that there can be a mismatch in the expectations of referral sources and service providers.

Silverman (1980) has collected data that suggest that a client's mode of referral and entry will influence both diagnosis and treatment. He drew a 10% sample of urban community mental health clients. People with behavioral disturbances, drug abuse, and suicidal tendencies were, for the most part, referred by hospitals and were typically treated with individual therapy or in specialized programs. Cognitive, interpersonal, and emotional disorders were referred by self, family, or friends and were typically treated by individual therapy and/or group, family, or couple therapy. These results are neither unreasonable nor unexpected since the data also showed the hospital referrals to be more socially isolated, with prevailing symptoms that gained them admission through the hospital. Nevertheless, one might ask whether the actual underlying problems might be the same for both groups, with social isolation and "choice" of symptoms leading to different forms of entry, expectations, and treatment.

More relevant for the current discussion is the fact that both the referral sources and the therapist often have formal and informal interlocking lines that influence who is referred where, as well as the nature of social pressures that are felt by the therapist. For example, several studies have found that more experienced therapists tend to be assigned cases with better prognosis that are more closely aligned with their particular specialty (Meyers & Auld, 1955; Sullivan et al., 1958). More recent studies appearing to support these earlier findings have been reviewed by Auerbach and Johnson (1977) and Parloff et al. (1978).

Bergin and Lambert (1978) reviewed the literature on client selection criteria set by the clinic in relation to the client acceptance of treatment. It is obviously a two-way street. The variables that seem to be related to the clinic's acceptance of the client are education, occupation, race, diagnosis, and type of treatment the client can afford. In the tight economy of the 1980s, the issue of what the client or the client's insurer can afford is a critical factor in the referral and triage process.

Assessment and Diagnosis

The second stage of the process is more directly under the control of the therapist, but not nearly so much as one might assume. Issues here include prior training, the therapist's personal history, years of experience, and success with each type of client, socioeconomic, and cultural differences and familiarity with the client, first- and third-party payment practices; supervision and quality assurance review practices; and so forth. All these facets contribute demands on and can influence the therapists' judgments and decisions at this early stage in the therapeutic process and reports of client status. Moreover, the judgments and decisions made at this point often have strong influence on the ensuing therapeutic processes and outcomes.

Before reviewing the literature on facets influencing clinical judgments and decisions made at this stage, we need to make a brief digression to introduce some basic concepts found in the human judgment literature. There are two general judgment strategies or "heuristics" that people appear to use (Kahneman & Tversky, 1973, 1979; Nisbett & Ross, 1980; Tversky & Kahneman, 1977). One is the "availability heuristic," and the other is the "representative heuristic." Although the use of these two heuristics appears to be prevalent, they are in and of themselves neither good nor bad. They simply represent the basic strategies used most often. There are, as we soon discuss, features of these judgment strategies that appear to set the stage for inaccurate or biased judgments.

AVAILABILITY HEURISTIC.   The availability heuristic plays an important role in those classes of judgment that require assessment of the relative frequency or probability of events. In simple terms, the availability heuristic is a strategy of judgment formulation based on relative frequency of the observed events. For example, the availability heuristic would be used for judgments made about the relative frequency of excessive mood swings and alcohol abuse accompanying the so-called "midlife crisis" of males between 40 and 50 years of age, relative to other age groups or females of the same age category. Another example might be judgments made about the prevalence of child and spouse abuse within a particular demographic subgroup. It is highly likely that such judgments can be influenced by the circumstances and recent experiences of the judge, particularly if the judgments of frequency set the stage for causality. Consider a classical example of bias offered in the literature (Nisbett & Ross, 1980; Tversky & Kahneman, 1977). The judgment of the unemployment rate is strongly influenced by whether the judge is unemployed. Whereas some would assume that unemployed people would guess that the unemployment rate is higher because of a psychodynamic "egocentric bias," the more likely reason for a judged higher frequency is that unemployed people tend to be aware of more instances of unemployment; that is, they are exposed more often to instances of unemployment.

There are comparable examples of bias due to the circumstances surrounding the therapist. For example, two therapists, one working in a private group practice in an affluent suburb and the other working at the university guidance clinic, would have sufficiently different first-hand experiences to suggest different relative frequencies of mood swings and alcohol abuse in 40- to 50-year-old males. Both therapists would very likely experience a high incidence of mood swings and alcohol abuse among their client populations, but the private practitioner would have greater exposure to the 40- to 50-year-old male population. A likely result would be to attribute "causality" of age and gender to mood swings and alcohol abuse. The inference of causality may or may not be warranted, but no experimental data exist to justify a causal judgment.

For the child and spouse abuse example, judgments might vary with different geographic settings. For example, in a blue-collar, high-employment area of suburban Memphis, Tennessee, there is a higher frequency of child and wife abuse cases treated at the local mental health center than is found in a comparable blue-collar area of Providence, Rhode Island. Conversations with staff at the Memphis mental health center about this relatively high frequency of child and wife abuse often include judgments of causality. The Memphis clinicians readily point to the "fact" that spanking of both children and wife is neither uncommon nor considered as "terrible" by local mores. This judgment of causality led to focusing of therapeutic efforts in treatment planning, supervision, and review, along with an effort for public education (through various organizations in the community dealing with the problems of child and wife abuse) on how the use of corporal punishment can be pushed too far. Thus inferences of causality set the stage for clinical and educational actions.

The availability heuristic often sets the occasion for judgments of causality (Fischoff, 1976; Fischoff & Beyth, 1975; Nisbett & Ross, 1980). Such judgments are not necessarily incorrect or "bad." Certainly it is appropriate for the clinician during the assessment and diagnosis stages of therapy to assess the probability, or relative frequency, of particular relationships and their underlying causes. Often the alternative to inferences of causality is the inference that there is "nothing to be done" since one does not know the "true" underlying causes. Humanely, one would hope that in instances of child and wife abuse, some therapeutic intervention would be devised on the basis of correlational hunches of causality.

The view of clinical judgments offered by an analysis of the availability heuristic and inferences of causality suggests that different clinical experiences would very likely lead to differences in expectations of normal and acceptable behavior. For example, one could offer the conjecture that a judgment of relative frequency for clinicians and attention to "abuse" symptoms differs for clinicians in the Memphis and the Providence settings. Moreover, these differences in the symptoms attended to and used may result in differences in proposed underlying causes and the program of treatments rendered. These differences may, in turn, lead to differences in outcomes.

Arkes (1981) has offered another insight on how the availability heuristic can be biased by what he calls "covariation misestimation" in clinical assessment judgments. Consider the arrangement given in Table 14.1. Note that there are four possible judgment–outcome combinations, each with different opportunities for feeding back the relative frequencies of correct or incorrect judgments to the therapist. The feedback from cell A is confirmatory of judging the symptom as a sign of the disorder. Cell B may or may not confirm the judgment. If the feedback does not correlate with the actual disorder, the clinical judge may realize that the selection of cues for symptom identification needs refinement; however, one may offer a cynical view and suggest that it is possible for a misjudgment by the therapist to result in the rapid "cure" of a nonexistent disorder, thereby confirming the contingencies that gave rise to the misjudgment. In terms of the availability heuristic, cells C and D offer the greatest problem. If the symptom is not identified, the client–patient probably will not be identified as having the disorder and not be treated appropriately, if treated at all. Because of nontreatment or inappropriate treatment, feedback of relative frequencies would be underestimates of the actual relative frequencies. Arkes's review of the literature suggests that raters perceive the events in cell C to be completely irrelevant to contingency estimates.

TABLE 14.1. Judgment of Symptom in Relation to Outcome

| | Outcome | |
Judgement	Disorder Present	Disorder Not Present
Symptom sign present	Cell A	Cell B
Symptom sign not present	Cell C	Cell D

Arkes and his associates have suggested that the therapists' use of the availability heuristic in their evaluations can offer both positive and negative influences on clinical judgments, depending on the availability and nature of the feedback (Arkes, 1981; Arkes et al., 1981).

THE REPRESENTATIVE HEURISTIC.   This judgment strategy has both positive and negative influences. The heuristic describes the degree to which the features of an object, event, or person are considered as similar to (i.e., representative of) the features or elements of an object, event, or person who does in fact belong to a particular category. This is the notion of labeling and diagnosis.

It is the representative heuristic that underlies many standardized assessment and diagnostic devices. The *Diagnostic and Statistic Manual For Mental Disorders*, Third Edition (DSM-III) is a prime example of an application of the representative heuristic. The clinician (typically a psychiatrist) is expected to go through a branching decision process to develop a diagnosis. At each step of the way, a judgment is made as to whether the characteristics of the client in question are more similar to one branch of the decision tree than another. The general format of DSM-III is to help the clinician to match the client along five axes (dimensions) to the representative model in discrete steps (Spitzer, 1980). The five axes of the DSM-III on which the clinician is to formulate a representativeness judgment are (I) clinical syndromes; (II) personality and developmental disorders; (III) physical disorders and conditions; (IV) severity of psychosocial stressors; and (V) highest level of adaptive functioning during the past year. Reports on the reliability of judgments on adult clients across the five axes are fair to good. High-reliability values would suggest that there is consistency in judgments of clients' correspondence to the representative model provided by DSM-III. When evaluating ratings across all disorders with Axes I and II, the kappa coefficients were .72 and .64, respectively. Specific disorders within each axis were much lower. The disorders that exhibited the lowest kappa coefficients were typically of low relative frequency in the sample used in the study, or required inferences about events for which the therapist could not obtain first-hand knowledge (e.g., disorders that derived from childhood remembrances). Ratings on Axes I and II for children and adolescents were less consistent than for adults (.52 and .55). The investigators do suggest that the reliability of Axes I and II ratings for children and adolescents is better than that for other psychiatric classification schemata developed for children (Beitchman, et al., 1978).

Ratings on Axes IV and V for adults resulted in relatively good reliability coefficients (.66 and .80, respectively) (Spitzer, 1980). The children and adolescent ratings were again found to be statistically significant, but only fair (.59 and .52, respectively) for Axes IV and V (Spitzer, 1980).

Most functioning scales use a representativeness strategy. One of the earliest scales used, the Menninger Health–Sickness scale, identifies global level of functioning by asking the rater to match the client's behavior and circumstances to those described in a brief vignette about a hypothetical patient functioning at that level (Luborsky, 1962; Luborsky & Bachrach, 1974). More detailed behavioral scales will typically ask the rater to match discrete behaviors to a model representing various levels of dysfunction, such as the Psychiatric Status Schedule (Spitzer et al., 1970).

There is also evidence from the study of medical diagnosis supporting the influence of a representativeness strategy in clinical assessment and diagnosis. Elstein et al. (1978) did a detailed content analysis of the diagnostic strategies of eight physicians on a fixed-content set of cases. They concluded that "problem formulations appear to be primarily a process of direct associative retrieval, rather than one of strategy-guided search" (Elstein et al., 1978, p. 197). Whereas Elstein et al. (1978) feel that this differs from Kleinmuntz's (1968) assertion that physicians tend to follow a "general to specific" search strategy, both investigators agree that a representativeness heuristic would describe many of the assessment and diagnostic formulations of the clinician.

A pervasive biasing influence on the representativeness heuristic has been described as "preconceived notions" (Arkes, 1981) or "dispositions" (Kaplan, 1975). This bias greatly influences ensuing judgments during treatment selection and provision as well as in outcome evaluation. This is critical for psychotherapy outcome research, since the literature suggests that once the therapist selects a representative model, the features of that model may overshadow and guide most, if not all, ensuing judgments. For example, Chapman and Chapman (1967) fabricated illusionary correlations between personality traits and facial features in drawings of faces (e.g., large eyes and suspicion) for their subjects. The result was a biasing of judgments about the pictured person even when other information suggested an inverse correlation between the facial features and the person's personality traits. Others have confirmed the finding of judgment bias by predisposition (Kaplan, 1975; Newman & Rinkus, 1978; Ross et al., 1977). Abramowitz and Herrera (1981), using medical students on psychiatric rotation, found that males tended to diagnose patients more severely than females. Newman and Rinkus (1978) found that a client's prior psychiatric hospitalization history differentially biases the level of functioning judgments of clinicians with different amounts of formal training. Therapists with doctoral degrees showed a reliable tendency to rate low- and middle-level-functioning clients with prior psychiatric hospitalization more severely than did their colleagues with less extended training (B.A., M.A., M.S.W.). For the lowest-functioning clients with no prior hospitalization history, the reverse was found; that is the doctoral-level staff rated no prior hospitalization history clients to be functioning at a higher level than did their colleagues with bachelors and masters degrees.

How the assessment scale is used also appears to influence rater reliability. Newman and Rinkus found that rater reliability was lower in those programs where the scale and its corresponding language of representativeness were not regularly used in case management, review, and supervision. Green et al. (1979) found that global scale rating reliability increased markedly when independent ratings from two judges were combined. Mariotto and Farrell (1979) also showed a corresponding increase in rater reliability on a multifaceted rating scale when the number of independent raters increased from one to two to seven. Although the expense of involving seven raters needs to be considered, the increased reliability of assessment with two raters is certainly worthy of consideration when symptom identification and diagnosis may lead to costly consequences.

Another issue here involves discerning the dimensions of the clients' behaviors and circumstances that therapists attend to in their assessments. Two multidimensional analysis studies (Giladi, 1981; Green, 1981) have converged on two dominant dimensions: (1) interpersonal functioning and (2) "readiness for psychological intervention." Because of differences in method, the two studies yielded different third dimensions. Green's study involved judgments of similarity between pairs of case vignettes that emphasized symptoms and not demographic characteristics or psychiatric history. The third dimension recommended by Green's analysis was described as hostility or aggression turned either inward or outward. Giladi's study had client demographic and historic information as the third dimension. Since the designs of the two studies differed, it is possible that both of their third dimensions are influential in clinicians' judgments.

In Giladi's study the clinicians rated each of 70 pieces of information about a hypothetical client according to whether they would use the information in assessment for the formation of a treatment plan and whether they would pursue that same information over the course of treatment. Thus, in Giladi's study, there was a great deal more information about the client than in the case vignettes used in Green's study. Therefore the differences in results were expected, given the design of the two studies.

The design of Giladi's study also permitted inquiries as to whether therapists of different theoretical orientations attended to and used the 70 elements of information differently. To investigate this facet, Giladi collected ratings from 132 therapists who identified themselves as either (1) psychodynamic, (2) behavioral, (3) family therapist, or (4) eclectic (between 32 and 46 per group). While the factor analysis suggested that all four groups attended to the same dimensions, they tended to use the information differently. For example, the psychodynamic therapists, relative to behavioral therapists, tended to place greater emphasis on personal, sexual, and marital history; family of origin; and assumption of responsibility. Behavior therapists also place less emphasis than do family and eclectic therapists on marital history, family of origin, and assumption of responsibility. Family and eclectic therapists tended to place greater emphasis on relationships with others outside of the client's family. From these data we can begin to understand what categories of preconceived notions may be biasing therapists of different theoretical orientations. Giladi's study does not provide an understanding of what the precise nature of bias is within each of the theoretical orientations, although it does suggest ways for us to pursue these issues.

The picture that emerges is that the representativeness heuristic is actively used, but preconceived notions can have a biasing influence. Data from Green and Giladi suggest that the major summary dimensions of the clinicians' preconceived notions are interpersonal functioning, readiness for psychological intervention or cooperativeness, personal demographic information, and tendencies toward hostility or aggression. These dimensions summarize and relate to most of the dimensions commonly attended to by therapists of different theoretical orientations, but the dimensions appear to be used in different ways.

REDUCTION OF BIAS.   The issue of bias reduction during the assessment and diagnosis stage is not commonly considered to be important to psychotherapy outcome research since outcome research usually involves the identification and quantification of one or two symptoms with no diagnosis. In the case of employing therapist assessments for outcome evaluations, symptom labeling and diagnosis at this point will establish a representative heuristic model that sets the judgment pattern through the remaining stages of the therapeutic process, including outcome assessment. If one can arrange to reduce bias and increase accuracy of judgments at this stage, the probability for accurate judgments at later stages increases.

A number of investigators have begun to study possible techniques to reduce bias in the assessment and diagnosis stage (Arkes, 1981; Einhorn & Hogarth, 1978; Fischhoff, 1977; Kaplan, 1975; Koriat et al., 1980; Kurtz & Garfield, 1978; Slovic & Fischhoff, 1977; Wood, 1978). The most intuitively obvious technique, informing someone of his or her bias, appears to have little impact. Arkes (1981) describes this approach as "worthless," and other reviews of research on this topic by Chapman and Chapman (1967), Fischhoff (1977), Kurtz and Garfield (1978), and Wood (1978) appear to support this conclusion.

The bias-reducing techniques that appear to have some efficacy seem to challenge the credibility of the rater's preconceived notion or disposition. Kaplan (1975), for example, found some diminution of preconceived notions when the subjects (college students making social trait judgments) were provided information that the subjects clearly understood as strongly weighted nonredundant information. Stated another way, the subjects had to clearly identify the information as being both new and important. This result is not always obtained in other situations. For example, Chapman and Chapman (1967) had little success in modifying preconceived notions of personality correlates by simply presenting evidence that was negatively correlated. A study by Koriat et al. (1980) seems to have provided some insight as to the underlying psychological processes that need to be understood in order to modify the biases. They investigated the reasons offered for or against a choice. Their data suggested that people have an extremely strong tendency to provide only supporting reasons for their choices and to avoid arguments against such choices. Once supportive reasons are established, two things happen: (1) subjects who are not required to offer reasons as to why they made a decision tend to have a higher degree of confidence that their decision was correct; and (2) a diminution in the confidence, when appropriate, is obtained only when the subjects are required to first offer reasons *against* their choice. If they were asked to supply both a reason for and a reason against, the diminution of judgment confidence does not occur.

The data offered by Koriat et al. (1980), and Kaplan (1975) confirm Arkes's arguments and offer a hint of what may be required for reducing bias. Specifically, some type of critical review of the possible outcomes of a set of decisions is needed before one alternative is selected. Moreover, if some information is ignored, deemphasized, or overemphasized, the diagnostician should be helped to modify his or her attention and information usage strategy.

If it is true that a prior decision critique is necessary for corrective feedback to be effective, there may be ways to accomplish this. One way would be to train the prospective diagnostician to withhold diagnostic judgment until he or she has developed an adequate set of hypotheses (Elstein et al., 1978). These investigators found more accurate symptom identification and diagnosis when the formulation of a medical diagnosis was delayed through the information acquisition stage. Moreover, the more accurate subjects tended to use five (±2) chunks of information [as recommended by Mandler's (1967) study]. Instructional feedback to medical students did result in improvement in both the number and accuracy of patient symptom and problem identification. Simple feedback of the "correct diagnosis" was better than process feedback, which involved their watching an experienced expert go through the deliberations in the formulation of the diagnosis.

A number of investigators have attempted to improve on the clinician's symptom selection and diagnostic accuracy by helping the clinician to more accurately assess the base rates of the probable incidence of each judgment given the circumstances (Galen & Gambino, 1975). This has not been a successful avenue in reducing bias.

One reason for the base rate bias to be so pervasive is the apparent heavy reliance of clinicians on their memory of past events (Arkes & Harkness, 1980; Fox, 1980). Fox's subjects (medical students) performing a diagnostic labeling task appeared to initially use an availability heuristic and then use a representative heuristic to fill in the gaps required for a diagnosis. Arkes and Harkness (1980) looked specifically at which events are recalled in a diagnostic labeling task. Their results suggests that it is highly probable that some events recalled may not have been present in the first place, but rather are events needed to fulfill the facets of the model representing the diagnosis label.

Arkes (1981) reports on an unpublished study by Shaklee and Mims [cited in Arkes (1981)], which showed that base rate judgments could be improved by presenting subjects with correct estimates of the data for all four cells shown in Table 14.1. One benefit of this approach is that it helps the judge synthesize the information into manageable chunks. This is important since it also appears that accuracy of judgments decreases as the amount of information increases (Leuger & Petzel, 1979).

Results that suggest that information needs to be synthesized for more accurate symptom selection and diagnosis is often countered with the problems inherent in "labeling" (Batson, 1975; Davis, 1979; Langer & Abelson, 1974; Snyder, 1977; Weiner, 1975). For example, in the Langer and Abelson (1974) study, clinicians from three academic training centers, which differed in theoretical orientation (one strongly psychodynamic, one less so, and one clearly behavioral) were asked to describe an individual being interviewed on film. For half of the clinicians, the target person was described as a job applicant, and for the other half, the target person was described as a patient. The results were that the main effect of how the target person was labeled (job applicant or patient) was significant. However, the clinicians who identified themselves as psychodynamic were more susceptible to the labeling effect than were those who identified themselves as behaviorists. The inference offered by Langer and Abelson (1974) was that behaviorists tend not to use labels as much as do psychodynamic therapists and thus would be less biased to false base rates imposed by labeling effects. Davis (1979) suggested that a Bayesian analysis of the base rate probabilities (of maladaptive behavior) given the label was very likely appropriate. That is to say, if the diagnostic label were correct, the identification of certain behavior patterns as maladaptive, rather than just job interview nervousness, would be correct. On the other hand, if the label of "patient" is inappropriate in the first place, then the labeling of the behavior patterns as maladaptive would also be inappropriate. Davis then concludes that we should concentrate on ensuring that appropriate diagnostic labeling is done in the first place. There are two reasons for this: (1) labeling (if correct) does lead to more efficient decision making; and (2) if there is a base rate bias on the part of the diagnostician, it is very difficult to modify. Two studies (Fischhoff et al., 1980; Hoffman et al., 1981) have shown that base rate assessments and their correlated influence on a judgment operated only under a condition where subjects were convinced to shift their *a priori* assumptions of outcome probability.

These results appear to support Kaplan's (1975) data, which suggested that the subjects had to agree that the feedback information is new, as well as being very important to the decision. The data also support the conclusions of Elstein et al. (1978) that diagnosticians ought to be trained to delay their diagnosis until all the information is assessed. It is possible that the general approach for client assessment proposed by Kiresuk and Sherman (1968), called "goal-attainment scaling," could offer many of the features that should avoid the biases of labeling. Although the goal attainment technique is not without its measurement difficulties (Cytrnbaum et al., 1979), it does force the clinician to completely assess the range of problems, along with the possible range of both bad and good consequences for the client before diagnostic and treatment decisions are made. This analysis of the goal-attainment scaling approach should not be construed as an unqualified endorsement of goal attainment scaling per se. There are indeed problems with some aspects of the approach that need to be resolved by further investigations. However, the technique's procedures for problem identification and potential outcome assessment do satisfy what is apparently needed to deal with the correction of judgment bias.

Hogarth (1981) reviewed the demand characteristics of the studies typically performed on the effects of feedback to improve on the correctness of the judgment heuristic. His review suggests that feedback has a mixed record of success in improving on judgments. Hogarth suggests that this is due to the demands of the designs of the studies. Specifically, most feedback studies treat the judgment task as static rather than dynamic. As a static event, feedback serves as a statement of correctness. But when feedback is part of a dynamic process, it can be considered as information concerning the relationship of cues in the environment and the criteria of success. As a cue in a dynamic event, the judge can use the information to adjust judgments. Whereas the clinical process is a mixture of dynamic and static circumstances (e.g., a discrete diagnosis must be offered an insurance carrier), the circumstances prior to the discrete events that terminate a particular stage of the therapeutic process can be viewed as dynamic. Certainly Hogarth would support Elstein, Shulman, and Sprafka's recommendation that the discrete decisions of symptom selection and diagnosis be delayed until sufficient information (cues) has been analyzed. Once these judgments have been formulated, the treatment plan and provision follow, setting the stages for outcome.

Therapeutic Plan

The majority of research on the development of the therapeutic plan has been embedded in outcome research. The focus of the research has been on the efficacy or cost-effectiveness of different therapeutic approaches to ameliorate the problems rather than the factors influencing treatment selection. Usually the outcome research provides careful controls over the selection of the treatment. A much smaller body of research, however, has been published on the facets that influence the therapist's selection of one therapeutic approach or another. Barlow (1981) has noted that it appears as if most clinicians tend to ignore the findings in the literature in the selection and refinement of their therapeutic technique. Instead, he suggests that most practicing clinicians use a trial and error approach in their selection of treatment procedures for their clients. But there are demands on the clinician that can influence treatment selection to be something other than just a simple trial and error strategy.

Ironically, one of the predominant influences has only an indirect clinical link. Funding and regulatory bodies (both public and private) do set standards or guidelines identifying which treatments are reimbursable or allowable for different diagnostic categories. That is, the amounts of dosage levels of allowable therapeutic interventions are often prescribed by funding and/or regulatory agencies. In Pennsylvania, for example, a maximum of 120 days of partial hospitalization services is allowed for a broad range of psychiatric diagnoses. But in Massachusetts, the amount of time spent in a day-treatment or partial hospitalization program is derived from baseline cost outcome data (Davenport, 1980). Whereas the Massachusetts reimbursement guidelines attempt to be data based, the Pennsylvania guidelines are based on a combination of what the state program budget could afford and what was negotiated as "reasonable" several years ago when an expenditure maximum was deemed necessary.

No experimental studies involving random assignment have been performed on the influence of funding contingencies; however, payment and accountability may be more motivating than scientific concerns to the therapist. Such cynicism about the clinician's selection of treatments, however, may not be warranted. DeMuth and Kamis (1980) performed a correlational analysis of the relationships between sources of fee payment, sociodemographic, service-provider characteristics, and services actually utilized by 321 admissions to a county mental health service program. These variables accounted for a very small amount of the variance (10%) relative to clinical considerations such as level of functioning and diagnosis (25%). The investigators studied both types of services provided and volume or dosage of service as related to level of functioning and diagnosis, relative to financial liability (i.e., whether public, private, or paid by the client). The number of clients who received individual and verbal therapies increased directly with level of functioning. As one might expect, the greatest proportion of clients to receive medication were at the lowest levels of functioning, and the second highest use of prescribed medication was at the highest levels of functioning. (From personal communication with the authors, it was learned that the medications provided to higher-functioning clients were usually mild tranquilizers.) The diagnostic data were strongly correlated with fees; that is psychotic diagnostic categories and related presenting problems and symptoms predominated for those clients who were receiving medicaid reimbursements. This latter result may or may not confirm the conjucture offered earlier, namely, that diagnosis may follow the clinician's desire for rendering a favored treatment. The data neither confirm nor refute this conjucture. What the DeMuth and Kamis investigation does suggest is that clinical considerations do appear to dominate over nonclinical factors in the selection of the type of treatment.

One debate in the literature concerns sex bias in the amount of psychotherapy provided. But the sex bias appears to be more a problem of symptom identification and diagnosis than an issue of treatment selection. Abramowitz et al. (1980) showed that the number of sessions in therapy was not significantly related to therapist or client gender. Instead, diagnosis and problem severity appeared to be the major determinants. Both male and female therapists tended to rate female clients' problems more severely than male clients. The female clients also showed a tendency to rate their own problems with the same level of severity as their therapists. The authors concluded that diagnostic and clinical information appears to be a major factor in the determination of type and amount of treatment rather than gender. These data may also indicate that the facets that appear to influence the assessment and diagnostic stage of therapy, such as symptom severity or level of functioning, also appear to persevere into the treatment planning stage.

Another issue concerns the influence of the therapist's theoretical orientation on treatment (e.g., behavioral or psychodynamic). Recall that Giladi found that orientation did influence what information they would pursue over the course of therapy. Certainly the information a therapist attends to during therapy will influence the outcome evaluation. The conclusion was that the preconceived notions (representations) did differ among clinicians who described their theoretical orientation as either behavioral, psychodynamic, family therapist, or eclectic. Cohen and Oyster-Nelson (1981) also found significant between-theoretical orientation differences. These investigators had 70 clinicians serve as peer reviewers for the American Psychological Association–Civilian Health and Medical Program of the Uniformed Services (APA–CHAMPUS). Each therapist reviewed three cases involving moderately severe levels of depression, supposedly a typical case reviewed by APA/CHAMPUS. The results were clear. Psychodynamic therapists, relative to behavioral and eclectic therapists, characterized the cases as being more disturbed and hence requiring more psychotherapy.

One additional question was raised by a review of the DeMuth and Kamis (1980) data on the the relationship of clinical and reimbursement factors to treatment selection. A combination of clinical and nonclinical variables accounted for only 35% of the total variance, suggesting that some other factors may be highly influential in the clinician's strategy of treatment selection. In other words, the contingencies that influence the clinician in treatment selection should be directly related to the strategy by which the clinician chooses a treatment. If clinical and financial factors do not account for a major portion of the variance, perhaps we need to consider the selection strategies themselves.

Unfortunately, work in the area of treatment selection strategy is in its infancy. Kleinmuntz (1968) and Fox (1980) attempted to describe the reasoning strategies of clinicians after the fact. Both investigators described the branching process as relying heavily on the availability heuristic for the selection of a branch and on the memory of a representative model for pursuing questions, gathering more information, and filling the information gaps. Arkes and Harkness (1980) suggested that the use of the representative heuristic and its reliance on memory may increase the potential for the clinician to remember "facts" that were not there in the first place but that would be there if the judge (clinician) were to complete the representative model.

Kleinmuntz and Kleinmuntz (1981) have performed a computer simulation study that raises the spector that the reward contingencies of a trial–error approach to treatment selection are sufficiently high to warrant it as a viable technique in treatment selection. Their data showed a high rate of good outcome with an approach they called "generate and test," which is similar to a trial–error approach as characterized by Barlow (1981). The high success rate was contrasted with a Bayesian optimal cure and a heuristic representation approach. Whereas both of the other procedures did better than the generate–test approach, the generate–test approach was sufficiently high as well as efficient in its use of time (200 to 240% faster) to suggest that its reward contingencies may be pervasive in its use as a treatment selection strategy. To continue with this line of speculation, it is also possible that therapists will be highly reinforced to attend to the symptoms that their favored treatments can modify, and this, in turn, will influence their evaluations of outcome.

Such speculation may, in fact, be reasonable. In circumstances that are commonly encountered by many therapists, there may be a good rationale for using a generate–test approach. As we discussed earlier, most clients come to a therapist because a referral agent has performed the preliminary diagnosis and feels that this particular therapist is probably the most appropriate professional to treat that individual. Thus the therapy (or a small set of therapies) that that therapist employs is, in the eyes of the referral agent, the most appropriate for dealing with that client. If the linkage of symptom to diagnosis to treatment is well understood by the referral agent, then, with the availability heuristic and a high level of positively reinforced feedback from client/patients, the therapist would probably continue to apply the techniques he or she uses most frequently. Under this strategy, the therapist would refer the client elsewhere only when his or her set of techniques is exhausted and the feedback is understood as extremely negative. Otherwise, discontinuation of therapy is the only means for the client to obtain treatments other than that in the repertoire of the therapist. In this light, the generate–test technique of treatment selection may be most efficient and effective when the initial diagnosis is accurate and when the linkage between a particular diagnosis and the best treatment is well known by the referral agent. One could speculate that since there are incomplete data on missed diagnosis and negative outcomes (Arkes, 1981), the frequency of positive reinforcement available to the therapist for using this sort of referral and treatment specialization mechanism is higher than it should be. In other words, clinicians may be reinforced with an artificially high frequency for using the generate–test technique of treatment selection. As Kleinmuntz and Kleinmuntz (1981) have speculated, clinicians probably use a combination of a heuristic and a generate–test strategy at different points in time as circumstances warrant. This was also the conclusion of Einhorn and Hogarth (1981) in their review of the behavioral decision literature. Or, as one colleague suggested, "If it ain't broke, don't fix it."

Treatment Provision

This chapter makes an artificial distinction between the treatment planning stage and the treatment provision stage, although many of the same issues arise in both stages. There is one important and distinctive demand characteristic of the treatment provision stage that is pervasive—namely the experiental effects of the therapist's interaction with the client. There are two interacting parts to which we need to attend: (1) the ongoing interaction of the client, the therapist, and auxiliary services and (2) the reassessment (and possible reformulation) of the problems, situation, supports, therapeutic goals, and therapeutic strategies.

The most extensive investigation of the experiential effects of therapy on the therapist was conducted by Orlinsky and Howard (1975). These investigators analyzed the reactions to psychotherapy sessions of 60 female clients and their respective therapists. Fifteen therapists were involved. One issue analyzed by Orlinsky and Howard was the degree to which the therapist can objectively and accurately relate what occurred in the therapy session. One measure of this would be the correlation of observations by both clients and therapists of what was said in therapy, as well as the correlations of the therapist's impressions of what the client felt with what the client claimed to feel. Table 14.2 summarizes the findings.

Orlinsky and Howard also found that there were relevent dimensions that dominated the therapist's reports of the sessions:

1. Depressive status versus effective movement (where depressive status is defined as resignation over impasse with a patient perceived as depressed and narcissistic; and effective movement is defined as a sense of progress with a patient seen as responsive and motivated).

2. Sympathetic involvement versus uncaring detachment (where the former is defined as active–supportive involvement with a patient seen as anxious and communicative and the latter is defined as passive–aggressive response to a patient felt to be intellectualizing).

3. Strengthening defenses versus stimulating insight.

4. Calm, frank facilitation (of the patient's hostility or withdrawal) versus intent supportiveness (of hostility or withdrawal).

5. Uneasy intimacy (e.g., uneasing of nurturing warmth when the patient is perceived as warm or seductive).

6. Engagement with a patient perceived as enthusiastic and open versus reserved with a patient perceived as feeling uncomfortable and mistrustful.

7. Cheerful warmth.

8. Collaborative relationship versus abiding a patient perceived as passively dependent.

9. Unresponsive activity with a patient perceived as feeling uncomfortably involved and mistrustful.

10. Sense of mutual failure.

11. Erotic countertransference.

These results are not in conflict with those of Giladi (1981), but rather provide greater detail of Giladi's three dimensions: client personal-history data; readiness for psychological intervention; and interpersonal relationships (including feelings and acts of hostility toward self and others).

Stiles (1980) sought to simplify the therapy session reports of Orlinsky and Howard. He developed a Session Evaluation Questionaire (SEQ) that includes 22 bipolar adjective scales presented in a seven-point semantic differential

TABLE 14.2.   Relationships Between Therapist's and Client's Perceptions of Psychotherapy Session

	Reliability R
Areas agreed as stated in session	
Childhood experiences with family members	.86
Sexual feelings and experiences	.76
Current relationships with parents or siblings	.73
Feelings toward therapist or feelings as a client	.72
Domestic concerns	.68
Work or school	.67
Dreams and fantasy	.62
Hopes or goals for the future	.61
Feelings of being close to or needing others	.57
Areas regarding client–patient's aims	
Client's goal to learn more about the therapist	.61
Hopes that the therapist will take the client's side	.53
Areas regarding client–patient's behavior	
Client acting in an independent manner	.50
Client acting distant or reserved	.40
Areas regarding client–patient feelings	
Playful	.72
Bored	.62
Cheerful	.59
Satisfied	.58
Optimistic	.58
Relieved	.56
Angry	.54
Embarrassed	.51
Relaxed	.45
Triumphant	.45
Areas of session's therapeutic development	
Eagerness in coming to the session	.57
Spontaneity and freedom of expression	.54
Clarity of focus on concerns	.54
Level of emotional–psychological functioning	.54
Noticeable areas that were not correlated	
Dialogue regarding	
Feelings and attitudes toward self	.01
Fears, inadequacies, and successes in getting along	.12
Social activities or relationships	.14
Client–patient's feelings regarding	
Tenseness	.24
Anxiety	−.14
Session's development regarding	
Degree of progress	.23
Global evaluations	.23

format. He reported the results of 113 sessions of individual psychotherapy, involving 12 private practice therapists (10 psychologists and 2 psychiatric social workers) and four staff of the university counseling center who were also graduate psychology students. The results showed that there was greater variance between therapy session than there was between therapists. The relative proportions of the variance between therapists and between sessions were similar to those found by Howard and Orlinsky. Thus one can use the results to characterize types of therapy sessions. Four types predominated, each containing a 2×2 typology:

Type of Session	Client Feels	Therapist Feels
1. Shallow—rough	Negative	Negative
2. Shallow—smooth	Positive (relaxed, defended)	Negative (bored, disappointed)
3. Deep—rough	Negative (shaken, vulnerable)	Positive (competent, intrigued)
4. Deep—smooth	Positive (good therapy hour)	Positive (good therapy hour)

Stiles draws parallels between his data and those due to Orlinsky and Howard (1975) and shows that there was a great deal of agreement when he employed the more easily administered SEQ.

The findings of Orlinsky and Howard (1975) and Stiles (1980) have not been integrated with the research on clinical judgment and decision making. That is, given the dimensions to which the clinician appears to be attending and what we know about the impact of feedback on the modification of judgments and decision making, what is to be learned about the possibility of clinicians by use of the information provided during the course of therapy to render reliable judgments about outcome and improvement? If they have a series of type 1 sessions, will they erroneously conclude that clients have not changed? At this point we have an understanding only as to which dimensions and information appear to hold the clinician's attention during therapy sessions. We do not have any evidence about what will influence the therapist to modify therapeutic goals or techniques. We could only guess that changes in judgment and treatment strategy would result under the condition described by Kaplan (1975) and Arkes (1981), as was discussed earlier.

Two additional demand characteristics should be acknowledged. Funding–reimbursement and review criteria often influence the length of treatment and could potentially influence the reports of outcome. The obvious reason why funding–reimbursement criteria influence length of treatment is that if there is no means of financing the therapy, it soon stops. The second demand characteristic originates from the author's personal experience in helping community mental health programs to establish quality assurance and utilization review procedures. When these procedures are linked to a general climate of urging clinical staff to move clients along toward termination, or a climate of negative feedback, there is a tendency for therapists to discharge patients before an in-depth review is invoked. The most blatant example of this was the case of an inpatient program of a community hospital where anyone occupying a bed for more than 14 days was reviewed by the hospital-wide utilization review committee dominated by staff from surgical and medical departments. In this case most patients were discharged to the partial hospitalization program within 10 to 12 days.

Termination and Follow-up

The last two stages, termination and follow-up, would appear to have their own demand characteristics, but again little research has been performed in these areas. Experience also suggests that in the majority of cases, termination is not initiated by the therapist, but rather by the client, third-party payer, or by other agency restrictions. The demand for follow-up with the client is usually initiated because of external requirements; that is some external agent (e.g., a review requirement) calls for a clinical care evaluation requiring follow-up contacts with the client. We know little about the influential demands on the therapist during these two last stages. For example, what level of awareness does the therapist have about clients who are about to discontinue therapy of their own volition? Are there any common characteristics of the interactions between the therapist and the client during the sessions immediately preceding client-initiated termination versus therapist-initiated termination? With regard to the follow-up, under what conditions would the therapist voluntarily recommend or initiate some type of follow-up with a client? What kinds of information and what kinds of contact procedure would be therapeutically beneficial to the client as well as informative to the therapist?

It is unfortunate that so little research has been performed on the demand characteristics on the therapist during the last three stages. Replication and extension of Orlinsky and Howard's (1975) and Stiles's (1980) investigations may help us to understand the parameters set up by the therapists for themselves. The dimensions to which they attend will filter what they see and hear of the client's process and progress in therapy. Kleinmuntz and Kleinmuntz's (1981) simulation study suggests that if the amount of effort (or financial resources available) is a major criterion in treatment selection, favored treatment procedures will be applied first. If there is a need for changing procedures, the therapist will require some information that they consider sufficiently new and important to warrant such changes (Kaplan, 1975). More research like that of Orlinsky and Howard (1975), Stiles (1980), and Giladi (1981) will help us understand the dimensions of feedback to which the therapist might attend. The feedback should come from data collected at termination and follow-up, yet the demands on the therapist are least understood for these stages. Orne's (1962) analysis of the demand characteristics and social psychology of the psychology experiment needs to be empirically extended to the demand characteristics of mental health and psychotherapy interventions. More efforts in these areas should be undertaken in the future.

Therapist Evaluation Techniques and Instruments

Systematic recording and storage of information into memory is one of the amazingly efficient and accurate processes the human can do. However, people appear to have problems with the retrieval of information after it is stored. In terms of the theme of the present chapter, our concern is to review the techniques and instruments that are useful for therapists to systematically retrieve information about their client–patients and the therapy sessions from their associative memories. No technique will generate data that are reliable, valid, and useful unless they aid the therapist to search for and retrieve information accurately and easily from his or her associative memory of the client–patient and the therapy sessions.

Raaijmakers and Shiffrin (1981) have introduced and tested a model to describe the means by which a person searchs associative memory during the retrieval process. The Search of Associative Memory (SAM) model presented fits well with the data discussed earlier on the use of the availability and representativeness heuristic strategies for assessment and diagnosis of clients. The general outline of the search strategy is as follows:

```
QUESTION ⟶ SELECT AND SET RETRIEVAL PLAN ⟶
         ⟶ ASSEMBLE PROBE CUES IN SHORT-TERM MEMORY ⟶
         ⟶ SEARCH LONG-TERM MEMORY {USING PLAN AND CUES} ⟶
         ⟶ STOP SEARCHING WHEN PLAN'S STOPPING RULE IS MET ⟶
         ⟶ EVALUATE TO DETERMINE IF MORE SEARCH IS NEEDED ⟶
         ⟶ DECISION TO CONTINUE SEARCH OR TO TERMINATE
```

Cues assembled in short-term memory and images in the long-term memory are matched in what Raaijmakers and Shiffrin call a "strength matrix" because the combinations of cues of memory images are weighted in a fashion that will influence their probability of recall (as is suggested by the availability heuristic).

Any systematic data collection technique serves as a means of cuing the therapist about the features of some representative model that may fit the characteristics of the client. If the technique's cues and retrieval plan are appropriate, the "strength matrix" will efficiently assist in an accurate recall of client characteristics. On the other hand, if the cues and retrieval plan inherent in the instrument's or techniques' structure are not representative of the therapist's memory, the data due to Raaijmakers and Shiffrin (1981) suggest that retrieval will be less accurate and slower.

Since the characteristics of the client and the experience of the therapy session is multivariate, any technique's retrieval plan should integrate the information in an efficient and useful fashion. A number of models of clinical information integration have been proposed (Anderson, 1974; Dawes, 1979; Tversky, 1977). Dawes (1979) argues that whereas there are probably some very sophisticated models that will represent the clinical judgment, even the most simple linear additive combination rule does a reasonably accurate job of retrieving and integrating information. Dawes also argues that the clinical judge ought not be left to integrate the information without direct application of an integrating rule. He sights a convincing array of evidence that clinical judges tend to be less accurate in combining information to form a judgment than will a simple linear combination rule that the judge has created. In one study Dawes cites, judges were asked to identify the facets they thought were essential to making an integrative judgment. The investigator then asked the judges to form integrative judgments about a set of cases containing all the necessary information. These judgments were then compared to judgments derived from an application of a linear combination of the facets that these same judges had created. The results were that the linear combination rule was more accurate than the intuitive integrative judgments. Although Dawes paints a disparaging picture of the clinical judge, a more positive view could be offered. That is, the judges could identify from their experiences what facets were essential, and with the aid of a guideline (rule) for information integration, their judgments could be considered to be quite good.

The model for integrating information used by Kaplan (1975) and one that appears useful for describing how information from global functioning and multivariate scales can be integrated (Newman, 1980) is an adaptation of Anderson's functional measurement model:

$$\begin{bmatrix} \text{Judgement of} \\ \text{problem or of} \\ \text{functioning} \end{bmatrix} = (\text{initial impression}) + \begin{bmatrix} \text{facets considered} \\ \text{relevant to the} \\ \text{judgment} \end{bmatrix}$$

$$J = (W_0 I_0) + W_1 P_1 + W_2 P_2 + \cdots + W_k P_k$$

where I_0 = the initial impression within the context that the impression is made

W_0 = the proportional level of credibility given to the initial impression I_0 relative to other information considered to be relevant

$P_i \, (i = 1, 2, \ldots, k)$ = the level of category intensity (e.g., problem severity) for those categories considered to be relevant to the judgment rating [usually three to nine problem categories are identified (Elstein et al., 1978; Mandler, 1967)]

$W_i \, (i = 1, 2, \ldots k)$ = the proportional weighting of the importance of each category to the overall judgment rating

The integration model provides a framework for identifying the major elements and their weighted importance that are part of the domain the therapist is thought to be evaluating in the formulation of a judgment. Moreover, it provides a framework for studying the facets influencing the therapist's judgments and use of an instrument; that is, it focuses on which cues were selected for the clinical assessment and what were the respective weightings. The features of the integration model also follow the same outline of a number of scales. For example, in goal attainment scaling (Kiresuk & Sherman, 1968), outcomes expected by the therapist are considered as a weighted average of the problems identified. When converted to a normal T distribution, goal attainment scaling is described as

$$T = \frac{50 + 10 \left(\sum_i W_i P_i \right)}{(1 - \rho)\sum_i W_i^2 + \rho \sum_i W_i^2}$$

where ρ is the interproblem correlation (usually assumed to be .3).

Global scales [e.g., Global Assessment Scale by Endicott et al. (1976), Menninger Health–Sickness Scale by Luborsky (1962), Level of Functioning Scales by Carter and Newman (1980)] are all considered integrated judgments of a number of subsets of, or domains, of client functioning. One of the cautions frequently offered to guard against misuse of global scales is that attention should be given to clearly identifying what domains of information are supposed to be considered, and integrated in the therapist's judgments. Reliability and validity decrease markedly when this is not done (Newman, 1980). In fact, the most frequent reason why global scales perform with low reliability has been that little or no effort was made for the proper training and supervision in the use of the scales to ensure that there was agreement as to which domains are represented in the scale. Hopefully, when two or more therapists use an instrument to search their memory, they would use the same cues with similar weighting. Thus the major advantage of reviewing therapist evaluation techniques in light of the Search of Associative Memory Model and the Information Integration Model is that it provides a framework for helping in the evaluation and selection of viable techniques.

A number of strategies for selecting therapist evaluation scales have been presented in the literature (Ciarlo et al., in press; Hargreaves et al. 1975; Newman, 1980; Waskow & Parloff, 1975). Ciarlo, with several colleagues (and two panels of measurements and user experts) developed an outcome measurement taxonomy that is designed for use in the selection of instruments. The taxonomy provides a practical outline for selecting appropriate measures. When the taxonomy outline is used along with the guideline that any instrument or technique should conform to the memory search and information integration capability of the therapist, instrument selection should be enhanced. A review of Ciarlo's (and colleagues) recommendations is thus useful for the present discussion.

First, Ciarlo et al. (in press) recommend that there are three questions that need to be asked at the outset (the questions have been modified to suit the present chapter's focus on therapist evaluations):

1. What are the principal purposes of collecting the therapist's evaluation?
2. What are the objectives of the therapeutic intervention being evaluated?
3. What specific "target population(s)" is involved?

Once these three questions have been addressed, the taxonomy contains a three-part outline that asks for the identification of:

1. Functional area–domain
   a. Individual–self focus
   b. Family–personal relations focus
   c. Community focus
2. Assessment approach
   a. Individualized (e.g., goal attainment scaling or target complaint)
   b. Partially standardized [e.g., specific types of goal attainment scale such as the Davis Outcome Assessment by Edwards (1974) or Level of Functioning Scales by Carter and Newman (1976)].
   c. Standardized [e.g., Endicott–Spitzer Global Assessment (1976), SCL-90 by Derogatis (1977), PARS by Elsworth et al. (1968), Denver Public System Dependability Scale by Ciarlo and Reihman (1977)].
3. Respondent
   a. Client
   b. Collateral–significant other
   c. Therapist
   d. Other observer (usually a trained independent observer)

Another view of the three major axes of the taxonomy is shown in Figure 14.1.

In addition, Ciarlo developed what is called an *Extended Format* for evaluating dozens of aspects of a scale from domain characteristics to psychometric characteristics to costs of administration and maintenance to uses by clinical and administrative personnel. Ciarlo then applied the Extended Format to the most prevalently used scales. He requested a panel of 12 experts (persons actively involved in both the development and use of outcome measurement) to identify and then to rate the assembled list of scales for prevalence of use. Over 100 scales were identified. The top twelve ranked therapist evaluation techniques are given in Table 14.3 along with the functional areas and domains covered. It should be noted that many of these techniques could be used by observers other than the therapist. In fact, some of the scales were originally intended for use by an impartial observer (e.g., goal attainment scaling) yet are now in prevalent use as a therapist evaluation technique.

All the scales have published results suggesting that, if properly applied, they can produce reliable and valid results. But there is a history of debate on the use of therapists' measures (Lorr, 1975; Mischel, 1968; Nelson, 1981; Newman, 1980; Strupp & Bloxom, 1975). Most criticism rests on the believed tendency for the therapist to generate a self-serving bias into the measures. There have been a number of studies that highlight the differences between the judgments of the therapist and that of the client [e.g., Orlinsky and Howard (1975)]. Nevertheless, recall that Mintz et al. (1973) found that the degree of unreliability was approximately the same for clients, therapists, and trained

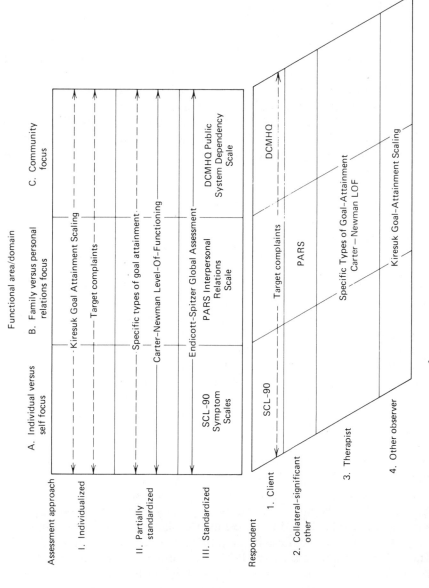

Figure 14.1. Basic taxonomy of client outcome measures.*
*(Ciarlo et al., in press)

TABLE 14.3.   Twelve Most Prevalently Used Therapist Evaluation Techniques (as Rated by a Panel of 12 Experts)

Techniques and Author(s) or Source	Domains[a]
Global Assessment Scale (Endicott et al., 1976)	A,B
Goal Attainment Scaling (Kiresuk & Sherman, 1968)	(A,B,C)
Brief Psychiatric Rating Scale (Overall & Gorham, 1962)	A
Level of Functioning (Carter & Newman, 1976)	A,B,C
Psychiatric Status Schedule & Psychiatric Evaluation Form (Spitzer et al., 1970)	A,B
Problem Oriented Records (Weed, 1969)	(A,B,C)
Discharge Readiness Inventory (Hogarty & Ulrich, 1972)	A,B,C
Clinical Global Impression Scale (Early Clinical Drug Evaluation Unit, NIMH, 1973)	A,B,C
Target Complaints (Battle et al., 1966)	(A,B,C)
Current and Past Psychopathology Schedule (Endicott & Spitzer, 1972)	A,B
Client Posttherapy Questionnaire, the therapist's version (Strupp et al., 1964)	(A,B,C)
Davis Goal Scaling Form (Edwards, 1974)	(A,B,C)

[a]Legend for domains: A, individual–self focus; B, family–personal relations focus; C, community focus; (A,B,C): any or all three domains may be used.

independent observers. The differences could be, and probably are, due largely to differences in the perspectives. The central theme of this chapter still holds: there is a significant amount of crucial information that the therapist can provide. Hopefully, one will select a technique for assisting the therapist to recall his or her judgments from memory as accurately as possible. There is ample evidence that when properly administered and used, therapists' evaluations have been informative. Moreover, there are techniques for detecting when and how extraneous facets are influencing therapists' evaluations.

Techniques for Detecting When and How Extraneous Facets Influence Therapists' Evaluations

The picture that emerges from the literature is that therapist evaluations can be fairly accurate and consistent when there is sufficient information and time to process the cues. Moreover, there are instruments and techniques for recording and using therapist evaluations that can provide a good insight into the therapeutic processes and products. But all these good, reliable, and valid therapist evaluations do not occur as frequently as they could. Instead, biased therapist evaluations have been all too common, even though we presently have the technology to obtain better data from therapists. Ordinarily, the demands for accurate reporting of therapeutic observations are not high. Hogarth (1981, p. 211) described it this way: "There is no need for organisms to respond at levels of accuracy exceeding task demands, nor would one expect them to learn how to do so." But when the task demands do suggest that a certain level of accuracy is warranted for outcome or evaluation research, we need techniques that can detect when and how facets are biasing the therapists' evaluations.

The most direct means of assessing whether certain facets are influencing judgments being used as dependent measures involves partitioning of potential sources of variance and estimating each component's relative contribution to the overall variance. This involves the use of a generalizability or kappa coefficient (Cronbach et al. 1972) that can describe the relative contribution of each facet to a particular domain's sources of variance. The basic concept underlying each of these coefficients when considering a particular facet suspected to be influencing therapist evaluations can be expressed as follows:

$$\text{Coefficient} = \frac{\hat{\sigma}^2_{\text{(facet of interest)}}}{\hat{\sigma}^2_{\text{(facet of interest)}} + \text{sum of weighted } \hat{\sigma}^2_k \text{ that are relevant}}$$
to generalization

The generalizability coefficient usually focuses on the dependability of the therapists' ratings and in its simplest form is the alpha coefficient used to describe reliability (Cronbach, 1970). Expressed in terms of components of variance, this would be

$$\text{Reliability coefficient} = \frac{\hat{\sigma}^2_{\text{(client)}}}{\hat{\sigma}^2_{\text{(clients)}} + \hat{\sigma}^2_{\text{(clients} \times \text{therapists)}}}$$

The interaction term $\hat{\sigma}^2$ (clients $\times$ therapists) is a pooling of all the facets that contribute to the unreliability of the therapists' ratings. To better understand what facets are contributing to the unreliability of ratings, one would want to partition and analyze the relative influences of each facet to either the overall interaction, to the (clients), or to some particular domain of facets to which one might wish to generalize the results. Once the facets potentially influencing the unreliability of therapists' ratings have been identified, it is a simple matter of partitioning components of variance and constructing ratios that suit the types of inference you wish to describe. Consider an example. Suppose that we are concerned that the evaluations of therapists working in an outpatient clinic are influenced by both their level of training (e.g., bachelor's, master's, or doctoral degree) and that symptoms of aggression (externally directed toward others or internally directed toward self) are influencing therapists' ratings on a depression scale. Each clinician is asked to rate the same set of client profiles presented in narrative form. The profiles have been selected because of their *a priori* diagnosis of moderately severe depression and their overt symptoms of either internally or externally directed aggression. The sources of variance identified in this example are given in Table 14.4.

Some interesting coefficients that can be derived from this design might be:

TABLE 14.4. Sources of Variance for an Example Clinical Judgment Study

Source of Variance	DF	Expected Mean Square[a]
Between clinicians	$(tr-1)$	
Training level (T)	$(t-1)$	$arc\,\Theta_T^2 + ca\,\sigma_{R/T}^2 + (\sigma_{(C/A)RT}^2 + \sigma_e^2)$
Clinicians/training level (R/T)	$t(r-1)$	$ca\,\sigma_{R/T}^2 + (\sigma_{(C/A)RT}^2 + \sigma_e^2)$
Within clinicians	$rt(a-1)$	
Client aggression level (A)	$(a-1)$	$crt\,\Theta_A^2 + c\sigma_{R\times A/T}^2 + rt\sigma_{C/A}^2 + (\sigma_{(C/A)RT}^2 + \sigma_e^2)$
Training × aggression levels (AT) or $A \times T$	$(a-1)(t-1)$	$cr\,\Theta_{AT}^2 + c\sigma_{R\times A/T}^2 + rt\sigma_{C/A}^2 + (\sigma_{(C/A)RT}^2 + \sigma_e^2)$
Clinician × aggression/training (RA/T) or $(R \times A)/T$	$t(r-1)(a-1)$	$c\sigma_{R\times A/T}^2 + rt\sigma_{C/A}^2 + (\sigma_{(C/A)RT}^2 + \sigma_e^2)$
Within cases/aggression level	$(c-1)art$	$(\sigma_{(C/A)RT}^2 + \sigma_e^2)$
Cases/aggression level (C/A)	$a(c-1)$	$rt\sigma_{C/A}^2 + (\sigma_{RC/(A/T)}^2 + \sigma_e^2)$
(Training × cases)/aggression level (TC/A) or $T \times C/A$	$(t-1)(c-1)a$	$r\sigma_{T\times C/A}^2 + (\sigma_{RC/(A/T)}^2 + \sigma_e^2)$
[Clinicians × (C/A)]/T [$R(C/A)/T$] or $R \times (C/A)/T$	$(r-1)(c-1)at$	$(\sigma_{RC/(A/T)}^2 + \sigma_e^2)$

[a]Legend: Θ^2, a fixed effect; σ^2, a random effect.

527

1. The relative influence of training independent of client aggression level:

$$\frac{\hat{\Theta}_T^2}{\hat{\Theta}_T^2 + \hat{\sigma}_{R/T}^2 + \hat{\sigma}_{(T \times C)/A}^2 + (\hat{\sigma}_{(R \times C)/(A/T)}^2 + \hat{\sigma}_e^2)}$$

2. The relative influence of training when client aggression level is involved:

$$\frac{\hat{\Theta}_T^2}{\hat{\Theta}_T^2 + \hat{\Theta}_A^2 + \hat{\Theta}_{A \times T}^2 + \hat{\sigma}_{R/T}^2 + \hat{\sigma}_{R \times A/T}^2 + (\hat{\sigma}_{(C/A)RT}^2 + \hat{\sigma}_e^2)}$$

3. The relative influence of aggression when training level is not involved:

$$\frac{\hat{\Theta}_A^2}{\hat{\Theta}_A^2 + \hat{\sigma}_{RA/T}^2 + \sigma_{C/A}^2 + (\hat{\sigma}_{RC/(A/T)}^2 + \hat{\sigma}_e^2)}$$

4. The relative influence of aggression when training level is involved:

$$\frac{\hat{\Theta}_A^2}{\hat{\Theta}_A^2 + \hat{\Theta}_T^2 + \hat{\Theta}_{AT}^2 + \hat{\sigma}_{R/T}^2 + \hat{\sigma}_{RA/T}^2 + (\hat{\sigma}_{(C/A)RT}^2 + \hat{\sigma}_e^2)}$$

5. The generalizability of ratings on client–patients across clinicians and levels of training independent of the fixed effects of aggression level (note that random effects involving aggression remain):

$$\frac{\hat{\sigma}_{TC/A}^2}{1/t(\hat{\Theta}_T^2 + \hat{\sigma}_{R/T}^2 + \hat{\sigma}_{(T \times C)/A}^2 + (\hat{\sigma}_{(R \times C)/(A/T)}^2 + \hat{\sigma}_e^2))}$$

6. The generalizability of ratings on client–patients across clients' levels of aggression independent of the fixed effects of training (note that the random effects involving training remain):

$$\frac{\hat{\sigma}_{C/A}}{1/a[\hat{\Theta}_A^2 + \hat{\sigma}_{C/A}^2 + (\hat{\sigma}_{RC/A/T}^2 + \sigma_e^2)]}$$

7. The generalizability of ratings on client–patients across levels of aggression and levels of clinician training and their interaction:

$$\frac{\hat{\sigma}_{TC/A}^2}{1/at\{\hat{\Theta}_A^2 + \hat{\Theta}_T^2 + \hat{\Theta}_{AT} + \hat{\sigma}_{R/T}^2 + \hat{\sigma}_{RA/T}^2 + (\hat{\sigma}_{(C/A)RT}^2 + \hat{\sigma}_e^2)\}}$$

A major issue in constructing a study designed to surface facets thought to influence clinicians' judgments is the judgment task itself. Should actual cases be used or should one use specially constructed cases that control the content of the information provided to the clinician? The studies that use specially constructed cases are called *analogue studies*. There are pros and cons for both approaches (Kazdin, 1978). Kushner et al. (1979) and Kushner (1978) have described how analogue studies do not adequately describe affective interactions that occur in actual cases. There is no evidence of inadequacy with regard to clinical judgments on analogue cases when the study does not deal with the affective interactions. This is not to say that no such inadequacy exists; however, there is no evidence offered in the empirical literature to believe that it does.

There are a number of practical reasons why analogue studies are used. First, one can control the content of the information (cues) provided the clinician. Because of this, the investigator can often surface the influence of facets that might otherwise be masked by other noisy information supplied by the client. Another reason is statistical tractability. That is, by having therapists all rate the same cases, the statistical analysis will be easier than if the error terms are based on different client–therapist pairs. A more complete description of how to construct case vignettes and analyze the results of generalizability studies is provided in a text by Newman and Sorensen (in press).

SOME CONCLUDING REMARKS

The therapist is a vital source of information about the therapeutic encounter with the client. Although the perceptions of others (client, significant others, and independent observers) are also important to assess, no one else can provide the perceptions of the therapist. In fact, there are some interesting issues about the therapeutic experience that require that the data be collected from the therapist (Orlinsky and Howard, 1975; Stiles, 1981). But the data derived from therapists' evaluations are not necessarily limited to phenomenological studies of the therapeutic experience. Mintz et al. (1973) have shown that the therapist's evaluations are apparently no less reliable than those of the client and trained, experienced independent observers. There are at least a dozen scales, with documented reliability and validity, that can be employed in an outcome study. The degree of reliability and validity will depend on the type and degree of experimental control exerted. For example, even with global scales, reputed to be grossly unreliable (Green et al., 1979), facets influencing decreases in reliability are usually present and can be identified and controlled (Newman, 1980) such that creditable outcome research can result (Mintz et al., 1979).

The major sources of bias appear to be derived from impressions made early in the therapeutic experience, such as during the assessment and diagnosis stage. Here prior experience appears to influence the base rates of which symptom signs the therapist attends to and which diagnostic representative models are employed in assessing the problems and selecting the therapeutic technique(s). It is often possible to uncover biases by having therapists provide independent ratings of a selected set of actual cases or specially constructed analogues that vary the facets that are suspected to be biasing therapists' judgments (Newman & Rinkus, 1978; Newman & Sorensen, in press). Control over biasing tendencies is potentially possible through training and supervision both before and during the conduct of the outcome research project. Feedback in training or supervision sessions on a bias (or biases) may be effective only if the contingencies of incorrect judgments are acknowledged prior to making the judgments (Arkes, 1981; Kaplan, 1975).

The bottom line in the use of therapist evaluations is that if properly collected, the data tend to be reliable. Moreover, if the technique for collecting the data is properly constructed to draw clinicians' responses that reflect the experimental or evaluation question, the data also tend to be valid.

REFERENCES

Abramowitz, S. I., Davidson, C. V., Greene, L. R., & Edwards, D. W. Sex role related countertransference revisited: A partial extension. *Journal of Nervous and Mental Disease*, 1980, **168**, 309–311.

Abramowitz, S. I., & Herrera, H. R. On controlling for patient psychopathology in naturalistic studies of sex bias: A methodological demonstration. *Journal of Consulting and Clinical Psychology*, 1981, **49**, 597–603.

Anderson, N. H. Algebraic models in perception. In E. C. Carterette & M. P. Friedman (Eds.), *Handbook of perception* (Vol. 2). New York: Academic Press, 1974.

Arkes, H. R. Impediments to accurate clinical judgment and possible ways to minimize their impact. *Journal of Consulting and Clinical Psychology*, 1981, **49**, 323–330.

Arkes, H. R., & Harkness, A. R. Effects of making a diagnosis on subsequent recognition of symptoms. *Journal of Experimental Psychology: Human Learning and Memory*, 1980, **6**, 568–575.

Arkes, H. R., Wortmann, R. L., Saville, P. D., & Harkness, A. R. Hindsight bias among physicians weighting the likelihood of diagnosis. *Journal of Applied Psychology*, 1981, **66**, 252–254.

Auerbach, A. H., & Johnson, M. Research on the therapist's level of experience. In A. S. Gurman & A. M. Razin (Eds.), *Effective psychotherapy: A handbook of research*. New York: Pergamon Press, 1977.

Barlow, D. H. On the relation of clinical research to clinical practice: Current issues, new directions. *Journal of Consulting and Clinical Psychology*, 1981, **49**, 147–155.

Batson, C. D. Attribution as a mediator of bias in helping. *Journal of Personality and Social Psychology*, 1975, **32**, 455–466.

Battle, C. C., Imber, S. D., Hoen-Saric, R., Stone, A. R., Nash, C., & Frank, J. D. Target complaints as criteria of improvement. *American Journal of Psychotherapy*, 1966, **20**, 184–192.

Beitchman, J. H., Dielman, T. E., Landis, J. R., Benson, R. M., & Kemp, P. L. Reliability of the Group for the Advancement of Psychiatry diagnostic categories in child psychiatry. *Archives of General Psychiatry*, 1978, **35**, 1461–1468.

Bergin, A. E., & Lambert, M. J. The evaluation of therapeutic outcomes. In S. L. Garfield & A. E. Bergin (Eds.), *Handbook of psychotherapy and behavioral change: An empirical analysis*. New York: Wiley, 1978.

Brown, J. H., & Brown, C. S. *Systematic counseling*. Champaign, Il.: Research Press, 1977.

Carter, D. E., & Newman, F. L. *A client oriented system of mental health service delivery and program management: A workbook and guide.* Rockville, Md.: Mental Health Service Systems Reports, Series FN No. 4, DHHS No. 80–307, 1980.

Chapman, L., & Chapman, J. Genesis of popular but erroneous psycho-diagnostic observations. *Journal of Abnormal Psychology*, 1967, **72**, 193–204.

Ciarlo, J. A., & Reihman, J. The Denver Community Mental Health Questionnaire: Development of a multidimensional program evaluation instrument. In R. Coursey, G. Spector, S. Murrell, & B. Hunt (Eds.), *Program evaluation for mental health: Methods, strategies, and participants.* New York: Grune and Stratton, 1977.

Ciarlo, J. A., Edwards, D. W., Kiresuk, T. J., Newman, F. L., & Brown, T. R. *The assessment of client/patient outcome techniques for use in mental health programs.* Rockville, Md.: NIMH Division of Biometry & Epidemiology, Mental Health Services Research Series, in press.

Cohen, L. H., & Oyster-Nelson, C. K. Clinicians' evaluations of psychodynamic psychotherapy: Experimental data on psychological peer review. *Journal of Consulting and Clinical Psychology*, 1981, **49**, 583–589.

Cronbach, L. J. *Essentials of psychological testing* (3rd ed.). New York: Harper & Row, 1970.

Cronbach, L. J., Gleser, G. C., Nanda, H., & Rajaratnam, N. *The dependability of behavioral measurement: Theory of generalizability of scores and profiles.* New York: Wiley, 1972.

Cytrnbaum, S., Ginath, Y., Birdwell, J., & Brant, L. Goal attainment scaling: A critical review. *Evaluation Quarterly*, 1979, **3**, 5–40.

Davenport, B. *Cost effectiveness of day treatment services: A pilot project.* Paper presented at the Eastern Psychological Association Meetings, Hartford, Connecticut, April, 1980.

Davis, D. A. What's in a name? A Bayesian rethinking of attributional biases in clinical judgment. *Journal of Consulting and Clinical Psychology*, 1979, **47**, 1109–1114.

Dawes, R. M. The robust beauty of improper linear models in decision making. *American Psychologist*, 1979, **34**, 571–582.

DeMuth, N. M., & Kamis, E. Fees and therapy: Clarification of the relationship of payment sources to service utilization. *Journal of Consulting and Clinical Psychology*, 1980, **48**, 793–795.

Derogatis, L. R. *SCL-90 administration, scoring and procedures manual.* Baltimore, Md.: Clinical Psychometrics Research, Johns Hopkins University Press, 1977.

Early Clinical Drug Evaluation Unit Program, *Clinical Global Impression Scale.* NIMH, Rockville, Md., 1973.

Edwards, D. W. Davis Outcome Assessment System (Version 2). Unpublished manuscript, Department of Psychiatry, University of California at Davis, (June) 1974.

Einhorn, H. J., & Hogarth, R. M. Behavioral decision theory: Processes of judgment and choice. In M. R. Rosenzweig, & L. W. Porter (Eds.), *Annual Review of Psychology* (Vol. 32). Palo Alto, Calif.: Annual Reviews, Inc. 1981.

Einhorn, H. J., & Hogarth, R. M., Confidence in judgment: Persistence in the illusion of validity. *Psychological Review*, 1978, **85**, 395–416.

Eisenberg, J. M. Sociologic influences on decision-making by clinicians. *Annals of Internal Medicine*, 1979, **90**, 957–964.

Elstein, A. S., Shulman, L. S., & Sprafka, S. A. *Medical problem solving: An analysis of clinical reasoning*. Cambridge, Mass.: Harvard University Press, 1978.

Elsworth, R. B., Foster, L., Childers, B., Arthur, G., & Kroeker, D. Hospital and community adjustments as perceived by psychiatric patients, their families and staff. *Journal of Consulting and Clinical Psychology (Monograph Supplement)*, 1968, **41**, 5–13.

Endicott, J., & Spitzer, R. L. Current and Past Psychopathology Scales (CAPPS): Rationale, reliability, and validity. *Archives of General Psychiatry*, 1972, **27**, 678–687.

Endicott, J., Spitzer, R. L., Fleiss, J. L., & Cohen, J. The Global Assessment Scale: A procedure for measuring overall severity of psychiatric disturbance. *Archives of General Psychiatry*, 1976, **33**, 766–771.

Fischhoff, B. Attribution theory and judgment under uncertainty. In J. H. Harvey, W. J. Ickes, & R. F. Kidd (Eds.), *New directions in attribution research*. Hillsdale, N. J.: Erlbaum, 1976.

Fischhoff, B. Perceived informativeness of facts. *Journal of Experimental Psychology: Human Perception and Performance*, 1977, **3**, 349–358.

Fischhoff, B., Slovic, P., & Lichtenstein, S. Knowing what you want: Measuring labile values. In T. S. Wallsten (Ed.), *Cognitive processes in choice and decision behavior*. Hillsdale, N. J.: Erlbaum, 1980.

Fischhoff, B. & Beyth, R. "I knew it would happen"—Remembered probabilities of once-future things. *Organizational Behavior and Human Performance*, 1975, **13**, 1–16.

Fox, J. Making decisions under the influence of memory. *Psychological Review*, 1980, **87**, 190–211.

Fromm-Reichmann, F. *Principles of intensive psychotherapy*. Chicago: University of Chicago Press, 1950.

Galen, R. S., & Gambino, S. R. *Beyond normality: The predictive value and efficiency of medical diagnoses*. New York: Wiley, 1975.

Giladi, D. *Differences among therapeutic approaches in the use of patient information*. Paper presented at the Society for Psychotherapy Research meeting, Aspen, Colorado, June, 1981.

Green, B. L., Gleser, G. C., Stone, W. N., & Seifert, R. F. Relationships among diverse measures of psychotherapy outcome. *Journal of Consulting and Clinical Psychology*, 1975, **43**, 689–699.

Green, R. S. *Deriving a mental health level of functioning scale by fitting the individual differences multidimensional scaling model to similarities data*. Paper presented at the joint meeting of the Evaluation Research Society and the Evaluation Network in Austin, Texas, October, 1981.

Green, R. S., Nguyen, T. D., & Attkisson, C. C. Harnessing the reliability of outcome measures. *Evaluation and Program Planning*, 1979, **2**, 137–142.

Hargreaves, W. A., Attkisson, C. C., Siegel, L. M., McIntyre, M. H., & Sorensen, J. E. *Resource materials for community mental health program evaluation: Part IV*

Evaluating the effectiveness of services. Rockville, Md.: NIMH, DHEW, No. 75-222, 1975.

Hoffman, P. J., Earle, T. C., & Slovic, P. Multidimensional functional learning (MFL) and some new conceptions of feedback. *Organizational Behavior and Human Performance*, 1981, **27**, 75–102.

Hogarth, R. M. Beyond discrete biases: Functional dysfunctional aspects of judgmental heuristics. *Psychological Bulletin*, 1981, **90**, 197–217.

Hogarty, G. E., & Ulrich, R. The Discharge Readiness Inventory. *Archives of General Psychiatry*, 1972, **26**, 419–426.

Kahneman, D., & Tversky, A. On the psychology of prediction. *Psychological Review*, 1973, **80**, 237–251.

Kahneman, D., & Tversky, A. Prospect theory: An analysis of decision under risk. *Econometrica*, 1979, **47**, 263–291.

Kaplan, M. F. Information-integration in social judgment: Interaction of judge and information components. In M. F. Kaplan & S. Schwartz (Eds.), *Human judgement and decision processes*. New York: Academic Press, 1975.

Kazdin, A. E. Evaluating the generality of findings in analogue research. *Journal of Consulting and Clinical Psychology*, 1978, **46**, 673–686.

Kiresuk, T., & Sherman, R. Goal attainment scaling: A general method for evaluating community mental health programs. *Community Mental Health Journal*, 1968, **4**, 443–453.

Kleinmuntz, B. The processing of clinical information by man and machine. In B. Kleinmuntz (Ed.), *Formal representations of human judgment*. New York: Wiley, 1968.

Kleinmuntz, D. N., & Kleinmuntz, B. Decision strategies in simulated environments. *Behavioral Science*, 1981, **26**, 294–305.

Koriat, A., Lichtenstein, S., & Fischhoff, B. Reasons for confidence. *Journal of Experimental Psychology: Human Learning and Memory*, 1980, **6**, 107–118.

Krumboltz, J. D., & Thoresen, C. E. *Behavioral counseling: Cases and techniques.* New York: Holt, Rinehart and Winston, 1969.

Kurtz, R. M., & Garfield, S. L. Illusionary correlation: A further exploration of Chapman's paradigm. *Journal of Consulting and Clinical Psychology*, 1978, **46**, 1009–1015.

Kushner, K. On the external validity of two psychotherapy analogues. *Journal of Consulting and Clinical Psychology*, 1978, **46**, 1394–1402.

Kushner, K., Bordin, E. S., & Ryan, E. Comparisons and Strupp and Jenkins' audiovisual psychotherapy and real psychotherapy interviews. *Journal of Consulting and Clinical Psychology*, 1979, **47**, 765–767.

Langer, E. J., & Abelson, R. P. A patient by any other name . . . : Clinician group differences in labeling bias. *Journal of Consulting and Clinical Psychology*, 1974, **42**, 4–9.

Lorr, M. Therapist measures of outcome. In I. E. Waskow & M. B. Parloff (Eds.), *Psychotherapy change measures*. Rockville, Md.: NIMH, DHEW, No. 74-120, 1975.

Luborsky, L. Clinician judgements of mental health: A proposed scale. *Archives of General Psychiatry*, 1962, **7**, 407–412.

Luborsky, L., & Bachrach, H. M. Factors influencing clinicians' judgements of mental health: Eighteen experiences with the Health-Sickness Rating Scale. *Archives of General Psychiatry*, 1974, **31**, 292–299.

Lueger, R. J., & Petzel, T. P. Illusory correlation in clinical judgment: Effects of amount of information to be processed. *Journal of Consulting and Clinical Psychology*, 1979, **47**, 1120–1121.

Mandler, G. Organization and memory, In K. W. Spence & J. T. Spence (Eds.), *The psychology of learning and motivation* (Vol. 1). New York: Academic Press, 1967.

Mariotto, M. J., & Farrell, A. D. Comparability of the absolute level of ratings on the Inpatient Multidimensional Psychiatric scale within a homogeneous group of raters. *Journal of Consulting and Clinical Psychology*, 1979, **47**, 59–64.

Meehl, P. E. *Clinical versus statistical prediction*. Minneapolis: University of Minnesota Press, 1954.

Meyers, J. K., & Auld, F. Some variables related to outcome of psychotherapy. *Journal of Counseling Psychology*, 1955, **11**, 51–54.

Miller, F. T. Mental health center versus community perceptions of mental health services. *Journal of Community Psychology*, 1981, **9**, 204–209.

Mintz, J., Auerbach, A. H., Luborsky, L., & Johnson, M. Patient's, therapist's, and observer's views of psychotherapy: A 'Rashomon' experience or a reasonable consensus? *British Journal of Medical Psychology*, 1973, **46**, 83–89.

Mintz, J., Luborsky, L., & Christoph, P., Measuring outcomes of psychotherapy: Findings of the Penn Psychotherapy Project. *Journal of Consulting and Clinical Psychology*, 1979, **47**, 319–334.

Mischel, W. *Personality and assessment*. New York: Wiley, 1968.

Nelson, R. O. Realistic dependent measures for clinical use. *Journal of Consulting and Clinical Psychology*, 1981, **49**, 168–182.

Newman, F. L. Strengths, uses and problems of global scales as an evaluation instrument. *Evaluation and Program Planning*, 1980, **3**, 257–268.

Newman, F. L., & Rinkus, A. J. Level of functioning, clinical judgement, and mental health service evaluation. *Evaluation and The Health Professions*. 1978, **1**, 175–194.

Newman, F. L., & Sorensen, J. E. *Creating your own client oriented system*. Belmont, Calif.: Lifetime Learning Division of Wadsworth, in press.

Nisbett, R. E., & Ross, L. *Human inference: Strategies and shortcomings of social judgment*. Englewood Cliffs, N. J.: Prentice-Hall, 1980.

Orlinsky, D. E., & Howard, K. I. *Varieties of psychotherapeutic experience*. New York: Teachers College Press, 1975.

Orne, M. T. On the social psychology of the psychological experiment: With particular reference to demand characteristics and their implications. *American Psychologist*, 1962, **17**, 776–783.

Overall, J. E., & Gorham, D. R. The Brief Psychiatric Rating Scale. *Psychological Reports*, 1962, **10**, 799–812.

Parloff, M. B., Waskow, I. E., & Wolfe, B. E. Research on therapist variables in relation to process and outcome. In S. L. Garfield & A. E. Bergin (Eds.), *Hand-*

book of psychotherapy and behavior change: An empirical analysis. New York: Wiley, 1978.

Raaijmakers, J. G. W., & Shriffrin, R. M. Search of associative memory. *Psychological Review*, 981, **88**, 93–134.

Rogers, C. R. *On becoming a person: A therapist's view of psychotherapy*. Boston: Houghton Mifflin, 1961.

Ross, L., Lepper, M. R., Strack, F., & Steinmentz, J. L. Social explanation and social expectation: The effects of real and hypothetical explanations upon subjective likelihood. *Journal of Personality and Social Psychology*, 1977, **35**, 817–829.

Shaklee, H., & Mims, M. Sources of error in judging event covariation: Effects of memory demands. (Unpublished ms cited in Arkes, 1981, ms can be obtained from senior author, Psychology Dept., University of Iowa.)

Shapiro, D. A., & Shapiro, D. Meta analysis of comparative therapy outcome studies: A replication and refinement. Paper presented at the Society for Psychotherapy Research, Aspen, Colorado, June, 1981.

Shrauger, J. S., & Osberg, T. M. The relative accuracy of self-predictions and judgments by others in psychological assessment. *Psychological Bulletin*, 1981, **90**, 322–351.

Silverman, W. H. Primary presenting problem and mental health service delivery. *Journal of Community Psychology*, 1980, **8**, 125–131.

Slovic, P., & Fischhoff, B. On the psychology of experimental surprises. *Journal of Experimental Psychology: Human Perception and Performance*, 1977, **3**, 544–551.

Smith, M. L., Glass, G. V., & Miller, T. I. *The benefits of psychotherapy*. Baltimore: Johns Hopkins University Press, 1980.

Snyder, C. R. "A patient by any other name" revisited: Maladjustment or attributional locus of problem? *Journal of Consulting and Clinical Psychology*, 1977, **45**, 101–103.

Spitzer, R. L. (Ed.). *Diagnostic and statistical manual of mental disorders* (3rd ed.). Washington, D.C.: American Psychiatric Association, 1980.

Spitzer, R. L., Endicott, J., Fleiss, J. L., & Cohen, J. The Psychiatric Status Schedule: A technique for evaluating psychopathology and impairment in role functioning. *Archives of General Psychiatry*, 1970, **23**, 41–55.

Stiles, W. B. Measurement of the impact of psychotherapy sessions. *Journal of Consulting and Clinical Psychology*, 1980, **48**, 176–185.

Strupp, H. H., & Bloxom, A. S. Therapists' assessments of outcome. In I. E. Waskow & M. B. Parloff (Eds.), *Psychotherapy change measures*. Rockville, Md.: NIMH, DHEW, No. 74-120, 1975.

Strupp, H. H., Wallach, M. S., & Wogan, M. Psychotherapy experience in retrospect: Questionnaire survey of former patients and their therapists. *Psychological Monographs*, 1964, **78** (Whole No. 588).

Sullivan, P. L., Miller, C., & Smelser, W. Factors in length of stay and progress in psychotherapy. *Journal of Consulting Psychology*, 1958, **22**, 1–9.

Tversky, A. Features of similarity. *Psychological Review*, 1977, **84**, 327–352.

Tversky, A., & Kahneman, D. Causal schemata in judgments under uncertainty. In M. Fishbein (Ed.), *Progress in social psychology*. Hillsdale, N. J.: Erlbaum, 1977.

VandenBos, G. R., & Pino, C. D. Research on outcome of psychotherapy. In G. R. VandenBos (Ed.), *Psychotherapy: Practice, research, policy*, Beverly Hills, CA: Sage, 1980, 23–69.

Waskow, I. E., & Parloff, M. B. *Psychotherapy change measures*. Washington, D.C.: DHEW, No. 74-120, 1975.

Weed, L. L. *Medical records, medical education, and patient care: The problem oriented record as a basic tool*. Cleveland: Case Western Reserve University Press, 1969.

Weiner, B. "On being sane in insane places": A process (attributional) analysis and critique. *Journal of Abnormal Psychology*, 1975, **84**, 433–441.

Wilkin, W. Expectations in therapy research: Discriminating among heterogeneous nonspecifics. *Journal of Consulting and Clinical Psychology*, 1979, **47**, 837–845.

Wood, G. The knew-it-all-along effect. *Journal of Experimental Psychology: Human Perception and Performance*, 1978, **4**, 345–353.

CHAPTER 15

Assessment of Psychotherapy Outcome from the Viewpoint of Expert Observer

ARTHUR H. AUERBACH

Look upon that last day always. Count no mortal happy till
He has passed the final limit of his life secure from pain.
SOPHOCLES

In this quotation from *Oedipus Rex* Sophocles reminds us that evaluation of someone's state of well-being has always been difficult. The hero you are assessing may, to all appearances, be happy and functioning well, but you never know what will happen next in his life, nor how the new events will interact with forces hidden within him to produce a totally different pattern of symptoms and role functioning.

In our present-day efforts to assess the results of psychotherapy, evaluation of the patient by a trained observer other than the therapist holds a respectable place. Common sense suggests the importance of a viewpoint different from that of the participants. So does current expert opinion: the Outcome Measures Project sponsored by the National Institute of Mental Health (Waskow & Parloff, 1975) recommended assessment by an independent evaluator as part of the core outcome battery.

Before discussing instruments that the observer can use, we shall review some aspects of the outcome concept that are often lost sight of in our concern with measuring devices. If by "true outcome" we mean, as we should, the total effect of the therapist on the patient, a full assessment is impossible. True outcome includes not only the changes that the patient decides have occurred

The author is grateful for the research and editorial assistance given by André Korogodon.

and can put into words, but also subtle or delayed effects such as an attitude conveyed by the therapist that meant little to the patient at the time but that later interacted with life events to become important in that patient's functioning. The number of such effects is large, their accessibility to language is often small, and their interactions are complex. To measure them is as difficult as it would be to assess the total impact of a love affair or other close relationship on each partner. Outcome should be viewed like the concept of a true score in classical test theory; it is known only to God. Our measurements of outcome are approximations, and because of the nature of personality and of psychotherapy, they are a good deal less precise than the determination of IQ.

We *assume* that our approximations are sufficiently accurate to have practical value. For some purposes they undoubtedly are. But there are a number of negative findings in psychotherapy research, some of them surprising, which could be explained by the invalidity of the usual outcome measures. When anything is correlated with outcome, the correlations tend to be low, specific effects seldom show up, and differences between groups are not striking. Thus trained therapists did not achieve better results than untrained professors (Strupp & Hadley, 1979); there is only meager evidence that experienced therapists do better than inexperienced ones (Auerbach & Johnson, 1977; Parloff et al., 1978); there is little evidence to indicate that any school of therapy gets better results than any other (Luborsky et al., 1975); and the outcome of therapy is difficult to predict (Luborsky et al., 1980).

Such findings call for an attitude of caution and suspended judgment in our decisions about outcome measurement. We must do that which is feasible and seems reasonable while remembering that the appearance of reasonableness may be deceptive. Thus, although it is reasonable to include the vantage point of an objective interviewer in the judgment of outcome, one must also entertain questions about the validity of the procedure. These issues are discussed below.

It should be noted that "assessment by an expert observer" could include a variety of measurements, such as psychological tests or observations of ward behavior by a nurse. For purposes of this chapter, the term is restricted to an interview with a patient conducted at the end of therapy by a trained interviewer in order to determine how the patient has changed during the course of therapy. The Psychotherapy Outcome Measures Project (Waskow & Parloff, 1975) similarly restricted its definition of "independent evaluator."

It seems that, no matter what problem in psychotherapy is explored, one is led back to a few fundamental issues. In the assessment of patients, the issue (and the researcher's choice) comes down to lifelike complexity versus reliability. Since humans are complex, the impulse of some researchers will be to make their assessments worthy of that complexity, which means that the assessments will suffer in precision. Other researchers, realizing that reliable measurements are an absolute necessity in the building of a science, will give highest priority to reliability, even if it means simplification of the phenomena.

"Lifelike complexity" is the more ambitious approach, not only because it aims at completeness, but because it usually involves explanation as well as description. But such complexity can, in general, be captured only by a prose description, although there have been a few ambitious attempts at descriptive systems that are standardized and yet do justice to the complexity of personality, such as the Minnesota-Hartford Personality Assay (Glueck et al., 1964). In prose descriptions of personality one finds selectivity, varying emphases, biases, connotations, ellipses, and inferences—all the untidy stuff of everyday judgment and literature.

On the other hand, when the highest priority is given to reliability, one assesses the patient with the help of an interview schedule that presents her with a set of standard stimuli in the form of preselected questions. The schedule also serves as an encoding device that, as Wiggins (1973, p. 306) has noted, provides a systematic frame of reference by which the observer can record her impressions and also usually contains rating scales that provide a metric for quantifying observations.

These considerations are related to that durable problem: the clinician versus the actuary (Holt, 1978; Meehl, 1954). In this connection, it is worth recalling Meehl's version of the black-box analogy. He imagined an opaque box, on one side of which is a row of 10 colored lights. The flashing of lights, in various patterns, is controlled by a complicated series of mechanical and electrical devices that are within the box and therefore hidden from the observer. The inner machinery is activated by a series of 10 buttons on the outside of the box, opposite to the lights. The box is stimulated by pressing any three of the buttons, and it responds by flashing some of the lights. Meehl's purpose was to dramatize the different understanding gained by the actuary and the clinician. The actuary, who sees only the outside of the box, learns empirically to connect certain patterns of button pressing with patterns of lights flashing. The clinician corresponds to a skilled mechanic who, having dismantled many such boxes, is familiar with their mechanisms. He is able, with a small number of button pressings and observations of the lights, to form a hypothesis about the inner structure.

The present author believes that this analogy has relevance to the assessment of patients by means of an interview. The approach to assessment will vary according to whether one believes that the interviewer is a skilled mechanic who should devise her own sequence of button pressings, or a relatively unskilled observer who should be instructed to follow a preset and fairly simple sequence.

Examples of each approach exist. Lifelike complexity, with the clinician as a skilled mechanic, is represented by the Menninger psychotherapy project (Kernberg et al., 1972). Emphasis on reliability, with the clinician as an actuary, is represented by the Denver Community Mental Health Questionnaire (Ciarlo & Reihman, 1977). It will be instructive to compare the advantages and limitations of each approach. The work of Ciarlo and his associates is only one instance of the modern trend toward standardization of clinical assessment. Another instance is the NIMH-sponsored psychotherapy of depression collaborative research program (1980, preprint, Reference Note 3 at end of chapter). Therefore, when we contrast the Menninger study with the modern trend, we are comparing the conventional wisdom of the past with that of the present.

Those who designed the Menninger study believed that the trained clinician has impressive perceptive and inferential powers; his judgments became the basic data for analysis. Therefore, the central method of the project was an unstructured interview of the patient (or of a relative or the therapist) by a clinician, after which the clinician would record his impressions. In the initial assessment of the patient there was not even a specific attempt to elicit information needed for judging the variables of research interest. The interviewer at that point was a staff member who did not know that the patient was in a research study. The designers of the study considered that the usual clinical evaluation would cover the required ground and that the evaluator's clinical write-up would provide enough information for the researchers to judge all the patient variables. By the end of treatment, the fact that the therapy was part of a research project was known, and the posttherapy interviews of the patient, significant relative, and therapist were carried out by a subgroup of the researchers known as the "termination team." They naturally knew what variables had to be judged, but their interviews were nevertheless unstructured. The metric used for quantifying judgments was the method of paired comparisons, in which every patient was compared with every other patient for each variable to be rated. These comparisons were made by the pooled judgments of the termination team and were arrived at in open discussion; there was (originally) no attempt at independent judgment or determination of interjudge agreement.

The termination team undertook a comprehensive description of the therapy experience. They noted all its features that were considered important. Examples are the mode of treatment (psychoanalysis or psychotherapy), the variations from the chosen mode that occurred and why they occurred, external circumstances that affected treatment, the therapeutic techniques used, the content and style of the patient's productions, the type of transference, the goals of treatment, and the extent to which the goals were attained (changes in symptoms, adaptive patterns, achievement of insight, etc.). Some of their judgments were theory-specific and inherently difficult to assess in after-the-fact interviews, such as "Extent to which inexact interpretations were employed to foster partial discharge of instinct derivatives" and "Extent, and in relationship to which manifestations, the transference was used as a vehicle and not interpreted."

This method of understanding the treatment permits ambitious syntheses. For example, one researcher subsequently wrote, with respect to one therapy:

For four years his analysis was essentially stalemated in an insoluble transference neurosis while he was awaiting a magical process of change. During this period there were no overtly psychotic developments except perhaps for the rigidity of his anaclitic attachment to the analyst. When the analyst finally gave up attempting to interpret the patient's largely ego-syntonic longing for nurturant protection from the analyst in favor of focusing upon the patient's rage and envy toward the father–analyst as this expressed itself in the masochistic–submissive transference, there ensued a psychotic regression during which the patient had delusional convictions about the analyst prohibiting him from having relationships with women, exercising control over all women, even including the patient's mother. (Horowitz, 1974, p. 73)

Such syntheses are open to numerous challenges and questions. If ever they were able to command the agreement of the majority of therapists, that day is past. The field has learned that clinicians often disagree even on much less inferential judgments than those in the example. It has also realized that reliable measurements are an essential foundation for progress in psychotherapy and that reliability of clinicians' judgments—in the form of interrater agreement—is difficult to achieve unless the judgments are confined to the patient's surface behavior. Therefore, the pendulum has swung away from complexity and toward reliability. Thus the Psychotherapy Outcome Measures project (Waskow & Parloff, 1975) recommended that the independent evaluator, in his interview with the patient, use the Psychiatric Status Schedule (PSS) (Spitzer et al., 1970), a rating form in which judgments are confined to observables. Speculations about nonobservable attitudes, motivations, and mechanisms of change are ruled out. An example of an item in the PSS is: "Mentions he feels people take advantage of him or push him around."

The Psychiatric Status Schedule is further discussed below. Here I wish only to raise a question that has not attracted much interest: the cost of restricting our interest to observables. The danger, of course, is that we may achieve reliability at the expense of validity. Items such as the one named above can be scored reliably, but how well do such items indicate psychotherapeutic change? Considering outcome as the total impact of the therapist on the patient, including subtle as well as obvious effects as discussed above, it would seem that outcome is not captured by such items. The clinician is likely to feel that the attempt to measure outcome purely by prespecified and objective bits of behavior implies an oversimplified view of psychotherapeutic changes, and of life. Some findings that support the clinician's sense are presented below.

Thus it seems that whether one inclines toward lifelike complexity or toward reliability, there are significant difficulties, which are of course of a different nature in the two cases. That is the central dilemma of outcome measurement. Whatever the ultimate solution to this problem, we may say that the limitations of rating instruments should not dictate a return to undisciplined clinical impressions. The imperative for reliable assessment is a strong one.

But what is needed are interview and assessment schedules that are valid as well as reliable. We thus turn to some considerations of validity.

VALIDITY OF ASSESSMENT INTERVIEWS

The ideal posttherapy assessment interview would cover three domains: how the patient is now; how the patient changed during therapy; and what, in the patient's view, were the therapeutic processes that fostered change. Many researchers would dispute the desirability of including the patient's view of the therapeutic process. Their implicit argument is that the posttherapy interview is like a snapshot at a particular time and that it is not the purpose of a snapshot to explain what produced the delineated features. I regard this view as narrow and excessively bound to the way things are now done, rather than the way they should be done. To further our understanding of psychotherapy, we should try to learn as much as possible from interviews with patients. They have not been sufficiently used as a source for teaching us about the process of therapy, even though a few researchers (Strupp et al., 1969) have been interested in the patient's point of view.

To continue with the validity of the ideal assessment instrument: the interview schedule would have content validity; that is, its items would fairly represent all aspects of the three domains. It would have concurrent validity; that is, its ratings would compare reasonably well with the assessment of change made by other reliable methods. It would have construct validity; that is, the constructs measured by the schedule would be those suggested by our theory of therapy. Finally, the schedule would be reliable.

When we look for these ideal qualities in the few interview schedules that have come to general attention and whose psychometric properties have been investigated, we realize how far we are from the goal. Regarding the domains of coverage, the well-known instruments inquire into the patient's present symptoms and role functioning. Change scores can be derived from pretherapy measurements of the same variables. No attention is paid to the therapeutic processes that foster change.

Regarding psychometric properties, those interview schedules that have achieved general usage—that is, beyond the group that originated them—have reported satisfactory reliability in the form of interrater agreement. Content validity seems satisfactory within the restricted domains (symptoms and specific role functioning) that the instruments cover. Concurrent validity appears satisfactory when the comparison is with other methods of obtaining the patient's word on how he is doing.

Construct validity may be considered from two points of view. If the constructs we are interested in are those that underlie symptoms and role functioning, it can be argued that the present instruments do a good job of measuring them. But if we are interested in the constructs that form a theory of therapy, the instruments are very inadequate. With few exceptions, the modern interview schedules have been constructed by methodologists rather than by exponents of particular schools of therapy. In the construction of these schedules, the implicit assumption has been either that the field is not ready for construct validation of therapy theories or that symptoms and role functioning are important phenomena in their own right. They are worthy of study either because they *are* the problem (as behavior therapists hold) or because they are good indicators of the patient's state of well-being (as most other therapists believe).

If this argument is granted, the next issue to be addressed is how well interview schedules measure symptoms and role functioning. There is no definite answer; one of the difficulties in determining the validity of an interview schedule is that there exists no adequate standard for assessing therapeutic change against which the new instrument can be compared. In discussing validity, we must, therefore, reason from our general knowledge of patients, therapy, and interviews.

Sources of Invalidity in Structured and Semistructured Interviews

The sources of invalidity may be classified into three groups, depending on whether they originate within the interviewer, within the patient, or within the interview schedule itself. The sources within the interviewer and patient are discussed here. Those within the interview schedule are discussed in connection with the specific instruments.

The interviewer's possible contribution to invalidity is greater when the schedule calls for her to make judgmental ratings than when it confines her to recording the patient's words. When she makes ratings, she is subject to the rating errors named by Guilford (1954, p. 267) and added to by Holt (1969, p. 592). These are:

1. *The halo effect or error.* The tendency to rate all traits in the direction of the general impression that the interviewer has. There are two related tendencies. In *stereotyping* the rater assigns the patient to a class and then makes ratings according to that class. In the *logical error* the tendency is to give similar ratings to traits that seem logically related, even though the traits may be independent.

2. *The leniency error.* The tendency to rate the patient as healthier or more improved than he actually is. A possible determinant of this rating tendency is the interviewer's wish to think of himself as a benign, accepting person. Other raters might show the opposite tendency, that is, the *severity error*.

3. *The central tendency error.* The tendency to use the middle categories of the rating scale, thus avoiding extreme judgments. This tendency may be reinforced by the rater's knowledge that the modal degree of improvement in psychotherapy is "some" to "moderate."

4. *The contrast error.*   The tendency to rate others in the opposite direction from the rater's own perceived position on the trait in question. For example, a rater may be struck by, and thus over-rate, any degree of impulsiveness in a patient if she herself has little of it.

5. *Errors arising from the rater's personality tendencies.*   For example, the tendency toward oversensitivity to hostility or, conversely, difficulty in perceiving hostility in others.

In addition to these errors, which are common to all rating tasks, there are certain specific problems in making clinical judgments of a patient's present functioning and extent of improvement. What is the clinician really judging? What cognitive activity is involved in that judgment? Sarbin et al. (1960) hold that clinical judgments are possible because the clinician has in mind certain schemata relevant to the judgment task. The schemata provide a frame of reference by which the various phenomena shown by the patient may be understood and discussed. The schemata for judging improvement are of necessity an ill-defined structure formed by the theory to which the clinician adheres, her own experiences as a patient and therapist, her personal idiosyncracies, and the common cultural values that she shares. These various factors, interacting in unknown ways in the clinician's mind, leave us uncertain of what is meant by a particular judge's rating of, for instance, "moderate improvement."

Sources of Invalidity Arising from the Patient

In assessment interviews the patient's mental set is a crucial determinant of his responses and thus deserves attention. The ideal patient would have no biasing mental sets. Such a patient would *want* to participate in the interview; would understand its purpose well; would have a clear-eyed, objective view of himself, sufficient intelligence, psychological mindedness, and verbal ability to communicate his experiences in ways that are meaningful to the interviewer; and would trust the interviewer enough to be completely open about himself. We would like his main motive for participating to be altruism—the desire to contribute to the understanding of psychotherapy. But what we often get is someone whose attitudes are influenced by various biases.

Why should a patient agree to an evaluation of herself and her therapy by a stranger? Perhaps she had to agree, as a condition for acceptance into the treatment program. Perhaps the authority of the clinic or of her therapist induced agreement. The patient knows that the interview is not primarily for her benefit. The demands of reliability—that is, ratings by another observer—involve some obvious breach of confidentiality, usually in the form of tape recording.

The patient will deviate in a number of ways from our ideal interview participant. Some deviations derive from his general personality characteristics, namely, those he would manifest in most situations. Some patients are reserved and inhibited; their inclination is to keep private matters to themselves, not to share them with a stranger. Some are not introspective and thus are not reliable informants of their inner psychological states. Some are suspicious rather than trusting. Some adjust to situations by very easily and readily assuming the role that they think is expected of them; the role then governs their responses.

Other deviations from the ideal role will result from the particular meaning that the patient places on the interview, which will be determined partly by the personality characteristics and manner of the interviewer. For the patient, the interview may have the meaning of close scrutiny to determine whether her belief that she has improved is valid. It thus becomes a test of her adequacy (the kind of person who would improve in therapy), and may stimulate her to put her best foot forward. Or the interviewer may be seen as an intruder into the patient's relationship with her therapist; the interview would then be a challenge to remain loyal to the therapist. Or the interviewer may be regarded as an authority to whom the patient can convey her resentment of the therapist— resentment arising from either realistic or unrealistic reasons.

Probably the patient's response in the interview represents some combination of his dominant mental set and the "truth" of the situation he is describing. Ordinarily, it is not possible to disentangle these factors. Once a mental set becomes dominant, it will easily and smoothly determine the patient's responses. Most patients learn in therapy how to render their experiences into words that carry conviction to clinicians. Herein lies the possibility for deception, which may be unconsciously motivated. Any therapist who has had occasion to get follow-up reports on his patients—either by design or by chance—knows that a certain percentage of cases present surprises, requiring revision of the previous view of the patient and how much he benefited in therapy.

Generalizability Theory

The above-mentioned points regarding reliability and validity may be summarized by considering the interview from the point of view of generalizability theory (Cronbach et al., 1972). This theory reminds us that the importance of any observation consists in the fact that we can generalize from it to certain classes of observations. A rating of a patient trait made by an interviewer may be generalized to various other conditions of observation—for example, to a similar rating made by another interviewer, to scores of that trait obtained by a different method, or to patient behavior in a nontest (real-life) situation. Each condition of observation can be regarded as a universe, of which the given observation is a sample. Thus the rating made by the second interviewer is a sample of the universe of ratings that might be made by all possible interviewers. Generalizability theory forces us to ask: "To what universe do we want to generalize this observation?" If we want to know how well we can generalize from the rating of the first interviewer to that of the second interviewer, we are asking about what classical test theory calls *reliability*. Generalization from the rating to the patient's behavior in a nontest situation is what classical test theory calls *validity*. As we discuss specific rating schedules, it will be seen that the psychometric data permit us to generalize with most confidence to the ratings of a second interviewer, next, to ratings made by the patient herself, next, at a substantially lower level of confidence, to the ratings of an informant, and finally to the ratings of another clinician judging the same trait but with a different instrument and in different circumstances.

INTERVIEW SCHEDULES AND RATING FORMS

Only a few interview schedules and rating forms have achieved general usage. The Psychotherapy Outcome Measures project (Waskow & Parloff, 1975) recommended that the Psychiatric Status Schedule (PSS) (Spitzer et al., 1970), used by the independent clinical evaluator, be part of the core battery of instruments.

The PSS is an interview schedule and rating form. It consists of questions designed to elicit the information needed to rate 321 items that are descriptive of behavior, thought, and feeling. The items are generally precise and specific in their coverage; an example would be "Mentions he feels people take advantage of him or push him around."

The PSS has been widely used, and its psychometric properties have been extensively investigated. For scoring, the items are grouped into 17 symptom and 6 role scales. The latter reflect the patient's functioning in common roles such as wage earner, parent, and so on. Spitzer et al. (1970) report that they have factor analyzed the 17 symptom scales into four second-level scales: subjective distress; behavioral disturbance; impulse control disturbance; and reality testing disturbance (no factor loadings are given). There is also a summary role scale that averages the ratings received by the patient on her individual role scales. The scales are independent of each other, relative to the correlations usually found among the scales of a rating instrument.

Reliability as judged by interrater agreement is quite good. Support for the concurrent validity of the PSS was obtained in the finding that most of its scales differentiated between hospitalized patients and normals. However, correlations between PSS ratings and those of other rating instruments made by other raters (therapist, patient, other interviewer, interviewer of patient's informant) were highly variable, depending on the particular scale being rated and the source of the other rating. In general, they were not persuasive that the same construct was being reliably rated across sources. Many of the PSS scales were found to be sensitive to the changes shown by inpatients four weeks after their admission, as well as to changes shown by manic–depressive patients in the phases of their illness.

These generally favorable psychometric properties prompted the Psychotherapy Outcome Measures project (Waskow & Parloff, 1975) to recommend the use of the PSS for both initial and posttherapy assessment of patients. A few reservations about the instrument were noted. These related to the PSS's devotion to the mental status examination and to the standard psychiatric nomenclature, as well as the fact that the instrument was originally developed to measure status, not change. No reservations were noted as to how the average psychotherapy patient would take to the PSS interview.

Ideally, the publication of the recommended core battery for psychotherapy outcome assessment (Waskow & Parloff, 1975) should have been followed by intensive testing of the recommended instruments. There should have been sufficient interest aroused to produce testing of the instruments, with exploration of their advantages and limitations. This did not occur, at least in any public way. There was not that critical mass of interest that would have produced a discussion of the issues in the scientific literature. One hears informally of researchers who have used the PSS, for example, but private efforts to learn potentially important results are not always successful.

The most notable study in which the PSS was used to assess outcome was the Vanderbilt study of specific versus nonspecific effects in psychotherapy (Strupp & Hadley, 1979). This was a study of psychotherapy with male college students who showed symptoms of depression, psychasthenia, and social introversion. They were assessed in a number of ways, including the PSS interview by a clinician at intake, termination of treatment, and at follow-up. Thanks to the kind cooperation of Drs. Strupp and Hadley (personal communications, 1980, 1981, Reference Notes 2 and 4 at end of chapter), certain valuable information about the PSS in their study was made available. It pertains to (1) the sensitivity of the instrument to change and (2) general impressions of the value of the PSS interview, and the patients' reaction to it.

Sensitivity to change may be measured by effect size, which is a standard measure of how much change is detected by the instrument (Smith et al., 1980). It is the ratio of the the average change during treatment to the standard deviation of the pretreatment scores. In the Vanderbilt study it is possible to compare the effect size shown by the PSS with that shown by the relevant MMPI scales (depression, psychasthenia, and social introversion) and with the following ratings made by the clinical interviewer: (1) Health Sickness Rating Scale (Luborsky,1962); (2) "clinical rating scales," covering anxiety, depression, guilt, enjoyment of life, self-esteem, optimism, and psychological distress; and (3) a rating of overall severity of problems.

As can be seen in Table 15.1, the effect size for the PSS scales was lower than that for the other instruments. Thus the PSS appears to be the least sensitive to change. The finding of a relatively low degree of sensitivity partially contradicts Spitzer et al.'s (1970) report of sensitivity of the PSS to change. The contradiction probably results from the fact that Spitzer et al. studied inpatients and manic–depressives, whereas outpatients were treated in the Vanderbilt study.

This finding of relatively low sensitivity to change corresponds to the general impression of the PSS formed by Strupp (personal communication, 1980) and

TABLE 15.1.   Effect Sizes of Pre–Post Measures in Vanderbilt Study

Instrument	Mean Effect Size[a]
MMPI (mean of 3 scales)	1.06
Health Sickness Rating Scale	1.03
Overall severity rating	.95
"Clinical rating scales" (7 variables)	.91
Psychiatric Status Schedule (mean of 3 scales)	.56

[a]Mean effect size for pretherapy to posttherapy measures in Vanderbilt psychotherapy study (Strupp & Hadley, 1979) for patients treated by therapists and alternate therapists. All ratings except those of the MMPI were made by the clinical interviewer.

Hadley (personal communication, 1981). They reported that the posttherapy evaluation was begun by a 15- or 20-minute unstructured clinical interview, before the interviewer turned to the PSS questions. Usually the unstructured period revealed more about how the patient had changed than did the longer structured interview. Furthermore, if the interviewer stuck closely to the PSS questions, observers felt that they did not understand the patient very well—in ordinary clinical terms. Finally, even though the PSS had been modified to make it more suitable for the patients under study (college students), the patients found the interview tedious and thought many of its questions inappropriate.

Indeed, many are inappropriate for the average nonpsychotic psychotherapy outpatient. This is because the PSS covers many of the same areas of disturbed functioning as does the psychiatric mental status examination, which was developed in hospital psychiatry: reality testing; orientation and memory; psychomotor disturbance; and so on. A count reveals that about 75 items of the PSS inquire into symptoms of overt psychosis or gross disturbance that are rare in psychotherapy outpatients.

The presence of this many inappropriate questions has implications beyond the time wasted. One must also consider the loss of rapport, which is vital if the patient is to convey anything of value about her therapeutic experience. Rapport and ease of interaction may also be injured by the specific nature of the required answers to many PSS questions. For example, with regard to the patient's mood, the indicated question is: "What kind of moods have you been in recently?" The answer, which is to be rated as yes or no, is: "Says he felt elated or 'high' (do not include mere good spirits)."

It should also be noted that Spitzer and Endicott (1975) state that the time required for the PSS interview varies from 30 to 50 minutes. If we consider that the average interview takes 40 minutes and that the average number of questions asked is about 270 (some questions are omitted for each patient because they do not pertain in that case), the time required for each question and answer would be about nine seconds. This is exclusive of the introductory interaction and of the probing, follow-up, and open-ended questions that the authors recommend as a supplement to the precoded questions, in order to further explore certain matters.

Three other interview guides and rating forms developed by Spitzer and Endicott and their colleagues at the New York State Psychiatric Institute may be mentioned. The Psychiatric Evaluation Form (PEF) (Endicott & Spitzer, 1972b), like the PSS, covers role behaviors as well as psychopathology found in neuroses, personality disorders, and psychotic disturbances. However, the raters' judgments are made, not on specific items of behavior as in the PSS, but on broader dimensions and inferred constructs such as "anxiety." The PEF interview guide is more flexible than that of the PSS and, therefore, not suitable for the inexperienced interviewer. The Current and Past Psychopathology Scale (CAPPS) (Endicott & Spitzer, 1972a) is similar to the PSS, but also has a section inquiring into the patient's past life from age 12 until 1 month ago. Like the PSS, the PEF and CAPPS seem oriented mainly toward inpatients. The present author is not aware that they have been used in psychotherapy evaluation studies.

The Schedule for Affective Diseases and Schizophrenia (SADS) (Endicott & Spitzer, 1978) was constructed in conjunction with the Research Diagnostic Criteria (RDC) (Spitzer et al., 1978). The RDC was developed as part of the NIMH Clinical Research Branch Collaborative Program on Psychobiology of Depression. It was an attempt to increase the reliability of psychiatric diagnoses by specifying the criteria for each diagnosis. The SADS interview schedule contains questions to elicit the necessary information, although the judgments are not to be based on the interview alone, but rather on all available sources of information such as case records and interviews with family members.

The SADS interview is modeled on a decision-tree approach to differential diagnosis: "The Schedule provides for a pregression of questions, items, and criteria that systematically rule out specific RDC diagnoses" (Endicott & Spitzer, 1978). The diagnostic criteria usually consist of observable psychopathology. It is recommended that the interviewer be a clinician. Endicott and Spitzer (1978) state that an experienced interviewer who is familiar with the SADS and RDC should be able to complete the interview in 1½ to 2 hours.

The interview questions and rating procedure seem more clinically meaningful than those of the PSS, and there is not the excessive specificity of required answers that characterizes the PSS. Symptoms are rated on 3 point to 7 point scales, rather than simply as present or absent.

Those considering the use of the SADS should be aware that the instrument was developed to achieve reliable diagnoses of major psychiatric disorders, with heavy emphasis on the functional psychoses. Thus the questions are designed to secure information that bears on the necessary and sufficient criteria for psychiatric disorders—criteria that were later formalized in the American Psychiatric Association Diagnostic and Statistical Manual for Mental Disorders, Third Edition (DSM-III, 1980). The criteria consist of items of descriptive psychopathology. A great many questions are needed to rule in or out the 24 diagnoses that are covered, some of which have subtypes. For example, there are eleven subtypes of a major depressive disorder. A patient with a generalized anxiety disorder must first be screened for schizophrenia, schizoaffective disorder, various types of manic and depressive disorder, and so on before questions relevant to the patient's condition are presented. Furthermore, it may seem a little unnatural to the clinician to secure only that information necessary for the diagnosis of generalized anxiety disorder (anxiety symptoms of at least two weeks duration and sufficiently severe to impair functioning or require treatment), and not to learn what the patient is anxious about. The SADS is brief and incomplete in its coverage of personality disorders and does not cover such conditions as adjustment disorder and marital disorder. Like the instruments discussed above, it is oriented toward, although not restricted to, inpatients.

The change version of the SADS (SADS-C) was designed to assess the patient's symptoms at some point after the onset of treatment, in order to learn how much change had taken place. It consists of 34 variables, a rating on the Global Assessment Scale, and a rating of the patient's degree of impaired functioning. These variables were taken from part one of the parent instrument, which permits a ready comparison with the initial assessment on the SADS. About one third of the variables consist of symptoms that one would expect to find in inpatients but not in outpatients.

THE STRUCTURED AND SCALED INTERVIEW TO ASSESS MALADJUSTMENT

The instruments discussed thus far were directed at the nature and intensity of the patient's symptoms. Another focus of psychotherapy is the patient's social adjustment, which may change independently of symptoms. Recent years have seen the development of instruments intended to judge social adjustment.

The Structured and Scaled Interview to Assess Maladjustment (SSIAM) is an interview guide and rating instrument. It covers five sectors of the patient's life: work; social; family; marriage; and sex. "Family" refers to family of origin. Each sector of the patient's life can be considered a role function. The instrument's developers (Gurland et al., 1972a) modified an idea of Parloff et al. (1954), namely, that there are different aspects of a person's role performance, and it is important to assess them. In the SSIAM the aspects of each role performance are: whether the patient's observable behavior is considered normal by the usual social standards; the degree of distress the patient experiences in that role; and how smooth the patient's interactions with others are while in that role function.

These three factors cut across all sectors, and questions were devised to inquire into each. Thus, with respect to the work sector, there are questions that deal with behavior (e.g., "Do you have difficulty holding a job?"), with interpersonal friction, and with the patient's distress (e.g., "Do you feel inferior at work?"). In addition, the rater makes global judgments of the degree of stress in the patient's environment; of factors affecting the patient's prognosis (duration of maladjustment, previous level of adjustment, willingness to change, and the pressure on her from others to change); and of the patient's assets, talents, and so on.

A factor analysis of the revised instrument (Gurland et al., 1972b) yielded a factor structure that was in part similar to and in part different from the *a priori* division of the instrument into five sectors. Median factor loadings for those items retained as factor markers was .43. Interrater reliability is not given for items of the SSIAM but is high for the factors (median intraclass correlation = .86). The factors are relatively independent of each other. Regarding validity, the ratings of the patient's interviewer were correlated with those of an informant's interviewer, thus providing a comparison of the patient's and informant's views. The median correlation for the six factors was .48.

The SSIAM was used to assess the adjustment of patients pre- and post-therapy (four months of therapy) in the Temple University study of psychotherapy and behavior therapy (Sloane et al., 1975). In computing the pre- and posttest scores, the researchers used only the first two of the SSIAM's six factors, namely, Social Isolation and Work Inadequacy. These factors consisted of five and four items, respectively. There were three groups of patients: those treated by behavior therapy, by psychotherapy, and a wait-list group that did not receive treatment. On the work inadequacy factor all three groups improved. For the behavior therapy group, the improvement was significant and for the other two groups it was "marginally significant," that is, significant by a one-tailed test. Similarly, all patients improved on the social isolation factor; the improvement reached significance for the behavior therapy and wait-list groups. An analysis of variance revealed no significant difference among the groups in the amount of improvement, nor was there any interaction between type of treatment received and initial level of neuroticism as measured by the Eysenck Personality Questionnaire.

On another measure of outcome, the patient's target complaints, there was a significant difference between the improvement achieved by patients who received treatment and those on the wait list. Thus the SSIAM failed to detect differential improvement that was apparent on another measure. It is not clear why the rating instrument differed from target complaints in this respect. The demand characteristics of the pre-post assessment tend to produce improvement in scores in controls as well as treated groups and thus are likely to erase between-group differences, but it is difficult to say why this factor should operate differently with the target complaints than with the adjustment ratings. One would normally expect symptoms to be more labile than adjustment level, and evidently the symptom change of the treated groups outstripped that of the controls.

At any rate, the results do not argue for great sensitivity to change on the part of the SSIAM. This impression is supported by a statement by Sloane et al. (1975, p. 92) that even one of the greatest changes shown by the SSIAM— by the behavior therapy patients on the social adjustment factor—"did not reflect the major shift which seemed clinically apparent."

SOCIAL ADJUSTMENT SCALE

The Social Adjustment Scale (SAS) (Wèissman et al., 1971, 1974) is derived from the SSIAM. Like it, the SAS rates the patient's adjustment in six sectors or roles, which in Weissman and Bothwell (1976) are named as work (including worker, housewife, or student roles), social and leisure activities, relationship with extended family, spouse role, parental role, and member of family unit. On the actual Social Adjustment Scale Questionnaire, the areas of inquiry are work, household, external (extended) family, social–leisure, and personal well-being. Forty-one questions inquire into these role functions. The variables are rated on five-point scales. There are also global judgments for each sector.

Like the SSIAM, the SAS inquires into both instrumental and affective aspects of the patient's role functioning: how well does he do it and how does he feel while doing it. Thus there are questions that assess the adequacy of the patient's functioning in each role, interpersonal friction in that role, and the distress experienced by the patient.

The information is obtained through a semistructured interview with the patient; that is, the first question is specified on the interview schedule, and the interviewer is to ask follow-up questions as needed. The interview is conducted by trained bachelor-level research assistants. It takes between 45 minutes and 1½ hours. The time period of reference is the most recent 2½ months of the patient's life. Weissman and Sholomskas (in press) state that in addition to its use with depressed outpatient woman, the SAS "has been used with non-psychiatric community populations and with suicide attemptors, alcoholics, methadone maintained patients and schizophrenics."

There is a kind of simplicity about the SAS questions that sometimes suggests that the instrument was designed for patients with only a high-school education. For example, questions addressed to a homemaker might be: "Have you been keeping up with the laundry? Has anyone run out of clean clothes?" Nevertheless, the questions are well thought out. They achieve a desirable balance between the objective and specifiable on one hand and the clinically important on the other. For example, the relationship between the patient and her "principal household member" (generally synonymous with the patient's significant other person) is explored by carefully worded questions that inquire into the amount of friction, emotional withdrawal, and communication of important matters and the patient's ability to emphathize with the other.

The original version of the SAS was used in the Boston–New Haven study of the maintenance treatment of depressed woman (Klerman et al., 1974; Weissman & Paykel, 1974; Weissman et al., 1974). In all the combinations permitted by a 2 × 3 design, depressed women who had responded favorably to antidepressant medication were given maintenance treatment consisting of psychotherapy, amitriptyline, a placebo, or no medication. It was for this study that the instrument was developed. Psychometric information for the first version is as follows: interrater reliability was tested under optimum conditions between two raters who trained together and who were both present during the interviews of patients, which were conducted by either of them. Pearson correlations for the SAS items ranged from .33 to .97, with a mean of .83. Factor analysis (Paykel et al., 1971) revealed one factor corresponding to a role function (work performance), one factor corresponding to an aspect of behavior cutting across a number of roles (interpersonal friction), and smaller, more specific factors.

Validity was supported by the ability of the SAS to distinguish between depressed women and normals (Weissman et al.,1971), and between women when acutely depressed and when recovered. Five out of the six factors significantly differentiated the patients when they were depressed and when they recovered, thus indicating that the instrument can detect change. The results of a different test of validity—the covariation of SAS factors with relevant variables assessed on different instruments—were not as encouraging (Weissman & Paykel, 1974, p. 234). Correlations were low, and in a few cases negative, between SAS factors and the apparently corresponding variables rated by the psychiatrist on the Clinical Interview for Depression scale (Paykel et al., 1970) and the Brief Psychiatric Rating Scale (Overall & Gorham, 1962).

The SAS also seemed able to discriminate psychotherapy patients from others. Those receiving psychotherapy improved significantly more than did those not receiving therapy on four of the six SAS factors (work performance, interpersonal friction, inhibited communication, and anxious rumination), as well as on the single score representing the mean of all six SAS scales and the rater's overall global evaluation. This difference was not apparent after four months of maintenance treatment, but it was after eight months. The ability of the instrument to differentially detect change is reassuring, although as Weissman et al. (1974) point out, there was the possibility that the psychotherapy patients had learned to be more comfortable with interviewers and that the interviewers were biased in favor of seeing good adjustment in therapy patients.

It should also be noted that Klerman et al. (1974) stated that there was no significant difference between the relapse rates for the psychotherapy patients and the drug patients. That is, although the psychotherapy patients reported a better adjustment at eight months, their relapse rate was the same as that of the drug patients. Furthermore, Weissman et al. (1981a) have subsequently reported that at the one-year follow-up the two groups showed no difference in social adjustment. Thus the social adjustment difference showed up on only one of a number of assessments.

The SAS was used in a second study of depression at Yale University (Weissman et al., 1979). Depressed outpatients received either amitriptyline, psychotherapy, combined treatment, or "nonscheduled treatment" (minimal contact). No differences were found in the patients receiving psychotherapy or pharmacotherapy after the four-month treatment period, but they were found at the one-year follow-up point. Differences between the two groups were reported (Weissman et al., 1981a) on three of the *a priori* role scales of the

SAS, namely, social and leisure activities, parental role, and member of family unit. In the earlier study, differences between the two groups were found in the *factors* of the SAS. On the question of why the results were reported in terms of the factors in one study and the *a priori* scales in the next, Weissman (personal communication, 1982, Reference Note 5) has stated that the data were analyzed according to both roles and factors but only one set was reported, since they correlated.

A self-report version of the SAS was developed (Weissman & Bothwell, 1976). The advantages of the self-report form are economy and ease of administration. It also facilitates case finding and longitudinal studies of patients. The self-report form is organized the same way as the interview version; its 42 questions inquire into the same six role functions. The time period of reference is the last two weeks.

The remarks made about the seeming simplicity of some of the SAS questions apply with added force to the self-report version. As on the parent instrument, the items are rated on a five-point scale. One of the problems with a self-report questionnaire is that the respondents have different internal standards and thus interpret scale point definitions differently. One patient's "much" may be equivalent to another patient's "moderate." The authors have attempted to solve this problem by making the scale point definitions roughly quantitative, which reduces the factor of idiosyncratic standards. Thus, with respect to Item 34 from the Social Adjustment Self-report Questionnaire ("Have you wanted to do the opposite of what your relatives wanted in order to make them angry during the last two weeks?"), the patient may answer (1) "I never wanted to oppose them."; (2) "Once or twice I wanted to oppose them"; (3) "About half the time I wanted to oppose them"; (4)" Most of the time I wanted to oppose them"; or (5) "I always oppose them."

The existence of the self-report form permits comparisons of the ratings made by both the interviewer and by the patient. This comparison constitutes a loose validity check of the interview rating—loose because the self-report ratings are not a standard, established instrument. The correlations for the six role areas range from .40 to .76, with a median of .54. This is relatively good agreement for across-viewpoint ratings and reflects the objective nature of the questions and scale point definitions of the items. An overall score was computed by simply calculating the mean of the SAS items. The self-report overall score correlated .72 with the rater's overall score.

One problem concerning the SAS has already been mentioned: the question of how to score it. Change was reported in factor scores in one study and in role scores in the second study. A second question, of a more impressionistic nature, concerns the kind of social adjustment it measures. It must be said that the instrument reflects not only a conventional view of adjustment, but a partly idealized conventional view. It was constructed with the modal good citizen in mind. There is no place in it for rating the patient's creativity nor, for that matter, her degree of occupational success. (Only her work impairment is rated.) The SAS appears to exclude homosexual relationships. This is not quite definite: there are questions pertaining to the patient's conjugal partner or to romantic involvements if there is no conjugal partner, but the associated questions about frequency of intercourse and type of birth control used indicate heterosexuality. Thus a sizable fraction of the population cannot be properly rated. One feels that Estragon and Vladimir in Beckett's play *Waiting for Godot* would get very low adjustment scores on the SAS. No doubt that is what they should get, but there are many life-styles intermediate between theirs and that of the idealized modal citizen whose adjustment will not be fully captured by the instrument.

In this connection, Platt's (1981) views should be mentioned, not that the present author necessarily endorses them, but because they represent a sociologist's perspective. He has criticized the concept of social adjustment as a criterion of treatment success—at least social adjustment as exemplified by the Structured and Scaled Interview to Assess Maladjustment and the Social Adjustment Scale. He states that these instruments make use of the sociologic concept of role but do so in a way that is not theoretically sound or practically useful. He raises the question of how the developers of the SAS decided on the number of roles to be assessed, their content, and the notion of what constitutes normal behavior within the role. His answer is that these ideas originated in the minds of the developers, that is, that they represent middle-class norms and do not take into account the cultural norms of the subjects to be rated. He recommends learning more about the expectations of these subjects' reference group and deriving one's norms empirically. "Reference group" includes the patient's own family; therefore, norms will vary from one patient to the next.

The psychotherapy researcher will not inevitably be aghast at the thought that a rating form represents middle-class norms. Such norms are not a bad place to start. Actually, the SAS probably does reflect the values of the population it is intended for, which is why it can discriminate depressed patients from normals, and the acutely depressed stage of the disorder from the recovered stage. It should also be noted that creating a separate reference group for each patient, as Platt seems to recommend, would mean using individualized measures, thus greatly reducing the possibility of across patient comparisons.

A more practical criticism of the SAS, in the author's opinion, is that it measures the lowest common denominator of social adjustment, which is why it seems oversimplified. But that is only to say that it is not a perfect instrument; it is limited, as all rating forms are. From the researcher's point of view, it represents a thoughtful attempt to make certain clinical judgments in a reliable way, and it has given some indication that it can do so, which is all we can ask.

DENVER COMMUNITY MENTAL HEALTH QUESTIONNAIRE

The Denver Community Mental Health Questionnaire (DCMHQ) (Ciarlo & Reihman, 1977) represents the field of program evaluation. Its goal is to assess treatment results on relatively large numbers of patients in order to evaluate the efficiency of an entire treatment program.

The questionnaire consists of 79 items that are rated by a trained, nonprofessional interviewer after an approximately 45-minute interview with the subject. The word "subject" is more accurate than "patient" because the interview is normally conducted with *ex*patients three or six months after their treatment. It is a follow-up interview, intended to learn the status of the subject's psychological functioning and degree of distress.

The questions are simple and specific, usually inquiring into behavior that can be reliably observed. There is a preference for behavioral acts that can be counted. For example, to "How many times do you visit or speak with friends who live away?" the subject may answer "once a day," "once or twice a week to once a month," "several times a year," or "never." There are also questions directed at feelings. For example, to "In the last couple of days how often have you felt fearful or afraid?" the subject may answer "never," "once or twice," "often," or "almost always." The interview is described as semistructured, although it in fact seems rather structured. The subject's answers to questions are recorded, rather than the interviewer's judgments based on the subject's responses.

The questionnaire is not routinely administered to pretherapy patients, although it has at times been given to patients seeking treatment at the Denver Northwest Community Mental Health Center for the purpose of establishing norms among incoming patients. The questions reflect the population for which the questionnaire was designed: applicants at a community mental health center. Thirty-two questions deal with alcohol and drug use. Nine questions ask about arrests and contacts with public agencies such as public assistance. There are also questions dealing with the subject's personal distress, relationships with family and friends, and degree of satisfaction with the service received at the mental health center. The items have been grouped by cluster analysis into 13 scales: psychological distress, interpersonal isolation from family, interpersonal isolation from friends, interpersonal aggression with friends, productivity (work), legal difficulties, public system dependence, alcohol abuse and negative consequences, drug abuse and negative consequences, frequency of hard drug use, frequency of soft drug use, client satisfaction, and productivity (home).

The scales have high coefficients of internal consistency (alpha) and are only slightly correlated with each other. Thus they appear to represent independent dimensions. Interrater agreement for an N of 18 was found to be exceedingly high, even considering that it was determined under optimal conditions (both raters present during the interview): Pearson correlations for 12 scales ranged from .85 to 1.00, with a median of .92. Ciarlo and Reihman (1977) state that present interrater agreement may be a little lower, which is reassuring.

The authors have explored validity in several ways.

1.   They compared the interviewer's own judgments with the subject's responses on an N of 349. These correlations, like those establishing interrater

reliability, are indecently high (from .79 to .97 for ten scales with a median of .94), indicating that the interviewers add virtually nothing of their own to the patients' responses.

2.   The responses of 91 subjects were compared with those of "collaterals" (informants). Correlations ranged from .52 to .87 for nine scales, with a median of .60.

3.   The DCMHQ ratings on eleven of the scales were compared with global ratings made by clinicians (nurse, social workers, paraprofessionals) at intake. The correlations ranged from −.03 to .63, with a median of .33. The authors explain the low correlations in a number of ways, including the fact that clinicians at intake tend to focus on the patient's main problem, rather than systematically evaluating that patient. Another possibility, not mentioned by the authors, is that the various clinicians may not have been making the ratings in a standardized way.

4.   The authors administered the DCMHQ to three samples, totaling 212 people chosen randomly from the population of Denver and thus were able to show that the mental health center clients differed significantly from the normals on every scale but one. This demonstration was not their only reason for obtaining normal standards. Since the purpose of treatment is to restore the client's functioning to normal levels, it becomes important to learn what those levels are. The authors converted the scale scores of the normal sample into standard scores with a mean of 50 and a standard deviation of 5. Subsequently, the scores of all subjects taking the DCMHQ were converted to these standard scores. The patient satisfaction with treatment items were not appropriate for the normal sample; these items were standardized by the first 100 patients who were followed up. Interestingly, they found that patient satisfaction is unrelated to patient self-reported functioning on all other scales. They conclude that the patient's satisfaction with the services received is not a satisfactory index of that patient's well-being.

Patients attending the mental health clinic have been divided into groups to study the pretreatment and post-treatment status of each group. The groups were formed according to the patients' "major problem category" (MPC), which was assigned by the intake clinician. There are eight MPC's: alcohol abuse, drug abuse, antisocial behavior, somatic complaints, disorganized thinking and behavior, emotional distress, maladaptive behavior, and personal–social handicap.

With this scheme for classifying patients, the authors constructed, for each group, a profile of its average scores on the DCMHQ scales. Profiles were drawn for each group at admission and at the three-month follow-up point. Each graph displays the Denver population mean (the value of 50) and the 45 point, which is one standard deviation below the mean, and which is the minimal level of functioning desired for the treated patient. Clinicians studying these graphs can easily see how well their patients are doing in relation to the population mean and the minimal desired goal.

The authors also present time series of outcome profiles, which means the profiles for successive cohorts of patients all measured at the three-month point. This provides a judgment of how well the patients—whose MPC is, for example, disorganized thinking and behavior—are doing, compared with how well previous groups with that MPC were doing at the three-month point. If the recent group is not doing as well as the former ones, recent clinic procedures may have been ineffective for some reason. The idea is that this information, clearly and graphically presented to the clinic staff, may induce corrective measures. If the recent group of patients is doing better than average, it will of course also be valuable for the clinic staff to obtain that feedback. One goal of the outcome evaluation and feedback is to stimulate managers and clinicians to try innovations that might improve outcome.

Ciarlo (1977) points out that this time series design is frequently used in other fields such as economic forecasting and financial monitoring by corporations. However, "the mere idea of continuously monitoring selected program data is quite new to mental health clinicians and clinically trained managers . . . . In order to capitalize on the informational opportunities inherent in an outcome information monitoring system program, managers and staff must adopt, at least periodically, a more tentative and less doctrinaire style of thinking about their professional activities than is customary" (Ciarlo, 1977, pp. 113, 114).

Finally, Ciarlo and Reihman (1977) have calculated the cost per interview of locating subjects and conducting the interviews, thus permitting some estimate of the cost-effectiveness of the outcome evaluation effort. The figure given for cost is $30 per interview. They state that community mental health centers should be willing to spend a portion of their budget on outcome evaluation and that 2 to 3% of the budget could purchase hundreds of interviews.

Ciarlo and his associates have opened some very interesting prospects. Their program has many important strengths: the development of a reliable and apparently fairly valid questionnaire designed for a specific population; the effort to learn the subject's reaction to the services received; the assessment of community norms; the setting of clear and reasonable treatment goals in relation to the community norms; the goal of assessing all patients, including dropouts; the identification of groups of patients according to their major problem category and the observation of their profiles at follow-up; and the graphic representation of results and the quick feedback to clinic staff.

The promises aroused by this research program are briefly discussed below. First, a few cautions about the DCMHQ. As indicated above, it taps relatively gross disturbances likely to be found in a community mental health clinic population, but not particularly characteristic of the clientele of other treatment facilities. The questionnaire does not ask about such matters as the subject's feelings of empathy toward friends, or sharing of important problems with them. If the DCMHQ claimed to be a comprehensive measure of psychological adjustment, that claim could be disputed. Questions about the narrow view of adjustment that were raised in connection with the Social Adjustment

Scale are even more pertinent here. But the DCMHQ does not claim to be a comprehensive measure, only that it can reliably distinguish between community mental health clinic patients and the general population.

Another question relates to the validity of the Major Problem Category groups. Each patient is assigned to a group by the intake clinician, a procedure of unknown reliability. We don't know how homogeneous the profiles of those patients sharing an MPC are, or how different they are from those of other patients. Nevertheless, the attempt to group patients according to their principal reaction tendencies is clinically sound; it corresponds to the impressions gained in clinical practice.

GLOBAL RATING SCALES

Mention should be made of global adjustment rating scales, that is, those that assign a patient a single number to indicate that patient's general level of adjustment. The appeal of such rating scales is that change can be expressed in the simplest possible way—as the numerical difference between posttherapy and pretherapy scores.

The Health Sickness Rating Scale (HSRS) (Luborsky, 1962) was devised for the Menninger Psychotherapy Project. It is a 100-point scale on which the patient's level of adjustment may be rated from the lowest conceivable (0) to an ideal state of complete mental health (100). In using the HSRS, one first rates the patient on seven scales, each of which contributes to the concept of mental health. These are (1) the patient's need to be protected and/or supported versus the ability to function autonomously, (2) the degree of severity of the symptoms, (3) the degree of subjective discomfort and distress, (4) the patient's effect on the environment (e.g. causing danger or discomfort), (5) the degree to which the patient can utilize his abilities, especially at work, (6) the quality of the patient's interpersonal relationships, and (7) the breadth and depth of the patient's interests.

These seven judgments influence the rater's decision about a final global rating for the patient, but that rating is made by comparison with two additional sets of standards: (1) the global scale has nine scale point definitions, consisting of both general behavioral descriptions and indications of where particular diagnostic categories should be placed; and (2) the patient to be rated is compared with 30 brief case vignettes. These vignettes, which serve as anchor points, describe people at varying levels of adjustment, from extremely low to extremely high. In rating a patient, one first decides what range of adjustment she falls in and then places her by comparison with the case descriptions of that range. For example, the rater may decide that the patient is better adjusted than case number 23 but not as well adjusted as case number 24.

Luborsky and Bachrach (1974) reviewed 18 studies that used the HSRS. In the ten studies in which raters independently made judgments of the HSRS, the interjudge agreement ranged from .65 to .94. The correlates of the Health

Sickness ratings were examined. The highest correlations were with other measures of overall adjustment. For example, in the Menninger Psychotherapy Study (Kernberg et al., 1972), Health Sickness ratings correlated .88 with ego strength. Lower, somewhat variable, correlations were found with measures of severity of symptoms and with quality of interpersonal relationships.

As an outcome measure, Health Sickness ratings correlate highly with other similar, clinical judgments. For example, Kernberg et al. (1972) reported that improvement on the HSRS correlated .81 with global judgment of improvement. How the HSRS would correlate with an independent assessment of improvement is not definitely known, although there is some evidence for moderate across-viewpoint agreement: in the University of Pennsylvania psychotherapy study (Luborsky et al., 1980), a cluster formed by the Health Sickness ratings and an adjustment score derived from the Prognostic Index (Auerbach et al., 1972) correlated .65 with a patient-judged cluster and .46 with a therapist-judged cluster.

The Global Adjustment Scale (GAS) (Endicott et al., 1976) is a modification of the HSRS. The GAS provides a single rating of the patient's level of adjustment from 1 to 100. Unlike the HSRS, the GAS does not have seven component scales (patient's need to be protected, etc.) or case vignettes. The judge's ratings are based only on the scale point definitions, which are brief and are worded only in terms of behavior, not diagnostic label. For example, the range from 71 to 80 on the scale is defined as "Minimal symptoms may be present but no more than slight impairment in functioning, varying degrees of 'everyday' worries and problems that sometimes get out of hand."

The psychometric properties of the GAS have been explored in more varied and rigorous ways than those of the HSRS (Endicott et al., 1976). Interjudge reliability was determined in five studies that varied in type of population and in conditions for making ratings. Intraclass correlations among the raters ranged from .61 to .91. When GAS ratings made by an interviewer were compared with those made by another observer based on different information (e.g., the therapist, or the interviewer of the family), correlations were naturally lower. They ranged from .45 to .67 six months after admission. On admission they were still lower because of the restricted range displayed by the patients in their level of adjustment at the time of admission. Correlations across viewpoints between GAS ratings and the summary scales of the Psychiatric Status Schedule ranged from .17 to .49 six months after admission; they were lower on admission.

The GAS was found to be sensitive to the change shown by inpatients from admission to the six-month point. Its sensitivity is comparable to that of the total score on the Psychiatric Status Schedule and is greater than that of the summary scales of the PSS.

In short, it seems possible for clinicians to use the GAS in a reasonably reliable and valid way, even though its scale point definitions are brief. There are a number of reasons why psychotherapy researchers should seriously consider using it or the HSRS:

1. Very little extra time is required. This is particularly true of the GAS, whose single rating is merely an expression of a judgment that every clinician speaking with a patient inevitably makes: "How disturbed is this person?"

2. A global rating provides a simple way of communicating to other researchers the range of adjustment level in the patients under study.

3. Change in therapy is expressed quite simply as post minus pre score (regressed change scores are, of course, possible).

4. It will be important to learn whether the satisfactory reliability and validity of these scales can be duplicated in the hands of researchers other than those who developed the instruments.

PROGNOSTIC INDEX FOR PSYCHOTHERAPY

Many other rating instruments have undoubtedly been used by interviewers in various projects but have not been developed to the point of achieving wide usage. One such is the Prognostic Index for Psychotherapy (PI) (Auerbach et al., 1972), which is briefly described not only because of the author's familiarity with it, but because it is an example of a rating instrument that was developed, tested, and used at modest expense. As the name implies, it was originally developed to assess patients on variables believed to be of prognostic significance in therapy. Its present version consists of 29 variables that are rated after a semistructured interview with the patient at the beginning of therapy. The interview is conducted by a trained professional and takes about 1 to 1½ hours. Some of the PI variables are objective, such as the patient's level of education. Some are clinically descriptive, concerning, for example, the amount of drug use. Some are clinical–inferential, such as the quality of the patient's interpersonal relationships. The instrument has been factor analyzed (Auerbach et al., 1972) yielding the following factors: level of adjustment (formerly called "general emotional health"), emotional freedom, aptitude for psychotherapy, acute depression, and intellectual achievement. A modified PI interview is conducted at the end of therapy in order to determine how the patient has changed. When rated pre and posttherapy, the PI can yield change scores. This is because some of its variables, although chosen from their prognostic potential, reflect present psychological health. These variables form the level of adjustment factor.

Since the rating of some of the PI variables requires inferential judgments, interrater reliability depends on the degree of training of the judges. With 7 to 10 hours of training, a median interjudge correlation of .78 for the PI variables was achieved (Auerbach & Alexander, in preparation, Reference Note 1). Without adequate training, median interjudge correlations fell to as low as .47 (Luborsky et al., 1980).

The PI was the main clinical assessment instrument used in the University of Pennsylvania Psychotherapy Study (Luborsky et al., 1980). The validity of its

Level of Adjustment factor in judging outcome was explored by examining its correlations with other outcome measures. As mentioned above, the level of adjustment factor correlated so highly (.84) with the Health Sickness rating in that study that the two measures were combined into a cluster, which was found to correlate .65 with a composite of patient ratings of posttherapy adjustment and .46 with a composite of therapist ratings. Comparison with the patient's viewpoint thus appears to be satisfactory, probably because the interviewer's ratings were made just after the PI interview with the patient, which enabled the interviewer to learn the patient's view of how he is doing. The therapist's judgments flowed from different kinds of information.

Regarding sensitivity to change, the level of adjustment factor of the PI showed an effect size of .54. This is essentially the same as the effect size for three subscales of the MMPI (hysteria, hypochondriasis, ego strength) that were used as pre- and postmeasures. The Hopkins Symptoms Checklist showed an effect size of .80.

Our experience with the PI indicates that it is possible, even with limited resources, to devise an interview guide and instrument for rating clinically meaningful variables. With appropriate attention to definitions of variables and with sufficient training of raters, one can achieve reliability and validity comparable to that of standard instruments. The implications of this fact are mentioned below.

CONCLUSIONS

The preceding brief survey of assessment procedures suggests the following conclusions:

1. *There is no wholly satisfactory rating instrument or assessment procedure.* As soon as a decision is made regarding the assessment approach to be used, certain limitations come into play. A highly objective questionnaire cannot get at the subtleties of the patient's inner experience. An in-depth interview cannot have the same reliability as an objective questionnaire.

2. *The value of standard, well-known instruments for interview assessment of psychotherapy outcome is probably overestimated.* The standard instruments may be well known for reasons other than their ability to validly detect psychotherapeutic change. The choice of the Psychiatric Status Schedule by the Outcome Measurements Project (Waskow & Parloff, 1975) illustrates this tendency. The problems resulting from its use have been described above. The fact that it was not selected for use in the NIMH collaborative study of the psychotherapy of depression is an acknowledgment of its limitations. The use of standard instruments lulls the researcher into a false sense of security. The reputable psychometric qualities of the standard instrument make its choice seem unassailable. But whereas the reliability of such instruments is usually satisfactory, validity is another matter. What the researcher sometimes loses sight of is the fact that although the validity data supplied by the test developer

may be the best that she might reasonably have been expected to provide, the test's validity may still not be good enough for the researcher's purposes.

Validity data may consist merely of satisfactory correlations between the ratings on the new instrument and those from a source not fundamentally different, such as patient self-reports and observer ratings made after an interview with the patient. Furthermore, these correlations were probably obtained under optimal conditions by a researcher with a strong commitment to the test. The prospective user of the instrument may be planning to apply it to a different population undergoing a different kind of treatment, and she cannot take its validity for granted. It should be noted that the Outcome Measurements Project conferees hoped that the tests selected for the core battery would be compared with other instruments favored by individual researchers, so that more would be learned both about the core battery and other instruments. If this has happened, it has not been to an extent sufficient to attract much notice.

3.   *The mental habits of researchers contribute to a less than optimal choice of assessment procedures.* Consider the ideal way of making such a choice, as it is set forth in the chapter entitled "Fantasied Dialogue With a Researcher" by Irene Elkin Waskow in *Psychotherapy Change Measures* (Waskow & Parloff, 1975), a chapter that every psychotherapy researcher should review periodically: the researcher and the research consultant discuss what the former wants to study. During this leisurely exploration, the researcher's originally rather general ideas become focused onto the kinds of change he expects to find in the patients under study, that is, the relevant constructs of therapeutic change. For each change construct, he is directed to review articles, handbooks, manuals, and other materials that describe the pertinent tests. One feels that this literature, plus the knowledge of the consultant, will provide a comprehensive overview of the domain, thus enabling the researcher to choose an appropriate test. The same process *might* occur in reality, but in practice it rarely does. More frequently, decisions are made fairly quickly under the pressure of a deadline for a grant request submission. The researcher may find that it is not easy to obtain an accurate overview of the domain of relevant tests. Reviews of some tests may be in conflict or may, by giving somewhat favorable and somewhat unfavorable reviews to a number of tests, leave the researcher in a quandary. Consultation with an expert is inherently unpredictable; its results will depend on the consultant's experience and biases. Under these circumstances, the researcher is apt to simply settle on a test that she has heard of frequently.

4.   *The fact that there is no wholly satisfactory instrument has its corollary: each instrument has its unique set of advantages.* Every rating scale carves out a domain somewhere along the continuum from real-life complexity to objectivity. A good instrument is one that exploits the advantages inherent in that domain. If it exploits the possibilities in a creative way, so much the better. In this respect the Denver Community Mental Health Questionnaire deserves mention. Its developers opted for a highly objective assessment of overt distur-

bances in a particular population. This is a relatively narrow focus, but it permitted the test developers to pursue such important and novel goals as learning the community norms, the results achieved with successive cohorts of patients, and graphic feedback to clinicians. The Social Adjustment Scale is commendable for achieving what appears to be the appropriate degree of objectivity in its exploration of clinically important matters. The approach taken by the Menninger Psychotherapy Study carries its own set of advantages. The intensive study of individual cases permits an assessment worthy of the complexity of real life, as well as inquiry into the mechanisms of change. These advantages were partly exploited. However, in retrospect the researchers seemed to have had excessive faith in their theory-bound clinical inferences and, in general, had insufficient awareness of the likelihood of much error variance in their judgments.

5. *The researchers should try to maintain perspective on current research trends, rather than be swept along by them.* Today's dominant trend is toward objectivity in assessment, and some of its accompanying costs have been mentioned above. A tribute to the strength of the objectivity trend is, in the author's opinion, the change that has occurred in the kinds of therapy that are done. Because it proved extremely difficult to objectively assess the results of the previously dominant therapy—long-term psychodynamic—we have changed the nature of the therapy we do in order to conform to what can be objectively assessed. Or, if we have not changed the therapy we *do*, we have changed the kind of therapy that is researched, written about, and thus popularized. The present vogue is for short-term therapy directed at symptoms or behaviors that can be objectively measured.

6. *Researchers should be interested in formulating and measuring the various dimensions of therapeutic change.* Waskow and Parloff (1975) were aware that the instruments recommended by the Outcome Measurements Project were directed mostly at symptom relief, with some attention paid to fairly gross indicators of social adjustment. Other possible psychotherapeutic dimensions are "growth" (i.e., change in personality) and change in self-concept, attitudes, and values. These considerations lead to the next conclusion.

7. *We will probably rediscover the fact that "outcome" is approximately as complex as human life.* There is a need for assessment methods to do justice to that complexity. We should remember that there have been previous efforts to find a method of measurement that would remain faithful to clinical judgments, such as the Minnesota–Hartford Personality Assay (Glueck et al., 1964), which attempted a comprehensive description of a person by means of a great many items, some descriptive and some deeper and explanatory; and the method of paired comparisons used in the Menninger Psychotherapy Study (Sargent, 1956), in which the metric consists of rankings of patients on important variables. These methods have their difficulties, which may explain why they are not used today. But they were good ideas, and they can serve as departure points for future good ideas. The basic task remains what it always has been: to convert the clinician's judgments, arrived at in an unstructured or

semistructured interview, into a reliable metric. A supplementary, and important, way of approaching true-life complexity is simply to do repeated assessments at intervals.

8.   *Our assessments should incorporate efforts to build theories of therapy.* Past theories, which originated in the armchair, were overly ambitious, were not sufficiently tied to data, and were instruments in the noisy competition among schools. What is now needed are more modest steps toward theory construction, beginning with empirical generalizations. Ideally, these efforts should be made in a spirit of impartiality.

9.   *Theorists will have to acknowledge the fact that patients respond differently to therapy.* This simple truth, which does not receive much emphasis these days, should resurrect our interest in the patient's personality—not in all-embracing theories of personality that attempt to explain everything, but in limited, empirically based theories of those aspects of personality that are important in psychotherapy. We are searching for interactions between personality dispositions and the events of therapy.

10.   *Researchers should at least consider constructing their own instruments if they do not find ones that meet their needs.* There are arguments on both sides of this issue. Cattell (1973) has argued, with respect to self-report questionnaires, that there is very little value in a home-made questionnaire consisting only of face-valid items. He states that extensive scale development and testing are needed before a test is useful. Furthermore, comparability across research centers is impossible when home-made tests are used. Finally, the researcher's decision to construct a test may merely reflect his unawareness that there already exists one that would serve his purposes.

On the other hand, there are some less obvious advantages in creating one's own test. The investigator, ideally, knows what she wants to measure, which may be a construct or dimension overlooked by everyone else. She knows the population of patients with whom she will be working. She can word the items in a way most appropriate to that population. Also, she *values* the test of her own devising. She will apply it skillfully, rather than in a perfunctory way. In response to Cattell's argument that merely face-valid items are not sufficient, it must be said that in regard to interview rating instruments, we are at an early stage of development in which even the standard instruments rely on face-valid items. It is probably not terribly difficult for a researcher to produce a test whose reliability and validity are comparable to that of the standard instruments. However, these psychometric properties cannot be taken for granted; they must be demonstrated.

REFERENCE NOTES

1.   Auerbach, A. H. and Alexander, L. A. *Psychometric Properties of the Prognostic Index for Psychotherapy.* (In preparation)
2.   Hadley, S. W. Personal communication, 1981.

3. Psychotherapy of Depression Collaborative Research Program, January 1980. *Revised Research Plan*. Psychosocial Treatments Research Branch, NIMH.
4. Strupp, H. H. Personal communication, 1980.
5. Weissman, M. M. Personal communication, 1982.

REFERENCES

Auerbach, A. H., & Johnson, M. Research on the therapist's level of experience. In A. S. Gurman & A. M. Razin (Eds.), *Effective psychotherapy*. Oxford: Pergamon Press, 1977.

Auerbach, A. H., Luborsky, L., & Johnson, M. Clinicians' predictions of outcome of psychotherapy: A trial of prognostic index. *American Journal of Psychiatry*, 1972, **128**, 830–835.

Cattell, R. B. *Personality and mood by questionnaire*. San Francisco: Jossey-Bass, 1973.

Ciarlo, J. A. Monitoring and analysis of mental health program outcome. *Data Evaluation: A Form for Human Service Decision Makers*. 1977, **4**, 109–114.

Ciarlo, J. A., & Reihman, J. The Denver Community Mental Health Questionnaire: Development of a multi-dimensional program evaluation instrument. In R. D. Coursy et al. (Eds.), *Program evaluation for mental health methods, strategies and participants*. New York: Grune & Stratton, 1977.

Cronbach, L. J., Gleser, G. C., Nanda, H., & Rajaratnam, N. *The dependability of mental measurements*. New York: Wiley, 1972.

Diagnostic and statistical manual for mental disorders (DSM-III). Washington, D.C.: American Psychiatric Association, 1980.

Endicott, J., & Spitzer, R. L. Current and Past Psychopathology Scales (CAPPS): Rationale, reliability and validity. *Archives of General Psychiatry*, 1972, **27**, 678–687. (a)

Endicott, J., & Spitzer, R. L. What! Another rating scale? The Psychiatric Evaluation Form. *Journal of Nervous and Mental Disease*, 1972, **154**, 88–104. (b)

Endicott, J., & Spitzer, R. L. A diagnostic interview—The Schedule for Affective Disorders and Schizophrenia. *Archives of General Psychiatry*, 1978, **35**, 837–844.

Endicott, J., Spitzer, R. L., Fleiss, J. L., & Cohen, J. The Global Assessment Scale—A procedure for measuring overall severity of psychiatric disturbance. *Archives of General Psychiatry*, 1976, **33**, 766–771.

Glueck, B. C., Meehl, P. E., Schofield, W., & Clyde, D. W. *Minnesota-Hartford Personality Assay*. Hartford, Conn.: Traucom, Inc., 1964.

Guilford, J. P. *Psychometric methods* (2nd ed.). New York: McGraw-Hill, 1954.

Gurland, B. J., Yorkston, N. J., Stone, A. R., Frank, J. D., & Fleiss, J. L. The Structured and Scaled Interview to Assess Maladjustment (SSIAM) I. Description, rationale, and development. *Archives of General Psychiatry*, 1972, **27**, 259–263.

Gurland, B. J., Yorkston, N. J., Goldberg, K., Fleiss, J. L., Sloane, R. B., & Cristol, A. H. The Structured and Scaled Interview to Assess Maladjustment (SSIAM) II. Factor analysis, reliability and validity. *Archives of General Psychiatry*, 1972, **27**, 264–267.

Holt, R. R. Assessing personality. In I. L. Janis, G. F. Mahl, J. Kagan, & R. R. Holt, (Eds.), *Personality: Dynamics, development and assessment:* New York: Harcourt, Brace, & World, 1969.

Holt, R. R. *Methods in clinical psychology.* New York: Plenum Press, 1978.

Horwitz, L. *Clinical prediction in psychotherapy.* New York: Jason Aronson, 1974.

Kernberg, O. F., Burstein, E. D., Coyne, L., Applebaum, A., Horwitz, L., & Voth, H. Psychotherapy and psychoanalysis—Final report of the Menninger Foundations' psychotherapy research project. *Bulletin of the Menninger Clinic,* 1972, **36**, 1–276.

Klerman, G. L., DiMascio, A., Weissman, M. M., Prusoff, B., & Paykel, E. S. Treatment of depression by drugs and psychotherapy. *American Journal of Psychiatry,* 1974, **131**, 186–191.

Luborsky, L. Clinicians' judgments of mental health: A proposed scale. *Archives of General Psychiatry,* 1962, **7**, 407–417.

Luborsky, L., & Bachrach, H. Factors influencing clinicians' judgments of mental health—Eighteen experiences with the Health-Sickness Rating Scale. *Archives of General Psychiatry,* 1974, **31**, 292–299.

Luborsky, L., Mintz, J., Auerbach, A., Cristoph, P., Bachrach, H., Todd, T., Johnson, M., Cohen, M., & O'Brien, C. P. Predicting the outcome of psychotherapy—Findings of the Penn Psychotherapy Project. *Archives of General Psychiatry,* 1980, **37**, 471–481.

Luborsky, L., Singer, B., & Luborsky, L. Comparative studies of psychotherapies: Is it true that "Everyone has won and all must have prizes"? *Archives of General Psychiatry,* 1975, **32**, 995–1008.

Meehl, P. E. *Clinical versus statistical predictions.* Minneapolis: University of Minnesota Press, 1954.

Overall, J. E., & Gorham, D. R. Brief psychiatric rating scale. *Psychological Reports,* 1962, **10**, 799–812.

Parloff, M. B., Kelman, H. C., & Frank, J. D. Comfort, effectiveness, and self-awareness as criteria of improvement in psychotherapy. *American Journal of Psychiatry,* 1954, **111**, 343–351.

Parloff, M. B., Waskow, I. E., & Wolfe, B. E. Research on therapist variables in relation to process and outcome. In S. L. Garfield & A. E. Bergin (Eds.), *Handbook of psychotherapy and behavior change* (2nd ed.). New York: Wiley, 1978.

Paykel, E. S., Klerman, G. L., & Prusoff, B. A. Treatment setting and clinical depression. *Archives of General Psychiatry,* 1970, **22**, 11–21.

Paykel, E. S., Weissman, M., Prusoff, B. A., & Tonks, C. M. Dimensions of social adjustment in depressed women. *Journal of Nervous and Mental Disease,* 1971, **152**, 158–172.

Platt, S. Social adjustment as a criterion of treatment success: Just what are we measuring? *Psychiatry,* 1981, **44**, 95–110.

Sarbin, T. R., Taft, R., & Bailey, D. E. *Clinical interference and cognitive theory.* New York: Holt, Rinehart and Winston, 1960.

Sargent, H. D. The psychotherapy research project of the Menninger Foundation: II. Rationale. *Bulletin of the Menninger Clinic,* 1956, **20**, 226–233.

Sloane, R. B., Staples, F. R., Cristol, A. H., Yorkston, N. J., & Whipple, K. *Psychotherapy versus behavior therapy.* Cambridge, Mass.: Harvard University Press, 1975.

Smith, M. L., Glass, G. V., & Miller, M. I. *The benefits of psychotherapy*. Baltimore: Johns Hopkins Press, 1980.

Spitzer, R. L., & Endicott, J. Psychiatric rating scales. In A. M. Freedman, H. I. Kaplan, & B. J. Sadock (Eds.), *Modern synopsis of comprehensive textbook of psychiatry*. Baltimore: Waverly Press, 1975.

Spitzer, R. L., Endicott, J., Fleiss, J. L., & Cohen, J. The Psychiatric Status Schedule: A technique for evaluating psychopathology and impairment in functioning. *Archives of General Psychiatry*, 1970, **23**, 41–55.

Spitzer, R. L., Endicott, J., & Robins, E. Research Diagnostic Criteria: Rationale and reliability. *Archives of General Psychiatry*, 1978, **35**, 773–782.

Strupp, H. H., Fox, R. E., & Lessler, K. *Patients' view of their psychotherapy*. Baltimore: John Hopkins Press, 1969.

Strupp, H. H., & Hadley, S. W. Specific vs. non-specific factors in psychotherapy—A controlled study of outcome. *Archives of General Psychiatry*, 1979, **36**, 1125–1136.

Waskow, I. E., & Parloff, M. B. (Eds.). *Psychotherapy change measures*. Rockville, Md.: NIMH, 1975.

Weissman, M. M., & Bothwell, S. Assessment of social adjustment by patient self-report. *Archives of General Psychiatry*, 1976, **33**, 1111–1115.

Weissman, M. M., & Paykel, E. S. *The depressed woman: A study of social relationships*. Chicago: The University of Chicago Press, 1974.

Weissman, M. M., & Shalomskas, D. The assessment of social adjustment by the clinician, the patient, and the family. In E. Burdock, W. Sudilonsky, & S. Gershon (Eds.). *Quantitative techniques for the evaluation of the behavior of psychiatric patients*. New York: Marcel Dekker, Inc., in press.

Weissman, M. M., Paykel, E. S., Seigel, R., & Klerman, G. L. The social role performance of depressed women: A comparison with a normal sample. *American Journal of Orthopsychiatry*, 1971, **41**, 390–405.

Weissman, M. M., Klerman, G. L., Paykel, E. S., Prusoff, B., & Hanson, B. Treatment effects on the social adjustment of depressed patients. *Archives of General Psychiatry*, 1974, **30**, 771–778.

Weissman, M. M., Prusoff, B., DiMascio, A., Neu, C., Goklaney, M., & Klerman, G. L. The efficacy of drugs and psychotherapy in the treatment of acute depressive episodes. *American Journal of Psychiatry*, 1979, **136**, 555–558.

Weissman, M. M., Klerman, G. L., Prusoff, B. A., Sholomskas, D., & Padian, M. S. Depressed outpatients—Results one year after treatment with drugs and/or interpersonal psychotherapy. *Archives of General Psychiatry*, 1981, **38**, 51–55.(a)

Weissman, M. M., Sholomskas, D., & John, K. The assessment of social adjustment. *Archives of General Psychiatry*, 1981, **38**, 1250–1258.(b)

Wiggins, J. S. *Personality and prediction: Principles of personality assessment*. Reading, Mass: Addison-Wesley, 1973.

CHAPTER 16

The Significant Other
as Data Source
and Data Problem in
Psychotherapy Outcome Research

CHRISTINE V. DAVIDSON AND RONALD H. DAVIDSON

The methodological traditions of the social and behavioral sciences are replete with instances of the use of significant others, whether they be anthropological or sociological "informants," historical "sources," or relatives or friends of the"subjects" in clinical or social psychological studies. Inasmuch as significant others may offer researchers a means of triangulating their own observations and subjects' self-reports with a third perspective, one based on first-hand knowledge of the subjects' real-world functioning and behavior, their utility as a fundamental data source for the study of human behavior would seem to be readily apparent. Generally speaking, the concept of the significant other as used in the social and behavioral sciences is taken to mean any individual— parent figure or surrogate, spouse, sibling, child, or other relative, peer, or friend—possessing pertinent information about the subject based on a history of relationship to, and/or interaction with, that person. It is further assumed that the significant other, because of his real-world involvement with the subject, has access to ecologically valid data that might ordinarily go unreported were the investigator to exclude this data source from his study. The operational assumption, therefore, is that the information derived from the use of significant others is of an order different from that yielded by the subject's self-report, expert opinion (e.g., therapist or teacher ratings) or the investigator's own observations.

Although such third-party perspectives offer numerous conceptual and methodological attractions to researchers, it must also be acknowledged that the information subsequently derived from these sources, as well as the process of information gathering itself, is apt to present the investigator with a variety of frequently hidden or half-understood obstacles. Erikson (1969), for example, in describing his psychohistorical reconstruction of the life of Gandhi, pointed to a number of such difficulties as he attempted to rely on interviews with former followers of the Mahatma:

> The psychoanalyst-turned-historian, then, must adapt himself to and learn to utilize a new array of "resistances" before he can confidently know that he is encountering those he is accustomed to. There is, first of all, the often incredible or implausible claim to having lost memorabilia—a claim which can be variably attributed to simple carelessness on the part of witnesses, or to a lack of aware-ness, or, indeed, an absence of candor. Deeper difficulties, however, range from an almost cognitively a-historical orientation—ascribed by some to Indians in general—to a highly idiosyncratic reluctance to lose the past by formulating it. . . . There are those whose lives became part of their leader's and who therefore had to incorporate him into their self-image. They must consider his image as well as their own an invested possession to be shared only according to custom and religion, personal style—and stage of life. Here it becomes especially clear that a man in the wake of great events will want to divest himself of his past only in order to cure, to purify, or to sell himself; wherefore the psycho-historian may do well to clarify his informant's general purpose—as well as his own. (pp. 66 – 67)

Taking Erikson's cogent example as a point of departure, the task of this chapter will be to examine those aspects of the research agenda of the psycho-therapy investigator where information obtained from patients' significant others may be relied on with confidence while nevertheless keeping in mind some of the inherent conceptual and methodological caveats regarding the use of this particular data source. In the course of this discussion, representative research in which the perspective of the signficant other was ascertained is examined, and some extant measures that may be useful for tapping that vantage point are also discussed.

THE SIGNIFICANT OTHER AS DATA SOURCE

The Unique Perspective of the Significant Other

It has by now become a commonplace conclusion among psychotherapy re-searchers that treatment-induced outcome effects must be examined in a multidimensional framework, taking into account the necessity for multiple criterion measures capable of gauging both the patient's internal state and outward functioning (Bergin, 1971; Bergin & Lambert, 1978). In addressing this issue, Strupp and Hadley (1977) have proposed a "tripartite model of mental health" for assessing psychotherapy outcome that attempts to more explicitly utilize the separate vantage points and values of all those who are in a position to judge mental health and therapy-induced change. Their model goes beyond the therapeutic dyad of the patient and the mental health professional to incorporate those representatives of society (including, but not limited to, significant persons in the patient's life) who have a stake in the outcome. Recognizing that "society is primarily concerned with the maintenance of social relations, institutions . . . , behavioral stability, predictability, and conformity to the social code" (p. 188), Strupp and Hadley reiterate the conceptual necessity of "considering fully and simultaneously the multiple values that may be brought to bear" (p. 191) on the issue of the subject's posttreatment status. Where the individual may be judged by others according to his ability to fulfill social expectations, the criteria that he applies for evaluating his own sense of well-being are understandably more egoistic, generally relying more on the goals of an increase in personal gratification and self-esteem, as well as a diminution of discomfort for oneself, than on an altruistic concern for these needs in others. Since the mental health professional tends to operate within a framework of dual loyalty to the individual patient and (at least certain minimal) social values, it is not surprising that most practitioners supplement their formulations regarding the individual with additional criteria based on social adaptation. Ultimately, however, the mental health professional's point of reference to a highly structured theoretical model of personality and behavior "may on occasion result in a diagnosis of mental health or pathology at variance with the opinion of society and/or the individual" (p. 189).

Apart from their divergent criteria for evaluating mental health and treatment outcome, these three "interested parties" clearly apply wholly different procedures for measuring their sometimes conflicting desiderata. In this sense, the patient's subjective perceptions form the data base for his self-reports and his relationship to external reality. These same subjective perceptions are also taken into consideration by the clinician and examined in the light of his presumably more objective measurement armamentarium, including structured behavioral observations and psychological tests; at the societal level (the domain of the significant other) the measurement of the patient's functioning is accomplished by reference to a range of observations and experiences of his behavior, especially the degree to which he meets his obligation to the social contract.

In outlining the research implications of these divergent perspectives on mental health, Strupp and Hadley's tripartite model provides a framework for examining the patient's functioning according to the level of agreement between the three interested parties. The possible outcomes thus range from total agreement at either end of the continuum (i.e., all parties agree that the person is either healthy or crazy) to every conceivable variation in between. For example, the significant others may judge the subject's behavior to be troubling, but the person's sense of well-being is experienced as intact and his personality is judged sound by the clinician, a situation not unlike that of many adolescents attempting to differentiate from family by adopting a temporarily rebellious life-style. On the other hand, a marginally integrated individual with a borderline personality disorder may be identified by a clinician as having certain impaired ego functions and poor coping mechanisms, although experience himself, and be experienced by his family, as not in need of mental health treatment. With respect to this tripartite frame of reference, therefore, each vantage point, whether objectively "true" or not, must be accorded a certain validity as an empirical indicator about the state of the subject.

In short, Strupp and Hadley's marching orders for psychotherapy researchers underscore the critical importance of evaluating and integrating all three facets of the tripartite model of functioning—behavior, affect, and inferred psychological structure. Equally importantly, they insist that "assessments of therapy outcome must be based whenever possible on standardized, generally accepted criteria of 'good functioning' in each of the three areas," and they draw our attention to the fact that "failure to implement these principles can only mean a continued proliferation of scattered pieces of knowledge that cannot be fitted into an integrated understanding of whether psychotherapy has any effects—either for good or ill—and how these effects are achieved" (p. 196).

Professional Accountability and Societal Criteria for Evaluating Psychotherapy Outcome

As controversy has raged over the "effectiveness" or "ineffectiveness" of psychotherapy in general (Bergin, 1971; Bergin & Lambert, 1978; Eysenck, 1952; Luborsky et al., 1975; Meltzoff & Kornreich, 1970), clinical researchers have been increasingly concerned with the importance of avoiding the design, implementation, and inferential flaws that handicapped previous work. The fact that the future of psychotherapy itself, to say nothing of psychotherapy research, has been called into question by the policy decisions of government funding agencies and third-party insurers has not been lost on the research community (Parloff, 1979). This situation has added a certain pragmatic urgency to the interests psychotherapy researchers had in attending to the perspective of the significant other in the first place. Since, as Parloff notes, "we can no longer be confident that our papers will be read only by fellow researchers" (p. 296), clinical investigators are confronted with the problem of not only "safeguarding" their tentative results from misinterpretation or misappropriation, but of finding ways to adapt themselves and their methods to address the legitimate concerns of these new colleagues. Insofar as the level of inquiry will undoubtedly tend to be phrased in societal terms—which is to say, with regard to social behavior and prevailing standards of conduct—then researchers may find that the most appropriate methodological response for measuring clinical outcome is one that offers a complementary framework for balancing these competing claims. From the standpoint of the social and institutional claim on the psychotherapeutic enterprise, the information provided by the patient's significant others is often of a value at least equal to that provided by the therapist (or other expert judge) or the patient himself.

Indications for Use with Specific Patient Populations

Without a doubt, certain clinical populations lend themselves more readily than others to inclusion of the perspective of the significant other, particularly, for example, in such areas where the patient is unable to comply with self-report measures because of a disabling level of psychopathology (i.e., the individual is overtly delusional, too disturbed to understand the nature of the questions, or openly seeks to falsify his responses) (Prusoff et al., 1972; Spitzer & Endicott, 1973; Weissman, 1975). The significant other's reports can also contribute in cases where there is other severe impairment, such as mental retardation or an organic mental disorder, including neurological damage, toxic states, or senium or presenium dementias (Kellett et al., 1975); in situations where the patient is too young to comprehend the nature of the presenting problem (and, in fact, is generally presented for evaluation by a significant other) (Achenbach, 1978; Barrett et al., 1978); and in those instances where the treatment regimen is interpersonally focused and requires the paticipation of the significant other (i.e., marital or family therapy) (Gurman & Kniskern, 1981).

The utility of gathering data from significant others in cases where the patient is psychotic seems rather straightforward and is, in fact, a fairly routine procedure in clinical practice. From the vantage point of the psychotherapy researcher, information from the significant others of psychotic patients is of particular value as it bears on psychosocial adaptation in the community, which is normally a major therapeutic goal in work with these patients. Similarly, information collected from significant others could also prove useful in those instances where certain patient populations are known to be characteristically unreliable informants about their behavior and external social adaptation or where there is a tendency to produce actual "disinformation" (e.g., juvenile delinquents and certain other adolescent populations, antisocial personalities). Thus data from family members in one study revealed manic symptoms not reported by the patients themselves, "especially so for excessive or inappropriate activities" (Braden et al., 1980, p. 226). In treatment studies of alcoholism, drug dependence, and cigarette smoking, behavior therapists have often called on significant others to corroborate subjects' self-reports of abstinence, since the validity of the latter has often been questioned with these populations (Maisto et al., 1979; McFall, 1978; Nathan & Lansky, 1978). Furthermore, asking patients' relatives and friends for information about life events can both quantitatively and qualitatively supplement the data base concerning the subjects' recent experiences and situational stressors (Schless & Mendels, 1978; Yager et al., 1981).

With respect to assessing children's "pathologies and competencies and measuring change in them," Achenbach (1978) argues that "the more diverse the sources of data (parents, teachers, peers, clinicians, self-reports) and the greater the focus on important life situations, the more useful such procedures are likely to be" (p. 773). Additionally, if we can assume that, in marital and family therapy, "a higher level of positive change has occurred when improvement is evidenced in systematic (total family) or relationship (dyadic) interactions than when it is evidenced in individuals alone" (Gurman & Kniskern, 1981, p. 765), then this, in itself, is a compelling enough reason for tapping family members' perceptions of one another as part of a standard outcome battery.

THE SIGNIFICANT OTHER AS DATA PROBLEM

Having considered the obvious conceptual and methodological assets that can accrue from the use of significant others as data sources, the investigator must also take into account a number of potential problems both at the level of data collection and with regard to the interpretation of the resultant data.

Availability, Cooperativeness, and Motivation of Significant Others in Providing Information

It may perhaps seem too elementary to remark, but the first consideration for engaging in data gathering from significant others ought to be a preliminary determination as to whether, for the particular patient population in question, there are indeed likely to exist cooperative and knowledgeable significant others in sufficient number to ensure reasonable feasibility for this mode of data collection. Two major factors must be kept in mind here: (1) that patients whose immediate social environment includes certain categories of significant others (e.g., patients who are married or who live in family settings) are likely to differ in various ways from those patients whose attachments to such significant others—whether because of geographic or emotional distance—are more tenuous (Clausen, 1972); and (2) even when a prospective pool of friends or relatives is available to the investigator, a further source of unknown bias lies in the likely differences between those significant others who are motivated to cooperate readily versus those who resist or refuse to participate—that is, the magnitude and direction of bias resulting from data drawn only from cooperating significant others needs to be ascertained (Mendlewicz et al., 1975).

With regard to the question of simple availability of significant others, Clausen (1972), in a review of methodological and conceptual problems in studies of community tenure of former mental patients, noted some examples in which the sampling of significant others was probably biased, so that data derived from their reports are probably of limited generalizability. In one study, for example, there was apparently some difficulty persuading the families of patients to accept them back home or persuading patients who had lived independently to return home. In these cases, arrangements for the patient to live at home for the duration of the study were contrived solely for the purpose of the research (Pasamanick et al., 1967), thereby raising the issue of whether reports from these family members can be said to be a genuine and knowledgeable representation of the patient's functioning. From a similar perspective, Clausen (1972) suggested "another instance where the use of a design requiring a significant other restricts the population studied . . .," noting that, "former patients who are psychologically dependent or compliant are likely to be over-represented" (p. 25).

Turning to another patient population, depressed women, Weissman and her colleagues chose not to use significant others' reports as a means of obtaining data on social adjustment, but to rely instead on patients' self-reports. This decision was related to two issues that commonly arise when considering significant others as a data source. Reliable informants for certain types of patients—in this case, unmarried, older women or women with "nonperceptive or hostile" spouses—would have been difficult to obtain. In addition, subjects were found to be "reluctant to have their spouses interviewed" (Weissman et al., 1974, p. 776).

We have already alluded to the question of the informant's motivations for supplying data concerning the patient's functioning. To elaborate further, the very reason that makes significant others so attractive a data source—their day-to-day proximity to and intimate relationship with the patient—also introduces a certain degree of contamination in their responses since their investment in the patient is more likely than not to be highly affectively charged, a situation not particularly suited to yielding reliable or unbiased reports. Data from significant others may be colored by a variety of biases in perception or reporting, including defensiveness, social desirability, projection, and negative labeling, to name only a few; in some cases, outright psychiatric disturbance in the respondent himself may render his observations of the subject invalid. To illustrate, the parents of a severely conduct-disordered child might defensively present his behavior as "mere rebelliousness" or, in more extreme instances, as an adequate and necessary self-protective response to a hostile peer environment. Generations of social caseworkers and juvenile authorities would probably bear witness to the questionable nature of reports based primarily on the perceptions of parents or other family network informants. Clearly, such motivational and perceptual factors skew not only the results of initial pre-treatment evaluations, but the posttreatment outcome and long-term follow-up findings as well. Indeed, Ross (1978) has commented that "investigators have repeatedly found that parents tend to evaluate treatment outcome more positively than either the therapists (O'Leary et al., 1973) or independent observers (Eyberg & Johnson, 1974; Patterson, 1974)" (p. 614). In the same vein, the collective folklore from the family therapy literature reiterates the well-known tendency of certain family systems to continue the stigmatization of the "identifiably" disturbed member as a means of preserving the unit's functioning. This complex of motivational and perceptual issues surrounding the reporting behavior of significant others must by systematically examined not only from the standpoint of their perspective on the patient, but also in terms of their own self-perceptions and self-presentations, all of which may otherwise eventually find their way into the investigator's data bank.

In sum, then, these examples illustrate rather clearly our earlier comments that many patient populations either cannot be expected to have available significant others or, if they do, that the data supplied by these informants often raise a host of unintended interpretive dilemmas. Such sampling restrictions will continue to be seen as a major stumbling block to the use of significant others as we proceed with this discussion.

Somewhat less obvious, although equally critical, is the necessity of tailoring the recruitment procedures and data collection procedures to the unique characteristics of the target informants. In large sample studies where the investigator must rely on mailed questionnaires, for example, as opposed to more individualized or socially intimate data collection procedures, it is important to be able to compensate for the loss of the ability to conduct face-to-face "checks" on the informant's capacity to simply understand what he or she is being asked to provide. This particular issue would certainly arise in studies involving some ethnic or minority populations where, on the one hand, language or reading skills might be limited, and, on the other hand, strong cultural proscriptions may exist regarding communication beyond the family or small group network. Thus any Census Bureau interviewer might readily attest to the doubtful feasibility of asking certain types of questions in particular neighborhoods (e.g., "tell me the names of the members of your household," might be considered an imprudent issue to raise in, say, a barrio in East Los Angeles known to have a high density of illegal immigrants). Perhaps one of the more ingenious methods of overcoming potential community/cultural resistance that we have encountered was devised by an anthropologist colleague of ours who was studying personality developent in rural Thailand, a technique that involved having the abbot of the local Buddhist monastery select by lottery those villagers who would be asked to be informants for the curious American professor (Phillips, 1970).

Language and cultural barriers, however, are generally less problematic in most studies than are issues regarding the ability of significant others to adequately and reliably make the sort of higher-order generalizations about the patient's behavior that may be required by the investigator. Commenting on this problem, McFall (1978) has suggested that "it may be useful to distinguish between differences in accuracy as a function of the type of data being collected," noting that in smoking cessation research, for example, "it probably would be easier for a collaborator to report accurately on a subject's abstinence than on the subject's smoking rate" (p. 707). Along the same lines, one might expect to be able to gather accurate data on "how many times" Mrs. Smith has taken an overdose, although family members might have considerable difficulty estimating her "level of depression," if, in fact, they even perceived her to be depressed. The situation is complicated all the more where, as is often the case, the clinical phenomena in question are more "elusive" or where, as mentioned earlier, a certain degree of anxiety or defensiveness might be expected to arise in response to the investigator's queries.

To recapitulate, briefly, we have outlined some of the preliminary factors to be evaluated whenever the use of significant others as potential data sources is contemplated in psychotherapy outcome research. These include (1) the likely existence and availability of relevant significant others, (2) the probable motivational or other situational biases of the informants and how these are likely to affect the data, (3) the appropriateness of the data collection instruments for the target informants with respect to language difficulty, cultural fit, and level of inference required of the informant, and (4) the informant's knowledge base concerning the patient, especially with regard to the type of information sought by the researcher. Considerable methodological and conceptual criteria for the use of significant other informants have been suggested by researchers in the area of social network analysis, and we return to this important topic later in the chapter.

Ethical and Human Subject Considerations

Among the most important concerns in research incorporating significant others, the investigator is confronted with a special obligation to all participants in the study, patient and informant alike, within the guidelines laid down by generally accepted human subjects procedures, and these restrictions may further narrow the design and the implementation of the data collection plan. Although the clinical research contract regarding confidentiality and other standards of professional conduct originates in the patient—therapist—investigator relationship, it by no means ends there since the significant other—investigator relationship is fraught with the same types of human subject risk, requiring that the significant others be fully informed as to the purpose of the research, the identity and the institutional affiliation of the investigator, and the steps that will be taken to safeguard their disclosures. At the same time, just as is routinely done with the patient, significant others must be apprised of any potentially harmful effects they may experience from cooperating with the research procedures, such as temporary increase in anxiety or embarrassment as they discuss the patient's behavior, and their relationship to the patient, with a stranger. In those instances in which the patient or others (e.g., therapist, social agencies, or legal authorities) may have access to the research materials, the significant other informants must clearly be notified of this in advance of their participation.

Showstack et al. (1978), in a study examining the relative effectiveness of short- versus long-term hospitalization with follow-up data collections at one and two years postadmission, commented directly on many of these issues. Noting the differential investment of each of their three sources of information (the patient, a significant other, and the clinician treating the patient at the time of follow-up), they suggested that "under ideal circumstances one should have not only each party's own consent to provide information, but each party's consent to contact the other two" (p. 41). The patient's permission to contact the informants was renewed at each follow-up point, so that an informant's name would be removed if the patient so wished. An additional area of concern related to the recent Freedom of Information Act, whereby under certain circumstances the patient would have the right to have access to any materials gathered about him. This was felt to raise the question of whether patient and informants should be advised of the patient's potential legal right to obtain the data; given this sensitive problem area, it was recommended that this information about disclosure be included in the written consent form.

Finally, a single remaining ethical issue may make all the above moot: namely, that the patient himself may not give permission to the investigator to gather data about him from his significant others, as in those instances where the patient simply may not want his friends and relatives to be aware of the fact that he is a patient. Here the investigator must exercise considerable professional judgment and restraint, balancing off his natural enthusiasm for completing a solid research task with the more important necessity of maintaining his independent ethical responsibilities to his subjects.

The Problem of Consensus

In commenting on Strupp and Hadley's (1977) tripartite model for evaluating psychotherapy outcome, Garfield (1980) raised the thorny issue of *who* will serve as referee when the interested parties—patient, clinician, and society— are at odds in their assessments, in short, "if the three modes of evaluation are discrepant, what kinds of judgment concerning the effectiveness of psychotherapy can be made?" Apart from the relative merits of a tripartite or multisource scheme of evaluation, Garfield underscores the point that such approaches "call into question the limitations of relying on a single source for data on outcome" and emphasizes the importance of systematically investigating "the basis for the differences among different sources of outcome evaluation" (p. 251).

In fact, a number of investigators have examined the degree of divergence of multisource outcome assessments, noting especially the ambiguous findings that contribute to somewhat equivocal interpretations regarding the presence or absence of patterns of agreement among sources. Although this body of research addresses the general issue with which we are concerned here—the degree of agreement among different parties in their evaluations of treatment efficacy—none of these major studies, however, actually included the perspective of the significant other. Garfield et al. (1971), for example, reported that they obtained "modest" intercorrelations ($r = .35$ to .44) among client, therapist, and supervisor global ratings of improvement but found that although both therapists and clients rated 80% of the clients as improved, the supervisors judged only 56% as improved. Commenting elsewhere on this study, they interpreted these findings as providing "more evidence for observer disagreement than observer agreement" (Garfield et al., 1974, p. 296). Other investigators have interpreted these same data as suggesting some consensus, albeit an understandably limited amount given the unique perspectives of the sources. Luborsky (1971) thus commented that, "considering the unreliability of (these

types of) single item ratings, the amount of the interrelationship among different criteria is not to be dismissed as slight" and further observed that "rotation
of their factor matrix showed patient, therapist, and supervisor ratings of
change loading the same factor" (p. 316). Leve (1974) likewise interpreted the
Garfield et al. data as indicating "substantial agreement" (p. 293).

The Garfield et al. study is one of several seminal investigations pertaining
to the issue of consensus among measures of treatment outcome (these studies
including Berzins et al., 1975; Cartwright et al., 1963; Green et al., 1975; Harty
& Horwitz, 1976; Mintz et al., 1979) and process (Mintz et al., 1973). Perhaps
the most generally held conclusion about the issue of intersource consensus is
that the amount of agreement is not substantial, a conclusion that Mintz and his
colleagues (Mintz et al., 1979) have challenged in their analysis of outcome
data from the Penn Psychotherapy Project and their reanalysis of the often
cited University of Chicago study data, reported in Cartwright et al. (1963).
Mintz et al. (1979) found that "relationships among similarly defined and
highly reliable measures of outcome across sources were substantial, and
conceptually meaningful composites with high reliability could be constructed." However, their data also demonstrated that "distinct viewpoints *do*
exist." To summarize their conclusions:

> That unique viewpoints exist is indisputable. But the correlations found in both
> the Penn Psychotherapy Project and the University of Chicago data were in the
> area of .5 and .6. Surely this represents substantial commonality of judgment
> concerning status and outcome. Berzins et al. (1975) have stressed the impor-
> tance of this consensus for establishing a foundation on which to base scientific
> evaluation of treatment outcome as well as ethical accountability of practitioners.
> (p. 331)

Returning to our specific concern with significant others as sources of
treatment evaluation data, it would appear reasonable to expect that their view
of the patient would be unique and hence somewhat different from that of the
patient, the therapist, or the independent clinical rater. This is not to imply that
the significant other would necessarily render opinions that are at odds with
those of the other parties, but only to suggest that he or she would contribute
complementary information based on a qualitatively different level of experience with the patient. Fiske (1975a), in an article cogently entitled "A Source
of Data is Not a Measuring Instrument," reminds us that sources of data in
psychotherapy research are "active agents in personality measurement" (p. 22)
with different capacities and dispositions as well as unique role relationships to
the patient. Although there are ways to increase agreement among sources—
such as asking for information about observable, concrete behavior as opposed
to opinions or judgment data that require higher-order inferences, minimizing
methods factors, and so forth—full consensus should not be expected. That is:

> a source of data yields observations from a distinctive role providing distinctive
> experience. When an observer representing a source makes judgments about the

complex variables of interest to current psychotherapeutic theory, he is actively processing his own experience. His observations may agree fairly well with parallel observers representing that source, but will not agree as well with observers from other sources. Nearly exact agreement can be obtained only from inanimate measuring instruments or from observers functioning like instruments. (p. 20)

This still, of course, leaves the investigator with the dilemma of how to most appropriately integrate the separate evaluations of the interested parties. Strupp and Hadley (1977) propose, and we agree, that "in the final analysis, this is an issue of human values and public policy, not of empirical research" (p. 196). Equally important for psychotherapy researchers to keep in mind, however, is that investigations aimed at systematically examining "the basis for the *differences* among *different* sources of outcome evaluation" [Garfield (1980, p. 251); italics ours] may prove more instructive in their own way than those that only address the issue of consensus per se. To be sure, although we found several calls in the literature for the study of perceptual and motivational factors that may affect significant others' evaluations, and even scattered pieces of data concerning consensus among sources (some of which are reviewed in the sections to follow on measures), the sort of systematic and concerted effort that is needed here has yet to be attempted.

Additional Problems in Data Collection and Interpretation

Not the least of the considerations that must be taken into account when the use of significant other informants is contemplated are the actual costs, in time as well as in research funds, incurred by what amounts to at least a doubling of one's sources—the patient and one or more of his significant others. Thus, when one calculates the time and funds expended in travel for home visits, telephone, and mail contacts, and especially in tracking informants to ensure an adequate rate of response for long-term follow-up—not to mention the vital necessity of maintaining a pool of well-trained interviewers to gather these data—the costs of this type of data collection may begin to look prohibitive for all but the most well-connected investigators. Fiske (1975b) has recommended that, whenever feasible, data should be obtained from at least two informants per patient, a refinement that would certainly allow for a closer examination of the motivational and relationship variables that may affect relative's reports about the patient's functioning, although again inflating the data collection burden and expense for the investigator.

Recalling our earlier discussion of the indications for the use of significant others with specific patient populations, it bears reiterating that this data collection strategy may not be appropriate, desirable, or even allowable with certain patient categories or therapeutic modalities. To illustrate, whereas one might not hesitate to ask the significant other of (an otherwise high-functioning) patient to corroborate the effects of short-term smoking-cessation treatment, an entirely different order of problems would arise in contacting these same informants for psychotherapy outcome data were the patient in intensive psychoanalysis, for example. This caveat applies to high-functioning patient populations in general, however, since available measures of social adjustment may not be phrased in such a manner as to capture changes relevant at their level. Where the aims of treatment with such populations tend to be oriented toward internal processes, feeling states, and higher-level life goals, neither the content nor the direction of social adjustment measures are pertinent and self-report instruments would, in fact, be more germane to the task of evaluating treatment efficacy. As has been documented elsewhere (Weissman et al., 1974), some patients will simply object to their relatives being involved in any phase of the treatment process or follow-up; patients frankly do not always care to have it known that they have been in psychotherapy for any reason, and these wishes must be respected by the investigator.

When interpreting the data derived from significant others' reports, it must also be kept in mind that these appraisals are likely to be vulnerable to an unknown range of expectancies that relatives may have concerning the probably impact of treatment on the target patient, since the informant would not likely be "blind" to the general fact that the patient had been in treatment (Fiske, 1975b), although in comparative outcome studies, the informant may not always be fully cognizant of the actual treatment condition. Finally, with regard to the issue of multiple data collection points (such as before and after therapy), Fiske has underscored the importance of making sure that the data are drawn from the same informant at both times, a factor that must be especially considered in collecting information by mail questionnaires. Likewise, in terms of being able to derive fullest meaning from the data, it is particularly imperative that the category of significant other chosen for inclusion in a study be consistent across subjects, in terms of either structural (e.g., parent, spouse, friend) or functional (e.g., expressive, supportive, or instrumental) relationship to the patient.

Having raised a number of methodological problems and limitations that might understandably give pause to an investigator in the planning stage of a new treatment outcome study, let us now attempt to revitalize the reader's interest in the appropriate use of significant others as data sources by examining the range of measures that have been developed in this area. It should be noted that we have not included here measures of outcome directed primarily at children, since we considered this topic to involve a host of conceptual and methodological issues (Achenbach, 1978; Weissman et al., 1980) that are beyond the scope of the present discussion, although the reader will recognize that many of the topics related to measures in adult treatment outcome research are equally pertinent for children's studies as well.

MEASURES

By and large, most of the instruments that have been developed for administration to significant others of adult patients have been oriented toward gauging social and community adjustment. These measures have attempted to assess not only symptomatic behavior, but performance in a general range of social roles, including employment, homemaking activities, management of money, use of recreational time, participation in interpersonal relationships, and other aspects of daily life thought to reflect on the nature of psychotherapeutic outcome. Some of the scales have also attempted to tap the informant's expectations concerning the patient's behavior and role performance as well as the situational and emotional impact of the patient's problems on the informant. In addition to the present chapter, several comprehensive review articles (Fiske, 1975b; Hogarty, 1975; Weissman, 1975; Weissman et al., 1981) in this area should provide the prospective investigator a well-grounded basis for selecting an appropriate instrument.

The Katz Adjustment Scale—Relative's Form

The most widely used and reported measure is the Katz Adjustment Scale—Relative's Form (KAS-R), developed nearly 20 years ago as a means of "describing and classifying patients in accordance with their behavior prior to entrance to the hospital and in the community follow-up evaluation and comparison of psychiatric treatments" (Katz & Lyerly, 1963, p. 503). It is instructive to note that the KAS-R was recommended for inclusion in the Core Battery generated by the NIMH Outcome Measures Project (Waskow & Parloff, 1975) and that it is part of the battery for the pilot study of the NIMH Psychotherapy of Depression Collaborative Research Program (Clinical Research Branch, NIMH, 1980).

The scale form is intended to be filled out by a relative, who has had close contact with the patient and who is asked to base the report on the previous three-week period. The KAS-R includes five sections: 127 items intended to tap psychiatric symptoms (e.g., "looks worn out," "says that people are trying to make him do things he doesn't want to do") and social behavior (e.g., "pleasant," "critical of other people"), 16 items intended to tap performance of socially expected activities (e.g., "helps with household chores," "works"), 16 items intended to tap the informant's expectation that the patient would engage in each of these same activities, 23 items intended to tap involvement in common free-time activities (e.g., "watch television," "takes rides"), and 23 items intended to tap the informant's satisfaction with the patient's level of involvement in each of these same free-time activities. The items are rated along Likert-type continua, with the four-point response format for the ratings of symptoms and social behavior, for instance, ranging from "almost never" to "almost always." Items are written in straightforward, everyday language, so that psychiatric jargon is avoided; as far as possible the items refer to concrete, observable behaviors, and are phrased in such a way as to minimize judgmental overtones. The scale should take from 30 minutes to 1 hour for most informants to complete. There is a similar form intended for administration to the patient.

The KAS-R yields several overall scale scores. Thus the 127 ratings of psychiatric symptoms and social behavior generate 13 clusters (belligerence, verbal expansiveness, negativism, helplessness, suspiciousness, anxiety, withdrawal and retardation, general psychopathology, nervousness, confusion, bizarreness, hyperactivity, and stability) and three general factors (social obstreperousness, acute psychoticism, and withdrawal–helplessness). There are also scale scores for performance of socially expected activities, expectations for their performance, involvement in free-time activities, and satisfaction with this involvement; a discrepancy measure indicative of dissatisfaction with expected role performance can also be calculated.

Certainly one of the most compelling reasons to choose this measure is the careful attention that was given to its psychometric development, by general agreement one of the more rigorous histories in this literature of studies of instrument reliability and validity. The preliminary work (Katz & Lyerly, 1963) established that the KAS-R could differentiate between previously hospitalized patients who had been judged by clinician raters to be well- versus poorly adjusted to the community. The item clusters for the measure of psychiatric symptoms and social behavior were derived with a sample of newly hospitalized patients, again primarily schizophrenic, and were found to have adequate internal consistency reliability (ranging from .61 to .87), a finding that was cross-validated with a larger sample of hospitalized acute schizophrenic subjects in the NIMH Collaborative Study of Drugs and Schizophrenia (the range of internal consistency coefficients showing "a slight . . . but consistent drop," p. 529). Intercorrelations among the clusters were stable across the two patient samples. Finally, using the data from the Collaborative Study sample, a factor analysis of the correlations among the clusters was conducted, which yielded the three general factors mentioned above. Thus, on the basis of this initial work, it was concluded that the instrument was "highly discriminative and capable of approximating expert clinical judgment" and that it yielded a "profile of measures of symptomatic and social behavior," with the specific clusters demonstrating "reasonably high internal consistency" and "stable relationships with the other measures in the set" (p. 532). Subsequent research has extended and reinforced these initial data; since the amount of data generated with this scale is voluminous, we discuss only those studies that addressed the most salient psychometric issues.

Crook et al. (1980) examined the interrater reliability of the KAS-R by comparing the responses of mothers and fathers of schizophrenics recently admitted to a psychiatric hospital. They found high agreement on the scales that gauge symptoms and social behaviors, with greater consensus on the measures of more directly observable behaviors (e.g., hyperactivity, $r = .74$; performance of socially expected activities, $r = .85$) than on those that tapped domains requiring more inference on the part of the informant (e.g., nervousness, $r = .33$). As would be expected, agreement on the two scales that basically tap the informant's attitudes—expectation for performance of socially-expected activities and dissatisfaction with expected role performance—was low ($r = .08$ and $.28$, respectively). With the exception of these latter correlations, the interrater reliabilities between the mothers and fathers ranged from .85 to .33, with a mean interrater correlation of .64.

There is suggestive, but as yet limited, evidence that the informant's relationship to the subject may affect scale scores, thereby detracting from interrater reliability. In the context of a field study to establish norms for the KAS-R for nonpatient and patient populations, Hogarty and Katz (1971) found that a group of adolescents who were rated by their mothers were described as less symptomatic than another group of adolescents who were rated by their siblings. Likewise, married women who were rated by their spouses were characterized differently from married women who were rated by nonspouses. A more direct test of the effect of the informant's relationship with the subject on KAS-R scores was made by comparing the ratings of cottage mothers of delinquent adolsecent boys to those of cottage fathers [data cited in Crook et al. (1980)]. The same boys were reported to have more obstreperous behavior by the cottage mothers than by the fathers, it being unclear, however, whether this was an artifact of differential perception of the boys or due to differential behavior on their part toward the mothers and fathers.

The KAS-R has been used in numerous treatment outcome studies (Caffey et al., 1971; Hargreaves et al., 1977; Levene et al., 1970; Schooler et al., 1967). For example, Hogarty et al. (1974) followed the course of nonrelapsed schizophrenic patients at 6, 12, 18, and 24 months after hospital discharge. The patients had been assigned to the following treatment conditions: chlorpromazine plus sociotherapy, drug alone, placebo plus sociotherapy; or placebo only. In addition to the KAS-R, the outcome battery included a variety of instruments completed by the patient and the treating psychiatrist and social worker. The investigators found that, among the drug-treated patients, those who had also received the sociotherapy demonstrated superior adjustment at 18 and 24 months. For our purposes, it is important to note that the data from the patients' significant others converged with those from the other sources. Thus "the effect is observed not only on measures obtained from the physician and social worker, but is also more consistently observed on self-report measures from the patient and on scales completed by the relative" (p. 612).

Other studies (Michaux et al., 1973) have examined the utility of relatives' reports, based on the KAS-R, in predicting response to treatment. Thus Sappington and Michaux (1975) attempted to differentiate between patients who relapsed (i.e., required hospitalization within a year following treatment) and those who did not. There were two subsamples of subjects, a group of patients who had been hospitalized and a group who were in day treatment. All the predictor instruments were administered when the patient began treatment. Relevant to our specific interests, the authors report that, "of the three groups of measures, those based on professional evaluation were least able to distinguish relapsed from nonrelapsed patients. On self-report and relative report measures, the scores of patients who relapse following day-care treatment resemble those of patients who succeed following hospital treatment and vice versa" (p. 904).

The KAS-R has demonstrated the ability to differentiate between target populations, including hospitalized versus day-treatment patients (Hogarty et al., 1968), types of depressed patients (Paykel, 1972), and drivers involved in fatal single or multiple car accidents (relative interview completed post-mortem) versus the general population (estimate based on norms for nonpatients) (Schmidt et al., 1972). It has shown utility in cross-cultural research on mental health (Katz, 1981), and it likewise appears to have applications for epidemiologic surveys of untreated psychiatric illness in the general population (Hogarty et al., 1967). Scores on the KAS-R have shown conceptually meaningful patterns of relationships with psychiatrists' reports of symptomatology (Katz et al., 1967) as well as with nurses' ratings of behavior on a psychiatric ward (Vestre & Zimmerman, 1969).

Even though this measure was developed with prepsychotic and psychotic populations in mind, with much of the initial psychometric study being done on such samples, it has subsequently been applied to a range of patient (Clum, 1976; Paykel, 1972) and nonpatient populations (Schmidt et al., 1972), with satisfactory results. One procedural caveat, nevertheless, should be noted when the KAS-R is being considered for use with other than severely disturbed patients. Some of the items geared toward measuring social behavior (e.g., "dresses and takes care of himself," "helps with family shopping") are clearly of doubtful use with more high-functioning, neurotic outpatient populations (Waskow, 1975), and this issue needs to be taken into account when constructing a battery. With regard to coverage of the range of functioning in certain areas (e.g., work, marital, parental roles) the KAS-R does not provide more than a rudimentary screening, so this, too, may limit its utility for some applications (Weissman, 1975). In addition, the patient self-report form of the KAS battery appears to have much less of a track record (Young & Meltzer, 1980), most reports on this battery having concentrated on the relative form, so that researchers desiring to obtain convergent data from the patient may also wish to choose a well-established self-report scale. For example, in the NIMH Psychotherapy of Depression Collaborative Research Program (Clinical Research Branch, NIMH, 1980), the Social Adjustment Scale (Weissman et al., 1971) was selected for completion by the patient and a clinical evaluator.

As Hogarty (1975) has noted, no method for detecting informants who give unreliable or invalid reports is built into the KAS-R, other than the interviewer's subjective assessment of the informant. Another problem, identified by both Hogarty (1975) and Fiske (1975b), is that research pertaining to informant biases is relatively limited. Fiske specifically recommends, in this regard, that data be collected from more than one informant and pooled, a recommendation that may not always be feasible to implement given the constraints placed on the investigator by such factors as informant availability and knowledgeability.

In sum, although the KAS-R is not without limitations, it is clearly a well-developed measure that covers a broad range of symptomatology, albeit a more restricted range of social behavior. The incorporation of indices of significant others' expectations of the patient adds greatly to its utility. Investigators interested in further information about the scale should especially consult two earlier reviews by Fiske (1975b) and Hogarty (1975), in addition to Katz and Lyerly (1963).

Other Informant Measures of Social Adjustment

Of course, the KAS-R is not the only available measure of social adjustment suitable for administration to the patient's significant others, although a perusal of sheer bulk of research in which this instrument has been used might give that impression. There are a number of other options that the investigator may choose, several of which we describe briefly here.

Psychological Adjustment to Illness Scale

Researchers in the area of behavioral medicine will be especially interested in the Psychological Adjustment to Illness Scale (Derogatis, 1976; Morrow et al., 1978). This inventory, administered as a semistructured interview with the interviewer assigning the scores, is suitable for use with both medical patients and their significant others. The specific illness-related issues tapped are health care orientation (i.e., attitudes toward physicians and treatment, information and expectancies about illness); psychological distress; and disruption in the areas of vocational environment, domestic environment, sexual relationships, extended family relationships, and social environment. Although the preliminary scale development research has concentrated on adult lung cancer patients and parents of children with Hodgkin's disease, this instrument appears to have applicability to most other major medical illnesses. The initial work on establishing reliability and validity has been encouraging, although it was concluded that "revision of items in the extended family relationships subscale, as well as possibly those in the vocational domain, could further strengthen the psychometric characteristics of this promising and important new instrument" (Morrow et al., 1978, p. 609).

Social Behaviour Assessment Schedule

This measure, developed by Platt and his colleagues (Platt et al., 1980, 1981) is intended to tap both changes in a patient's behavior related to mental or medical illness as well as the impact of these changes and events on the patient's family. The scale gives extensive coverage to this latter domain, including the more objective (e.g., changes in health and life-styles of household members) and the more subjectively experienced (e.g., distress) effects on the patient's household. The social network support system available to the family is also tapped. Items are rated by an interviewer on the basis of the informant's report. Initial data, including information as to reliability and validity, have been reported.

Social Adjustment Self-Report Scale and Social Adjustment Scale-II

There are at least a half-dozen other inventories of social adjustment that may be used effectively with psychiatric populations. Both the Social Adjustment Self-Report Scale (SAS-SR) (Weissman et al., 1978) and the Social Adjustment Scale-II (SAS-II) (Glazer et al., 1980) have been administered to patients' significant others. The SAS-SR, and the earlier interview measure (Weissman & Paykel, 1974) from which it was derived, was originally intended for use with depressed outpatients but has subsequently been applied to a broad range of subjects (e.g., normals in the community, alcoholics, and schizophrenics). The SAS-II is a revision designed specifically for use with schizophrenic patients and takes into account the typical characteristics "in schizophrenics' lives such as unemployment, lack of spouse and children, special living arrangements, and poor living skills" (Glazer et al., 1980, p. 494). The scale is administered as an interview, again with the interviewer rendering the actual scores. Items gauge instrumental and expressive role performance in eight areas: "work as a housewife, student, or wage earner; relationship with principal household member; parental role; relationships with external family; social and leisure activities; conjugal and nonconjugal heterosexual behavior; romantic involvement; and, finally, an area called personal well-being which includes such items as appearance, grooming, and ability to care for oneself" (p. 494). The SAS-SR, on the other hand, covers instrumental and expressive functioning in the domains of work, social and leisure activities, relationship with extended family, marital role as spouse, parental role, and membership in the family unit. The SAS-II differs from the SAS-SR, then, primarily in its inclusion of the personal well-being items as well as in the lessened attention paid to the family unit as the principal interpersonal context. Unlike the KAS-R (Katz & Lyerly, 1963) and the Social Behaviour Assessment Schedule (Platt et al., 1980, 1981), neither of these measures directly evaluate the informant's attitudes toward the patient; psychiatric symptoms are also not directly covered.

Initial data regarding the use of the SAS-II with patients' significant others have revealed generally high agreement between patient and informant, although the pattern of findings across the different areas tapped by the scale raised some suspicion that scores may be influenced by interpersonal dynamics between these two parties, such as "burden, expressed emotion, collusion to present a nice picture, and expectation" (Glazer et al., 1980, p. 497). Weissman and Bothwell (1976) found adequate consensus between reports by depressed patients and their significant others on the SAS-SR, although agreement was slightly attenuated when functioning was gauged at recovery than when it was measured during the acute phase of the depression.

Structured and Scaled Interview to Assess Maladjustment

This instrument, although originally developed for administration to patients, has also been given to significant other informants (Gurland et al., 1972a; Sloane et al., 1975). An interview, from which ratings are made, covers five areas of functioning: work, social, family, marriage, and sex. Additionally, within each of these areas are items pertinent to the patient's deviant behavior, level of distress, and the friction between the patient and others (Gurland et al., 1972b). It bears emphasis here that this scale has been applied with high-functioning populations, notably in the comparative outcome study of psycho-analytically oriented psychotherapy versus behavior therapy conducted by Sloane and his colleagues (Sloane et al., 1975). It should also be noted that the Social Adjustment Scale, described above, was derived in large measure from the Structured and Scaled Interview to Assess Maladjustment (SSIAM).

Psychiatric Status Schedule, Psychiatric Evaluation Form, Current and Past Psychopathology Scales, and Family Evaluation Form

The well-developed and widely used scales published by Spitzer and Endicott's research group are also applicable for use with patients' significant others. The Psychiatric Status Schedule (PSS) (Spitzer et al., 1966, 1970) covers psychiatric symptoms as well as functioning in major roles (wage earner, housekeeper, student, parent, mate), leisure time activities, daily routine, and alcohol and drug use. Content coverage in the Psychiatric Evaluation Form (PEF) (Endicott & Spitzer, 1972b) is similar; the main differences between the instruments are that the PSS employs a highly structured interview schedule and collects precise information about specific behaviors, whereas the PEF interview is less structured (and optional) and the assessment focuses on broader dimensions of behavior. In addition to gauging present mental status and social adjustment, the Current and Past Psychopathology Scales (CAPPS) (Endicott & Spitzer, 1972a) cover relevant historical material (e.g., antisocial traits in childhood, adolescent friendship patterns, and school performance). The Family Evaluation Form (FEF) (Spitzer et al., 1971) taps aspects of the psychosocial and economic impact of the patient's mental illness on the significant other informant, so it is conceptually similar in this regard to the Social Behaviour Assessment Schedule (Platt et al., 1980, 1981).

Personal Adjustment and Role Skills

It should be noted that both Hogarty (1975) and Fiske (1975b) had high regard for this instrument and recommended it as an alternative to the KAS-R (Katz & Lyerly, 1963) for inclusion in the Core Battery of the NIMH Outcome Measures Project (Waskow & Parloff, 1975). The Personal Adjustment and Role Skills (PARS) scale was originally developed by Ellsworth and his colleagues (Ellsworth et al., 1968) to evaluate the community adjustment of hospitalized schizophrenic male veterans. It has since undergone two revisions, both of which were oriented toward broadening the scale's applicability to other populations and to supplementing the range of issues covered. The most recent version, PARS-III (Ellsworth, 1975), was developed with a community clinic sample and has separate forms for men and women. The version for men yields seven general factors: interpersonal involvement, confusion, anxiety, agitation–depression, alcohol–drug abuse, employment, and outside social activities. Parenthood skills can also be scored if appropriate. The factors generated by the form for women are interpersonal involvement, confusion, agitation, alcohol–drug abuse, household management, and outside social activities; optional additional areas that can also be scored are employment and parenthood skills. There are short forms of the PARS-III as well, with a score for household management having been added to the form for men. The PARS is completed directly by the informant, as opposed to being scored by an interviewer, and has, in fact, been used by Ellsworth and his colleagues as a mailed questionnaire.

As is the case with the KAS-R, the PARS has undergone ample research aimed at establishment of reliability and validity [see Ellsworth (1975) for a summary]; it has also been used in recent outcome research (Evans et al., 1973; Fontana & Dowds, 1975; Penk et al., 1978), although it has by no means achieved the sort of high visibility given the KAS-R. To be sure, in some ways, the coverage of topics provided by the PARS is more limited; the most notable deficit (relative to the KAS-R) is the absence of an assessment of the informant's attitudes toward and expectations concerning the target patient. On the other hand, however, the PARS does yield separate factor scores for the various role activities gauged, while the KAS-R does not.

Further Options

We have described a number of instruments whose psychometric properties and utility for psychotherapy or other outcome research have either been well-established or look promising. Space does not permit as extensive a summary of some of the other measures of social adjustment that have appeared in the literature, although the reader may find many of them potentially useful for his or her special purposes. The *Social Adjustment Inventory* (Berger et al., 1963, 1964, 1965) has been used, for example, in a study of crisis-oriented family therapy for hospitalizable patients (Langsley & Kaplan, 1968). It covers community adaptation in the areas of social and family relationships, work adjustment, self-care practices, and antisocial tendencies but has the chief limitation of not including a measure of the types of psychiatric symptom that are of general interest. This same shortcoming applies as well to Clare and Cairns's (1978) scale, the *Standardized Interview to Assess Social Maladjustment*, which gauges material conditions, social management, and satisfaction in the areas of housing, finance, occupation, social and leisure activities, and relationships with significant others. The *Freeman and Simmons Interview Schedule* (Freeman & Simmons, 1963), on the other hand, has been noted to give especially thorough coverage in the area of family expectations (Hogarty, 1975), although it has also been criticized on a number of grounds, including lack of information on scale properties and the fact that the scores are "not so fully determined by the significant other as one might wish" (Fiske, 1975b, p. 192) since an interviewer renders the actual judgments. The *Social Ineffectiveness Scale* (Stone et al., 1961) is of primarily historical interest in that it "laid the groundwork for the development of later scales," although, according to Weissman (1975), the authors of the instrument do not themselves "recommend its use currently because of the cumbersome interview method and the reliance on clinical impressions for ratings." (p. 360).

In the event that none of the measures of behavior, psychiatric symptoms, and social adjustment that we have mentioned here fit the particular needs of the reader, it should be pointed out that a number of patient measures may have the potential to be creatively modified or adapted for use with informants. The reviews by Weissman and her colleagues (Weissman, 1975; Weissman et al., 1981) may be especially helpful in this regard.

Finally, perhaps even more interesting from a historical perspective, Fiske (1975b) has commented on Carl Rogers's (1954) use of the *Willoughby Scale of Emotional Maturity*, developed in 1932, in a study of significant others' perceptions of change following psychotherapy. After having reviewed dozens of contenders for inclusion in the present chapter, we found Fiske's remarks about Rogers and the Willoughby both wistful and cogent and certainly reflective of our own sense of frustration with a few of the other measures that we encountered in the literature in this area—namely, that whereas "the scale has many desirable features, including the care with which it was originally constructed by Willoughby . . . ," and whereas "it appears to cover much appropriate content . . . , one might wish, however, that there were further evidence about it from other studies and that one knew more about it" (p. 193).

CONCEPTUAL AND METHODOLOGICAL DIRECTIONS FOR FUTURE RESEARCH

Although substantial interest has been shown in the last few years in evaluating the psychometric properties of these measuring instruments and in utilizing such scales to broaden the scope of psychotherapy research, we are nevertheless left with the impression that the most salient issues for investigators concerned with applying a psychosocial perspective to their work are less methodological than conceptual and theoretical in nature. This is not to say, with respect to the appropriate exploitation of data derived from significant others, that the important task of refining and amending these measuring instruments has been achieved; it decidedly has not, nor do we wish to minimize the problems involved in this domain. Moreover, although most of the major investigators whose work we have reviewed here have contributed much in the way of innovative research directions, certainly increasing the explanatory power of their evaluation models by incorporating a social framework, the field of psychotherapy research as a whole often seems to display a curious ambivalence around the reference to such extratherapeutic factors. It is no longer uncommon, for example, to encounter studies that have given prominent focus to significant others as data sources, although it is indeed unusual when a study goes beyond the operational utility of the specific criteria at hand and addresses the broader theoretical implications of social phenomena for understanding psychotherapy.

The point we would raise here for consideration is simply that attempts to enrich and expand the empirical observation of psychotherapy outcome—in the matter at hand, by way of examining its social ecological context—cannot rightly be expected to yield much beyond rather prosaic, one-dimensional data so long as psychotherapy researchers proceed "as if" such material could be treated straightforwardly like the other criteria with which they are familiar. In fact, neither the conceptual underpinnings for the study of significant other data (e.g., the notions of social adjustment, social support systems, social networks) nor the theoretical and disciplinary traditions from which they are derived (e.g., network analysis, social role theory, social anthropology, and the sociology of mental illness) are likely to prove sufficiently fruitful for psychotherapy researchers without a certain degree of reorganization or "translation" at the level of our organizing problem–statements or conceptual paradigms. Although he had a purpose in mind quite different from that of the problems of studying treatment outcome, psychotherapy researchers may still appreciate Kuhn's (1970) description of the broader issues involved when members of different scientific communities attempt to "translate the other's theory and its consequences into [their] own language and simultaneously to describe in [their] language the world to which that theory applies." In pursuing the issue of interdisciplinary communication, Kuhn pointed out that "locutions that present no . . . difficulties may be homophonically translated . . . ," while also recognizing that "terms and locutions that, used unproblematically within each community, are nevertheless foci of trouble for inter-group discussions" (p. 202).

We are not suggesting here that the problem–statements of psychotherapy research should be upended whenever recourse is made to other than psychological constructs, nor that socially phrased observations must necessarily be directly linked to an organizing matrix of social theory before they can be gainfully employed within clinical investigations. Yet, if we may be allowed by way of illustration to rather loosely apply the clinical notion of "resistance" to the normal processes of the scientific enterprise, it strikes us that the latent ambivalence or dissatisfaction that many psychotherapy researchers have professed with regard to socially phrased measures, for example, may also reflect precisely those areas where they have allowed their own methodology to outrun the intended function of the original theoretical construct. In other words, what was assumed to be a "homophonic" translation—"normative social adjustment," for instance—may actually serve to mask the fact that a particular construct or instrument is inadequate to the task *because* inadequate attention was paid to assuring that, indeed, nothing was lost in the process of translation. Although there is no theory-independent way to utilize the descriptive or "puzzle-solving" (Kuhn, 1970) ability of such parallel interdisciplinary constructs without exacerbating a number of thorny problems, a greater awareness of this issue on the part of psychotherapy investigators might contribute to a more informed process of translation when socially phrased measures are introduced; such attention, in turn, could profitably lead to a readjustment not only in the general consensus on the acceptable range of research methods, but, equally valuable, in our perspective on the appropriate territorial boundaries for psychotherapy research as well.

Whether this process also involves an element of actual interdisciplinary collaboration at the design and implementation stages is a pragmatic matter of policy for the individual investigator, although we have consistently found this to be a rewarding and instructive exercise. On the other hand, when the matter involves the use of not only, say, "social adjustment" measures or "social network" data, but their application with cross-cultural or cross-ethnic types of studies as well, we consider it imperative to include a sociologist or anthropologist colleague as a research consultant; this is nowhere more critical than when significant others' reports are being relied on as part of an attempt to utilize multiple-outcome measures that, among other things, purport to reflect appropriate relationship variables and change goals with these populations (Lambert, 1981).

Similarly, a review of the social network literature, especially that area dealing with certain aspects of the measurement problem from a sociological perspective, may suggest further enhancements to the multiple-outcome criteria generally used by psychotherapy researchers. Recalling our earlier comments to the effect that one of the initial tasks for the investigator ought to be a preliminary determination of whether a relevant pool of significant others, in fact, exists for the target population, we have been impressed by a number of measures described in this literature that would certainly seem to fulfill this requirement admirably. Moreover, we would point to a range of well-developed social network measures that would also seem to offer considerable flexibility and depth in examining numerous related issues concerning the use of significant other data in treatment outcome research.

As a start, we would draw attention to a recent report prepared for the Task Force on Environmental Assessment, a committee of the National Council of Community Mental Health Centers (Mitchell & Trickett, 1980), that attempted to order (by degree of inclusiveness) the range of operational definitions of criteria that behavioral scientists have employed for social network membership, while also describing not only the multiple determinants underlying social network formation but "what effects these networks have on individuals in terms of such substantive areas as help-seeking or general psychological adjustment" (p. 33). In another review of social network theory related to the study of schizophrenic patients and their social support systems, Hammer (1981) describes the utility of a number of measures of "clustering" in the interpersonal network of this patient population; one main structural measure of network density that we find especially intriguing for possible adaptation in treatment outcome research was cited because it "indicates the extent to which the individuals connected to a focal individual are also connected to each other" (p. 52), although it should also be noted that there are some limitations with density measures regarding range of variation across populations.

Likewise, Garrison and Podell (1981), in a discussion of a semistructured clinical interview format, the *Community Support Systems Assessment*

(CSSA), outlined many of the problems that traditional quantitative instruments or more structured interviews often entail for the investigator, including the fact that

> such instruments also assume the supportive significance of persons in labeled roles (e.g., "family," "friends," and "neighbors") that can be counted or of supportive functions (e.g., instrumental and affective supports) that can be provided by various persons and rated for quantity and quality by respondents . . ., suppositions [that] impose categories on the patient which might not be relevant and which might exclude other categories of greater supportive importance. (p. 101)

Pointing out that these supportive categories may be expected to vary widely with cultural background, socioeconomic level, and psychiatric disease category—and that, at any rate, the notion of "support" can often present a misleading clinical picture (e.g., the "schizophrenogenic" parent or "supportive but abusive" husband)—Garrison and Podell argue that an appropriate clinical assessment of a patient's social support system "requires knowledge of normative social participation patterns, role expectations, and available alternatives within the patient's subculture and community, and that these must be assessed with consideration of the patient's usual level of functioning" (p. 102). In addition to having intake workers gather the standard demographic background information on the patient, Garrison and Podell report on the experimental introduction of a new role on the treatment–research team, that of the "culture specialist," whose task it is to conduct a "more thorough exploration of the social network and support system" using the CSSA and who has also been "trained extensively in the theory, empirical research, and hypotheses on which [this instrument] is based" (p. 102). The central focus of the CSSA is the "expanded genogram," or social network diagram, that is worked out with the patient in the course of the semistructured interview, a representation of the patient's perceived affective support network. Follow-up questioning (e.g., "Who do you count on when you are sick . . . have financial problems . . .? Who do you confide in?") elicits more detailed information on the linkages between the patient and these significant others. Additional probing on the patient's use of time and space over the course of a "reconstructed week" yields an even more objective assessment of the social world, one that is often at odds with the patient's subjective self-portrayal of the moment (e.g., "I have no friends") or his accounting based on the genogram alone. Garrison and Podell comment that such interviews have "also sometimes influenced a change in the assessment of the clinical picture from, for example, one of schizophrenic withdrawal to one of the disaffected state associated with depression" (p. 104).

From another perspective, Sokolovsky and Cohen (1981) have discussed some of the methodological dilemmas of social network mapping suggested by anthropological theorists, including an analysis of the "synchronic" versus "diachronic" frames of reference that psychotherapy researchers may find applicable to their own work, and they have offered a *Network Analysis Profile* that appears to hold some promise along these lines for follow-up outcome studies with discharged mental patients. Pattison and Pattison (1981) have also provided an interesting account of "network intervention" in the psychotherapy of a schizophrenic girl, a technique they derived from the empirical study of the social network paradigm using their *Psychosocial Kinship Inventory*.

At the same time, Linn et al. (1981) have also examined the conceptual grounding for the notion of social support, including the issues of reliability and validity of its measures, and have reviewed a number of relevant instruments derived from community survey research involving the use of significant others. Of particular interest to psychotherapy researchers attempting to assess the simple availability of significant others, for example, are the battery of items that these authors selected from a series of widely used social support scales.

Operating from a more traditional psychiatric perspective, Brown et al. (1972), on the other hand, not only gathered information about the patient's social network and work impairment from his family members, but drew on their structured interview materials to construct an index of the quality of the emotional responses of these significant others toward the patient, later using them as a means of predicting symptomatic relapse following discharge.

Finally, Platt (1981)—in a paper pointedly subtitled "Just What Are We Measuring?"— has directly (if in a somewhat overstated fashion) raised some of the sociological objections to the "deficiencies in conceptualization and operationalization" of social role adjustment criteria in treatment outcome research. Taking his review of three measurement instruments—the Normative Social Adjustment Scale, the Structured and Scaled Interview to Assess Maladjustment, and the Social Adjustment Scale—as a point of departure, Platt argues that whereas each of these instruments "adopts an explicitly sociological approach to adjustment, using the concepts and language of role analysis, . . . this approach is insufficiently sophisticated at the theoretical level and abandoned de facto at the operational level," and he charges that "operationally, all three schedules fail to give any consideration to the actual expectations of relevant audiences or to locate the individual in his own social context" (p. 106). Platt suggests that much of the efforts of psychotherapy researchers to establish measurable norms of social adjustment instead reflect basic misconceptions of the sociology of role behavior, and he underscores the critical necessity of "taking into account the views of the subject's significant others in arriving at both a description and an evaluation of role performance" (p. 108). Katz and Lyerly's (1963) work with the KAS-R receives some acknowledgment from Platt as at least heading in the right direction, sociologically speaking, although even this measure is ultimately rejected as "unavoidably ambiguous."

We have by no means attempted to present here an exhaustive selection of the extant measures available in the social network or sociology literature. A good many of the measures described in this literature have already seen duty in psychological research of one form or another and are directly applicable to the treatment outcome issues that we have discussed above, whereas others may require considerable translation by the investigator. Rather, our intention in pursuing this particular detour was primarily to examine some of the conceptual and methodological issues that surround the use of social or psychosocial instruments, point out some of the sociological objections that have been raised, and illustrate a number of areas where psychotherapy researchers might expect to find a few rich veins of thought waiting to be tapped. It is our impression that investigators looking for innovative approaches to old problems in psychotherapy research will find much of value in this area.

SUMMARY AND RECOMMENDATIONS

To summarize briefly, we have discussed in this chapter both the major advantages and the obstacles surrounding the use of significant others as focal data sources in treatment outcome studies, and we have suggested ways in which theoretical constructs from related social science approaches can further enrich and expand this measurement perspective for psychotherapy researchers. We have also reviewed at varying lengths the most useful, frequently used, or promising measuring instruments; however, we have attempted to avoid a "cookbook" attitude to these empirical methods. To be sure, we trust that those investigators simply seeking a useful compendium of scales that can be administered to patients' significant others will not be disappointed, although we have placed at least equal emphasis on the methodological limitations and caveats attached to this measurement strategy in general.

Chief among the drawbacks are the availability of a knowledgeable and cooperative relative or friend, the motivational or perceptual biases of the informant that may color his or her report, the problems of constructing or choosing a data collection instrument appropriate to both the characteristics of the patient population and to the abilities of the significant other informants, the possibly prohibitive costs associated with this type of data collection, the ethical ramifications of assuring informed consent of all participants, and the interpretive problems of evaluating outcome when the appraisal of the significant other does not converge with the judgments of the other interested parties—that is, the patient and the therapist.

Assuming that the investigator has been able to allay whatever misgivings we may have provoked by our critical assessment of the opportunities for empirical research involving these data sources, the advantages of achieving a multidimensional perspective on the effects of psychotherapy should more than compensate for the added burden of ensuring that one's data collection methods are actually adequate to the task. Having decided on the necessity of supplementing data drawn from patient self-reports or therapist ratings, the investigator will find that significant others' observations open up a considerably more complex and socially relevant level of analysis and one that is especially pertinent to those patient populations for which improved social adjustment and role performance are treatment desiderata. In addition to addressing the problems inherent in obtaining the informant's report *about* the patient's behavior, we have emphasized the importance of eliciting data concerning his expectations *of* the patient (in terms of behavior, ability to function in certain roles, and so forth).

The utility of this assessment approach could be further enhanced by research specifically aimed at examining the contributions of motivational and relationship variables to informants' reports. Special attention must also be paid to the conceptual and methodological underpinnings of socially phrased treatment outcome criteria and to the various disciplinary traditions that lay competing claims to these constructs, since there continue to be numerous indications for rewarding interdisciplinary collaboration in the study of psychotherapy outcome.

REFERENCES

Achenbach, T. M. Psychopathology of childhood: Research problems and issues. *Journal of Consulting and Clinical Psychology*, 1978, **46**, 759–776.

Barrett, C. L., Hampe, I. E., & Miller, L. C. Research on child psychotherapy. In S. L. Garfield & A. E. Bergin (Eds.), *Handbook of psychotherapy and behavior change: An empirical analysis* (2nd ed.). New York: Wiley, 1978.

Berger, D. G., Rice, C. E., Sewall, L. G., & Lemkau, P. V. Factors affecting the adequacy of patient community adjustment information obtained from the community. *Mental Hygiene*, 1963, **47**, 452–460.

Berger, D. G., Rice, C. E., Sewall, L. G., & Lemkau, P. V. The post-hospital evaluation of psychiatric patients: The Social Adjustment Inventory method. *Psychiatric Studies and Projects*, 1964, **2**, 1–31.

Berger, D. G., Rice, C. E., Sewall, L. G., & Lemkau, P. V. The impact of psychiatric hospital experience on the community adjustment of patients. *Mental Hygiene*, 1965, **49**, 83–93.

Bergin, A. E. The evaluation of therapeutic outcomes. In A. E. Bergin & S. L. Garfield (Eds.), *Handbook of psychotherapy and behavior change: An empirical analysis*. New York: Wiley, 1971.

Bergin, A. E., & Lambert, M. J. The evaluation of therapeutic outcomes. In S. L. Garfield & A. E. Bergin (Eds.), *Handbook of psychotherapy and behavior change: An empirical analysis* (2nd ed). New York: Wiley, 1978.

Berzins, J. I., Bednar, R. L., & Severy, L. J. The problem of intersource consensus in measuring therapeutic outcomes: New data and multivariate perspectives. *Journal of Abnormal Psychology*, 1975, **84**, 10–19.

Braden, W., Bannasch, P. R., & Fink, E. B. Diagnosing mania: The use of family informants. *Journal of Clinical Psychiatry*, 1980, **41**, 226–228.

Brown, G. W., Birley, J. L. T., & Wing, J. K. Influence of family life on the course of schizophrenic disorders: A replication. *British Journal of Psychiatry*, 1972, **121**, 241–258.

Caffey, E. M., Galbrecht, C. R., & Klett, C. J. Brief hospitalization and aftercare in the treatment of schizophrenia. *Archives of General Psychiatry*, 1971, **24**, 81–86.

Cartwright, D. S., Kirtner, W. L., & Fiske, D. W. Method factors in changes associated with psychotherapy. *Journal of Abnormal and Social Psychology*, 1963, **66**, 164–175.

Clare, A. W., & Cairns, V. E. Design, development and use of a standardized interview to assess social maladjustment and dysfunction in community studies. *Psychological Medicine*, 1978, **8**, 589–604.

Clausen, G. T. Some problems of design and inference in studies of community tenure. *Journal of Nervous and Mental Disease*, 1972, **155**, 22–35.

Clinical Research Branch, NIMH. *Psychotherapy of depression collaborative research program (pilot phase): Revised research plan.* Washington, D.C.: NIMH, 1980.

Clum, G. A. Role of stress in the prognosis of mental illness. *Journal of Consulting and Clinical Psychology*, 1976, **44**, 54–60.

Crook, T., Hogarty, G. E., & Ulrich, R. F. Inter-rater reliability of informants' ratings: Katz Adjustment Scales, R Form. *Psychological Reports*, 1980, **47**, 427–432.

Derogatis, L. R. *Scoring and Procedures Manual for PAIS.* Baltimore: Clinical Psychometric Research, 1976.

Ellsworth, R. B. Consumer feedback in measuring the effectiveness of mental health programs. In M. Guttentag & E. L. Struening (Eds.), *Handbook of evaluation research* (Vol. 2). Beverly Hills, Calif.: Sage Publications, 1975.

Ellsworth, R. B., Foster, L., Childers, B., Arthur, G., & Kroeker, D. Hospital and community adjustment as perceived by psychiatric patients, their families and staff. *Journal of Consulting and Clinical Psychology Monograph*, 1968, **32** (5, Pt. 2).

Endicott, J., & Spitzer, R. L. Current and Past Psychopathology Scales (CAPPS). *Archives of General Psychiatry*, 1972, **27**, 678–687.(a)

Endicott, J., & Spitzer, R. L. What! Another rating scale? The Psychiatric Evaluation Form. *Journal of Nervous and Mental Disease*, 1972, **154**, 88–104.(b)

Erikson, E. H. *Gandhi's truth.* New York: Norton, 1969.

Evans, J. R., Goldstein, M. J., & Rodnick, E. H. Premorbid adjustment, paranoid diagnosis, and remission: Acute schizophrenics treated in a community mental health center. *Archives of General Psychiatry*, 1973, **28**, 666–672.

Eyberg, S. M., & Johnson, S. M. Multiple assessment of behavior modification with families: Effect of contingency contracting and order of treated problems. *Journal of Consulting and Clinical Psychology*, 1974, **42**, 594–606.

Eysenck, H. J. The effects of psychotherapy: An evaluation. *Journal of Consulting Psychology*, 1952, **16**, 319–324.

Fiske, D. W. A source of data is not a measuring instrument. *Journal of Abnormal Psychology*, 1975, **84**, 20–23.(a)

Fiske, D. W. The use of significant others in assessing the outcome of psychotherapy. In I. E. Waskow & M. B. Parloff (Eds.), *Psychotherapy change measures.* Washington, D.C.: DHEW, 1975.(b)

Fontana, A. F., & Dowds, B. N. Assessing treatment outcome. I. Adjustment in the community. *Journal of Nervous and Mental Disease*, 1975, **161**, 221–238.

Freeman, H. E., & Simmons, O. G. *The mental patient comes home.* New York: Wiley, 1963.

Garfield, S. L. *Psychotherapy: An eclectic approach.* New York: Wiley, 1980.

Garfield, S. L., Prager, R. A., & Bergin, A. E. Evaluation of outcome in psychotherapy. *Journal of Consulting and Clinical Psychology*, 1971, **37**, 307–313.

Garfield, S. L., Prager, R. A., & Bergin, A. E. Some further comments on evaluation of outcome in psychotherapy. *Journal of Consulting and Clinical Psychology*, 1974, **42**, 296–297.

Garrison, V., & Podell, J. Community Support Systems Assessment for use in clinical interviews. *Schizophrenia Bulletin*, 1981, **7**, 101–108.

Glazer, W. M., Aaronson, H. S., Prusoff, B. A., Williams, D. H. Assessment of social adjustment in chronic ambulatory schizophrenics. *Journal of Nervous and Mental Disease*, 1980, **168**, 493–497.

Green, B. L., Gleser, G. C., Stone, W. N., & Seifert, R. F. Relationships among diverse measures of psychotherapy outcome. *Journal of Consulting and Clinical Psychology*, 1975, **43**, 689–699.

Gurland, B. J., Yorkston, N. J., Goldberg, K., Fleiss, J. L., Sloane, R. B., & Cristol, A. H. The Structured and Scaled Interview to Assess Maladjustment (SSIAM). II. Factor analysis, reliability, and validity. *Archives of General Psychiatry*, 1972, **27**, 264–267.(a)

Gurland, B. J., Yorkston, N. J., Stone, A. R., Frank, J. D., & Fleiss, J. L. The Structured and Scaled Interview to Assess Maladjustment (SSIAM). I. Description, rational, and development. *Archives of General Psychiatry*, 1972, **27**, 259–264.(b)

Gurman, A. S., & Kniskern, D. P. Family therapy outcome research: Knowns and unknowns. In A. S. Gurman & D. P. Kniskern (Eds.), *Handbook of family therapy.* New York: Brunner/Mazel, 1981.

Hammer, M. Social supports, social networks, and schizophrenia. *Schizophrenia Bulletin*, 1981, **7**, 45–57.

Hargreaves, W. A., Glick, I. D., Drues, J., Showstack, J. A., & Feigenbaum, E. Short vs. long hospitalization: A prospective controlled study. VI. Two-year follow-up results for schizophrenics. *Archives of General Psychiatry*, 1977, **34**, 305–311.

Harty, M., & Horwitz, L. Therapeutic outcome as rated by patients, therapists, and judges. *Archives of General Psychiatry*, 1976, **33**, 957–961.

Hogarty, G. E. Informant ratings of community adjustment. In I. E. Waskow & M. B. Parloff (Eds.), *Psychotherapy change measures.* Washington D.C.: DHEW, 1975.

Hogarty, G. E., Dennis, H., Guy, W., & Gross, G. M. "Who goes there?"—A critical evaluation of admissions to a psychiatric day hospital. *American Journal of Psychiatry*, 1968, **124**, 94–104.

Hogarty, G. E., Goldberg, S. C., & Schooler, N. R. Drug and sociotherapy in the aftercare of schizophrenic patients. III. Adjustment of nonrelapsed patients. *Archives of General Psychiatry*, 1974, **31**, 609–618.

Hogarty, G. E., & Katz, M. M. Norms of adjustment and social behavior. *Archives of General Psychiatry*, 1971, **25**, 470–480.

Hogarty, G. E., Katz, M. M., & Lowery, H. A. Identifying candidates from a normal population for a community mental health program. In R. R. Monroe, G. D. Klee, & E. B. Brody (Eds.), *Psychiatric epidemiology and mental health planning: Psychiatric Research Report No. 22.* Washington, D.C.: American Psychiatric Association, 1967.

Katz, M. M. Evaluating drug and other therapies across cultures. In A. J. Marsella & P. B. Pederson (Eds.), *Cross-cultural counseling and psychotherapy*. New York: Pergamon, 1981.

Katz, M. M., Lowery, H. A., & Cole, J. O. Behavior patterns of schizophrenics in the community. In M. Lorr (Ed.), *Explorations in typing psychotics*. New York: Pergamon, 1967.

Katz, M. M., & Lyerly, S. Methods for measuring adjustment and social behavior in the community: I. Rationale, description, discriminative validity and scale development. *Psychological Reports*, 1963, **13**, 503–535.

Kellett, J. M., Copeland, J. R. M., & Kelleher, M. J. Information leading to accurate diagnosis in the elderly. *British Journal of Psychiatry*, 1975, **126**, 423–430.

Kuhn, T. S. *The structure of scientific revolutions* (2nd ed.). Chicago: University of Chicago Press, 1970.

Lambert, M. J. Evaluating outcome variables in cross-cultural counseling and psychotherapy. In A. J. Marsella & P. B. Pederson (Eds.), *Cross-cultural counseling and psychotherapy*. New York: Pergamon, 1981.

Langsley, D. G., & Kaplan, D. M. *The treatment of families in crisis*. New York: Grune and Stratton, 1968.

Leve, R. M. A comment on Garfield, Prager, and Bergin's evaluation of outcome in psychotherapy. *Journal of Consulting and Clinical Psychology*, 1974, **42**, 293–295.

Levene, H. I., Patterson, V., Murphey, B. G., Overbeck, A. L., & Veach, T. L. The aftercare of schizophrenics: An evaluation of group and individual approaches. *Psychiatric Quarterly*, 1970, **44**, 296–304.

Linn, N., Dean, A., & Ensel, W. M. Social support scales: A methodological note. *Schizophrenia Bulletin*, 1981, **7**, 73–89.

Luborsky, L. Perennial mystery of poor agreement among criteria for psychotherapy outcome. *Journal of Consulting and Clinical Psychology*, 1971, **37**, 316–319.

Luborsky, L., Singer, B., & Luborsky, L. Comparative studies of psychotherapies. *Archives of General Psychiatry*, 1975, **32**, 995–1008.

Maisto, S. A., Sobell, L. C., & Sobell, M. B. Comparison of alcoholics' self-reports of drinking behavior with reports of collateral informants. *Journal of Consulting and Clinical Psychology*, 1979, **47**, 106–112.

McFall, R. M. Smoking-cessation research. *Journal of Consulting and Clinical Psychology*, 1978, **46**, 703–712.

Meltzoff, J., & Kornreich, M. *Research in psychotherapy*. New York: Atherton, 1970.

Mendlewicz, J., Fleiss, J. L., Cataldo, M., & Rainer, J. D. Accuracy of the family history method in affective illness: Comparison with direct interviews in family studies. *Archives of General Psychiatry*, 1975, **32**, 309–314.

Michaux, M. H., Chelst, M. R., Foster, S. A., Pruim, R. J., & Dasinger, E. M. Postrelease adjustment of day and full-time psychiatric patients. *Archives of General Psychiatry*, 1973, **29**, 647–651.

Mintz, J., Auerbach, A. H., Luborsky, L., & Johnson, M. Patient's, therapist's, and observers' views of psychotherapy: A "Rashomon" experience or a reasonable censensus? *British Journal of Medical Psychology*, 1973, **46**, 83–89.

Mintz, J., Luborsky, L., & Christoph, P. Measuring the outcomes of psychotherapy: Findings of the Penn Psychotherapy Project. *Journal of Consulting and Clinical Psychology*, 1979, **47**, 319–334.

Mitchell, R. E., & Trickett, E. J. Task force report: Social networks as mediators of social support. An analysis of the effects and determinants of social networks. *Community Mental Health Journal*, 1980, **16**, 27–44.

Morrow, G. R., Chiarello, R. J., & Derogatis, L. R. A new scale for assessing patients' psychosocial adjustment to medical illness. *Psychological Medicine*, 1978, **8**, 605–610.

Nathan, P. E., & Lansky, D. Common methodological problems in research on the addictions. *Journal of Consulting and Clinical Psychology*, 1978, **46**, 713–726.

O'Leary, K. D., Turkewitz, H., & Taffel, S. J. Parent and therapist evaluation of behavior therapy in a child psychological clinic. *Journal of Consulting and Clinical Psychology*, 1973, **41**, 279–283.

Parloff, M. B. Can psychotherapy research guide the policymaker? A little knowledge may be dangerous. *American Psychologist*, 1979, **34**, 296–306.

Pasamanick, B., Scarpitti, F. R., & Dinitz, S. *Schizophrenics in the community*. New York: Appleton-Century-Crofts, 1967.

Patterson, G. R. Interventions for boys with conduct problems: Multiple settings, treatments, and criteria. *Journal of Consulting and Clinical Psychology*, 1974, **42**, 471–481.

Pattison, E. M., & Pattison, M. L. Analysis of a schizophrenic psychosocial network. *Schizophrenia Bulletin*, 1981, **7**, 135–143.

Paykel, E. S. Correlates of a depressive typology. *Archives of General Psychiatry*, 1972, **27**, 203–210.

Penk, W. E., Charles, H. L., & Van Hoose, T. A. Comparative effectiveness of day hospital and inpatient psychiatric treatment. *Journal of Consulting and Clinical Psychology*, 1978, **46**, 94–101.

Phillips, H. P. *Thai peasant personality: The patterning of interpersonal behavior in the village of Bang Chan*. Berkeley: University of California Press, 1970.

Platt, S. Social adjustment as a criterion of treatment success: Just what are we measuring? *Psychiatry*, 1981, **44**, 95–112.

Platt, S. D., Hirsch, S. R., & Knights, A. C. Effects of brief hospitalization on psychiatric patients' behaviour and social functioning. *Acta Psychiatrica Scandinavica*, 1981, **63**, 117–128.

Platt, S. D., Weyman, A. J., Hirsch, S. R., & Hewett, S. The Social Behaviour Assessment Schedule (SBAS): Rationale, contents, scoring and reliability of a new interview schedule. *Social Psychiatry*, 1980, **15**, 43–55.

Prusoff, B. A., Klerman, G. L., & Paykel, E. S. Pitfalls in the self-report assessment of depression. *Canadian Psychiatric Association Journal*, 1972, **17**, 101–107.

Rogers, C. R. Changes in maturity of behavior as related to therapy. In C. R. Rogers & R. F. Dymond (Eds.), *Psychotherapy and personality change: Coordinated research studies in the client-centered approach*. Chicago: University of Chicago Press, 1954.

Ross, A. O. Behavior therapy with children. In S. L. Garfield & A. E. Bergin (Eds.), *Handbook of psychotherapy and behavior change: An empirical analysis* (2nd ed.). New York: Wiley, 1978.

Sappington, A. A., & Michaux, M. H. Prognostic patterns in self-report, relative report, and professional evaluation measures for hospitalized and day-care patients. *Journal of Consulting and Clinical Psychology*, 1975, **43**, 904–910.

Schless, A. P., & Mendels, J. The value of interviewing family and friends in assessing life stressors. *Archives of General Psychiatry*, 1978, **35**, 565–567.

Schmidt, C. W., Jr., Perlin, S., Townes, W., Fisher, R. S., & Shaffer, J. W. Characteristics of drivers involved in single-car accidents. *Archives of General Psychiatry*, 1972, **27**, 800–803.

Schooler, N. R., Goldberg, S. C., Boothe, H., & Cole, J. O. One year after discharge: Community adjustment of schizophrenic patients. *American Journal of Psychiatry*, 1967, **123**, 986–995.

Showstack, J. A., Hargreaves, W. A., Glick, I. D., & O'Brien, R. S. Psychiatric follow-up studies: Practical procedures and ethical concerns. *Journal of Nervous and Mental Disease*, 1978, **166**, 34–43.

Sloane, R. B., Staples, F. R., Cristol, A. H., Yorkston, N. J., & Whipple, K. *Psychotherapy versus behavior therapy*. Cambridge: Harvard University Press, 1975.

Sokolovsky, J., & Cohen, C. I. Toward a resolution of methodological dilemmas in network mapping. *Schizophrenia Bulletin*, 1981, **7**, 109–116.

Spitzer, R. L., & Endicott, J. The value of the interview for the evaluation of psychopathology. In J. Hammer, K. Salzinger, & S. Sutton (Eds.), *Psychopathology: Contributions in the biological, behavioral, and social sciences*. New York: Wiley, 1973.

Spitzer, R. L., Endicott, J., & Cohen, G. *Psychiatric Status Schedule: Informant Form*. New York: Biometrics Research, New York State Department of Mental Hygiene, 1966.

Spitzer, R. L., Endicott, J., Fleiss, J. L., & Cohen, J. The Psychiatric Status Schedule: A technique for evaluating psychopathology and impairment in role functioning. *Archives of General Psychiatry*, 1970, **23**, 41–55.

Spitzer, R. L., Gibbon, M., & Endicott, J. Family Evaluation Form. *Biometric Research*, New York State Psychiatric Institute, 1971.

Stone, A. R., Frank, J. D., Nash, E. H., & Imber, S. D. An intensive five year follow-up study of treated psychiatric outpatients. *Journal of Nervous and Mental Disease*, 1961, **113**, 410–422.

Strupp, H. H., & Hadley, S. W. A tripartite model of mental health and therapeutic outcomes with special reference to negative effects in psychotherapy. *American Psychologist*, 1977, **32**, 187–196.

Vestre, N. D., & Zimmerman, R. Validity of informants' ratings of the behavior and symptoms of psychiatric patients. *Journal of Consulting and Clinical Psychology*, 1969, **33**, 175–179.

Waskow, I. E., & Parloff, M. B. *Psychotherapy change measures*. Washington, D.C.: DHEW, 1975.

Weissman, M. M. The assessment of social adjustment: A review of techniques. *Archives of General Psychiatry*, 1975, **32**, 357–365.

Weissman, M. M., & Bothwell, S. Assessment of social adjustment by patient self-report. *Archives of General Psychiatry*, 1976, **33**, 1111–1115.

Weissman, M. M., Klerman, G. L, Paykel, E. S., Prusoff, B. A., & Hanson, B. Treatment effects on the social adjustment of depressed patients. *Archives of General Psychiatry*, 1974, **30**, 771–778.

Weissman, M. M., Orvaschel, H., & Padian, N. Childrens' symptom and social functioning self-report scales: Comparison of mothers' and children's reports. *Journal of Nervous and Mental Disease*, 1980, **168**, 736–740.

Weissman, M. M., Paykel, E. S., Siegel, R., & Klerman, G. L. The social role performance of depressed women: Comparisons with a normal group. *American Journal of Orthopsychiatry*, 1971, **41**, 390–405.

Weissman, M. M., & Paykel, E. S. *The depressed woman: A study of social relationships*. Chicago: The University of Chicago Press, 1974.

Weissman, M. M., Prusoff, B. A., Thompson, W. D., Harding, P. S., & Myers, J. K. Social adjustment by self-report in a community sample and in psychiatric outpatients. *Journal of Nervous and Mental Disease*, 1978, **166**, 317–326.

Weissman, M. M., Sholomskas, D., & John, K. The assessment of social adjustment: An update. *Archives of General Psychiatry*, 1981, **38**, 1250–1258.

Yager, J., Grant, I., Sweetwood, H. L., & Gerst, M. Life event reports by psychiatric patients, nonpatients, and their partners. *Archives of General Psychiatry*, 1981, **38**, 343–347.

Young, M. A., & Meltzer, H. Y. The relationship of demographic, clinical, and outcome variables to neuroleptic treatment requirements. *Schizophrenia Bulletin*, 1980, **6**, 88–101.

CHAPTER 17

Institutional Measures of Treatment Outcome

STEPHEN A. MAISTO AND CHRISTINE A. MAISTO

During the 1970s, increasing attention was paid to accountability of psychological treatment programs. The term "accountability" refers in part to treatment program effects or the consequences of treatment, which may be evaluated at both program and individual levels (Guess & Tuchfeld, 1977). This chapter deals primarily with the effects of psychological treatments on individual client behaviors. The use of the scientific method to correlate an individual's functioning at a given time to treatment interventions is the subject of treatment outcome research.

Application of the scientific method to evaluating treatment effects raises the question of methods of how to measure an individual's life functioning. In this regard, Hersen and Bellack (1976) suggested that psychological measures may be broadly classified into three categories. First, self-report measures involve directly asking clients about their behavior. For example, a measure of vocational functioning may be the client's report of the number of days spent in employment during the last six months. Another category is behavioral measures, which are systematic observations of a client's overt behavior pertinent to an outcome criterion. For instance, phobic clients may be observed approaching the object(s) that aroused sufficient fear to bring them to treatment. Finally, physiological measures involve use of psychophysiological recording equipment to assess an individual's physical arousal in a situation that is pertinent to treatment goals. Physiological arousal may be measured at post-treatment in an alcoholic client as that client approaches an alcoholic beverage.

These types of measure are always recorded with the intention of using them specifically for research or evaluation purposes. In the context of treatment outcome, such measures are taken as part of conducting a particular evaluation study. Thus clients typically are not interviewed following their treatment as part of a treatment program's routine. Rather, personal interviews (to elicit self-reports of functioning) would be planned especially for purposes of evaluation research. This contrasts with another type of measure that psychologists often overlook [with some notable exceptions (Webb, et al., 1966)] called *institutional measures*, which may be defined as data obtained from records maintained primarily for the internal use of an organization or agency. Importantly, these records, which are commonly used in the other social and behavioral science disciplines, such as sociology and epidemiology, are *not* set up for research purposes. As we discuss below, there are many sources of institutional data that bear on a client's functioning, such as treatment programs, welfare agencies, schools, employment offices, and law enforcement and correctional facilities on both the local and federal levels (Ball & Brown, 1977, p. 98). Furthermore, institutional records can pertain to individual clients or to an aggregate of individuals that may be used as a comparison group in an evaluation. Although there has been only limited use of these records in outcome studies, we feel that their status as measures of life functioning should be reassessed. Good treatment outcome research methodology involves using data from as many sources as possible in order to capture the broad spectrum of changes produced by treatment. In addition, the validity of outcome data would be strengthened by using a variety of methods to measure life functioning.

The purpose of this chapter is to provide an overview of the uses of institutional measures in the evaluation of clients following treatment.[*] The first section of the chapter is a discussion of the sources of institutional measures and the types of data that can be obtained from them. A presentation of examples of the use of institutional measures in various phases of an outcome study follows. The third part of the chapter concerns the advantages and disadvantages of using institutional measures. In the final section, the effects of rights of privacy and client confidentiality legislation on using institutional measures are reviewed.

---

[*]The three most common types of treatment outcome evaluation designs published in the psychological literature include prospective–current clients, prospective–noncurrent clients, and retrospective–current or noncurrent clients. In the first type of design, clients admitted to treatment typically are evaluated from the point of admission, through their treatment experiences, and for some time following formal termination of treatment. This is often considered the ideal method of outcome evaluation. In the second design, longitudinal data are analyzed, but only through past records. For example, police records may contain an individual's criminal behavior for 10 successive years, which would allow an analysis of recidivism rates. Another example is that the progress of former psychiatric inpatients may be evaluated through use of hospital records. Finally, in the last, generally least desirable design from a methodological viewpoint, former clients are asked to report on their behavior over a given (past) period, and longitudinal inferences are drawn from such reports. Similarly, an individual may report on his or her present functioning, and determinants of that level of functioning are inferred from records or reports of past events. Because retrospective designs have many problems of interpretation and their primary value is for exploring new hypotheses, this chapter is concerned generally with prospective study of individuals.

SOURCES OF INSTITUTIONAL MEASURES AND TYPES OF DATA

Institutional measures may be obtained from a variety of sources. Franklin and Thrasher (1976) noted that almost all programs and organizations collect a considerable amount of data pertinent to treatment outcome. Similarly, Berelson and Steiner (1964) suggested the following sources of data may be used in an outcome study: census information; life insurance records; medical facility records; prison, church, and school records; and business records. Shyne (1975) wrote that the Department of Health, Education, and Welfare (or Health and Human Services) uses both the National Center for Health Statistics and the Bureau of Labor Statistics as its major sources of statistics relevant to social work research. The National Center for Health Statistics publishes vital statistics that may be of particular use to the outcome researcher, including information on birth, death, marriage and divorce rates. Furthermore, vital statistics are available at the level of local government (Webb et al., 1966). Although there are severe restrictions on accessibility of records that identify individuals, the Social Security Administration (SSA) provides data that are applicable to various stages of a treatment outcome study (Alexander & Jabine, 1978). For example, SSA records include data on living persons who are currently paying into its fund for workers, are drawing disability or retirement benefits on their own account, or are receiving supplemental security income payments. Furthermore, since information about the deceased is not covered by the Privacy Act of 1974, the SSA does release records of the facts and circumstances of death of individuals. In the specific context of drug abuse treatment outcome, Ball and Brown (1977) argued that treatment program agency records, published national and regional statistics on drug treatment populations, and demographic and census data are often useful to the outcome researcher. In summary, the sources of institutional measures seem to be limited only by the circumstances of data collection and the ingenuity of the researcher.

A good idea of the variety of sources of institutional measures and types of data that they provide may be obtained from a review of published treatment research literature. Therefore, we sampled the literature for outcome studies that included institutional measures. These studies are listed in Table 17.1 and may be classified into three client populations: adolescent, substance abuse, and general psychiatric. Often the authors of the reports failed to specify what outcome variables they were attempting to measure. In such cases the word "outcome" is noted as the variable measured. In addition, some of the studies were not concerned with the outcome of current clients, but they did involve the evaluation of outcome of past clients with records of their treatment history. It should be noted that this sample of studies is not meant to be exhaustive but to illustrate how institutional measures have been used to index psychological constructs. Furthermore, only outcome studies were included in the sample. Therefore, studies that may have involved, for example, estimates of alcoholism rates in a region on the basis of records indicating death by cirrhosis of the liver were not included. Also excluded were the numerous studies in which institutional records have been examined to determine incidence or prevalence rates (MacEachron, 1979).

Table 17.1 shows that a wide variety of record data have been used in outcome research and that the data are on both individual and aggregate levels. The frequency and variety of measures used seem to be related to the disorder treated. In this regard, the substance abuse outcome researchers in our sample of studies apparently have made the most extensive use of institutional measures. This is likely due to the nature of problems substance abuse clients bring to treatment and, relatedly, treatment goals. Thus alcohol and drug abusers frequently have a history of involvement with the legal system and of medical problems. Legal status and physical health are thus frequently among outcome variables, and record data may be used as relatively direct measures of such outcomes. Similarly, the type of measure used depends on the population tested. School records as measures of academic performance are used commonly in the studies of outcome in adolescent samples at risk for deviant behavior or classified as delinquent, but such measures are rarely used with the other client groups.

There are several other features of the studies listed in Table 17.1 that are worth noting because they accent some important points about using institutional measures of outcome. The authors of many of the reports listed in Table 17.1 did not make explicit their assumptions concerning the relationship between a particular institutional measure and the outcome variables of interest. Therefore, at times the reasons for choosing an institutional measure were not apparent. However, as with any other type of measure, its connection to a variable or construct should be clear to allow interpretation of a pattern of results. Another feature of the studies in Table 17.1 is that sometimes institutional records were the only type of data used. As we have stated earlier and repeat in this chapter, reliance on one type of data is to be avoided in favor of using multiple methods of measurement. This approach is essential to determining the validity of data relating to outcome variables that lack a definitive criterion (Waskow & Parloff, 1975).

The fact that sources of institutional measures of outcome are limited only by the conditions of data collection and the goals of treatment is illustrated by categorizing the sources of data listed in Table 17.1. In Table 17.1 we found 24 different sources of data among the relatively small number of studies that were sampled. For heuristic purposes, these were divided into five categories of data sources, including government (federal, state, and local), educational institutions (schools and universities), private sector (businesses), medical and psychological treatment settings, and the legal–correctional system. Many types of data were associated with each source. For example, "government" included census data, welfare records, and vital statistics, and "educational institutions" included grades, achievement test scores, and attendance and

Table 17.1. Sample Outcome Studies in Which Institutional Measures Were Successfully Used

References	Population Tested	Institutional Measures Used	Construct or Variable Measured
ADOLESCENT			
Allerhand et al., 1966	Institutionalized, emotionally disturbed youths (12–16 years old)	Lengthy past records (not specified); numerous psychological tests, and staff reports by cottage workers, teachers, and caseworkers; all data collected post treatment	Adaptability and adaptation of the children outside the institution
Berleman & Steinburn, 1969	High risk (of antisocial behavior) junior-high-school boys	Record search: juvenile court records; police, school and school disciplinary files searched; also, school grades; citizenship patterns, school attendance, health records	Delinquency
Garber, 1972	Adolescent psychiatric population (hospitalized)	Hospital records examined for identifying data, diagnostic impressions, therapists, school and program notes	Current function; functioning during hospital stay
Goldenberg, 1971	Low-SES male adolescents	Work attendance, performance on the job, advancement, and income obtained from employer; number of arrests, time in jail obtained from police	Assess vocational behavior and change; community behavior and change
Kent & O'Leary, 1977	Behavior problem children	Academic performance as measured by California Achievement Test and school grades	(Improvement in) academic performance
Lewis et al., 1979	Delinquent children	Children's hospital records examined (for seriousness and frequency of medical problems); state records examined for parent criminality	Parental criminality; children's health history

(continued)

Table 17.1. *(continued)*

Maas, 1969	Young adults who had been separated from home at an early age and placed in a nursery	Nursery records examined; collateral agencies' records examined (social and medical agencies)	Effect of childhood separation on adult adjustment (their feeling for life, inner controls, relationship patterns, role performance, and intellectual functioning)
Massimo & Shore, 1963	Adolescent delinquent boys	WAIS scores, Metropolitan Achievement Tests, school performance; legal status (obtained from probation officers as well as police records); work history	Records of anti-social behavior used to select subjects for study; also used to assess pretreatment functioning
Meyer et al., 1969	High-school girls, at risk for delinquency	School records examined for grades, attendance, conduct marks, health records; authorities contacted about subjects' legal status	Prevention of more "serious problems" later on
Snyder & White, 1979	Behaviorally disturbed, institutionalized adolescents	Class absences collected from teachers; number of observed incidents involving drug taking, physical aggression toward residents or staff, or destruction of property kept as a daily record	Social responsibility; impulsive behavior
SUBSTANCE ABUSE Caplovitz, 1976	Heroin addicts in treatment	Information on addicts in New York City obtained from the research office of the state's addiction agency; demographic data such as age, sex, marital status, ethnicity, and similar data from the 1970 census obtained	Wanted to measure characteristics of the working addict

Gearing, 1974	Heroin addicts admitted to a methadone maintenance program	Intake interview forms of a cohort of patients; unit director's monthly reports of employment status, schooling, or training, criminal problems; incarceration and arrest data obtained from the police department records; welfare records examined; employment status checked with paycheck stubs	Social productivity, antisocial behavior and detoxification—all measures that should relate to treatment success
Miller, 1978	Problem drinkers in treatment program	Driver's records of court-referred clients examined	Recidivism
Nash et al., 1976	Drug addicts in either methadone maintenance or drug-free treatment programs	Arrest data obtained from the records of the New Jersey state police; prison records checked; death records checked with the Bureau of Vital Statistics in the New Jersey Department of Health	Abatement in criminality
Sechrest & Dunckley, 1975	Drug addicts in a methadone maintenance treatment program	Data on number of arrests, type of conviction, type of sentence collected from the California Department of Justice, Bureau of Criminal Statistics; data on employment (determined by data on unemployment and disability insurance benefits) obtained from the "Base Wage File" of the California Department of Human Resources	Social responsibility
Simpson et al., 1979	Drug abuse clients in a wide variety of programs	Arrests and incarcerations determined from the criminal justice records; treatment files examined	Social responsibility

(Continued)

Table 17.1. *(continued)*

Vaillant, 1973	Heroin addicts out of treatment	Arrest and incarceration data obtained from the New York City police records; Bureau of Narcotic & Dangerous Drugs files searched; FBI criminal sheets obtained to check for convictions; files of drug treatment centers searched; vital statistics obtained from New York City Department of Health Records; data about employment checked with unemployment records	Life functioning of addicts
PSYCHIATRIC			
Evans et al., 1973	Schizophrenics (hospitalized for the first time)	Hospital treatment records examined to determine length of stay, medication, etc.	Relationship between premorbid adjustment, diagnosis, and outcome examined
Matthews & Burkhart, 1977	Outpatient psychiatric population; therapists also included in study	Files of patients reviewed; pretreatment MMPI scores examined; number of sessions clients attended	Client improvement as a function of type of therapist
Reinhart et al., 1972	Students hospitalized for psychiatric problems	SAT, ACE scores, GPA obtained from university academic records; diagnosis, length of hospitalization, kind of treatment collected from the hospital records	Impact of neuropsychiatric hospitalization on an individual's college career
Schwartz et al., 1973	Inpatient schizophrenics	Retrospective data (diagnosis, symptomatology, and treatment history) collected from hospital records	Maladjustment

disciplinary records. The "private sector" typically was used to evaluate employment functioning and involved measures such as paycheck stubs on employer reports or work records. "Medical and psychological treatment settings" were used, as would be expected, very often and included any data that were entered on a client's record of treatment. Thus diagnostic information, psychological test scores, physical health, and mental health status were obtained. Another common source was the "legal–correctional system," which typically provided arrest records and prison records.

It is important to realize that institutional measures have not typically been viewed as a method of assessing a client's behavior, at least in prospective studies. Most of the research is retrospective. Rather, they have most frequently been cited as a method for corroborating client's self-reports of their functioning in a variety of areas of life health (Hubbard, et al., 1976; Sobell & Sobell, 1980). For example, Sobell and Sobell (1978) used driver's records, arrest records, and hospital records to corroborate alcoholic clients' self-reports of possession of a valid driver's license and number of arrests and hospitalizations, respectively. Similarly, Robins (1966) used arrest records, jail records, and divorce records to corroborate personal interview data obtained from clients who were diagnosed as sociopathic personalities.

Although it is sound practice to substantiate self-report data, the more general principle to follow is to use as many methods as possible to measure outcome variables. The consistency across each measure then can be evaluated and confidence in conclusions drawn from the data can then be appraised accordingly. Institutional measures clearly may be one valuable method among a collection of outcome measures.

Interpretation of Institutional Measures

If institutional data are viewed like other types of data, then they can be interpreted with only limited background information. First, it is necessary to be aware of the goals of treatment and the individual client's history. A variable that is often measured with institutional data, recidivism (repetition of the problem that brought the client to treatment) provides a good example (Solomon & Doll, 1979). Assume that a treatment agency record is obtained indicating that an individual has reentered treatment during follow-up after the initial treatment has been terminated. Whether this event is interpreted as a positive or negative outcome can be determined only with information about the client's past and current behavior. Readmission to treatment may be viewed as an adaptive way of coping with current stresses, rather than as "relapsing" psychological problems. On the other hand, a different evaluation might follow if a client reentered treatment under coercion of the legal system for a drunk driving arrest. Another example is marital status, which is also commonly measured with institutional data. If is is discovered through use of vital statistics that a client is divorced during follow-up, this outcome can be interpreted only in the context of that client's past and present behavior.

Changes in a client's life should be evaluated with reference to that client's history and probable future trends without intervention.

The second important factor to consider in interpreting institutional measures is the confidence in the data. We are referring to the relationship between methods and measures used in one study and similar empirical studies. Thus, like any other type of measure, the reliability and validity of the data are critical. In this regard, treatment outcome research is notorious for its lack of attention to reliability and validity. Determination of the replicability of a result may be prohibitive given the time, effort, and expense of even a small outcome project. However, when measures are not carefully chosen in view of past research and theory, the interpretability of a specific finding is reduced.

Summary

In this section typical sources of institutional measures and the type of data that they provide were reviewed. It was shown that there is a wide variety of sources available, each associated with different types of data. A relatively small sample of outcome studies was presented that included 24 different sources of institutional measures. These sources were categorized into government, educational institutions, private sector, treatment settings, and legal–correctional system. Finally, it was argued that institutional measures should be viewed as a measure of outcome to be interpreted in the context of other types of measures (such as self-report) of the client's past and current behavior, and with due regard for their reliability and validity.

DESCRIPTIONS OF USE OF INSTITUTIONAL MEASURES IN OUTCOME RESEARCH

The variety of institutional measures on both the individual subject and aggregate levels may be applied to the different steps comprising a treatment evaluation. Such application ranges from design of the outcome study to assessment of client functioning during various periods following the termination of formal treatment. Indeed, although the psychological treatment literature shows that institutional measures have been used infrequently, illustrations of their application to most phases of outcome research can be found.

Use of Institutional Measures in the Design of Samples

Part of designing a treatment outcome evaluation concerns, of course, sampling of subjects for study. One aspect of sampling is representativeness of some population on specified characteristics (Borus, 1970; Riecken & Boruch, 1974; Shyne, 1975). For example, researchers may attempt to stratify their samples so that they are representative of the clients who come to specific treatment program with a particular diagnosis. The program's past treatment records could provide the required information in aggregate form. Another possibility is that researchers may want to assess how their own samples of clients compare on certain demographic characteristics to members of the community in which treatment is administered. The Census Bureau is one source of such grouped data.

Siegel and Goodman (1976) provided an illustration of the use of institutional data to define the different characteristics of clients and their communities covered by East Coast community mental health centers. Four centers participated in an attempt to develop an evaluation methodology that could be based on data that the centers collected routinely on individual clients. Important to the present discussion is the authors' attempt to define different "social areas" in order to classify the types of communities from which center clients were drawn. Census data were used to measure a community's social rank, lifestyle, and ethnicity. Social rank was measured by the census variables median house value and median rent. The census factor percent of persons living in overcrowded housing was used to assess lifestyle or urbanization, and ethnicity was assessed by information on the percentage of nonwhites in the population.

Use of Institutional Measures as Response or Behavior Measures

Selection of dependent measures is, of course, basic to any research endeavor. Such measures are used to characterize a client's functioning (behavior) during all phases of outcome research, from pretreatment to various times following treatment. Depending on the goals of treatment, institutional measures provide a valuable means for assessment of client functioning.

Table 17.1 showed the diverse sources and types of institutional data useful to assess client outcomes. A study by Sobell and Sobell (1973) is an excellent example of taking full advantage of institutional measures in assessing the functioning of clients following treatment for alcohol abuse. Furthermore, institutional records were used as measures of outcome, as corroboration of client self-reports, and as a method to virtually eliminate client attrition from the follow-up study. The subjects were 70 hospitalized chronic alcohol abusers, many of whom had had a history of treatment failures and a high level of transience. Multiple dimensions of outcome were measured. The major variables included (1) drinking behavior, (2) psychological adjustment, (3) vocational status; (4) driver's license status, (5) residential status, and (6) use of outpatient treatment supports.

Sobell and Sobell (1973, p. 601) described their use of institutional measures in the follow-up data collection and included the following: (1) data were obtained every two months during the follow-up interval, and the "rap sheets" (criminal records obtained from the California Bureau of Criminal Identification and Investigation and the Federal Bureau of Investigation) were studied; (2) each subject's driver's record was obtained from the California Department of Motor Vehicles (the record included out-of-state traffic violations, accidents, arrests); (3) all jail and hospital incarcerations of subjects were verified by contacting the appropriate facility (this procedure also permitted determination of the relationship between the incarceration and drinking); and (4) a multitude of public and private agencies were contacted to obtain information on subjects. These included the California Department of Human Resources Development, credit bureaus, the Veterans Administration, telephone companies, the Social Security Administration, Bureaus of Vital Statistics and Records, Welfare Departments, municipal courts, and the California Bureau of Biostatistics.

In summary, the Sobell and Sobell (1973) study is exemplary because it demonstrates the flexibility and value of institutional measures when they are used by diligent researchers in obtaining sound outcome data. Institutional measures were used jointly as (1) direct measures of client functioning and as corroboration of client self-reports and (2) as a way to keep track of a clinical population during follow-up that has always been considered extremely difficult to locate. This was reflected in the authors' success in obtaining follow-up data on 69 of 70 clients. Similar procedures were used to collect two and three-year outcome data (Caddy, 1980). Therefore, institutional measures may be used as an integral component of outcome data that have empirically demonstrated validity.

Use of Institutional Measures During Follow-Up

In addition to assessing a client's behavior, institutional measures may be incorporated into at least two other features of the follow-up design. One application that has received little attention among psychologists is the use of institutional measures on the aggregate level to define the community to which the client returns following treatment. Siegel and Goodman's (1976) use of census data to define social areas, for example, could easily be made part of a follow-up design. When therapy is conducted on an out-patient basis, this application would also be pertinent to measurement of client functioning during treatment.

The argument for including such measurement is based on the assumption that the most sensitive analysis of a individual's behavior may be one that is interpreted within the context of the environment in which that behavior occurs. Thus institutional data can be extremely useful in providing a background against which behavior change can be viewed. For example, if one goal of treatment were full-time employment and job satisfaction, it would be important to know the unemployment rate of the community where the client resides. Such measures could be used to provide a specific reference point for making comparisons (Simon, 1969). For instance, knowledge of the unemployment rate of adolescents in a community would be useful to researchers interested in the effects of a job training program on adolescent's vocational status. Or an evaluation of the divorce rate among psychiatric clients can be aided by examining the divorce rate in the community as a whole. In the case of alcoholic samples, assessment of a client's drinking behavior following treatment for alcohol abuse may be facilitated if the researcher were aware of the availability of alcohol in the client's community. Information such as the distribution of beverage alcohol outlets, sales of alcohol beverages, and drunk driving offense enforcement rates are a few types of institutional data that the researcher may easily access. Similarly, the availability of drugs in a community may be estimated by examining police departments records for illicit drug selling and use.

Finally, as noted earlier, institutional measures may also be used during follow-up to limit sample attrition, a serious threat to the external validity of outcome data. Attrition is an especially acute problem when the sample is drawn from typically mobile populations, such as alcohol and drug abusers and young adults. O'Donnell (undated) described the use of various institutional measures in his successful efforts to follow drug abusers after they leave treatment. Some of the techniques that O'Donnell discussed are similar to those used by Sobell and Sobell (1973) and involve the use of data that are easily accessed, and others currently require the client's informed consent. (Informed consent procedures are discussed in a later section of this chapter). Of course, the way to ensure that certain types of data may be accessed during follow-up is to obtain the client's informed consent at the beginning of the evaluation study. The researcher must be careful not to abuse the principle of informed consent in such efforts [see also Caddy (1980)].

Some of the sources of data that O'Donnell presented are as follows:

1. *Post office.* At minimal cost a card may be sent to a client's old address, and it will be returned either with a check that the address is still correct or with a forwarding address. Local post offices typically retain forwarding addresses for one year.

2. *Record checks.* Individuals may be located through files of utility companies, local hospital records, welfare records, state employment agencies, schools, voter registration lists, state departments of motor vehicles, libraries, and military base locators. For certain samples, law enforcement records may be valuable, such as local police, sheriff, jail, and bail bondman records, probation and parole records, and state police and prison records. City directories are another obvious source of information.

3. *Telephone directories.* The telephone directory and cross directory may be useful in obtaining current phone numbers and addresses.

Summary

In this section we have shown that institutional records can be extremely useful in all phases of treatment outcome research. Specifically, institutional records may be used in designing a sampling plan so that research participants are representative on selected variables, in providing measures of client behavior to be used jointly with other types of measure such as client self-reports, in providing an environmental context for interpreting an individual's behavior, and in locating clients during follow-up. We argued that diligent use of institutional measures in treatment outcome research can add depth to outcome data and substantially increase their validity.

ADVANTAGES AND DISADVANTAGES OF USING INSTITUTIONAL MEASURES IN OUTCOME RESEARCH

It would be possible to list advantages and disadvantages that are associated with each source of institutional measures or types of data that are obtained from them. If such a task were completed, it would be clear that there would be much overlap between different sources and the records that they provide. Furthermore, the value of the data depend very much on the conditions under which they were recorded and collected. Therefore, it appears that it would be more useful to discuss the *general* features of institutional data that any researcher who elects to use them should be aware of.

In our literature review we discovered several authors who commented on the utility of institutional data (Riecken & Boruch, 1975; Selltiz et al., 1976; Shyne, 1975; Webb et al., 1966; Weiss, 1972; Weissman, 1975). Across these references different advantages and disadvantages can be discerned in using institutional data either on the aggregate or the individual level. These are listed in Table 17.2

It is useful to briefly describe the individual entries in Table 17.2. Among the

Table 17.2.   Advantages and Disadvantages of Using Institutional Measures

Advantages	Disadvantages
1. Nonreactive	1. May be irrelevant to treatment goals
2. Low cost and little time to collect data	2. Susceptible to random error and systematic biases
3. Ability to study hypotheses (in field experiments) as external conditions vary over time	3. Recording errors unknown
4. Grouped data are relatively easily obtained	4. May not be representative because of inaccuracy or missing data
5. May be used to limit sample attrition in treatment outcome studies	5. Differences in definition of terms during different historical periods
6. Can provide more objective, quantifiable measures of change in life functioning	6. May not be up-to-date
7. Could provide information about treatment effects that were not foreseen or expected	7. May not be consistently available

advantages, perhaps the most important (and the one for which institutional measures are best known) is nonreactivity. A nonreactive measure is one that is obtained without the individual's awareness of any special observations. Therefore, the pitfalls of an individual's awareness of being observed, such as biased reporting or behavior, are avoided. Low cost and little time required for collection of the data are straightforward and will apply if the researcher plans the data collection adequately. The ability to study hypotheses as external conditions change over time refers to the opportunity to conduct "natural experiments" regarding, for example, the effects of some social policy or legal innovations. Furthermore, when data are desired on the aggregate level, minimal cooperation is required from the subjects of investigation. As we have shown, institutional records can considerably aid location of clients during follow-up. Advantage 6 in Table 17.2 related to nonreactivity and refers to the increased scientific value that institutional measures may lend to outcome data. Finally, institutional measures may allow detection of effects of a treatment that might not be discovered in data that are more limited by a researcher's expectations of the results of treatment.

Among the disadvantages appearing in Table 17.2, five refer to problems in reliability and validity (items 2 to 6) that *may be* side effects of the nonreactivity of the measures. That is, for the very reason that institutional measures are nonreactive—the data were collected independent of a particular study—the accuracy and completeness of the data are not under the researcher's control. Relevance to treatment goals suggests that, because record data likely were not designed to answer the same questions immediately concerning the researcher, they may not be directly related to treatment goals and outcomes. Another possible problem is that definitions of terms used in records may not be specified and could differ from what a researcher assumes. Researchers must also be aware that the availability of records could be unexpectedly limited as a result of conditions imposed by an institution.

All the above disadvantages point to problems in the interpretation of the findings of research. In fact, their difficulties may be taken to mean that the problems in institutional measures prohibit their use. Indeed, some outcome researchers have expressed this view (Weissman, 1975). However, it is essential to remember that the same limitations can apply to other data sources, depending on the conditions under which the data were collected. For example, client's self-reports of behavior, if not verified, cannot be assumed to be accurate. We see little conceptual difference between the problems with using institutional measures and with the use of any other type of measure. Furthermore, under some circumstances, the advantages of institutional measures may be seen as essential to a researcher's goals. In this regard, measures of outcome must be obtained under conditions that allow the highest likelihood of their reliability and validity (Maisto et al., 1979). One important step is to be as clear as possible about the conditions under which the record data were collected and the reasons for collecting the data (Selltiz et al., 1976). In this way the researcher can learn such important information as definitions of categories and terms in the data, as well as possible sources of error in recording. In short, the limitations of the data can be evaluated. Webb et al. (1966) also suggested that internal analyses of the data may be conducted in order to handle problems of selective deposit and survival. Such analyses would ordinarily consist of dividing the data into subclasses and making cross-checks.

Finally, we have noted that a long-standing problem is that psychotherapy outcome research lacks the ultimate criterion, one that yields a definitive measure of outcome. Each type of measure that has been used in outcome research has specific strengths and weaknesses that must be identified. Therefore, the best available procedure for ensuring valid results is to use multiple measures, including institutional measures, if relevant, of the same outcome variables. For instance, if a researcher decides that institutional measures may contribute to her understanding of outcome, there are some important questions that may determine whether the advantages of these measures can be realized:

1. How direct a measure of the outcome variables does the recorded data provide? Does their connection to outcome require some unvalidated assumptions?
2. Under what conditions were the data collected?
3. What kind of record-keeping system does the relevant institution have? Is record keeping a routine procedure? Is it systematic and up-to-date?
4. To what extent does the content of the record depend on the recorder? For instance, is the record a subjective entry such as a psychiatric diagnosis or test interpretation, or something more objective, such as the dates that an individual participated in a treatment program? If subjective factors are heavily involved in the record data, it may be even more important to know several details concerning the conditions of data entry.
5. Have there been any changes in the system of record keeping during the time of interest?

As can be seen from these questions, the extent and value of what can be gained from using institutional measures (as with other types of measure) depend ultimately on the diligence and foresight of the researcher. Clearly, institutional measures provide numerous advantages to the treatment outcome researcher who needs interpretable measures of outcome.

INSTITUTIONAL MEASURES AND CLIENT CONFIDENTIALITY

Researchers typically have relatively easy access to institutional data that have already been summarized by the granting institution. That is, when data are requested in a form so that individuals are not directly identified and there is little potential for them to be identified indirectly, data can be obtained for legitimate purposes with relatively little requirement on the researcher's part. This can be done through normal institutional channels or through the Freedom of Information Act (Boruch & Cecil, 1979). In this regard, researchers may request information from an institution by writing a letter specifying what data are desired and how the data will be used. Furthermore, this is the type of request for information in which the subjects need not be contacted and thus not required to cooperate with the researcher.

However, many of the advantages in using institutional measures in outcome studies derive from the unique contributions such measures make to information about individual clients. Therefore, the researcher is placed in the position of requesting records that will reveal something about the history of specific, identifiable individuals. This context of data collection greatly differs from the case in which individuals are not identified and is associated with many more restrictions in data accessibility to people outside of the granting institution or agency.[*] This has been a subject of increasing sensitivity over the last 10 years and is closely related to questions of an individual's right to privacy and to client confidentiality (Panel on Privacy and Behavioral Research, 1967; Riecken & Boruch, 1974).

Although questions concerning the individual's right to privacy have received wide publicity only recently, it has been suggested that privacy between client and clinician has long been tacitly acknowledged as an essential part of their relationship (Hagedorn et al., 1976). Boruch and Cecil (1979, p. 23) defined privacy as a state of the individual, that is, "whether the individual's attitudes and experiences are known to another." Furthermore, the right of privacy "concerns the individual's control over whether and to what extent information about himself or herself will be shared with anyone else" (Boruch & Cecil, 1979, p.23). Clinicians and researchers honor rights to privacy by eliciting any personal data about individuals only in the context of voluntary disclosure.

Confidentiality is closely related to privacy. Information that one individual conveys to another is confidential when it is assumed that such information will not be disclosed with identifying data to third parties. Identifiers may include names, addresses, and other unique tags. Psychological researchers and clinicians are, of course, ethically obligated to respect the confidentiality of their subjects and clients.

Increasing concern about violation of individuals' right to privacy and threats to confidentiality from accumulation of sophisticated computer data banks led to the Federal Privacy Act of 1974 (PL 93-579). This legislation, which originally was passed to protect federal agency records, has considerably altered researchers' accessibility to information that identifies individuals. For example, Alexander and Jabine (1978) noted how the Privacy Act markedly

---

[*] An exception to these restrictions is information that is part of the public record. These include, for example, certain vital statistics such as information surrounding an individual's death and arrest records of a local police department.

restricted the Social Security Administration's release of data to individuals outside of that agency.

As summarized by Bower and de Gasparis (1978), the act stipulates that federal agencies identify their record systems annually and establish minimum standards to regulate data collection, use, and security. Individuals are also permitted access to their own records and to challenge the accuracy of the data contained in such records. Most important for the outcome researcher, the act states that unless the individual gives informed consent, no agency is permitted to release records unless exceptions or conditions specified in the act apply. Informed consent is defined as " 'the knowing consent of an individual or his legally authorized representative, so situated as to be able to exercise free power of choice without undue inducement or any element of force, fraud, deceit, duress, or other form of constraint or coercion' " (Bower & de Gasparis, 1978, p. 8). Another important feature of the Privacy Act is that release of records is also the discretion of the agency possessing the records. Thus, if an agency desires to maintain confidentiality of its records, it is free to resist researchers' requests.

It has been argued (Bower & de Gasparis, 1978) that there are several elements of the Privacy Act that weaken its protection of identifiable records. First, the act controls only records maintained by federal agencies. Private record systems and those maintained by local and state governments that do not receive federal funding are not covered by this act. Furthermore, the act stipulates a number of exceptions to its protection. These include disclosures to employees of the agency for reasons consistent with which the records were collected, to the Census Bureau, to the National Archives when preservation is appropriate, to agencies to facilitate law enforcement, to Congressional committees, to the comptroller or pursuant to court order, and when there are questions of the individual's health and safety. Finally, even nonfederal employees have access to agency records for the purposes of "routine" statistical use.

Despite stipulations that weaken the Privacy Act, it still has made researchers' access to identifying data considerably more difficult than it was previously. Before passage of the act, researchers were able to obtain individual records relatively easily through the Freedom of Information Act, if it was for legitimate reasons and did not present an undue violation of individual rights to privacy and confidentiality. Furthermore, although the Privacy Act pertains only to federal agencies and to institutions receiving federal support, it covers a wide body of data that are useful to outcome researchers. At the least, the scope of identifying records that the outcome researcher has free access to has been substantially narrowed.

Therefore, legislation passed during the 1970s has made it incumbent on the researcher to obtain a client's informed consent to obtain information if institutional measures are to be used in outcome studies. In this regard, stipulations about the confidentiality of alcohol and drug abuse clients' records (Department of Health, Education, & Welfare, 1975) illustrate elements of a client's formal release of information about him or herself: (1) the name of the program that is to make the disclosures; (2) the name or title of the person who is to make the disclosure; (3) the client's name; (4) the purpose of the disclosure; (5) the nature and extent of information to be disclosed; (6) a statement that the consent is subject to revocation at any time and a specification of the date, event, or condition on which it will expire without expressed revocation; (7) the date on which the consent is signed; and (8) the client's signature and, in the case of minors, the signature of a person authorized to provide a signature in lieu of the client.

Researchers must guard against several problems in obtaining informed consent. It violates the spirit and letter of the law to obtain blanket consent forms, which refer to a client's authorizing release of his or her records without knowing what information those records contain (Ellis, 1977; Smith, 1981). Researchers should also be aware of the special provisions regarding access to the records of minors and to protect minors' rights to privacy and confidentiality (Lister et al., 1975) when working with such populations. Finally, there is ambiguity in the concept of informed consent, which often does not allow assurance that clients are being protected. Essentially, the definitions of "informed" and "consent" are not absolute (Bower & de Gasparis, 1978). In many instances subjects do not have the background to fully understand the purposes of the research in which they are participating and the ramifications of their consent to its various requirements. For example, Bower and de Gasparis (1978) cited a study (Gray, 1974) in which it was found that 39% of the research subjects in a hospital setting recognized that they were participating in a medical study only by talking to the author. These subjects had given their "informed" consent to participate in the study. To date there has been virtually no work in the treatment outcome area on the extent of clients' understanding of the ramifications of their agreeing to participate in a study, but it appears to be a central question for outcome researchers.

Summary

It is important to distinguish between levels of data in accessing institutional records. Researchers typically can access data from institutions relatively easily if those data are in a form preventing identification of individuals. Access can be achieved by formal written request to the institution. In the case of data pertaining to individuals, it is necessary to further distinguish between records obtained from an institution that the researcher is formally affiliated with and records of outside institutions. Researchers have fairly easy access to an agency's data regarding individuals if the individual is affiliated with that agency and can justify a need for the data. However, access to data on individuals included in records held by an outside (the researcher's) agency requires the client's informed consent. In prospective outcome studies, therefore, it is necessary to obtain the client's voluntary informed consent to obtain information about him or her from specified sources at the beginning of the evaluation effort. In this regard, the researcher is obligated not to violate the spirit or letter of the law in obtaining informed consents. Thus the researcher should ensure as much as possible that the client is aware of what he or she is consenting to and the ramifications of that consent. Furthermore, under no circumstances should clients be asked to grant blanket consent, which would amount to noninformed consent.

GENERAL SUMMARY AND CONCLUSIONS

This chapter was designed to provide a survey of the use of institutional measures in treatment outcome research and focused on measuring treatment outcome of individuals. The first section of the chapter delineated the sources of institutional measures and the types of data that can be obtained from them. This discussion included guidelines in interpreting institutional data. The next section of the chapter was a description of uses of institutional data in published outcome research. The major aspects of an outcome study were covered, including sample selection, measuring client behavior, and procedures for tracking clients during follow-up. The last sections of the chapter reviewed the advantages and disadvantages of using institutional data in outcome evaluations and their application in the current legal environment.

Institutional measures are best seen as one method, among others, with unique advantages in measuring outcome. These advantages include nonreactivity, prevention of subject attrition, and interpretability, which are strong reasons for using institutional measurements to facilitate specification of the effects of treatment.

If institutional measures are used in view of their pitfalls as well as strengths, they can provide the outcome researcher with a relatively cheap, nonreactive addition to that researcher's collection of outcome indices. Given the continued increased costs associated with conducting outcome research, institutional measures should be considered as one valuable source of information, usable during the design and implementation of an outcome study.

REFERENCES

Alexander, L., & Jabine, T. Access to Social Security microdata files for research and statistical purposes. *Social Security Bulletin*, 1978, **41**, 3–17.

Allerhand, M., Weber, R., & Haug, M. *Adaptation and adaptability: The Bellefair follow-up study*. New York: Child Welfare League of America, 1966.

Ball, J., & Brown, B. S. Institutional sources of data. In U. S. Department of Health, Education and Welfare, *Conducting follow-up research on drug treatment programs*, 1977.

Berelson, B., & Steiner, G. *Human behavior: An inventory of scientific findings*. New York: Harcourt, Brace, & World, 1964.

Berleman, W. C., & Steinburn, T. W. The execution and evaluation of a delinquency prevention program. In P. Fellin, T. Tripodi, & H. Meyer (Eds.), *Exemplars of social research*. Itasca, Ill.: Peacock, 1969.

Boruch, R. F., & Cecil, J. S. *Assuring the confidentiality of social research data*. Philadelphia: University of Pennsylvania Press, 1979.

Borus, M. Using employment insurance wage reports as a data source. *Monthly Labor Review*, 1970, **93**, 66–68.

Bower, R. T., & de Gasparis, P. *Ethics in social research*. New York: Praeger, 1978.

Caddy, G. R. A review of problems in conducting alcohol treatment outcome studies. In L. C. Sobell, M. B. Sobell, & E. Ward (Eds.), *Evaluating alcohol and drug abuse treatment effectiveness*. New York: Pergamon, 1980.

Caplovitz, D. *The working addict*. White Plains, N. Y.: M.E. Sharpe, Inc., 1976.

Department of Health, Education, and Welfare. Confidentiality of alcohol and drug abuse patient records. *Federal Register*, 1975, **40**, 27802–27821.

Ellis, J. W. Patient rights in program evaluation. In R.D. Coursey, G. A. Specter, S. A. Murrell, & B. Hunt (Eds.), *Program evaluation for mental health*. New York: Grune & Stratton, 1977.

Evans, J., Goldstein, M., & Rodnick, E. Premorbid adjustment, paranoid diagnosis, and remission: Acute schizophrenics treated in a community mental health center. *Archives of General Psychiatry*, 1973, **28**, 666–672.

Franklin, J., & Thrasher, J. *An introduction to program evaluation*. New York: Wiley, 1976.

Garber, B. *Follow-up study of hospitalized adolescents*. New York: Brunner/Mazel, 1972.

Gearing, F. Methadone maintenance treatment five years later—where are they now? *American Journal of Public Health Supplement*, 1974, **64**, 44–50.

Goldenberg, I. *Build me a mountain: Youth, poverty, and the creation of new settings*. Cambridge, Mass.: MIT Press, 1971.

Gray, B. *Social control by peer review: The case of human experimentation*. Paper presented at the Annual Meeting of the American Sociological Association, Montreal, Canada, May 1974.

Guess, L. L., & Tuchfeld, B. S. *Manual for drug abuse treatment program evaluation*. Rockville, Md.: National Institute on Drug Abuse, 1977.

Hagedorn, H. J., Beck, K. J., Neubert, S. F., & Werlin, S. H. *A working manual of simple program evaluation techniques for community mental health centers*. Rockville, Md.: National Institute of Mental Health, 1976.

Hersen, M., & Bellack, A. S. *Behavioral assessment: A practical handbook*. New York: Pergamon, 1976.

Hubbard, R. L., Eckerman, W. C., & Rachal, J. V. Methods of validating self-reports of drug use: A critical review. *Proceedings of the American Statistical Association*, 1976.

Kent, R., & O'Leary, D. Treatment of conduct problem children: BA and/or PhD therapists. *Behavior Therapy*, 1977, **8**, 653–658.

Lewis, D., Shanok, S., & Balla, D. Parental criminality and medical histories of delinquent children. *American Journal of Psychiatry*, 1979, **136**, 288–292.

Lister, C., Baker, M. A., & Milhaus, R. L. Record keeping, access, and confidentiality. In N. Hobbs (Ed.), *Issues in the classification of children* (Vol. 2). San Francisco: Jossey-Bass, 1975.

Maas, H. S. The young adult adjustment of twenty wartime residential nursery children. In P. Fellen, T. Tripodi, & H. Meyer (Eds.), *Exemplars of social research*. Itasca, Ill.: Peacock, 1969.

MacEachron, A. E. Mentally retarded offenders: Prevalence and characteristics. *American Journal of Mental Deficiency*, 1979, **84**, 165–176.

Maisto, S. A., Sobell, M. B., & Sobell, L. C. Comparison of alcoholics' self-reports of drinking behavior with reports of collateral informants. *Journal of Consulting and Clinical Psychology*, 1979, **46**, 106–112.

Massimo, J., & Shore, M. The effectiveness of a comprehensive vocationally oriented psychotherapeutic program for adolescent delinquent boys. *American Journal of Orthopsychiatry*, 1963, **33**, 634–642.

Matthews, J., & Burkhart, B. A-B therapist status, patient diagnoses and psychotherapy outcome in a psychiatric outpatient population. *Journal of Consulting and Clinical Psychology*, 1977, **45**, 475–482.

Meyer, H. J., Borgatta, E. F., & Jones, W. C. An experiment in prevention through social work intervention. In P. Fellen, T. Tripodi, & H. Meyer (Eds.), *Exemplars of social research*. Itasca, Ill.: Peacock, 1969.

Miller, W. Behavioral treatment of problem drinkers: A comparative outcome study of three controlled drinking therapies. *Journal of Consulting and Clinical Psychology*, 1978, **46**, 74–86.

Nash, G., Foster, K., & Lynn, R. *The impact of drug abuse treatment upon criminality: A look at 34 programs in New Jersey*. Unpublished manuscript, 1976.

O'Donnell, J.A. *Locating subjects and obtaining cooperation*. Unpublished manuscript, University of Kentucky, undated.

Panel on Privacy and Behavioral Research: Report. *Science*, 1967, **155**, 535–538.

Reinhart, M., Lohr, N., Schaefer, D., Berlinger, N., & Huddlestone, J. Evaluation of academic performance in a neuropsychiatric hospitalized population. *Archives of General Psychiatry*, 1972, **26**, 68–70.

Riecken, H., & Boruch, R. *Social experimentation: A method of planning and evaluating social intervention*. New York: Academic Press, 1974.

Robins, L. *Deviant children grown up*. Baltimore: Williams & Wilkins, 1966.

Schwartz, C., Myers, J., & Astrachan, B. The outcome study in psychiatric evaluation research. *Archives of General Psychiatry*, 1973, **29**, 98–102.

Sechrest, D., & Dunckley, T. Criminal activity, wages earned, and drug use after two years of methadone treatment. *Addictive Diseases*, 1975, **1**, 491–512.

Selltiz, C., Wrightsman, L., & Cook, S. *Research methods in social relations*. New York: Holt, Rinehart & Winston, 1976.

Shyne, A.M. Exploiting available information. In N. Polansky (Ed.), *Social work research: Methods for the helping professions*. Chicago: The University of Chicago Press, 1975.

Siegel, C., & Goodman, A. An evaluative paradigm for community mental centers using an automated data system. *Community Mental Health Journal*, 1976, **12**, 215–227.

Simon, J. L. *Basic research methods in social science: The art of empirical investigation.* New York: Random House, 1969.

Simpson, D., Savage, J., & Lloyd, M. Follow-up evaluation of treatment of drug abuse during 1969 to 1972. *Archives of General Psychiatry*, 1979, **36**, 772–780.

Smith, D. Unfinished business with informed consent procedures. *American Psychologist*, 1981, **36**, 22–26.

Snyder, J., & White, M. The use of cognitive self-instruction in the treatment of behaviorally disturbed adolescents. *Behavior Therapy*, 1979, **10**, 227–235.

Sobell, L. C., & Sobell, M. B. Validity of self-reports in three populations of alcoholics. *Journal of Consulting and Clinical Psychology*, 1978, **46**, 901–907.

Sobell, L. C., & Sobell, M. B. Convergent validity: An approach to increasing confidence in treatment outcome conclusions with alcohol and drug abusers. In L. C. Sobell, M. B. Sobell, & E. Ward (Eds.), *Evaluating alcohol and drug abuse treatment effectiveness.* New York: Pergamon, 1980.

Sobell, M. B., & Sobell, L. C. Alcoholics treated by individualized behavior therapy: One year treatment outcome. *Behavior Research and Therapy*, 1973, **11**, 599–618.

Solomon, P., & Doll, W. The varieties of readmission: The case against the use of recidivism rates as a measure of program effectiveness. *American Journal of Orthopsychiatry*, 1979, **49**, 230–239.

Vaillant, E. 20-Year follow-up of New York narcotic addicts. *Archives of General Psychiatry*, 1973, **29**, 237–241.

Waskow, I. E., & Parloff, M. B. (Eds.). *Psychotherapy change measures.* Rockville, Md.: National Institute of Mental Health, 1975.

Webb, E. J., Campbell, D. T., Schwartz, R. D., & Sechrest, L. *Unobtrusive measures: Nonreactive research in the social sciences.* Chicago: Rand McNally, 1966.

Weiss, C. H. *Evaluative research: Methods for assessing program effectiveness.* Englewood Cliffs, N.J.: Prentice Hall, 1972.

Weissman, M. The assessment of social adjustment. A review of techniques. *Archives of General Psychiatry*, 1975, **32**, 357–365.

PART FIVE

Summary

CHAPTER 18

Assessing the Effects of Psychological Treatments: A Summary

M. J. LAMBERT AND E. R. CHRISTENSEN

The assessment of changes in patients following psychological treatments has a relatively short history. However, there has been considerable progress in assessment, in terms of the quality, quantity, and variety of devices, as well as the methodology involved in their use. Assessment procedures are becoming more comprehensive, more complex, and relying more heavily on standardized instruments that deal with specific kinds of change. The preceeding chapters are a testimony to these trends. There is a growing sensitivity to the fact that change is multidimensional and that the results of evaluations are dependent on the source from which data are collected; there is also an increasing awareness of methods that are used, the content area that is being tapped, and the implicit associated values underlying the available devices.

TOWARD SPECIFICITY

As with the treatment of medical disorders, where greater specificity and more reliable and valid measures exist, the trend in psychological treatments is toward greater specificity. The major thrust of research at this time should continue to be on identifying measures that are uniquely appropriate to assessing changes in the specific problems and disorders that particular treatments are aimed at changing. This kind of specificity will eventually result in the identification of the most powerful and useful treatment methods. Although not comprehensive, the chapters included in the present text have covered a broad range of patient populations and disorders. The kind of specificity called for has resulted in a variety of recommendations that cannot be briefly summarized. A few general observations, however, seem appropriate.

Measurements of outcome in specific populations cannot be accomplished with a single core battery of devices. Although most clinical populations share

629

the symptoms of increased anxiety and poor morale or depressed mood, these are by no means the most important or central symptoms in all groups. For example, patients entering treatment at a crises center, correctional populations, schizophrenics in outpatient treatment, and adolescents vary a great deal in the degree to which they can be appropriately assessed with standardized measures of these symptoms.

Sabalis (Chapter 8, this volume), for example, has clearly indicated the complexity of assessing sexual behavior. An exhaustive analysis of change in this domain would include biological changes (biochemistry, physiology), psychological (desire for sexual activity, sexual thoughts, sexual knowledge, sexual attitudes, subjective emotional satisfaction, sexual activity), interpersonal (expectations for interpersonal sexual situation, partners' emotional and sexual responses, nature of the interpersonal relationship), and societal (prosocial behavior). Recognition of the complexity of extensively measuring changes in specific disorders makes one aware of the limitations and even the inadequacies of less compulsive approaches to the problem.

The kinds of assessment tool that are used with various populations are highly dependent on the resources and purposes of evaluations. A particular assessment tool that is appropriate with chronic outpatients, such as those discussed by Wallace and Haas, may be practical and highly valuable in a study aimed at program evaluation but inappropriate for a more tightly controlled study with a more scientific purpose. A study aimed at changes in sexual functioning may extensively investigate biological, interpersonal, and intrapersonal changes or be limited to assessment of increased orgasmic response. Clearly, the scientific community and public policy makers need to be sensitive to the limitations that result from narrow purposes and limited resources. Chapters 5 through 12 provide the researcher with a starting point for future investigations of changes in many of the most important and challenging patient populations.

DIRECTIONS FOR FUTURE RESEARCH

Research on psychotherapy outcome is of potentially great value. If the treatments people receive and pay for are to be improved, the improvement will be in no small way related to this type of research. Before outcome research can live up to its promise and our high expectations, the quality of dependent measures must be high. Therefore, outcome research must show more than a passing interest in instrument and method quality.

There is an urgent need for studies that deal directly with the interrelationship of instruments that purport to measure the same dimensions. One step in this research would be to focus on the interrelationship of devices within a source of assessment such as self-report or significant-other report. Another step would be to examine the interrelationship of devices that purport to measure the same content but are derived from different sources.

In situations where broad conclusions—ranging across many specific studies on sets of data—are desired, data aggregation techniques or meta analysis may become increasingly important. Research should pay careful attention to variables that interact with source of measurement. Of primary importance would be the method of measurement—descriptive data, judgmental data, performance data, and status data (see Chapter 1). In addition, researchers may also find it productive to make judgments about the content of data. Does it assess functioning mainly in the affective, cognitive, social, or conative domain?

At this time there has not been any systematic research on instrumentation that has conceptualized outcome measures in such an exhaustive fashion. Whether research based on such a conceptualization will prove beneficial remains to be seen. We are optimistic that it will solve some of the more recalcitrant problems facing the field and move psychotherapy research further along its present stage of development.

Appendix A

CONFIDENTIAL: THERAPIST(S) WILL NOT SEE THIS FORM

I.D. Number_____   Date_____

It is important for us to find out how you feel about your experiences at our mental health center. If you will answer the questions below, it will help us to improve our services. Both positive and negative feelings about your experiences will be helpful. Please check the box which most closely matches your feelings.

1. The problems, feelings or situations that brought me to the Mental Health Center are:
   ☐ A. Much Improved
   ☐ B. Improved
   ☐ C. About the same
   ☐ D. Worse
   ☐ E. Much Worse

2. Because of therapy, I understand the problem well enough to manage it in the future:
   ☐ A. Strongly agree
   ☐ B. Agree
   ☐ C. Neither agree nor disagree
   ☐ D. Disagree
   ☐ E. Strongly disagree

3. I think my therapist(s) has been:
   ☐ A. Very easy to talk with
   ☐ B. Somewhat easy to talk with
   ☐ C. Neither easy nor hard to talk with
   ☐ D. Somewhat hard to talk with
   ☐ E. Very hard to talk with

4. I feel that the orientation I received about therapy and related services was:
   ☐ A. Very satisfactory
   ☐ B. Somewhat satisfactory
   ☐ C. Neither satisfactory nor unsatisfactory
   ☐ D. Somewhat unsatisfactory
   ☐ E. Very unsatisfactory

5. I feel that the information I received about fees and payment for services was:
   ☐ A. Very satisfactory
   ☐ B. Somewhat satisfactory
   ☐ C. Neither satisfactory nor unsatisfactory
   ☐ D. Somewhat unsatisfactory
   ☐ E. Very unsatisfactory

6. I found the Center staff other than therapists (for example secretaries, intake interviewers, etc.) to be:
   ☐ A. Very helpful and pleasant
   ☐ B. Somewhat helpful and pleasant
   ☐ C. Neither helpful and pleasant nor unhelpful and unpleasant
   ☐ D. Somewhat unhelpful and unpleasant
   ☐ E. Very unhelpful and unpleasant

7. If I needed help in the future, I would come back to the Mental Health Center.
   ☐ A. Definitely yes
   ☐ B. Probably yes
   ☐ C. Maybe
   ☐ D. Probably not
   ☐ E. Definitely not

8. I would recommend the Mental Health Center to others needing help
   ☐ A. Definitely yes
   ☐ B. Probably yes
   ☐ C. Maybe
   ☐ D. Probably not
   ☐ E. Definitely not

9. The interest shown by my therapist(s) in helping me solve my problems has been:
   ☐ A. Very satisfactory
   ☐ B. Satisfactory
   ☐ C. Neither satisfactory nor unsatisfactory
   ☐ D. Unsatisfactory
   ☐ E. Very Unsatisfactory

10. Are you still receiving therapy at the Center?
   ☐ A. Yes
   ☐ B. No

11. If no, how long has it been since your last visit?
   ☐ A. Less than one month
   ☐ B. One or two months
   ☐ C. Three to five months
   ☐ D. Six months or more

COMMENTS:
_____
_____
_____
_____
_____
_____

UMHPEC/3-79   WE WOULD APPRECIATE ANY ADDITIONAL COMMENTS ON REVERSE SIDE OF THIS PAGE

Appendix B

SERVICE EVALUATION QUESTIONNAIRE

Please help us improve our program by answering some questions about the services you have received. We are interested in your honest opinion, whether they are positive or negative. *Please answer all of the questions.* We also welcome your comments and suggestions. Thank you very much, we really appreciate your help.

CIRCLE YOUR ANSWER

1. How would you rate the quality of service you have received?

4	3	2	1
Excellent	*Good*	*Fair*	*Poor*

2. Did you get the kind of service you wanted?

1	2	3	4
No, definitely not	*No, not really*	*Yes, generally*	*Yes, definitely*

3. To what extent has our program met your needs?

4	3	2	1
Almost all of my needs have been met	*Most of my needs have been met*	*Only a few of my needs have been met*	*None of my needs have been met*

4. If a friend were in need of similar help, would you recommend our program to him or her?

1	2	3	4
No, definitely not	*No, I don't think so*	*Yes, I think so*	*Yes, definitely*

5. How satisfied are you with the amount of help you have received?

1	2	3	4
Quite dissatisfied	*Indifferent or mildly dissatisfied*	*Mostly satisfied*	*Very satisfied*

6. Have the services you received helped you to deal more effectively with your problems?

4	3	2	1
Yes, they helped a great deal	*Yes, they helped somewhat*	*No, they really didn't help*	*No, they seemed to make things worse*

7. In an overall, general sense, how satisfied are you with the service you have received?

4	3	2	1
Very satisfied	*Mostly satisfied*	*Indifferent or mildly dissatisfied*	*Quite dissatisfied*

8. If you were to seek help again, would you come back to our program?

1	2	3	4
No, definitely not	*No, I don't think so*	*Yes, I think so*	*Yes, definitely*

Appendix C

CLIENT SURVEY

12.81

Confidential: Therapists will not see your answers

ID # _____   DATE _____

It is important for us to find out how you feel about your experiences at our mental health center. If you will answer the questions below, it will help us improve our services. Both **positive** and **negative** feelings about your experiences will be helpful. Please check the blank which most closely matches your feelings.

1. The problems, feelings or situations that brought me to the mental health center are:

☐ A. Much improved
☐ B. Improved
☐ C. About the same
☐ D. Worse
☐ E. Much worse

2. Because of therapy I feel:

☐ A. Self-confident and good about myself.
☐ B. Better about myself.
☐ C. The same about myself.
☐ D. Worse about myself.
☐ E. Much worse about myself.

If you could make changes in the mental health center, which of the following would you change to improve services? (Check any items you feel need improvement)

☐ 3. The communication between myself and my therapist.
☐ 4. The information I received about what to expect from therapy.
☐ 5. My therapist taking an interest in my problems.
☐ 6. The amount of paperwork I had to do.
☐ 7. The friendliness and courtesy of center staff other than my therapist; for example, secretaries, receptionist, etc.
☐ 8. The location and surroundings of the place I went for therapy.
☐ 9. My therapist being on time and keeping appointments.
☐ 10. The way medications were handled. Explain _____
☐ 11. The information I received about fees for services.
☐ 12. The professional skills of my therapist.
☐ 13. The accuracy of bills I received.
☐ 14. The hours the center was open.
☐ 15. The distance I had to travel to get to services.
☐ 16. The amount of time I had to wait for my first visit.
☐ 17. The understanding and reassurance given by my therapist.
☐ 18. Other _____

19. Please list any part of your mental health services that was particularly good and worthy of praise.

_____

_____

Please mark all of the following statements indicating whether you **agree** or **disagree** with the statement. If a statement does not apply, leave it blank.

Agree	Dis-agree	
☐	☐	20. My experience with mental health was not good or bad.
☐	☐	21. If the center published a monthly bulletin about mental health, I would like to receive it.
☐	☐	22. Because of therapy I have made a better adjustment to my family.
☐	☐	23. If a friend needed help, I would refer him or her to the center.
☐	☐	24. I would like the name of someone I could tell about my mental health service complaints.
☐	☐	25. I would be willing to help out occasionally with mental health activities if I were called.
☐	☐	26. I would be willing to sign a petition that would raise taxes to support mental health activities.
☐	☐	27. I would donate money to help support mental health activities.
☐	☐	28. Because of therapy I can better cope with my job or school.
☐	☐	29. My experience with mental health was a waste of time.

30. Other comments: _____

_____

_____

Appendix D

WEBER MENTAL HEALTH CENTER: BRIEF SERVICE SURVEY

A. I felt my experience with the Weber Mental Health Center was:

[ ] 1. Very satisfactory.
[ ] 2. Somewhat satisfactory.
[ ] 3. Neither satisfactory or unsatisfactory.
[ ] 4. Was somewhat unsatisfactory.
[ ] 5. Very unsatisfactory.

B. Please check any items that you feel led to your brief contact with the Weber Mental Health Center:

[ ] 1. Therapy was completed.
[ ] 2. The problem improved on its own.
[ ] 3. Therapy was not what I expected.
[ ] 4. I felt I could get better help elsewhere.
[ ] 5. I was not treated in a professional manner.
[ ] 6. There was too much paperwork.
[ ] 7. The fees were too high.
[ ] 8. I had difficulty with transportation.
[ ] 9. My work or daily schedule prevented me from attending.
[ ] 10. Members of my family objected.
[ ] 11. My immediate crisis was resolved.
[ ] 12. I had to wait too long for someone to see me.
[ ] 13. Other activities kept me from attending.
[ ] 14. I sought other help.
[ ] 15. I didn't feel comfortable with the therapist that was assigned.
[ ] 16. The stigma of coming to the Weber Mental Health Center discouraged me.
[ ] 17. My friends put me down for seeking help.
[ ] 18. Another family member(s) would not attend with me.
[ ] 19. I felt overwhelmed by the whole thing.
[ ] 20. I could not attend during the hours you were open.
[ ] 21. I didn't care for the location.

C. Please make any comments that you feel would help us improve services:

_____

_____

_____

_____

Author Index

Numbers in parentheses are reference numbers and indicate that the author's work is referred to although his name is not mentioned in the text. Numbers in *italics* show the pages on which the complete references are listed.

Subject Index